THE LIBRARY OF CHRISTIAN CLASSICS

GENERAL EDITORS

JOHN BAILLIE
Principal, New College,
Edinburgh

JOHN T. McNEILL
Auburn Professor of Church History,
Union Theological Seminary,
New York

HENRY P. VAN DUSEN
President, Union Theological Seminary,
New York

THE LIBRARY OF CHRISTIAN CLASSICS

Volume

VOLUME II

ALEXANDRIAN CHRISTIANITY

THE LIBRARY OF CHRISTIAN CLASSICS

Volume II

ALEXANDRIAN CHRISTIANITY

Selected Translations
of Clement and Origen
with Introductions and Notes by

JOHN ERNEST LEONARD OULTON, D.D.
Regius Professor of Divinity in the University of Dublin;
Chancellor of St. Patrick's

and

HENRY CHADWICK, B.D.
Fellow and Dean of Queens' College,
Cambridge

Philadelphia
THE WESTMINSTER PRESS

Published simultaneously in Great Britain and the United States of America
by the S.C.M. Press, Ltd., London, and The Westminster Press, Philadelphia

First published MCMLIV

Library of Congress Catalog Card Number . . 54–10257

Printed in the United States of America

GENERAL EDITORS' PREFACE

GENERAL EDITORS' PREFACE

The Christian Church possesses in its literature an abundant and incomparable treasure. But it is an inheritance that must be reclaimed by each generation. THE LIBRARY OF CHRISTIAN CLASSICS is designed to present in the English language, and in twenty-six volumes of convenient size, a selection of the most indispensable Christian treatises written prior to the end of the sixteenth century.

The practice of giving circulation to writings selected for superior worth or special interest was adopted at the beginning of Christian history. The canonical Scriptures were themselves a selection from a much wider literature. In the Patristic era there began to appear a class of works of compilation (often designed for ready reference in controversy) of the opinions of well-reputed predecessors, and in the Middle Ages many such works were produced. These medieval anthologies actually preserve some noteworthy materials from works otherwise lost.

In modern times, with the increasing inability even of those trained in universities and theological colleges to read Latin and Greek texts with ease and familiarity, the translation of selected portions of earlier Christian literature into modern languages has become more necessary than ever; while the wide range of distinguished books written in vernaculars such as English makes selection there also needful. The efforts that have been made to meet this need are too numerous to be noted here, but none of these collections serves the purpose of the reader who desires a library of representative treatises spanning the Christian centuries as a whole. Most of them embrace only the age of the Church Fathers, and some of them have long been out of print. A fresh translation of a work already

9

translated may shed much new light upon its meaning. This is true even of Bible translations despite the work of many experts through the centuries. In some instances old translations have been adopted in this series, but wherever necessary or desirable, new ones have been made. Notes have been supplied where these were needed to explain the author's meaning. The introductions provided for the several treatises and extracts will, we believe, furnish welcome guidance.

JOHN BAILLIE
JOHN T. MCNEILL
HENRY P. VAN DUSEN

CONTENTS

CLEMENT OF ALEXANDRIA

ORIGEN

Professor Oulton has written or translated those portions of the book marked with a †, Mr. Chadwick those marked with an*, except that the translation of Stromateis, VII, is that of J. B. Mayor, revised.

CLEMENT OF ALEXANDRIA

General Introduction

I

CHRISTIANITY MUST HAVE TAKEN ROOT EARLY AT Alexandria. It was the second city of the Roman Empire, the centre of much trade and commerce, with a population reckoned at about half a million. There was a large Jewish population there. The learned Jew Philo, elder contemporary of Paul, says that the Jews in Alexandria and all Egypt totalled a million.[1] It was the home of that hellenistic Judaism of which Philo's works are the outstanding monument. Nevertheless, we have no reliable information concerning the way in which the young Christian movement developed there. The fourth-century historian Eusebius of Caesarea reports that Mark was the first Bishop of Alexandria, a statement which does not take us beyond the realm of legend. But it is highly probable that there were Christians there in apostolic times. In the Acts of the Apostles (18:24 ff.) Luke tells of Apollos who was an Alexandrian; he may well have learnt there such knowledge of Jesus as he possessed before he met Aquila and Priscilla.

It is only towards the end of the second century that the Christian community at Alexandria emerges from its shroud of darkness. Earlier in the second century during the latter part of Hadrian's reign there flourished at Alexandria a distinguished Christian teacher named Basilides. Soon after him there followed the even more eminent Valentine, who moved to Rome, where, it seems, he very nearly succeeded in becoming Pope.

[1] Philo, in *Flaccum*, 43; cf. the commentary in H. Box's edition (London, 1939), p. 94. On the history of the Jewish colony at Alexandria see also H. B. Swete, *Introduction to the Old Testament in Greek* (1902), pp. 1 ff.; H. I. Bell, *Jews and Christians in Egypt* (1924), pp. 10 ff., and his recent Forwood Lectures, *Cults and Creeds in Graeco-Roman Egypt* (1953).

15

Both these teachers, however, were prominent in the so-called "gnostic" movement of the period, and their opinions were not acceptable to the Church at large. To these men Clement of Alexandria owed much, both as provoking reaction and as commanding assent.

Of the life of Clement himself not much is known. He was born about the middle of the second century, probably in Athens, of pagan parents. His father may have been a descendant of a freedman of the Titus Flavius Clemens who shared the consulship with the emperor Domitian in A.D. 95. Like many men of that age, he travelled about to receive instruction from various teachers. In a famous passage he tells us about his education (Strom., I, 11): "This book is not written to show off my skill as a writer; it is rather that I am treasuring up notes for my old age, a remedy for forgetfulness.[2] They are intended simply as a picture and rough sketch of those clear and living teachings and of those blessed and truly honourable men whom I was privileged to hear. Of them one was an Ionian who taught in Greece. Others were in Magna Graecia [i.e., Southern Italy]; of them one came from Coele-Syria, the other from Egypt. Others lived in the East; of these one was an Assyrian, one a Palestinian Hebrew. After I met the last (who was first of them in importance) I abandoned further search, having discovered him hiding in Egypt. A truly Sicilian bee, he drew honey from the flowers in the meadow[3] of the apostles and prophets, and implanted in the souls of his pupils pure knowledge."

The identity of Clement's last teacher is not in doubt. He was Pantaenus, described here as "a truly Sicilian bee." The best honey came from Sicily,[4] so that this is Clement's way of complimenting him upon the brilliance of his lectures. (The phrase gives us no compelling reason for supposing, as has been thought by many writers on Clement, that Pantaenus was a Sicilian.) Pantaenus was head of the Christian school at Alexandria, and before his conversion was said to have been a Stoic (Eusebius, H.E., V, 10); we are also told that he had visited India. Little is known of his teaching, and it has proved a forlorn undertaking to attempt any reconstruction of his ideas from Clement's works.

Clement met Pantaenus perhaps about A.D. 180. Not long

---

[2] A commonplace; cf. Cicero, pro Sulla, 45.
[3] A reminiscence of Euripides, Hippolytus, 76 ff. (cf. W. Telfer, in J.T.S., XXVIII (1927), p. 169).
[4] Varro, de Re Rustica, III, 16:4; Pliny, Nat. Hist., XI., 13:32. That Clement here refers to Pantaenus is indicated by Eusebius, H.E., V, 11:2.

afterwards he succeeded Pantaenus at the Christian school, and proceeded to give lectures and to write works intended to win over to the Church the educated classes óf Alexandria.

Clement's chief extant writings are his great trilogy: (a) "The Exhortation to the Greeks" (Protrepticus) in one book: (b) "The Instructor" (Paedagogus) in three books; (c) "The Miscellanies" (Stromateis). The title Stromateis was not uncommonly used in Clement's age for writings without any strict order and containing varied subject-matter.[5] In the manuscripts there are eight books of the Stromateis, and Eusebius of Caesarea thought the whole work was complete in the eight books before him.[6] But the eighth book was evidently not intended for publication, and consists of notes of a preparatory nature on which Clement draws in the first seven books. Probably it was appended to the incomplete work after Clement's death. How many books Clement meant to write we cannot tell. At the end of Book VII (cf. also VII, 89) he writes of continuing further.

The only other complete work from Clement's pen is the tractate on the rich young ruler (Quis Dives Salvetur?),[7] written to reassure his wealthy and cultured Christian pupils that Christ condemned only the wrong attitude to wealth, not wealth as such.

Numerous fragments of other works are quoted in later writers, and the manuscripts also preserve two works which throw important light on gnosticism entitled "Selections from the Prophetic Sayings" (Eclogae Propheticae) and "Epitomes from the Writings of Theodotus and the so-called Eastern Teaching of the Time of Valentinus" (Excerpta ex Theodoto). Of the latter there is an edition with English translation and notes by Dr R. P. Casey (1934).[8] It is scarcely intelligible without an extensive commentary.

II

Clement's life work was a war, waged on two fronts; unlike other such conflicts, it ended in success. The gnostic teachers

---

[5] On the title see J. B. Mayor, Clement of Alexandria : Miscellanies, Book VII, pp. xi–xxi.   [6] Eusebius, H.E., VI, 13:1.

[7] This work is excellently translated by G. W. Butterworth in the Loeb Classical Library. In the Ante-Nicene Christian Library, Vols. IV and XII, W. Wilson translates the trilogy, excepting Strom., III, which is given in Latin.

[8] Recently a French edition has been produced by F. Sagnard (Paris, 1948); thereon see A. J. Festugière in Vigiliae Christianae, III (1949), pp. 193–207.

had tended to approximate Christianity to notions drawn from Graeco-Oriental syncretism and heterodox Judaism. These sects had given ordinary church folk such a fright that they had come to fight shy of any form of Christianity which claimed philosophical support. That philosophy was the mother of all heresy was the firm conviction of Tertullian of Carthage, Clement's contemporary. He remarks that the heretics quote "Seek and ye shall find" to defend their curiosity. But for Tertullian Christian believers have already found the object of their search: "after one has believed there is but one thing more to be believed, namely that there is nothing more to believe" (*de Praescr.*, 9). The pagan critic of Christianity Celsus, writing about A.D. 177–180, probably at Alexandria or perhaps at Rome, says that while indeed there are some educated Christians, the majority commonly say: "Do not ask questions, only believe. Faith will save you. Wisdom is an evil thing and foolishness good."[9] Galen, the distinguished medical writer of this time, caustically remarks: "If I had in mind people who taught their pupils in the same way as the followers of Moses and Christ teach theirs—for they order them to accept everything on faith —I should not have given you a definition."[10] Distrust of learning and argument was evidently characteristic of much Christian feeling at this period. The most Tertullian was prepared to give in justification of his belief was *Credo quia absurdum*. And the Roman Hippolytus, Clement's junior contemporary, constructed his refutation of all heresies on the assumption that each heretic derived his ideas from some pagan philosopher—an assumption for which classical scholars have every reason to be grateful to him, since he thus preserves valuable fragments of early philosophers like Heraclitus.

Accordingly, in the eyes of many Christians it was doing the devil's work to pretend that anything more than simple faith was required. Such an attitude did nothing to commend Christianity to educated people. Clement conceives of his task as a vocation to see to it that the Church is made safe for a more positive evaluation of Greek philosophy. For him it is a pastoral necessity arising directly out of his work among the cultured classes of Alexandria. To tell a well-educated catechumen that even the greatest of Greek poets and philosophers were inspired by the devil, would be catastrophic. "The earth is the Lord's and the fullness thereof," quotes Clement in self-justifica-

[9] Origen, *contra Celsum*, I, 9.
[10] See R. Walzer, *Galen on Jews and Christians* (1949), pp. 15, 48–56.

tion; "and anyone who seeks to help catechumens, especially if
they are Greeks, must not shrink from scholarly study."[11] "But
the multitude are scared of Greek philosophy, as children are of
masks, fearing that it will lead them astray."[12] Like the com-
panions of Odysseus passing the Sirens, "they stop up their ears
because they know that if they once allow themselves to listen to
Greek learning they will not be able afterwards to find their way
home again."[13] "I am well aware of what is said by some who
stupidly take fright at any noise. They assert that one must concern oneself only with what is necessary and is bound up with
faith, that we ought to pass by anything outside this as superfluous because it distracts us to no purpose and absorbs our
energies in studies which are of no help towards our ultimate
end. There are others who even think that philosophy was
introduced into human life by some evil inventor for the ruin of
men."[14]

The existence of such critics makes Clement cautious in his
expressions. It has even been suggested that only this obscurity
of his style prevented Clement from suffering condemnation like
Origen in later centuries.[15] The *Miscellanies* is a baffling and
enigmatic work to read because Clement is constantly passing
from one subject to another, leaving hints and allusions unex-
plained and undeveloped. He himself makes it clear that this is
a deliberate attempt to cover his tracks.[16] He wishes to be con-
ciliatory to his opponents, and never lashes them with scorn.
At most he allows himself a gentle irony.[17] To his critics he
admits that pagan philosophy is a harlot. But the scripture says:
"Be not much with a strange woman" (Prov. 5:20). "This is an
admonition that we are to use but not to linger and spend too
much time with worldly culture."[18]

Clement believes that philosophy is of divine origin. In an
important passage he discusses various possible explanations of
the origin of philosophy:[19] "They may say that it is mere chance
that the Greeks have expressed something of the true philosophy.

11 *Strom.*, VI, 89.   12 *Ibid.*, VI, 80.
13 *Ibid.*, VI, 89.   14 *Ibid.*, I, 18.
15 A. Jülicher, art. "Clemens Alexandrinus," in Pauly-Wissowa, *Realenc.*,
  IV (1901), col. 13. Photius (*cod.* 109, 111) utters a word of warning about
  Clement's unsoundness.
16 Clement is explicit on this point (*Strom.*, I, 20–21, 56; IV, 4; VI, 2; VII,
  110–111).
17 Cf. *Strom.*, I, 43; VI, 80, cited above.   18 *Strom.*, I, 29.
19 *Ibid.*, I, 94. Valuable comments on this passage by E. Molland in *Sym-
  bolae Osloenses*, XV–XVI (1936), pp. 57 ff.

But that chance is subject to divine providence. For no one will make chance into a god merely in order to get the better of their argument with us. Or they may call it a happy coincidence. Or in the next place it may be said that the Greeks possessed an idea of the truth implanted by nature. But we know that the Creator of nature is one only. . . . And if it is said that they had a common mind, let us examine who is author of it and of the righteousness which is apparent in the distribution of mind to all men.[20] But if anyone says that the cause of this anticipation in Greek philosophy is a 'previous proclamation' or says that it is due to a coincidental agreement, he is implying that it is a form of prophecy. Moreover, others affirm that many teachings of the philosophers arise from a reflection of the truth " (i.e., by introspection the philosopher contemplates the image of God within himself, which is a reflection of God; cf. I Cor. 13:12). It is with the last view that Clement associates himself. But it is characteristic of him not to be too decided on the point. And elsewhere he alludes favourably to the view that Greek philosophy goes back to the fallen angels of Genesis, ch. 6, who were supposed to have imparted their secrets to their women folk, so that the truth, albeit in distorted form, had come down to men (*Strom.*, V, 10; cf. I, 81). He is particularly attracted by the theory, taken over from traditional Jewish apologetic, that the Greek philosophers had plagiarized Moses. The Lord had said, "All who came before me were thieves and robbers." Clement devotes inordinate space to proving the priority of Moses and to arguing that the Greeks had stolen their ideas from the Old Testament. And in a long section (*Strom.*, V, 89–139) he even argues that this is only to be expected, since the Greeks were in the habit of plagiarizing from one another. It is necessary to observe that much of this section, like other parts of the *Miscellanies*, seems itself to have been a compilation drawing on earlier sources.[21]

Clement's debt to other writers is so great that some modern scholars have treated him as if he had not a single idea of his own and was merely a compiler of other men's work. If Clement were no more than an expert with scissors and paste he would scarcely merit Jerome's high praise that of all the Fathers he was the most learned (*Epist.*, LXX, 4). It is of course demonstrable that he draws much from elsewhere. For his too-numerous poetic

[20] Allusion to Plato, *Laws*, 714 A.
[21] For a recent discussion see K. Ziegler's article "Plagiat" in Pauly-Wissowa, *Realenc.*, XX, 2 (1950), cols. 1984–1991.

quotations he uses anthologies, and for his philosophy he uses the current handbooks of "potted" philosophy, summarizing the opinions of the various schools;[22] the same practice was adopted by many others of his time, both pagan and Christian. There can, however, be no question that he had an excellent first-hand knowledge of most of the classics of Greek literature. He knew well Homer and Euripides, Plato and the Stoics. Platonic allusions are particularly frequent, and probably even now not all of them have been noticed and identified. Equally familiar to him were the writings of Philo of Alexandria, from whom he quotes almost as often as from Plato. Philo provided him with a ready-made attitude to Greek philosophy; he had interpreted the story of Hagar and Sarah as an allegory of the relations of philosophy and theology, to show that the former is to be the handmaid of the latter.[23] It is an attitude Clement is glad to make his own.

Paul had spoken of the Law of Moses as a *paidagogos* until the coming of Christ (Gal. 3:24). Clement would attribute the same role to Greek philosophy: "Even if Greek philosophy does not comprehend the truth in its entirety and, in addition, lacks the strength to fulfil the Lord's command, yet at least it prepares the way for the teaching which is royal in the highest sense of the word, by making a man self-controlled, by moulding his character, and by making him ready to receive the truth" (*Strom.*, I, 80). "Greek philosophy, as it were, provides for the soul the preliminary cleansing and training required for the reception of the faith, on which foundation the truth builds up the edifice of knowledge" (*Strom.*, VII, 20).

III

If, on the one hand, Clement is anxious to vindicate for Christian teachers the right to study the Greek philosophers and poets, on the other hand he wishes to make it clear that this does not leave the door open for unorthodox gnostic speculations. Between Clement and the gnostics there were two chief points

---

[22] H. Diels, *Doxographi Graeci*, pp. 244 ff.
[23] Philo, *de Congressu Eruditionis gratia*, freely pillaged by Clement, *Strom.*, I, 28–32.

The Jewish Wisdom-literature was also of great importance to Clement in enabling him to bridge the gulf between the biblical theology of church tradition and the rational inquiry of philosophy. Cf. W. Völker, "Die Verwertung der Weisheit-Literatur bei den christlichen Alexandrinern," in *Zeits. f. Kirchengeschichte*, LXIV (1953), pp. 1–33.

at issue: their pessimistic view of the world, and their denial of the part played by free will in the attainment of salvation.

The gnostics took so pessimistic a view of the created world that they refused to recognize in its Creator the God and Father of our Lord Jesus Christ. This present evil world must be the work of an inferior, perhaps even of an evil, power; it certainly could not have been made by the supreme God, of whom it was entirely unworthy. It followed from this that the Old Testament which was inspired by the Creator must be similarly inferior, and could tell us little or nothing about the God revealed in Jesus Christ.

In the third book of his *Miscellanies* Clement has a full-scale discussion of the implications of this view of the world. The gnostic estimate of the world led to two opposed attitudes to sex and marriage. Clement himself divides his opponents into two groups, the extreme ascetics and the licentious (*Strom.*, III, 40). Of the former class the most prominent representatives are Marcion and Tatian. Although in other respects Marcion stood apart from the "gnostic" movement, he shared their idea of the Old Testament and the Creation. The inferior Creator-God had given the command: "Increase and multiply and replenish the earth" (Gen. 1:28). The good Marcionite would therefore do nothing whatever to assist the Creator in his business. In fact, in Marcion's eyes the methods chosen by the Creator for replenishing the world were as nasty as could be. Marcion's language about sex and the process of reproduction shows him to have been a psychopathic case; the contemplation of sex overwhelmed him with a sense of nausea. No member of the Marcionite church was allowed to be married.

A similarly ascetic line was adopted by Tatian, former pupil of the apologist Justin Martyr. There is all too little evidence of the details of the heretical doctrines he came to hold. Irenaeus has three complaints to make against him: (*a*) he adopted Valentinian ideas about invisible aeons; (*b*) he called marriage fornication, like Marcion and Saturninus; (*c*) he denied that Adam could be saved.[24] He evidently came to attribute an inferior status to the Creator and the created world, since he interpreted "Let there be light" (Gen. 1:3) as a request from the Creator, who found himself in darkness and had to ask the supreme God for light so that he could see to make the world.[25] In *Strom.*, III, 80–81 Clement quotes from Tatian's work en-

[24] Irenaeus, *adv. Haer.*, I, 28, quoted by Eusebius, *H.E.*, IV, 29:1.
[25] See Prof. Oulton's note on Origen, *de Orat.*, XXIV, 5 (p. 358 below).

titled "On Perfection according to the Saviour." It was probably the ascetic tendency of this work which led to Tatian's
separation from the Church. His excommunication is dated by
Eusebius in A.D. 172.[26] When the church at Rome became too
hot to hold him, he returned to his native land, Mesopotamia,
where he exercised wide influence and would, it seems, have
found many like-minded persons who held the married state to
be incompatible with the Christian profession.[27] His "Harmony
of the Gospels" (*Diatessaron*) remained in general use, especially
in the Syrian church for which it was originally composed. A
Greek version was soon made for the many Greek-speaking
Christians of the Eastern provinces.[28] Whether the *Oration to the
Greeks*, for which he is chiefly known, was written at Rome or in
Mesopotamia is not certain. If, as has recently been urged,[29] it
was written late in 177 or early in 178, then it is clear that even
after his separation from the Church Tatian remained faithful
to the apologetic tradition he had inherited from Justin.

It is interesting that Clement's quotations from Tatian's
work "On Perfection according to the Saviour" show that he
expounded Paul, and give no hint that he rejected the apostle's
writings. His followers, however, according to the statements of
Hippolytus and Origen, rejected the Pauline epistles, and
Eusebius says that they also rejected the Acts.[30]

Of the ascetic wing of the "gnostic" movement Clement's
third representative is Julius Cassianus. We know nothing about
him other than what we are told by Clement (Jerome's statements about him are wholly dependent on Clement). We learn
that he was the originator of Docetism—a statement which
cannot be accepted in view of the New Testament evidence for
the prevalence of this tendency before the end of the first century
(I John 4:1 ff.). In the first book of the *Miscellanies* Cassian is
mentioned with respect in company with Tatian as having
proved in his "commentaries" the priority of Moses to Greek

26 Eusebius, *Chronicle*, p. 206, ed. Helm.
27 Epiphanius, *Panarion*, XLVI. Cf. F. C. Burkitt in *Camb. Anc. Hist.*, XII,
p. 499.
28 See P. E. Kahle, *The Cairo Geniza* (1947), pp. 197 ff.; A. Vööbus, *History
of the Gospel Text in Syriac* (1951).
29 R. M. Grant, "The Date of Tatian's Oration," in *Harvard Theological Review*, XLVI (1953), pp. 99–101. J. Geffcken, *Zwei griech. Apologeten*
(1907), pp. 105–106, dates Tatian's *Oration* after his break with the
Church. Cf. also Grant in *J.T.S.* n.s. V (1954), pp. 62–68.
30 Hippolytus, *Refut.*, VIII, 20:1; Origen, *contra Celsum*, V, 65; Eusebius,
H.E., IV, 29:5.

philosophers (*Strom.*, I, 101). He was at one time a Valentinian, but fell out with the school perhaps because of his extreme docetic opinions and his rejection of marriage (*Strom.*, III, 92).

At the opposite extreme to the ascetic sects were the Carpocratians. This sect is a peculiar phenomenon even in the curious penumbra of eccentric sects which gathered round the Church in the second century and claimed the name of Christian. The evidence concerning the sect is not a little obscure. The origin of the sect is ascribed by Clement and Irenaeus to a man Carpocrates, but his historical existence has been doubted. We have to examine the possibility that Clement and Irenaeus assumed that the sect was founded by a man of this name, just as Tertullian invents a mythical Ebion as founder of the Ebionites.

The earliest writer to speak of the sect is Celsus, the pagan critic of Christianity whose *True Doctrine* was probably written about A.D. 177–180. He enumerates several Christian sects, observing that none is willing to co-operate with any other. There are, he says, 'Marcellians who follow Marcellina, and Harpocratians who follow Salome, and others who follow Mariamme, and others who follow Martha." The immorality of some of these groups is even more shameful, he thinks, than that associated with the hero-cult paid to Hadrian's favourite Antinous. For his factual information about these sects Celsus seems to have been dependent not upon a first-hand acquaintance but upon some orthodox Christian pamphlet (elsewhere his remarks about Marcion strongly suggest that such anti-heretical literature lay before him; cf. Origen, *contra Celsum*, VI, 53, with my note thereon). He goes on to observe that some of these heretics are called (presumably by their orthodox critics) "Circes and wily agitators," and others "Sirens . . . who seal the ears of their converts and make their heads like pigs."[31]

Contemporary with Celsus is the bare mention of the Carpocratians in the *Memoirs* of Hegesippus (in Eusebius, *H.E.*, IV, 22:5), but this tells us nothing of the doctrine of the sect.[32]

---

[31] Origen, *contra Celsum*, V, 62–64. For " Circes " cf. Clem. *Strom.*, VII, 95.

[32] Bishop Lightfoot, *St. Clement of Rome*, I (1890), pp. 328 ff., tried to prove that the account of the Carpocratians in Epiphanius, *Panarion*, XXVII, 6, was based on the lost *Memoirs* of Hegesippus. His view was accepted by Zahn (*Forsch. z. Gesch. d. N. T. Kanons*, VI (1900), pp. 258 f.), Harnack (*Chronologie*, I (1897), pp. 184 f.), and H.J. Lawlor (*Eusebiana* (1912), pp. 73 ff.). This view, however, has not survived the criticisms of Karl Holl in his notes on this passage in his edition of Epiphanius (Vol. I (1915), pp. 308–309), which make it clear that Epiphanius gives no evidence of having had any sources in front of him other than Irenaeus and Eusebius.

According to the summary of Irenaeus, reproduced in essentials by most of the later anti-heretical writers,[33] Carpocrates believed that the world was created by inferior angels. Jesus, son of Joseph, however, exercising his Platonic powers of *anamnesis*, remembered what he had seen in the divine sphere, and on this account power came upon him from the Father to enable him to escape from the world-creators. Souls like Jesus can similarly overcome the world, being visited by the same power which they can obtain by magic. Those who possess it can indulge in any practice without danger, since right and wrong are merely human conventions. It is by faith and love that we are saved. If it is to avoid reincarnation the soul must have experience of everything, this being the meaning of Jesus' words, "Thou shalt not go forth thence till thou hast paid the last farthing."

Irenaeus concludes his account of the Carpocratians by observing that one group of them was led by a lady named Marcellina who came to Rome in the time of Pope Anicetus (c. A.D. 155–166). This group had a ceremony of initiation which was a literal baptism by fire; initiates were branded with a hot iron at the back of the lobe of the right ear. Irenaeus' information thus fills out and substantiates the obscure references in Celsus. The Carpocratian ceremony of baptism by branding the ear is also mentioned by the Valentinian Heracleon.[34]

Hitherto the evidence considered is reasonably coherent and self-consistent. But some modern writers doubt whether Clement's information in the third book of the *Miscellanies* is equally reliable. Clement gives here substantial quotations from a book attributed to Carpocrates' son Epiphanes entitled *Concerning Righteousness*. This work merely consists of the scribblings of an intelligent but nasty-minded adolescent of somewhat pornographic tendencies. The work attempts to justify extreme sexual licence by a communistic theory: the existence of private property is of human invention and has no divine sanction; communism is therefore to be practised in sexual relationships.

33 Irenaeus, *adv. Haer.*, I., 25; Hippolytus, *Refut.*, VII, 32; Tertullian, *de Anima*, 23 and 35; Eusebius, *H.E.*, IV, 7:9 f.; Ps.-Tertullian, *adv. Omn. Haer.*, 3; Filastrius, 35; Theodoret, *Haer. Fab. Comp.*, I, 5; Augustine, *de Haer.*, 7; Didymus, *de Trinitate*, III, 42; Ps.-Anthimus of Nicomedia (? = Marcellus of Ancyra), *de Sancta Ecclesia*, 6 (*Studi e Testi*, V, 1901).

34 "Some brand with fire the ears of those whom they seal" (ap. Clem. Alex., *Ecl. Proph.*, XXV, 1). See F. J. Dölger, "Die Sphragis als religiöse Brandmarkung im Einweihungsakt der gnostischen Karpokratianer," in *Antike und Christentum*, I (1929), pp. 73–78.

The difficulty, however, lies in Clement's remarkable account of the posthumous cult of Epiphanes. He affirms that Epiphanes' father, Carpocrates, was an Alexandrian. His mother, named Alexandria, came from the town of Same in the island of Cephallenia in the Ionian islands. After their son died at the tender age of seventeen they founded a temple in his honour at Same, and the islanders used to gather once a month for a religious beano in celebration of the hero's birthday.

Volkmar entirely disbelieved in the existence of such a person as Epiphanes. He held that Clement had totally misunderstood a new moon festival at Same, in some account of which the new moon was entitled *epiphanes*.[35] A modified form of this radical hypothesis was accepted by Lipsius.[36] He saw that there must have been an Alexandrian gnostic named Epiphanes who was author of the book *Concerning Righteousness*, but this person has no connection with the moon-god worshipped on Cephallenia.

Celsus calls the sect "Harpocratians." From this the conclusion has been drawn that the name of the sect was not taken from any man Carpocrates, but from the Egyptian deity Horus, son of Isis and Osiris, who was worshipped by the Greeks under the name Carpocrates or Harpocrates (both forms of the name occur in inscriptions). Egyptian deities were worshipped in Asia Minor and the Greek islands.[37] Harpocrates may well have been worshipped at Cephallenia, although no inscriptions have been found there to prove it.[38] He may there have been associated with a feminine consort named after the city Alexandria, and his cult fused with a local cult of some Cephallenian deity, *theos epiphanes*.[39]

[35] G. Volkmar, "Über die Häretiker Epiphanes und Adrianus," in *Monatsschrift des wissenschaftlichen Vereins in Zürich*, I (1856), pp. 276–282, criticized by Hilgenfeld briefly in *Zeitschr. f. wiss. Theol.*, V (1862), p. 426, n. 2, and at length in his *Die Ketzergeschichte Urchristentums* (1884), pp. 402 f. For a good summary in English see G. Salmon in *Dict. Chr. Biogr.*, s.v. "Epiphanes."

[36] R. A. Lipsius, *Zur Quellenkritik des Epiphanios* (Vienna, 1865), p. 161.

[37] See T. A. Brady, *The Reception of Egyptian Cults by the Greeks* (Univ. of Missouri Studies, X (1935)); M. P. Nilsson, *Geschichte der griechischen Religion*, II (1950), p. 118; D. Magie, "Egyptian Deities in Asia Minor in Inscriptions and on Coins," in *Amer. Journ. Arch.*, LVII (1953), pp. 163–187.

[38] The poverty of epigraphical evidence of any kind from Same is remarked by G. Klaffenbach, "Bericht über eine epigraphische Reise durch Mittelgriechenland und die Ionischen Inseln," in *Sitzungsberichte d. preuss. Akad. d. Wiss.* (1935), pp. 691–726, at pp. 711 f. For a dedication to Isis and Sarapis at nearby Corcyra, cf. *Inscr. Gr.*, IX, 716.

[39] W. Schultz, *Dokumente der Gnosis* (1910), pp. lxviii, 160; H. Leisegang, *Die*

Against this view we have to reckon the explicit and detailed statements which Clement makes, even to the inclusion of the precise age at which Epiphanes died. Clement's story is circumstantial. And as a general rule it is safe to say that Clement is the most reliable of all early Christian writers on gnosticism. On Basilides and Valentine he is extremely well informed. It would be remarkable if he were to be completely mistaken in this instance. In a recent attempt to discredit Clement's evidence Heinz Kraft has emphasized the silence of Clement regarding Marcellina and the ceremony of branding the ear with hot iron. But this proves nothing. In any event Clement is in entire accord with both Celsus and Irenaeus in representing the sect as wholeheartedly licentious.

Clement's only statement about the metaphysics of the Carpocratians is that they believed in "the monadic gnosis." This is not supported by Irenaeus or Hippolytus, but it is curiously echoed by two Latin Christian writers who have been suspected of using a lost work of Hippolytus.[40] And it is entirely in Clement's manner to concentrate attention upon the ethics rather than the metaphysics of the heretical sects. Basilides is treated in exactly this way. The cryptic statement that the doctrine of the Monad was important for the Carpocratians is perhaps explained by the quotation Clement makes (*Strom.*, III, 29) from a lost apocryphal work and which he regards as "the mother of their licentiousness." It is an account of the origin of the world: the Monad was alone at first, but since it seemed good to its unity not to be alone an Idea came forth from it, and from the intercourse of Monad and Idea came the invisible powers of the cosmos. Clement observes that the Valentinian doctrine is superficially akin to this, but that in Valentine's system the union of the pairs in the Pleroma is wholly "spiritual," whereas the licentious sects have understood the union in crudely physical terms.

Clement's statement that Epiphanes' birthday was celebrated

Gnosis (3rd edn., 1941), pp. 257 ff. The case has been argued with at least the maximum of plausibility by H. Kraft, "Gab es einen Gnostiker Karpokrates?" in *Theol. Zeitschr.*, VIII (1952), pp. 434–443. The position of de Faye (*Gnostiques et Gnosticisme* (1925), pp. 413–419) is agnostic: there is no proof that the Carpocratian sect was founded by Epiphanes' father; it may have been another man named Carpocrates, but we really have no certain knowledge about the sect whatever. The reliability of Clement's statements is upheld by Hilgenfeld, *Ketzergeschichte*, p. 403; H. Liboron, *Die karpokratianische Gnosis* (1938), pp. 10 ff.

[40] *Strom.*, III, 5. Cf. Ps.-Tertullian, *adv. Omn. Haer.*, 3; Filastrius, 35.

monthly offers no ground for supposing that he was really a moon-god. There is plenty of evidence that in antiquity birthdays were celebrated monthly.[41]

The story of the posthumous cult of Epiphanes at Same is certainly remarkable. Clement evidently thought so, or he would not have reported the details. The cult does not appear to be more remarkable than the hero-cult paid to Hadrian's favourite, the boy Antinous who was drowned in the Nile in A.D. 130. The emperor believed the boy had become a star.[42] The celebrations at Antinoopolis in Egypt were attended by nocturnal orgies so notorious that they were generally deplored by such writers as Celsus and were a godsend to critics of paganism like the Christian apologists. Indeed, when Celsus compares the licentiousness of the Carpocratians with that of the revellers of the cult of Antinous he may have been nearer the truth than he knew. It is not impossible that the Carpocratians modelled their practice on the recently founded cult of Hadrian's favourite. The activities of Carpocrates are no doubt rightly dated by Theodoret in the time of Hadrian. And it would not be a unique case of cultus offered to a young child early ripened for heaven. A famous inscription found on the island of Thera records that a *Mouseion* was built by a husband and wife, whose impulse to found the place came from the early death of their young son. An annual sacrifice was offered and a meal eaten there in memory of dead members of the family.[43] Clement does not say that the Carpocratian sect flourished in Cephallenia. But that Epiphanes' parents founded a temple there in his memory and venerated him as a hero is not inconceivable. Nor is it incredible that a seventeen-year-old boy of some ability, even if of little moral education, should have written the work *Concerning Righteousness*.

Clement makes the Carpocratians responsible for bringing

[41] See E. Schürer, "Zu II Macc. 6, 7 (monatliche Geburtstagfeier)," in *Zeitschr. f. d. N. T. Wiss.*, II (1901), pp. 48–52; G. Wissowa, "Monatliche Geburtstagfeier," in *Hermes*, XXXVII (1902), pp. 157–159; E. Rohde, *Psyche* (Eng. tr., 1925), p. 197.

[42] Dio Cassius, 69, 11; Tatian, *Oratio ad Graecos*, 10. For the widespread ancient belief that a dead child became a star and for the practice of offering sacrifice to such, cf. F. Cumont, *Lux Perpetua* (1949), pp. 183–184.

[43] The comparison between Epiphanes and the Thera inscription (*Inscr. Gr.*, XII, 3:330) is made by Usener, *Das Weihnachtsfest* (2nd edn., 1911), p. 114, n. 10, though Usener could not believe that the Cephallenian Epiphanes is identical with the author of the book *Concerning Righteousness*. On the Thera inscription, cf. also Wilamowitz, *Glaube der Hellenen* (1932), II, p. 140, n. 2.

upon the Christians the popular scandal that they indulged in immorality. This charge is often rebutted by the apologists of the second century, though Celsus is sufficiently well informed to know that there is no truth in the story. Origen (who thought the story was put into circulation by the Jews) tells us that in his time "these allegations are now condemned even by the multitude and by people entirely alien to our religion as being a false slander against the Christians." But in the second century the scandal was widely believed. "This malicious rumour," Origen observes, "some time ago exercised an unreasonable influence on a very large number and persuaded people knowing nothing of the gospel that this really was the character of Christians. And even now it still deceives some who by such stories are repelled from approaching Christians even if only for a simple conversation."[44] When the rumour began it is not possible to say, but it is certainly earlier than the Carpocratians. The language of Tacitus and of the younger Pliny about "the vices with which the name Christian is associated"[45] suggests that it was current by the end of the first century.

Three other groups of licentious gnostics are mentioned by Clement. Of those whom he calls *Antitactae* nothing is known from elsewhere. The Nicolaitans (cf. Rev. 2:6) claimed to follow Nicolas the proselyte of Antioch. Clement disputes this claim; some scholars have thought him correct, and have explained the name "Nicolaitans" as due to the common anxiety of heretics to father their opinions on some New Testament personage. On the other hand, it is obvious that Clement's remarks about Nicolas are whitewash. Clement was anxious to clear a prominent person of the apostolic age from any responsibility for those who claimed his authority, just as he also argues that the Cephas with whom Paul had a battle royal at Antioch (Gal. 2:11 f.) was not Simon Peter the apostle but another disciple of the same name who was one of the seventy sent out by Jesus.[46] As late as the fifth century John Cassian attacks people who deny that the Nicolas of Acts, ch. 6, is to be identified with the leader of the Nicolaitan sect.[47]

[44] Origen, *contra Celsum*, VI, 40, and 27.
[45] Pliny, *Epist.*, X, 96: *flagitia cohaerentia nomini*. Tacitus (*Ann.*, XV, 44) similarly says that the Christians were "hated for their vices" (*per flagitia invisos*).
[46] Clement in Eusebius, *H.E.*, I, 12:1 f.
[47] *Coll.*, XVIII, 16:6. Further material on the Nicolaitans in Harnack, *Geschichte der altchr. Litt.*, I, p. 156; M. Goguel, "Les Nicolaites," in *Revue de l'hist. des religions*, CXV (1937), pp. 5–36.

Prodicus (*Strom.*, III, 30) is a shadowy figure of uncertain date, and most of what we know about him is derived from Clement. Besides his immoral teaching he denied the utility of prayer on the ground that since God already knows all our needs there is not the slightest reason to inform him of them (*Strom.*, VII, 41), an opinion dealt with by Origen (*de Orat.*, V, 1). Clement also says that his followers prided themselves on possessing some writings of Zoroaster (*Strom.*, I, 69); we know from Porphyry's *Life of Plotinus* (c. xvi) that "apocalypses of Zoroaster" were current among the gnostics.[48] The followers of Prodicus knew themselves to be saved and that nothing could interfere with the predeterminate counsel of God; they therefore held that apostasy in persecution was a matter of no moral significance for the elect.[49] This is about the sum of our knowledge about the sect. Apart from this there is only the dubious statement of Theodoret that Prodicus was leader of the Adamite sect, a group of nudist encratites of whom Epiphanius gives an account based on hearsay in his "Medicine-Chest for the Cure of all Heresies."[50]

Between the two extremes, the rigidly ascetic and the freely licentious, there stand the two most prominent Christian gnostics, Basilides and Valentine.

Basilides and his son Isidore held marriage to be no sin, and allowed it on the apostolic ground that it was indeed better to marry than to burn. But it was to be avoided by the man who was ambitious to attain perfection. The followers of Basilides in the next generation after his death departed from their master's teaching and fell into licentious ways (*Strom.*, III, 3). When Irenaeus accuses Basilides of immorality, the charge is evidently not true of the master himself, though we have Clement's testimony that it was true of the Basilidians of his own time. Irenaeus, however, is not well informed about the teaching of the historical Basilides.

The Valentinians were distinguished from other gnostics by their warm approval of monogamous marriage. For Valentine there was no question of any licentiousness, nor of any frowning disapproval, much less outright rejection, of the married state. According to Tertullian the Valentinians accounted the unmarried as on a lower level than the married (*adv. Val.*, 30), a

---

[48] Cf. H. C. Puech in *Coptic Studies in Honor of W. E. Crum* (Boston, Mass., 1950), pp. 107–108, 132–134.
[49] Tertullian, *Scorpiace*, 15 (cf. *adv. Prax.* 3).
[50] Theodoret, *Haer. Fab. Comp.*, I, 6; Epiphanius, *Panarion*, 52.

view which was hardly likely to recommend Valentinianism to the North African rigorist.[51] This feature is the more remarkable in that of all the gnostic teachers Valentine was the most deeply influenced by Platonism, which might have encouraged in him a pessimistic view of the world. His approval of marriage was grounded upon his fantastic metaphysics, to which the Hellenistic commonplace idea that things on earth have their counterpart of things in heaven is integral. The Godhead, the *Pleroma* or fullness, consists of thirty spiritual beings called aeons. The *Pleroma* begins with Depth (*Bythos*) and his consort Silence (*Sige*), whose marriage produces Mind and Truth. These in turn beget Word and Life, to whom are born Man and Church. These eight form the Ogdoad. In the same kind of way the rest of the *Pleroma* gradually evolves until the full number of thirty aeons is attained. We need not stop here on the further development of the system. The sacred marriages of the aeons in the Godhead (cf. *Strom.*, III, 29) are for Valentine the model for earthly activity. The marriage of the Valentinian bridegroom with his Valentinian bride is the earthly counterpart of the whole process of evolution enacted in the very life of God, who is the *Pleroma*. It is a foretaste, therefore, of that final bliss in the heavenly marriage feast to which all the saved (i.e. the Valentinians) are invited, when they are to strip themselves of their souls, their wedding garments, and pass into the bridal chamber, the *Pleroma* itself, where they enjoy unutterable union and the beatific vision.[52]

With the teaching of Basilides and more especially of Valentine Clement found himself in a fair degree of sympathy. Both are men of eminence whom he always regards with respect, even though he is aware of important differences. His main complaint is against the general gnostic tendency to adopt extreme predestinarian views. Most of the sects held that they alone were the saved, they alone had the divine spark within. The Naassene sect is quoted by Hippolytus as saying, "We alone of all men are Christians"(*Ref.*, V, 9:22).[53] Basilides

---

51 According to Irenaeus (I, 6:4) the Valentinians taught that marriage was indeed a mark of the elect "pneumatic." But continence has to be practised by the "psychic" if he wished to be saved.

52 Clement, *Exc. Theod.*, LXIII–IV; Heracleon in Origen, *Comm. in Evang. Ioannis*, X, 19; XIII, 52; Irenaeus, I, 7:1.

53 The pagan Celsus says of the Christian sects: "They slander one another with dreadful and unspeakable words of abuse; and they will not make even the least concession to reach agreement, for they utterly detest each other" (Origen, *contra Celsum*, V, 63; cf. III, 10–12).

stood far nearer to orthodox Christianity than the Naassenes, whose connections with the faith were, to say the least, thin. He seems to have held a rigorous division of mankind into the saved and the lost in accordance with a "supra-cosmic election" (*Strom.*, II, 10; V, 3; IV, 165). But we are not told that he identified his own adherents with the saved exclusively. Valentine was more explicit. He divided mankind into three classes, following Paul's tripartite division of man into body, soul, and spirit (I Thess. 5:23). Humanity consisted of those whose essential nature was spirit, the pneumatics; those whose nature was of soul-stuff, the psychics; and those who were merely of the earth, earthy. The pneumatics with whom the Valentinians naturally identified themselves were wholly predetermined to gain complete salvation and incorporation into the *Pleroma*. The earthy class were equally absolutely predestined for hell. The middle class, however, the psychics, consisted of the ordinary members of the Christian Church who did not attend Valentine's conventicle. The Valentinian was permitted to hope for their salvation; they might be saved or they might be lost; everything depended on their use of free will.

This threefold division Valentine takes right through his entire system. He found the middle or "psychic" category particularly useful for his Christology. Jesus' body, he held, was not purely spiritual, as the cruder docetists had taught. Nor, on the other hand, was it of earthy matter, as simple church teachers believed. It was made of soul-stuff; it was psychic. Clement regards this idea with some anxiety as being at least in principle docetic; for in *Strom.*, III, 102 he remarks that because they regard birth into a material body as an evil thing Cassian and Marcion hold their docetic opinions—"and even Valentine indeed teaches that Christ's body was psychic." Nevertheless, Clement is able to quote with approval Valentine's letter to one Agathopus, saying that Jesus "ate and drank in a manner peculiar to himself and the food did not pass out of his body." There was no normal digestive process (*Strom.*, III, 59).[54] Elsewhere Clement advances a similar view on his own, when he remarks that Jesus certainly ate and drank, not because he needed to do so, for his body was sustained by divine power, but

[54] Origen attacks Valentinus' Christology in his Commentary on Galatians (quoted in Pamphilus' *Apology for Origen*: Lommatzsch, XXIV, 365 ff.). "... Si vero quis indignas obscoenasque ad haec proferat inquisitiones, requirens si etiam digestiones in corpore fiebant, nihil absurdum videtur fateri secundum consequentiam naturae corporeae."

because he wished to forestall the Docetists (*Strom.*, VI, 71).
Valentine's concession to the docetic spirit in admitting that the
body of Jesus was not of common matter but was psychic led to
trouble in the Valentinian school. If psychic, why could it not
be pneumatic? According to Hippolytus (*Ref.*, VI, 35:5–7) this
problem led to a split in the Valentinian ranks: the Italian
school led by Ptolemy and Heracleon held that the body was
psychic, the Eastern School led by Axionicus of Antioch and
Bardesanes of Edessa that it was pneumatic.

IV

Clement's personal attitude to marriage is curiously confused. Against the heretics he has to give a positive evaluation
of marriage as the creation of a beneficent Creator. And in this
spirit he can say that the unmarried man is inferior to the married man, because he tends to be more selfish and has fewer
opportunities of self-denial; the married man, on the other hand,
can show his mettle "by rising superior to every temptation that
assails him through his children and his wife, his servants and
possessions" (*Strom.*, VII, 70). Again, he remarks that the married and unmarried states are alike gifts of God (III, 79). Echo-
ing Stoic teaching, he insists that marriage is to be undertaken
for patriotic reasons and for the maintenance of the human
race (II, 140). The first-century Stoic Musonius Rufus asks:
"Is it fitting for each man to act for himself alone or to act in
the interest of his neighbour also, not only that there may be
homes in the city but also that the city may not be deserted and
that the common good may best be served? If you say that each
one should look out for his own interests alone, you represent
man as no different from a wolf. . . . It is each man's duty to
take thought for his own city, and to make of his home a rampart for its protection. But the first step toward making his home
such a rampart is marriage. Thus whoever destroys human
marriage destroys the home, the city, and the whole human
race. For it would not last if there were no procreation of
children and there would be no just and lawful procreation of
children without marriage."[55] Clement resists the gnostic
world-denying understanding of the New Testament, insisting
that the apostles themselves were married. Even Paul, he thinks,

[55] Musonius, frag. 14 Hense. I cite the translation of Cora E. Lutz in *Yale
Classical Studies*, 10 (1947), pp. 92–93. The "patriotic" motive for marriage is attacked by Tertullian, *Exh. Cast.*, 12.

was married, and "the only reason why he did not take her about with him was that it would have been an inconvenience for his ministry" (*Strom.*, III, 53).[56]

On the other hand, he often expresses himself in terms which are scarcely consistent with so positive an attitude. Indeed, although the apostles, as Paul tells us (I Cor. 9), took their wives about with them that the gospel might be preached in the women's quarters without scandal,[57] they lived with their consorts as brother and sister. When the heretics who reject marriage affirm that they are living now the life of the world to come where there is no marriage (*Strom.*, III, 48),[58] Clement replies that to be consistent they ought equally to abstain from food and drink. Yet when he himself speaks of the spiritual perfection of the true gnostic, he can say that his passionless life, in that he lives with his wife as with a sister, is a realization on earth of the resurrection state (VI, 100). In short, the best Christians in Clement's view are those who are married but have no sexual relations with their wives.[59] The degree to which he shared his opponents' presuppositions is shown by his distinction between the pagan ideal of self-control and the Christian ideal. The difference is that while the pagan ascetic feels desire and does not give in to it, the Christian is not to feel anything at all (*Strom.*, III, 57–58).

Thus Clement's position is vacillating. Despite his anxiety to vindicate marriage as created by God, at heart he shared the idea that sex relations are to be avoided. The notion that defilement attaches to sexual relations is ancient enough, and is prominent in much ancient religion. The Christians took it over, so that Origen, for example, directs that prayer should not be made in bed, since the marriage union takes place there (*de Orat.* XXXI, 4). Like Ignatius of Antioch, Origen also enjoins continence before receiving the eucharistic bread.[60] And he declares expressly that he cannot think of the presence of the Holy Spirit at the time of sexual union: "Lawful marriages are not

---

[56] No doubt she would not have fitted comfortably into the basket when her husband escaped from Damascus over the city wall.

[57] Similarly *Didascalia Apost.*, 16 (ed. R. H. Connolly, p. 148).

[58] That the celibate lives an angelic life on earth is commonplace in later ascetic writings: Basil of Ancyra, *de Virginitate*, 51 (Migne, *P.G.*, XXX, 772 A); Jerome, *adv. Iovin.*, I., 36; Augustine, *de Bono Coniug.*, 8; *de Sancta Virg.*, 4 and 12, etc.

[59] Similarly Methodius, *Symposium*, IX, 4:252.

[60] Ignatius, *Ep. ad Polyc.*, V, 2; Origen, *in I Cor.*, VII, 5 (ed. Jenkins, *J.T.S.*, IX (1908), p. 502).

sinful; but at the time when the sex act is performed the Holy
Spirit will not be given, even if it were a prophet doing the act
of generation. Moreover, there are many other things for which
only human power is required, and for which neither does the
act itself need, nor is it proper for it to have, the presence of the
Holy Spirit."[61] Even Clement implies as much when he observes that after intercourse Christians need no ceremonial
washing such as that prescribed in Leviticus, since they are
cleansed once for all by their baptism for every such occasion
(*Strom.*, III, 82).

The most obvious outcome of this tendency is the demand for
clerical celibacy which becomes prominent in the fourth century. Since the clergy offer the Church's sacrifice, they must
always be free from defilement; therefore they must abstain
from all sexual intercourse. The argument is explicit in Ambrose
of Milan (*de Officiis*, I, 50:258), and the contemporary Pope
Siricius, Bishop of Rome 384–399, did all in his power to enforce the celibate ideal on the same ground. Chastity is required
of "bishops, presbyters, and deacons, who take part in the
divine sacrifices, by whose hands both the grace of baptism is
given and the body of Christ made."[62] Paul, according to
Siricius, teaches in I Cor. 7:5 that the laity must be continent if
their prayers are to be heard—"How much more ought a priest
to be ready at any moment, without anxiety whether he is pure
and clean, in case he should either offer the sacrifice (of the
eucharist) or be compelled to give baptism? If he should be con-
taminated by carnal desire, what is he to do? Is he to excuse
himself?"[63] The movement furthered with enthusiasm by Ambrose and Siricius was in full accord with the ascetic ideals of
the age. Although the laity continued to express their preference
for married clergy, it was explained that they did not know
what was good for them.[64]

The third and seventh books of Clement's *Miscellanies* are
documents of the first importance for understanding the origins
of Christian asceticism. The tremendous strength of the gnostic
position against which Clement contends lay in its not unjusti-
fied appeal to the world-denying strain in New Testament

[61] Origen, *Hom. in Num.*, VI, 3.
[62] Siricius, *Ep.* 10 *ad Gallos episcopos*, of A.D. 391 (*P.L.*, XIII, 1184 B). Cf.
Jerome, *c. Iovin*, I, 34. For a full account of the development of clerical
celibacy see H. Leclercq's article "Célibat" in *Dict. d'archéol. chrét. et de
liturgie*, II, 2 (1910), cols. 2802–2832.
[63] Siricius, *Ep.* 5 *ad episcopos Africae* (*P.L.*, XIII, 1160).
[64] Jerome, *c. Iovin.*, I, 34.

thought. If redemption is made the focal point of theology at the expense of the doctrine of Creation, this present world can hardly seem other than something from which we must pray to be delivered at an early opportunity. So long as the Gospel remained on Palestinian soil, it was controlled by the tradition of Judaism which was very different from that of the Graeco-Oriental world. Dr. K. E. Kirk has written: "Judaism . . . was too deeply committed to the doctrine of the goodness of all God's creation, and the divine authority for peopling the world and reaping the fruits of the earth, to admit any large element of asceticism or self-mortification into its constitution, even when it thought of the coming Day of the Lord."[65] But when with Paul, a hellenistic Jew of the Dispersion, the Gospel is launched on the hellenistic world, this world-denying strain in the New Testament meets, so to speak, with a resonant sounding-board upon which the gospel of redemption from sin becomes vastly magnified and filled out to be redemption from this material world, the body, and all the ills that flesh is heir to.

The Christian apologists of the second century were well aware that they were addressing a world in which renunciation of marriage was highly regarded. They could point with no little pride to Christian men and women devoted to lifelong chastity.[66] The fact that Christian virgins had such a considerable "sales value" is in itself highly significant. We have the testimony of the medical writer Galen concerning the impression which such remarkable chastity made on his mind. He writes of the Christians as follows: "Their contempt of death is patent to us every day, and likewise their restraint in cohabitation. For they include not only men but also women who refrain from cohabiting all through their lives; and they also number individuals who, in self-discipline and self-control in matters of food and drink, and in their keen pursuit of justice, have attained a pitch not inferior to that of genuine philosophers."[67] The inconveniences and encumbrances of married life are a matter of frequent comment in ancient writers. "From a dislike of its inconveniences the Greeks have made many adverse observations about the birth of children," remarks Clement

[65] *The Vision of God*, p. 61.
[66] Justin, *Apol.*, I, 15:6; Tatian, XXXII, 2; Athenagoras, *Leg.*, XXXIII, 1; Minucius Felix, XXXI, 5; Tertullian, *Apol.*, IX, 19; Eusebius of Caesarea, *Laus Const.*, XVII, 6; Origen, *contra Celsum*, VII, 48.
[67] I quote the translation of R. Walzer, *Galen on Jews and Christians* (1949), p. 15 (see his discussion, pp. 56 ff.).

(*Strom.*, III, 22). The works of Theophrastus and Seneca on marriage, and above all the writings of the third-century Neoplatonist Porphyry, who collected together an enormous amount of material from earlier writers on this theme, illustrate Clement's observation. The Christian writers on asceticism in the fourth century drew heavily on Porphyry, undeterred by the fact that he was the most prominent and dangerous critic of Christianity of his time. Jerome plunders his work *On Abstinence* to refute the claim of Jovinian that virginity was in no degree superior to marriage; he does not dare to make any acknowledgment of his borrowings from such a source.[68] Porphyry also exercised some influence upon the ascetic ideals of Basil the Great.[69] We find frequent occurrence of the argument that if even good pagans practise the ascetic life, the chastity of Christians must at least exceed theirs.[70]

Towards second marriage Clement shares the widespread early Christian feeling that it is best avoided, but with Paul he allows it on the ground that "it is better to marry than to burn." If a man makes use of the concession allowed by the apostle, "he does not commit any sin according to the Old Testament (for it was not forbidden by the Law) but he does not fulfil the heightened perfection of the gospel ethic" (*Strom.*, III, 4 and 82). That second marriage is only tolerable as the lesser of two evils is a very general notion in Christian writers of this period, including the Shepherd of Hermas (*Mand.*, IV, 4), Justin Martyr (*Apol.*, I, 15:5), and Athenagoras, who describes it as "fair-seeming adultery" (*Leg.*, 33:2). The Montanists altogether excommunicated those who contracted second marriages, whether clerical or lay (see Tertullian, *de Monogamia*). But the Church at large took Paul to tolerate, though not to approve, the practice in the case of laymen.[71]

A passage from one of Origen's sermons on St. Luke may illustrate Christian feeling in this matter: "Just as not only fornication but marriage is a disqualification for ecclesiastical

---

[68] E. Bickel, *Diatribe in Senecae Philosophi Fragmenta*, I (Leipzig, 1915), pp. 129–220; P. Courcelle, *Les Lettres grecques en Occident de Macrobe à Cassiodore* (Paris, 1948), pp. 325 ff.

[69] D. Amand, *L'ascèse monastique de saint Basile* (Maredsous, 1949), p. 71 ff.

[70] E.g., Basil of Ancyra, *de Virgin.*, 67 (*P.G.*, XXX, 805 B).

[71] Origen comments in this sense on I Cor. 7:8–12 (*J.T.S.*, IX (1908), p. 504). We may also note that the rigorist Novatianists of the East altogether rejected the twice married (canon 8 of Nicaea), but their Western brethren freely received such people to communion (Socrates, *H.E.*, V, 22:60–61).

office, for neither bishop, nor presbyter, nor deacon, nor widow can be twice married: so also perhaps the twice-married will be expelled from the assembly of the firstborn and of the unspotted members of the Church that has no spot or blemish—not that he will be sent into eternal fire, but he will have no part in the kingdom of God. I remember that when I was expounding the word written to the Corinthians 'The church of God which is at Corinth with all who call upon him,' I said that there is a difference between the Church and those who call upon the name of the Lord. For I think that the once married and the virgin and he who perseveres in continence are of the Church of God. He who is twice married may live a good life and have other virtues, but he is not of the Church, of that number who have neither spot nor blemish nor any such thing; he is rather of the second grade, of those who call on the name of the Lord and are saved in the name of Jesus Christ, but are certainly not crowned by him."[72]

It would be difficult to exaggerate the influence of Clement and Origen upon later Christian ideas of the ascetic life. The Alexandrian spiritual ideals were taken to the Western Church by John Cassian and so passed to Benedict.[73] In the East the line of direct influence proceeds through Origen's enthusiastic admirer and defender, Eusebius of Caesarea,[74] to the group of conservative theologians led by Basil of Ancyra and Eustathius of Sebaste, whose watchword that the Son was "of like essence" with the Father was to play a vital part at a crucial stage of the Arian controversy (A.D. 356–361). The tradition was inherited by Basil the Great, whose organization of monasticism was to prove decisive for the Eastern Church.

The seventh book of the *Stromateis* shows Clement setting forth his ascetic theology at its most impressive. The Christian life is conceived of as a ladder of ascent. The soul progresses from faith to knowledge; by suppression of the unreasoning passions and by works of love it mounts to union with God and the beatific vision. Dominant in Clement's thought is the idea of sanctification. The true "gnostic" advances by a continuous moral progress until, "leaving behind all hindrances and scorn-

---

[72] Origen, *Hom. in Lucam*, XVII.

[73] W. O. Chadwick, *John Cassian* (Cambridge, 1950). The spiritual ideals of Clement and Origen have been studied in two fine books by W. Völker, *Das Vollkommenheitsideal des Origenes* (1931), and *Der wahre Gnostiker nach Clemens Alexandrinus* (1952).

[74] Eusebius summarizes his ideas about marriage in *Demonstratio Evangelica*, I, 8–9.

ing all the distractions of matter, he cleaves the heaven by his wisdom, and having passed through the spiritual entities and every rule and authority, he lays hold of the throne on high, speeding to that alone, which alone he knows" (*Strom.*, VII, 82).

Admittedly Clement sets out his mystical ideal with more than half an eye on his rivals outside the Church. The heretical systems had great attractions for those who wanted to know the details of the heavenly hierarchy, and to learn by heart the passwords and correct amulets which would enable them at death to ascend through the planetary spheres to the supreme God. Clement's language is frequently reminiscent of "gnosticism" of a less orthodox stamp. His anxiety is to go one better than the sects. Accordingly, he describes the perfection of the true, orthodox "gnostic" in such absolute terms that it is hard to feel that he is in close touch with realities.

In the last section of the seventh book (89 ff.) Clement turns to the problem of Christian disunity. The existence of many warring sects raised in an acute form the question of the definition of orthodoxy. The problem of defining authentic Christianity raises questions of perennial interest in the history of the Church. This issue was never more acute than during the second century, when the "gnostic" sects were at their height.

The translation of the third book of the *Miscellanies* has been made from the text of O. Stählin in the Berlin Corpus (1906), and has been revised by comparison with Stählin's translation in the *Bibliothek der Kirchenväter* (2. Reihe, Band xvii, Munich, 1936). The translation of the seventh book is taken from the edition by F. J. A. Hort and Joseph B. Mayor (London, Macmillan, 1902). Mayor's translation has been revised at some places in accordance with the text of Stählin.

On Marriage

Miscellanies, Book III

THE TEXT

CHAPTER I

1. The Valentinians, who hold that the union of man and woman is derived from the divine emanation in heaven above, approve of marriage. The followers of Basilides, on the other hand, say that when the apostles asked whether it was not better not to marry, the Lord replied: "Not all can receive this saying; there are some eunuchs who are so from their birth, others are so of necessity."[1] And their explanation of this saying is roughly as follows: Some men, from their birth, have a natural sense of repulsion from a woman; and those who are naturally so constituted do well not to marry. Those who are eunuchs of necessity are those theatrical ascetics who only control themselves because they have a passion for the limelight. [And those who have suffered accidental castration have become eunuchs of necessity.][2] Those, then, who are eunuchs of necessity have no sound reason for their abstinence from marriage. But those who for the sake of the eternal kingdom have made themselves eunuchs derive this idea, they say, from a wish to avoid the distractions involved in marriage, because they are afraid of having to waste time in providing for the necessities of life.

2. And they say that by the words "it is better to marry than to burn"[3] the apostle means this: "Do not cast your soul into the fire, so that you have to endure night and day and go in fear lest you should fall from continence. For a soul which has to

---

1 Matt. 19:11 f.

2 This sentence may be a scribe's marginal note which has crept into the text. The ground for suspecting it is that, except here, Basilides' exegesis of Matt. 19:12 assumes that in all three instances "eunuch" is used figuratively rather than literally and simply means "celibate."

3 I Cor. 7:9.

concentrate upon endurance has lost hope." In his *Ethics* Isidore says in these very words: "Abstain,[4] then, from a quarrelsome woman[5] lest you are distracted from the grace of God. But when you have rejected the fire of the seed, then pray with an undisturbed conscience. And when your prayer of thanksgiving," he says, "descends to a prayer of request, and your request is not that in future you may do right, but that you may do no wrong, then marry. But perhaps a man is too young or poor or suffers from weak health, and has not the will to marry as the apostle's saying suggests. Such a man should not separate himself from his brother Christian. He should say, I have come into the sanctuary, I can suffer nothing. And if he has a presentiment that he may fall, he may say, Brother, lay your hand on me lest I sin, and he will receive help both spiritually and physically. Let him only wish to accomplish what is right and he will achieve his object.

3. "Sometimes, however, we say with our mouth 'I wish not to sin' while our mind is really inclined towards sin. Such a man does not do what he wishes for fear lest any punishment should be in store for him. Human nature has some wants which are necessary and natural, and others which are only natural. To be clothed is necessary and natural; sexual intercourse is natural but not necessary."[6]

I have quoted these remarks to prove in error those Basilidians who do not live purely, supposing either that they have the power even to commit sin because of their perfection, or indeed that they will be saved by nature even if they sin in this life because they possess an innate election. For the original teachers of their doctrines do not allow one to do the same as they are now doing. They ought not, therefore, to take as a covering cloak the name of Christ and, by living lewder lives than the most uncontrolled heathen, bring blasphemy upon his name. "For such people are false apostles, deceitful workers" as far as the words "whose end shall be like their works."[7]

4. Continence is an ignoring of the body in accordance with the confession of faith in God. For continence is not merely a matter of sexual abstinence, but applies also to the other things for which the soul has an evil desire because it is not satisfied with the necessities of life. There is also a continence of the tongue, of money, of use, and of desire.[8] It does not only teach

---

[4] Adopting Epiphanius' reading.   [5] Cf. Prov. 21:19.
[6] Cf. Epicurus, *frag.* 456, Usener.   [7] II Cor. 11:13, 15.
[8] Cf. Aristotle, *Nicomachean Ethics*, 7:4. *Strom.*, III, 59, below.

us to exercise self-control; it is rather that self-control is granted to us, since it is a divine power and grace.[9] Accordingly I must declare what is the opinion of our people about this subject. Our view is that we welcome as blessed the state of abstinence from marriage in those to whom this has been granted by God. We admire monogamy and the high standing of single marriage, holding that we ought to share suffering with another and "bear one another's burdens,"[10] lest anyone who thinks he stands securely should himself fall.[11] It is of second marriage that the apostle says, If you burn, marry.[12]

Chapter II

5. But the followers of Carpocrates and Epiphanes[13] think that wives should be common property. Through them the worst calumny has become current against the Christian name. This fellow Epiphanes, whose writings I have at hand, was a son of Carpocrates and his mother was named Alexandria. On his father's side he was an Alexandrine, on his mother's a Cephallenian. He lived in all only seventeen years, and at Same in Cephallenia was honoured as a god. There a temple of vast blocks of stone was erected and dedicated to him, with altars, sacred precincts, and a "museum." The Cephallenians gather at the temple every new moon and celebrate with sacrifices the day when Epiphanes became a god as his birthday; they pour libations to him, feast in his honour, and sing his praises. He was educated by his father in the general education and in Platonism, and he was instructed in the knowledge of the Monad, which is the root-origin of the Carpocratians' heresy.[14]

6. This is what he says, then, in the book *Concerning Righteousness*: "The righteousness of God is a kind of universal fairness and equality. There is equality in the heaven which is stretched out in all directions and contains the entire earth in its circle. The night reveals equally all the stars. The light of the sun, which is the cause of the daytime and the father of light, God pours out from above upon the earth in equal measure on all who have

---

[9] Cf. *Strom.*, III, 57, below. That continence is a gift is a common idea in early Christian writers, e.g., I Clement, 38:2; Ignatius, *ad Polyc.*, 5:2; and Augustine's famous prayer (*Conf.*, 10:40) "Grant that which thou commandest, and command what thou wilt. Thou dost command us to be continent." It goes back to Wisdom of Solomon 8:21.

[10] Gal. 6:2.   [11] I Cor. 10:12.

[12] I Cor. 7:9; cf. *Strom.*, III, 82, below.   [13] See Introduction, pp. 24 ff.

[14] Cf. the apocryphal work quoted below, III, 29.

power to see. For all see alike. There is no distinction between
rich and poor, people and governor, stupid and clever, female
and male, free men and slaves. Even the irrational animals are
not accorded any different treatment; but in just the same way
God pours out from above sunlight equally upon all the animals.
He establishes his righteousness to both good and bad by seeing
that none is able to get more than his share and to deprive his
neighbour, so that he has twice the light his neighbour has. The
sun causes food to grow for all living beings alike; the universal
righteousness is given to all equally. In this respect there is no
difference between the entire species of oxen and any individual
oxen, between the species of pigs and particular pigs, between
the species of sheep and particular sheep, and so on with all the
rest. In them the universality of God's fairness is manifest.
Furthermore all plants of whatever sort are sown equally in the
earth. Common nourishment grows for all beasts which feed on
the earth's produce; to all it is alike. It is regulated by no law,
but rather is harmoniously available to all through the gift of
him who gives it and makes it to grow.

7. "And for birth there is no written law (for otherwise it
would have been transcribed). All beings beget and give birth
alike, having received by God's righteousness an innate equality.
The Creator and Father of all with his own righteousness appointed this, just as he gave equally the eye to all to enable them
to see. He did not make a distinction between female and male,
rational and irrational, nor between anything and anything
else at all; rather he shared out sight equally and universally.
It was given to all alike by a single command. As the laws (he
says) could not punish men who were ignorant of them, they
taught men that they were transgressors. But the laws, by pre-
supposing the existence of private property, cut up and destroyed
the universal equality decreed by the divine law." As he does
not understand the words of the apostle where he says "Through
the law I knew sin,"[15] he says that the idea of Mine and Thine
came into existence through the laws so that the earth and
money were no longer put to common use. And so also with
marriage. "For God has made vines for all to use in common,
since they are not protected against sparrows and a thief; and
similarly corn and the other fruits. But the abolition, contrary
to divine law, of community of use and equality begat the thief
of domestic animals and fruits.

8. "God made all things for man to be common property.
                    15 Rom. 7:7.

He brought female to be with male and in the same way united all animals. He thus showed righteousness to be a universal fairness and equality. But those who have been born in this way have denied the universality which is the corollary of their birth and say, 'Let him who has taken one woman keep her,' whereas all alike can have her, just as the other animals do." After this, which is quoted word for word, he again continues in the same spirit as follows: "With a view to the permanence of the race, he has implanted in males a strong and ardent desire which neither law nor custom nor any other restraint is able to destroy. For it is God's decree."

And how can this man still be reckoned among our number when he openly abolishes both law and gospel by these words. The one says: "Thou shalt not commit adultery."[16] The other says: "Everyone who looks lustfully has already committed adultery."[17] The saying in the law, "Thou shalt not covet,"[18] shows that one God is proclaimed by law, prophets, and gospel; for it says: "Thou shalt not covet thy neighbour's wife." But for a Jew the "neighbour" is not a Jew, for he is a brother and has the same spirit. Therefore it remains that "neighbour" means one of another race. But how can he not be a neighbour who is able to share in the same spirit? For Abraham is father not only of the Hebrews, but also of the Gentiles.[19]

9. If the adulteress and he who committed fornication with her are punished with death,[20] clearly the command which says "Thou shalt not covet thy neighbour's wife" speaks of the Gentiles, in order that anyone who, as the law directs, abstains from his neighbour's wife and from his sister may hear clearly from the Lord, "But I say unto you, Thou shalt not lust." The addition of the word "I," however, shows the stricter force of the commandment, and that Carpocrates fights against God, and Epiphanes likewise. The latter in the same notorious book, I mean *Concerning Righteousness*, writes in one passage as follows: "Consequently one must understand the saying 'Thou shalt not covet' as if the lawgiver was making a jest, to which he added the even more comic words 'thy neighbour's goods'. For he himself who gave the desire to sustain the race orders that it is to be suppressed, though he removes it from no other animals. And by the words 'thy neighbour's wife' he says something even more ludicrous, since he forces what should be common property to be treated as a private possession."

[16] Exod. 20:14.   [17] Matt. 5:28.   [18] Exod. 20:17.
[19] Cf. Rom. 4:16 f.; Gen. 17:5.   [20] Cf. Lev. 20:10 Deut. 22:22.

10. These then are the doctrines of the excellent Carpocratians. These, so they say, and certain other enthusiasts for the same wickednesses, gather together for feasts (I would not call their meeting an Agape), men and women together. After they have sated their appetites ("on repletion Cypris, the goddess of love, enters,"[21] as it is said), then they overturn the lamps and so extinguish the light that the shame of their adulterous "righteousness" is hidden, and they have intercourse where they will and with whom they will.[23] After they have practised community of use in this love-feast, they demand by daylight of whatever women they wish that they will be obedient to the law of Carpocrates—it would not be right to say the law of God. Such, I think, is the law that Carpocrates must have given for the copulations of dogs and pigs and goats. He seems to me to have misunderstood the saying of Plato in the *Republic*[24] that the women of all are to be common. Plato means that the unmarried are common for those who wish to ask them, as also the theatre is open to the public for all who wish to see, but that when each one has chosen his wife, then the married woman is no longer common to all.

11. In his book entitled *Magica* Xanthus says: "The Magi think it permissible to have sexual intercourse with mothers and daughters and sisters, and that wives are to be held in common, not by force and in secret, but both parties may agree when one man wishes to marry another's wife."[25] Of these and other similar sects Jude, I think, spoke prophetically in his letter— "In the same way also these dreamers" (for they do not seek to find the truth in the light of day) as far as the words "and their mouth speaks arrogant things."[26]

CHAPTER III

12. If Plato himself and the Pythagoreans, as indeed later also the followers of Marcion,[27] regard birth as something evil

---

[21] Euripides, *frag. inc.*, 895.
[23] Cf. Origen, *contra Celsum*, VI, 40, and note thereon in my translation.
[24] *Rep.*, 457 D, similarly interpreted by Epictetus, 2, 4:8–10. (Cf. also Epictetus, *frag.* 15, Schenkl.)
[25] Xanthus of Lydia, *frag.* 28, Müller (*F.H.G.*, I, p. 43). On his work see J. Bidez and F. Cumont, *Les Mages hellénisés* (1938), I, p. 5 ff.; II, p. 82, n. 1.
[26] Jude 8–16.
[27] Cf. A. von Harnack, *Marcion*² (1924), pp. 273*–277*. For the Marcionite view of marriage cf. Origen, *in I Cor.*, VII, 7:18–20 (*J.T.S.*, IX (1908), pp. 503, 507).

(though the last named was far from thinking that wives were to be held in common), yet by the Marcionites nature is regarded as evil because it was created out of evil matter and by a just Creator. On this ground, that they do not wish to fill the world made by the Creator-God, they decide to abstain from marriage. Thus they are in opposition to their Maker and hasten towards him who is called the good God, but not to the God, as they say, of the other kind. As they wish to leave nothing of their own behind them on this earth, they are continent, not of their own free choice, but from hatred of the Creator, being unwilling to use what he has made. But these folk, who in their blasphemous fight against God have abandoned natural reasoning, and despise the long-suffering and goodness of God, even if they do not wish to marry, use the food made by the Creator and breathe his air; for they are his works and dwell in his world.[28] They say they have received the gospel of the knowledge of the Strange God;[29] yet at least they ought to acknowledge gratitude to the Lord of the world because they receive this gospel on this earth.

13. But we shall give a detailed answer to these people when we discuss the doctrine of First Principles.[30]

The philosophers whom we have mentioned, from whom the Marcionites blasphemously derived their doctrine that birth is evil, on which they then plumed themselves as if it were their own idea, do not hold that it is evil by nature, but only for the soul which has perceived the truth. For they think the soul is divine and has come down here to this world as a place of punishment. In their view souls which have become embodied need to be purified. But this doctrine is not that of the Marcionites, but of those who believe that the souls are enclosed in bodies and change from this prison and undergo transmigration. There will be an opportunity to reply to these when we come to speak about the soul.[31]

14. It is clear that Heraclitus regards birth as something evil when he says: "When men are born they are fain to live and suffer death," or rather go to their rest, "and they leave children

---

[28] Clement adapts a pagan argument against the Christian refusal to worship pagan deities; cf. Celsus as quoted by Origen, *contra Celsum*, VIII, 28.
[29] Cf. Celsus in Origen, *contra Celsum*, VI, 53.
[30] Cf. *Strom.*, III, 21; IV, 2, 16; V, 140; VI, 4; *Quis dives*, 26:8. Stählin (introduction to his translation, p. 40) rightly observes that this was not a special work, but an intended section of the *Miscellanies*. The extant books do not contain this section.   [31] Cf. *Strom.*, II, 113; V, 88.

who also suffer death."[32] Empedocles is obviously in agreement
with him when he says:

> "When I saw the place, so strange it was, I wept and
> wailed."

And further:

> "For out of the living he made the dead, changing their
> forms."

And again;

> "O woe, unhappy race of mortals, wretched men!
> Out of what kind of dissensions and groans were you
> born!"[33]

And the Sibyl also says:

> "Mortal men are ye, and fleshly, being nothing,"[34]

like the poet who writes:

> "Earth nurtures nothing weaker than a man."[35]

15. Moreover Theognis shows that birth is evil when he
speaks as follows:

> "For mortals best it is not to be born at all
> And never to see the rays of the bright sun,
> But if born to pass the gates of Hades as soon as possible."[36]

With this agrees also the tragic poet Euripides when he writes:

> "When a man is born we ought to assemble only to bewail
> His lot in coming into so much evil.
> But when one dies and comes to the end of troubles
> Then we should rejoice and praise his happy departure."[37]

And again he says the same in these words:

> "Who knows if life be not in truth but death
> And death be life."[38]

16. Herodotus, it is clear, makes Solon say the same as this:
"O Croesus, every man is a misfortune."[39] And his myth about

---

[32] Heraclitus, *frag.* 20, Diels.   [33] Empedocles, *frags.* 118, 125, 124, Diels.
[34] *Orac. Sib. frag.* 1:1 (=Theophilus of Antioch, *ad Autolycum*, 2:36).
[35] Homer, *Odyssey*, 18:130.   [36] Theognis, 425–427.
[37] Euripides, *Cresphontes, frag.* 449.   [38] Euripides, *Polyidos, frag.* 638.
[39] Herodotus, 1:32.

Cleobis and Biton[40] has obviously no other intention than to disparage birth and praise death. "As scattered leaves, so is mankind," says Homer.[41] And in the *Cratylus* Plato attributes to Orpheus the doctrine that the soul in this body is suffering punishment. This is what he says: "Some say that the body is a tomb of the soul, as being buried in it for the present life. And because the soul expresses (*sēmainei*) by this body whatever it may wish to express, so it is rightly called a tomb (*sēma*). The Orphics, in particular, seem to have given it this name, as they think the soul suffers punishment for its misdeeds."[42]

17. It is also worth mentioning the remark of Philolaus. This Pythagorean speaks as follows: "The ancient theologians and seers testify that the soul is conjoined to the body to suffer certain punishments, and is, as it were, buried in this tomb."[43] And Pindar speaks of the Eleusinian mysteries as follows: "Blessed is he who has seen before he goes under the earth; for he knows the end of life and knows also its divine beginning.[44] Similarly in the *Phaedo* Plato does not hesitate to write as follows: "And these men who established our mysteries . . ." down to the words "and will dwell with the gods." And what when he says, "As long as we have still the body and our soul is involved in such evil, shall we never have sufficient possession of that which we desire?"[45] Does he not hint that birth is the cause of the worst evils? And in the *Phaedo* he bears witness again: "All who have rightly been concerned with philosophy run the risk that other men will fail to notice that their sole object is to pursue death and dying."[46]

18. And in another place: "Accordingly here the soul of the philosopher mostly disregards his body and flees from it, and seeks to be existent by itself."[47] Does he not agree to some extent with the divine apostle when he says, "O wretched man that I am, who shall deliver me from this body of death?"[48] unless he speaks of "body of death" in a figurative sense to refer to the agreement of those who have been enticed into evil. And that sexual intercourse, as the cause of birth, was rejected long before Marcion by Plato is clear from the first book of the *Republic*. For after praising old age he continues: "Mark it well, for me the more the other pleasures of the body fade away, the

---

40 Herodotus 1:31; cf. Plutarch, *Solon*, 27; *Mor.*, 58 E.
41 *Iliad*, 6:146.   42 Plato, *Crat.*, 400 BC.
43 *Frag.* 14, Diels.   44 *Frag.* 137a, Schröder.
45 Plato, *Phaedo*, 69 C; 66 B.   46 *Phaedo*, 64 A.
47 *Ibid.*, 65 CD.   48 Rom. 7:24.

more grow the desires and pleasures of rational enquiry."
And with reference to sex relations: "Be silent, O man, it is with
the greatest joy that I escaped from it—as if I had escaped from
a wild and raging tyrant."[49]

19. Again in the *Phaedo* he disparages birth when he writes of
"the doctrine which is secretly taught about this that we men
are in a sort of prison." And again, "Those who are manifestly
distinguished for their holiness of life are liberated from these
places on earth and are set free as if this earth were a prison, and
go to the pure home above." Nevertheless, although he says
this, he perceives that the administration of this world is good,
and says: "One ought not to set oneself free and run away."[50]
And to sum up briefly, he has given Marcion no opening for his
view that matter is evil, when he himself reverently says of the
world, "All that is good the world has received from him who
has composed it; but from its previous state arise all the recal-
citrant and unjust things in the heaven and from this it derives
these elements and causes them in living beings."

20. With even greater clarity he adds: "The cause of these
things was the material element in the world's constitution,
which was at one time bound up with its ancient nature. For
before it came into its present ordered state it was in a condition
of great chaos."[51] To the same effect in the *Laws* he laments the
race of men saying: "The gods had mercy on mankind which
was born for trouble, and to give them rest from their labours
appointed the changing cycle of feasts."[52] And in the *Epinomis*
he discusses the causes of this pitiful condition and says this:
"From the beginning birth was difficult for every human being;
first to get to the state of being an embryo, then to be born, and
then to be nourished and educated, all this is attended by countless pains, as we all agree."[53]

21. What then? Does not Heraclitus call birth death, just as
Pythagoras and Socrates in the *Gorgias*,[54] when he says: "Death
is what we see when we are awake; and what we see in our sleep
is a dream."[55]

But enough of this. When we discuss First Principles[56] we
shall consider the difference between the views of the philosophers and those of the Marcionites. But I think I have shown
clearly enough that Marcion took from Plato the starting-point

[49] *Rep.*, 328 D, 329 C.
[50] *Phaedo*, 62 B, 114 BC.
[51] Plato, *Polit.*, 273 BC.
[52] *Laws*, 653 CD.
[53] *Epinomis*, 973 D.
[54] Plato, *Gorg.*, 492 E.
[55] Heraclitus, *frag.* 21, Diels.
[56] Cf. *Strom.*, III, 13, above.

A.C.—4

of his "strange"[57] doctrines, without either grateful acknowledgment or understanding.

22. Now we may continue our discussion about continence. We were saying that from a dislike of its inconveniences the Greeks have made many adverse observations about the birth of children, and that the Marcionites have interpreted them in a godless sense and are ungrateful to their Creator. For the tragedy says:

> "For mortals it is better not to be born than to be born;
> Children I bring to birth with bitter pains;
> And then when I have borne them they lack under-
>   standing.
> In vain I groan, that I must look on wicked offspring
> While I lose the good. If the good survive,
> My wretched heart is melted by alarm.
> What is this goodness then? Is it not enough
> That I should care for one alone
> And bear the pain for this one soul?"[58]

And further to the same effect

> "So now I think and have long so thought
> Man ought never children to beget,
> Seeing into what agonies we are born."[59]

But in the following verses he clearly attributes the cause of evil to the primal origins, when he speaks as follows:

"O thou who art born for misfortune and disaster, thou art born a man, and thine unhappy life thou didst receive from the place where the air of heaven, which gives breath to mortals, first began to give food for all. Complain not of thy mortal state, thou who art mortal."[60]

23. Again he puts the same idea in these words:

> "No mortal is content and happy
> Nor is any born free from sorrow."[61]

---

[57] Marcion's good God was called by him the "Stranger."
[58] Euripides, *frag. inc.*, 908.
[59] *Tragicorum Graecorum Fragmenta*, ed. Nauck, *Adesp.*, 111.
[60] *Ibid.*, *Adesp.*, 112 (probably Euripides).
[61] Euripides, *Iphigeneia in Aulis*, 161–163.

And then again:

> "Alas, alas, how many are the chances of mortal calamity!
> How many forms it takes! None can tell the end."[62]

And further likewise:

> "Of what is mortal there is nothing which is happy without end."[63]

24. It is asserted that on this ground the Pythagoreans exercised abstinence. But to me, on the contrary, it seems that they marry for the sake of procreating children, but after they have begotten children they desire to control sexual indulgence. That is why they give the mysterious command to abstain from beans, not because pulse leads to flatulence and is indigestible and causes troubled dreams,[64] nor because the bean is shaped like a man's head; as the verse has it, "It is alike to eat beans and the head of one's parents."[65] The real reason is that if beans are eaten they make women barren. At any rate Theophrastus in the fifth book of his *Causes of Plants*[66] relates that if the pods of beans are put round the roots of newly planted trees the shoots dry up and that if birds that live round houses are continuously fed on beans they become unable to lay eggs.

CHAPTER IV

25. Of the heretics we mentioned Marcion of Pontus as forbidding the use of this world's goods on the ground of opposition to the Creator. The Creator himself is thus the reason for his continence, if this can be called continence; for this giant who thinks he can resist God is not continent by an act of free choice, in that he attacks the creation and the process by which man is formed. If they quote the Lord's words to Philip, "Let the dead bury their dead, but do thou follow me,"[67] they ought to consider that Philip's flesh is also formed in the same way; his body is not a polluted corpse. How then could he have a body of flesh which is not a corpse? Because he rose from the tomb

---

[62] Euripides, *Antiope, frag.* 211.   [63] Euripides, *Hiketides*, 269 f.
[64] Cf. Plutarch, *Mor.*, 286 DE.
[65] Cf. Mullach, *Fragmenta Philos. Graec.*, I, 200.
[66] Theophrastus, *de Caus. Plant.*, V, 15:1. Clement draws this section, with the quotation from Theophrastus, from Apollonius, *Mirabilia*, 46.
[67] Matt. 8:22; Luke 9:60 (not ascribed to Philip).

when the Lord killed his passions, and he began to live unto Christ. We also mentioned the blasphemous immorality of Carpocrates. But when we spoke about the saying of Nicolaus[68] we omitted to say this. Nicolaus, they say, had a lovely wife. When after the Saviour's ascension he was accused before the apostles of jealousy, he brought his wife into the concourse and allowed anyone who so desired to marry her. For, they say, this action was appropriate to the saying: "One must abuse the flesh." Those who share his heresy follow both his action and his words simply and without qualification by indulging in the gravest enormity.

26. I am informed, however, that Nicolaus never had relations with any woman other than the wife he married, and that of his children his daughters remained virgins to their old age, and his son remained uncorrupted. In view of this it was an act of suppression of passion when he brought before the apostles the wife on whose account he was jealous. He taught what it meant to "abuse the flesh" by restraining the distracting passions. For, as the Lord commanded,[69] he did not wish to serve two masters, pleasure and God. It is said that Matthias also taught that one should fight the flesh and abuse it, never allowing it to give way to licentious pleasure, so that the soul might grow by faith and knowledge.[70]

27. There are some who call Aphrodite Pandemos[71] [i.e., physical love] a mystical communion. This is an insult to the name of communion. To do something wrong is called an action, just as also to do right is likewise called an action. Similarly communion is good when the word refers to sharing of money and food and clothing. But they have impiously called by the name of communion any common sexual intercourse. The story goes that one of them came to a virgin of our church who had a lovely face and said to her: "Scripture says, 'Give to every one that asks you.'"[72] She, however, not understanding the lascivious intention of the man gave the dignified reply: "On the subject of marriage, talk to my mother." What godlessness! Even the words of the Lord are perverted by these immoral

---

[68] *Strom.*, II, 118.   [69] Matt. 6:24; Luke 16:13.

[70] Evidently from the *Traditions of Matthias* (cf. *Strom.*, VII, 82), a work current among the followers of Basilides (Hippolytus, *Refut.*, VII, 20:1). See M. R. James, *Apocryphal New Testament*, p. 12 f. It appears that a Coptic version of this lost work has been found in the gnostic library discovered recently at Nag-Hammadi. Cf. H. C. Puech, in *Coptic Studies in honor of W. E. Crum* (1950), p. 120.

[71] Plato, *Symposium*, 180 E ff.   [72] Luke 6:30; Matt. 5:42.

fellows, the brethren of lust, a shame not only to philosophy but to all human life, who corrupt the truth, or rather destroy it, as far as they can. These thrice wretched men treat carnal and sexual intercourse as a sacred religious mystery, and think that it will bring them to the kingdom of God.

28. It is to the brothels that this "communion" leads. They can have pigs and goats as their associates. Those who have most to hope from them are the public harlots who shamelessly receive all who want to come to them. "But you have not so learned Christ, if you have heard him and have been taught by him as the truth is in Christ Jesus; put off with the ways of your former life your old man which is corrupted by the deceitful lusts. Be renewed in the spirit of your mind and put on the new man which after God is created in righteousness and true holiness," so as to be made like unto God. "Be therefore imitators of God, as dear children, and walk in love as Christ also loved us and gave himself for us as an offering and sacrifice to God for a sweet smelling savour. But fornication and all impurity and covetousness and shamefulness and foolish talk, let them not be mentioned among you as is fitting for saints."[73] Moreover, the apostle teaches us to be chaste in speech when he writes, "Know this well that no fornicator . . ." and so on as far as the words "but rather expose them."[74]

29. They derived their doctrines from an apocryphal work.[75] I will quote the text which is the mother of their licentiousness. And whether they themselves, I mean the authors of the book, are responsible (see their madness, for by their licence they do grievous wrong to God) or whether they derived their ideas from some others whom they fell in with, they have taken a sound doctrine and perversely misapplied it. The passage reads as follows: "All things were one; but as it seemed good to its unity not to be alone, an idea came forth from it, and it had intercourse with it and made the beloved. In consequence of this there came forth from him an idea with which he had intercourse and made powers which cannot be seen or heard . . ." down to the words "each by her own name."

If these people spoke of acts of spiritual union like the Valentinians,[76] perhaps one could accept their view. But to suppose that the holy prophets spoke of carnal and wanton intercourse is the way of a man who has renounced salvation.

[73] Eph. 4:20–24. [74] Eph. 5:1–4, 5–11.
[75] The work is lost except for this quotation.
[76] See Introduction, p. 31.

30. These are also the doctrines of the adherents of Prodicus,[77] who falsely entitle themselves gnostics, asserting that they are by nature sons of the first God. But they misuse their noble birth and freedom and life as they desire. And their desire is for pleasure, thinking that no one is superior to them, as they are lords of the sabbath and are royal sons far above the rest of mankind. To a king, they say, there is no law prescribed. But in the first place they cannot do all they desire since there is much to prevent them, however much they desire and essay to do it. And even what they can do, they do not like kings, but like cringing slaves. For it is only in secret that they commit adultery, as they are scared of being caught. They want to avoid condemnation and are afraid of punishment. What freedom is there in their licence and filthy talk? "Everyone who sins is a slave,"[78] says the apostle.

31. The Lord has said: "But I say unto you, you shall not lust."[79] How then can he live according to God's will who surrenders himself to every desire? And is a man to decide of his own free will that he can sin, and lay it down as a principle that one may commit adultery and revel in sin and break up other men's marriages, when we even take pity on others if they fall into sin against their will? And if they regard the world into which they have come as an alien country they will not possess the truth if they have not been faithful in that which is another's.[80] Does a foreign visitor insult the citizens and do them injury? Does he not rather behave as a guest[81] and conform to the necessary rules, living without causing offence to the citizens? And how can they say that they alone know God when they do the same things as those who are loathed by the heathen because they do not do what the laws direct, that is, as the wicked and incontinent and covetous and adulterous? They ought to live good lives even while they are dwelling in an alien country, to manifest their truly kingly nature.

32. But because they have chosen to disobey the laws, they make themselves objects of hatred both to human lawgivers and to the law of God. At any rate in Numbers the man who thrust his spear into the fornicator is evidently blessed by God.[82] And John says in his epistle: "If we say that we have fellowship with him and walk in darkness, we lie and do not the truth; but if we walk in the light as he is in the light, we have fellowship with him, and the blood of Jesus his Son cleanses us from sin."[83]

[77] See Introduction, p. 30. [78] John 8:34; cf. Rom. 6:16. [79] Matt. 5:28.
[80] Cf. Luke 16:12. [81] Cf. I Peter 2:11. [82] Num. 25:8. [83] I John 1:6 f.

33. How then are they who do these things superior to
worldly men when they behave like the very worst men of this
world? Those whose actions are alike are in my opinion of like
nature. Those who think they are superior to others by their
nobility of birth ought to be superior to them also in their moral
characters, that they may escape incarceration in the prison.[84]
For indeed as the Lord said: "Except your righteousness exceed
that of the scribes and Pharisees, you shall not enter the kingdom
of God."[85] However, abstinence from food is exemplified in the
book of Daniel.[86] And to sum up in a word, concerning obedience David speaks in the Psalms: "How shall a young man correct his way?" And at once he hears "by keeping thy word with
his whole heart."[87] And Jeremiah says: "Thus saith the Lord,
You shall not walk in the ways of the heathen."[88]

34. Because of this certain other depraved and worthless
fellows have been impelled to assert that man was formed by
various powers, and that down as far as the navel his body
shows the work of godlike craftsmanship, but his lower parts
indicate inferior workmanship.[89] In consequence of the latter
man has a sexual impulse. They fail to observe that the upper
parts also want food and in some men are lustful. And they
contradict Christ when he said to the Pharisees that the same
God made both our outer and our inner man.[90] Moreover, desire is not a bodily thing, though it occurs because of the body.[91]

Certain others, whom we may call *Antitactae* [i.e., opponents],
assert that the God of the universe is our Father by nature, and
all that he has made is good. But one of the beings made by him
sowed tares and so caused the origin of evils. He involved us all
in them and so made us opponents of the Father. Therefore
even we ourselves are set in opposition to him to avenge the
Father, and act contrary to the will of the second. Since, then,
the latter has said, "Thou shalt not commit adultery,"[92] let us,
say they, commit adultery to abolish his commandment.

35. To them we would say: We have been taught to recognize by their works false prophets and all who merely pretend
to the truth.[93] And your works tell against you. How can you
still assert that you adhere to the truth? For either nothing evil

[84] Cf. I Peter 3:19.   [85] Matt. 5:20.   [86] Dan. 1:10.
[87] Ps. 119: 9 f.   [88] Jer. 10:2.
[89] Epiphanius (*Panar. haer.*, 45:2) says this view was held by the Severians.
Even Basil of Ancyra (*de Virginitate*, 7, Migne, *P.G.*, XXX, 684 A) suggests that God made man like a centaur, his upper parts rational, lower
bestial.   [90] Luke 11:40.
[91] Plato, *Phil.*, 35 C.   [92] Ex. 20:14.   [93] Cf. Matt. 7:16.

exists, in which case there is no question of finding fault with him whom you attack as being in opposition to God, and he is not the originator of anything evil (both the fruit and the tree are done away together), or, if wickedness really does exist, let them tell us what they have to say of the commandments given to us about righteousness, self-control, patience, longsuffering, and other such virtues, whether they think them bad or good? If the command is bad which forbids one to do almost all that is disgraceful, then evil must enact laws against itself in order to destroy its own fruit, which is impossible. If it is good, by opposing good commandments they must confess that they are opposing what is right and doing wrong.

36. But the Saviour himself, whom alone they think one should obey, has forbidden hatred and reviling[94] and says: "When you go with your adversary to court, try to achieve a friendly reconciliation with him."[95] Accordingly, they will either refuse to accept Christ's exhortation, in that they are in opposition to the adversary, or they will become his friends and cease to oppose him. What then? Do you not realize, my worthy friends (I speak as if you were present with me) that by conflict with these excellent commandments you fight against your own salvation? You overturn yourselves, not these beneficial instructions. The Lord said, "Let your good works shine out."[96] But you make your licentiousness manifest to all. Besides, if your aim is to destroy the lawgiver's commands, why is it the commands "Thou shalt not commit adultery" and "Thou shalt not corrupt boys,"[97] and all the commandments enjoining purity, which through your incontinence you seek to destroy? Why do you not abolish winter, which he made, and make it summer when it is still midwinter, and make dry land navigable and the sea passable on foot,[98] as the historians say Xerxes the barbarian desired to do?[99]

37. Why do you not oppose all the commandments? For he says, "Increase and multiply."[1] You who are opposed to him ought to abstain from sexual relations altogether. And if he says, "I have given you all things for food and enjoyment,"[2] you ought to enjoy nothing at all. Moreover, he says, "An eye for an eye."[3] You ought not, therefore, to repay opposition with

[94] Cf. Matt. 5:44.   [95] Matt. 5:25.   [96] Matt. 5:16.
[97] Cf. *Didache*, 2:1; *Ep. Barnab.*, 19:4.
[98] II Maccabees 5:21 (of Antiochus Epiphanes).
[99] Herodotus, 7:54.   [1] Gen. 1:28; 9:1.   [2] Gen. 1:29; 9:3.
[3] Ex. 21:24.

opposition. If he tells the thief to restore fourfold,[4] you ought even to give something to the thief. Similarly again, you who oppose the command "Thou shalt love the Lord"[5] ought not to love the God of the universe at all. And if he says, "Thou shalt not make any graven or molten image,"[6] it follows that you ought to bow down to graven images. Are you not blasphemous, therefore, when you oppose, as you say, the Creator, and endeavour to do the same as fornicators and adulterers? Do you not perceive that you make him all the greater whom you regard as weak if what is taking place is what he wishes and not what the good God wills? For, on the contrary, your father, as you call him, is shown to be weak by you yourselves.

38. These folk also collect extracts from the prophets, making a selection and mischievously stringing them together. They interpret in a literal sense sayings intended to be understood allegorically. It is written, they say, "They resisted God and were saved."[7] But they add the "shameless" God, and interpret this saying as if it gave them advice, thinking it will bring them salvation if they resist the Creator. In fact, scripture does not mention the " shameless" God. And if it did, you fools, you should have understood the word "shameless" to refer to him who is called the devil, either because he slanders men, or because he accuses sinners, or because he is an apostate. The people to whom the passage refers were unwilling to be punished for their sins, and they spoke the words quoted in a spirit of complaining and grumbling, on the ground that other nations were not punished when they transgressed, and that on every occasion they alone were humiliated, so that even Jeremiah said, "Why is the way of the ungodly easy?"[8] Similar in sense to this is the saying in Malachi which has been quoted: "They resisted God and were saved." In uttering their oracles the prophets do not only say that they have heard some message from God; it is also evident that they take up phrases in common use among the people and reply to them, as if they were reporting certain questions raised by them. The saying under discussion is an instance of this.

39. Perhaps it is such people that the apostle attacks in the epistle to the Romans when he writes: "And not as we are blasphemously accused and some assert that we say, Let us do evil that good may come, an argument which is rightly condemned."[9] These are they who when reading the Bible pervert

---

[4] Ex. 22:1.   [5] Deut. 6:5.   [6] Deut. 27:15.
[7] Mal. 3:15.   [8] Jer. 12:1.   [9] Rom. 3:8.

the sense to their own desires by their tone of voice, and by changing certain accents and marks of punctuation[10] twist words that are wise and useful to conform to their own lusts. "You who provoke God with your words," says Malachi, "have even said Wherein have we provoked him? In this, that you have said, Anyone who does evil is good in the Lord's sight, and he is well pleased with them; and, Where is the God of righteousness?"[11]

Chapter V

40. It is not our aim to pursue this subject in further detail and to mention further senseless heresies. To put them to shame we should be forced to deal with each one, and to state our objections to each point, which would extend these notes to an unconscionable length. Accordingly we may divide all the heresies into two groups in making answer to them. Either they teach that one ought to live on the principle that it is a matter of indifference whether one does right or wrong, or they set a too ascetic tone and proclaim the necessity of continence on the ground of opinions which are godless and arise from hatred of what God has created. First we may discuss the former group. If it is lawful to live any sort of life one likes, obviously one may live in continence; or if any kind of life has no dangers for the elect, obviously one of virtue and self-control is far less dangerous. If the "lord of the sabbath"[12] has been given the right to pass uncorrected if he lives an immoral life, *a fortiori* there will be no correction for him who behaves decently. "All things are lawful, but all things are not expedient,"[13] says the apostle. If all things are lawful, obviously this includes self-control.

41. Therefore if one who uses his power to live a virtuous life receives praise, then much more worthy of reverence and honour is he who has given us this free and sovereign power and has allowed us to live as we choose, not allowing us to become enslaved and subjected to necessity by our acts of choice and rejection. But if both can have no anxiety, he who chooses incontinence and he who chooses abstinence, yet the honour is not equal. He who indulges his pleasures gratifies his body; but he who is controlled liberates from its passions his soul which is master of the body. And if they tell us that we are called to freedom, only let us not use our freedom as an opportunity for the flesh, as the

10 For the accentuation of the scriptures cf. Epiphanius, *de Mens. et Pond.*, 2.
11 Mal. 2:17.   12 Matt. 12:8. Cf. *Strom.* III, 30 above.   13 I Cor. 6:12; 10:23.

apostle says.[14] If lust is to be gratified and a life of sin regarded as morally neutral, as they say, either we ought to indulge our desires in every direction and, if this is our desire, do the most lascivious and immoral acts, in that we are following our instincts in every way; or we may suppress certain desires and live no longer a life which recognizes no distinction of right and wrong, nor be absolute slaves to our most dishonourable members, the stomach and the private parts, gratifying our carcase for the sake of desire. For desire is nourished and invigorated if it is encouraged in indulgence, just as, on the other hand, it loses strength if it is kept in check.

42. But how is it possible to become like the Lord and have knowledge of God if one is subject to physical pleasures? Every pleasure is the consequence of an appetite, and an appetite is a certain pain and anxiety, caused by need, which requires some object.[15] In my opinion those who choose this kind of life are simply "suffering pain to their shame," as the well-known verse puts it,[16] choosing evil which they bring upon themselves,[17] now and hereafter. If, then, all things were lawful and one need have no fear that because of one's wicked deeds one's hope of salvation would be lost, perhaps they might have some excuse for living this wicked and wretched life. But through the commandments a life of blessedness is shown to us. We must all keep to them without misinterpreting any of the words or neglecting any of our duties, however minute. We must follow where the word leads; and if we depart from it, we must fall into "endless evil."[18] And by following the divine scripture, the path by which believers travel, we are to be made like unto the Lord as far as possible. We must not live as if there were no difference between right and wrong, but, to the best of our power, must purify ourselves from indulgence and lust and take care for our soul which must continually be devoted to the Deity alone. For when it is pure and set free from all evil the mind is somehow capable of receiving the power of God and the divine image is set up in it. "And everyone who has this hope in the Lord purifies himself," says the Scripture, "even as he is pure."[19]

43. To attain the knowledge of God is impossible for those who are still under the control of their passions. Therefore they

[14] Cf. Gal. 5:13.
[15] A traditional dictionary definition; cf. Andronicus, *de affect.*, p. 124, Kreuttner.
[16] Hesiod, *Works and Days*, 211.   [17] Homer, *Odyssey*, 18:73.
[18] Homer, *Odyssey*, 12:118.   [19] I John 3:3.

cannot attain the salvation they hope for as they have not obtained any knowledge of God. He who fails to attain this end is clearly subject to the charge of being ignorant of God, and ignorance of God is shown by a man's manner of life. It is absolutely impossible at the same time to be a man of understanding and not to be ashamed to gratify the body. Nor can the view that pleasure is the supreme Good be reconciled with the view that only the beautiful is good, or that only the Lord is beautiful, and God alone is good and is alone to be loved. "You are circumcised in Christ with a circumcision not done with hands, which consists rather in the putting away of the carnal body, in the circumcision of Christ." "If you then are risen with Christ, seek those things which are above; have in mind higher things, not earthly things. For you are dead, and your life is hid with Christ in God"—but not the fornication which they practise. "Mortify therefore your earthly members, fornication, uncleanness, passion, lust; for on account of these wrath is coming." Let them also therefore "put away anger, wrath, wickedness, blasphemy, filthy talk from their mouth, putting off the old man with its lusts, and putting on the new man which is renewed to possess full knowledge according to the image of him who created it."[20]

44. It is the manner of life which shows up those who know the commandments; for as a man's word is, so is his life. The tree is known by its fruit,[21] not by its blossom and leaves. Knowledge, then, comes from the fruit and from behaviour, not from talk and from blossom. We say that knowledge is not mere talk, but a certain divine knowledge, that light which is kindled in the soul as a result of obedience to the commandments, and which reveals all that is in a state of becoming, enables man to know himself and teaches him to become possessed of God. What the eye is in the body, knowledge is in the mind.[22] Let them not call bondage to pleasure freedom, as if bitterness were sweet. We have learnt to recognize as freedom that which the Lord alone confers on us when he liberates us from lusts and desires and the other passions. "He who says, I know the Lord, and does not keep his commandments, is a liar and the truth is not in him," says John.[23]

---

[20] Col. 2:11; 3:1–3, 5–6, 8–10.   [21] Matt. 7:16.
[22] Cf. Aristotle, *Nicomachean Ethics*, 1:4 (1096b, 29) "As sight is in the body, so mind is in the soul." Cf. Aristotle, *Top.*, 1:18 (108a, 11); Celsus in Origen, *contra Celsum*, VII, 45.
[23] I John 2:4.

CHAPTER VI

45. To those, on the other hand, who under a pious cloak blaspheme by their continence both the creation and the holy Creator, the almighty, only God, and teach that one must reject marriage and begetting of children, and should not bring others in their place to live in this wretched world, nor give any sustenance to death, our reply is as follows. We may first quote the word of the apostle John: "And now are many antichrists come, whence we know that it is the last hour. They went out from us, but they were not of us. For if they had been of us, they would have remained with us."[24] Next we may destroy their case on the ground that they pervert the sense of the books they quote, as follows. When Salome asked the Lord: "How long shall death hold sway?" he answered: "As long as you women bear children."[25] Her words do not imply that this life is evil and the creation bad, and his reply only teaches the ordinary course of nature. For birth is invariably followed by death.[26]

46. The task of the law is to deliver us from a dissolute life and all disorderly ways. Its purpose is to lead us from unrighteousness to righteousness, so that it would have us self-controlled in marriage, in begetting children, and in general behaviour. The Lord is not "come to destroy the law but to fulfil it."[27] "To fulfil" does not imply that it was defective, but that by his coming the prophecies of the law are accomplished, since before the law the demand for right conduct was proclaimed by the Logos to those also who lived good lives. The multitude who know nothing of continence live for the body, not for the spirit. But the body without spirit is "earth and ashes."[28] Now the Lord judges adultery which is only committed in thought.[29] What then? Is it not possible to remain continent even in the married state and not to seek to "put asunder what God has joined together"?[30] For such is the teaching of those who divide the yoke of marriage, by reason of whom the Christian name is blasphemed. If it is the view of these people who themselves owe their existence to sexual relations that such relations are

---

24 I John 2:18 f.
25 Cf. *Strom.*, III, 63 f., 66, 92; *Exc. Theod.*, 67. Clement quotes the Gospel according to the Egyptians, for which cf. M. R. James, *Apocryphal New Testament*, p. 10 f.
26 For this commonplace cf. *Strom.*, III, 64, below, and my note on Origen, *contra Celsum*, III, 43.   27 Matt. 5:17.   28 Gen. 18:27.
29 Matt. 5:28.   30 Matt. 19:6.

impure, must not they be impure? But I hold that even the seed of the sanctified is holy.

47. In us it is not only the spirit which ought to be sanctified, but also our behaviour, manner of life, and our body. What does the apostle Paul mean when he says that the wife is sanctified by the husband and the husband by the wife?[31] And what is the meaning of the Lord's words to those who asked concerning divorce whether it is lawful to put away one's wife as Moses commanded? "Because of the hardness of your hearts," he says, "Moses wrote this; but have you not read that God said to the first man, You two shall be one flesh? Therefore he who divorces his wife except for fornication makes her an adulteress."[32] But "after the resurrection," he says, "they neither marry nor are given in marriage."[33] Moreover, concerning the belly and its food it is written: "Food is for the belly and the belly for food; but God shall destroy both the one and the other."[34] In this saying he attacks those who think they can live like wild pigs and goats, lest they should indulge their physical appetites without restraint.

48. If, as they say, they have already attained the state of resurrection,[35] and on this account reject marriage let them neither eat nor drink. For the apostle says that in the resurrection the belly and food shall be destroyed. Why then do they hunger and thirst and suffer the weaknesses of the flesh and all the other needs which will not affect the man who through Christ has attained to the hoped for resurrection? Furthermore those who worship idols abstain both from food and from sexual intercourse.[36] "But the kingdom of God does not consist in eating and drinking,"[37] he says. And indeed the Magi make a point of abstaining from wine and the meat of animals and from sexual intercourse while they are worshipping angels and daemons.[38] But just as humility consists in meekness and not in treating one's body roughly, so also continence is a virtue of the soul which is not manifest to others, but is in secret.

49. There are some who say outright that marriage is fornication and teach that it was introduced by the devil.[39] They

---

[31] I Cor. 7:14. [32] Matt. 19:3–9. [33] Matt. 22:30.
[34] I Cor. 6:13. [35] Cf. Introduction, p. 34.
[36] Cf. Origen, in I Cor., VII, 5 (Journ. Theol. St., IX (1908), 501–502): "If pagans sometimes abstain from sexual relations for the worship of idols, how much more should you do so who pray to the supreme God!"
[37] Rom. 14:17.
[38] Cf. Porphyry, On Abstinence, IV, 16, copied without acknowledgment by Jerome, c. Jovin., II, 14.
[39] Clement is probably thinking of Tatian; cf. III, 81–82, 89, below.

proudly say that they are imitating the Lord who neither married nor had any possession in this world, boasting that they understand the gospel better than anyone else. The Scripture says to them: "God resists the proud but gives grace to the humble."[40] Further, they do not know the reason why the Lord did not marry. In the first place he had his own bride, the Church; and in the next place he was no ordinary man that he should also be in need of some helpmeet[41] after the flesh. Nor was it necessary for him to beget children since he abides eternally and was born the only Son of God. It is the Lord himself who says: "That which God has joined together, let no man put asunder."[42] And again: "As it was in the days of Noah, they were marrying, and giving in marriage, building and planting, and as it was in the days of Lot, so shall be the coming of the Son of man."[43] And to show that he is not referring to the heathen he adds: "When the Son of man is come, shall he find faith on the earth?"[44] And again: "Woe to those who are with child and are giving suck in those days,"[45] a saying, I admit, to be understood allegorically. The reason why he did not determine "the times which the Father has appointed by his own power"[46] was that the world might continue from generation to generation.

50. Concerning the words, "Not all can receive this saying. There are some eunuchs who were born so, and some who were made eunuchs by men, and some who have made themselves eunuchs for the sake of the kingdom of heaven; let him receive it who can receive it,"[47] they do not realize the context. After his word about divorce some asked him whether, if that is the position in relation to woman, it is better not to marry; and it was then that the Lord said: "Not all can receive this saying, but those to whom it is granted." What the questioners wanted to know was whether, when a man's wife has been condemned for fornication, it is allowable for him to marry another.

It is said, however, that several athletes abstained from sexual intercourse, exercising continence to keep their bodies in training, as Astylos of Croton and Crison of Himera.[48] Even the cithara-player, Amoebeus, though newly married, kept away from his bride.[49] And Aristotle of Cyrene was the only man to disdain the love of Lais when she fell for him.

40 James 4:6; I Peter 5:5.   41 Gen. 2:18.   42 Matt. 19:6.
43 Matt. 24:37-39.   44 Luke 18:8.   45 Matt. 24:19.
46 Acts 1:7.   47 Matt. 19:11 f.
48 Plato, Laws, 840 A, and the scholiast thereon.
49 The same story in Aelian, Nat. Anim., 6:1; Var. Hist., 3:30.

51. As he had sworn to the courtesan that he would take her to his home country if she rendered him some assistance against his antagonists, when she had rendered it, he kept his oath in an amusing manner by painting the closest possible likeness of her and setting it up in Cyrene. The story is told by Istros in his book on *The Peculiarity of Athletic Contests*.[50] Therefore there is nothing meritorious about abstinence from marriage unless it arises from love to God. At any rate the blessed Paul says of those who revile marriage: "In the last times some shall depart from the faith, turning to spirits of error and doctrines inspired by daemons, forbidding to marry and commanding abstinence from food."[51] And again he says: "Let no one disqualify you by demanding self-imposed ascetic practices and severe treatment of the body."[52] And the same writer has this also: "Are you bound to a wife? Do not seek to be separated from her? Are you free from any wife? Do not seek to find one." And again: "Let every man have his own wife lest Satan tempt you."[53]

52. How then? Did not the righteous in ancient times partake of what God made with thanksgiving? Some begat children and lived chastely in the married state. To Elijah the ravens brought bread and meat for food.[54] And Samuel the prophet brought as food for Saul the remnant of the thigh, of which he had already eaten.[55] But whereas they say that they are superior to them in behaviour and conduct, they cannot even be compared with them in their deeds. "He who does not eat," then, "let him not despise him who eats; and he who eats let him not judge him who does not eat; for God has accepted him."[56] Moreover, the Lord says of himself: "John came neither eating nor drinking, and they say, He has a devil. The Son of man came eating and drinking and they say, Behold a gluttonous man and a wine-bibber, a friend of publicans and a sinner."[57]

Or do they also scorn the apostles? Peter and Philip had children, and Philip gave his daughters in marriage.

53. Even Paul did not hesitate in one letter to address his consort.[58] The only reason why he did not take her about with him was that it would have been an inconvenience for his

---

[50] Istros, *frag.* 48, Müller (*F.H.G.*, I, 424). Aelian, *Var. Hist.*, 10:2, tells a similar story of Eubotas.
[51] I Tim. 4:1, 3.   [52] Col. 2:18, 23.   [53] I Cor. 7:27, 2, 5.
[54] I Kings 17:6.   [55] I Sam. 9:24.   [56] Rom. 14:3.
[57] Matt. 11:18 f.
[58] Clement so understands Phil. 4:3: "I beseech thee also, true yokefellow, help these women . . ." (R.V.).

ministry. Accordingly he says in a letter: "Have we not a right to take about with us a wife that is a sister like the other apostles?"[59] But the latter, in accordance with their particular ministry, devoted themselves to preaching without any distraction, and took their wives with them not as women with whom they had marriage relations, but as sisters, that they might be their fellow-ministers in dealing with housewives. It was through them that the Lord's teaching penetrated also the women's quarters without any scandal being aroused. We also know the directions about women deacons which are given by the noble Paul in his second letter to Timothy.[60] Furthermore, the selfsame man cried aloud that "the kingdom of God does not consist in food and drink," not indeed in abstinence from wine and meat, "but in righteousness, peace, and joy in the Holy Spirit."[61] Which of them goes about like Elijah clad in a sheepskin and a leather girdle? Which of them goes about like Isaiah, naked except for a piece of sacking and without shoes? Or clothed merely in a linen loincloth like Jeremiah?[62] Which of them will imitate John's gnostic way of life? The blessed prophets also lived in this manner and were thankful to the Creator.

54. The "righteousness" of Carpocrates, however, and those like him who pursue immoral "communion" is to be refuted by an argument along the following lines. Immediately after the words "Give to him that asks you," he continues: "And do not turn away from him who wishes to borrow."[63] Thus it is this kind of communion which he is teaching, not the immoral kind. How can there be one who asks and receives and borrows unless there is someone who possesses and gives and lends? What, then, is the position when the Lord says, "I was hungry and you fed me, I was thirsty and you gave me drink, I was a stranger and you took me in, naked and you clothed me," after which he adds "inasmuch as you did it to one of these little ones, you did it to me"?[64] And does he not lay down the same principle in the Old Testament? "He who gives to the poor lends to God," and "Do not avoid giving to the needy,"[65] he says.

55. And again: "Let not your almsgiving and faithfulness lapse." And: "Poverty brings a man low, but the hands of the energetic are made rich." And he adds: "Behold the man who has not given his money on usury is accepted." And does he not

---

[59] I Cor. 9:5.   [60] I Tim. 5:9 f.   [61] Rom. 14:17.
[62] I Kings 19:13; II Kings 1:8; Isa. 20:2; Jer. 13:1.
[63] Matt. 5:42; cf. *Strom.*, III, 27, above.
[64] Matt. 25:35 f., 40; cf. *Quis dives*, 13:30.   [65] Prov. 19:17; 3:27.

declare expressly, "A man's wealth is judged to be his soul's ransom"?[66] Just as the world is composed of opposites, of heat and cold, dry and wet, so also is it made up of givers and receivers. Again when he says, "If you would be perfect, sell your possessions and give to the poor,"[67] he convicts the man who boasts that he has kept all the commandments from his youth up. For he had not fulfilled "Thou shalt love thy neighbour as thyself." Only then was he taught by the Lord who wished to make him perfect, to give for love's sake.

56. Accordingly he has not forbidden us to be rich in the right way, but only a wrongful and insatiable grasping of money. For "property gained unlawfully is diminished." "There are some who sow much and gain the more, and those who hoard become impoverished." Of them it is written: "He distributed, he gave to the poor, his righteousness endures for ever."[68] For he who sows and gathers more is the man who by giving away his earthly and temporal goods has obtained a heavenly and eternal prize; the other is he who gives to no one, but vainly "lays up treasure on earth where moth and rust corrupt"; of him it is written: "In gathering money, he has gathered it into a condemned cell."[69] Of his land the Lord says in the gospel that it produced plentifully; then wishing to store the fruits he built larger storehouses, saying to himself in the words dramatically put into his mouth "You have many good things laid up for many years to come, eat, drink, and be merry. You fool," says the Lord, "this night your soul shall be required of you. Whose then shall be the things you have prepared?"[70]

CHAPTER VII

57. The human ideal of continence, I mean that which is set forth by Greek philosophers, teaches that one should fight desire and not be subservient to it so as to bring it to practical effect. But our ideal is not to experience desire at all. Our aim is not that while a man feels desire he should get the better of it, but that he should be continent even respecting desire itself. This chastity cannot be attained in any other way except by God's grace. That was why he said "Ask and it shall be given you."[71] This grace was received even by Moses, though clothed in his needy body, so that for forty days he felt neither thirst nor

66 Prov. 3:3; 10:4; Ps. 15:5; Prov. 13:8.   67 Matt. 19:19–21.
68 Prov. 13:11; 11:24; Ps. 111:9; cf. Clement, *Paedag.*, III, 35:5.
69 Hag. 1:6.   70 Luke 12:16–20.   71 Matt. 7:7; cf. *Strom.*, III, 4.

hunger.[72] Just as it is better to be in good health than for a sick man to talk about health, so to be light is better than to discuss light, and true chastity is better than that taught by the philosophers. Where there is light there is no darkness. But where there is inward desire, even if it goes no further than desire and is quiescent so far as bodily action is concerned, union takes place in thought with the object of desire, although that object is not present.

58. Our general argument concerning marriage, food, and other matters, may proceed to show that we should do nothing from desire. Our will is to be directed only towards that which is necessary. For we are children not of desire but of will.[73] A man who marries for the sake of begetting children must practise continence so that it is not desire he feels for his wife, whom he ought to love, and that he may beget children with a chaste and controlled will. For we have learnt not to "have thought for the flesh to fulfil its desires." We are to "walk honourably as in the way", that is in Christ and in the enlightened conduct of the Lord's way, "not in revelling and drunkenness, not in debauchery and lasciviousness, not in strife and envy."[74]

59. However, one ought to consider continence not merely in relation to one form of it, that is, sexual relations, but in relation to all the other indulgences for which the soul craves when it is ill content with what is necessary and seeks for luxury. It is continence to despise money, softness, property, to hold in small esteem outward appearance, to control one's tongue, to master evil thoughts. In the past certain angels became incontinent and were seized by desire so that they fell from heaven to earth.[75] And Valentine says in the letter to Agathopus:[76] "Jesus endured all things and was continent; it was his endeavour to earn a divine nature; he ate and drank in a manner peculiar to himself, and the food did not pass out of his body. Such was the power of his continence that food was not corrupted within him; for he himself was not subject to the process of corruption." As for ourselves, we set high value on continence which arises from love to the Lord and seeks that which is good for its own sake, sanctifying the temple of the Spirit. It is good if for the sake of the kingdom of heaven a man emasculates himself from all desire, and "purifies his conscience from dead works to serve the living God."[77]

---

[72] Ex. 24:18.   [73] Cf. John 1:13.   [74] Rom. 13:13–14.
[75] Gen. 6:2; cf. Clement, *Paedag.*, III, 14:2; *Strom.*, V, 10:2.
[76] See Introduction, p. 32. Nothing is known of Agathopus.   [77] Heb. 9:14.

60. But those who from a hatred for the flesh ungratefully long to have nothing to do with the marriage union and the eating of reasonable food, are both blockheads and atheists, and exercise an irrational chastity like the other heathen. For example, the Brahmans neither eat animal flesh nor drink wine. But some of them take food every way, as we do, while others do so only on every third day, as Alexander Polyhistor says in his *Indian History*.[78] They despise deaths and reckon life of no account. For they are persuaded that there is a regeneration. The gods[79] they worship are Heracles and Pan. And the Indians who are called Holy Men go naked throughout their entire life. They seek for the truth, and predict the future, and reverence a certain pyramid beneath which, they think, lie the bones of a certain god.[80] Neither the Gymnosophists nor the so-called Holy Men have wives. They think sexual relations are unnatural and contrary to law. For this cause they keep themselves chaste. The Holy Women are also virgins. They observe, it seems, the heavenly bodies and from what they indicate foretell future events.

Chapter VIII

61. Those who hold that for them there is no difference between right and wrong force a few passages of Scripture and think they favour their own immoral opinions. In particular they quote the saying: "Sin shall not have dominion over you; for you are not under the law but under grace," and others of this sort, which there is no reason to add, for I am not proposing to fit out a pirate ship. Let us then briefly put a stop to their argument. The noble apostle himself refutes the charge against him implied in their false exegesis by the words with which he continues after

---

[78] Alexander Polyhistor, *frag.* 95, Müller (*F.H.G.*, III, 236) =*frag.* 18, Jacoby (*Fr. gr. Hist.*, III A (1940), p. 99). On the abstinence of the Brahmans and Samanaeans, cf. Porphyry, *On Abstinence*, IV, 17-18. For their scorn of death cf. *Strom.*, IV, 17, 50.

[79] Read *theous de* with Münzel and Stählin's translation.

[80] The pyramid is obviously the Buddhist *stupa* (for which cf. H. Kern, *Manual of Indian Buddhism* (1896), pp. 91-96). Clement mentions the Buddhists in *Strom.*, I, 71: "Among the Indians there are also adherents of the precepts of Buddha, whom because of his exceeding holiness they have honoured as a god." But his account here seems somewhat confused, since in Buddhism nakedness is regarded with horror; nakedness suggests perhaps a Jainist community. For a recent discussion cf. E. Benz, "Indische Einflüsse auf die frühchristliche Theologie," in *Abhandlungen der Akademie der Wissenschaften und der Literatur, Geistes- und sozialwissenschaftlichen Klasse* (Mainz, 1951), No. 3.

the saying just quoted: "What then? Shall we sin because we are not under the law but under grace? God forbid."[81] In this inspired and prophetic way he at once destroys the device of these licentious sophists.

62. They fail to understand, it seems, that "we must all stand before the judgment seat of Christ that each man may be rewarded for what he has done with his body, whether it is good or bad," that is, in order that a man may receive his reward for what he has done by means of his body. So then, "if any man be in Christ he is a new creation," no longer inclined to sin; "old things are passed away," we have washed off the old life; "behold new things have happened,"[82] there is chastity instead of fornication, continence instead of incontinence; righteousness instead of unrighteousness. "What is there in common between righteousness and lawlessness? Or what fellowship between light and darkness? Or what harmony between Christ and Belial? What community is there between a believer and an unbeliever? What agreement between the temple of God and idols? Having then these promises let us cleanse ourselves from all defilement of flesh and spirit, perfecting holiness in the fear of God."[83]

CHAPTER IX

63. Those who are opposed to God's creation, disparaging it under the fair name of continence, also quote the words to Salome which we mentioned earlier.[84] They are found, I believe, in the Gospel according to the Egyptians. They say that the Saviour himself said "I came to destroy the works of the female," meaning by "female" desire, and by "works" birth and corruption. What then would they say? Has this destruction in fact been accomplished? They could not say so, for the world continues exactly as before. Yet the Lord did not lie. For in truth he did destroy the works of desire, love of money, contentiousness, vanity, mad lust for women, paederasty, gluttony, licentiousness, and similar vices. Their birth is the soul's corruption, since then we are "dead in sins."[85] And this is the incontinence referred to as "female." Birth and the corruption chiefly involved in the creation must necessarily continue until the achievement of complete separation and the restoration of the elect, on whose account even the beings mingled with this world are restored to their proper condition.

[81] Rom. 6:14–15.   [82] II Cor. 5:10, 17.   [83] II Cor. 6:14–16; 7:1.
[84] Cf. *Strom.*, III, 45, above.   [85] Eph. 2:5.

64. It is probably therefore with reference to the consummation that Salome says: "Until when shall men die?" The Scripture uses the word "man" in two senses, the outward man and the soul,[86] and again of him who is being saved and him who is not; and sin is said to be the death of the soul. That is why the Lord gave a cautious answer—"As long as women bear children," that is, as long as the desires are active. "Therefore, as through one man sin entered into the world, and through sin death came to all men, in that all sinned, and death reigned from Adam to Moses,"[87] says the apostle. By natural necessity in the divine plan death follows birth, and the coming together of soul and body is followed by their dissolution.[88] If birth exists for the sake of learning and knowledge, dissolution leads to the final restoration. As woman is regarded as the cause of death because she brings to birth, so also for the same reason she may be called the originator of life.

65. In fact the woman who first began transgression was named "Life"[89] because she became responsible for the succession of those who were born and fell into sin, the mother of righteous and unrighteous alike, since each one of us makes himself either righteous or disobedient. On this account I for my part do not think the apostle was expressing disgust at life in the flesh when he said: "But with all boldness both now and ever Christ shall be magnified in my body, whether by life or by death. For to me to live is Christ and to die is gain. If, however, it is to be life in the flesh, that also means for me fruitful work. I do not know which I prefer. I am constrained on both sides: I have a desire to depart and to be with Christ, which is far better; but to abide in the flesh is more needful for your sakes."[90] Here he showed clearly, I think, that the perfect reason for departing from the body is love for God, and that if one is to be in the flesh one should thankfully remain here for the sake of those who need salvation.

66. But why do they not go on to quote the words after those spoken to Salome, these people who do anything rather than walk according to the truly evangelical rule? For when she says, "I would have done better had I never given birth to a child," suggesting that she might not have been right in giving birth to a child, the Lord replies to her saying: "Eat of every plant, but eat not of that which has bitterness in it." For by this saying also he indicates that whether we are continent or married is a matter

[86] II Cor. 4:16.   [87] Rom. 5:12, 14.   [88] Cf. Plato, *Phaedo*, 67 D.
[89] Gen. 3:20.   [90] Phil. 1:20–24.

for our free choice and that there is no absolute prohibition which would impose continence upon us as a necessity. And he further makes it clear that marriage is co-operation with the work of creation.

67. Therefore a man ought not to think that marriage on rational principles is a sin, supposing that he does not look on the bringing up of children as being bitter (on the contrary to many childlessness is most grievous); but if a man regards the rearing of children as bitter because it distracts him from the things of God on account of the time it takes up, he may yet desire to marry because he does not take easily to a bachelor's life. What he wants to do is not harmful if it is done with self-control; and each one of us is master of his own will in deciding whether to beget children. But I am aware that because of marriage there are some who have kept clear of it and against the principles of holy knowledge have lapsed into hatred of humanity so that the spirit of charity has departed from them. There are others who have become absorbed by marriage and fulfil their desires in the indulgence which the law permits,[91] and, as the prophet says, "have become like beasts."[92]

CHAPTER X

68. But who are the two or three gathered in the name of Christ in whose midst the Lord is?[93] Does he not by the "three" mean husband, wife, and child?[94] For a wife is bound to her husband by God.[95] If, however, a man wishes to be undistracted, and prefers to avoid begetting children because of the business it involves, "let him remain unmarried," says the apostle, "even as I am."[96] They explain that what the Lord meant was this. By the plurality he means the Creator, the God who is the cause of the world's existence; and by the one, the elect, he meant the Saviour who is Son of another God, the good God. But this is not correct. Through his Son, God is with those who are soberly married and have children. By the same mediation the same God is also with the man who exercises continence on rational grounds.

According to another view the three may be passion, desire,

91 The Greek phrase occurs in an Epicurean fragment on papyrus (*P. Oxy.*, 215). 92 Ps. 48:13, 21.
93 Matt. 18:20. 94 Cf. Origen, *Comm. in Matt.*, 14:2.
95 Prov. 19:14. 96 I Cor. 7:8.

and thought;[97] another interpretation makes them flesh, soul, and spirit.[98]

69. Perhaps the triad mentioned refers to the called, and in the second place to the chosen, and in the third place to the race appointed to receive the greatest honour.[99] With them is the power of God watching over all things which is indivisibly divided among them. He, then, who uses the soul's natural powers as is right, desires those things which are appropriate, and hates what is harmful, as the commandments prescribe: "Thou shalt bless him who blesses thee and curse him who curses thee."[1] But when he has risen above these, passion and desire, and in very deed has begun to love the creation of the God and Creator of all things, then he will live a gnostic life, as he has become like the Saviour and has attained to a state of continence no longer maintained with difficulty. He has united knowledge, faith, and love. Thenceforth he is one in his judgment and truly spiritual, wholly incapable of thoughts arising from passion and desire, one who is to be made perfect after the image of the Lord by the artist himself, a perfect man, already worthy to be called a brother to the Lord[2] as well as his friend and son. Thus the "two" and the "three" come together into one and the same thing—a gnostic man.

70. The agreement of many, which is indicated by the number "three," with whom the Lord is present, might also be the one Church, the one man, and the one race. Or could it mean this? The Lord when he gave the law was with the one, that is the Jew. Later when he inspired the prophets and sent Jeremiah to Babylon[3] and, moreover, called believers from the Gentiles by the teaching of the prophets, he brought the two peoples together. And was not the third the one which is made out of the two into a new man[4] in which he walks and dwells, in the Church itself?[5] And the law, the prophets, and also the gospel were brought together in Christ's name into a single knowledge. Accordingly, those who from hatred do not marry or from desire use the flesh as if it were not a matter of right and wrong,[6] are not in the number of the saved with whom the Lord is present.

---

[97] Cf. Clement, *Paedag.*, III, 1:2; *Strom.*, III, 93, below.
[98] I Thess. 5:23, quoted with the same reference by Origen, *Comm. in Matt.*, 14:3.
[99] The angels.
[2] Heb. 2:11.
[4] Eph. 2:15.
[6] Cf. *Strom.*, II, 118; III, 25, 26.
[1] Gen. 12:3; 27:29.
[3] Probably just a mistake.
[5] II Cor. 6:16.

CHAPTER XI

71. The demonstration of these matters being concluded, let us now quote all the Scriptures which oppose these heretical sophists, and show the right rule of continence that is preserved on grounds of reason. The man of understanding will find out the particular Scripture which deals with each individual heresy, and at the right time will quote it to refute those who teach doctrines contrary to the commandments. Right from the beginning the law, as we have already said,[7] lays down the command, "Thou shalt not covet thy neighbour's wife,"[8] long before the Lord's closely similar utterance in the New Testament, where the same idea is expressed in his own mouth: "You have heard that the law commanded, Thou shalt not commit adultery. But I say, Thou shalt not lust."[9] That the law intended husbands to cohabit with their wives with self-control and only for the purpose of begetting children is evident from the prohibition which forbids the unmarried man from having immediate sexual relations with a captive woman.[10] If the man has conceived a desire for her, he is directed to mourn for thirty days while she is to have her hair cut; if after this the desire has not passed off, then they may proceed to beget children, because the appointed period enables the overwhelming impulse to be tested and to become a rational act of will.

72. For this reason you could not point to any place in Scripture where one of the ancients approached a pregnant woman;[11] later, after the child is born and weaned, you might find that marriage relations of husbands and wives were resumed. You will find that Moses' father kept this principle in mind. After Aaron's birth three years passed before Moses was born.[12] Again, the tribe of Levi observed this law of nature given by God, although they were fewer in number than any others which came into the promised land.[13] For a tribe does not easily grow to great numbers if their men have intercourse only within the legal marriage relationship and then wait until the end not only of pregnancy but also of breast-feeding.

73. It was, therefore, reasonable when Moses in his attempt to bring the Jews to continence by degrees, directed that after sexual intercourse they must abstain for three days before they

---

[7] *Strom.*, III, 9.   [8] Ex. 20:17.   [9] Matt. 5:27 f.
[10] Deut. 21:11–13; cf. *Strom.*, II, 88–89.   [11] Cf. *Paedag.*, II, 92.
[12] Ex. 7:7.   [13] Num. 3:39.

heard the divine words.[14] "We are God's temples; as the prophet said, I will dwell among them and walk among them, and I will be their God, and they shall be my people," if our behaviour conforms to the commandments both as individuals and also as a society, as the Church. "Wherefore come out from among them and be separate, saith the Lord, and touch not the unclean thing, and I will receive you and be to you a Father, and you shall be my sons and daughters, saith the Lord Almighty."[15] He prophetically commands us to be separate not from those who are married, as they assert, but from the heathen who are still living in immorality, and also from the heretics we have mentioned, as unclean and godless persons.

74. Hence Paul speaks against people who are like those I have mentioned, saying: "You have then these promises, beloved; let us cleanse ourselves from all defilement of flesh and spirit, perfecting holiness in the fear of God."[16] "For I am jealous for you with a divine jealousy, for I betrothed you to one husband to present a pure virgin to Christ."[17] The Church cannot marry another, having obtained a bridegroom; but each of us individually has the right to marry the woman he wishes according to the law; I mean here first marriage.[18] "I am afraid lest, as the serpent in his craftiness deceived Eve, so also your thoughts may be corrupted from the simplicity which is toward Christ,"[19] said the apostle as a very careful and conscientious teacher.

75. So also the admirable Peter says: "Beloved, I exhort you as strangers and pilgrims, to abstain from carnal lusts, which war against the soul, and conduct yourselves well among the heathen; for this is the will of God that by doing good you should put to silence the activity of foolish men, as free and not using your freedom as a covering for evil, but as God's slaves."[20] Likewise also Paul in the Epistle to the Romans writes: "We who are dead to sin, how shall we any longer live in it? Because our old man is crucified with him, that the body of sin might be destroyed," down to the words, "do not present your members as instruments of unrighteousness to sin."[21]

76. While on this point I think I must not omit mention of the fact that the apostle declares that the same God is the God of the law, the prophets, and the gospel. In the Epistle to the Romans he quotes the gospel saying "Thou shalt not lust" as

[14] Ex. 19:15.   [15] II Cor. 6:16–18.   [16] II Cor. 7:1.
[17] II Cor. 11:2.   [18] Cf. *Strom.*, III, 4; 82.   [19] II Cor. 11:3.
[20] I Peter 2:11 f., 15 f.   [21] Rom. 6:2, 13.

if it were from the law, knowing that it is the one Father who is preached by the law and the prophets. For he says: "What shall we say? Is the law sin? God forbid. I had not known sin except through the law; and I had not known lust unless the law had said, Thou shalt not lust."[22] Even if the heretics who are opposed to the Creator suppose that in the next sentence Paul was speaking against him when he says, "I know that in me, that is in my flesh, there dwells no good thing," yet let them read what precedes and follows this. For before it he says, "But sin which dwells in me," which explains why it was appropriate for him to say, "in my flesh dwells no good thing."[23]

77. In what follows he continues, "But if I do that which I do not wish to do, it is no longer I that do it, but sin which dwells in me," which being at war with the law of God and "of my mind," he says, "makes me captive by the law of sin which is in my members. O wretched man that I am, who shall deliver me from this body of death."[24] And again (for he does not become in the least weary of being helpful) he does not hesitate to add, "For the law of the Spirit has set me free from the law of sin and death," since by his Son "God condemned sin in the flesh that the righteousness of the law might be fulfilled in us who walk not after the flesh but after the Spirit."[25] In addition to this he makes the point still clearer by saying emphatically, "The body is dead because of sin," indicating that if it is not the temple,[26] it is still the tomb of the soul.[27] For when it is dedicated to God, he adds, "the spirit of him who raised Jesus from the dead dwells in you, who shall also make alive your mortal bodies through his Spirit dwelling in you."[28]

78. Again his remarks are directed against libertines when he continues as follows: "The mind of the flesh is death because those who live according to the flesh mind the things of the flesh, and the mind of the flesh is enmity against God. For it is not subject to the law of God. Those who are in the flesh cannot please God," not in the sense in which some teach, but in the sense which we have already explained. Then by contrast to this he says to the Church: "But you are not in the flesh but in the spirit, if the Spirit of God dwells in you. If any man has not Christ's Spirit, he is none of his. But if Christ be in you, the body is dead because of sin, the Spirit is life because of righteousness. So then, brethren, we are under an obligation, not to the flesh

---

22 Rom. 7:7.   23 Rom. 7:17–18.   24 Rom. 7:20, 23 f.
25 Rom. 8:2–4.   26 Cf. I Cor. 3:16; 6:19.
27 Cf. Plato, *Crat.*, 400 BC; cf. *Strom.*, III, 16.   28 Rom. 8:10 f.

to live after the flesh. If you live after the flesh you shall die. But if by the Spirit you mortify the deeds of the body, you shall live. For all who are led by the Spirit of God are sons of God."[29] And against the "nobility of birth" and the "freedom"[30] abominably taught by the heretics who make a boast of their licentiousness, he goes on to say: "You have not received the spirit of bondage that you should again be in fear, but you have received the spirit of sonship by which we cry, Abba, Father."[31] That is, we have received the Spirit for this purpose, that we may know him to whom we pray, the true Father, the only Father of all that is, him who like a father educates us for salvation and destroys fear.

Chapter XII

79. If by agreement marriage relations are suspended for a time to give opportunity for prayer,[32] this teaches continence. He adds the words "by agreement" lest anyone should dissolve his marriage, and the words "for a time" lest a married man, brought to continence by force, should then fall into sin; for if he spares his own wife he may fall into desire for another woman. On this principle he said that the man who thinks he is not behaving properly if he brings up his daughter to be unmarried, does right to give her in marriage.[33] Whether a man becomes a celibate or whether he joins himself in marriage with a woman for the sake of having children, his purpose ought to be to remain unyielding to what is inferior. If he can live a life of intense devotion, he will gain to himself great merit with God,[34] since his continence is both pure and reasonable. But if he goes beyond the rule he has chosen to gain greater glory, there is a danger that he may lose hope.[35] Both celibacy and marriage have their own different forms of service and ministry to the Lord; I have in mind the caring for one's wife and children. For it seems that the particular characteristic of the married state is that it gives the man who desires a perfect marriage an opportunity to take responsibility for everything in the home which he shares with his wife. The apostle says that one should appoint bishops who by their oversight over their own house have learned to be in charge of the whole church.[36] Let each

---

[29] Rom. 8:5–7, 9–10, 12–14.   [30] Cf. *Strom.*, III, 30, above.
[31] Rom. 8:15.   [32] I Cor. 7:5.   [33] I Cor. 7:36.
[34] Cf. Shepherd of Hermas, *Simil.*, V, 3:3 "If you do a good deed outside God's command, you gain for yourself greater glory . . ."
[35] Cf. Basilides in *Strom.*, III, 2, above.   [36] I Tim. 3:4 f.

man therefore fufil his ministry by the work in which he was called,[37] that he may be free[38] in Christ and receive the proper reward of his ministry.

80. Again when speaking about the law he makes use of an illustration saying: "The married woman is by law bound to her husband while he is alive"[39] and the following words. And again: "The wife is bound to her husband so long as he is alive, but if he dies, she is free to marry, only in the Lord. But she is happier in my judgment if she remains as she is."[40] Moreover in the former passage he says, "You are dead to the law," not to marriage, "that you may belong to another who was raised from the dead," as Bride and Church. The Church must be chaste, both from inward thoughts contrary to the truth and from outward tempters, that is the adherents of the sects who would persuade her to commit fornication against her one husband, Almighty God, lest as the serpent deceived Eve,[41] who is called Life, [42] we too should be led to transgress the commandments by the lewd craftiness of the sects. The second passage teaches single marriage. One should not suppose, as some have expounded the text, that when Paul says the wife is bound to her husband he means that flesh is involved in corruption.[43] He is attacking the notion of the godless men who attribute the invention of marriage directly to the devil,[44] a notion which dangerously blasphemes the Lawgiver.

81. I believe Tatian the Syrian made bold to teach these doctrines. At any rate he writes these words in his book *On Perfection According to the Saviour*:[45] "While agreement to be continent makes prayer possible,[46] intercourse of corruption destroys it. By the very disparaging way in which he allows it, he forbids it.[47] For although he allowed them to come together again because of Satan and the temptation to incontinence, he indicated that the man who takes advantage of this permission will be serving two masters,[48] God if there is 'agreement,' but,

---

[37] I Cor. 7:24. [38] I Cor. 7:22. [39] Rom. 7:2.
[40] I Cor. 7:39 f. [41] II Cor. 11:3. [42] Gen. 3:20.
[43] Epiphanius (*Panarion*, 46:2 f.) attributes this view to Tatian.
[44] Cf. Strom., III, 49:81.
[45] The title is drawn from Luke 6:40. Rendel Harris, "Tatian: Perfection according to the Saviour," in *Bulletin J. Ryl. Libr.*, VIII, 1 (Jan. 1924), translates an Armenian fragment which he would identify as coming from this work, but his evidence is not cogent. [46] Cf. I Cor. 7:5.
[47] Cf. Tertullian, *ad Uxorem*, I, 3: "Some things are not to be sought after because they are not forbidden even though in a certain sense they are forbidden when other things are valued more highly." [48] Matt. 6:24.

if there is no such agreement, incontinence, fornication, and the devil." This he says in expounding the apostle. But he falsifies the truth in that by means of what is true he tries to prove what is untrue. We too confess that incontinence and fornication are diabolical passions, but the agreement of a controlled marriage occupies a middle position. If the married couple agree to be continent, it helps them to pray; if they agree with reverence to have sexual relations it leads them to beget children. In fact the right time to procreate is said in Scripture to be knowledge[49] since it says: "And Adam knew his wife Eve, and she conceived and bore a son, and they called him by the name of Seth. For God has raised up for me other seed instead of Abel."[50] You see who is the object of the blasphemy of those who abuse sober marriage and attribute birth to the devil? The Scripture here does not speak simply of a God, but of *the* God, indicating the Almighty by the addition of the definite article.

82. The point of the apostle's addition "And then come together again because of Satan" is to stop the husband from ever turning aside after other women. A temporary agreement, although for the moment intercourse is not approved, does not mean that the natural instincts are completely removed. Because of them he again restores the marriage bond, not so that husband and wife may be incontinent and fornicate and do the devil's work, but to prevent them from falling into incontinence, fornication, and the devil. Tatian also separates the old man and the new,[51] but not as we understand it. We agree with him that the law is the old man and the gospel the new, and say the same ourselves, but not in the sense in which he takes it since he would do away with the law as originating from another God. But it is the same man and Lord who makes the old new, by no longer allowing several marriages (for at that time God[52] required it when men had to increase and multiply), and by teaching single marriage for the sake of begetting children and looking after domestic affairs, for which purpose woman was given as a "helpmeet."[53] And if from sympathy the apostle allows a man a second marriage because he cannot control himself and burns with passion,[54] he also does not commit any sin according to the

---

[49] Cf. *Strom.*, III, 94, where Adam's fall consisted in having intercourse before the proper time.

[50] Gen.4:25.   [51] Cf. Rom. 7:2.

[52] Perhaps by a change of text (L. Früchtel in *Würzb. Jahrb.*, II (1947), p. 149) read "for then the time required it . . ."

[53] Gen. 2:18.   [54] Cf. I Cor. 7:9, 36, 39 f.; *Strom.*, III, 4.

Old Testament (for it was not forbidden by the Law), but he does not fulfil the heightened perfection of the gospel ethic. But he gains heavenly glory for himself if he remains as he is,[55] and keeps undefiled the marriage yoke broken by death, and willingly accepts God's purpose for him, by which he has become free from distraction for the service of the Lord.[56] But the providence of God as revealed by the Lord does not order now, as it did in ancient times, that after sexual intercourse a man should wash.[57] For there is no need for the Lord to make believers do this after intercourse since by one Baptism he has washed them clean for every such occasion, as also he has comprehended in one Baptism the many washings of Moses.

83. In ancient times the law directed washing after the emission of the generative seed because it was foretelling our regeneration by speaking of fleshly birth, not because it held human birth to be a defilement. For that which after birth appears as a man is effected by the emission of the seed. It is not frequent intercourse of the parents which produces birth, but the reception of the seed in the womb. In the workshop of nature[58] the seed is transformed into an embryo. How then can marriage be a state only intended for ancient times and an invention of the law, and marriage on Chrisitian principles of a different nature, if we hold that the Old and the New Testaments proclaim the same God? "For what God has joined together no man may ever put asunder"[59] for any good reason; if the Father commanded this, so much the more also will the Son keep it. If the author of the law and the gospel is the same, he never contradicts himself. For there is life in the law in that it is spiritual[60] and is to be gnostically understood. But "we are dead to the law by the body of Christ, that we should belong to another, to him who was raised from the dead" and was prophesied by the law: "that we might bear fruit unto God."[61]

84. Therefore "the law is holy and the commandment holy, righteous, and good."[62] We, then, are dead to the law, that is to sin of which the law makes us aware; the law indicates it, it does not give rise to it; by telling us what we ought to do and prohibiting what we ought not to do, the law shows up the sin which lies underneath "that sin may be manifest."[63] But if marriage according to the law is sin, I do not know how anyone

---

55 Cf. *Strom.*, III, 79. 56 I Cor. 7:35. 57 Lev. 15:18.
58 Cf. *Strom.*, IV, 150: Philo, *de Aetern. Mundi*, 66; *de Sp. Leg.*, 3:109; *Leg. ad G.*, 56. 59 Matt. 19:6. 60 Rom. 7:14.
61 Rom. 7:4. 62 Rom. 7:12. 63 Rom. 7:13.

can say he knows God when he asserts that the command of God is sin. If the law is holy, marriage is holy. This mystery the apostle refers to Christ and the Church.[64] Just as "that which is born of the flesh is flesh, so that which is born of the spirit is spirit"[65] not only in respect of its birth but also of what is acquired by learning. Thus "the children also are holy,"[66] they are well-pleasing to God, in that the Lord's words bring the soul as a bride to God. Fornication and marriage are therefore different things, as far apart as God is from the devil. "And you are dead to the law through the body of Christ so that you might belong to another, to him who was raised from the dead."[67] It is to be understood here that you become closely obedient, since it is also according to the truth of the law that we obey the same Lord whose commands are given to us from a distance.[68]

85. And no doubt of such people it is reasonable when, "the Spirit says expressly that in the last times some shall depart from the faith, giving heed to spirits of error and the teaching inspired by daemons, through hypocritical sophists who are seared in conscience and forbid marriage, and demand abstinence from foods which God created to be eaten with thanksgiving by believers who know the truth. Everything created by God is good, and none is to be rejected but accepted with thanksgiving. For it is sanctified by the Word of God and by prayer."[69] It necessarily follows, then, that it is wrong to forbid marriage and indeed eating meat or drinking wine. For it is written: "It is good to eat no meat and to drink no wine"[70] if it causes offence to do so, and that it is "good to remain as I am."[71] But both he who eats with thanksgiving and he who does not eat, who also offers thanksgiving[72] and has a continent enjoyment, should live in accordance with reason.

86. In general all the epistles of the apostle teach self-control and continence and contain numerous instructions about marriage, begetting children, and domestic life. But they nowhere rule out self-controlled marriage. Rather they preserve the harmony of the law and the gospel and approve both the man who with thanks to God enters upon marriage with sobriety and the man who in accordance with the Lord's will lives as a celibate, even as each individual is called, making his choice without blemish and in perfection. "And the land of Jacob was praised above all other lands," says the prophet, glorifying the vessel of his

[64] Eph. 5:32.	[65] John 3:6.	[66] I Cor. 7:14.
[67] Rom. 7:4.	[68] Cf. Isa. 46:11.	[69] I Tim. 4:1–5.
[70] Rom. 14:21.	[71] I Cor. 7:8.	[72] I Tim. 4:4; Rom. 14:6.

spirit.[73] But a certain man[74] who disparages birth, speaking of it as corrupt and destined for abolition, and does violence to the Scripture, saying that the Lord was referring to procreation in the words that on earth one ought not to "lay up treasure where moth and rust corrupt."[75] And he is not ashamed to add to this the quotation from the prophet: "You all shall wax old like a garment and moth shall eat you."[76] But we do not contradict the Scripture. Our bodies are corruptible and by nature subject to continual change.[77] Perhaps the prophet was foretelling destruction to those whom he was addressing because they were sinners. But the Saviour did not refer to begetting children, but was exhorting those who wished only to possess large wealth and not to help the needy, to share their goods with others.

87. That is why he says: "Work not for the food which perishes, but for that which abides unto eternal life."[78] Similarly they quote the saying: "The children of the age to come neither marry nor are given in marriage."[79] But if anyone thinks carefully about this question concerning the resurrection of the dead and those who asked it, he will find that the Lord is not rejecting marriage, but ridding their minds of the expectation that in the resurrection there will be carnal desire. The phrase "the children of this age" is not meant to make a contrast with the children of some other age, but is equivalent to saying "those who are born in this age," who are children because of birth; they beget and are begotten since without birth no one will come into this life. But this birth, which must expect a corresponding corruption,[80] no longer awaits him who has once departed from this life. "Your father in heaven is one," but he is also father of all men by creation. "Therefore call no man your father on earth,"[81] which is as if he said: Do not reckon him who begat you by fleshly generation to be the cause of your being, but as the one who co-operated in causing your birth, or rather as a subordinate helper to that end.

88. He thus wishes us to turn ourselves again and become as children[82] who have come to know the true Father and are reborn through water by a generation different from birth in the created world. Yes, he says, "the unmarried cares for the things

[73] The source of the quotation is unknown; the entire sentence is cited by Clement from the *Epistle of Barnabas* (11:9).
[74] Schwartz (in his edition of Tatian, p. 49) thinks this is not Tatian.
[75] Matt. 6:19.   [76] Isa. 50:9.   [77] Cf. *Harv. Theol. Rev.*, XLI (1948), p. 87.
[78] John 6:27.   [79] Luke 20:35.
[80] A philosophical commonplace; cf. *Strom.*, III, 45, 64, above.
[81] Matt. 23:9.   [82] Matt. 18:3.

of the Lord, but he who is married how he can please his wife."[83] What then? Is it not lawful also for those who wish to please their wives according to the will of God to give thanks to God? Is it not allowable for both the married man and his wife to care for things of the Lord together? But just as "the unmarried woman cares for the things of the Lord, that she may be holy both in body and spirit,"[84] so also the married woman cares in the Lord for the things of her husband and the things of the Lord, the one as a wife, the other as a virgin. But to put to shame and to discourage those inclined to contract a second marriage the apostle appropriately uses strong language and says at once: "Every other sin is external to the body, but he who commits fornication sins against his own body."[85]

89. But if anyone dares to call marriage fornication, he again falls into blasphemy against the law and the Lord. For as covetousness is called fornication because it is opposed to contentment with what one possesses, and as idolatry is an abandonment of the one God to embrace many gods, so fornication is apostasy from single marriage to several. For, as we have remarked, the apostle uses the words fornication and adultery in three senses.[86] On this matter the prophet says: "You were sold to your sins." And again: "You were defiled in a foreign land."[87] Here he regards as defilement an association which is bound up with a strange body and not with that which in marriage is bestowed for the purpose of procreation. That is why the apostle also says: "I wish then that the younger women marry, bear children, look after their houses, and give the adversary no occasion for abuse; for some have already turned aside after Satan."[88]

90. And indeed he entirely approves of the man who is husband of one wife, whether he be presbyter, deacon, or layman, if he conducts his marriage unblameably.[89] "For he shall be saved by child-bearing."[90] Again when the Saviour calls the Jews "a wicked and adulterous generation"[91] he teaches that they did not know the law as the law intended; by following the tradition of the elders and the commandments of men,[92] they were committing adultery against the law, as they did not accept "the husband and lord of their virginity."[93] But perhaps he also knew that they were enslaved by alien desires, on account of

---

[83] I Cor. 7:32 f. [84] I Cor. 7:34. [85] I Cor. 6:18.
[86] Cf. Strom., VII, 75, below. [87] Isa. 50:1; Baruch 3:10.
[88] I Tim. 5:14 f. [89] I Tim. 3:2, 12; Titus 1:6.
[90] I Tim. 2:15. [91] Matt. 12:39. [92] Matt. 15:2, 9. [93] Jer. 3:4.

which they were in continual bondage to their sins and were sold to foreigners, since among the Jews at least no public harlots existed and adultery was forbidden. But he who said, "I have married a wife and therefore I cannot come"[94] to the divine supper was an example to convict those who for pleasure's sake were abandoning the divine command; for if this saying is taken otherwise, neither the righteous before the coming of Christ nor those who have married since his coming, even if they be apostles, will be saved. And if they again bring forward the point that the prophet also said, "I have become old among all my enemies,"[95] by "enemies" they ought to understand sins. It is not marriage that is a sin but fornication, since otherwise they must say that birth and the creation of birth are sinful.

CHAPTER XIII

91. Such are the arguments of Julius Cassianus,[96] the originator of docetism. At any rate in his book *Concerning Continence and Celibacy* he says these words: "And let no one say that because we have these parts, that the female body is shaped this way and the male that way, the one to receive, the other to give seed, sexual intercourse is allowed by God. For if this arrangement had been made by God, to whom we seek to attain, he would not have pronounced eunuchs blessed; nor would the prophet have said that they are 'not an unfruitful tree,'[97] using the tree as an illustration of the man who chooses to emasculate himself of any such notion."

92. And striving still further to support his godless opinion he adds: "Could not one rightly find fault with the Saviour if he was responsible for our formation and then delivered us from error and from this use of the generative organs?" In this respect his teaching is the same as Tatian's. But he departed from the school of Valentine. On this account he says: "When Salome asked when she would know the answer to her questions, the Lord said, When you trample on the robe of shame, and when the two shall be one, and the male with the female, and there is neither male nor female."[98]

93. In the first place we have not got the saying in the four Gospels that have been handed down to us, but in the Gospel according to the Egyptians. Secondly Cassian seems to me not to know that it refers to wrath in speaking of the male impulse

94 Luke 14:20.   95 Ps. 6:7.   96 See Introduction, p. 23,
97 Isa. 56:3.   98 Cf. II *Clement*, XII, 2; *Strom.*, III, 45, above.

and to desire in speaking of the female. When these operate, there follow repentance and shame. But when a man gives in neither to wrath nor to desire, both of which increase in consequence of evil habit and unbringing so as to cloud and obscure rational thought,[99] but puts off from him the darkness they cause with penitence and shame, uniting spirit and soul in obedience to the Word, then, as Paul also says, "there is among you neither male nor female."[1] For the soul leaves this physical form in which male and female are distinguished, and being neither the one nor the other changes to unity.[2] But this worthy fellow thinks in Platonic fashion that the soul is of divine origin and, having become female by desire, has come down here from above to birth and corruption.[3]

CHAPTER XIV

94. He then does violence to Paul, making him hold that birth originated from deceit because he says: "I am afraid lest, as the serpent deceived Eve, your thoughts should be corrupted from the simplicity which is towards Christ."[4] But the Lord, as all agree, came to that which was astray,[5] but it had not strayed from above into earthly birth (for birth is created and the creation of the Almighty who would never bring the soul down from what is good to what is bad). The Saviour came to men who were astray in their thoughts, to us whose minds were corrupted as a result of our disobeying the commandments because we were lovers of pleasure, and perhaps also because the first man of our race did not bide his time, desired the favour of marriage before the proper hour, and fell into sin by not waiting for the time of God's will;[6] "for every one who looks upon a woman to lust after her has already committed adultery with her."[7]

95. It was the same Lord who at that time also condemned the desire which preceded marriage. When, therefore, the apostle says, "Put on the new man which is created after God,"[8] he speaks to us who were formed as we are by the will of the Almighty. In speaking of the old man and the new he is not referring to birth and rebirth respectively, but to manner of life, the one being disobedient, the other obedient. The "coats of

[99] Cf. Plato, *Rep.*, 492 A, 495 A.
[1] Gal. 3:28.   [2] Cf. *Strom.*, III, 69, above.
[3] Cf. *Strom.*, III, 13; IV, 83; Plato, *Phaedo*, 81 C; *Phaedr.*, 248 C.
[4] II Cor. 11:3.   [5] Matt. 18:11.   [6] Cf. *Strom.*, III, 81.
[7] Matt. 5:28.   [8] Eph. 4:24.

skins" in Cassian's view are bodies.[9] That both he and those who teach the same as he does are wrong here we will show later when we undertake an explanation of the birth of man after the necessary preliminary discussion. He further says: "The subjects of earthly kings both beget and are born, 'but our citizenship is in heaven, from whence also we look for the Saviour.'"[10] That this remark also is right we recognize, since we ought to behave as strangers and pilgrims, if married as though we were not married, if possessing wealth as though we did not possess it, if procreating children as giving birth to mortals, as those who are ready to abandon their property, as men who would even live without a wife if need be, as people who are not passionately attached to the created world, but use it with all gratitude and with a sense of exaltation beyond it.

CHAPTER XV

96. And again when the apostle says, "It is good for a man not to touch a woman; but because of the risk of immorality let each man have his own wife," he explains it, as it were, by the further words "lest Satan tempt you."[11] In the phrase "because of incontinence"[12] he speaks not to those who chastely use marriage for procreation alone, but to those who were desiring to go beyond procreation, lest the adversary should raise a stormy blast and arouse desire for alien pleasures. But perhaps because Satan is zealously hostile to those who live rightly and contends against them, and wishes to bring them over to his own side, he aims to give them occasions for falling by making it difficult for them to be continent.

97. Accordingly the apostle rightly says, "It is better to marry than to burn,"[13] that the husband may give to the wife her due and the wife to the husband, and that they should not deprive one another of help given by divine providence for the purpose of generation. "But whosoever shall not hate father or mother or wife or children," they quote, "cannot be my disciple."[14] This is not a command to hate one's family. For he says: "Honour

---

[9] Gen. 3:21. Among the gnostics this interpretation of the coats of skins is common; it was also attributed to Origen, who certainly regarded it as a possible interpretation but does not definitely declare himself. Cf. my note on Origen, *contra Celsum*, IV, 40. Philo understood them in this sense (*Leg. Alleg.*, III, 69; *de Post. Caini*, 137) and also Porphyry (*de Abst.*, I, 31, probably following Numenius).   [10] Phil. 3:20.

[11] I Cor. 7:1 f., 5.   [12] I Cor. 7:5.

[13] I Cor. 7:9.   [14] Luke 14:26.

thy father and thy mother that it may be well with thee."[15] But what he means is this: Do not let yourself be led astray by irrational impulses and have nothing to do with the city customs. For a household consists of a family, and cities of households, as Paul also says of those who are absorbed in marriage that they aim to "please the world."[16] Again the Lord says, "Let not the married person seek a divorce, nor the unmarried person marriage,"[17] that is, he who has confessed his intention of being celibate, let him remain unmarried.

98. To both the same Lord gives the corresponding promises by the prophet Isaiah in the following words: "Let not the eunuch say, I am dry wood. To eunuchs the Lord says this, If you keep my sabbaths and do all that I command you, I will give you a place better than sons and daughters."[18] For a eunuch is not justified merely because he is a eunuch, and certainly not because he observes the sabbath, if he does not keep the commandments. And for the married he goes on to say, "My elect shall not labour in vain nor bear children to be accursed; for they are a seed blessed by the Lord."[19] For him who begets children and brings them up and educates them in the Lord, just as for him who begets children by means of the true teaching, a reward is laid up, as also for the elect seed. But others hold that procreation is a curse and do not understand that the Scripture speaks against them. Those who are in truth the Lord's elect neither teach doctrines nor beget children to be accursed, as the sects do.

99. A eunuch, then, does not mean a man who has been castrated, nor even an unmarried man, but a man who is unproductive of truth. Formerly he was "dry wood," but if he obeys the word and observes the sabbaths by abstaining from sins and keeps the commandments, he will be in higher honour that those who are educated in word alone and fail to do what is right. "Little children," says our teacher, "a little while longer I am with you."[20] That is why Paul also instructs the Galatians in these words: "My little children, with whom I travail in birth again until Christ be formed in you."[21] And again he writes to the Corinthians: "For though you may have ten thousand instructors in Christ, yet you have not many fathers. For in Christ I have begotten you through the gospel."[22] On this account a

---

[15] Ex. 20:12.   [16] I Cor. 7:33.
[17] Cf. I Cor. 7:27, 32–36. The quotation may be taken from the Gospel according to the Egyptians.   [18] Isa. 56:3–5.   [19] Isa. 65:23.
[20] John 13:33.   [21] Gal. 4:19.   [22] I Cor. 4:15.

eunuch "shall not enter into God's assembly,"[23] that is, the man who is unproductive and unfruitful both in conduct and in word; but blessed are those who have made themselves eunuchs, free from all sin, for the sake of the kingdom of heaven by their abstinence from the world.[24]

Chapter XVI

100. When Jeremiah says, "Cursed be the day in which I was born, and let it not be longed for," he is not saying simply that birth is accursed, but is in despair at the sins and disobedience of the people. In fact he goes on, "Why was I born to see labour and pain and my days accomplished in shame?"[25] All those who preach the truth are persecuted and in danger because of the disobedience of their hearers. "Why did not my mother's womb become my tomb, that I might not see the distress of Jacob and the toil of the nation of Israel?" says Esdras the prophet.[26] "No one is pure from defilement," says Job, "not even if his life last but one day."[27] Let them tell us how the newly born child could commit fornication, or how that which has done nothing has fallen under the curse of Adam. The only consistent answer for them, it seems, is to say that birth is an evil, not only for the body, but also for the soul for the sake of which the body itself exists. And when David says: "In sin I was born and in unrighteousness my mother conceived me,"[28] he says in prophetic manner that Eve is his mother. For "Eve became the mother of the living."[29] But if he was conceived in sin, yet he was not himself in sin, nor is he himself sin.

101. But on the question whether everyone who turns from sin to faith turns from sinful habits to life as though born of a mother, I may call as witness one of the twelve prophets who said: "Am I to give my firstborn for my impiety, the fruit of my womb for the sin of my soul?"[30] This is not an attack on him who said: "Increase and multiply."[31] Rather he calls the first impulses resulting from birth, by which we do not know God, "impiety." If on this basis anyone maintains that birth is evil, let him also on the same ground hold that it is good, since in it we

[23] Deut. 23:1.
[24] An allusion to a saying ascribed to Jesus, not in the canonical gospels; cf. Oxyrhyncus Logia (P. Oxy., i); Clement, Ecl. Proph., 14:1.
[25] Jer. 20:14. [26] II Esdras 5:35. [27] Job. 14:4 f.
[28] Ps. 51(50):5. [29] Gen. 3:20. [30] Micah 6:7.
[31] Gen. 1:28.

recognize the truth. "Be sober as is right, and sin not; for some have not the knowledge of God,"[32] that is, those who sin. "For we wrestle not against flesh and blood, but against spiritual powers."[33] But "the rulers of darkness" have power to tempt us. That is why concessions are made.[34] Therefore also Paul says: "I buffet my body and bring it into subjection." "For everyone who wishes to take part in a contest is continent in all things" (the words "he is continent in all things" really mean that, though he does not abstain from everything, yet he is self-controlled on such things as he thinks fit). "They do it to obtain a corruptible crown, but we an incorruptible,"[35] if we conquer in the struggle, though there is no crown for us if we do not put up any fight at all. There are also some now who rank the widow higher than the virgin in the matter of continence, on the ground that she scorns pleasure of which she has had experience.[36]

CHAPTER XVII

102. If birth is something evil, let the blasphemers say that the Lord who shared in birth was born in evil, and that the virgin gave birth to him in evil. Woe to these wicked fellows! They blaspheme against the will of God and the mystery of creation in speaking evil of birth. This is the ground upon which Docetism is held by Cassian and by Marcion also, and on which even Valentine indeed teaches that Christ's body was "psychic."[37] They say: Man became like the beasts when he came to practise sexual intercourse. But it is when a man in his passion really wants to go to bed with a strange woman that in truth such a man has become a wild beast. "Wild horses were they become, each man whinnied after his neighbour's wife."[38] And if the serpent took the use of intercourse from the irrational animals and persuaded Adam to agree to have sexual union with Eve, as though the couple first created did not have such union by nature, as some think, this again is blasphemy against the creation. For it makes human nature weaker than that of the brute beasts if in this matter those who were first created by God copied them.

---

[32] I Cor. 15:34.   [33] Eph. 6:12.   [34] Cf. I Cor. 7:6.
[35] I Cor. 9:27, 25.
[36] Cf. *Strom.*, VII, 72, 76. Tertullian, *ad Uxorem*, I, 8. The opposite view is taken by Augustine, *de sancta Virginitate*, 46.
[37] Cf. Introduction, p. 32.
[38] Jer. 5:8.

103. But if nature led them, like the irrational animals, to procreation, yet they were impelled to do it more quickly than was proper because they were still young and had been led away by deceit. Thus God's judgment against them was just, because they did not wait for his will. But birth is holy. By it were made the world, the existences, the natures, the angels, powers, souls, the commandments, the law, the gospel, the knowledge of God. And "all flesh is grass, and all the glory of man as the flower of grass. The grass withers, the flower falls; but the word of the Lord abides"[39] which anoints the soul and unites it with the spirit. Without the body how could the divine plan for us in the Church achieve its end? Surely the Lord himself, the head of the Church,[40] came in the flesh, though without form and beauty,[41] to teach us to look upon the formless and incorporeal nature of the divine Cause. "For a tree of life" says the prophet, "grows by a good desire,"[42] teaching that desires which are in the living Lord are good and pure.

104. Furthermore they wish to maintain that the intercourse of man and wife in marriage, which is called knowledge,[43] is a sin; this sin is referred to as eating of the tree of good and evil, and the phrase "he knew"[44] signifies transgression of the commandment. But if this is so, even knowledge of the truth is eating of the tree of life.[45] It is possible for a sober-minded marriage to partake of that tree. We have already observed that marriage may be used rightly or wrongly;[46] and this is the tree of knowledge, if we do not transgress in marriage. What then? Does not the Saviour who heals the soul also heal the body of its passions? But if the flesh were hostile to the soul, he would not have raised an obstacle to the soul by strengthening with good health the hostile flesh. "This I say, brethren, that flesh and blood cannot inherit the kingdom of God nor corruption incorruption."[47] For sin being corruption cannot have fellowship with incorruption which is righteousness. "Are you so foolish?" he says; "having begun in the Spirit are you now to be made perfect by the flesh."[48]

Chapter XVIII

105. Some, then, as we have shown,[49] have tried to go beyond what is right and the concord that marks salvation which is holy

---

[39] Isa. 40:6–8. [40] Eph. 1:22; 5:23. [41] Isa. 53:2.
[42] Prov. 13:12. [43] Cf. *Strom.*, III, 81. [44] Gen. 2:9.
[45] Gen. 2:9; 3:22. [46] *Strom.*, III, 96. [47] I Cor. 15:50.
[48] Gal. 3:3. [49] *Strom.*, III, 40.

and established. They have blasphemously accepted the ideal of continence for reasons entirely godless. Celibacy may lawfully be chosen according to the sound rule with godly reasons, provided that the person gives thanks for the grace God has granted,[50] and does not hate the creation or reckon married people to be of no account. For the world is created: celibacy is also created. Let both give thanks for their appointed state, if they know to what state they are appointed. But others have kicked over the traces and waxed wanton, having become indeed "wild horses who whinny after their neighbour's wives."[51] They have abandoned themselves to lust without restraint and persuade their neighbours to live licentiously; as wretches they follow the Scripture: "Cast your lot in with us; let us all have a common purse and let our moneybag be one."[52]

106. On account of them the same prophet gives us advice saying: "Go not in the way with them, withdraw thy foot from their steps. For not unjustly are nets spread out to catch birds; for they are guilty of bloodshed and treasure up evil for themselves"[53]—that is, they seek for immorality and teach their neighbours to do the same. According to the prophet they are "fighters struck with their own tails"[54] (*ourai*), to which the Greeks give the name *kerkoi*. Those to whom the prophecy refers might well be lustful, incontinent, men who fight with their tails, children of darkness[55] and wrath, bloodstained suicides and murderers of their neighbours. "Purify out the old leaven, that you may be a new lump,"[56] cries the apostle to us. And again in anger at such people he directs that we should "have no fellowship with any one called a brother if he is a fornicator or covetous man or idolater or reviler or drunkard or robber; with such a man one ought not even to eat."[57] "For I through the law am dead to the law," he says, "that I may live unto God. I am crucified with Christ; it is no longer I that live," meaning that I used to live according to my lusts, "but Christ lives in me," and I am pure and blessed by obeying the commandments; so that whereas at one time I lived in the flesh carnally, "the life which I now live in the flesh I live by faith in the Son of God."[58]

107. "Go into no way of the heathen and enter no city of the Samaritans,"[59] says the Lord, to keep us away from society

50 Cf. I Cor. 7:7.   51 Jer. 5:8.   52 Prov. 1:14.
53 Prov. 1:15–18.   54 The origin of the quotation is unknown.
55 Eph. 2:3.   56 I Cor. 5:7.   57 I Cor. 5:11.
58 Gal. 2:19–20.   59 Matt. 10:5.

contrary to his will. "For the end of the lawless man is evil. And these are the ways of all those who do lawless deeds."[60] "Woe to that man," the Lord says, "it were well for him if he had never been born, than that he should cause one of my little ones to stumble. It were better for him that a millstone were hung about him and he cast into the sea than that he should pervert one of my elect."[61] "For the name of God is blasphemed because of them."[62] Therefore the apostle nobly says, "I wrote to you in my letter to have no company with fornicators," as far as the words "but the body is not for fornication but for the Lord, and the Lord for the body." And to show that he does not regard marriage as fornication he goes on: "Do you not know that he who is joined to a harlot is one body with her?"[63] Or who will assert that before she is married a virgin is a harlot? "And do not deprive one another," he says, "except by agreement for a time," indicating by the word "deprive" the obligation of marriage, procreation, which he has set forth in the preceding passage where he says: "Let the husband give the wife her due and likewise also the wife to the husband."[64]

108. In fulfilling this obligation she is a helpmeet in the house and in Christian faith. And the apostle expresses the same point even more clearly as follows: "To the married I direct, yet not I but the Lord, that the wife be not separated from her husband (and if she is separated, let her remain unmarried or be reconciled to her husband) and that the husband should not leave his wife. But to the rest I say, not the Lord: If any brother . . .," down to the words "but now are they holy."[65] What have they to say to these words, these people who disparage the law and speak as if marriage were only conceded by the law and is not also in accord with the New Testament? What reply to these directions have those who recoil from intercourse and birth? For he also lays down that the bishop who is to rule the Church must be a man who governs his own household well. A household pleasing to the Lord consists of a marriage with one wife.[66]

109. "To the pure," he says, "all things are pure: but to the defiled and unbelieving nothing is pure, but their mind and conscience are polluted."[67] With reference to illicit indulgence he

---

[60] Prov. 1:18 f.
[61] The gospel sayings (Matt. 26: 24; 18:6 f.; Mark 9:42; Luke 17:2) are quoted from I *Clement*, 46:8.   [62] Rom. 2:24.
[63] I Cor. 5:9; 6:13, 16. Cf. *Strom.*, III, 49.   [64] I Cor. 7:5, 3.
[65] I Cor. 7:10–12, 14.   [66] Cf. I Tim. 3:2–4; Titus 1:6; *Strom.*, III, 79, 90.
[67] Titus 1:15.

says: "Make no mistake: neither fornicators nor idolaters nor adulterers nor effeminate men nor homosexuals nor covetous men nor robbers nor drunkards nor revilers nor thieves shall inherit the kingdom of God. And we," who used to indulge in such practices, "have washed ourselves."[68] But they have a purification, with a view to committing this immorality; their baptism means passing from self-control to fornication. They maintain that one should gratify the lusts and passions, teaching that one must turn from sobriety to be incontinent. They set their hope on their private parts.[69] Thus they shut themselves out of God's kingdom and deprive themselves of enrolment as disciples,[70] and under the name of knowledge, falsely so called, they have taken the road to outer darkness.[71] "For the rest, brethren, whatever is true, whatever is holy, whatever is righteous, whatever is pure, whatever is attractive, whatever is well spoken of, whatever is virtuous, and whatever is praiseworthy, think on these things. And whatever you have learnt and received and heard and seen in me, this do. And the God of peace shall be with you."[72]

110. And Peter in his epistle says the same: "So that your faith and hope may be in God, because you have purified your souls in obedience to the truth,"[73] "as obedient children, not behaving after the fashion of the lusts in which in your ignorance you formerly indulged; but as he who has called you is holy, so also must you be holy in all your conduct; as it is written, Be ye holy for I am holy."[74]

But our polemic, though necessary against those who masquerade under the false name of knowledge, has carried us beyond the limit and made our discussion lengthy. Accordingly this is the end of our third miscellany of gnostic notes in accordance with the true philosophy.

---

[68] I Cor. 6:9–11. 　　　[69] Phil. 3:19. 　　　[70] Cf. Rev. 20:12, 15; 21:27.
[71] Cf. Matt. 8:12. 　　　[72] Phil. 4:8 f. 　　　[73] I Peter 1:21 f.
[74] I Peter 1:14–16 (Lev. 11:44; 19:2; 20:7).

On Spiritual Perfection

Miscellanies, Book VII [1]

THE TEXT

CHAPTER I

1. It is now time for us to prove to the Greeks that the gnostic alone is truly devout, so that the philosophers, learning what sort of person the true Christian is, may condemn their own folly for their careless and indiscriminate persecution of the name of Christian, while they irrationally abuse as atheists those who have the knowledge of the true God. And in addressing philosophers I think one should employ ratiocination as more convincing, since they are better trained to understand it from their previous course of instruction, even if they have not yet shown themselves worthy to participate in the power to believe. Of the sayings of the prophets [2] we will make no mention at present, intending hereafter to avail ourselves of the Scriptures on the fitting occasions. For the present we will only give a summary indication of what is declared by them, in the form of a sketch of the Christian religion, in order that we may not break the thread of the discourse by constant references to the Scriptures, especially when addressing those who do not yet understand their phraseology. When we have shown their general purport, the exhibition of the testimonies shall be superadded afterwards on their believing. And if our words seem to some of the uninstructed to be different from the Lord's Scriptures, let them know that it is from the Scriptures that they draw their life and breath, and that it is their object, taking these as their starting-point, to set forth, not their phraseology, but their meaning only. For further elaboration being unseasonable would with good reason seem superfluous, while on the other hand it would be a very careless and unsatisfactory way of

---

1 The translation of Book VII is that of J. B. Mayor, revised.
2 I.e., the Scriptures as a whole (so often in Clement).

treating the subject if we were to omit all consideration of that which is of pressing importance. And blessed indeed are they who search out the testimonies of the Lord: with their whole heart they will seek him.[3] Now they which testify of the Lord are the law and the prophets.[4]

2. It is our business then to prove that the gnostic alone is holy and pious, worshipping the true God as befits him; and the worship which befits God includes both loving God and being loved by him. To the gnostic every kind of pre-eminence seems honourable in proportion to its worth. In the world of sense rulers and parents and elders generally are to be honoured; in matters of teaching, the most ancient philosophy and the earliest prophecy; in the spiritual world, that which is elder in origin, the Son, the beginning and first-fruit of all existing things, himself timeless and without beginning; from whom the gnostic believes that he receives the knowledge of the ultimate cause, the Father of the universe, the earliest and most beneficent of all existences, no longer reported by word of mouth, but worshipped and adored, as is his due, with silent worship and holy awe; who was manifested indeed by the Lord so far as it was possible for the learners to understand, but apprehended by those whom the Lord has elected for knowledge, those, says the apostle, who have their senses exercised.[5]

3. The gnostic therefore pays service to God by his constant self-discipline and by cherishing that which is divine in himself in the way of unremitting charity. For as regards the service of men, part may be classed as meliorative treatment and part as ministrative service. Thus the medicinal art is meliorative of the body and philosophy of the soul; but that which parents receive from children and rulers from subjects is ministrative aid. Similarly in the Church the meliorative service is imaged in the presbyters, the ministrative in the deacons. As both these services are performed by the ministering angels for God in their administration of earthly things, so they are also performed by the gnostic himself, while on the one hand he serves God, and on the other hand sets forth his meliorative philosophy to men, in whatsoever way he may be appointed to instruct them with a view to their improvement. For he alone is truly devout who ministers to God rightly and unblameably in respect to human affairs. For, as the best treatment of plants is that whereby the fruits grow and are gathered in by the science and art of hus-

[3] Ps. 119 (118):2, I Peter 1:10.
[4] John 5:39, Rom. 3:21 (cf. Acts 10:43).   [5] Heb. 5:14.

bandry, supplying to men the benefit derived from the fruits; so the best ingathering which the devoutness of the gnostic can accomplish by means of his art is the appropriation of the fruits of all who have come to believe through him, as one after another becomes possessed of knowledge and is thus brought into the way of salvation. And if by godliness we understand the habit of mind which preserves the fitting attitude towards God,[6] then the godly alone is dear to God. And such would be he who knows what is fitting both in theory and in life, as to how one should live who will one day become god, aye and is even now being made like to God.[7]

4. Thus he is before all things a lover of God. For as he who honours his father is a lover of his father, so he who honours God is a lover of God. Hence too the gnostic faculty seems to me to reveal itself in three achievements: (1) in the knowledge of the facts of the Christian religion, (2) in the accomplishment of whatever the Word enjoins, (3) in the capacity to impart to others after a godly manner the hidden things of truth. How then can he who is convinced that God is almighty, and who has learnt the divine mysteries from his only-begotten Son—how can such an one be an atheist? An atheist is one who does not believe in the existence of God, while we call by the name of superstitious him who fears the demons and who deifies everything down to stocks and stones, having brought into slavery the spirit and the inner man which lives in accordance with reason.

CHAPTER II

5. The first proof that one knows God, after one has put confidence in the Saviour's teaching, is that one in no way does wrong, in the conviction that this befits the knowledge of God. Thus the most excellent thing on earth is the most devout of men, and the most excellent in heaven is the angel, who is nearer in place to the deity and already more purely participant of the eternal and blessed life. But most perfect and most holy of all, most sovereign, most lordly, most royal, and most beneficent, is the nature of the Son, which approaches most closely to the One Almighty Being. The Son is the highest pre-eminence, which sets in order all things according to the Father's will,[8] and steers the universe aright, performing all things with unwearying energy, beholding the Father's secret thoughts through his

6 A Stoic definition.   7 Plato, *Theaet.*, 176 A, B.
8 Matt. 7:21; 12:50; John 6:40.

working. For the Son of God never moves from his watchtower,[9] being never divided, never dissevered, never passing from place to place, but existing everywhere at all times and free from all limitations. He is all reason, all eye, all light from the Father, seeing all things, hearing all things[10] knowing all things, with power searching the powers. To him is subjected the whole army of angels and of gods—to him, the Word of the Father, who has received the holy administration by reason of him who subjected it to him;[11] through whom also all men belong to him, but some by way of knowledge,[12] while others have not yet attained to this; some as friends,[13] some as faithful servants,[14] others as servants merely.

6. This is the Teacher who educates the gnostic by means of mysteries, and the believer by means of good hopes, and him who is hard of heart with corrective discipline acting on the senses. He is the source of Providence both for the individual and the community and for the universe at large. And that there is a Son of God, and that this Son is the Saviour and Lord that we assert him to be, is directly declared by the divine prophecies. Thus the Lord of all, whether Greek or barbarian, uses persuasion to those who are willing; for it is not his way to compel one who is able of himself to obtain salvation by the exercise of free choice and by fulfilling all that is required on his part[15] so as to lay hold on the hope.[16] This is he who bestows on the Greeks also their philosophy through the inferior angels. For by an ancient and divine ordinance angels are assigned to the different nations; but to be the Lord's portion[17] is the glory of the believers. Here we have the following alternatives: either the Lord cares not for all men—which might arise from incapacity (but this it is forbidden to say, for incapacity is a mark of weakness), or from want of will on the part of one possessed with power (but such an affection is incompatible with goodness; in any case he who for our sake took upon him our flesh with its capacity for suffering is not rendered indifferent to others' sorrow by self-indulgence)—or he has regard for us all, which also beseems him who was made the Lord of all. For he is the Saviour not of one here and another there, but, to the extent of each man's fitness, he distributed his own bounty both to Greeks and

---

[9] Plato, *Polit.* 272 E.
[10] Xenophanes ap. Sext. Emp., *adv. Math.*, IX, 144.
[11] Rom. 8:20.   [12] Cf. Rom. 10:2.   [13] John 15:14, 15.
[14] Heb. 3:5.   [15] Plato, *Rep.*, 620 E.   [16] Heb. 6:18.
[17] Deut. 32:8, 9.

to barbarians, and to the faithful and elect,[18] who were fore-ordained out of them and were called[19] in their own season. 7. Neither again could envy be the impelling principle with him, who has called all alike, though he has assigned special honours to those who have shown special faith; nor could the Lord of all be hindered by opposition from without, especially when he is carrying out the will of the good and almighty Father.[20] No, as the Lord himself is absolutely inaccessible to envy, being eternally free from passion, so neither is man's state such as to be envied by the Lord. It is another who envies, who is also acquainted with passion.[21] Nor yet can it be said that the Lord from ignorance did not will to save mankind, because he knew not how to take care of each. For ignorance touches not the Son of God, who was the Father's counsellor[22] before the foundation of the world,[23] the Wisdom in which the Almighty God rejoiced.[24] For the Son is the power of God,[25] as being the original Word of the Father, prior to all created things: and he might justly be styled the Wisdom of God[25] and the Teacher of those who were made by him. Neither indeed could he ever abandon his care for mankind through the distraction of any pleasure, seeing that, after he had taken upon him our flesh, which is by nature subject to passion, he trained it to a habit of impassibility. And how could he be Saviour and Lord, if he were not Saviour and Lord of all—Saviour of those who have believed, because they have determined to know, Lord of those who have been disobedient, until they have been enabled to confess their sins, and have received the grace which comes through him, in the way adapted and corresponding to their state? But all the activity of the Lord is referred to the Almighty, the Son being, so to speak, a certain activity of the Father.

8. The Saviour then could never be a hater of men, seeing that it was owing to his abounding love for man that he scorned not the weakness of human flesh, but having clothed himself with it, has come into the world for the common salvation of men. For faith is common to all who choose it. No, nor could he ever neglect man, his peculiar work, seeing that into man alone of all animals has an idea of God been instilled at his creation. Neither could there be any better government of men, or one more consonant to the divine nature, than that which has been

---

[18] Rev. 17:14. [19] Rev. 17:14. [20] Matt. 7:21; 12:50; John 6:40.
[21] I.e., the devil (cf. Wisdom of Solomon 2:24).
[22] Job 15:8; Isa. 40:13; Rom. 11:34. [23] Eph. 1:4.
[24] Prov. 8:22–30. [25] I Cor. 1:24.

ordained. At any rate it always belongs to him who is naturally superior to direct the inferior, and to him who is able to manage anything well, that he should have received the government of it as his due. But the true Ruler and Director is the Word of God and his Providence, superintending all things and neglecting the charge of none of her household. And such would be they who have chosen to attach themselves to the Word, viz., those who are being perfected through faith. Thus, by the will of the Almight Father,[26] the Son, who is the imperceptible power of primaeval motion,[27] is made the cause of all good things. For he was not seen in his true nature by those who could not apprehend it owing to the infirmity of the flesh, but having taken upon him a body which could be seen and handled, he came into the world to reveal what was possible to man in the way of obedience to God's commandments.

9. Being then the power of the Father, he easily prevails over whomsoever he will, not leaving even the smallest atom of his government uncared for: else the universe of his creation would have been no longer good. And I think the greatest power is shown where there is an inspection of all the parts, proceeding with minute accuracy even to the smallest, while all gaze on[28] the supreme Administrator of the universe, as he pilots all in safety according to the Father's will,[29] rank being subordinated to rank under different leaders, till in the end the great High Priest[30] is reached. For on one original principle, which works in accordance with the Father's will,[29] depend the first and second and third gradations;[31] and then at the extreme end of the visible world there is the blessed ordinance of angels; and so, even down to ourselves, ranks below ranks are appointed, all saving and being saved by the initiation and through the instrumentality of One. As then the remotest particle of iron is drawn by the influence of the magnet extending through a long series of iron rings,[32] so also through the attraction of the Holy Spirit the virtuous are adapted to the highest mansion,[33] and the others in their order even to the last mansion: but they that are wicked from weakness, having fallen into an evil habit owing to unrighteous greed, neither keep hold themselves nor are held by another, but collapse and fall to the ground, being entangled in

[26] Matt. 7:21; 12:50; John 6:40.   [27] Plato, *Leg.*, X, 897 A.
[28] Heb. 12:2.   [29] See above, p. 95.   [30] Heb. 4:14.
[31] Plato, *Epist.*, II, 312 E. For the idea, cf. A. O. Lovejoy, *The Great Chain of Being* (1934).
[32] *Ibid.*, *Ion*, 533 D, E, 535 E, 536 A.   [33] John 14:2.

their passions. For this is the law from the beginning, that he who would have virtue must choose it.

10. Wherefore also both the commandments according to the law and the commandments previous to the law, given to those who were not yet under law[34]—for law is not enacted for a just man[35]—ordained that he who chose should obtain eternal life and a blessed reward, and on the other hand permitted him who delighted in wickedness to consort with what he chose. Again they ordained that the soul that at any time improved as regards the knowledge of virtue and increase in righteousness, should obtain an improved position in the universe, pressing onwards[36] at every step to a passionless state, until it comes to a perfect man,[37] a pre-eminence at once of knowledge and of inheritance. These saving revolutions are each severally portioned off, according to the order of change, by variety of time and place and honour and knowledge and inheritance and service, up to the transcendent orbit which is next to the Lord, occupied in eternal contemplation. And that which is lovely has power to draw to[38] the contemplation of itself every one who through love of knowledge has applied himself wholly to contemplation.

11. Therefore the commandments given by the Lord, both the former and the latter, all flow from one source, for neither did he negligently suffer those who lived before the law to be altogether without law,[39] nor on the other hand did he permit those who were ignorant of the barbarian (i.e., Jewish) philosophy to run wild. For, by giving to the Jews commandments and to the Greeks philosophy, he confined unbelief[40] until the period of his own presence on earth, in which every one who believed not is without excuse.[41] For he leads men by both ways of advance, whether Greek or barbarian, to the perfection which is through faith. But if any of the Greeks dispenses with the preliminary guidance of the Greek philosophy and hastens straight to the true teaching, he, even though he be unlearned, at once distances all competition, having chosen the short-cut to perfection, viz., that of salvation through faith.[42]

12. Accordingly he made all things to be helpful for virtue, in so far as might be without hindering the freedom of man's choice, and showed them to be so, in order that he who is indeed the One Alone Almighty might, even to those who can only see

---

34 I Cor. 9:21.   35 I Tim. 1:9   36 Phil. 3:14.
37 Eph. 4:13.   38 Plato, Rep., 525; Symp., 204 C.
39 I Cor. 9:21.   40 Rom. 11:32; Gal. 3:19–24.
41 Rom. 1:20.   42 Eph. 2:8.

darkly, be in some way revealed as a good God, a Saviour from age to age through the instrumentality of his Son, and in all ways absolutely guiltless of evil.[43] For by the Lord of the universe all things are ordered both generally and particularly with a view to the safety of the whole. It is the work then of saving righteousness always to promote the improvement of each according to the possibilities of the case. For the lesser things also are managed with a view to the safety and continuance of the superior in accordance with their own characters. For instance, whatever is possessed of virtue changes to better habitations, the cause of the change being that independent choice of knowledge with which the soul was gifted to begin with; but those who are more hardened[44] are constrained to repent by necessary chastisements, inflicted either through the agency of the attendant angels or through various preliminary judgments or through the great and final judgment, by the goodness of the great Judge whose eye is ever upon us.

CHAPTER III

13. As to the rest I keep silent,[45] giving glory to God: only I say that those gnostic souls are so carried away by the magnificence of the vision that they cannot confine themselves within the lines of the constitution by which each holy degree is assigned and in accordance with which the blessed abodes of the gods have been marked out and allotted; but being counted as holy among the holy,[46] and translated absolutely and entirely to another sphere, they keep on always moving to higher and yet higher regions, until they no longer greet[47] the divine vision in or by means of mirrors,[48] but for loving hearts feast for ever on the uncloying, never-ending sight, radiant in its transparent clearness, while throughout the endless ages they taste a never-wearying delight, and thus continue, all alike honoured with an identity of pre-eminence. This is the apprehensive vision of the pure in heart.[49] This, therefore, is the life-work of the perfected gnostic, viz., to hold communion with God through the great High Priest,[50] being made like the Lord, as far as may be, by means of all his service towards God, a service which extends to the salvation of men by his solicitous goodness towards us and also by public

43 Plato, *Rep.*, 617 E; *Tim.*, 42 D.   44 Eph. 4:19.
45 Cf. Euripides, *Iphigeneia in Tauris*, 37.   46 Isa. 57:15.
47 Heb. 11:13.   48 I Cor. 13:12.   49 Matt. 5:8.
50 Heb. 4:14.

worship and by teaching and active kindness. Aye, and in being thus assimilated to God,[51] the gnostic is making and fashioning himself and also forming those who hear him, while, so far as may be, he assimilates to that which is by nature free from passion that which has been subdued by training to a passionless state: and this he effects by undisturbed intercourse and communion with the Lord.[52] Of this gnostic assimilation the canons, as it appears to me, are gentleness, kindness and a noble devoutness.

14. These virtues I affirm to be an acceptable sacrifice with God,[53] as the Scripture declares that the unboastful heart joined with a right understanding is a perfect offering to God,[54] since every man who is won over for holiness is enlightened into an indissoluble unity. For both the Gospel and the apostle command us to bring ourselves into capitivity[55] and put ourselves to death,[56] slaying the old man which is being corrupted according to its lusts[57] and raising up the new man[58] from the death of our old perversion, laying aside our passions and becoming free from sin. This it was which was signified also by the law when it commanded that the sinner should be put to death,[59] viz., the change from death to life, that is, the "apathy" which comes from faith. But the expounders of the law, not understanding this, took the law to be jealous, and have thus given a handle to those who without ground endeavour to discredit it.

It is for this reason that we fitly refrain from making any sacrifice to God, who has provided all things for all, being himself in need of nothing; but we glorify him who was consecrated for us, by consecrating ourselves also to ever higher degrees of freedom from want and from passion. For God takes pleasure only in our salvation. Fitly therefore do we abstain from offering sacrifice to him who cannot be swayed by pleasures, bearing in mind also that the smoke of the sacrifice reaches those whom it does reach, i.e., the demons, in some low region far beneath the densest clouds.

15. The Divine Nature then is neither wanting in anything nor is it fond of pleasure or gain or money, being of itself full and affording all things to every creature which is in need. Nor again is the Divine Nature propitiated by sacrifices or offerings or by glory and honour, nor is it allured by such things: it shows itself to the virtuous alone, who would never betray justice either on

---

[51] Plato, *Rep.*, X, 613 B.   [52] I Cor. 7:35.   [53] Phil. 4:18.
[54] Ps. 51(50):16, 17.   [55] II Cor. 10:5.   [56] Matt. 16:25.
[57] Eph. 4:22.   [58] Eph. 4:24.   [59] Deut. 13:8, 9; Ezek. 18:4.

account of threatened terrors or from a promise of greater gifts. Those however who have not observed the freedom of man's spirit and its unfettered action in respect to choice of life, chafe at what is done by unchastened injustice, and disbelieve in the existence of God. Like to them in opinion are they who, from their incontinence in pleasure, being involved both in cross accidents and pains out of the common course, and losing heart at their calamities, say that there is no God, or that, if he exists, he is not the overseer of all. Another class consists of those who are persuaded that the gods of common belief are to be propitiated with sacrifices and gifts, being accomplices, so to speak, in men's own wickednesses, and who are even unwilling to believe that he alone is the true God who is unchangeably the same in his just beneficence.[60]

16. We are justified therefore in ascribing piety to the gnostic, whose care is first for himself and then for his neighbours with a view to our attaining the highest standard of excellence. For so the son tries to please a good father by showing himself virtuous and like his father, and likewise the subject to please a good ruler; since belief and obedience are in our own power. But the cause of evils one might find in the weakness of matter, and the random impulses of ignorance and the irrational forces to which we fall victims from our incapacity to learn; whereas the gnostic gets the better of these wild elements by his learning, and benefits all who are willing, to the best of his power, in imitation of the divine purpose for men. Should he ever be placed in authority, he will rule, like Moses, with a view to the salvation of his subjects, and will quell what is savage and faithless by showing honour to the best, and by punishing the bad, punishment that is rightly classed under the head of education. For above all things, the soul of the just man is an image divine, made like to God himself,[61] seeing that in it is enshrined and consecrated, by means of obedience to his commands, the Ruler of all mortals and immortals, the King and Parent of all that is noble, who is indeed Law and Ordinance and Eternal Word, the one Saviour both for each individually and for all in common. He is in truth the Only-begotten,[62] the express image of the glory[63] of the universal King and almighty Father, stamping on the mind of the gnostic the perfect vision after his own image; so that the divine image is now beheld in a third embodiment, assimilated as far as possible to the Second Cause, to him, namely, who is

[60] Cf. Plato, *Laws*, 885 B, 907 A, 908 BC.
[61] Nauck, *Fragm. Trag.* 688.   [62] John 1:18.   [63] Heb. 1:3.

the Life indeed,[64] owing to whom we live the true life, copying the example of him who is made to us knowledge,[65] while we converse with the things which are stable and altogether unchangeable.

17. Being ruler therefore of himself and of all that belongs to him the gnostic makes a genuine approach to truth, having a firm hold of divine science. For the name science would fitly be given to the knowledge and firm hold[66] of intellectual objects. Its function in regard to divine things is to investigate what is the First Cause and what that through which all things were made and without which nothing has been made,[67] what are the things that hold the universe together partly as pervading it and partly as encompassing it, some in combination and some apart, and what is the position of each of these, and the capacity and the service contributed by each: and again in things concerning man, to investigate what he himself is, and what is in accordance with, or is opposed to his nature; how it becomes him to act and be acted on, and what are his virtues and vices, and about things good and evil and the intermediates, and all that has to do with manhood and prudence and temperance, and the supreme all-perfect virtue, justice. Prudence and justice he employs for the acquisition of wisdom, and manhood not only in enduring misfortunes, but also in controlling pleasure and desire and pain and anger, and generally in withstanding all that sways the soul either by force or guile. For we must not endure vices and things that are evil, but must cast them off, and reserve endurance for things that cause fear. At any rate even suffering is found to be useful alike in medicine and in education and in punishment, and by means of it characters are improved for the benefit of mankind.

18. Forms of manhood are fortitude, high-spirit, magnanimity, generosity, magnificence. It is owing to this that the gnostic takes no notice either of blame or of ill-repute from the world, nor is he in subjection to good opinions or flatteries of others. In the endurance of labours he shows himself amongst other men as a man indeed, being always occupied in some good work at the same time that he is manfully surmounting difficulties of every kind. Again he is temperate owing to his abiding good sense[68] combined with tranquillity of soul; his readiness to take to himself the promises as his own being in proportion to his

---

[64] I Tim. 6:19.   [65] I Cor. 1:30; Col. 2:2, 3.
[66] Sext. Emp., *Adv. Math.*, VII, 151.   [67] John 1:3.
[68] Cf. Plato, *Crat.*, 411 E; Aristotle, *Eth. N.*, VI, 5 (1140 b, 11).

shrinking from base things as alien. He is a citizen of the world, and not of this world only, but of a higher order, doing all things in order and degree, and never misbehaving in any respect. Rich he is in the highest degree because he covets nothing, having few wants and enjoying a super-abundance of every good, owing to his knowledge of the absolute Good. The first effect of his justice is that he loves to be with those of kindred spirit, and to commune with them, both on earth and in heaven.

19. For this reason also he is ready to impart to others of all that he possesses: and being a lover of men he has a profound hatred of the wicked through his abhorrence of every kind of evil doing, having learnt that one should be faithful both to oneself and to one's neighbours, as well as obedient to the commandments. For he who is willingly led on by the commandments may be called God's servant;[69] but he who is already pure in heart,[70] not because of the commandments, but for the sake of knowledge by itself—that man is a friend of God. For neither are we born virtuous, nor is virtue a natural after-growth, as are some parts of the body (for then it would have been no longer voluntary or praiseworthy); nor yet is it acquired and perfected, as speech is, from the intercourse of those who live with us (for it is rather vice which originates in this way). Nor again is knowledge derived from any art connected with the supplies of life or the service of the body, nor yet from the ordinary course of instruction: for we might be well satisfied if this could but prepare and sharpen the soul. The laws of the state, it is true, might perhaps be able to restrain evil practices. 20. Again, mere persuasive arguments are too superficial in their nature to establish the truth on scientific grounds, but Greek philosophy does, as it were, provide for the soul the preliminary cleansing and training required for the reception of the faith, on which foundation the truth builds up the edifice of knowledge.

Here it is we find the true wrestler, who in the amphitheatre of this fair universe is crowned for the true victory over all his passions. For the president is God Almighty, and the umpire is the only-begotten Son of God, and the spectators are angels and gods, and our great contest of all arms is not waged against flesh and blood, but against the spiritual powers[71] of passionate affections working in the flesh. When he has come safe out of these mighty conflicts, and overthrown the tempter in the combats to which he has challenged us, the Christian soldier

[69] Cf. John 15:15.   [70] Matt. 5:8.   [71] Eph. 6:12.

wins immortality. For the decision of God is unerring in regard to his most righteous award. The spectators then have been summoned to view the contest; the wrestlers are contending in the arena, and now the prize is won by him amongst them, who has been obedient to the orders of the trainer. For the conditions laid down by God are equal for all, and no blame can attach to him; but he who is able will choose,[72] and he who wills prevails. It is on this account also that we have received the gift of reason, in order that we may know what we do. And the maxim "Know thyself"[73] means in this case, to know for what purpose we are made. Now we are made to be obedient to the commandments, if our choice be such as to will salvation. This, I think, is the real *Adrasteia*, owing to which we cannot escape from God.[74]

21. Man's work then is submission to God, who has made known a manifold salvation by means of commandments, and man's acknowledgment thereof is God's good-pleasure. For the benefactor is the first to begin the kindness, and he who accepts it heartily, keeping due reckoning, and observes the commandments—such an one is faithful; but he who goes on to return the kindness to the best of his power by means of love, rises to the dignity of friend. And the one most appropriate return from man is to do those things which are pleasing to God. Accordingly the Master and Saviour accepts as a favour and honour to himself all that is done for the help and improvement of men, as being his own creation and in a certain respect an effect akin to its Cause; just as he accepts the wrongs done to those who have believed upon him, regarding such wrongs as instances of ingratitude and dishonour to himself.[75] For what other dishonour could affect God? Wherefore it is impossible for so great a gift to make a return in full, corresponding to the benefit received from God, as measured by the worth of salvation. But, as they who injure the cattle put a slight on the owners, and those who injure the soldiers put a slight on their captain, so it shows disrespect for the Lord, when injury is done to those who are devoted to him. For as the sun not only lights up the heaven and the whole world, shining on land and sea alike, but also darts his rays through windows and every little cranny into the innermost chambers, so the Word being shed abroad in all directions observes even the minutest details of our actions.

---

72 Plato, *Rep.*, 617 E.
73 Chilon, *ap.* Stob. *Anth.*, III, 79.
74 A Stoic etymological explanation of *Adrasteia* (=inescapable necessity).
75 Cf. Matt. 25:34 ff.

Chapter IV

22. But the Greeks assume their gods to be human in passions as they are human in shape; and, as each nation paints their shape after its own likeness (according to the saying of Xenophanes, the Ethiopians black with turned up nose, the Thracians with red hair and blue eyes),[76] so each represents them as like itself in soul. For instance, the barbarians make them brutal and savage, the Greeks milder, but subject to passion. Hence the conceptions which the wicked form about God must naturally be bad, and those of the good must be excellent. And on this account he who is a gnostic and truly royal in soul[77] is both devout and free from superstition, persuaded that the only God is alone meet to be honoured and reverenced, alone glorious and beneficent, abounding in well-doing, the author of all good and of nothing that is evil.[78] As for the superstitions of the Greeks I think sufficient evidence has been adduced in my discourse entitled *Protrepticus*, where the necessary investigation is given at great length.

23. What need is there then "the tale once clearly told to tell again"?[79] But as we are on this topic it will be enough just to give a small sample for proof, with a view to show that those are atheists who liken the Divinity to the worst of men. For either they make the gods injured by men, which would show them to be inferior to man as being capable of receiving injury from him; or, if this is not so, how is it that they are embittered at what is no injury, like an old shrew losing her temper, as they say Artemis was wroth with the Aetolians on account of Oeneus? Being a goddess, how did she fail to reflect that it was not from contempt for her, but either from forgetfulness,[80] or because he had previously sacrificed, that he neglected her worship? Again, Augé, in pleading against Athena, because she was wroth with her for having given birth to a child in her temple, well says:

> Spoils of dead mortals thou delight'st to see
> And corpses strewn: these thou dost not abhor:
> But this new birth thou deem'st a sacrilege.[81]

And yet no fault is found with other animals when they bring forth in the temples.[82]

---

[76] *Frag.* 16 Diels.
[78] Plato, *Rep.*, 379 B.
[80] Homer, *Iliad*, IX, 533.
[82] An opinion of the Stoic Chrysippus (Plutarch, *Mor.*, 1045 A).

[77] Plato, *Phileb.*, 30 D.
[79] Homer, *Odyssey*, XII, 453.
[81] Euripides, *Frag.* 268, Nauck.

24. In their dealings therefore with beings who are so quick to wrath men naturally become superstitious, and think that whatever happens is a sign and cause of evil. "If a mouse digs through an altar of clay or gnaws through a sack for want of something better, or if a cock that is being fattened begins to crow in the evening, they take it as a portent of something."(83) Menander ridicules a fellow of this stamp in his play entitled *The Superstitious Man*.(84) "Heaven send me good luck! In putting on my right shoe I broke the thong. Of course you did, you noodle, because it was worn out, and you were too miserly to buy a new pair." That was a pleasant saying of Antiphon's,(85) when one made an omen of a sow's devouring her young: seeing that the sow was a mere skeleton from her owner's niggardliness, "Well for you," said he, "that the omen did not take the form of her devouring your own children in her hunger." And, "What wonder is it," says Bion, "if the mouse, finding nothing to eat, gnawed through the sack? The wonder would have been if, as Arcesilaus[86] jestingly retorted, the sack had eaten the mouse."(87)

25. Excellent too was the reply of Diogenes to him who marvelled because he found the snake coiled round the pestle. "Marvel not," said he, "for it would have been far more surprising if you had seen the snake erect and the pestle coiled up round it."(88) For the irrational animals too have to run and eat and fight and breed and die; and these things being according to nature for them can never be unnatural for us. "Moreover many birds beneath the sunlight range,"(89) from which omens may be derived. Follies of this sort are caricatured by the comic poet Philemon.(90) "When I behold," says he, "a slave on the watch to see who sneezes, or who speaks, or who comes out of his house, I offer him at once to the first bidder. It is to himself that each of us walks and speaks and sneezes, and not to all the city. Things happen as 'tis their nature to." And then we find them praying for health when sober, but bringing on diseases by cramming and drinking themselves drunk at the festivals. Many too have a superstitious fear of the mottoes that are written up.

26. It was a witty remark of Diogenes, when he found the house of a man of bad character bearing the inscription, "Here

(83) Kock, *Com. Att. Frag.*, III, 471.   (84) *Ibid.*, 33.
(85) Antiphon, *Test.*, 8, Diels.   86 Founder of the Middle Academy.
(87) Bion of Borysthenes, *frag.* 45, Mullach.
(88) Diogenes, *frag.* 282, Mullach.   (89) Homer, *Odyssey*, II, 181.
(90) Kock, *Com. Att. Fr.*, II, p. 510. For sneezing as an omen, see A. S. Pease's Commentary on Cicero, *de Divinatione*, II, 40:8.

dwells the victorious Heracles: let no wickedness enter": "How then," said he, "is the master of the house to enter?"[91] And the same people worship every stock and every shining stone, as the phrase is, and are in awe of red wool and grains of salt and torches and squills and brimstone, being bewitched by the sorcerers according to certain impure purifications. But the true God regards nothing as holy but the character of the just man, nothing as polluted but what is unjust and wicked. At any rate you may see the eggs, which have been removed from the body of those who have undergone purification, hatched by warmth, and this could not have happened, if they had contracted the ills of the person purified.[92] And so the comic poet Diphilus[93] pleasantly satirizes the sorcerers in these words: "He purifies the daughters of Proetus with their father, the son of Abas, and an old crone besides to make up five—so many mortals with a single torch, a single squill, and brimstone and asphaltus of the boisterous surge, gathered from the deep pools of the soft-flowing ocean.[94] But, O blessed Air, send Anticyra[95] from heaven that I may change this bug to a stingless drone."

27. Menander[96] too says well, "If you were suffering from any real evil, Pheidias, you ought to have sought a real remedy for it. But as that is not so, I have devised a remedy as imaginary as the evil: simply imagine that it does you some good. Let the women rub you down and fumigate thoroughly: then sprinkle yourself with water from three springs, throwing in salt and beans." Every one is pure whose conscience is free from guilt. So in the tragedy[97] we read:

> "Orestes, say, what canker saps thy life?
> Conscience, which tells me of a dark deed wrought."

For indeed purity is no other than the abstaining from sin. Well therefore says Epicharmus, "If your mind is pure your whole body is pure too."[98] Certainly it is our rule to begin by cleansing our souls from bad and wicked opinions by means of right reason, and then, after that, to turn to the mention of the more excellent principles; for so too, in the case of those who are about to be initiated, it is thought right to apply certain puri-

---

[91] Diogenes, *frag.* 118, Mullach. Cf. Diog. Laertius 6:39, 50.
[92] For use of eggs for purification, cf. Juvenal 6:518, etc.
[93] Kock, *Com. Att. Fr.*, II, 577.   [94] Homer, *Iliad*, VII, 422.
[95] I.e., hellebore, which came from Anticyra.
[96] Kock, *Com. Att. Fr.*, III, 152 *seq.*
[97] Euripides, *Orest.*, 395.   [98] *Frag.* 269, Kaibel.

fications before the communication of the mysteries, on the ground that the godless opinion must be got rid of before they are ready to have the truth communicated to them.[99]

CHAPTER V

28. Surely it cannot be denied that we are following right and truth when we refuse to circumscribe in a given place him who is incomprehensible, and to confine in temples made with hands[1] that which contains all things. And what work of builders and masons and of mechanic art could be called holy? Were not they more in the right who held that the air and the circumambient ether, or rather the whole world and the universe itself, were worthy of the divine dignity? It would indeed be ridiculous, as the philosophers themselves say, that man being but a toy of God[2] should make God, and that God should come into being through the play[3] of human art. For that which is produced resembles, and is indeed the same as, that from which it is produced: thus, what is made of ivory is ivory, and what is made of gold is golden; and in like manner statues and temples executed by the hands of mechanics, being composed of lifeless matter, must themselves also be lifeless and material and profane; and even though you should carry your art to perfection, they still retain something of the mechanical. This being so, we cannot regard works of art as sacred and divine.

Again, among the heathen enshrinement is supposed to be essential to deity.[3] But what is it which could be localized in a shrine, if there is nothing unlocalized to start with (on the assumption that all things are in space)? And further, that which is enshrined has received enshrinement from something else, being itself previously unenshrined. If then God has received enshrinement from men, he was previously unenshrined and therefore non-existent. For by the hypothesis it is only the non-existent which was unenshrined, seeing that it is always the non-existent which undergoes the process of localization by enshrinement. And that which exists could not be localized by that which is non-existent, nor yet by anything else that exists:

[99] Cf. Celsus in Origen, *contra Celsum*, III, 59.
[1] Acts 17:24. In this and the following paragraphs Clement seems to be following a sceptical argument, probably of Academic origin: if enshrinement is essential to the pagan god, that is evidence that the god does not exist.   [2] Plato, *Laws*, 803 C, 889 C–E.
[3] Dedication ceremonies included elaborate magical rites to force the god to inhabit his shrine. Cf. Numenius, quoted by Origen, *contra Celsum*, V, 38.

for it is itself also in existence and therefore already localized in common with all other existing things. 29. It remains therefore that it must be enshrined by itself. But how is a thing to beget itself? Or how is the self-existent to localize itself in a shrine? Was it formerly unlocalized and did it afterwards localize itself? No, in that case it could not even have existed, since it is the non-existent which is unlocalized. And how could that which is supposed to have been localized make itself subsequently what it already was? Or that to which all existing things belong, the self-existent Deity, be itself in need of anything?

Again, if the Deity is in human shape, he will need the same things as man needs, food and covering and a house and all things belonging to them. For beings of like form and like passions will require the same kind of life. And if the word "holy" is taken in two senses, as applied to God himself and also to the building raised in his honour, surely we should be right in giving to the Church, which was instituted to the honour of God in accordance with sanctified wisdom, the name of a holy temple of God, that precious temple built by no mechanic art, no, nor embellished by any common vagabond, but made into a shrine by the will of God himself. I use the name Church now not of the place, but of the congregation of saints. This is the shrine which is best fitted for the reception of the greatness of the dignity of God. For to him who is all-worthy, or rather in comparison with whom all else is worthless, there is consecrated that creature which is of great worth owing to its pre-eminent holiness. And such would be the gnostic, who is of great worth and precious in the sight of God, he in whom God is enshrined, i.e., in whom the knowledge of God is consecrated. Here too we should find the likeness, the divine and sanctified image—here in the righteous soul, after it has been itself blessed, as having been already purified and now performing blessed deeds. Here we find both that which is enshrined and that which is in process of enshrinement, the former in the case of those who are already gnostics, the latter in those who are capable of becoming so, though they may not yet be worthy to receive the knowledge of God. For all that is destined to believe is already faithful in the eye of God and consecrated to honour, an image of virtue dedicated to God.

Chapter VI

30. As then God is not circumscribed in place, nor made like to the form of any creature, so neither is he of like passions, nor

lacks he anything after the manner of created things, so as from hunger to desire sacrifices for food. Things that are capable of suffering are all mortal; and it is useless to offer meat to that which is in no need of sustenance. The famous comic poet Pherecrates in his *Deserters*[4] wittily represents the gods themselves as finding fault with men for their offerings. "When you sacrifice to the gods, first of all you set apart what is customary for the priests first among you, and then—shame to say—do you not pick the thigh-bones clean to the groin and leave the hip-joint absolutely bare, assigning to us gods nothing but the dogs' portion, a back-bone polished as with a file, which you then cover with thick layers of sacrificial meal to save appearances?" And another comic poet, Eubulus, writes as follows about the sacrifices: "To the gods themselves you offer nothing but the tail and the thigh, as though they were enamoured of these."[5] And, where he brings on Dionysus in his *Semele*,[6] he represents him as distinguishing: "First of all, when any sacrifice to me, they sacrifice blood and bladder—don't mention heart or caul —the gall and thigh-bones are no food for me." 31. And Menander[7] has written of "the scrag end of the rump, the gall and dry bones, which," says he, "they set before the gods, while they consume the rest themselves." Why, the smoke of burnt sacrifices is intolerable even to the beasts. If, however, this smoke is really the meed of the gods of Greece, no time should be lost in deifying the cooks also (since they are deemed worthy of the same happiness) and in worshipping the stove itself, when it becomes an altar closely connected with the precious smoke. Hesiod[8] somewhere says that: "Zeus, being outwitted in some division of the flesh of the sacrifice by Prometheus, chose the white bones of the ox craftily concealed in the glistening lard: and from that time the tribes of men on earth burn to the immortals white bones on fragrant altars." Still they altogether deny that God's partaking of nourishment could be explained by the craving which grows out of want. Accordingly they must suppose him nourished without appetite like plants or hibernating bears. At all events they say that these are not impeded in their growth, whether it be that they are nourished from the density of the air, or even from the exhalation arising from their own body. And yet, if they hold that the Deity is nourished without needing it, what is the use of nourishment to one who

---

[4] Cf. Kock, *Com. Att. Frag.*, I, 151.
[6] *Ibid.*, 197.
[8] *Theog.*, 556.
[5] Kock, *Com. Att. Frag.*, II, 210.
[7] *Ibid.*, III, 39.

needs it not? But if the Deity, being by nature exempt from all need, rejoices to be honoured, we have good reason for honouring God by prayer, and for sending up most rightly this sacrifice, the best and holiest of sacrifices when joined with righteousness,[9] venerating[10] him through whom we receive our knowledge, and through him glorifying him (i.e., the Father) whom we have learnt to know. At any rate our altar here on earth is the congregation of those who are devoted to the prayers, having, as it were, one common voice and one mind.

As to the kinds of nutrition received through the sense of smell, though they may be less unworthy of the deity than those received through the mouth, still they witness to respiration. 32. What then is the worshippers' idea as to the breathing of God? Is it by means of transpiration as in the demons? or by inspiration only, as in fishes through the dilatation of their gills? or by circumspiration, as in insects, through the pressure of the membranes on the waist? No, they would not liken God to any of these, if they were in their senses. But as for creatures that live by respiration, they draw in the air by rhythmic beats corresponding to the counter-dilatation of the lungs against the chest. Then if they assign viscera and arteries and veins and sinews and members to God, they will exhibit him as in no respect differing from man. The word "conspiration" is that which is properly used of the Church. For the Church's sacrifice is indeed speech rising, like incense, from holy souls, while every thought of the heart is laid open to God along with the sacrifice. They are fond of talking about the purity of the most ancient altar at Delos, that altar which, we are told, was the only one approached by Pythagoras, because it was unpolluted by slaughter and death: will they then refuse credence to us when we say that the truly hallowed altar is the righteous soul, and the incense which ascends from it, the prayer of holiness? Sacrifices, I believe, are an invention of mankind to excuse the eating of flesh, though, even apart from such idolatry, it was always possible for one who wished it to partake of flesh. The Mosaic sacrifices symbolize Christian piety; for instance the dove and the pigeon offered for sins show that the purging away of the irrational part of the soul is acceptable to God. But if any of the righteous refuses to weigh down his soul by the eating of flesh, he does this on some reasonable ground, not as Pythagoras and his school from some dream as to the transmigration of souls.[11]

9 Ps. 4:5.   10 Plato, *Leg.*, 799 A.
11 Similarly Origen, *contra Celsum*, VIII, 30.

Xenocrates in a special treatise on animal food and Polemon[12] in his book on Life according to Nature, seem to lay it down clearly that a flesh diet is inexpedient, as it has already passed through a process of digestion and been thus assimilated to the souls of irrational creatures.

33. On this ground especially the Jews abstain from swine's flesh, considering that this animal is unclean because it roots up and destroys the fruits more than any other. But if it is argued that the animals have been given to men, we too agree in this, only we say that they are not given entirely, nor indeed all, for the purpose of eating, but only those that do no work. Wherefore the comic poet Plato in his play *The Feasts*[13] well says: "Hereafter 'twere well to kill no beast but swine, for they are excellent eating, and we get nothing out of them but bristles and mire and squealing." Hence it was well said by Aesop that "the reason why pigs make such an outcry when they are being dragged away is because they are conscious that they are good for nothing but to be sacrificed."[14] And so Cleanthes says that in them the soul takes the place of salt to prevent the flesh from putrefying.[15] Some then eat it because it is useless, and others because it injures the fruits; while others again abstain from eating it because of its immoderate salacity. For the same reason the law never requires the sacrifice of a goat except with a view to banishing evils, since pleasure is the fountainhead of vice. Further, they tell us that the eating of goats' flesh conduces to epilepsy. And they say that the largest amount of nutriment is supplied from pork, for which reason it is of use to those who practise bodily training, but, owing to the sluggishness produced by eating flesh, it is of no use to those who try to encourage the growth of the soul. A gnostic might therefore abstain from flesh, both for the sake of discipline and to weaken the sexual appetite. For, as Androcydes says, "wine and fleshly gorging make the body strong, but the soul more sluggish."[16] Such a diet does not tend to precision of thought. Wherefore also the Egyptians in their purifications forbid their priests to eat flesh, and they themselves live on fowl as the lightest diet and abstain from fish for various fanciful reasons and especially from the idea that such food makes the flesh flabby. 34. Besides this, the life of beasts and

---

12 Polemon succeeded Xenocrates as head of the Platonic Academy.
13 Kock, *Com. Att. Fr.*, I, 607.
14 Cf. Aelian, *Var. Hist.*, 10:5.   15 Cleanthes, *frag.* 516, Arnim.
16 Cf. Plutarch, *Mor.*, 472 B, 995 E; Pliny, *N.H.*, 14:58; 17:240. Androcydes
  was a Pythagorean.

birds is supported by breathing the same air as our souls, their soul being akin to the air; but we are told that fishes do not even breathe our air, but that air which was infused into water, as into the other elements, on its first creation, which is also a proof of the fact that air pervades all matter.

"It is not then expensive sacrifices that we should offer to God, but such sacrifices as are dear to him,"[17] viz., that composite incense of which the Law speaks,[18] an incense compounded of many tongues and voices in the way of prayer, or rather which is being wrought into the unity of the faith[19] out of divers nations and dispositions by the divine bounty shown in the Covenants, and which is brought together in our songs of praise by purity of heart and righteous and upright living grounded in holy actions and righteous prayer. For (to add the charm of poetry) "what man is there so unwise and beyond measure credulous as to expect that, at the burning of bare bones and gall, which even hungry dogs would refuse, the gods would all rejoice, and accept this as their due meed";[20] aye, and would show their gratitude to the celebrants, though they might be pirates or robbers or tyrants? The Christian teaching is that the fire sanctifies, not flesh or sacrifice, but sinful souls, understanding by fire not the all-devouring flame of common life, but the discerning flame[21] which pierces through[22] the soul that walks through fire.[23]

CHAPTER VII

35. Further, we are bidden to worship and honour the Son and Word, being persuaded that he is both Saviour and Ruler, and to honour the Father through him, doing this not on special days, as some others do, but continuously all our life through, and in all possible ways; (though it is true the chosen race,[24] being justified by obedience to the precept, say, "Seven times a day did I praise thee").[25] Wherefore it is neither in a definite place or special shrine, nor yet on certain feasts and days set apart, that the gnostic honours God, returning thanks to him for knowledge bestowed and the gift of the heavenly citizenship;[26]

---

[17] Theophrastus, *ap.* Porph. *Abst.*, II, 19.   [18] Ex. 30:25.
[19] Eph. 4:13.   [20] Kock, *Com. Att. Fr.*, III, 606.
[21] Clement's use of this Stoic distinction (cf. Cleanthes in Cicero, *de Nat. Deor.*, II, 15:41) is important for the origins of the doctrine of purgatory.
[22] Heb. 4:12.   [23] Isa. 43:2.   [24] I Peter 2:9.
[25] Ps. 119 (118):164.   [26] Phil. 3:20. Cf. p. 324 f.

but he will do this all his life in every place, whether he be alone by himself or have with him some who share his belief. And if the presence of some good man always moulds for the better one who converses with him, owing to the respect and reverence which he inspires, with much more reason must he, who is always in the uninterrupted presence of God by means of his knowledge and his life and his thankful spirit, be raised above himself on every occasion, both in regard to his actions and his words and his temper. Such is he who believes that God is everywhere present, and does not suppose him to be shut up in certain definite places, so as to be tempted to incontinence by the imagination, forsooth, that he could ever be apart from God whether by day or night. Accordingly all our life is a festival: being persuaded that God is everywhere present on all sides, we praise him as we till the ground, we sing hymns as we sail the sea, we feel his inspiration in all that we do. And the gnostic enjoys a still closer intimacy with God, being at once serious and cheerful in everything, serious owing to his thoughts being turned towards heaven, and cheerful, as he reckons up the blessings with which God has enriched our human life.

36. But the pre-eminence of knowledge is plainly set forth by the prophet in the words "Teach me goodness and instruction and knowledge,"[27] where he presents in an ascending scale the guiding principle of perfection. Here then we truly have the royal man, the holy priest of God—a combination which is still retained even at the present time among the most enlightened of the barbarians, who employ the priestly caste for government.[28] Such a one is far from surrendering himself to the mob-government which tyrannizes over the theatres; and as for the things which are there said and done and seen with a view to the allurements of pleasure, he repudiates them even in a dream. He repudiates therefore both these spectacular pleasures and the other refinements of luxury, such as costly perfumes flattering the sense of smell, or combinations of meats and the attractions of various wines enticing the palate, or fragrant wreaths of a variety of flowers which enfeeble the soul through the sense. Enjoying all things soberly, he refers his enjoyment in every case to God as its author, whether it be of food or drink or ointment, and offers to the Giver first-fruits of the whole, using the speech which he has bestowed, to thank him both for the gift and for the use of it. But he seldom appears at convivial entertainments

---

27 Ps. 119 (118):66 (LXX).   28 The Egyptians (Plato, *Polit.*, 290 D, E).

unless the banquet invites his attendance by promise of friendly
intercourse with those of like mind. For he is persuaded that
God knows all things, and hears not only the voice but the
thought, since even in our own case the hearing, though set in
action by means of the passages of the body, causes apprehension, not by the power of the body, but by a certain mental impression and by the intelligence which distinguishes between
significant sounds.

37. There is consequently no need for God to be in human
shape in order that he may hear, nor does he need senses, as the
Stoics held,[29] especially hearing and sight, dependent on the
sensitiveness of the air (as though he would otherwise be incapable of apprehension): but indeed the instantaneous perception
of the angels, and the power of conscience touching the soul—
these recognize all things with the quickness of thought by
means of some indescribable faculty apart from sensible hearing.
Even if one should say that it was impossible for the voice,
rolling in this lower air, to reach God, still the thoughts of the
saints cleave, not the air alone,[30] but the whole universe as well.
And the divine power instantly penetrates the whole soul, like
light. Again do not our resolves also find their way to God,
uttering a voice of their own? And are not some things also
wafted heaven-ward by the conscience? Moreover can we conceive that he who has known his elect according to his eternal
purpose,[31] and known before its birth[32] that which was to be,
as already existing, must wait for the sound of a voice? Is it not
true that the light of power shines forth in all directions even to
the very bottom of the soul, since the candle of power, as the
Scripture says, searches the secret chambers?[33] God is all ear
and all eye,[34] if one may make use of these expressions.

38. Where then there is an unworthy conception of God,
passing into base and unseemly thoughts and significations, it is
impossible to preserve any sort of devoutness either in hymns or
discourses or even in writings or doctrines. For which reason
what most men call reverence is indistinguishable from irrever-
ence, owing to their ignorance of the truth. Now the objects of
the appetites and desires and of impulses generally are also the
objects of our prayers. Wherefore no one desires drink in the
abstract but to drink, nor an inheritance, but to inherit; and in

---

[29] Clement makes a slip. He means the Epicureans.
[30] Cf. Ecclesiasticus 32(35):21.   [31] Rom. 8:28, 29; 9:11.
[32] Susanna, 42.   [33] Prov. 20:27.
[34] See above, VII, 5.

like manner no one desires knowledge, but to know; no, nor a right constitution, but to live under such a constitution. We pray therefore for the same things that we request, and we request the same things that we desire; and praying and longing are on the same footing as regards the possession of good things and the benefits attached to their acquisition. Accordingly the gnostic makes his prayer and request for the things that are really good, i.e., those pertaining to the soul, and he prays, and joins his own efforts as well, that he may no longer have his good things attached to him like ornaments, but may be himself good.

39. Hence too prayer is most fitting for those who have a right knowledge of the Divinity and that excellence of character which is agreeable to him, i.e., for those who know what are the things which are truly good, and what should be asked for, and when, and how, in each case. But it is the height of folly to ask of those who are not gods as if they were gods, or to ask what is inexpedient (i.e., what is evil for oneself), under the impression that it is good. Since then the good God is one,[35] we and the angels are right in praying that we may receive from him alone either the bestowal or continuance of good things. But we do not ask alike, for it is not the same thing to ask that the gift may be continued, and to strive to obtain it in the first instance.[36] Prayer for the avoidance of evil is also a kind of prayer. But we must never employ a prayer of this kind for the injury of other men, except where the gnostic might adapt his request so as to contrive for those who were hardened their return to righteousness. Prayer, then, to speak somewhat boldly, is converse with God. Even if we address him in a whisper, without opening our lips, or uttering a sound, still we cry to him in our heart. For God never ceases to listen to the inward converse of the heart.

40. For this reason also we raise the head and lift the hands towards heaven,[37] and stand on tiptoe as we join in the closing outburst of prayer, following the eager flight of the spirit into the intelligible world: and while we thus endeavour to detach the body from the earth by lifting it upwards along with the uttered words, we spurn the fetters of the flesh and constrain the soul, winged[38] with desire of better things, to ascend into the holy place.[39] For we are well assured that of his own will the

---

[35] Matt. 19:17.
[36] Clement seems to mean that the angels only pray for the continued enjoyment of what is already theirs.
[37] Cf. Origen, de Orat., XXXI, below, p. 322 ff.
[38] Plato, Phaedr. 246.   [39] Heb. 9:25.

gnostic leaves this world behind him, just as the Jews did Egypt, showing in the plainest way that he was destined to be as near as possible to God. And if there are any who assign fixed hours to prayer,[40] such as the third and the sixth and the ninth, yet the gnostic at all events prays all his life through, striving to be united with God in prayer, and, in a word, to have done with everything that is useless for that higher life, as one who has already attained here below the perfection of one who in love is full-grown. However, the triple distribution of the hours and their observance by corresponding prayers is also familiar to those who are acquainted with the blessed triad of the holy mansions.[41]

41. At this point I am reminded of the opinions which are being secretly propagated by certain heterodox persons, belonging to the heresy of Prodicus, against the use of prayer.[42] In order that they may not pride themselves on this their godless wisdom as though it were something novel, let these men learn that they are only following in the steps of the so-called Cyrenaic school.[43] The refutation however of the impious knowledge of these falsely called gnostics[44] I reserve to its proper season, in order that the censure, which must be somewhat protracted, may not steal into my notes at this point and so interrupt the subject we have in hand; which is a demonstration that only he who is a gnostic according to the rule of the Church is really pious and devout, and that he alone has his petitions, whether spoken or unspoken,[45] granted according to the will of God. For as God is able to do every thing that he wills, so the gnostic receives every thing that he may ask.[46] For God knows generally those that are worthy to receive good things and those that are not; whence he gives to each what belongs to him. For this reason if request were made by unworthy persons he would often refuse to give it, but would give unasked provided they were worthy. Yet the petition is not superfluous, even though good things be granted without petition made. For instance, both thanksgiving and prayer for the conversion of his neighbours are the duty of the gnostic. Thus the Lord also prayed, returning

---

[40] Cf. Tertullian, *Orat.*, 25; *Ieiun.*, 10.
[41] Cf. above, VII, 9, and *Strom.*, VI, 114: The three grades of believers (the thirty-, sixty-, and hundred-fold of the parable of the sower) have different mansions according to their merits.
[42] Cf. Origen, *de Orat.*, V, 1, below, p. 247.
[43] Cf. Diogenes Laertius, 2:97.   [44] I Tim. 6:20.
[45] See below, VII, 73.   [46] Matt. 21:22.

thanks for the accomplishment of his ministry[47] and praying that as many as possible might share in knowledge,[48] in order that God, who alone is good, alone is Saviour, may be glorified through his Son,[49] in those who are being saved through the salvation which is according to knowledge,[50] and that the knowledge of him may grow from age to age. Howbeit the mere faith that one will receive is itself also a kind of prayer stored up in a gnostic spirit.

42. But if prayer is thus an occasion for converse with God,[51] no occasion for our approach to God must be neglected. Certainly the holiness of the gnostic, being bound up with the Divine Providence through a voluntary acknowledgment on his part, shows the beneficence of God in perfection. For the holiness of the gnostic is, as it were, a return back on itself of Providence and a responsive feeling of loyalty on the part of the friend of God. For neither is the goodness of God involuntary like the warmth of fire (but his imparting of good things is voluntary, even though he should wait to be asked); nor on the other hand will the man who is being saved be saved without his will, for he is no lifeless machine, but will most assuredly hasten to salvation with eager alacrity. It is on this account that the commandments were given to man as to a being who would be spontaneously impelled to whichever he might choose, whether of things eligible or ineligible. God therefore does not do good of necessity, but of his own free will he befriends those who turn to him of their own accord.[52] For the providence that comes to us from God is not ministrative,[53] as though it proceeded from inferiors to superiors; but it is from pity of our weakness that the nearer dispensations of Providence are set in motion, like the care of shepherds for their sheep and that of a king towards his subjects; while we ourselves also are submissive to our superiors, who govern us in an orderly manner according to the commission with which they were entrusted by God. They therefore are ministers and worshippers of the Divinity who offer the freest and most royal worship, viz., that which is rendered by devoutness both of purpose and of knowledge.

43. Every place then and every time at which we entertain the thought of God is truly hallowed;[54] but when he who is at once right-minded and thankful makes his request in prayer, he

---

47 John 17:4.
49 Matt. 19:17; John 17:1.
51 See above, VII, 39.
53 See above, VII, 3.

48 John 17:19, 23.
50 John 17:3.
52 Cf. Origen, de Orat., XXIX, 15.
54 Cf. Origen, de Orat., XXXI, 4.

in a way contributes to the granting of his petition, receiving with joy the desired object through the instrumentality of his prayers. For when the Giver of all good meets with readiness on our part, all good things follow at once on the mere conception in the mind. Certainly prayer is a test of the attitude of the character towards what is fitting. And if voice and speech are given to us with a view to understanding, how can God help hearing the soul and the mind by itself, seeing that soul already apprehends soul, and mind apprehends mind? Wherefore God has no need to learn various tongues, as human interpreters have, but understands at once the minds of all men; and what the voice signifies to us, that our thought utters to God, since even before the creation he knew that it would come into our mind. It is permitted to man therefore to speed his prayer even without a voice, if he only concentrates all his spiritual energy upon the inner voice of the mind by his undistracted turning to God.

And since the east symbolizes the day of birth, and it is from thence that the light spreads, after it has first "shone forth out of darkness,"[55] aye, and from thence that the day of the knowledge of the truth dawned like the sun upon those who were lying in ignorance,[56] therefore our prayers are directed towards the rise of dawn.[57] It was for this reason that the most ancient temples looked toward the west in order that they who stood facing the images might be taught to turn eastwards. "Let my prayer ascend up as incense before thee, the lifting up my hands be an evening sacrifice"[58] is the language of the Psalms.

44. In the case of the wicked then prayer is most hurtful not only to others, but even to themselves. At any rate, if in answer to prayer they were to receive what they call pieces of good fortune, they are injured by receiving them, because they know not how to use them. For they pray to obtain what they have not got, and they ask for apparent, not real good. The gnostic, on the other hand, will ask for a continuance of the things he possesses and fitness for what is about to happen, and indifference as to what shall be denied; but as for the things that are really good, i.e., those pertaining to the soul, his prayer is that they may both be granted to him and may continue. Thus he does not even desire anything which he has not, being contented with his present lot. For he is not lacking in the good things that are proper to him, being already sufficient to himself through

[55] II Cor. 4:6.   [56] Matt. 4:16.
[57] Origen, *de Orat.*, XXXII, below, p. 327. Cf. F. J. Dölger, *Sol Salutis*[2] (1925), p. 146.   [58] Ps. 141:2.

the Divine grace and knowledge. But, having his resources in himself and being independent of others, and having learnt to know the omnipotent Will, so that he no sooner prays than he receives, he is brought close to the Almighty Power and, by his earnest striving after spirituality, is united to the Spirit through the love that knows no bounds. This is the man of lofty mind, who by the way of science has acquired the most precious and best of all possessions, being on the one hand quick to apply the faculty of contemplation, while on the other hand he retains permanently in his soul the power over the objects of contemplation, i.e., the keen clearness of science. This power he strives to the utmost to acquire by gaining the mastery over all that wars against the reason[59] and persisting in uninterrupted contemplation, while he exercises himself in the discipline which teaches the curbing of pleasures and the right direction of action. Besides this, from his wide experience, gathered both from study and from life, he has acquired freedom of speech, not the power of a mere random fluency, but the power of straightforward utterance, keeping back nothing that may be spoken in fitting time before a right audience, either from favour or fear of influential persons.

45. At any rate he who has received a clear conception of the things concerning God from the mystical chorus of the truth itself, makes use of the word of exhortation, exhibiting the greatness of virtue according to its worth, both in itself and in its effects, being united as intimately as possible with things intellectual and spiritual in the way of knowledge along with an inspired exaltation of prayer. Hence he is always meek and gentle, affable, easy of access, forbearing, considerate, conscientious. In him we have a severity of virtue, such as is not only proof against corruption, but proof against temptation also. He presents a soul altogether unyielding and impregnable whether to the assaults of pleasure or of pain. If reason calls him to it, he is an unswerving judge, in no respect indulging his passions, but keeping inflexibly to the path in which it is the nature of justice to walk, being fully persuaded that all things are admirably ordered, and that, for the souls which have made choice of virtue, progress is always in the direction of what is better, until they arrive at the Absolute Goodness, being brought close to the great High Priest,[60] in the vestibule,[61] so to speak, of the Father. This is the faithful gnostic who is fully persuaded

59 Rom. 7:23.   60 Heb. 4:14; cf. Strom., VII, 9 and 13, above.
61 Plato, Phileb., 64 C.

---

122   CLEMENT OF ALEXANDRIA

that all things in the world are ordered for the best. Certainly he is well pleased with all that happens.

46. He is right therefore in not seeking anything further when he is once supplied with the necessaries, being persuaded that God, who knows all things, supplies whatever is expedient to the good, even without their asking. For as the artificer, I suppose, has each request granted to him in the way of his art, *qua* artificer, and the heathen *qua* heathen, so the gnostic has his in the way of knowledge *qua* gnostic. And he that turns to God from among the heathen will ask for faith, but he that aspires to knowledge will ask for the perfection of love.[62] And when he has now reached the summit, the gnostic prays that the power of contemplation may grow and abide with him, just as the common man prays for a continuance of health. Aye, and he will pray too that he may never fall away from virtue, co-operating to the best of his power that he may end his life without a fall. For he knows that even of the angels some, having slipped back to the ground from carelessness, have never yet succeeded in extricating themselves completely out of their tendency to duplicity into the former singleness of heart. But, to him who has been trained here below to the highest point of knowledge, and the supreme elevation of a perfect man, all incidents of time and space are favourable; for he is fixed to one unchanging course of life both by choice and practice, owing to his uniform stability of purpose. But in those who have still some corners[63] of depressing languor that weighs them down,[64] the soaring impulse of faith also flags. In him, then, who has rendered his virtue indefectible by discipline based upon knowledge, habit is changed into nature; and in such a one his knowledge becomes an inseparable possession, like weight in a stone, not involuntarily, but of his own free will, by the power of reason and knowledge and forethought.

47. And since that which has not been lost may be raised to a state of indefectibility by carefulness and consideration, the gnostic will hold fast to carefulness with a view to avoid sin, and to consideration with a view to the indefectibility of virtue. Now knowledge seems to be the parent of consideration, because it teaches us to discern the things which can help to the permanence of virtue. But it will be granted that the knowledge of God is the most important of all things. Wherefore in this way also

---

62 Cf. John 14. 17.
63 Since in the Platonic or Stoic view the perfect shape was the sphere, any angular corner was imperfect.   64 Plato, *Phaedr.*, 247.

the indefectibility of virtue is assured. And he who knows God is holy and pious. We have proved therefore that the gnostic alone is pious. He rejoices in his present blessings and delights himself in those that are promised, as though they were already present—for he has not lost sight of them as if they were still absent—because he already knows of what nature they are. Being therefore convinced by his knowledge that each of the things that shall be, really is, he virtually possesses each. And this is enough for man; for sufficient and insufficient are measured by that which is normal in each case. At any rate, if the gnostic is possessed of wisdom, and wisdom is divine, he who partakes of what has no defect must himself be without defect. For the communication of wisdom is not the resultant of energy on the part of the giver and inertia on the part of the recipient, nor is any abstraction or deficiency caused by it; at any rate the energy is shown to be undiminished by the very fact of the communication. Thus then our gnostic has all good in potentiality, though not yet in full tale; since he would otherwise have been incapable of change in reference to the inspired progresses and orderings which are still due to him by God's decree.

48. God also assists him, honouring him with a closer oversight. For is it not the case that all things have been created for the sake of good men and for their use and benefit or, rather we should say, salvation? He would not therefore deprive of the rewards of virtue those for whom all things exist. For it is plain that he valued highly their good disposition and their holy choice, seeing that he breathes into those that have taken on themselves a good profession, strength for the completion of their salvation, in some cases by simple exhortation, but also by actual help in the case of those who have proved themselves worthy of their own efforts. For to the gnostic every kind of good comes as an accessory,[65] seeing that his chief end is in each case knowledge and action in accordance with knowledge. And as the physician provides health for those who co-operate with him for health, so also God provides eternal salvation for those who co-operate with him for knowledge and right action; and the moment that we do any one of the things in our power, which are enjoined by the commandments, the promise also receives its fulfilment. I like that story which is told among the Greeks of a famous athlete of former days, who had trained himself for feats of manhood by a long course of discipline. Having gone up to the Olympian games he turned to the image of Pisaean Zeus

65 A Stoic phrase (Cicero, de Finibus, III, 32).

and uttered these words: "If I, O Zeus, have now done all that was fitting on my part in preparation for the contest, do thou make haste to bestow the victory I deserve." For just so does the gnostic, when he has thoroughly and conscientiously performed his part with a view to learning and discipline and with a view to doing good and pleasing God, find the whole world contributing to perfect his salvation. The things then that are required of us are those which are in our own power, viz., choice and desire and acquisition and use and distribution of the things which concern us, according as they are present or absent.

49. Wherefore also he who holds intercourse with God must have his soul undefiled and absolutely pure, having raised himself to a state of perfect goodness if possible, but at any rate both making progress towards knowledge and longing for it, and being entirely withdrawn from the works of wickedness. Moreover it is fitting that he should offer all his prayers in a good spirit and in concert with good men, for it is a dangerous thing to countenance the errors of others. The gnostic will therefore share the prayers of ordinary believers in those cases in which it is right for him to share their activity also. But all his life is a holy festival. For instance, his sacrifices consist of prayers and praises and the reading of the Scriptures before dining, and psalms and hymns during dinner and before going to bed, aye and of prayers again during the night. By these things he unites himself with the heavenly choir, being enlisted in it for ever-mindful contemplation, in consequence of his uninterrupted thought of heaven while on earth. Again, is he not acquainted with that other sacrifice which consists in the free gift both of instruction and of money among those who are in need? Certainly he is. On the other hand he is not wordy in his uttered prayers,[66] since he has been also taught by the Lord what to ask for. Accordingly he will pray in every place, not however publicly or for all to see; but in every sort of way his prayer ascends, whether he is walking or in company or at rest or reading or engaged in good works; and though it be only a thought[67] in the secret chamber[68] of the heart, while he calls on the Father[69] in groanings which cannot be uttered,[70] yet the Father is nigh at hand,[71] even before he has done speaking.[72] Of the three ends of action, the honourable, the expedient and the pleasant, he

[66] Matt. 6:7.
[67] See the quotation in para. 73 below, and *Strom.*, VI, 78.
[68] Matt. 6:6. [69] I Peter 1:17. [70] Rom 8:26.
[71] Ps. 145:18. [72] Isa. 65:24; Dan. 9:21.

makes the two former his rule, and leaves it to those who follow the common life to be guided in any action by the third motive of pleasure.

CHAPTER VIII

50. He whose life is characterized by piety of this kind has little temptation to lying and swearing. For an oath is a definitive compact in which God is called to witness. And how could one who has once for all proved himself faithful, make himself unfaithful so as to stand in need of an oath, instead of allowing his life to carry with it the security and definiteness of an oath?[73] Both in his life and in his intercourse with others he shows the faithfulness of his promise by unfailing steadfastness both of life and speech. And, if injustice consists in the determination of the doer and speaker, and not in the suffering of the aggrieved person, he will refrain both from lying and forswearing himself, not with an idea that he is doing injury to God (since he knows that God is naturally incapable of receiving injury); but also for his neighbour's sake he will refuse to lie or break any agreement, seeing that he has learnt to love him,[74] even though he may not be a personal friend; and still more for his own sake he will refrain both from lying and from perjury, seeing that he would never, if he could help it, be found guilty of wronging himself. Nay, he will not even swear at all, preferring simply to use the particle "yes" in case of affirmation, and "no"[75] in case of denial. For to swear is to use an oath or its equivalent with intent to inspire confidence. 51. It is enough for him therefore to add the words "I speak the truth" either to his assent or denial, in order to give confidence to those who are too obtuse to see that his answer may be depended on. For, as regards those who are without, I think his life should be worthy of trust, so that they should not even ask for an oath; but as regards his own family and those who have a right understanding[76] there should be confidence in his fairness, i.e., in his unforced desire to do right. In any case the gnostic is true to his oath, but slow to swear, since he rarely comes forward to take an oath, and that only as we have stated. Still to be true to one's oath is a part of the harmony of truth; so that the observance of an oath follows the rule for the performance of ordinary duties. Where then is there any further need for the oath to one who lives according

---

73 Cf. Isocrates, 1:22.   74 Matt. 19:19.
75 Matt. 5:37.   76 Prov. 8:9.

to the highest standard of truth? He who does not even swear will be far indeed from perjuring himself, and he who observes every clause of his contracts would never swear at all, seeing that it is actions that decide whether contracts are broken or fulfilled; just as the question of falsehood and perjury is decided by speaking and swearing contrary to right. But he that lives justly, without violating any duty, is proved by his actions, wherein the judgment of the truth is sifted, to be true to his oath. The evidence of the tongue is therefore superfluous in his case. Being then persuaded that God is always present everywhere, and being ashamed not to tell the truth, and knowing that, not to speak of perjury, even a lie is unworthy of himself, he is satisfied with the witness of God and of his own conscience only. So, while on the one hand he neither lies nor does anything contrary to his agreements, on the other hand he neither takes an oath when it is demanded of him, nor denies what he has done, being resolute to be clear of lying, even though he should die under torture.

CHAPTER IX

52. But the dignity of the gnostic is carried to an even further pitch by him who has undertaken the direction of the teaching of others, assuming the management in word and deed of that which is the greatest blessing on earth, by virtue of which he becomes a mediator to bring about a close union and fellowship with God. And as they that worship earthly things pray to the images as though they heard them, confirming their covenants before them; so the true majesty of the word is received from the trustworthy teacher in the presence of men, the living images of God, and the benefit done to them is referred to the Lord himself, after whose likeness the true man creates and moulds the character of the man under instruction, renewing him to salvation. For, as the Greeks call iron by the name of Ares and wine by that of Dionysus (according to the figure which carries back the effect to the cause), so the gnostic who regards good done to his neighbours as his own salvation, might well be called a living image of the Lord, not according to the particular outward form, but in so far as he symbolizes his power and resembles him in preaching the gospel.

53. Whatever then he has in his mind, that he has also on his tongue, when addressing those who are worthy to hear it from their agreement with him, since both his word and his life are in harmony with his thought. For he not only thinks what is true,

but he also speaks the truth, except it be medicinally, on occasion; just as a physician, with a view to the safety of his patients, will practise deception or use deceptive language to the sick, according to the sophists.[77] For instance, the great apostle circumcised Timothy,[78] though he proclaimed aloud and in writing that circumcision made with hands profiteth not.[79] But fearing that, if he were all at once to withdraw from the law to the circumcision of the heart which is by faith,[80] he might drive the Hebrew disciples who were still restive to break off from the congregation, accommodating himself to the Jews, he became a Jew that he might gain all.[81] He then who stoops to accommodation merely for the salvation of his neighbours, i.e., for the salvation of those for whose sake he practises accommodation, not dissembling under stress of the danger which threatens the righteous from those who are jealous of them—such a one can by no means be said to act under compulsion; though, solely for the good of his neighbours, he will do some things, which would not be done by him in the first instance, were it not for them. He offers himself in behalf of the Church, in behalf of the disciples whom he has himself begotten[82] in the faith, for a pattern to those that are capable of succeeding to the exalted office of a teacher filled with love to God and love to man, for confirmation of the truth of his words, for the manifestation of his love to the Lord. He is not enslaved in fear, he is patient in toil, true in word, shrinking from falsehood even in the outward utterance, and herein always attaining strict accuracy, since a lie in his eyes is no idle word, but is active for wickedness, as being the expression of a kind of treachery. 54. So then it is the gnostic alone that witnesses to the truth[83] in every way both by word and deed: for he is altogether right in all things, in word and act and even in thought itself.

Such then is a brief account of Christian devoutness. If now the Christian does these things fittingly and in accordance with right reason, he is acting piously and justly. And if this is so, the gnostic alone would be really pious and just and devout. The Christian therefore is no atheist—for this is what we proposed to prove to the philosophers—so that nothing bad or mean, i.e.,

---

[77] Cf. Plato, *Rep.*, 382 C; 389 B; 459 C, D; Origen, *contra Celsum*, IV, 18–19.
[78] Acts 16:3.
[79] Rom. 2:25; Eph. 2:11. Porphyry, in his attack on Christianity, accuses Paul of inconsistency in circumcising Timothy (*frag.* 27, Harnack).
[80] Rom. 2:29; 3:30.   [81] I Cor. 9:19 f.
[82] I Cor. 4:15.   [83] John 5:31; 18:37.

nothing unjust, will ever be done by him in any wise. It follows from this that neither is he impious; rather it is he alone that is truly pious, fitly and piously worshipping after the rule of a true devotion him who is in very deed the All-ruling God and Almighty King.

CHAPTER X

55. For the knowledge of insight (*gnosis*) is, so to speak, a kind of perfection of man as man, harmonious and consistent with itself and with the divine word, being completed, both as to the disposition and the manner of life and of speech, by the science of divine things. For it is by insight that faith is made perfect,[84] seeing that the man of faith only becomes perfect in this way. Now faith is a certain inward good: without making search for God, it both confesses his existence, and glorifies him as existent. Hence a man must start with this faith, and having waxed strong in it by the grace of God, must thus attain to insight concerning him, so far as is possible. We distinguish however between insight and the wisdom which is implanted by teaching. For in so far as anything deserves to be called insight, so far it is certainly wisdom also; but in so far as a thing is wisdom, it is not certainly insight. For the meaning of the term wisdom is shown only in the use of the spoken word: while the foundation of insight, on the other hand, lies in having no doubt about God, but trusting him implicitly; and Christ is both the foundation and the superstructure—Christ, through whom are both the beginning and the end. Now the extremes, i.e., the beginning and the end, I mean faith and love, are not matters of teaching; but knowledge (*gnosis*), being handed down by tradition according to the grace of God, is entrusted as a deposit to those who show themselves worthy of the teaching; and from this teaching the worth of love shines forth in ever-increasing light. For it is said, to him that hath, shall be added,[85] knowledge added to faith and love to knowledge, and to love, the heavenly inheritance.

56. This takes place whenever any one hangs upon the Lord by means of faith and knowledge and love, and ascends up with him to the presence of the God and guardian of our faith and love; who is the ultimate source from which knowledge is imparted to those who are fitted and approved for it, because they need further preparation and training both for the hearing of the words spoken, and with a view to soberness of life and to their

[84] James 2:22.   [85] Luke 19:26.

careful advance to a point beyond the righteousness of the law.[86] This knowledge leads us on to that perfect end which knows no end, teaching us here the nature of the life we shall hereafter live with gods according to the will of God, when we have been delivered from all chastisement and punishment, which we have to endure as salutary chastening[87] in consequence of our sins. After this deliverance rank and honours are assigned to those who are perfected, who have done now with purification and all other ritual, though it be holy among the holy; until at last, when they have been made pure in heart[88] by their closeness to the Lord, the final restoration attends on their everlasting contemplation of God. And the name of gods is given to those that shall hereafter be enthroned with the other gods, who first had their station assigned to them beneath the Saviour.[88a] Knowledge therefore is swift to purify, and suitable for the welcome change to the higher state. 57. Hence, too, it easily transplants a man to that divine and holy state which is akin to the soul, and by a light of its own carries him through the mystic stages, till it restores him to the crowning abode of rest, having taught the pure in heart to look upon God[89] face to face[90] with understanding and absolute certainty. For herein lies the perfection of the gnostic soul, that having transcended all purifications and modes of ritual, it should be with the Lord[91] where he is, in immediate subordination to him.

Faith then is a compendious knowledge of the essentials, but knowledge is a sure and firm demonstration of the things received through faith, being itself built up by the Lord's teaching on the foundation of the faith, and carrying us on to unshaken conviction and scientific certainty. As I mentioned before, there seems to me to be a first kind of saving change from heathenism to faith, a second from faith to knowledge; and this latter, as it passes on into love, begins at once to establish a mutual friendship between that which knows and that which is known. And perhaps he who has arrived at this stage has already attained equality with the angels.[92] At any rate, after he has reached the final ascent in the flesh, he still continues to advance, as is fit, and presses on through the holy Hebdomad into the Father's house, to that which is indeed the Lord's abode,[93] being destined there to be, as it were, a light standing and abiding for ever, absolutely secure from all vicissitude.

[86] Matt. 5:20; Rom. 10:5.   [87] Heb. 12:7.   [88] Matt. 5:8.
[88a] I.e. the angels. Cf. Origen, contra Celsum, III, 37.   [89] Matt. 5:8.
[90] I Cor. 13:12.   [91] I Thess. 4:17.   [92] Luke 20:36.   [93] John 14:2.

58. The first mode of the Lord's working gives evidence of the above-mentioned reward following on devoutness. Out of many testimonies I will adduce one, thus summarily stated by the prophet David: "Who shall ascend into the hill of the Lord? or who shall stand in his holy place? He that hath clean hands and a pure heart; who hath not lifted up his soul unto vanity, nor sworn deceitfully to his neighbour. He shall receive a blessing from the Lord and mercy from God his Saviour. This is the generation of them that seek the Lord, that seek the face of the God of Jacob."[94] The prophet is here briefly describing the gnostic, and in passing, as it seems, he shows that the Saviour is God, calling him the face of the God of Jacob, i.e., one who preached and taught concerning the Father. Wherefore also the apostle used the phrase "impress of the Father's glory"[95] in reference to the Son, who taught the truth concerning God and gave this mark, that one alone is God and Father,[96] viz., the Almighty, whom no one knew but the Son, and he to whom the Son shall have revealed him.[97] That God is one is also declared by the phrase seeking the face of the God of Jacob, whom alone, being God the Father, our Saviour and God characterizes as good.[98] But the generation of them that seek him is the chosen race[99] which seeks with a view to knowledge.

59. For this reason also the apostle says: "I shall profit you nothing unless I speak unto you either in the way of revelation or of knowledge or of prophesying or of teaching."[1] And yet some things are done rightly, though not on rational grounds, even by those who are not gnostics, as in the case of courage. For some men, being by nature full of spirit and having fostered this quality without the use of reason, act for the most part by irrational impulse and do the same sort of things as brave men, so as at times to exhibit the same height of virtue, as for instance to endure tortures calmly; but this is neither from the same cause nor even with the same purpose as the gnostic, even though they should give up their whole body;[2] for, as the apostle says, they have not the love which proceeds from knowledge. All the action then of a man of understanding is of the nature of well-doing and all the action of him who is without understanding is ill-doing, even though he should be maintaining a principle, since his courage does not proceed from reason, nor does he direct his action for any useful purpose, such as has its

94 Ps. 24:3–6.   95 Heb. 1:3.   96 Eph. 4:6.
97 Matt. 11:27.   98 Matt.19:17.   99 I Peter 2:9.
1 I Cor. 14:6.   2 I Cor. 13:3.

end in virtue.[3] The same thing may be said of the other virtues and therefore by analogy in the case of piety. Accordingly we shall find the gnostic to be such not in holiness only; but, in regard to the rest of his conduct also, his professions are in accordance with his enlightened piety. For it is the life of the gnostic which it is our purpose now to describe, and not to give a systematic view of his beliefs which we shall afterwards set forth at the fitting season, preserving the sequence of thought.

CHAPTER XI

60. The gnostic then has a true and noble conception of the universe, as might be expected from one who has comprehended the divine teaching. Starting with that admiration[4] for the creation which he brings with him as an evidence of his capacity to receive knowledge, he becomes an eager disciple of the Lord, and the moment he hears of God and Providence, his admiration prompts him to believe. Proceeding from this point he does his best to learn in every way, employing every means to obtain the knowledge of those things which he longs for (and longing joined with seeking arises as faith increases), that is, to be made worthy of such high and glorious contemplation. Thus the gnostic will taste of the will of God. For he lends, not his ears, but his soul, to the facts indicated by the spoken words. Since then what he receives through the words are realities and the facts themselves, he naturally brings his soul to his duties, understanding the commands Do not commit adultery, Do not kill,[5] in a special sense, as they are addressed to the gnostic and not as they are apprehended by the rest of the world.

61. Training himself in scientific contemplation, he goes on to contend on the strength of these higher and more universal truths, being fully assured that "he who" (according to the prophet) "teaches man knowledge is the Lord,"[6] the Lord using man's mouth as his organ. Wherefore also he has taken human flesh. With good reason therefore he never prefers what is pleasant to what is expedient, not even though he should be taken at a disadvantage and vehemently urged by the harlot arts of some fair wanton; for neither could Joseph be seduced from his firm purpose by his master's wife, but when she kept hold of his garment, he left it in her hands, being thus denuded

---

3 This is Stoic teaching (Arnim, *S.V.F.*, III, 511).
4 Plato, *Theaet.*, 155 D. 5 Ex. 20:13, 15; Matt. 5:21, 27.
6 Ps. 94:10, 11.

of sin, but clothing himself in modesty. For, though the eyes of his master, I mean the Egyptian, did not see Joseph, yet the eyes of the Almighty were watching him. For we men hear the voice and see the bodily form, but the Lord searcheth the spirit,[7] from which both speech and sight proceed. In like manner, whether disease or accident befall the gnostic, aye, or even death the most terrible of all things, he continues unchanged in soul, knowing that all such things are a necessary result of creation, but that, even so, they are made by the power of God a medicine of salvation,[8] benefiting by discipline those who are disposed to rebel against amendment, being distributed according to desert by a truly merciful Providence.

62. The gnostic then uses God's creatures, when, and so far as, it is reasonable, in a spirit of thankfulness to the Creator, and so gains the mastery over his enjoyment of them. He never bears a grudge, is never angry with anyone, even though he should deserve hatred for his conduct; for he worships the Creator and loves his fellow man, pitying him and praying for him on account of his ignorance. Moreover, though he shares in the affections of the body, naturally sensitive as it is, in which he is imprisoned, yet he is not primarily affected by passion. At any rate, in the accidents which befall him against his will, he raises himself from his troubles to his native element, and is not carried away by things which have nothing to do with true self, but accommodates himself to the necessities of the case, so far as it does not interfere with the welfare of the soul. For he does not wish to be faithful only in reputation or indeed in outward seeming, but in knowledge and in truth, that is to say, in consistent action and effectual speech. Wherefore he not only praises what is noble, but himself strives to be noble, passing from the condition of a good and faithful servant[9] to that of a friend[10] by means of love, owing to the perfection of the virtuous habit which he acquired in its purity by true instruction and long training.

63. As one then who would force his way to the pinnacle of knowledge, orderly in character, sober in bearing, he possesses all the advantages which mark the true gnostic, fixing his eyes on noble images, on the many patriarchs who have fought their fight before him, on a still greater multitude of prophets, on angels beyond our power to number, on the Lord who is over all, who taught him, and made it possible for him to attain that

---

[7] I Sam. 16:7; Jer. 17:10, etc.   [8] Euripides, *Phoen.*, 893.
[9] Matt. 25:23.   [10] John 15:15.

crowning life. For this reason he loves none of the fair things that the world holds out to him, fearing lest they should tie him to the ground; but he loves the things which are hoped for, or rather are already known, but whose possession is hoped for. Thus he endures his labours and tortures and afflictions, not, like the brave men whom the philosophers talk of, from hope that the present evils will cease, and that he will again have a share of pleasures; no, knowledge has begotten in him a persuasion, surer than any hope, of the reaping of rewards to come. Wherefore he despises not only the persecutions, but also all the pleasures of this world. So we are told that the blessed Peter, when he beheld his wife on her way to execution,[11] rejoiced on account of her call and her homeward journey, and addressed her by name with words of exhortation and good cheer, bidding her "remember the Lord."

64. Such was the marriage of those blessed ones and such their perfect control over their feelings even in the dearest relations of life. So too the apostle says, "Let him that marrieth be as though he married not,"[12] requiring that marriage should not be enslaved to passion nor distracted from the love to the Lord;[13] to which love the wife, when departing from this life to the Lord, was exhorted to cling by him who showed himself a husband indeed. Was not the faith in the hope after death clearly manifested by those who, even in the very height of persecution, could return thanks to God? The reason, I suppose, was the steadfastness of their faith, which was accompanied by acts of corresponding faithfulness. So in every difficulty the soul of the gnostic proves its strength, being in first-rate condition and vigour, like the body of the athlete. For it is well-advised in the affairs of men, measuring what has to be done by the rule of justice, having received its principles from God in the first instance, and having attained to moderation in the pleasures and pains of the body, in accordance with the divine likeness; thus he rises up against his fears with good courage, putting his trust in God. Accordingly the gnostic soul is just an earthly image of the divine Power, adorned with perfect virtue, built up by the combined action of nature, discipline, and reason. The soul thus beautified becomes a temple of the Holy Spirit,[14] when it has acquired a temper of mind corresponding to the gospel in every relation of life.

65. Such a one rises up against every fear and all that is

[11] That Peter's wife was martyred is a story told only by Clement.
[12] I Cor. 7:29.   [13] I Cor. 7:35.   [14] I Cor. 6:19.

terrible, not death alone, but poverty and disease and disgrace and whatever is akin to these, being invincible by pleasure and master of the irrational appetites. For he knows well what ought and what ought not to be done, having a thorough understanding of what is really formidable and what is not. Hence he undertakes with intelligence what reason dictates as right and fitting for him to do, distinguishing intelligently things that are really encouraging, i.e., good things,[15] from those which only seem to be so, and that which is formidable from that which appears formidable, such as death and disease and poverty, which pertain rather to seeming than to truth. This is the truly good man who stands outside the passions, having risen above the whole life of passion by the habit or disposition of the virtuous soul. For him, all depends upon himself for the attainment of the end. For the so-called dangers of fortune are not formidable to the good man, because they are not really evil; but real dangers are foreign to the gnostic Christian, since, as evil, they are directly opposed to what is good; and it is "impossible that opposites can happen simultaneously to the same thing in the same respect and at the same time."[16] Thus, playing irreproachably whatever part in life God may have assigned to him to act, he perceives both what he ought to do and what he ought to endure.

66. Does cowardice then arise in any other way except through ignorance of what is, and what is not, to be feared?[17] If not, the gnostic alone is of good courage, because he perceives what is good both in the present and in the future, and combines with this, as I said, the knowledge of the things which are not really to be feared. For, being convinced that vice alone is hostile and destructive to those who are on the road to knowledge, he wars against it, as such, being fortified with the armour of the Lord. (For it does not follow that, if an action has its rise in folly and the operation, or rather co-operation, of the devil, it is to be at once identified with folly or the devil; (because no operation is prudence; for prudence is a habit, and no operation is a habit): so neither is the action that originates in ignorance to be forthwith styled ignorance: it is a bad action caused by ignorance, not ignorance pure. For not even passions or sins are vices, thought they proceed from vice.) No one, therefore, who is irrationally brave is a gnostic. Else we might be told that children are brave when they face dangers from ignorance of

15 Plato, *Laches*, 198 C.   16 Plato, *Rep.*, IV, 436 B.
17 Cf. Plato, *Prot.*, 360 C.

the grounds of fear—for instance they will even play with fire—and we may be told that wild beasts are virtuous when they rush upon the spears, being irrationally brave. On the same principle they will perhaps tell us that jugglers are brave when they have learnt the trick of tumbling among the swords, practising a base art for a miserable pittance. But he who is truly brave, though the peril arising from popular fury is plain before his eyes, awaits with confidence whatever comes. Herein is he distinguished from other so-called martyrs, in that they provide occasions for themselves by exposing themselves to dangers for whatever reason (for we must avoid harsh language); but the others, taking precautions in accordance with the dictates of reason, and then cheerfully offering themselves, when God really calls them, both make their calling sure,[18] from the consciousness that they have not been guilty of any rash act, and give opportunity for testing their manhood by their truly rational courage.

67. It is therefore neither through "enduring lesser terrors from fear of greater"[19] (as other people do), nor again through apprehension of fault-finding from people of their own station and way of thinking, that they abide by the confession of their calling: no, they willingly obey the divine call owing to their love to God, not for the sake of the prizes of the contests, since they prefer no other aim to the doing of that which is well-pleasing to God. For those that endure from love of glory, or from fear of some severer punishment, or with a view to any joys or pleasures after death, these are mere children in faith, blessed indeed, but not having attained to manhood, like the gnostic, in their love to God—for the Church too has its crowns both for men and for boys, just as the gymnasium has—but love is to be chosen for its own sake, not for any other reason. It may be said therefore that the gnostic's perfection of courage grows with the growth of knowledge out of the discipline of life, because he has always studied how to control his passions. Love then, by her anointing and training, makes her own champion fearless and intrepid and full of trust in the Lord, just as righteousness wins for him the power of life-long truthfulness. For in the phrase "Your yea shall be yea and your nay nay,"[20] there was given an abstract of righteousness. And the same may be said of self-control also. For a man is not made really self-controlled through ambition, as in the case of the athlete, for the sake of crowns and glory; nor again through covetousness,

[18] II Peter 1:10. [19] Plato, *Phaedo*, 68 D. [20] James 5:12.

as some feign, pursuing a good end by means of a fatal passion; no, nor yet through the desire of bodily health, nor from boorish insensibility enabling him to abstain from pleasures for which he has no taste.[21] Certainly those who live a life of toil, when they get a taste of pleasure, presently break down the rigour of their self-restraint in regard to pleasure. Such too are those who are kept in check only by law and by fear; for when they get a chance they evade the law, deserting the side of honour. But temperance that is chosen for her own sake, being perfected according to knowledge and taking up her abode in the heart, gives a man authority and makes him independent; so that the gnostic is temperate and passionless, proof against pleasures and pains, as, they say, the adamant is against fire.

68. The cause of these things is love, love surpassing all knowledge in holiness and sovereignty. For by it the gnostic, owing to his worship of the best and highest, the stamp of which is unity, is made friend[22] and son[23] at once, a perfect man indeed, grown to the full measure of stature.[24] Aye, and concord also is defined to be agreement about the same thing, and by "the same thing" we mean unity; and friendship is brought about by similarity, because fellowship lies in unity. The gnostic therefore, being naturally disposed to love God who is truly one, is himself a truly perfect man and a friend of God, being ranked and reckoned as a son. These are names expressive of nobility and knowledge and perfection, in accordance with that vision of God which is the crowning height attainable by the gnostic soul, when it has been perfectly purified, being now deemed worthy to behold for ever the Almighty, face to face.[25] For having been made entirely spiritual it departs to its kindred sphere and there, in the spiritual Church, abides in the rest of God.

CHAPTER XII

69. So much then for these things. But the gnostic, being such as we have described him in body and soul, is found to be fair alike towards all his neighbours, whatever their legal position, whether servant or foeman or whatever it be. For he does not neglect him who, according to the divine law, stands to him in the relation of brother by the same parents; certainly, when he is in distress, he relieves him by consolations and encouragements and by making provision for the needs of daily life. While

[21] Cf. Aristotle, *Eth. Nic.*, II, 2:2 (1004 A, 24).   [22] John 15:15.
[23] John 1:12.   [24] Eph. 4:13.   [25] I Cor. 13:12.

he gives to all who are in need, he does not do it to the same extent, but in accordance with justice and proportionately; moreover he gives even to one who persecutes and hates him, if he stands in need of it, caring little for those who insinuate that fear was his motive, provided that he was doing it not from fear, but only from a wish to help. For if a man is liberal and forgiving in dealing with enemies, how much more will he be loving to his friends? Such an one will proceed from this point to an exact understanding as regards the person, the amount, the time and the manner in which liberality would be best dispensed. And who could reasonably be the enemy of a man who affords no possible excuse for enmity? Perhaps as, in speaking of God, we say that God is opposed to none and the enemy of none (for he is Creator of all things and there is no existing thing that he does not love, but we call those his enemies who are disobedient and do not walk according to his laws, as for instance those who hate his covenant); so we might find the same disposition in the case of the gnostic. For he himself could never be in any way hostile to any one, but they who take the contrary course might be thought hostile to him. Besides, even if our habit of freely sharing with others is called justice, still the habit which makes proportionate distinction of less or more in cases where distribution should be scientific, is a form of highest justice. There are indeed cases in which right is done, as in abstaining from pleasures, from vulgar motives. For, as among the heathen some practise abstinence from present pleasures, both through inability to obtain what they desire,[26] and through fear of man, while there are others who abstain for the sake of greater pleasures;[27] so also in the faith some are continent either on account of the promise or through fear of God.

70. Still even such continence as this serves as a foundation of knowledge and an introduction to what is better and a movement towards perfection. For the fear of the Lord is said to be the beginning of wisdom.[28] But he that is perfect beareth all things and endureth all things[29] for love's sake, not as pleasing man, but God.[30] Yet praise too attends him by way of natural consequence, not for his own benefit, but for the imitation and use of those who bestow the praise. The word meaning continent is used in another sense also, not of him who only conquers his

[26] A quotation from Theognis (Aristotle, *Eth. Nic.*, I, 9, 1099 A, 25 f.; *Eth. Eud.*, I, 1, 1214 A, 6).
[27] The Epicurean view. Cf. Origen, *contra Celsum*, VII, 63.
[28] Prov. 9:10.   [29] I Cor. 13:7.   [30] I Thess. 2:4.

passions, but of him also who has become possessed of good and has a firm hold of the treasures of understanding, from which spring the fruits of virtuous activity. Thus the gnostic never departs from his own set habit in any emergency. For the scientific possession of good is fixed and unchangeable, being the science of things divine and human.[31] Knowledge therefore never becomes ignorance, nor does good change to evil. Hence with him eating and drinking and marrying are not the main objects of life, though they are its necessary conditions. I speak of marriage sanctioned by reason and in accordance with right: for being made perfect he has the apostles as his patterns.[32] And true manhood is shown not in the choice of a celibate life; on the contrary the prize in the contest of men is won by him who has trained himself by the discharge of the duties of husband and father and by the supervision of a household, regardless of pleasure and pain—by him, I say, who in the midst of his solicitude for his family shows himself inseparable from the love of God and rises superior to every temptation which assails him through children and wife and servants and possessions. On the other hand he who has no family is in most respects untried. In any case, as he takes thought only for himself, he is inferior to one who falls short of him as regards his own salvation, but who has the advantage in the conduct of life, in as much as he actually preserves a faint image of the true Providence.

71. In any case it is our duty to provide the most varied training for the soul so as to make it impressible for the reception of knowledge. Do you not see how wax is softened and copper refined that it may receive the stamp impressed upon it? Further, as death is a separation of soul from body, so knowledge is, as it were, a rational death, leading off the soul from its passions and separating it from them, and leading it on to the life of virtuous activity, in order that it may then say with boldness to God, "I live as thou wouldst have me." For he who makes it his aim to please men,[33] cannot please God,[34] since the mass of men choose not the things that are expedient, but the things that are pleasant; but if one pleases God, he becomes incidentally well pleasing to good men. How then could such an one any longer take delight in eating and drinking and sexual pleasure, when he is suspicious even of discourse that is productive of pleasure, and of any mental excitement and exercise of will that causes delight? For "no man can serve two masters, God and

---

[31] Stoic definition of wisdom.   [32] Cf. III, 52–53.
[33] Gal. 1:10.   [34] Rom. 8:8.

mammon."[35] This he says, not meaning money simply, but the provision that money supplies for the various kinds of pleasure. For indeed it is impossible for him who has a high and true knowledge of God to be a slave to the pleasures that are contrary to him.

72. There is then one alone who is free from desire to begin with, viz., the Lord, who is the lover of men, who for our sakes became man; but all that are eager to be assimilated to the stamp given by him, strive to become free from desire by training. For he who has felt desire and has gained the mastery over himself, like the widow also, becomes virgin again through chastity. This is the reward of knowledge[36] to the Saviour and Teacher, which he himself asked for his own, viz., abstinence from all evil and activity in well-doing, by which means salvation is procured. As, then, they that have learnt the arts get their livelihood by the training they underwent, so the gnostic gets spiritual life by his knowledge and is saved. For he who refuses to eradicate the passion of his soul causes his own death. But ignorance, as it seems, is the starvation of the soul and knowledge its sustenance. And the gnostic souls are those which the gospel likened to the sanctified virgins who wait for their Lord.[37] For they are virgins as having abstained from evil and awaiting their Lord through love, and they are wise souls, since they kindle their own light to see the real facts, saying, "We long to receive thee, O Lord, at last: we have lived according to thy commandments, we have transgressed none of thy precepts: wherefore also we claim thy promises; and we pray for what is expedient for us, feeling that it is unfitting for us to ask of thee the highest rewards: even though they may seem to be evil, we will receive as expedient all the trials that meet us, whatever they may be, which thy ordering employs for our training in steadfastness."

73. The gnostic indeed has risen to such a pitch of holiness that he is ready rather to pray and fail than to succeed without prayer. For all his life is prayer and communion with God, and if he is free from sins he will assuredly receive what he desires. For God says to the righteous: "Ask and I will give to thee; think and I will do it."[38] If, then, what he asks is expedient, he will receive it at once; but things inexpedient he will never ask

---

[35] Luke 16:13.
[36] John 4:36; I Cor. 9:18; cf. Isa. 53:11; John 17:3, 15, 17.
[37] Matt. 25:1 ff.
[38] The same quotation occurs in *Strom.*, VI, 78; 101; cf. VII, 49.

for, and therefore will never receive: so he will always have what he desires. And if we should be told that sinners sometimes succeed in their prayers, on the one hand this occurs but rarely, because God's goodness is always just, and on the other hand it is to those who are able to benefit others that this favour is shown. Hence the gift is not bestowed for the sake of the petitioner, but the divine ordering has a foresight of the person who will be saved by his means, and thus reasserts the character of justice in the benefit imparted. But to such as are worthy, the things that are truly good are granted even without the asking. When, then, a man is righteous, not from compulsion or fear or hope, but of choice, this is called the King's high-way[39] traversed by the King's seed; but the others are all by-ways, slippery and precipitous. At any rate, if the motives of fear and honour were removed, I know not whether our brave outspoken philosophers would still be able to hold out against their troubles.

74. Now lusts and other sins have been called briars and thorns.[40] The gnostic therefore toils in the Lord's vineyard,[41] planting,[42] pruning, watering, being indeed a divine husbandman for those who have been planted in the faith. They, then, who have not done evil expect to receive a reward for doing nothing, but he who has done good from choice alone claims the reward as a good labourer. Doubtless he will receive also a double reward, partly for what he has not done and partly in return for his good actions. Such a gnostic is tempted by none, except it be through divine permission, and that for the benefit of his associates. At any rate they are encouraged to believe, being cheered by his manly endurance. Doubtless it was for this cause also that the blessed apostles were brought to give proof and witness of perfection with a view to establishing and confirming the churches. Since the gnostic, then, has ringing in his ears the voice which says, "Do thou show pity to him whom I shall smite,"[43] he prays for the repentance even of those that hate him. For the punishment of criminals, which is carried out in the amphitheatre, is a spectacle unsuited even for children. As for the gnostic it is impossible that he should be instructed or delighted with such shows, since he has trained himself of set purpose to be noble and good, and has thus become insensible to pleasure. As he never falls under the power of sins, he is not corrected by examples of other men's evils. Much less can *he* be

39 Num. 20:17.　　　　　　40 Jer. 4:3; Matt. 13:7; Heb. 6:8.
41 Isa. 5:7; Matt. 21:33.　　　42 I Cor. 3:6.
43 Cf. perhaps Job 19:21; Ps. 69:27.

satisfied with the pleasures and spectacles of earth, who thinks little even of the promises, divine though they be, of worldly blessings. "Not everyone" therefore "that saith Lord, Lord, shall enter into the kingdom of God, but he that doeth the will of God."[44] And such would be the gnostic labourer, who has the mastery over his worldly desires[45] even while he is still in the flesh, and is so fully persuaded with regard to the unseen future which he knows, that he holds it to be more immediately present than the things which are actually before him.

75. This is the capable labourer, who rejoices in his knowledge, but humbles himself for his entanglements in the necessities of life, being not yet held worthy of the active participation in those things which he knows. Thus he uses this life as something foreign to him, merely as an unavoidable necessity. He understands too the hidden meanings of the fasting of these days, I mean of Wednesday and Friday:[46] for the one is dedicated to Hermes, the other to Aphrodite. At any rate he makes his life a fast both from love of money and love of pleasure, which are the springs of all the vices; for I have often ere now pointed out[47] that, according to the apostle, the generic varieties of fornication are three, viz., love of pleasure, love of money and idolatry.

76. Accordingly he fasts both from evil deeds according to the law and from wicked thoughts according to the perfection of the gospel. He is also subjected to trials, not for his own purification, but, as we said,[48] for the benefit of his neighbours, if, after experience of labours and troubles, he is seen to despise and disregard them. The same is to be said about pleasure: the great thing is to abstain from pleasure after having had experience of it. For what credit is it to practise self-control, where pleasure is unknown? The gnostic carries out the evangelical command and makes that the Lord's day on which he puts away an evil thought and assumes one suited for the gnostic, doing honour to the Lord's resurrection in himself. Moreover when he gets hold of a scientific principle, he believes that he sees the Lord, while he directs his eyes to the unseen; and if he fancies that he sees what he is unwilling to see, he chides the faculty of vision whenever he is conscious of a feeling of pleasure at the visual impression; since he desires to see and hear nothing but what beseems him. For instance, while contemplating the souls of his brethren, he sees also the beauty of the flesh with the

44 Matt. 7:21. 45 Tit. 2:12. 46 Cf. Didache, 8:1.
47 Strom., III, 89:1; VI, 147:1; Eph. 5:5. 48 Cf. above, para. 74.

soul itself, which has been trained to look on beauty alone apart from fleshly pleasure.

77. And brethren indeed they are according to the elect creation and the similarity of disposition and the character of their actions, where thought and word and deed manifest that same holiness and beauty which the Lord willed them, as elect, to have in mind. For faith is shown in the choice of the same things, and knowledge in having learnt the same and keeping them in mind, and hope in desiring the same. And if, owing to the necessities of life, some slight portion of his care is occupied about food, he thinks he is defrauded by such distraction. Thus he never sees even a dream which is unsuited to an elect soul. For verily a stranger and pilgrim[49] all his life through is every one who, dwelling in a city, despises the things that others admire in it, and lives in it as though it were in a desert, that he may not be constrained by locality, but that his own free will may show him to be just. To sum up, such a gnostic fills the vacant place of the apostles by his upright life, his exact judgment, his assistance of the deserving, by removing mountains[50] from the hearts of his neighbours and casting down the inequalities of their souls; though indeed each one of us is his own vineyard and his own labourer. He however, even in his best actions, desires to escape the eyes of men, as long as he persuades the Lord and himself that he lives according to the commandments, preferring those things on which he believes that his life depends. "For where a man's heart is," says one, "there is his treasure also."[51] Through the perfection of his love he impoverishes himself that he may never overlook a brother in affliction, especially if he knows that he could himself bear want better than his brother.

78. At any rate he esteems the other's grief as his own pain: and if he suffers any inconvenience through his kindness in making provision out of his own deficiency, he is not vexed at this, but only increases his bounty still further. For he has a faith unmixed with doubt, faith concerning the realities, while he commends the gospel both in his actions and in his thoughts. And verily the praise he reaps is not from men but from God,[52] as he fulfils the Lord's instructions. Being attracted by the eternal hope, he tastes not the fair things of this world, but disdains all that belongs to this life. He pities those who undergo discipline after death and are brought to repentance against their will by

[49] Heb. 11:13.   [50] I Cor. 13:2.   [51] Matt. 6:21.
[52] Rom. 2:29; John 5:41–44.

means of punishment, while he is himself of good conscience as regards his departure and is ever ready for it as being a pilgrim and a stranger[53] to this present world, remembering only his own inheritance and regarding all things here as alien. And, as he not only admires the commandments of the Lord, but is made, so to speak, a partner of the Divine Will by actual knowledge, he is a true intimate of the Lord and of his commandments, elect as righteous, fitted as gnostic for rule and sovereignty, despising all the gold that is upon the earth and under the earth, and the sovereignty which extends from one end of the ocean to the other, so as to hold fast to the one service of God. Wherefore also both in eating and drinking and in marrying, if reason so dictates, and even in his dreams, his actions and his thoughts are holy, so that he is always purified for prayer. He prays also with angels, as being already equal to angels,[54] and never passes out of the holy keeping; even if he prays alone he has the chorus of saints banded with him. Such a man is aware of a twofold energy, the one that of him who believes, the other the deserved pre-eminence of him who knows, since righteousness also is twofold, the one caused by love, the other by fear.

79. Certainly we are told that the fear of the Lord is pure, enduring for ever.[55] For they who turn to faith and righteousness from fear endure for ever. For instance fear brings about abstinence from evil, while love prompts us to do good, building us up to a willing mind, in order that one may hear from the Lord the words, "No longer do I call you servants, but friends,"[56] and may thenceforward join with confidence in the prayers. And the form of his prayer is thanksgiving for what is past and what is present and what is future, as being already present through his faith: and this is preceded by the acquisition of knowledge. Moreover he prays that he may so live his appointed time in the flesh as a gnostic and as one free from the flesh, and that he may obtain the best things and escape the worse: aye, and he prays for us, that we may be comforted about our sins and may be converted to knowledge. No sooner does he hear the the Master's call to depart, than he follows it; nay, owing to his good conscience even leads the way so to speak, hastening to offer his sacrifice of thanksgiving, and being joined with Christ there, to make himself worthy from his purity to receive by inward union the power of God which is supplied through Christ. For he does not desire to be warm through borrowed warmth or

53 Heb. 11:13. 54 Luke 20:36. 55 Ps. 19:9. 56 John 15:15.

luminous through borrowed fire, but to be altogether light himself. Such an one knows accurately the word that is spoken, Unless ye hate your father and mother, aye, and your own life also, and unless ye bear the sign.[57] For he both hates the lusts of the flesh with their potent spell of pleasure, and disdains all that belongs to handicraft and the support of the flesh; nay he rises up against the corporeal soul, putting a bit in the mouth of the irrational spirit when it breaks loose, because the flesh lusteth against the spirit.[58] But to bear the sign[59] is to carry about death[60] whilst still alive, having renounced all,[61] since higher love is due to him who created the soul for knowledge than to him who begot the body.

80. When he has once formed the habit of doing good, the gnostic loses no time in benefiting others also, praying that he may be reckoned as sharing in the sins of his brethren[62] with a view to the repentance and conversion of his kinsfolk, and eager to impart his own good things to those whom he holds dearest. And his friends for their part feel the same for him. Thus he helps the growth of the seeds deposited with him according to the husbandry enjoined by the Lord, and continues without sin and acquires self-control and lives in the spirit with those who are like him in the choirs of the saints, even though he be still detained on earth. Throughout the day and night he is filled with joy uttering and doing the precepts of the Lord, not only at dawn on rising, and at midday, but also when walking and lying down, dressing and undressing; and he teaches his son,[63] if his child be of that sex, never losing hold of the commandment and the hope, giving thanks always to God, like the creatures which give glory to God in Isaiah's allegory.[64] Patient under every trial he says: "The Lord gave, the Lord hath taken away."[65] For such also was Job, he who despising the loss of his outward prosperity, surrendered everything else along with his bodily soundness, owing to his love to the Lord. For it says he was upright and holy and eschewed all evil.[66] But the word "holy" implies that his whole management of life was just in things pertaining to God; and his knowledge of these things made him a gnostic. For neither, if good things come, should a man be engrossed by them, seeing they are merely human, nor again should he quarrel with them, if evil, but should be superior to both, treading the one under his feet, and passing

[57] Luke 14:26, 27.   [58] Gal. 5:17.   [59] Luke 14:27.   [60] II Cor. 4:10.
[61] Luke 14:33.   [62] Cf. Ex. 32:32; Rom. 9:3   [63] Deut. 6:7; 11:19.
[64] Isa. 6:3.   [65] Job 1:21.   [66] Job 1:1.

on the other to those who are in need. But let the gnostic be guarded in accommodating himself to others, lest accommodation should imperceptibly change into inclination.

CHAPTER XIII

81. He never remembers those who have sinned against him, but forgives them; wherefore also he has a right to pray: "Forgive us, for we forgive."[67] For this too is one of the things which God desires, that we should covet nothing and hate none,[68] for all mankind are the work of one Will. And perhaps our Saviour, in desiring that the gnostic should be perfect as the Father in heaven,[69] that is, as himself—our Saviour, who says, "Come ye children and I will teach you the fear of the Lord"[70]—desires that the gnostic should no longer need the help given through the angels,[71] but being made worthy should receive it from himself, and have his protection from himself by means of his obedience. The prayer of such an one is the claiming of a promise from the Lord. And in the case of his brethren who are in need the gnostic will not ask a superfluity of wealth for himself to distribute, but will pray that there may be to them a supply of what they need. For so he not only gives his prayer to the needy, but he provides that which comes through prayer in a secret and unostentatious manner. Poverty indeed and disease and such-like trials are often used for admonition, with a view to produce both amendment of the past and care for the future. In virtue of the prerogative of knowledge, such an one becomes an instrument of the Divine Goodness by asking for relief for the sufferers, and himself does the kind action, not from vainglory, but simply because he is a gnostic.

82. We are told in the Traditions that the apostle Matthias[72] was wont to say on occasion: "If the neighbour of an elect person sins, it is the fault of the elect; for if he had conducted himself as reason dictates, his neighbour's reverence for such a life would have prevented him from sinning." What shall we say then about the gnostic himself? "Know ye not," says the apostle, "that ye are the temple of God?"[73] The gnostic therefore is already holy and divine, carrying God within him and being carried by God. Certainly the Scripture represents sin as something

---

[67] Matt. 6:12. [68] Cf. Basilides in *Strom.*, IV, 86:1.
[69] Matt. 5:48. [70] Ps. 34:11. [71] Ps. 91:11.
[72] Cf. *Strom.*, III, 26, above; VII, 108, below. [73] I Cor. 3:16.

alien, where it sells to the strangers those that fall away.[74] And
by the words "Look not with desire on another man's wife,"[75]
it tells us in plain terms that sin is alien and contrary to the
nature of the temple of God. Now the temple is either large like
the Church or small like the individual who keeps safe the seed
of Abraham.[76] He then who has God enthroned within him will
not desire anything else. At any rate, leaving behind all hindrances and scorning all the distractions of matter, he cleaves
the heaven by his wisdom, and having passed through the
spiritual entities and every rule and authority,[77] he lays hold of
the throne on high, speeding to that alone, which alone he
knows. So blending the serpent with the dove[78] he lives perfectly and with a good conscience, faith being mixed with hope
as regards the expectation of that which is to come. For he feels
that he has been made worthy to obtain the gift which he received, and that he has been translated from servitude to sonship[79] in accordance with his understanding, being on the one
hand not without a knowledge of God (or rather being known
by him),[80] and on the other hand showing in the end the effects
thereof in a manner worthy of the grace received. For works
follow knowledge, as the shadow the body.

83. Being then fully assured that it will be better for him
after his decease, he has good reason for not being troubled at
anything that happens, nor is he suspicious of any of those
things which come to pass for good according to the divine
order; and since his conscience is void of offence, he does not
shrink from appearing before the unseen powers after his death,
having been purged, so to speak, from every stain of the soul.
Hence he never prefers the pleasant or the expedient to the
divine order, but trains himself by means of the commandments
that he may be both well-pleasing to the Lord in all things and
praiseworthy as regards the world, since all things rest upon the
one Almighty God. It was to his own, we read, the Son of God
came and his own received him not.[81] Wherefore also in his use
of the things of the world he is not only full of thankfulness and
of admiration for the creation, but he also receives praise himself for using it as he ought, since it is through intelligent action,
in obedience to the commands, that the gnostic arrives at the
goal of contemplation. From this point he advances, ever gathering from science new food for contemplation, and having em-

---

[74] Cf. Judg. 2:11–14, etc.   [75] Cf. Matt. 5:28; Prov. 6:24, 25.
[76] John 8:33 f.; Gal. 3:29, etc.; I John 3:9.
[78] Matt. 10:16.   [79] Rom. 8:15.   [80] Gal. 4:9.   [77] Eph. 1:21; 6:12.
                                                          [81] John 1:11.

braced with enthusiasm the great idea of knowledge, till at last he receives the holy reward of his translation[82] hence. For he has heard the psalm which says, "Walk about Sion and encompass it, declare in the towers thereof ";[83] the meaning of which is, I suppose, that those who receive the word in a lofty spirit will be lofty as towers, and will stand securely both in faith and in knowledge.

CHAPTER XIV

84. Let thus much be said in the briefest possible terms about the gnostic to the Greeks as seed for further thought. Though the simple believer may succeed in one or other of the points mentioned, yet it must be remembered that he cannot do so in all, nor with perfect science like the gnostic. And further, of our gnostic's apathy, if I may use the term, according to which the perfecting of the believer advances through love, till it arrives at the perfect man, at the measure of the stature,[84] being made like to God and having become truly equal to the angels[85]— of this apathy many other evidences from Scripture occur to me which I might adduce, but I think it better to defer so ambitious an attempt owing to the length of the discussion, leaving the task to those who are willing to take pains in elaborating the doctrines by extracts from Scripture. One Scripture however I will briefly refer to, so as not to leave the topic altogether unnoticed. The divine apostle says, in his earlier epistle to the Corinthians, "Dare any of you, having a matter against another, go to law before the unjust, and not before the saints? Know ye not that the saints shall judge the world, etc.?"[86] As the paragraph is very long, I will set forth the meaning of the apostle's utterance by making use of such of the apostolic expressions as are most to the point, giving in the most concise language a rapid paraphrase of the passage where he describes the perfection of the gnostic. For he not only defines the gnostic's position as consisting in submitting to wrong rather than in inflicting wrong on another, but he also teaches him to forget injuries, not even allowing him to pray against him who has done the wrong; for he knows that the Lord also gave a plain command that we should pray for our enemies.[87] The assertion then that the injured party goes to law before the unjust,[88] shows nothing else than a desire to retaliate and a willingness to commit a second

82 Heb. 11:5. 83 Ps. 48:12. 84 Eph. 4:13. 85 Luke 20:36.
86 I Cor. 6:1, 2. 87 Matt. 5:44. 88 I Cor. 6:6.

wrong, that is, to be himself equally in fault. But the statement that some wish to go to law before the saints indicates those who ask in prayer that their oppressors may be requited for their extortion; it shows too that though the latter are better than the former, still they are not yet free from passion, unless they entirely forget their wrongs and pray even for their enemies, according to the teaching of the Lord.

85. It is well then that they should also come to a better mind by repentance to faith. For if the truth seems to have enemies in those who provoke her to jealousy,[89] still she is in no wise hostile to any herself. For as "God causes his sun to shine upon the just and the unjust,"[90] aye, and sent the Lord himself to just and unjust, so he who strives to be made like to God through the absence of all malice "forgives seventy times seven times"[91] (i.e., as one might say, throughout his whole life and the entire cosmical revolution signified by the reckoning of sevens) and shows kindness to every one, even though some continue to ill-treat the gnostic all the time of their life here in the flesh. For it is not only the judgment of those who have wronged him that the apostle requires the virtuous man to leave to others; he even desires that the just man should ask from those judges the forgiveness of their sins for those who have offended against him; and with good reason, seeing that they who attempt injustice damage only what is external and concerned with the body, even though it should go to the extent of death; but none of such things properly belongs to the gnostic. And how could one judge the apostate angels[92] if he is himself an apostate from the gospel rule that we are to forget injuries? "Why do ye not rather take wrong?" he continues, "why do ye not rather suffer yourselves to be defrauded? Nay, ye do wrong" (namely, by praying against those who offend in ignorance) and, so far as in you lies, "ye defraud" of the goodness and kindness of God those against whom ye pray, "and that your brethren"[93] (referring hereby, not only to those who are brethren by faith, but to those also who are strangers among you). 86. For we know not yet whether even he who is at present hostile may not hereafter believe. From which we clearly gather, if not that all are brethren, yet that to us they should seem such. And further, that all men are the work of one God, invested with one likeness upon one nature (though in some the likeness may be more confused than in others) —the recognition of this is reserved for the

[89] Deut. 32:21; I Cor. 10:22.   [90] Matt. 5:45.   [91] Matt. 18:22.
[92] I Cor. 6:3.   [93] I Cor. 6:7, 8.

man of understanding, who through the creation adores the Divine energy, through which again he adores the Divine Will.

"Or know ye not that wrong-doers shall not inherit the kingdom of God?"[94] He then is a wrong-doer who retaliates either by deed or word or by the wish in the heart, which is excluded by the Gospel after the schooling of the law.[95] "And such were some of you"—such, manifestly, as those still are whom you refuse to pardon—"but ye washed yourselves,"[96] not simply like the rest, but with knowledge you cast off the passions of the soul, so as to become assimilated to the goodness of the Divine Providence, to the best of your power, both by long-suffering and by forgiveness, causing the gentleness of your word and deeds to shine like the sun upon just and unjust[97] alike. The gnostic will attain this result either by his own greatness of mind, or by imitation of one who is better than himself; and there is a third cause denoted by the word: "Forgive and it shall be forgiven you,"[98] where the command seems to compel to salvation through its exceeding goodness. But ye were sanctified.[99] For he who has attained such a habit as this, must necessarily be holy, never falling into any passion in any way, but being, as it were, already freed from the flesh and having reached a holiness above this world.

87. Wherefore, he says, "ye were justified by the name of the Lord";[99] ye were, so to speak, made by him to be just, as he is just, and ye were intimately joined with the Holy Spirit, so far as it is possible for man. For does he not say, "All things are lawful for me, but I will not be brought under the power of any,"[1] so as to do or think or speak anything contrary to the gospel? "And meats are for the belly and the belly for meats, but the Lord shall destroy them,"[2] that is, all who so reason and live as if they were born for eating, instead of eating to live as a subordinate aim, but devoting themselves to knowledge as their principal aim. And perhaps he means that these are, as it were, the fleshy parts of the Holy Body, the Lord's Church being figuratively described as a body,[3] viz., that spiritual and holy choir, of whom those who are only called by the Name and do not live accordingly constitute the flesh. But this spiritual body, i.e., the holy Church, is not for fornication nor must it be connected in any possible sort or way with the apostasy from the gospel to the life of the heathen.

94 I Cor. 6:9.   95 Gal. 3:24.   96 I Cor. 6:11.   97 Matt. 5:45.
98 Matt. 6:14; Polyc., *Phil.*, 2; Clem. Rom., *Ep. ad Cor.*, I, 13.
99 I Cor. 6:11.   1 I Cor. 6:12.   2 I Cor. 6:13.   3 Eph. 1:23.

88. For he who behaves like a heathen in the Church, whether in act or word or even merely in thought, commits fornication against the Church and against his own body.[4] He that is joined to this harlot[5] (viz., the activity which is contrary to the covenant), for one flesh[6] and for a heathenish life and another hope, becomes another body which is not holy; but he that is joined to the Lord after a different kind of union, in spirit, is a spiritual body. He is wholly a son, a holy man, passionless, gnostic, perfect, being formed by the Lord's teaching, in order that he may be brought close to him in deed and word and in his very spirit, and may receive that mansion[7] which is due to one who has thus approved his manhood.

This may serve as a sample for those that have ears. For we must not divulge the mystery, but only indicate it so far as to recall it to those who have been partakers in knowledge, who will also understand what is the meaning of the Lord's saying, "Be ye perfect as your Father is perfect,"[8] perfectly forgiving sins and forgetting injuries, and being habitually free from passion. For as we speak of a perfect physician and a perfect philosopher, so, I suppose, we may speak of a perfect gnostic; but none of these perfections, to whatever height it may attain, is regarded as coming into comparison with God. For we do not agree with the impious opinion of the Stoics as to the identity of human and divine virtue.[9] Perhaps, then, we ought to be as perfect as the Father wishes us to be: for it is impracticable and impossible that any one should be as perfect as God *is*; but our Father wishes that we should arrive at an unimpeachable perfection by living according to the obedience of the gospel. If then, since the saying is incomplete, we supply what is wanting for the completion of the passage, the explanation of which has been left to those who are capable of understanding, we shall both recognize the will of God and shall live a life of piety and aspiration, in a manner worthy of the commandment.

CHAPTER XV

89. The next thing is to reply to the charges brought against us by Greeks and Jews. And since the different schools in other departments of learning take their part in some of the difficulties raised, similarly to the above mentioned, it may be well to begin by clearing away obstacles and then to proceed to the next

[4] I Cor. 6:18.   [5] I Cor. 6:16.   [6] I Cor. 6:16.   [7] John 14:2.
[8] Matt. 5:48.   [9] Cf. Origen, *contra Celsum*, IV, 29; VI, 48.

Miscellany fully prepared for the solution of the difficulties. The first charge they allege is this very point, that the diversity of sects shows belief to be wrong, for the voice of truth is drowned amid the din of conflicting assertions. To whom we reply that, both among you Jews and among the most approved of the Greek philosophers, there have been multitudes of sects, yet of course you do not say that one should hesitate to be a philosopher or a follower of the Jews on account of the internal discord of your sects.[10] In the next place it was prophesied by the Lord that the seed of heresy would be sown upon the truth like tares upon wheat[11] (and what was prophesied cannot but come to pass), the cause of this being that the beautiful is always shadowed by its caricature.[12]

90. What then? If some one is guilty of breaking his engagements[12a] and neglecting his agreement with us, shall we let go the truth ourselves on account of him who has been false to his agreement? No, the good man must be true to his word and not belie any promise, however much others may break their engagements. And just so, we ought in no way to transgress the rule of the Church. Above all the confession which deals with the essential articles of the faith is observed by us, but disregarded by the heretics. Those, then, are to be believed who hold firmly to the truth. Using this defence broadly we are now entitled to reply to them, that physicians also, though holding different opinions in accordance with their particular schools, are still equally engaged in the practice of healing. Does then any one who is suffering in body and needs medical treatment refuse to call in a physician owing to the diversity of medical schools? So neither should he who is diseased in soul and full of idols plead the heresies as his excuse in regard to the recovery of health and conversion to God. Aye, and we are told that heresies are for the sake of those who are approved;[13] and by "approved" is meant either those who are coming to the faith, if they show unusual discrimination in approaching the teaching of the Lord (like the approved money-changers[14] who distinguish the spurious from the legal coin by the false stamp), or

---

10 Cf. Origen, *contra Celsum*, III, 12.
11 Matt. 13:25.
12 Clement seems to be quoting some tag.
12a Cf. *Strom.* VII, 51 and note on Origen, *Dial. c. Heracl.* 130 (below, p. 440).
13 I Cor. 11:19.
14 Clement quotes a saying of Jesus not recorded in the Gospels but frequently cited by early Christian writers (cf. Resch, *Agrapha*, 116–127).

those who are in the faith itself, and have already approved themselves therein, both by their life and their knowledge.

91. It is for this reason therefore that we need more attention and consideration to determine how we should live with strictness, and what is true piety. For it is evident that the trouble and difficulty of ascertaining the truth have given rise to questionings, from whence spring vain and self-willed heresies, when man have not learnt or really received knowledge, but have merely got a conceit of it. We must therefore spend more thought in searching for the very truth, which alone has for its subject the very God. And sweet are the discovery and the remembrance which attend on toil. The effect of the heresies should therefore be to make one buckle to the toil of discovery and not to abandon it altogether. So too, if we have set before us on the one hand ripe natural fruit, and on the other fruit of wax made to resemble it as closely as possible, we ought not to abstain from both on account of their similarity, but to distinguish the real from the apparent both intuitively and by strict process of reasoning. And just as, if there were only one royal road, but many by-roads, some leading to a precipice, some to a rushing torrent, or deep sea, a man would not hesitate to travel because of this diversity, but would make use of the king's safe highway; so we must not give up our search because there are different views as to the truth, but must hunt all the more earnestly for the most exact knowledge concerning it. For even among the herbs of the garden weeds spring up, but the husbandmen do not therefore desist from gardening. Since then nature supplies us with many helps for testing the things we are told, we ought also to discover the harmony of the truth. Hence we are rightly condemned if we withhold our assent to the things which we ought to believe, because we fail to distinguish what is incongruous and unseemly and unnatural and false from what is true and consistent and seemly and natural; and these helps we should make full use of in order to gain a knowledge of the real truth.

92. This is therefore an idle excuse on the part of the Greeks: for those who desire it will be able also to discover the truth, while those who put forward irrational grounds have no excuse for their judgment.[15] For what is their view of demonstration? Do they deny that there is such a thing or do they admit it? I suppose all would admit it except those who deny the evidence of the senses. But if there is such a thing as demonstration they

15 Rom. 2:1.

must descend to investigation and be taught demonstratively from the Scriptures themselves how the heretical schools went astray, and how it is only in the true and the ancient Church that there is the most exact knowledge and the really best school of thought. But of those who turn aside from the truth some try to deceive themselves only; others to deceive their neighbours as well. They, then, who are termed "wise in their own conceit," those, I mean, who think they have discovered the truth without any true demonstration; these men deceive themselves, thinking to have attained rest: and of such persons there is no small number, men that avoid inquiry for fear of being refuted and also flee from instruction because it condemns themselves. But those who try to impose on their followers are utterly unscrupulous, who, being well aware that they are absolutely without knowledge, nevertheless darken the truth with plausible sophisms. But in my opinion, the nature of such sophisms is entirely distinct from that of true arguments. Further, we know that it is necessary to give the terminology of the heresies in order that the truth may be clearly distinguished from them. For the sophists steal certain fragments of the truth for the injury of mankind and bury them in the human systems they have themselves devised, and then glory in presiding over what is rather a school than a Church.

Chapter XVI

93. But they who are willing to work for the noblest prizes will not relinquish their search for truth, until they obtain the proof from the Scriptures themselves. Now there are certain criteria common to all men, such as the senses; while the other technical criteria acquired by thought and reasoning, to distinguish between true and false arguments, are confined to those who have made truth their aim and practice. But the chief thing is to get rid of self-conceit, taking a position midway between exact science and rash opinionativeness, and to recognize that he who hopes for the eternal rest knows also that the entrance to it is toilsome and strait.[16] But let not him who has once received the gospel and, as it says, embraced salvation with joy[17] in the hour when he became acquainted with it—let not him, I say, "turn back like Lot's wife,"[18] nor recur to his former life which was devoted to the things of sense, nor yet to the heresies, for they in a sort imitate the heathen, not knowing the true God. For "he

16 Matt. 7:14.   17 Matt. 13:20.   18 Luke 17:31, 32.

that loveth father or mother more than me,"[19] i.e., than the true Father and teacher of the truth, who regenerates and re-creates and nourishes the elect soul—"he," saith he, "is not worthy of me," worthy, that is, to be a son of God and at once a disciple and friend and kin to God. For "no man who looks backward and puts his hand to the plough is fit for the kingdom of God."[20]

But, just as most people even now believe, as it seems, that Mary ceased to be a virgin through the birth of her child, though this was not really the case—for some say that she was found by the midwife to be a virgin after her delivery[21]—(94) so we find it to be with the Lord's Scriptures, which bring forth the truth and yet remain virgins, hiding within them the mysteries of the truth. "She has brought forth and has not brought forth,"[22] says the Scripture, speaking as of one who had conceived of herself and not from another. Wherefore the Scrip-tures are pregnant to the gnostics, but the heretics, not having examined them, dismiss them as barren. And though all men have the same faculty of judgment, some find their grounds for belief in following the dictates of reason, while others surrender themselves to pleasures and wrest the Scripture to suit their desires. But, methinks, the lover of truth needs energy of soul; for they who set themselves to the greatest tasks must meet the greatest disasters, unless they have received the canon of the truth from the truth itself. And such persons, having fallen away from the right path, generally go wrong in particulars also, as might be expected, because they have no criterion of truth and falsehood accurately trained to make the right choice. Otherwise they would have believed the divine Scriptures.

95. As if, then, one were to become a beast instead of a man, like those who were changed by Circe's drugs,[23] so is it with him who has spurned the tradition of the Church and has sud-denly taken up with the fancies of human sects; he has lost the character of a man of God, and of enduring trust in the Lord. But he who has returned from this deceit, after hearing the

---

[19] Matt. 10:37.   [20] Luke 9:62.
[21] For the story of the midwife, cf. Protevangelium of James, 19-20 (M. R. James, *Apocr. N.T.*, 46); for perpetual virginity of Mary, Origen, *in Matt.*, X, 17.
[22] Cf. Tertullian, *De Carne Christi*, 23, "legimus apud Ezechielem de vacca illa quae peperit et non peperit." (Probably from the apocryphal Ezekiel; M. R. James, *J.T.S.*, XV (1914) 240; Karl Holl, *Gesammelte Aufsätze*, II, 36.)
[23] Homer, *Odyssey*, X, 235 f.

Scriptures, and has turned his life to the truth, such an one becomes in the end as it were a god instead of a man. For in the Lord we have the first principle of instruction, guiding us to knowledge from first to last "in divers ways and divers portions"[24] through the prophets and the gospel and the blessed apostles. And, if any one were to suppose that the first principle stood in need of something else, it could no longer be really maintained as a first principle. He then who of himself believes the Lord's Scripture and his actual voice is worthy of belief, being one who would be naturally moved by the Lord to act for the benefit of men. Certainly we use it as a criterion for the discovery of the real facts. But whatever comes into judgment is not to be believed before it is judged, so that what is in need of judgment cannot be a first principle. With good reason therefore having apprehended our first principle by faith without proof, we get our proofs about the first principle *ex abundanti* from the principle itself, and are thus trained by the voice of the Lord for the knowledge of the truth. For we pay no attention to the mere assertions of men, which may be met by equally valid assertions on the other side. If, however, it is not enough just simply to state one's opinion, but we are bound to prove what is said, then we do not wait for the witness of men, but we prove the point in question by the voice of the Lord, which is more to be relied on than any demonstration, or rather which is the only real demonstration. From this science it comes that, while they who have but tasted of the Scriptures are believers, the gnostics, who have made further progress, are accurate judges of the truth; since even in the ordinary concerns of life craftsmen have an advantage over laymen, and give shape to finer models far surpassing common ideas.

96. So too we, obtaining from the Scriptures themselves a perfect demonstration concerning the Scriptures, derive from faith a conviction which has the force of demonstration. And though it be true that the heretics also have the audacity to make use of the prophetic Scriptures, yet in the first place they do not use them all, and in the second place they do not use them in their entirety, nor as the general frame and tissue of the prophecy suggest; but picking out ambiguous phrases, they turn them to their own opinions, plucking a few scattered utterances, without considering what is intended by them, but perverting the bare letter as it stands. For in almost all the passages they employ, you will find how they attend to the words

24 Heb. 1:1.

alone, while they change the meaning, neither understanding them as they are spoken, nor even using in their natural sense such extracts as they adduce.

But the truth is discovered not by altering the meanings of words (for by so doing they will subvert all true teaching), but by considering what is perfectly fitting and appropriate to the Lord and the Almighty God, and by confirming each thing that is proved according to the Scriptures from similar passages of the Scriptures themselves. Hence they are neither ready to turn to the truth, being ashamed to derogate from their own importance, nor have they any way of setting forth their own opinions but by doing violence to the Scriptures. Having hastily published to the world their false doctrines, which are palpably at variance with almost all the Scriptures, and being always confuted by our opposing arguments, they still even now persist in their refusal to accept some of the prophetic writings; while on the other hand they accuse us of inability to understand what is peculiar to them, as though we were quite of another nature; and at other times they are driven to deny even their own doctrines, being ashamed to confess openly what in private they boast of teaching.

97. For so we shall find it to be in all the heresies, when we examine the iniquities of their doctrines. When they are refuted by plain proof on our part that they are opposed to the Scriptures, you may see the upholders of the doctrine in question taking one or other of two courses: they either make light of the consistency of their own doctrines, or they make light of prophecy itself, in other words, of that which constitutes their own hope; preferring on each occasion that which commends itself to their own reason, rather than that which was spoken by the Lord through the prophets and is attested and confirmed by the gospel as well as by the apostles. Perceiving, then, that it was not merely a single doctrine which was at stake, but the keeping up of their heresies, and having no desire to discover the truth—for after reading the books we commonly use in public, they despised them as worthless—and aiming simply to exceed the common rule of the faith, they abandoned the truth. For being ignorant of the mysteries of the knowledge of the Church, and incapable of apprehending the grandeur of the truth, they were too sluggish to penetrate to the bottom of the matter, and so laid aside the Scriptures after a superficial reading.

98. Being elated therefore by a conceit of wisdom they are constantly quarrelling, showing that they care more to be

thought philosophers than to be[25] so in reality. For instance, though they lay no foundation of necessary principles, but are moved simply by the opinions of men, yet afterwards they labour to make the conclusion follow necessarily on their premises, and, for fear of being confuted, keep sparring with those who pursue the true philosophy. And their vanity impels them to endure everything, and stir every stone, as the phrase is, even going to the length of impiety through disbelieving the Scriptures, rather than surrender their heresy and the much-talked-of precedence in their assemblies, for the sake of which they so eagerly affect the first couch[26] in the drinking-bout of their mis-named Agapé.[27] But the knowledge of truth, which is found among us Christians, supplies, from what is already believed, faith for what is not yet believed—faith which is, so to speak, the substance of demonstration. On the other hand, it seems that heresy of every kind has absolutely no ear for what is expedient, but listens only to what is pleasurable; otherwise a heretic might have been healed, if he had only been willing to obey the truth. Now conceit, like every other ailment, requires a three-fold treatment: there must be a knowledge of the cause, and of the way in which this may be removed, and thirdly there must be discipline of the soul and the training which enables us to follow what is judged to be right.

99. For, as a clouded eye, so too the soul that is confused by unnatural opinions is unable to discern accurately the light of truth, but sees amiss even what lies before it. Certainly we are told that eels also lose their sight and are easily caught in turbid water.[28] And just as naughty children lock out their tutor, so the heretics shut out the prophecies from their church, holding them in suspicion because they convict and admonish them. I grant they patch up many lying inventions to give a sort of decent excuse for their neglect of the Scriptures; and herein they show their want of piety, quarrelling as they do with the divine commands, that is, with the Holy Spirit. And as we call almonds empty, not only when they have nothing in them, but when what is in them is worthless, so we say that the heretics are empty of the divine purposes and of the traditions of Christ,

---

[25] Aesch., *Sept. c. Th.*, 577; cf. Plato, *Rep.*, 361 B. For the quarrelsome behaviour of the heretical sects, cf. Celsus in Origen, *contra Celsum*, III, 10; V, 63.

[26] Matt. 23:6.

[27] On the riotous love-feasts of the sects, cf. *Strom.*, III, 10; *Paedag.*, II, 4:3–4.

[28] Aristotle, *Hist. Anim.*, VIII, 2 (592 A, 6 f.).

because they are the authors of dogmas which are in truth as bitter as the wild almond, except in so far as the clearness of the truth made it impossible for them to set aside or conceal it.

100. As, then, in war the soldier must not leave the post assigned to him by the general, so neither must we leave the post to which we are appointed by the Word, whom we have received as our captain both of knowledge and of life. But the greater part of men have not inquired whether they ought to follow any guide, and, if so, when and how he should be followed. For as is the word, such too should the life[29] of the believer be, so as to be able to follow God, as he holds his unswerving path[30] in all things from the beginning. But when a man breaks his word and so sins against God, if his weakness was due to a sudden impression, he must take care to have reasonable impressions in readiness; but if he is mastered by a habit that has gained dominion over him, and has so become what the Scripture calls gross,[31] he must put an absolute stop to the habit and train his soul to resist it. And if there are some who seem to be attracted by contradictory opinions, they must gradually get rid of them, and resort to those who can introduce harmony[32] of opinions, those who can charm the timid and inexperienced with the spell of the divine Scriptures, making the truth plain by means of the agreement of the Testaments. But, as it seems, we incline rather to the common opinion, though it may involve contradiction, than to the truth with its sternness and severity.

Again of the three different mental conditions, ignorance, conceit, knowledge, ignorance is the characteristic of the heathen, knowledge of the true Church, conceit of the heretics. 101. Certainly one does not find scientific men making more positive and definite assertions about the objects of their knowledge, than these men about their opinions, so far as depends on unproved assertion. At any rate they despise and laugh at one another; and it sometimes happens that the same interpretation is held in the highest honour by one set and regarded as insane by another. And further we have learnt that there is a difference between voluptuousness, which must be assigned to the heathen, and strife which we must adjudge to the heresies, and on the other hand between joy which one must appropriate to the Church, and gladness which must be imputed to the true gnostic. And just as Ischomachus will make those who attend

29 Stoic maxim.   30 Plato, *Legg.*, 716 A.
31 Ex. 1:7.   32 Matt. 5:9.

to his instructions husbandmen, and Lampis sea-captains, and Charidemus commanders, and Simon horsemen, and Perdix hucksters, and Crobylus cooks, and Archelaus dancers, and Homer poets, and Pyrrho wranglers, and Demosthenes orators, and Chrysippus logicians, and Aristotle men of science, and Plato philosophers,[33] so he who obeys the Lord and follows the prophecy given through him, is fully perfected after the likeness of his teacher, and thus becomes a god while still moving about in the flesh.

It is from such a height, then, that they fall who do not follow God wherever he may lead them, and he leads them by way of the inspired writings.[34] Certainly, though the number of human actions is infinite, it may be said that there are only two causes of all failure, both of which are in our own power, viz., ignorance and weakness on the part of those who are neither willing to learn nor to gain the mastery over their desires. The former makes men judge wrongly, the latter prevents them from following out right judgments; for neither could any one act rightly if he were deceived in his judgment, even though he were perfectly able to carry out his determinations; nor on the other hand would he show himself blameless if he were a weakling in act, whatever might be his capacity to discern what was right.

102. Corresponding to these there are also two kinds of discipline provided, suitable for either class of failings; for the one, knowledge and the plain proof derived from the witness of the Scriptures; for the other, training according to reason controlled by faith and fear: and both of these grow up into perfect love. For the end of the gnostic on earth is in my opinion twofold, in some cases scientific contemplation, in others action.

Would that even these heretics would take a lesson from these suggestions and be reformed and turn to the Almighty God! But if, like deaf adders, they refuse to listen to the charm,[35] new in form, but most ancient in substance, may they at any rate undergo the divine discipline, submitting to the corrections of their heavenly Father before the Judgment, until they become ashamed and repent, instead of rushing headlong into utter condemnation through their stubborn disobedience! For there are also partial forms of discipline, which are called chastisements, into which most of us, who have trespassed from among the Lord's people, slip and fall. But as children are chastened

33 Similar list of teachers in Aelian, *Var. hist.*, IV, 16 (perhaps from the same source as that followed by Clement).
34 Cf. II Tim. 3:16.   35 Ps. 58:4, 5.

by their teacher or their father, so are we by Providence. For God does not take vengeance (for vengeance is a retaliation of evil), but he chastens with a view to the good, both public and private, of those who are chastened. These things I have set forth, desiring to turn aside from their proclivity to heresy those who are eager to learn; but as for others, I have used these arguments out of a longing desire to make them cease from the prevailing ignorance or stupidity or ill condition or whatever it is to be called, and endeavouring to persuade and bring over to the truth those who are not yet altogether incurable.

103. For there are some who absolutely refuse to give ear to those who urge them to seek the truth: aye, and they aim at smartness, pouring out blasphemous words against the truth, while they credit themselves with the possession of the highest knowledge, though they have not learnt or sought or laboured or discovered the harmony of truth—men who excite our pity rather than our hate for such perverseness. But if any one is still curable, able to endure the plain-speaking of the truth, when it burns and cuts away their false opinions, like the cautery or the knife, let him lend an attentive ear. And this will be so unless, in their slothfulness, they thrust away the truth, or through ambition press after novelties. For those are slothful who, having it in their power to provide the fitting proofs for the Divine Scriptures from the Scriptures themselves, nevertheless select what is exclusively favourable to their own pleasures; and those are ambitious who, of set purpose, explain away by other spurious arguments the beliefs which attach to the inspired words, beliefs handed down by the blessed apostles and teachers, and thus oppose divine tradition with human doctrines in order to establish their heresy. For indeed what place was left among the great men of old—I mean, according to the judgment of the Church—for Marcion, say, or Prodicus[36] or the like, who walked not along the straight road? For they could not have surpassed in wisdom the men that went before, so as to discover something beyond what had been truly spoken by them; but might have been well content if they had been able to understand what had been already handed down.

104. We find, then, that the gnostic alone, having grown old in the study of the actual Scriptures, guards the orthodox doctrine of the apostles and the Church and lives a life of perfect rectitude in accordance with the gospel, being aided by the Lord to discover the proofs he is in search of both from the law and the

[36] Cf. above III, 30; VII, 41.

prophets. For the life of the gnostic, as it seems to me, is nothing else than deeds and words agreeable to the tradition of the Lord. "But knowledge belongeth not to all."[37] "For I would not have you ignorant," says the apostle, "that all were under the cloud and partook of spiritual meat and drink,"[38] evidently arguing that not all who hear the word have been capable of understanding the greatness of knowledge, both in deed and word. Wherefore also he added, "But he was not well pleased with all."[39] Who is meant by "he"? It is he who said, "Why call ye me 'Lord,' and do not the will of my Father?"[40] the teaching, that is, of the Saviour, which is our spiritual food[41] and a drink that knows no thirst,[42] the water of gnostical life.[43] "Aye," say they, "we are told that 'Knowledge puffeth up.'"[44] To whom we reply, perhaps seeming knowledge is said to puff up, if it is supposed that the interpretation of the word is self-conceit. But if, as is rather the case, the apostle's language means to have lofty and true thoughts, then the objection vanishes. Let us however confirm what has been said by following the Scriptures.

105. "Wisdom," says Solomon, "inspirited her own children."[45] Assuredly the Lord did not infuse conceit by means of the particular courses of instruction; but faith in truth and confidence in the knowledge handed down through the Scriptures, make a man disdain the seductions to sin; and it is this disdain that is signified by the term "inspirited": it teaches the sublimity of the wisdom implanted in children by learning. At any rate the apostle says, "And I will know not the speech of them that are 'inspirited,' but the power,"[46] whether ye have a lofty, that is, a true understanding of the Scriptures[47] (for nothing is higher than truth); for herein lies the power of the "inspirited" children of wisdom; meaning something of this sort, "I shall know whether ye take a just pride in knowledge." For, as David says, "In Judah is God known,"[48] i.e., to those who are Israelites according to knowledge. For Judah is by interpretation "Confession." With reason therefore has it been said by the apostle, "This, thou shalt not commit adultery, thou shalt not steal, thou shalt not covet, and if there be any other command, it is briefly comprehended in this saying, Thou shalt love thy neighbour as thyself."[49] For we must never adulterate the truth, nor steal the rule of the Church, as those who follow the

---

37 I Cor. 8:7.   38 I Cor. 10:1–4.   39 I Cor. 10:5.
40 Luke 6:46; Matt. 7:21.   41 I Cor. 10:3.   42 John 4:14.
43 Rev. 22:17.   44 I Cor. 8:1.   45 Ecclesiasticus 4:11.
46 I Cor. 4:19.   47 Luke 24:45.   48 Ps. 76:1.   49 Rom. 13:9.

heresies, gratifying our own desires and ambitions with a view to the deception of our neighbours, whom we ought to love above every thing and teach to cling to the truth itself. At any rate it has been expressly said, "Tell among the heathen his doings,"[50] in order that those who have been thus forewarned may not be judged, but may be converted. But as many as flatter with their tongues[51] have their punishments prescribed.

CHAPTER XVII

106. They, then, who engage in impious words and introduce them to others, and make no good use, but an utterly wrong use, of the divine words, such men "neither enter themselves into the kingdom of God, nor permit"[52] those whom they have deceived to attain to the truth. Nay, they have not even got the key[53] of the door themselves, but only a false or, as it is commonly called, a skeleton key, which does not enable them to throw open the main door,[54] and enter, as we do, through the tradition of the Lord; but they cut a side door and break secretly through the wall of the Church; and so overstepping the bounds of truth, they initiate the soul of the impious into their mysteries. For it needs no long discourse to prove that the merely human assemblies which they have instituted were later in time than the Catholic Church. For the teaching of our Lord, during his life upon earth, begins under Augustus and Tiberius, and is completed in the middle of the reign of the latter, and the preaching of his apostles, at least up to the end of Paul's ministry, is completed under Nero; while the heresiarchs began quite late, about the time of the emperor Hadrian, and lasted to the age of Antoninus the elder, as was the case with Basilides, in spite of his claiming to have been taught by Glaucias, whom they themselves boast to have been the interpreter of Peter. So too they report that Valentinus heard Theodas, who was a disciple of Paul. 107. For Marcion, who lived about the same time, associated with them as an elder with his juniors. After him Simon was for a short time a hearer of Peter.[54a]

Such being the case, it is evident that these later heresies and those which are still more recent are spurious innovations on the oldest and truest Church. From what has been said I think it

[50] Ps. 9:11.   [51] Ps. 5:9.   [52] Matt. 23:14.
[53] Matt. 16:19; Luke 11:52.   [54] John 10:1 ff.
[54a] Cf. Acts 8. "After him" is probably corrupt. Read perhaps "Only Simon . . ." (Wilamowitz). Nothing is known of Theodas or Glaucias.

has been made plain that unity is a characteristic of the true, the really ancient Church, into which those that are righteous according to the divine purpose are enrolled. For God being one and the Lord being one, that also which is supremely honoured is the object of praise, because it stands alone, being a copy of the one First Principle: at any rate the one Church, which they strive to break up into many sects, is bound up with the principle of Unity. We say, then, that the ancient and Catholic Church stands alone in essence and idea and principle and pre-eminence, gathering together, by the will of one God through the one Lord, into the unity of the one faith, built upon the fitting covenants (or rather the one covenant given at different times) all those who are already enlisted in it, whom God foreordained, having known before the foundation of the world[55] that they would be righteous. And, further, the pre-eminence of the Church, like the principle of its constitution, is in accordance with the Monad, surpassing all other things and having nothing like or equal to itself.

108. Of this we shall speak on a future occasion. But of the heresies some are called after the name of the founder, as that which is called after Valentinus, and Marcion, and Basilides, though the last sect professes to cite the opinion of Matthias.[56] I say "professes," for, as the teaching, so also the tradition of all the apostles has been one and the same. Other heresies are called from the place where they arose, as the Peratici; others from their nationality, as the Phrygian heresy; others from their practice, like the Encratites; others from peculiar opinions, as the Docetae and Haematitae; others from the personages they admire, as the Cainites and those who are styled Ophites; others from their unblushing immoralities, as the so-called Entychitae among the Simonians.

Chapter XVIII

109. Before closing my discourse I should like, for the benefit of the more speculative members of the Church, to throw a little light from the sacrificial law, concerning clean and unclean beasts, in reference to the ordinary Jews and the heresies which are mystically distinguished, as unclean, from the Church of God. We are taught by the Scriptures that the victims which divide the hoof and chew the cud are clean[57] and acceptable to God, implying that the righteous make their approach to the

[55] Eph. 1:4-5.   [56] Cf. note on *Strom.*, VII, 82, above.   [57] Lev. 11:3 f.

Father and the Son through their faith—for in this consists the stability of those that divide the hoof—and that they study and ruminate the oracles of God[58] by night and day[59] in the mental receptacle of knowledge, which being also a kind of gnostic discipline, is figuratively described in the law as the chewing of the cud by a clean animal. But those who are wanting in both or even in one of these qualifications are rejected. For instance, those which chew the cud without dividing the hoof signify the Jews generally, who have the oracles of God[58] in their mouth, but have not the firm footing of faith stayed upon truth, which carries them to the Father through the Son. Whence this class of creatures is liable to slip, as is natural where the foot is not parted and they are not stayed upon the doubleness of faith. For we read: "No one knows the Father but the Son, and he to whom the Son may reveal him."[60] On the other hand, those too are unclean which divide the hoof without chewing the cud. For this phrase denotes the heretics who take their stand on the name of the Father and of the Son, but have no power to bring out the exact perspicuity of the oracles by subtle distinctions and by smoothing away of difficulties, while their prosecution of the works of righteousness, if they prosecute them at all, is rough and careless rather than exact.

110. It is to some such persons that the Lord says: "Why call ye me Lord, Lord, and do not the things which I say?"[61] But those who do not divide the hoof nor chew the cud are utterly unclean. As Theognis says, "You Megarians are neither in the third class, nor even the twelfth, nor in any number or account whatever; but are like the chaff which the wind scattereth from the face of the earth,[62] and as a drop of a bucket."[63],[64]

Having completed this introduction, and given a summary outline of ethical philosophy, wherein we have scattered the sparks of the doctrines of the true knowledge dispersedly here and there, as we promised, so that it should not be easy for the uninitiated who came across them to discover the holy traditions; let us pass on to our general argument.

111. Now it seems that what are known as *Miscellanies* are not to be compared to ornamental parks with rows of ordered

---

[58] Rom. 3:2; Num. 24:16.   [59] Ps. 1:2.   [60] Luke 10:22.
[61] Luke 6:46.   [62] Ps. 1:4   [63] Isa. 40:15.
[64] The quotation is wrongly ascribed to Theognis. The Megarians asked the oracle who were the most important people in Greece, and were told they were not in the reckoning at all. Cf. H. Chadwick on Origen, *contra Celsum*, IV, 31.

plantations to please the eye, but rather to some thickly wooded hill, overgrown with cypresses and planes and bay-tree and ivy, and at the same time planted with apple-trees and olives and figs, the cultivation of fruit-bearing and of woodland trees being intentionally mingled together, since the Scripture desires to withdraw from observation on account of those who venture secretly to steal its fruits. It is by transplanting the suckers and trees from these preserves that the gardener will furnish a beautiful park and pleasure-ground. Our *Miscellanies* therefore make no pretence of order or of choice diction, seeing that in this kind of composition the Greeks purposely object to over-sweetness of style, and sow their doctrines secretly and not in a plain, unmistakable manner, seeking to exercise the diligence and ingenuity of the readers, if there should be such. For we must provide a large variety of baits owing to the varieties of fish.

And now, having concluded our seventh *Miscellany*, we will make a new start in our discussion of what is to follow.[65]

[65] Clement wrote no more of the *Stromateis*, for what reason we do not know. The so-called VIIIth book is not a continuation, and consists of notes, perhaps a rough draft for lectures. It does not bear signs of having been intended for publication.

ORIGEN

ABBREVIATIONS

The following abbreviations have been used, in addition to others which it is unnecessary to explain.

A.N.F.—*Ante-Nicene Fathers*, ed. A. Roberts and J. Donaldson, Edinburgh, 1864, and Buffalo, 1885.

Anonymous—Notes on the *De Oratione* of Origen by an anonymous English scholar, included in the edition of W. Reading.

Bigg—C. Bigg, *The Christian Platonists of Alexandria*, Oxford, 1913.

C.B.—(*Corpus Berolinense*): *Die griechischen christlichen Schriftsteller der ersten drei Jahrhunderte*, Berlin, 1897.

C.V.—(*Corpus Vindobonense*): *Corpus Scriptorum Ecclesiasticorum Latinorum*, Vienna, 1866.

D.A.C.L.—*Dictionnaire d'Archéologie Chrétienne et de Liturgie*, ed. F. Cabrol and H. Leclerq, Paris, 1907.

D.C.B.—*Dictionary of Christian Biography*, ed. W. Smith and H. Wace, London, 1877.

de Faye—E. de Faye, *Origène, Sa Vie, Son Œuvre, Sa Pensée*, 3 vols., Paris, 1923–1928.

Diels—*Doxographi Graeci*, collegit H. Diels, Berlin, 1879.

H.D.B.—J. Hastings, *Dictionary of the Bible*, Edinburgh, 1898.

H.E.—Historia Ecclesiastica.

I.C.C.—*International Critical Commentary*, Edinburgh.

J.T.S.—*Journal of Theological Studies*, London, 1899.

Koetschau—P. Koetschau, Introduction to, and Text of, the *De Oratione* of Origen in *C.B.* ii, pages lxxv–xc, and iii, pages 297–403, Berlin, 1899.

Lawlor and Oulton—Eusebius, *The Ecclesiastical History and The Martyrs of Palestine*, H. J. Lawlor and J. E. L. Oulton, 2 vols., London, 1927–1928.

Moulton—Milligan—J. H. Moulton and G. Milligan, *Vocabulary of the Greek New Testament, illustrated from the Papyri and other non-literary Sources*, London, 1914.
N.P.N.F.—*Nicene and Post-Nicene Fathers*, ed. H. Wace and P. Schaff, Oxford and New York, 1890.
P.G.—J.-P. Migne, Patrologia, Series Graeca, Paris, 1857.
P.L.—J.-P. Migne, Patrologia, Series Latina, Paris, 1844.
Rahlfs—Septuaginta, ed. A. Rahlfs, third edition, Stuttgart, 1949.
Reading—Gulielmus Reading, *Origenis de Oratione Liber*, London, 1728.
T—Codex in the Library of Trinity College, Cambridge, containing the Greek text of the *De Oratione* of Origen, complete apart from a few lacunae.
T.W.N.T.—*Theologisches Wörterbuch zum neuen Testament*, ed. G. Kittel, Stuttgart, 1933.
von Arnim—*Stoicorum Veterum Fragmenta*, collegit Ioannes ab Arnim, 4 vols., Leipzig, 1903–1924.

References to the following editions are to be assumed:
Irenaeus, *Adversus Haereses*: W. W. Harvey, Cambridge, 1857.
Origen:
  In Joh. A. E. Brooke, Cambridge, 1896.
  Philocalia. J. A. Robinson, Cambridge, 1893.

General Introduction

THE MAIN FACTS OF ORIGEN'S LIFE ARE WELL
known to students of the history of the early Church, and
a critical examination of them in detail is not called for
here, in a context which is concerned rather with one of his
writings. Inasmuch, however, as this is a devotional work, it
may be appropriate, in a rapid sketch of his career, to dwell
upon those facts in it which testify to that rich inner experience
of which the treatise *On Prayer* is a notable expression. Origen
was born about the year 186, and most probably in Alexandria,
although we are never told so in so many words. The name
"Origen" has been derived by some from the name of the
Egyptian god Horus, the suggestion being that he was born on
the anniversary day of that god; and, if this be correct, it would
go far to show that at the time of his birth, his parents, or at least
his father, were pagans. That this was probably so, other facts
serve to suggest. When in 202 a persecution against Jews and
Christians suddenly burst out at Alexandria, Leonides, Origen's
father, was arrested. Now this persecution, under Septimius
Severus, was not aimed at extirpating Judaism or Christianity,
but rather at propaganda at these religions making converts.
Spartian[1] says that under a grave penalty Severus forbade Jews
to make proselytes, and also issued a similar order against
Christians. If then Leonides was a convert to Christianity of
only a few years standing (for Origen was little more than a boy
when the persecution broke out), we can understand how such a
decree might, retrospectively, fall harshly upon such as he. In
any case we may detect in the picture that Eusebius draws of
Leonides[2] the fervent zeal of one who had come to embrace a

[1] *Severus*, 16 f.   [2] VI, 1:2, 1–13.

new faith. He was at great pains not only to instruct the boy in the Scriptures, but also to give them a primary place in his studies. The boy's early proficiency in sacred learning filled the father with a delight which was none the less sincere because he felt it prudent to conceal it. Like many a parent, before and after him, he recognized with wonderment and yet with humble thankfulness that God had chosen him to be the father of a saint.[3] It is not difficult, in any case, to see in Leonides the primary, human, source from which Origen drew that fervent devotion to God to which the pages of *On Prayer* bear so eloquent a testimony.

Of Origen's mother, and the part she played in his Christian upbringing, we know nothing. It can scarcely be urged against the sincerity of her faith that she strove to prevent her son from achieving his desire for martyrdom by the effective, if somewhat crude, method of hiding his clothes so that he could not leave the house by day. For indeed, at that early age—he was not yet seventeen when his father suffered martyrdom—Origen was filled, as Eusebius says, with "a zeal intense beyond his years."[4] This manifested itself in various ways: in his refusal to have anything to do with heretics or heresies, even at the risk of offending a generous benefactress of his; in his open espousal of the cause of martyrs, on trial or in prison; and especially in his asceticism. De Faye, indeed, affirms that this was not derived from Christianity, but from philosophy. Asceticism was "in the air," he says, an element in that religious syncretism which was so marked a feature of the Egypt of that time: and Origen in this followed the example of his day.[5] It is true that in describing Origen's asceticism Eusebius speaks of him as "living like a philosopher."[6] But he also expressly states that certain elements, at any rate, in his manner of life at that time found their express sanction in the gospel—those sayings which exhort us not to provide two coats nor to use shoes, nor indeed to be worn out with thoughts of the future.[7] It was not, as we shall see, the only occasion on which a literal following of an evangelical command guided his conduct.

Origen's gifts, and the need for their use at that time, decided at once what his career should be. The origins of the Catechetical School at Alexandria are obscure, but they seem to have been fortuitous. All we know is that a person named Pantaenus gathered round him a number of young men for the study and

[3] See the passage quoted on p. 186.   [4] *H.E.*, VI, 2:6.   [5] I, 13.
[6] *H.E.*, VI, 3:9.   [7] *Ibid.*, VI, 2:10: cf. Matt. 10:10, 6:34.

exposition of the Scriptures. Among them was Clement, who had arrived at Alexandria on his travels in search of knowledge, and having discovered Pantaenus had attached himself to this group of students. On the death of Pantaenus, Clement undertook the direction of the "School." Such a voluntary association of learners was not novel in the world of that day. We are not to think of it as a university or theological college in the modern sense of the term. All was free and unofficial. The authority exercised by the Head was *auctoritas* rather than *potestas*: the authority of the expert, of the teacher whose reputation, learning and skill in teaching were sufficient to create his clientele. Clement had chosen Pantaenus as his teacher for that reason. And when Clement fled from Alexandria on the persecution of Severus (202–203), Origen was selected as his successor. It may be that the circumstances of the time created a limited choice. But in any case Origen was known to be Clement's most brilliant pupil, although apparently only his pupil for a short time. He was then under eighteen years of age; but all accounts speak of his precocity. His competence as a teacher was already recognized. His zeal was undaunted by the dangers that confronted an open profession of the Christian way of life. And so this boy succeeded to the "chair" of a venerable and learned teacher of over fifty years of age.

From the first Origen appears to have been successful as Head of the School; and as time went on his reputation increased and more and more pupils came to him. Had the state of the Church at Alexandria been normal, the free and independent position that Pantaenus and Clement had enjoyed might have been his too. But persecution had driven from the city those to whom the instruction of catechumens would naturally have been entrusted; and in their absence Demetrius, the Bishop of Alexandria, committed to Origen alone that task.[8] Even then, all went happily at first, and none could have foreseen that the direct link with ecclesiastical authority would have had such tragic consequences. The School attracted pupils of greater proficiency and learning, so much so that whereas Origen had previously eschewed the teaching of pagan letters, and indeed is said to have sold off his "classical" books, he was now compelled to resume the study of Greek philosophy,[9] place it upon his curriculum, and assign the teaching of the less mature pupils to an assistant named Heraclas.

It would appear to be during this period of expansion,

8 Eusebius, *H.E.*, VI, 3:8.   9 *Ibid.*, ch. 15, 18, 19.

probably before 210, that Origen performed the act which was to be used by his subsequent detractors to his lasting disadvantage. Finding that pupils of both sexes were coming to his classes, "he took the saying *There are eunuchs which made themselves eunuchs for the kingdom of heaven's sake* in too literal and extreme a sense."[10] It has been frequently remarked how strange it was that Origen, the allegorizer *par excellence* of the Scriptures, should in this instance have fallen into the opposite error. We have seen, however, that previously he had based ascetic practices upon a literal interpretation of sayings in the Gospel; and few are absolutely consistent when it comes to applying Biblical principles to their own case. The truth probably is that by nature and disposition Origen was inclined towards "severity to the body," and this tendency was reinforced by his Platonic idealism. Nor have we reason to believe that in the Alexandria of his day, or at any rate in the circle in which he moved, his action would necessarily be censured. Eusebius indeed says that "Demetrius got to know of it later . . . and while he marvelled exceedingly at him for his rash act, he approved the zeal and sincerity of his faith, bade him be of good cheer, and urged him to attach himself now all the more to the work of instruction."[11]

The story of the worsening in relations between Demetrius and Origen cannot be told in detail, for sufficient materials are lacking, and we can only put forward probable reasons. Clearly the bishop had a right to supervise Origen's movements, since preparation of the catechumens (apart from the other teaching of the School) was a matter for which the Church authorities were ultimately responsible. But Origen's fame was now becoming world-wide. He was invited to pay visits to other parts of the world, for example, to Arabia and Palestine; and when at Caesarea, although still a layman, was requested to discourse and expound the Scriptures publicly in the church there. We are left in no doubt of the fact that Demetrius resented this permission being given. He wrote that "such a thing had never been heard of, nor taken place hitherto, that laymen should preach in the presence of bishops." In defence of their action, Alexander, Bishop of Jerusalem, and Theoctistus, Bishop of Caesarea, point out that Demetrius's statement was incorrect, and from their own knowledge cite other instances of laymen being allowed by bishops to preach.[12]

This "incident," which took place about 215, passed off. Demetrius recalled Origen by letter, sending messengers to urge

[10] Eusebius, *H.E.*, VI, 8:2.   [11] *Ibid.*, 8:3.   [12] *Ibid.*, 19:17, 18.

his speedy return: and he resumed the work of the School as diligently as before. Clearly, however, Demetrius felt that his authority was being challenged; and it may be also that he was jealous of Origen's fame. A further reason for the bishop's action may have lain in the development of church order at that time at Alexandria. According to the famous, if much disputed, statement of Jerome,[13] down to the episcopates of Heraclas (the successor of Demetrius) and Dionysius the presbyters at Alexandria always chose one of their number and styled him "bishop," apparently without consecration. If this be so, it may well be that during the long term of office of Demetrius (190–233), things at Alexandria were already moving towards such a system of monarchical episcopacy as encouraged Demetrius to emphasize his authority.

The order of incidents connected with Origen's final departure from Alexandria is uncertain, since the evidence of Eusebius and Photius and others does not tally at every point; but of the main facts, and their permanent result, we are left in little doubt. It is clear that even before he left Alexandria for good, considerable tension prevailed. The year was 231–232. Origen had then got as far as the fifth "tome" of his Commentary on *John*, and though, as he says,[14] "the storm at Alexandria" seemingly hindered his work, he succeeded in dictating what was given him to say, "for Jesus rebuked the winds and the waves of the sea." When he had proceeded some way upon the sixth tome, he "was rescued from Egypt, God who had brought out his people thence, delivering" him. It seems on the whole most probable that this deliverance came to him through a call to important work in Greece, to which he travelled by way of Palestine.[15] But while at Caesarea a momentous thing happened. He was ordained presbyter by the bishops there; and if we are to follow at this point the translation, or paraphrase, of the *Church History* of Eusebius made by Rufinus, they were about to raise him to the episcopate,[16] when Demetrius, hearing of what was afoot, spread the information about his act of self-mutilation when a young man, for the purpose not only of stopping Origen's consecration but also of censuring even those who had raised him to the presbyterate. The action taken by Demetrius in Alexandria itself is obscure in its details, but it would appear that he summoned one or two synods of bishops,

13 *Ep.*, CXLVI, 1.   14 *In Joh.*, VI, 2.
15 Eusebius *H.E.*, VI, 23:4: Lawlor and Oulton, II, 218.
16 "summo eum sacerdotio iam iamque dignum probarent." *Ibid.*, VI, 8:4.

the upshot of which was that Origen was not only excluded
from Alexandria but also deprived of the priesthood. His
degradation was communicated to all bishops, and Jerome is
our authority for stating that all endorsed it, with the exception
of the Bishops of Palestine, Arabia, Phoenicia, and Achaia.[17]

This was the greatest spiritual crisis in Origen's life; and it is
worthy of note that he met it like a true Christian philosopher.
Though "the enemy" (i.e., Demetrius) "made war most bitterly
against us by means of his new letters which were truly at enmity with the gospel, and though he stirred up against us all the
winds of wickedness, reason[18] called me to stand firm for the
contest and to preserve the inner self,[19] lest haply evil thoughts
should have power to bring the storm against my soul also,
rather than to compose the rest of the book out of season before
my mind had recovered its calm."[20] In other words, Origen's
chief concern, in this situation, was to preserve his spiritual
forces unbroken. De Faye has expressed this with sympathy and
insight. "What appears to have caused him the most anxiety
was not so much the consequences that might result from the
furious campaign of Demetrius, as the effect that might be produced in his own thoughts by so bitter and odious a conflict.
Origen trembled, as he says, for his own soul. It might founder
in the tempest. Elsewhere, he expresses himself more directly.
He was afraid of being embittered, of getting into a passion, of
replying by the same methods to the malicious insinuations and
calumnies. Nevertheless, he emerged from the tempest intact.
What was it that preserved him? He tells us with a clarity which
leaves no room for any doubt. It was his mystical faith in Jesus.
That, he is fully aware, lifted him above sentiments and passions
which an injustice of this kind might easily have engendered in
him."[21]

That Origen was successful in achieving this spiritual conquest is also evident not only from his resumption of literary
work generally but also from the treatise *On Prayer* in particular,
which, as we shall see,[22] was composed in 233 or 234, that is,
within a year or so of "the storm" at Alexandria which caused
him to leave it and its old associations for ever and to settle down
eventually at Caesarea. As he says himself,[23] the fiery darts of

---

[17] *Ep.*, 33:5; 84:10; but see p. 432 and the arguments there put forward for
holding another view of the reasons for Origen's condemnation.
[18] Or "the Word." [19] Lit., "the guiding principle."
[20] *In Joh.*, VI, 2. [21] *Origène*, I, 38, 39.
[22] P. 181. [23] *In Joh.*, VI, 2.

the wicked had been quenched by God, his soul had become accustomed to what had happened, he had learned to bear with equanimity the attacks of his enemies, and, as it were, a period of calm weather had set in. And, as we shall also see, one of the features of the treatise is its insistence upon the right disposition of him who engages in prayer: he must come to it without distraction, without anger, without malice.

The remainder of Origen's life can be summarized briefly here. Eventually he settled at Caesarea in Palestine and made it his home, certainly before 240. The intervening years were marked by much travelling, in the course of which he visited Athens, Ephesus, Antioch, Caesarea in Cappadocia, and also Tyre, with which he appears to have been associated more definitely. His reputation in general does not seem to have suffered as a result of "the storm" at Alexandria. Demetrius died soon afterwards, in 233, and he was succeeded by Origen's old assistant in the School, Heraclas. Origen established another School at Caesarea, to which he attracted some of the most brilliant Christian pupils of that day, who were afterwards destined as bishops to mould the theology of succeeding centuries— Gregory Thaumaturgus, Bishop of Neocaesarea in Pontus, who has left us a panegyric of his master,[24] his brother Athenodorus, Firmilian of Caesarea in Cappadocia, and others. He was also sought after as a consultant theologian on many occasions. We hear of him being called in to refute the errors of Beryllus, Bishop of Bostra, in Arabia, concerning the Person of Jesus Christ; and again, also in Arabia, about the soul and the resurrection.[25] Within recent years the record[26] has been discovered of a discussion also held by Origen with a bishop named Heracleides and other bishops associated with him, *coram populo*, on the Father, the Son, and the soul. The editor[27] supposes that this also took place in Arabia. In all these it seems to have been assumed that Origen was the right person to give the correct and orthodox answers on the points in dispute. (Whether those answers would satisfy the Church today is another matter.) At the same time it would appear that Origen's soundness in the faith was not everywhere unchallenged. According to Eusebius, "he wrote to Fabian, and to very many other rulers of Churches, with reference to his orthodoxy."[28] It is scarcely sufficient to

[24] See below, p. 179.   [25] Eusebius, *H.E.*, VI, ch. 33, 37.
[26] A translation, with introduction and notes, by the Rev. Henry Chadwick, is included in this volume.   [27] J. Scherer, Cairo, 1949.
[28] *H.E.*, VI, 36:4.

A.C.—12

suppose, as de Faye does,[29] that this was merely to repudiate falsifications of what he had actually said in public discussions. That he was sometimes misrepresented is undoubtedly true. But the phrase "very many other rulers of Churches"[30] suggests, on the evidence of his warm admirer, that Origen's teaching had, even in his own lifetime, given rise to widespread questioning.

We need not seek to give a detailed account of Origen's life after his departure from Alexandria. Indeed the evidence upon which such an account could be based is lacking. It was, however, the period of his most prolific literary activity. He had begun to write in 218, and even before 231 portions of two important works, the *De Principiis* and the Commentary on *John*, had been completed. But after 231 not only were these works finished, but a great number of other commentaries were written, and, in addition, special works such as the treatise *On Prayer*, the treatise *On Martyrdom* and the long and important book *Contra Celsum*. Moreover, Origen had always been a fluent *viva voce* expounder of Scripture; but it was not until he was sixty years of age (c. 246) that he allowed his *Homilies*, as he called them, to be taken down in shorthand and published. These were of a simpler, more popular character, and were intended for those who could not follow the more difficult commentaries, from which, however, they differed in presentation rather than in fundamental ideas or doctrine. It is certain that only a fraction, perhaps one-third, of his enormous literary output is extant.

The treatise *On Martyrdom*, written in 235, makes it clear that Origen, now a man of fifty, had not changed in his ideas since a boy as concerning the highest form of Christian witness. Martyrdom was in his opinion the supreme achievement of the Christian life. There can be little doubt that he would have desired this end for himself. But if martyrdom, in the commonly accepted sense of the term, was denied him, he may certainly be ranked high among the confessors. The persecution of Decius broke out in 249, and under it Origen suffered all but the extreme penalty. Eusebius speaks[31] of what he endured for the word of Christ, chains and tortures, punishments inflicted on his body, punishments as he lay in irons and in the recesses of his dungeon, and cruel stretching of his legs for many days on end in the stocks. But he survived all this, and so was enabled to encourage others, and especially the faint-hearted, by his ex-

[29] I, 43.   [30] De Faye omits to take in consideration these words.
[31] *H.E.*, VI, 39:4.

ample and his helpful words. No doubt his sufferings hastened his end, which took place, probably at Tyre, in 255, when he was sixty-nine years of age.

De Faye says, of the treatise *On Martyrdom*, "veut-on connaître le chrétien qu'était Origène, c'est là qu'il faut le chercher."[32] The same might be said of the *De Oratione*, which reveals Origen as a man of prayer, who was not content simply to deal with the matter of prayer in general (as he might have done in the circumstances), but was also anxious to speak of Christian prayer as taught by the Saviour, his words and his example, and what it involves for us who engage in it, both in the inner life and in the life of action. This, we hope, will be made plain in the Introduction and in the Treatise itself. But it may be well to illustrate this aspect of Origen from another source; and for this we may select the panegyric on Origen by Gregory Thaumaturgus, to which we have already referred. There is much in this composition which is artificial, rhetorical, and even fulsome. We cannot read it aright unless we relate it to similar compositions of the schools. Nevertheless, it is impossible not to recognize, under its exuberant verbiage, the genuine love of the writer for Origen as a teacher and a man. Here it will be sufficient to quote the closing section,[33] which has a special appropriateness when we consider that it is addressed to the author of the *De Oratione*. Gregory and his brother, after many years of instruction under Origen, are about to leave for their own country; and Gregory bids his master farewell in these words: "Do thou, dear heart, arise and when thou hast prayed send us on our way. Having kept us safely when we were with thee by thy holy teaching, so continue to keep us safely when we are away from thee by thy prayers. Do thou commit and commend us continually; or rather commit us to him who led us to thee, even God, giving him thanks for all that has been granted us in the past, and imploring him still to lead us by his hand, to watch over us always in the days to come, to instil into our minds his precepts, and to fill us with that godly fear which will be the best guide of our steps in the future. For when we are gone from thee our service of him will lack that freedom which it had in thy company. Implore him to vouchsafe us some encouragement when we lose thy presence, to send us an angel to be our good conductor upon the way. And entreat him also to turn our steps and bring us back to thee; for that is the one thing above all else which should prove our consolation."

[32] I, 45.   [33] *In Origenem Oratio Panegyrica*, ch. xix (*P.G.*, X, 1101).

On Prayer

INTRODUCTION

THE OCCASION OF THE TREATISE ON PRAYER

THE TREATISE *On Prayer* AND *The Exhortation to Martyrdom* are distinctive among the extant works of Origen as being occasional in respect of their composition, that is to say, they were called forth by the special needs of a particular incident. De Faye[1] styles them, happily enough, *Écrits de Circonstance*. It was otherwise with the *De Principiis*, in which Origen deliberately attempted to give a systematic exposition of theology, or the *Hexapla*, the fruit of his textual studies, or the commentaries and homilies which he poured forth during his lifetime as an expounder of Holy Scripture. The *Contra Celsum*, although it was an answer to a particular book, the *True Word* of the philosopher Celsus, can hardly be ranked as an occasional writing, since it was composed about seventy years after the book to which it was a reply. But the *Exhortation to Martyrdom* was written for the immediate object of consoling and exhorting two of his friends who had been cast into prison for their faith. And the treatise *On Prayer* arose, similarly, out of a particular occasion. Just as I Corinthians may be said to have been written, at any rate in part, in order to answer certain questions put to Paul by the Corinthian Church or individuals in it, so also *On Prayer* arose, as we shall see, out of a specific question about prayer. In both cases, the answer in scope and fullness far transcended the limits which the particular situation necessitated.

The year when *On Prayer* was written can be determined with more or less exactitude.[2] A topical allusion has been usually found in the language of XXVIII, 10: "Certain persons, I know

[1] I, 190.
[2] See Koetschau, I, lxxv–lxxvii. De Faye follows Koetschau in the matter of date (I, 190, 191).

not how, arrogating to themselves powers beyond the priestly office, perhaps because they have no accurate grasp of the knowledge that a priest should possess, boast that they are able to pardon even idolatry and to absolve adultery and fornication, on the ground that by means of prayer offered for those who have committed these deeds even *the sin unto death* is absolved."

The most obvious reference in this is to be found, not to powers exercised by martyrs and confessors (who were not necessarily priests), but to Callistus, Bishop of Rome (c. 217–223), who was accused by the rigorist party of that day, and notably by Hippolytus, of laxity in the matter of pardons and absolutions; and since the plural ("certain persons") is used, the reference is extended to include the successors of Callistus, namely, Urbanus (223–230) and Pontianus (230–235), under whom the Hippolytean schism is supposed to have continued. With this controversy, at any rate in its earlier stages, Origen was personally acquainted, for he visited Rome about the year 212, and listened, at least on one occasion to the preaching of Hippolytus, who at that time was engaged in his feud against Zephyrinus, the predecessor of Callistus, whom Zephyrinus had made his archdeacon.[3] Origen's temperament would naturally lead him to support the rigorist party.

Literary allusions in the treatise serve to date it more exactly. (1) In XXIII, 4, Origen refers to his comment on the passage Gen. 3:8, 9. Now the Commentaries on Genesis were begun at Alexandria, and eight volumes were written there,[4] the remaining four being added at Caesarea. In the twelve volumes he only covered the first four chapters of Genesis.[5] The comment on Gen. 3:8, 9 can hardly therefore have been in one of the earlier volumes; and in any case he speaks of the Commentaries on Genesis as a completed work: "we have treated these matters at length in our Commentaries on Genesis." This places the treatise *On Prayer* after his removal to Caesarea, i.e., after 231 or 232. (2) There is a reference in XV, 1, in the words "as is shown elsewhere," to the tenth tome of the Commentary on *John*.[6] The present tense is taken by Koetschau and de Faye to indicate that this Commentary was still in process of being written. In any case tomes vi–xxii were written, after Origen had left Alexandria, in Caesarea, and, according to Koetschau, between 232 and 235. Therefore 233 or 234 may be conjectured as the date of the composition of the treatise *On Prayer*. (3) Further, in this

---

3 Lawlor and Oulton, II, 201.   4 Eusebius, *H.E.*, VI, 24.
5 *Contra Celsum*, VI, 49.   6 X, 37 (21); Brooke, I, 230.

treatise there is no reference to martyrdom, although the opportunity to do so is not lacking.[7] This is a reason for placing its composition before the persecution of Maximin (235–237).

The immediate occasion of the treatise was a letter addressed to Origen by his friend Ambrose, in association with a lady named Tatiana, which stated, either on their own behalf or on that of others, certain objections and difficulties in regard to the practice of prayer.[8] From this letter Origen quotes a passage which makes it quite clear what was the nature of the difficulties urged against it. "First: if God knows the future beforehand, and it must come to pass, prayer is vain. Secondly: if all things happen according to the will of God, and if what is willed by him is fixed, and nothing of what he wills can be changed, prayer is vain."[9]

Had Origen been acquainted with Milton, he might have pointed out to Ambrose and Tatiana that such questions were discussed and discussed in vain by the fallen angels, who:

> reasoned high
> Of Providence, foreknowledge, will, and fate,
> Fix'd fate, free will, foreknowledge absolute,
> And found no end, in wandring mazes lost.[10]

But to evade a difficulty, or to give it up as insoluble, was never Origen's way; and least of all could he have adopted such a method towards a request made by Ambrose. He was, of course, none other than his devoted patron, friend, and admirer, to whom he owed both the incentive to produce books (if indeed Origen needed any such incentive) and also the abundant means to produce them. As to the incentive, Origen playfully refers to Ambrose as his task-master or slave-driver (ἐργο-διώκτης: Ex. 3:7; 5:6–14); and in a fragment of a letter printed by Delarue (I, 3) gives a lively picture of his importunities. "The holy Ambrose . . . supposing that I am a zealous worker and utterly athirst for the word of God, convicted me by his own zeal for work and passion for sacred studies . . . for neither when we are engaged in collating can we take our meals, nor, when we have taken them walk and rest our bodies. Nay, even at the times set apart for these things we are constrained to discourse learnedly and to correct our manuscripts. Neither can we sleep at night for the good of our bodies, since our learned discourse extends far into the evening. I need not mention that

[7] E.g., XXV, 3; XXIX, 2.   [8] II, 1; V, 1, 6.
[9] V, 6.   [10] *Paradise Lost*, II, 558–561.

our morning studies also are prolonged to the ninth, at times to the tenth, hour."[11] Ambrose was equally insistent in supplying Origen unstintingly (for he was a wealthy man) with the means to produce his commentaries, and also, we cannot doubt, such a treatise as the present one. Thanks to his liberality, as Origen dictated "there were ready at hand more than seven shorthand writers, who relieved each other at fixed times, and as many copyists, as well as girls skilled in penmanship."[12] The picture reminds us of a professor today in a university in the New World, who can command unlimited resources in respect of money and material and helpers for the production of learned works covering a vast field of inquiry. Therefore we can understand how Origen, even when engaged on a large and important work such as the Commentaries on *John*, could at the same time break in upon it and also produce a treatise which not only answered the particular questions propounded to him by his friends, but also (as we shall see) went on to deal with prayer in general and to give a lengthy exposition of the Lord's Prayer. His mind, through long training and practice, was fully equipped with a working knowledge of the principal philosophical systems. His knowledge of Holy Scripture was unrivalled. As an exegete his skill was remarkable. With all this knowledge and capacity in himself, he had only to dictate what flowed from his teeming brain to the shorthand writers. Eusebius notes that there were more than seven of them and that they relieved one another at fixed times. No doubt when Origen was dictating such an arrangement was as humane as it was necessary. Then the "copyists" transcribed the shorthand into longhand. And finally the girl scribes produced neatly written copies of the work.

Later on we shall give an analysis of the treatise. It is sufficient to say here that Origen himself gives a brief description of its contents in ch. XXXIV when he speaks of having treated (1) the problem of prayer, and (2) the prayer that is found in the Gospels, and the preceding context in Matthew. We must add, however, to these a third section containing a supplement to the general discussion of prayer, which should more appropriately have come after section (1). The work was, in fact, somewhat hastily put together, and Origen seems to have been aware of this, for in his concluding words he expresses the hope that he may be able "to treat again of these same matters with greater

---

[11] See Lawlor and Oulton, II, 213 f.
[12] Eusebius, *H.E.*, VI, 23. Cp. J. de Ghellinck, *Patristique et Moyen Age*, II, 215 f.

breadth and elevation and clarity," and adds "for the present you will read this book with indulgence." Furthermore we can detect throughout the composition signs which indicate a diversity of aim. Origen, in fact, wished at one and the same time to answer the questions of Ambrose and Tatiana and dissipate their doubts, to handle the subject of prayer generally, and finally to give an exposition of the Lord's Prayer. As a result, both here and in the treatise *On Martyrdom*, matter which should have been combined is broken up, and Origen repeats himself.[13] These faults in structural arrangement, however, do not seriously detract from the general "effect" of the treatise, which is perhaps the most readable of his works,[14] and reveals attractively many of his characteristic qualities. To these we shall now turn.

General Characteristics of Origen

To a student of Church History, the most obvious aspect of Origen is that he represents the Greek element in Christianity, as did also his predecessor in the Catechetical School at Alexandria, Clement. We cannot, however, simply leave the matter there, but rather must go on to ask, which characteristics in the Greek genius does he exemplify? The moment this question is asked, we begin to see that we must qualify such a general description and distinguish between certain elements within it. Origen shows, for example, little appreciation of Greek literature as such.[15] In his day, at Alexandria, Homer was the bible and the foundation of secular letters. His poetry represents, perhaps better than any other writer, the soul of the Greek genius and the imagination of the race. Origen cites him frequently in his other works, and calls him "the best of poets,"[16] but he shows little appreciation of his purely poetical qualities. It is the same with the other, rather few, Greek poets that he quotes from or refers to, such as Hesiod, Euripides, Aristophanes, Callimachus, Apollonius Rhodius. The references to Hesiod are particularly significant, as de Faye points out.[17] This poet inspires in him no admiration. He makes fun of Celsus because he calls him a divine poet. He appears to find no grace or beauty

---

[13] Koetschau, I, lxxxi.
[14] "No writing of Origen is more free from his characteristic faults, or more full of beautiful thoughts." B. F. Westcott in *D.C.B.*, IV, 124.
[15] See de Faye, I, ch. 14.   [16] *Contra Celsum*, VII, 6.
[17] I, 215.

in the description of the formation of Pandora, which he transcribes. In fact, Hesiod is for him only a retailer of myths. For the prose writers of Greece in the day of its glory Origen shows no greater appreciation, nor for its art.

Neither does Origen exhibit the Greek genius in his style and method of composition. Not for him the "nothing too much" or "the half is greater than the whole." On the contrary, he is diffuse, discursive, repetitive. His immense erudition, and especially his Biblical knowledge, frequently leads him aside into irrelevant digressions. The torrent of words and exuberance of ideas are at times reminiscent of the opening chapter of Ephesians. They certainly do not recall the reticence and restraint and economy of the classical period of Greek literature. If Greek "balance" is to be seen at all in Origen, it is in his grasp of the Christian revelation as a number of related truths. His *De Principiis* is the first and perhaps the greatest work on systematic theology. But this attempt "to see life steadily, and see it whole" was due, I imagine, less to an inner sense of artistic completeness than to a grasp of divine revelation as a unifying principle. That God shall be all in all was the vision which dominated his thinking and gave form to his conception of all things whether in heaven or on earth.

The Greek element in Origen is most truly seen in his love of inquiry and speculation. His training in philosophy and his subsequent teaching of it implanted in him the habit, which became a second nature, of asking questions, of probing into the meaning of things, and of conjecturing when no certain answer could be found. As a Biblical student, he is never tired of wresting from a passage its inner meaning, of comparing one passage with another and of confronting difficulties that may thereby arise. After the manner of the schools his custom is to bring forward an objector imaginary or real. This method of conducting an argument occurs again and again. Perhaps we owe Paul's doctrine of the resurrection body to the question of an inquiring and quick-witted Greek: *But some one will say, How are the dead raised?* [18] We meet the same kind of thing frequently even in a treatise such as *On Prayer*. [19] And this is not surprising because for Origen Christianity was chiefly an illumination of the reason, which by itself and without revelation was incapable of knowing God, and growth in grace was a deeper and deeper apprehension of divine mysteries and of the Logos as he communicates himself more and more to the soul of man. So it was that living

[18] I Cor. 15:35. [19] See p. 270.

in a day when few, at any rate in Alexandria, questioned the
validity of the allegorical method of interpreting the Scriptures,
Origen regarded it as one of the highest achievements to pierce
beneath the outward and obvious meaning of a passage to the
hidden and esoteric meaning that lay beneath. And even if such
a meaning escapes our present understanding, Origen is sure
that it exists and is known to the divine Logos "who has contemplated the Father's will."[20]

It would be a great mistake, however, to picture Origen as a
mere intellectualist and his religion as simply and solely a kind
of higher *gnosis*. The intellectual side of him was balanced by
purity of soul, flame of devotion and virtue of life. "Dedicated
to God" or "genuinely devoted to God"[21] was for him a description of the true Christian. If, on the one hand, he seems to lay
much stress upon prayer as contemplation of God, on the other
he speaks "of the whole life of the saint as one great unbroken
prayer," since he "combines with the prayer the needful deeds
and the prayer with the fitting actions."[22] Again and again he
reminds us of the duty of love and forgiveness, a virtue which, in
view of his cruel wrongs, he had himself much occasion to practise.[23] From boyhood his soul was aflame for martyrdom; and
there is little doubt that the end of his life was hastened by the
tortures he endured for the name of Christ. Origen was indeed
one of those rare souls whose light "shineth more and more unto
the perfect day."[24] Whether his doctrine of the pre-existence of
souls is true or false, it seemed from the first that his body was
inhabited by something from another sphere. "It is said that
many a time his father would stand over the sleeping boy and
uncover his breast, as if a divine spirit were enshrined therein,
and kissing it with reverence count himself happy in his goodly
offspring."[25]

In his capacity for combining as a unity in himself intellectual
passion with warm personal devotion to God in Christ and the
practical virtues of a Christian, Origen is perhaps unique among
the Fathers. He had many disciples, and has had many followers, but never one of them who equalled him in this. Arno-
bius could write a long work without revealing a distinctively
Christian spirit. Boethius could keep his philosophy and
theology apart, and write *The Consolations of Philosophy* without
betraying that he was a Christian. We have only to reflect for

[20] XXVII, 14.   [21] IX, 2; XIII, 5.
[22] XII, 2.   [23] See IX, 3; XXVIII, 7, 8.
[24] Prov. 4:18.   [25] Eusebius, *H.E.*, VI, 2:11.

a moment to see that such detachment would be impossible for
Origen. John Scotus Erigena is a kind of "throw-back" to
Origen across a gulf of some six hundred years, and like Origen
was a great intellectualist: but we have no reason to suppose
that he matched him as a devotional or practical Christian.
Hence, to follow Origen in his never-resting spirit of inquiry
concerning all things would inevitably involve for lesser mortals
a less sure grasp of Christianity as a way of personal life. This
thought has been beautifully expressed in the lines of Isaac
Williams in the *Lyra Apostolica*:

> Into God's word, as in a palace fair,
> Thou leadest on and on, while still beyond
> Each chamber, touched by holy wisdom's wand,
> Another opes, more beautiful and rare:
> And thou in each art kneeling down in prayer,
> From link to link of that mysterious bond
> Seeking for Christ: but oh, I fear thy fond
> And beautiful torch, that with so bright a flare
> Lighteth up all things, lest the heaven-lit brand
> Of thy serene Philosophy divine
> Should take the colourings of earthly thought,
> And I, by their sweet images o'erwrought,
> Led by weak Fancy, should let go Truth's hand,
> And miss the way into the inner shrine.[26]

THE TREATISE ON PRAYER AND ORIGEN'S ORTHODOXY

The concluding words of the poem just quoted lead us naturally to consider those questions concerning Origen's orthodoxy
that arise out of the *Treatise On Prayer*. The first of these is concerned with the Person to whom prayer should be addressed.
It is commonly stated that Origen teaches that prayer is to be
made to God alone, and not to Christ. This is not quite accurate.
Origen, following I Tim. 2:1, makes a distinction between four
forms of prayer, namely, "supplications, prayers, intercessions,
thanksgivings" (XIV, 2). Of these, he says, "intercession and
thanksgiving" may be addressed to all men, Christians ("saints")
or not, while "supplication" may be made to "saints" only
(XIV, 5). It follows, then, *a fortiori*, that "thanksgiving" and
"intercession" (and "supplication") may be addressed to

26 I owe this reference to A. R. Whitham, *History of the Christian Church*,
138.

Christ, "who has wrought such benefits for us by the will of the
Father"; and indeed Origen quotes from Scripture an example
of intercession to Christ, namely, the words of Stephen, "Lord,
lay not this sin to their charge."[27]

It is only, then, "prayer" in the special sense of the term that
is to be addressed to the Father alone. Origen defines this kind
of prayer as follows. "Prayer," he says, "is offered in a dignified
manner with ascription of praise by some one concerning matters
of importance."[28] He gives two examples of this, which, however, do not quite seem to square with his own definition: (1)
"A prayer of Habakkuk the prophet, with a song. O Lord, I
have heard thy voice, and was afraid: O Lord, I perceived thy
works and was astounded; in the midst of two living creatures
thou shalt be known, when the years draw nigh thou shalt be
observed."[29] (2) "Jonah prayed unto the Lord his God out of
the fish's belly, and he said, I called in my affliction unto the
Lord my God, and he heard me; out of the belly of hell thou
heardest my crying, even my voice. Thou didst cast me forth
into the depths of the heart of the sea, and the rivers were round
about me."[30] But in the first of these it is not easy to see what
are "the matters of importance" concerning which the prayer
is offered; and in the second there is no ascription of praise. It
would seem, therefore, that Origen has not quite clearly thought
out the distinctions he is endeavouring to make. Still, however,
the fact remains that in the *De Oratione* he does not allow
"prayer" as he defines it to be offered to Christ, but to the
Father only. And it is this limitation, chiefly, that caused the
treatise to be under a cloud, and added yet another reason for
holding its author suspect.

The point obviously raises the whole question of Origen's
doctrine of God, upon which, I suppose, the last word will never
be said. The matter is further complicated by the fact that often
we cannot be at all certain what Origen actually did write, for
many of his works are extant only in the Latin translation of
Rufinus, who is notoriously and admittedly unreliable as a
translator. It cannot be doubted that he frequently altered
Origen's language in a more orthodox direction. I have showed
that he did this also with some phrases of Eusebius of a doubtful
theological character.[31] Hence only those passages of Origen of
which the original Greek is extant can be safely trusted to give
his meaning. But it is not difficult to see that Origen's language

[27] Acts 7:60.   [28] XIV, 2.   [29] Hab. 3:1, 2 (LXX).
[30] Jonah 2:1, 2, 3.   [31] *J.T.S.*, XXX, 153–156.

concerning the relation of the Son (or the Word) to the Father must fail to be satisfactory from an orthodox point of view. Origen started from the conception of an absolutely transcendent God. God is intelligence, simple, invisible, incorporeal, or even beyond intelligence and being (substance), and cannot be comprehended save by him who was after the image of his intelligence.[32] God is above truth, wisdom, light,[33] and even above eternal life.[34] Elsewhere[35] Origen discusses whether God is not also beyond substance, and leans to the conclusion that he is; for we cannot say that he partakes of substance: rather, he causes all beings, the Logos included, to partake of it.[36]

On these premisses, such a conception as that of the Logos was essential, on the one hand, if revelation were to become possible for man; and, on the other, it was very difficult in relating the Logos (or Son, for the terms for Origen are interchangeable) to God to maintain their co-equality. In fact, Origen postulates a real subordinationism; and the logical outcome of it all is seen in the present passage, in which he teaches that "prayer" is to be directed to the Father alone.

In respect of this matter, two extreme attitudes towards Origen have been taken in later times. Some have aimed at establishing his orthodoxy in the terms of the Nicene Faith, labouring in the effort to explain or explain away everything that seems to point in the opposite direction; and such defenders have also brought to their aid the works of Origen known only in the Latin translation of Rufinus, although it is certain that Rufinus made them appear more orthodox than they really were. The opposite school has roundly accused Origen of heresy.

Both of these have forgotten that Origen was the child of his environment and of his age. His philosophic background at Alexandria provided him with a conception of God into which it was very difficult, if not impossible, to fit a doctrine of the essential Trinity. And, secondly, Origen lived before the controversies and the great conciliar decisions of the fourth and fifth centuries had given formal expression to the Catholic Faith. At the begining of the third century thought was fluid on these matters.

In his endeavour to systematize and state Christian theology Origen was a pioneer, and made the mistakes of a pioneer, especially as he was a daring pioneer. Many of his speculations

[32] *Contra Celsum*, VII, 38.
[33] *In Joh.*, II, 23 (18).
[34] *Ibid.*, XIII, 3.
[35] *Contra Celsum*, VI, 64.
[36] De Faye, III, 31, 32.

were simply speculations, upon which the Church has not pronounced an opinion; and we may let them pass. In other matters, including the doctrine in question, Origen failed to reach
the position which was afterwards seen to be orthodox. But
Origen never intended heresy, or to set his opinions against
those of the Church.[37] Eusebius tells us that when only seventeen
or thereabouts Origen could not be persuaded to associate in
prayer with a certain heretic named Paul "keeping the rule of
the Church, even from boyhood, and 'loathing'—the very word
he himself uses somewhere—the teachings of the heretics." And
it is interesting to note that—to go no further than this present
treatise—Origen refers to heretics and heretical teaching in a
way that betrays no sympathy with them or it, but very much
the contrary; and he certainly would have been distressed beyond measure, had he been told that one day he would be
classed among them. For example, in XXII, 3, he speaks of
"numbers of heretics" who for their own purposes say *Jesus is
Lord*. In XXIV, 5, he refers to the "most impious conceptions"
and "godless thought" contained in Tatian's interpretation of
Let there be light. In XXIX, 10, we have a vigorous passage,
denouncing those who misinterpreting the Scriptures fall into
error concerning the Son and the Father. In XXIX, 13, we
have a clear reference to the Marcionites, who "have imagined a
God other than the creator of heaven and earth because they
find many such things in the Law and the Prophets and have
taken offence against him as not good who utters such sentiments." And lastly, when in V, 1, he is dealing with objections
to prayer, he roundly denounces those who reject prayer completely as "downright atheists" who "deny the existence of God"
or else as people "who go as far as to accept the name of God
but do away with his Providence." These passages make it clear
that Origen was definitely on the side of orthodoxy as he conceived it.

Moreover, Origen was essentially a Biblical theologian, and
his subordinationism sprang not only from his conception of
Deity but also from what he conceived the Scriptures to teach.
Texts that he quoted for this purpose were, "The Father is
greater than I" (John 14:28); "That they should know thee,
the only true God" (John 17:3); "Why callest thou me good?"
(Mark 10:18); and especially I Cor. 15:28: "And when all
things have been subjected unto him, then shall the Son also
himself be subjected to him that did subject all things unto him,

[37] *H.E.*, VI, 2:14.

that God may be all in all."[38] Similarly, in support of prayer to God alone he turns to Scripture.[39] If prayer is to be offered to the Father, it is to be offered in the name of Christ, as taught in John 16:23, 24. Christ is the high priest (Heb. 2:17, etc.), and therefore prayer is not offered apart from him. Christ is also the brother of those who pray (Heb. 2:12); and "it is not reasonable that those who have been deemed worthy to have one Father should pray to a brother."[40] It is not suggested that Origen always drew the correct conclusions from these passages. But it is clear that he wrestled with Scripture as concerning the relationship of the Son to the Father, and that he believed that he had extracted its true meaning. The moral to be drawn from the whole controversy is that though Origen failed to satisfy Catholic orthodoxy, as it was expressed later, it still remains to examine Scripture more closely in order to discover from it such an exegesis as is consistent with the doctrine of the essential Trinity. Origen's mistakes will not have been in vain, if they lead us to a fresh investigation of this matter.

The second point which threw suspicion on the orthodoxy of the treatise On Prayer is one which will not cause us so much concern today. In XXXI, 3, Origen says that it has been shown by those who have treated of the matter that the bodies of heavenly beings are spherical. The sources from which he drew this conclusion are given elsewhere.[41] The modern Church may be disposed to receive such a notion with humorous indulgence. But it was not so in earlier times when Origenistic controversies waxed hotly.[42] As we shall see, the Emperor Justinian included this opinion among the nine tenets for which he anathematized Origen; and it is also to be found among the fifteen "Anathemas against Origen" which, though not properly part of the proceedings of the Fifth General Council, contain contemporaneous matter discussed and circulated at that time. The opinion, therefore, that heavenly bodies are spherical severely damaged the treatise in orthodox eyes, especially as Origen goes so far as to say that the opinion had been "demonstrated."[43] No doubt, opposition to the notion was bound up with a literalistic conception of the resurrection of the body or flesh which prevailed in the early Church; and as Origen was supposed to be unsound on this matter generally, the particular fancy concerning the sphericity of celestial bodies was fastened on by his opponents in an age when orthodoxy and dogmatism were often confused.

38 Cf. XXV, 2.   39 XV, 1, 2.   40 XV, 4.   41 See pp. 381, 382.
42 See p. 232.   43 The word he uses is ἀποδεδειγμένων.

CHARACTERISTIC IDEAS OF ORIGEN IN THE *De Oratione*

Besides the two particular ideas mentioned above, the treatise
On Prayer also contains much of Origen's characteristic outlook.

1. *Relation between body and soul, seen and unseen, earthly and heavenly*

As a Platonic idealist, the whole thought of Origen is dominated by the conviction of the inferiority of the material and visible as compared with the immaterial and invisible, and consequently by the dualism involved in this outlook. Characteristically, at the outset of the treatise[44] he quotes the words of Wisdom of Solomon 9:15.

> A corruptible body weigheth down the soul,
> And the earthy frame lieth heavy on a mind that is full of cares;

and he speaks of the human mind as "still imprisoned in the body."[45] The same conviction appears also, under various forms, in his treatment of the supposed saying of the Lord: "Ask for the great things, and the little things shall be added unto you; ask for the heavenly things, and the earthly things shall be added unto you."[46] He invariably interprets the "great" and "heavenly" things as spiritual blessings, the "little" and "earthly" things as material blessings. "It is clear," he says,[47] "that all symbolical and typical things are 'small' and 'earthly' in comparison with the true and spiritual things." It is thus that we are to interpret passages in the Old Testament which speak of the saints there as requesting material blessings: "In all likelihood the divine word . . . indicates the 'heavenly' and 'great' things by means of matters connected with 'earthly' and 'little' things, saying [to us], 'Ye who desire to be spiritual ask in prayer, so that having received them as 'heavenly' ye may inherit the kingdom of heaven, and as 'great' ye may enjoy the greatest blessings; but the 'earthly' and 'little' things, of which ye are in want for bodily necessities, the Father will supply unto you in accordance with the measure of your need." In accordance with this principle, Hannah, Hezekiah, Judith, Jonah, and the Three Holy Children, although Holy Scripture speaks of them as having received earthly benefits or deliverance, received in reality spiritual blessings which far outweighed the former.[48] We can obtain today such spiritual blessings as the

[44] I, 1.   [45] XVII, 2.   [46] II, 2.   [47] XIV, 1.   [48] XVI, 3.

Old Testament spoke of in type.[49] Earthly blessings are indeed
only the "shadow" of spiritual blessings; and just as the sun may
not cast a shadow at all in certain circumstances and at certain
latitudes, so some spiritual blessings are accompanied by no
earthly blessing.[50] Those on earth are hampered by certain impressions arising from attendant circumstances and so have a
tendency to follow the worse course, but this is not so with those
in heaven, who possess a soul that is perfected by reason and
alien to the influence of these impressions, and make use of a
body that is ethereal and absolutely pure.[51] One of the benefits
of prayer for us is that "the eyes of the understanding are lifted
up, away from converse with earthly things and occupation
with material impressions," and therefore they "can transcend
created things."[52] And finally this principle governs entirely
Origen's exegesis of "Give us this day our daily bread."[53] As we
shall see when we come to consider his exposition of the Lord's
Prayer clause by clause, the bread that Origen would have us
pray for is no material substance.[54] Origen appears to indicate
the philosophical basis of his conviction concerning the inferiority of material things in ch. XXI, 2. "No material or
bodily thing is single; but every one of them, though reckoned
single, is split up and cut in pieces and divided into several
parts, having lost its unity." And since, in accordance with
Greek belief, "virtue is one, vice is many," therefore the multi-
plex character of material things demonstrates this imperfec-
tion. Consistently with his general position, Origen quotes[55]
from Ignatius[56] with approval the saying "nothing that is seen
is good." But Origen, nor yet Ignatius, did not push this statement to its logical conclusion. Just as Ignatius vigorously asserts,
in reply to gnostic error, the reality of the Eucharist, so Origen[57]
attacks "those who completely reject objects of sense, and use
neither Baptism nor Eucharist." Such persons, according to
him, are influenced by the persuasions of Satan.

2. Immateriality of God

This follows from the foregoing. It was one of Origen's firmest
beliefs, and duly finds a place in this treatise, especially in
ch. XXIII in connection with the words "which art in heaven."
"When the Father of the saints is said to be in heaven, we are

[49] XIII, 3, 4, 5.   [50] XVII, 1, 2.   [51] Ch. VII.
[52] IX, 2.   [53] Ch. XXVII.   [54] See pp. 212, 218 ff., 361 ff.
[55] XX, 2.   [56] Romans, 3.   [57] V, 1.

not to suppose that he is circumscribed in bodily fashion and
dwells in heaven; otherwise, if the heaven contained him, God
would be found less than, because contained by, the heaven; but
we must believe that by the ineffable power of his Godhead all
things are contained and held together by him." Simple folk,
however, take in a literal sense phrases in Scripture which seem
to assert that God is in a place; and such passages must be given
their true meaning. Thus, for example, when in St. John's Gospel
the Lord speaks of "departing out of this world to the Father," of
"coming forth from God, and going to God," and so forth, and
of the Father and the Son "coming" unto the believer and
"making our abode with him," these sayings, according to
Origen, "do not conceive of a local departure of the Father and
the Son to him who loves the word of Jesus, nor are they to be
taken in a local sense." Similarly, the words at the end of the
same Gospel, "Touch me not; for I am not yet ascended to the
Father" are to be taken in a mystical sense as an ascent of
the mind rather than of the body. Again, we cannot take literally
the passage (Gen. 3:8) which speaks of the Lord God "walking
in the garden." Is a literal garden so much larger than God that
it contains him as he "walks" in it? We are, rather, to compare
the passage "I will dwell in them, and walk in them" (II Cor.
6:16). God's "walking" in the garden is of the same kind as his
"walking" in the saints. And, on the other hand, every sinner,
like Adam and Eve, "hides" himself from the presence of God,
avoids his visitation, and shuns open speech with him, just as
Cain "went out from the presence of God" (Gen. 4:16). Again,
in ch. XXV, Origen teaches that "the kingdom of God" is immanent and spiritual. The Saviour says (Luke 17:20, 21), "The
kingdom of God cometh not with observation: neither shall they
say, Lo, here! or, Lo, there! but the kingdom of God is within
you"; and to this Origen adds the saying in Deuteronomy
(30:14), "for the word is very nigh, in thy mouth, and in thy
heart." This is comparable to the saying quoted above: "We
will come unto him, and make our abode with him." Every
saint who takes God as his king and obeys the spiritual laws of
God dwells in himself as in a well-ordered city. By God's kingdom is meant the blessed state of the reason and the ordered
condition of wise thoughts.[58]

58 See further, pp. 216 ff.

3. Angels, heavenly powers and departed saints

It is not surprising that Origen, for whom the unseen world was the great reality, should give the place he does to the ministry of angels and of those who have passed within the veil. Chapter XI is devoted to this thought. Angels ministered to Jesus when he was on earth, and no doubt they still minister to him as he carries out his work for the salvation of men. Moreover, Scripture speaks of the angels in heaven rejoicing over the sinner that repenteth, and of the ministry of Raphael, as recorded in the Book of Tobit, in helping forward the prayers of Tobit and Sarah. So, according to Origen, we may assume that angels, who watch over things and minister to God, are at times brought into the presence of this or that man who is praying in order that they may join in his requests. Each one's guardian angel also joins in our prayers and gives us his aid.

With regard to the ministry of departed saints, Origen's line of thought is as follows. Love to one's neighbour, we are taught in God's Word, is one of the chiefest virtues. Care for the members of the body, the Church, is a mark of that love: and it is not only by those in this life that such love is exercised. Rather, "we must hold that the saints who have fallen asleep before us exercise it towards those who are struggling in this life much more than do they who are compassed about with human weakness and are struggling in company with feebler folk."

Similar thoughts are to be found in ch. XXXI, 5, 6, 7; only here it is not a question of the individual and his need of assistance, but of the Church when assembled for worship. On such occasions there is an invisible, as well as a visible, company present. Each worshipper's guardian angel is there to help him whom he is charged to guard, so that there is a double church, the one of men, the other of angels; and there are present also the spirits of those who are fallen asleep. The spot, therefore, where believers come together in one place, has a peculiar sacredness. There is a power, not of this world but derived from things invisible, present to that assembly, which is not to the same extent to be found in prayer offered by the individual believer.

4. Evil spiritual powers

Belief in evil spiritual powers is correlative to the foregoing, and like it is based on Scriptural language. With Paul, Origen is convinced that "our wrestling is not against flesh and blood, but against the principalities, against the powers, against the world-rulers of this darkness, against the spiritual hosts of wickedness in the heavenly places."[59] In XXVI, 3 he takes up the concluding words in this sentence. Why are we told to pray, "Thy will be done, as in heaven, so on earth," if in heaven there are these malevolent powers opposed to the will of God? An answer to this is put forward in XXVI, 5, 6. "The mind is its own place." He who has his citizenship in heaven, though literally on earth, is no longer of the earth, but of heaven and the heavenly world. Similarly, the spiritual hosts of wickedness that still reside in the heavenly places have their citizenship on earth, and because of their evil disposition dwell no longer in heaven; for they have fallen in mind with him who fell from heaven after the manner of lightning. Again, just as in an assembly of Christians for worship there is a twofold company, of holy men and of blessed angels, so there may be also in such an assembly a double gathering of a different sort, of wicked men and of bad angels: for church assemblies are not entirely composed of men genuinely devoted to God, but also, it may be, include some who have given themselves up to angels of the devil through their sins and wicked disregard of God.[60] Finally, Origen finds no difficulty in the concluding words of the Lord's Prayer, "Deliver us from the evil one." The presence and power of a personal devil was well within the content of his beliefs. He finds Scriptural warrant for it in the account of the temptations of Job, and those of the Saviour, and in the words of Paul already quoted—"the fiery darts of the evil one."

5. Ascetic view of life

That Origen lived a disciplined and ascetic life is plainly stated for us by Eusebius.[61] At any rate in his earlier days, "he continued to live like a philosopher, putting aside everything that might lead to youthful lusts; all day long his discipline was to perform labours of no light character, and the greater part of the night he devoted himself to studying the divine Scriptures; and he persevered, as far as possible, in the most philosophic manner of life, at one time disciplining himself by fasting, at another measuring out the time for sleep, which he was careful to take, never on a couch, but on the floor. . . . He is said, for example, to have walked for many years without using a shoe of any description, yea more, to have refrained for a great many

[59] Eph. 6:12.   [60] XXXI, 6.   [61] *H.E.*, VI, 3:9–12.

years from the use of wine and all except necessary food, so that he actually incurred the risk of undermining and destroying his constitution."

The treatise *On Prayer*, though not concerned with prescribing any particular mode of life, is entirely consistent with the description of its author as given by Eusebius. It is the work of a man for whom, as we have pointed out above, the body and bodily things held a negligible place. The conviction that the life of the spirit is everything is expressed in an eloquent passage in XVII, 1. "If spiritual things are present to us and we are being enlightened by God in the complete possession of what is truly good, we shall not waste words about the paltry thing that is the shadow. For all material and bodily things, of whatever kind they may be, have the value of an unsubstantial and feeble shadow, and can in no way be compared with the saving and holy gifts of the God of the universe. What sort of comparison can there be between bodily riches and the riches in all utterance and in all wisdom? Who that is not a madman would compare health of flesh and bones with a healthy mind and a robust soul and a balanced reason?" Again, in ch. XXIX, on "Bring us not into temptation," life is depicted as what Keats calls "a vale of soul-making." The whole of human life upon earth is a temptation. No one can escape from this discipline, rich or poor, high or low, healthy or sick. In this way God in his mercy shows us our weakness that we may discover his power, and gives us satiety of sin that we may be purified and come to hate what we formerly desired and retrace the path towards holiness. Even when temptation is not present, "in the times between successive temptations, we ought to take a firm stand against what is impending, and prepare ourselves for anything that may possibly happen, so that, whatever it may be, we shall not be proved unready, but shall be made manifest to have disciplined ourselves with the utmost care."[62] In addition to this general teaching there are also a few particular references which indicate the ascetic trend of Origen's mind. Prayer "as we ought" is hindered unless in the performance of the ineffable mysteries of marriage due regard is paid to gravity, infrequency, and the absence of passion.[63] "It is a question whether it is a holy and pure thing to intercede with God in the place where sexual intercourse occurs—I do not mean unlawful intercourse, but that which is allowed by the apostolic word 'by way of permission, not of commandment.' For if it is not possible to give

[62] XXIX, 19.   [63] II, 2.

oneself to prayer as one ought, unless given over to it by consent for a season, perhaps the same consideration should be applied, if possible, to the place."[64] He who has perceived what the beauty of the heavenly Bride and Bridegroom is will be ashamed to honour even with the same name of beauty the bodily beauty of woman or boy or man. Flesh does not contain beauty in the true sense of the word, seeing that all of it is shameful.[65] But a more modest expression of self-control is found in XXVIII, 2: "We are debtors in what we owe to ourselves in so using the body that we do not waste its strength through love of pleasure."

6. Allegory

Speaking of the treatise On Prayer, Westcott[66] says that "no writing of Origen is more free from his characteristic faults." And if we count excessive allegorism as one of these, this opinion can be endorsed; for as compared with most of his other works he here indulges to a far less degree his flights of exegetical fancy. This is no doubt partly due to the fact that he is treating a subject, not commenting directly upon a Biblical text. Occasionally, however, in this treatise he betrays his penchant for this kind of thing. In XXVI, 3, in the petition "Thy will be done, as in heaven, so on earth," "heaven" and "earth" are allegorized as "Christ" and "the Church" respectively. The text in Proverbs (15:17), "Better a dinner of herbs where friendship and grace are than a stalled ox and hatred therewith," is interpreted as follows: The simple-minded Christian who cannot receive the stronger and more important points of doctrine, is to be preferred to him who though more skilful and quick-sighted yet fails to see clearly what concerns the peace and harmony of the whole, and indulges in high-flown words exalted against the knowledge of God.[67] When the three men turned in and lodged with Abraham and partook of food with him (Gen. 18:2–6), perhaps this is to be taken quite figuratively, for the saints are able to partake on occasion of spirtual and reasonable food with diviner powers, and the angels in turn are glad and nourished therewith and co-operate the more readily with him who nourishes them with the nutriment of teachings formerly prepared.[68] The exegesis of the dragon and the Ethiopians in Ps. 73:13, 14 (LXX) and of Peter's vision in Acts, ch. 10, may also be referred to as curiosities.[69] In XXVII, 14, Origen does

[64] XXXI, 4.   [65] XVII, 2.   [66] D.C.B., IV, 124.
[67] XXVII, 6.   [68] XXVII, 11.   [69] XXVII, 12.

not doubt that there are hidden meanings connected with certain Jewish ordinances such as the feast of the seven weeks and
of the seventh month, and with the seven years of the freedom
of the Hebrew servants and with the Jubile, and so forth, but
these are part of the Father's unsearchable judgments and his
ways past finding out, and are known only to the mind of
Christ, who has contemplated the Father's will concerning his
ordinances in all ages. A similar thought—that the inner
mysteries underlying certain ordinances are things beyond man
in this life—appears again afterwards in XXVII, 16. But
Origen's most characteristic effort in the matter of exegesis in
this treatise is to be found in XXIX, 9. According to the LXX
of Canticles 2:9, 10, the beloved is to be found "glancing
through the meshes" ("he sheweth himself through the lattice,"
Revised Version). The beloved is, of course, the Saviour. The
meshes are the meshes of temptation, which the Saviour entered
for the sake of those who were caught in them aforetime. He
now promises deliverance to his bride, the Church, when he
says: "Rise up, come, my near one, my fair one, my dove." On
the other hand, Origen occasionally manifests a strange, almost
grotesque, literalism in expounding words of Scripture, as for
example in VII, 1, when he argues that the sun and moon have
a certain free will, because the Psalmist says, "Praise ye him,
sun and moon."

7. Different grades of hearers

One of Origen's most frequently expressed opinions is that
there are two classes of Christians, the less mature and the more
mature, to whom respectively teaching must be adapted according to their spiritual capacity to receive it. This idea he derived
ultimately from the New Testament.[70] And he found it suited
admirably his style of Biblical interpretation. The "babes in
Christ" could receive and understand the plain, literal meaning
of Scripture; but the inner, allegorical meaning could be imparted only to those who were spiritually "fullgrown." This idea
finds its place in the treatise On Prayer, as in all his writings. In
II, 4, he suggests that even John the Baptist observed such a
distinction, imparting certain teaching about prayer to some
only of his followers. "Simple folk,"[71] when they read "Our
Father, which art in heaven," imagine that God is in a place;
whereas this, and other passages open to a like misinterpretation,

[70] I Cor. 3:2; Heb. 5:13, 14; cf. I Cor. 2:6.   [71] XXIII, 1.

must be taken "in a loftier and more spiritual sense."[72]
The discussion on "the daily bread" also gives Origen ample
opportunity to express the idea of classes of hearers. The Word,
which nourishes us is varied and diverse, for not all are able to
be nourished with "the solidity and vigorous force of the divine
teachings."[73] Those who are "more perfect," when they read of
"bread," will understand it of "the bread which came down out
of heaven; not as the fathers did eat, and died." Then Origen
goes on to quote I Cor. 3:1–3 and Heb. 5:12–14, and in their
light to interpret Rom. 14:2: "One man hath faith to eat all
things: but he that is weak eateth herbs." This saying is not
principally concerned with bodily nourishment, but rather
with the words of God that nourish the soul: the stronger
man is able to partake of all teachings, the weaker and less perfect is content with simpler instruction. A similar thought is
found in XXVII, 9: "When the word of God is given either as
'milk' suitably for 'babes,' or as 'herbs' suitably for them that
are 'weak,' or as 'flesh' seasonably for those who are contesting,
each of those who are nourished, in proportion as he has offered
himself to the word, can accomplish this or that thing, or becomes such or such a person."

On the other hand, in another passage in this context, Origen
betrays an anxiety, based no doubt upon experience, that
dangers may lurk for those who pursue such higher interpretations, for they may give rise to "high-flown words" proclaiming
"a doctrine foreign to the Father of our Lord Jesus who has
given the Law and the Prophets" (the followers of Marcion
seem to be intended). And this is indicated in Prov. 15:17:
"Better a dinner of herbs where friendship and grace are (i.e.,
simpler teachings) than a stalled ox and hatred therewith (i.e.,
heretical presumptions)."

8. *Free Will*

That man and all creatures of reason possess free will is a
fundamental point in Origen's whole theological system, and is
affirmed in all his writings.[74] He believed in a pre-mundane
Fall, that is to say, that in the transcendent world a conscious
act of will on the part of spiritual beings took place, whereby
they fell from their high estate; and, further, that the return to
God, in the case of such beings, will be achieved also by an act
of free will. Moreover, since for Origen the action of God upon

[72] XXIII, 5.   [73] XXVII, 4.   [74] De Faye, III, 214.

human souls, in respect of their redemption and uplift, is always educative and disciplinary, it follows that God must have free creatures to respond to such education. It is not surprising, then, that when Origen is discussing the difficulties concerning prayer which his friends had brought to his notice (see p. 250), he should place in the forefront his reasons for believing in free will.[75] These will be examined later on in this volume.[76] Towards the end of the treatise[77] the same conviction receives characteristic expression: "I verily believe that God orders every rational soul with a view to its eternal life, and that it always maintains its free will, and of its own motion either mounts ever higher and higher until it reaches the pinnacle of virtue, or on the contrary descends through carelessness to this or that excess of wickedness." Then, in this latter case, after being glutted with sin, men may "hate what they formerly welcomed, and so when they are healed they can possess more securely the health that comes to their souls by being healed." In XXIX, 15, we are told that "God does not wish that good should come to anyone as of necessity, but of free will."

9. *Universalism*

There are only a few allusions to this doctrine in the treatise. In XXVII, 15, Origen says that "in the ages to come God will 'shew the riches of his grace in kindness':[78] when the greatest sinner, who has spoken ill of the Holy Spirit, and is under the power of sin throughout the present age, will, I know not how, be under treatment from beginning to end in the ensuing age that is to come." It is implied that this "treatment" will be successful. Purification after this life is over is referred to in XXIX, 14, and in the following section the cleansing of even the most reprobate sinners.

10. *Church Ordinances and Worship*

As a general rule Origen has little to say about these in his writings, and the present treatise is no exception, the greater part of which is concerned with private, individual prayer to God. Here and there, however, there are a few references to the visible order of the Church. In V, 1, Origen, when roundly denouncing certain persons who think that they ought not to pray, says that "the champions of this opinion" (which Origen

[75] Chs. VI–VIII, 1.   [76] See pp. 336 ff.
[77] XXIX, 13.   [78] Eph. 2:7.

attributes to the Evil One) "are those who completely reject objects of sense, and use neither Baptism nor Eucharist." In XV, 4, he speaks of those who have received through regeneration the spirit of adoption that they may be called sons of God: but the reference to Baptism is not actually made explicit. In XXVIII, 4, Origen speaks of the responsibilities of the several orders of ministers. "There is a certain debt . . . due from a deacon, and another from a presbyter, but the debt due from a bishop is the heaviest, since it is demanded of him by the Saviour of the whole Church, and retribution follows if it be not paid." Later on in the same chapter (sections 9 and 10) occurs the passage, to which reference is made elsewhere,[79] about priestly absolution. Chapter XXXI, 5–7, is the only passage that treats of prayer in the public assembly of the Church. In this Origen touches on the superiority of public over private prayer, as arising from the probability that in the former there are also present invisible, angelic powers and spirits of departed church members, not to speak of the power of the Lord and Saviour himself. But the passage throws no light upon the nature of the worship or the order of service.

ANALYSIS OF THE TREATISE

Introduction

Chapters I and II

What is impossible for man alone is made possible by the grace of God in Christ. Paul, who says that we know not what we ought to pray for as we ought, also says that the Spirit helps us to pray. The insufficiency of man's power was perceived by the disciple who besought the Lord for teaching on prayer.

Discussion of Prayer in General

Chapters III to XVII

THE WORDS EUCHE AND PROSEUCHE

Chapters III and IV

OBJECTIONS TO PRAYER

Chapter V

(a) By those who reject God altogether, or at any rate the idea of Providence.

[79] Pp. 180 ff., 372 ff.

(*b*) By those who though they accept God and Providence yet maintain that everything is known to God beforehand and predetermined by him.

ANSWER TO THESE OBJECTIONS
Chapters VI to VIII, 1

(*a*) Free will is proved by the power of motion: to deny free will to man would mean that he was neither a living creature nor a rational being.

(*b*) In every day life we act on the assumption that we and others possess free will.

(*c*) Foreknowledge and free will are shown to be not incompatible.

ADVANTAGES OF PRAYER
Chapters VIII, 2 to X, 2

The Scriptures are opposed to the foregoing objectors in that they speak in many places of the blessings that flow from prayer.

THE ANGELS, AS WELL AS CHRIST, PRAY WITH US
Chapter XI

OUR WHOLE LIFE OUGHT TO BE A PRAYER
Chapters XII to XIII, 1

(*a*) The meaning of "Pray without ceasing."

(*b*) The example of Jesus in prayer.

EXAMPLES FROM SCRIPTURE OF ANSWERED PRAYER
Chapter XIII, 2

Examples given are Hannah, Hezekiah, Mordecai, and Esther, Judith, the Three Holy Children, Jonah.

SIMILAR PRAYERS ARE ANSWERED TODAY
Chapter XIII, 3–5

The material blessings obtained by the foregoing saints in the Old Testament are types of the greater, spiritual blessings that come to Christians by the Holy Spirit.

PRAYER: (*a*) CONTENT (*b*) FORM (*c*) TO WHOM ADDRESSED

Chapters XIV to XVII

(*a*) What we ought to ask for is made clear in the saying: "Ask for the great things, and the little things shall be added unto you" (chs. XIV, 1, XVI,1–XVII, 2).

(*b*) Forms of prayer: these are indicated in the four expressions, "supplications," "prayers," "intercessions," "thanksgivings," in I Timothy 2:1 (ch. XIV, 2–5).

(*c*) Prayer, in the proper sense of the term, is to be directed to God alone, through Christ (chs. XIV, 6–XV, 4).

Discussion of the Lord's Prayer
Chapters XVIII to XXX

THE TEXTS OF THE LORD'S PRAYER
Chapter XVIII, 2, 3

Matthew and Luke do not hand down the same prayer.

THE INTRODUCTION TO THE PRAYER IN MATTHEW
Chapters XIX to XXI

Jesus teaches us where and how we ought to pray:

(*a*) Not in the streets or in the synagogues (chs. XIX, XX).
(*b*) Nor with vain repetitions (ch. XXI).

OUR FATHER WHICH ART IN HEAVEN
Chapters XXII, XXIII

HALLOWED BE THY NAME
Chapter XXIV

THY KINGDOM COME
Chapter XXV

THY WILL BE DONE, AS IN HEAVEN, SO ON EARTH
Chapter XXVI

GIVE US THIS DAY OUR DAILY BREAD
Chapter XXVII

(*a*) By "bread" the Logos according to John is to be understood.

(*b*) The word for, "daily" (*ἐπιούσιος*) is to be derived from
οὐσία, not from ἐπιέναι.

(*c*) "This day" signifies the whole of this age.

FORGIVE US OUR DEBTS
AS WE ALSO HAVE FORGIVEN OUR DEBTORS
Chapter XXVIII

(*a*) We have obligations to men and to God.

(*b*) We are debtors all the time; similarly others are in debt
to us.

(*c*) We must forgive in order to be forgiven: but sins unto
death are not to be forgiven.

BRING US NOT INTO TEMPTATION
BUT DELIVER US FROM THE EVIL ONE
Chapters XXIX, XXX

(*a*) All life is a temptation.

(*b*) Therefore the petition to be delivered from it is that we
should not be overcome by it.

(*c*) How can the good God bring us into temptation?

(*d*) The advantage of temptation is clear.

(*e*) But also the petition to be delivered from it is well
grounded.

Supplement to General Discussion on Prayer
Chapters XXXI to XXXIII

DISPOSITION AND POSTURE IN PRAYER
Chapter XXXI, 1-3

THE PLACE WHERE ONE OUGHT TO PRAY
Chapter XXXI, 4-7

THE SUPERIORITY OF PRAYER TOWARDS THE EAST
Chapter XXXII

THE SUBJECTS OF PRAYER
Chapter XXXIII

Conclusion
Chapter XXXIV

ORIGEN'S CONCEPTION OF PRAYER IN GENERAL

The theological starting point in Origen's treatment of the subject of Prayer is to be found in the absolute transcendence of God and the impossibility that man can know him or his will unaided.[80] "What man shall know the counsel of God? Or who shall conceive what the Lord willeth? Hardly do we divine the things that are on earth. But the things that are in the heavens, who ever traced out?"[81] Of ourselves, therefore, we do not know what we ought to say, when we pray, or how we should dispose ourselves to pray. But revelation has come to our assistance. The Scriptures tell us "what we ought" to pray about, and "how we ought" to pray. More particularly, there is the passage which declares that the Spirit himself maketh intercession to God on our behalf, as we address ourselves to prayer.[82] And Origen also recalls how one of Christ's disciples, recognizing his human weakness and ignorance in the matter of prayer, said to the Master, "Lord, teach us to pray."[83] Therefore, as he begins his difficult task, Origen knows that he needs the illumination of the Father, the teaching of the first-begotten Word, and the operation of the Spirit, if he is to treat worthily so weighty a matter, and accordingly he opens with a prayer that he may be able to speak rightly about prayer and to interpret rightly the prayers that are recorded in the Gospels.[84]

This introduction displays at the outset what is the outstanding feature of the treatise *On Prayer* and of all Origen's works, namely, their unvarying Biblical character. No one else in the early Church had so intimate and profound a knowledge of Holy Scripture or was so unremitting in using it as the basis of all his teaching. It is not surprising, therefore, that with this strong Biblical background Origen should go on to speak of some of the words used for prayer in the Greek Bible, Old and New Testaments. In point of fact, however, this is the least valuable part of the treatise. The discussion in chs. III and IV on the words *euche* and *proseuche* fails to throw much light on the difference between them. The passage seems to have been hastily composed, and to be based upon reminiscences of certain texts rather than on a careful study of the terms in question.[85] Of greater value is Origen's discussion, in XIV, 2–5, of the four words used in I Tim. 2:1, namely, "supplication" ($\delta\epsilon\eta\sigma\iota s$), "prayer" ($\pi\rho\sigma\sigma\epsilon\nu\chi\eta$), "intercession" ($\epsilon\nu\tau\epsilon\nu\xi\iota s$) and "thanks-

[80] I, 1.   [81] Wisdom of Solomon 9:13, 16.   [82] Rom. 8:26, 27.
[83] Luke 11:1.   [84] II, 6.   [85] See note, p. 334.

giving" *(εὐχαριστία)*. He notes, correctly, that "supplication" is a petition offered for the obtaining of some particular thing, and that *ἔντευξις* (which does not necessarily mean what the English word "intercession" does—prayer in relation to others) involves the notion of a free or "bold" approach to God. "'Intercession,' he says, is a request to God for certain things made by one who possesses more than usual confidence." Origen also notes the fact that "prayer"*(προσευχή)* is a word reserved for address to *God*; whereas the other three, "supplication," "intercession," "thanksgiving," may not unsuitably be addressed to holy men also.

But "prayer," according to Origen, is not simply asking God for something, nor are its benefits to be confined to the obtaining of what we ask for. On this point he is insistent: and indeed some of the most eloquent sentences in the treatise are devoted to expressing it. Great benefit, he says, results simply from a proper disposition or preparation for prayer. "Without doubt he whose mind is set on prayer is in some measure profited merely by the settled condition involved in praying, when he has disposed himself to approach God and speak in his presence as to one who watches over him and is present."[86] "The greatest benefits result from the attitude of, and preparation for, prayer, considered simply by themselves, of the man who has dedicated himself to God."[87] The calling to mind of a wise and famous man may check evil impulses and stir up to emulation. How much more profitable is it to recollect God, in whom we have put our trust, who knows the secrets of our heart, and is present with us![88] And not only in the mere disposition for prayer is there a looking up to God, there is also a looking away from earthly things and bodily impressions. Quoting the words of the Psalmists, "Unto thee have I lifted up mine eyes, O thou that dwellest in the heaven,"[89] and "Unto thee have I lifted up my soul, O God,"[90] Origen goes on to say, "When the eyes of the understanding are lifted up, away from converse with earthly things and occupation with material impressions, and when they are elevated so high that they can transcend created things and fix themselves solely upon the contemplation of God and of reverent and seemly intercourse with him who hears, it must needs be that the eyes themselves derive the greatest benefit, when 'with unveiled face they reflect as in a mirror the glory of the Lord, and are transformed into the same image from glory to glory.'[91]

[86] VIII, 2. [87] IX, 2. [88] VIII, 2.
[89] Ps. 123:1. [90] Ps. 25:1. [91] II Cor. 3:18.

. . . Moreover, when the soul is lighted up and follows the spirit and severs itself from the body . . . it must needs be that laying aside the nature of a soul it becomes spiritual."[92] He who prays must follow the precept of Christ,[93] and enter into his own inner chamber, shutting himself in upon the riches laid up in store, "the treasures of wisdom and knowledge."[94] He must never bend outside or gape at the things outside, but "shut every door of the faculties of sense, so that he may not be enticed by the impressions of sense and their image may not penetrate into his mind."[95]

But the mind of him who sets himself to pray has not merely to be free from sense impressions. He must also put away all angry or licentious thoughts.[96] He must bear no malice or hatred in his heart. Thus he will observe the commandment of the Saviour when he says, "If ye stand praying, forgive, if ye have aught against anyone."[97] By such preparation for prayer it is clear that we have already obtained the greatest benefits. And, further, he must not approach God in prayer with a heart that is secretly discontented, grumbling against Providence and murmuring at its lot. Those who do this are like wicked servants who, though they do not openly cavil at their master's orders, nevertheless among themselves mutter their displeasure at them. We are warned against this sort of thing in Deuteronomy[98] in the saying, "Beware that there be not a hidden word in thine heart, a lawless thing." On the other hand, it is written of one who was sorely tempted by the trials of life to murmur:[99] "In all these happenings did not Job sin with his lips before God."

This emphasis upon contemplation of God, apart from petition, and its benefits to the soul, is characteristic of one aspect— the mystical side—of Origen, which has been recently the object of numerous studies.[1] By its means, he says, by this mental *catharsis*, he who prays becomes more capable of union with God, and participates in the prayer of our Advocate, the Word of God, who stands in the midst even of those who know him not, and never fails the prayer of anyone.[2] No doubt, for Origen, it was a stage on the way towards the heavenly vision, the *epopteia* of the Mysteries, which was and is the goal of all mystical aspiration. But it would be a complete mistake to suppose that Origen is unpractical and merely visionary in his treatment of the subject of prayer. Quite the contrary. It has been said that

[92] IX, 2.   [93] Matt. 6:6.   [94] Col. 2:3.   [95] XX, 2.   [96] IX, 1.
[97] Mark 11:25.   [98] Deut. 15:9.   [99] Job 2:10.
[1] Cf. J. Daniélou, *Origène*, 287 f.   [2] X, 2.

mystics are among the most practical of people, and Origen appears to be an example of this fact, if it be a fact. For few writers have more definitely connected prayer with life, the vision of God with daily work, than he has in this treatise. He discusses[3] the meaning of Paul's command: "Pray without ceasing."[4] And it is to be noted that he makes no attempt to evade the difficulty evolved in it. Actual prayer, he says, ought to be engaged in not less than three times every day, citing the examples of Daniel[5] and Peter[6] and referring to relevant passages in the Psalms. We can, however, regard "Pray without ceasing" as a practicable saying if we include the performance of good deeds and the fulfilling of commandments as part of the prayer. "That man 'prays without ceasing' who combines with the prayer the needful deeds and the prayer with the fitting actions." In other words, prayer and action based on it are not to be regarded as two things but as one, joined indissolubly together. Thus we can "speak of the whole life of the saint as one great unbroken prayer." No other saying about prayer links up prayer so closely with practical duties. It is not as if we said *laborare est orare* or *orare est laborare*, as if the one could be regarded as an equivalent substitute for the other; but rather that both form part of a connected whole. Nor is it a saying which strives to balance the two sides of the Christian life—the devotional and the practical—and secure a fitting proportion between them: its purpose is rather to infuse new meaning into each of them, when it is shown that they are so interrelated as to form an integrated whole. Later on in the treatise,[7] in speaking about the opening words of the Lord's Prayer, he returns to this thought, which was evidently for him no passing phrase. "Do not let us think," he says, "that we are taught to say actual words at a certain fixed time of prayer. If we understand what has been said above in our discussion about 'praying without ceasing,' our whole life as we 'pray without ceasing'[8] shall say, 'Our Father which art in heaven':[9] its 'citizenship' shall in no wise be on earth but in every way 'in heaven,'[10] which is the 'throne'[11] of God, for the kingdom of heaven is seated in all those who 'bear the image of the heavenly,'[12] and are therefore themselves heavenly."

Origen's treatment of the practical benefits to be derived

3 XII, 2.
6 Acts 10:9–11.
9 Matt. 6:9.
12 I Cor. 15:49.

4 I Thess. 5:17.
7 XXII, 5.
10 Phil. 3:20.

5 Dan. 6:10.
8 I Thess. 5:17.
11 Cf. Isa. 66:1.

from prayer, as apart from its contemplative side, is enriched
and fortified by the examples he gives from the Bible of the personal advantages of prayer. In XIII, 2, he names, for example,
Hannah, Hezekiah, Mordecai and Esther, Judith, the Three
Holy Children, and Jonah. In all these cases the results of
prayer were manifest and notable. And he prefaces them by
reference to the supreme example,[13] Jesus, who prayed and did
not pray in vain, obtaining what he asked for, and on one occasion testifying to the Father "I knew that thou hearest me
always."[14]

If, as we have noted,[15] Origen begins his treatise with the
thought of an absolutely transcendent God, he certainly does
not leave us baffled and helpless when faced with God's awful
remoteness. Origen, for all his transcendence, was no Deist. It
is indeed rather from the intellectual aspect that he speaks of
the vast gulf that separates God from men. Unaided, man can
in no wise apprehend divine wisdom. But his doctrine of revelation is as clear and unhesitating as his doctrine of transcendence.
What is impossible for man alone becomes possible through the
grace of our Lord Jesus Christ and his Holy Spirit.[16] Through
these channels mediation, illumination, grace, stream down
from him who is above all. So it is that Origen's doctrine of
prayer, and its benefits, is warm, rich and personal. To reject
prayer, he says, is the tenet either of those who are downright
atheists and deny the existence of God, or else of those who go
as far as to accept the name of God, but do away with Providence.[17] On the other hand, the prayers commended by him
are the prayers of those "who are confident in themselves that
they stand before and speak to God as one who is present and
hears."[18] It is evident that Origen was touched to the quick by
the opinions subversive of prayer which his friends had communicated to him.[19] And this was so because Origen the intellectualist, the critic, the speculator, was also Origen the mystic,
the devoted disciple and the practical Christian. The latter
aspect of him is, naturally enough, prominent in this treatise,
which for this reason is indispensable if we are to form a
balanced view of the man as a whole.

Where Origen falls short of the richness of Bible teaching
about prayer is in connection with the range of things for which
the Christian ought to pray. As a Platonist he is convinced concerning the inferiority of the material world. It is shadowy, un-

[13] XIII, 1.   [14] John 11:42.   [15] p. 330.   [16] I, 1.
[17] V, 1.   [18] VIII, 2.   [19] See pp. 247, 250.

substantial and of small account as compared with the true, substantial and abiding invisible realities. Consequently, the things that we can see, hear and touch with the bodily senses, indeed the whole life of the body, are comparatively of little moment. And when we approach the invisible God in prayer, it is not for these bodily things that we are to pray, but for the spiritual only. As we have noted elsewhere,[20] it is thus that Origen interprets the saying traditionally supposed to come from the Lord: "Ask for the great things, and the little things shall be added to you; and ask for the heavenly things, and the earthly things shall be added unto you"[21]—the "little" and "earthly" things being, of course, the things of the body. Accordingly, "earnest seekers after spiritual life in Christ" should "turn away from prayer for trivial and earthly things," and pursue instead things mystical, of which the aforesaid are types.[22] The Old Testament, indeed, tells of material benefits bestowed upon the saints in answer to their prayers; but these only foreshadow the greater, immaterial blessings that flow, under the New Covenant, to the Christian through prayer. If Hannah in her barrenness was given a child in answer to her prayer,[23] so also "souls that have long been sterile, perceiving the barrenness of their own reason and the sterility of their own mind, have by the Holy Spirit through persistent prayer conceived and given birth to saving words."[24] Similarly, the deliverances from bodily dangers and death, vouchsafed to Hezekiah, Esther, Judith, the Three Holy Children, and Jonah, are but types of deliverances today from the spiritual hosts of wickedness. It is on these lines that, in XVI, 2, Origen answers an objection that may be made to his treatment of this matter, namely that the Bible tells of things pertaining to the body as being granted to prayer, and the Saviour speaks of such things as being "added" unto us. Take an illustration, he says, from ordinary life. "If some one were to give us a bodily object of any kind whatsoever, we should not say that such a one bestowed upon us the shadow of the bodily object. For in giving the bodily object he did not design to give two things, the object and its shadow, but the design of the giver was to give the bodily object: it followed, however, that with the gift of the object we also received its shadow. Similarly, when our understanding has grown in stature and we note what are the gifts which are pre-eminently given us by God, we shall say that bodily things are

[20] Pp. 331 f.   [21] II, 2.   [22] XIII, 4.
[23] XIII, 2.   [24] XIII, 3.

the most natural accompaniments of the great and heavenly gifts."

In XVII, 1, Origen continues the same line of thought, and this time employs an illustration from the sun-dial. In some latitudes and seasons, he says, the gnomon of the dial casts no shadow. This causes no concern to the man who rejoices in the sunlight. "If a man who seeks the rays of the sun has this indispensable thing, he is neither rejoiced nor grieved by the presence or absence of bodily shadows. . . . So also, if spiritual things are present to us and we are being enlightened by God in the complete possession of what is truly good, we shall not waste words about the paltry thing that is the shadow. For all material and bodily things, of whatever kind they may be, have the value of an unsubstantial and feeble shadow, and can in no way be compared with the saving and holy gifts of the God of the universe." Likewise, the petitionary part of the model prayer outlined in XXXIII, 1, is to be concerned with "great and heavenly things."

This point of view is carried by Origen to its logical conclusion in his treatment of the petition: "Give us this day our daily bread."[25] "Some suppose," he says, "that we are told to pray concerning material bread." But the opinion is false and must be refuted. The Lord who has taught us elsewhere to pray for "great" and "heavenly" things cannot forget here his own teaching, and command us to ask the Father for a "small" and "earthly" thing. The true interpretation, according to Origen, is along the lines of certain sayings in John, ch. 6, as for example: "Work not for the meat which perisheth, but for the meat which abideth unto eternal life."[26] This spiritualizing of what seems on the face of it to be a petition for bodily sustenance is comparable with Clement of Alexandria's treatment of the "riches" which the young man in the Gospels was told to give up. "So with regard to the rich, who shall hardly enter the kingdom, we must understand the word in the spirit of disciples, and not clumsily, rudely, or literally; for it is not spoken thus."[27] Both passages illustrate the weakness of the Alexandrines in the lengths to which they will push their interpretation of Scripture in the interests of their philosophy of life.

Towards the end of the treatise Origen turns to particulars concerning the posture and the subjects of prayer. When we are praying, he says, "that attitude in which the hands are stretched out and eyes lifted up is to be preferred to all others."[28] This

[25] XXVII, 1.   [26] John 6:27.   [27] *Quis Dives*, 18.   [28] XXXI, 2.

is an image of the qualities suitable to the soul and mind, by virtue of which the soul is intent upon its object and the mind directed to God. Standing (which Origen assumes to be the normal posture in prayer) is also a symbol, signifying that the reason is not earth-bound but lifted up towards the Lord of all. There is, however, a kind of prayer which demands that we should kneel.[29] "When one is about to accuse oneself of his sins before God, supplicating him for healing therefrom and for forgiveness thereof," then kneeling "is a symbol of the man who is abject and submissive." But it is not clear if this refers to a particular prayer of an especially penitentiary character or to the penitential part of the model prayer that he outlines later on.[30] In praying, we should turn towards the east.[31] It is the quarter in which the sun rises: therefore prayer in that direction is symbolical of the soul looking to the rising of the true light.

Prayer, says Origen, ought to fall into four parts according to subject.[30] First, in the beginning or preamble, God is to be glorified through Christ in the Holy Spirit. Next comes thanksgiving, both general and particular. In the third place comes confession of sin, followed by prayer for deliverance from the habit of sin and for forgiveness of the past. In the fourth place, he who prays should "add his request for great and heavenly things, his own and general, and also for his family and his dearest." Finally, the prayer should end as it began, by glorifying God through Christ in the Holy Spirit. Characteristically, Origen bases these subjects of prayer on Holy Scripture, and gives examples therefrom of each of the four subjects.

ORIGEN'S TREATMENT OF THE LORD'S PRAYER
Chapters XVIII to XXX

As a textual scholar Origen carefully distinguishes between the forms of the Prayer as found in Matthew and Luke, respectively. It might seem, he says, to most people that these Evangelists record the same prayer. But he rejects this point of view on two grounds: first, on account of their differences; and, secondly, because the prayers are found in two different contexts: Matthew placing it in the Sermon on the Mount, Luke as the answer to a disciple who asked the Lord, "Teach us to pray." So he thinks that perhaps the preferable view of the matter is that "the prayers are different, though they have some parts common."[33]

[29] XXXI, 3.   [30] XXXIII, 1.   [31] XXXII.   [33] XVIII, 2, 3.

It is characteristic also that before he speaks about the Prayer itself he should expatiate on the introduction to the Prayer in Matthew, with its teaching on *how* we are to pray— this point being a feature of this treatise. Indeed Origen himself reminds us that he has already dealt with the manner of our approach to prayer. Accordingly he has a good deal to say about the Lord's teaching concerning the manner of praying, as given in Matthew 6:5–9, upon which he comments at large in his usual discursive manner.

The texts, as given by Origen, in XVIII, 2, are, with one trifling exception,[34] identical with those that underlie the rendering of the Revised Version. So the prayers are as follows:

> Our Father which art in heaven.
> Hallowed be thy name.
> Thy kingdom come.
> Thy will be done, as in heaven, so on earth.
> Give us this day our daily bread.
> And forgive us our debts, as we also have forgiven our
>   debtors.
> And bring us not into temptation.
> But deliver us from the evil one.[35]

and

> Father,
> Hallowed be thy name.
> Thy kingdom come.
> Give us day by day our daily bread.
> And forgive us our sins;
> For we ourselves also forgive every one who is indebted to
>   us.
> And bring us not into temptation.[36]

There is no reference to the variant "Let thy Holy Spirit come upon us and cleanse us" (in place of "Thy kingdom come" or "Hallowed be thy name") which is attested by Origen's disciple Gregory of Nyssa among others, nor, of course, to the much later doxology. After dealing with the Introduction to the Prayer as given in Matthew, Origen proceeds to comment, at varying lengths, upon each petition separately.

---

34 In the Lukan version Origen has τῷ ὀφείλοντι instead of ὀφείλοντι.
35 Matt. 6:9–13.   36 Luke 11:2–4.

OUR FATHER WHICH ART IN HEAVEN
Chapters XXII, XXIII

Origen notes from his express examination of the Scriptures for this point that to address God as Father in prayer is a distinctively Christian attitude, as distinguished from the usage of the Old Testament, where indeed God is often styled "Father" and men his "sons," but not in a prayer. The use of "Father" in prayer by our Lord indicates a confident, firm and unchangeable affirmation as concerning our relationship to God. But a *caveat* is necessary. Sonship, according to Origen, is not simply a *status*, it involves character, good works, and a state of progressive conformation to the divine image. On the other hand, "he that doeth sin"[37] has within him the seed of the devil, and so long as it is inherent in the soul he cannot "right himself." It is when the Word of God dwells in him that it is possible for the works of the devil to be destroyed, for the evil seed to be done away with, and for him to become the child of God.

The words "which art in heaven" give Origen an opportunity which he is by no means loath to take of denying that God is circumscribed in bodily fashion and dwells locally in heaven. If this were so, it would follow that God was less than, because contained by, "heaven." Such an idea arises from a too literal interpretation of these and other words in the Bible on the part of simple folk. But these passages must be understood in a manner that befits grand and spiritual conceptions of God. Origen then proceeds to mention some of them and to expound them in a spiritual sense. And he points out further that to suppose that God is in a place after the manner of a body leads to the most impious opinions, namely, that he is a body, and therefore divisible, material and corruptible. This vigorous passage shows us Origen at his best as an interpreter of Scripture. It has also an historical significance, inasmuch as in later times, in the fifth century, some of his most ignorant opponents—certain monks—attacked him on the score of his teaching that God must not be thought of as possessing anything like a human form.[38]

HALLOWED BE THY NAME
Chapter XXIV

As arising out of this petition, Origen asks three questions: (1) Can a man ask that the name of God be hallowed, as if it

37 I John 3:8.   38 F. J. Foakes Jackson, *History of the Christian Church*, 445.

had not been hallowed? (2) What is the "name" of the Father? (3) What is its hallowing? The second question is answered first. A "name" is "a compendious appellation manifesting the individual quality of the being named. For example, Paul the apostle has a certain individual quality; a quality of soul, which makes it of a certain kind; a quality of mind, which makes him capable of contemplating certain kinds of things; a quality of body, which makes it of a certain kind. The individuality of these qualities, which is incommunicable to another (for no being is exactly similar to Paul) is indicated by the name 'Paul.'" To apply this to God—the idea that we are taught to have within us of God is that he is holy, and this conception of God is manifested to us in his several actions, when "he creates, foresees, judges, chooses, forsakes, receives, turns away from, deems worthy of honour, punishes each one according to his deserts." In this way the individual quality of God is characterized for us: and we have what is called the "name of God" in the Scriptures. Anyone who connects the idea of God with things that are not fitting "takes the name of the Lord in vain." On the other hand, he who by his words refreshes, encourages or edifies the soul of another, is able to do this because of the "name": for the character of God is seen in his action upon men for their own good and that of their fellows. So we come to question (3), What is the "hallowing" of God's name? Origen quotes Ps. 34:3: "Let us exalt his name together." We are commanded here, he says, "to haste unto the true and lofty knowledge of the distinctive being of God." "To exalt the name of God" is when "a man partaking of Deity exalts that very power of God of which he has partaken." The answer to question (1) is left to the end of the chapter. When we say, "Hallowed be thy name," though the verb is in the imperative mood, the meaning is optative "may thy name be hallowed." This usage, says Origen, occurs frequently in the Septuagint. Tatian, in fact, imagined wrongly, from its frequent use, that it was always so, and accordingly fell into error concerning expressions in the first chapter of Genesis.

THY KINGDOM COME

Chapter XXV

For Origen the kingdom of God is immanent and spiritual. He has no qualms, as some moderns seem to have, about accepting the saying in Luke "the kingdom of God cometh not with observation: neither shall they say, Lo, here! or Lo, there! but the kingdom of God is within you."[39] Indeed, he combines with this the saying in Deuteronomy,[40] "the word is very nigh, in your mouth, and in your heart." "I think," he says, "that by God's kingdom is meant the blessed state of the reason and the ordered condition of wise thoughts." "Every saint who takes God as his king and obeys the spiritual laws of God dwells in himself as in a well-ordered city." He draws a distinction between the kingdom of God and the kingdom of Christ. The latter is rather a saving power that goes forth into the world and is seen in action. "By Christ's kingdom is meant the words that go forth for the salvation of those who hear them and the works of righteousness and the other virtues which are being accomplished." This distinction helps Origen to lead up eventually to one of his favourite texts, which speaks of the time when Christ "shall deliver up the kingdom to God, even the Father . . . that God may be all in all."[41]

But the use of this text also indicates that for Origen the eschatological element in the kingdom of God was not entirely lacking. Indeed, when he speaks of the kingdom as being within us, he acknowledges that he may be met with the objection, Why, then, should we pray: "Thy kingdom come"? How shall a man "still fittingly pray concerning things that are present already as if they were not present"? The answer is that spiritual knowledge and understanding (with which Origen's conception of "salvation" is largely bound up) must be a growing thing. We have "the word of knowledge" and "the word of wisdom" even now, but we nevertheless pray for these things, to receive more and more of them, so that in this present life our knowledge "in part" will become as great as may be. When, however, "that which is perfect is come," the mind without sense perception will come in contact with spiritual realities, and without this the perfection of the "kingdom" cannot be. Our journey, therefore, in this life is "unto perfection";[42] and as we advance unceasingly the kingdom of God that is in us will reach its highest point when the saying of I Cor. 15:28 is fulfilled. So we may fittingly here and now pray, "Thy kingdom come," even though "the kingdom of God is within us." Similarly also, in the moral life the work of God within us, begun now, will be perfected when our corruptible has put on incorruption, and the mortal has put on immortality.

[39] Luke 17:20, 21.   [40] Deut. 30:14.
[41] I Cor. 15:24, 28.
[42] Heb. 6:1.

THY WILL BE DONE, AS IN HEAVEN SO ON EARTH
Chapter XXVI

Origen points out that the words "as in heaven, so on earth" are to be taken not only with "Thy will be done," but also with "Hallowed be thy name" and "Thy kingdom come."

When we do the will of God when on earth, he says, we are made like unto those in heaven, inasmuch as we bear, as they do, the image of the heavenly and shall inherit heaven.

An objection to the petition is next considered. We are told that there are spiritual hosts of wickedness in the heavenly places,[43] who bring about evil things on earth. If therefore we pray that God's will be done on earth as it is in heaven, we may unwittingly pray that these opposing forces may remain on earth, to which they came from heaven. A solution to this difficulty is ready to hand if we allegorize "heaven" and "earth," understanding "heaven" as "Christ" and "earth" as "the Church." We shall then be praying that even as Christ accomplished the Father's will in its entirety, so we, the members of the Church, being joined to Christ and become one spirit[44] with him, may likewise achieve it. (It is no objection to this that Christ says he has been given all authority in heaven and on earth;[45] for Christ is both man and Saviour, man mingled with Deity, and therefore, both realms being his, he takes as his fellow-workers his disciples that he may bring the things on earth to a blessed issue.) But it still remains, on the ordinary interpretation, to explain how the will of God is done in heaven, when the spiritual hosts of wickedness are in the heavenly places, wrestling against those on earth. Origen replies, in effect, "Because the mind is its own place." These hosts do not really dwell in heaven, because of their evil disposition; and therefore when we pray, "Thy will be done, as in heaven, so on earth," it is not to be reckoned that they are in heaven, since they have fallen in mind with Satan who fell from heaven like lightning.[46] Similarly, he whose citizenship is in heaven, though still on earth, is no longer of the earth in the world below, but of heaven and of the heavenly world that is better than this one.

GIVE US THIS DAY OUR DAILY BREAD
Chapter XXVII

This is one of the longest chapters on the Lord's Prayer, and certainly the least satisfactory. Dominated, as we have already

[43] Eph. 6:12. [44] I Cor. 6:17. [45] Matt. 28:18. [46] Luke 10:18.

remarked,[47] by the Platonic conception of the material world, Origen dismisses the plain, literal meaning of this petition. In fact he asserts that it is a false opinion, to be refuted, to suppose that we are here told to pray concerning material (lit. "bodily") bread.[48] Accordingly, the "bread" we pray for is not the bread that is to lie on our tables, but the meat which abideth unto eternal life, which the Son of man shall give. To feed on it is to feed on the spiritual teachings of Christ. "What is more nourishing to the soul than the Word, and what is more precious to the mind of him who makes room for it than the Wisdom of God? And what is more appropriate to the rational soul than truth?"[49]

Scripture, however, calls every kind of food "bread," and therefore the Word which nourishes is varied and diverse, for not all are able to be nourished by the solidity and vigorous force of the divine teachings.[50] Thus Origen introduces us to one of his favourite thoughts, as we have seen,[51] that of different grades of hearers who live on different levels of spiritual apprehension, and must be treated by the teacher accordingly.[52]

The unusual word for "daily" (ἐπιούσιος) bread next claims Origen's attention. He gives his view that it was coined by the evangelists.[53] He derives it from *epi* and *ousia*:[54] (the bread that comes together) into substance, and he compares *periousios laos*,[55] the people (dwelling) around substance.

The mention of the word *ousia* is sufficient to set Origen off into a philosophical disquisition,[56] and he now proceeds to give an account of the views of different schools of thought on "substance." This done, he shows that there must be a kinship in "substance" between the bread given and the person who receives it. The bread, as he believes to have shown, is "spiritual." Therefore *epiousios* bread[56] "is that which is best adapted to a reasonable nature and akin to it in its very substance: it provides at once health and strength and vigour to the soul, and imparts a share of its own immortality (for the word of God is immortal) to him who eats of it."[57] He ends this part of the discussion by references from the Bible to food partaken in common

47 See pp. 210 f.   48 XXVII, 1.
49 XXVII, 2.   50 XXVII, 4.
51 See pp. 199 f.   52 XXVII, 4–6.
53 See note, p. 363.
54 Elsewhere (section 13) he rejects the derivation from *epienai* "to come close upon."
55 Ex. 19:5.   56 XXVII, 8.
57 XXVII, 9.

by men on the one hand and greater and inferior spiritual powers on the other.[58] There is no reference to the Eucharist. The remainder[59] of the chapter is concerned with the meaning of "today" and "day by day," which Origen interprets as this present age and successive ages, respectively.

FORGIVE US OUR DEBTS, AS WE ALSO HAVE FORGIVEN
OUR DEBTORS

Chapter XXVIII

In contrast to his treatment of the foregoing petition, Origen expounds this one with refreshing realism. We all owe debts to one another, he says, not only in respect of money, but also in respect of particular actions, and gentle speech, and a charitable disposition. Further, there are debts to be paid because we are in a certain relationship to others—debts to our brethren in Christ, and debts due from us as citizens, as husband or wife, as a widow cared for by the Church, as a deacon, or presbyter, or bishop, and we have a debt to ourselves so to use the body that we do not waste its powers in pleasure. And, above all, we owe it to God to love him with all our heart and strength and mind; we are debtors to Christ, since he has bought us with a price, and also to the Holy Spirit. We are debtors also to our guardian angel, even though we do not know precisely who he is.

Others are in debt to us: but we must be gentle towards them, when they are slow in paying back, remembering the parable of the unmerciful servant. There is a limitation, however, in respect of our forgiveness of others, says Origen: and with this point he closes the chapter. It might seem, when Luke adds "for we ourselves also forgive everyone that is indebted to us," that there is no such limitation. But the Lord said to the apostles, "whose soever sins ye retain, they are retained,"[60] and John says: "There is a sin unto death: not concerning this do I say that he should make request."[61] In the law also a sacrifice might not be offered for presumptuous sins. It follows, then, that the Christian also, the true follower of Jesus, forgives what God forgives, and retains such sins as God retains. This leads Origen on to refer to those persons[62] who have arrogated to themselves powers beyond the priestly office and boast that they are able to pardon even idolatry and forgive even such deadly sins as adultery or fornication.

[58] XXVII, 10–12.   [59] XXVII, 13–16.   [60] John 20:23.
[61] I John 5:16.   [62] See p. 310.

BRING US NOT INTO TEMPTATION
Chapter XXIX

It is not surprising to anyone who knows Origen that he at once faces the obvious difficulty confronting the interpretation of this petition. How can we be bidden, he asks, to use these words in prayer, when the whole of human life upon earth is a temptation?[63] While on earth we are compassed about with the flesh that warreth against the spirit,[64] and we wrestle, not only with the flesh, but also against the spiritual hosts of wickedness?[65] And Paul tells the Corinthians, not that God will not suffer them to be tempted, but that he will not suffer them to be tempted beyond their power.[66] Other passages of Scripture are brought in for the purpose of proving the inevitability of temptation. Even the apostles were not free from it, as is clear from Paul's account, in the Epistles to the Corinthians, of his trials and sufferings. Moreover, temptation assails men in every condition of life—the poor, the rich, the sick, the whole, persons of low as well as those of high degree, the abject and those who are held in high esteem among men. Even the Saviour was tempted, and like the bridegroom in the Song of Songs, looking at us through the meshes of temptation, bids us arise.[67] Indeed, temptation lurks even in the reading of the Holy Scriptures, as is evident from the errors of those who, like the Marcionites,[68] misinterpret the doctrine of God as it is set forth in the Old and New Testaments.

The true meaning, therefore, of the petition in the Lord's Prayer is "not that we may not be tempted (for that cannot be), but that we may not be encompassed by temptation, a thing that happens to those who are held fast in it and overcome." (Similarly, Origen interprets the warning "not to enter into temptation"[69] as meaning to avoid being encompassed by temptation.)

It is impossible, then, to think that the good God should encompass anyone with evil and cause him to be held fast by it. It may be said, however, that the Lord in giving the Prayer was speaking to men of prayer and exhorting them to prayer against temptation. What of those who do not pray, or those whose prayer cannot be heard? Can God lead them into temptation in the sense of being brought under its domination? This question

---

[63] Quoting Job 7:1.   [64] Gal. 5:17.   [65] Eph. 6:12.
[66] I Cor. 10:13.   [67] See pp. 376 f.
[68] They are not actually named.   [69] Cf. Luke 22:40.

is suggested by such phrases as are found in the first chapter of Romans with reference to persons of dissolute character. "God gave them up in the lusts of their hearts unto uncleanness"; "God gave them up unto vile passions"; "God gave them up unto a reprobate mind." The Marcionites cannot maintain that these words are used of the God of the law (who, they mistakenly suppose, is other than the good Father of our Lord Jesus Christ) and therefore they must find in them a stumbling-block to their notions. Nevertheless, the difficulty in such phrases as "God gave them up unto vile passions," as well as in "Bring us not into temptation," remains. How is it to be overcome? Origen puts forward the following solution.[70]

"I verily believe that God orders every rational soul with a view to its eternal life, and that it always maintains its free will, and of its own motion either mounts higher and higher until it reaches the pinnacle of virtue, or on the contrary descends through carelessness to this or that excess of wickedness." If the soul chooses the downward grade, and falls into a sinful state, it may be that a rapid and brief cure will cause it to regard lightly the disease into which it has fallen, so that after being restored to health it may fall the second time into the same condition. Therefore in such cases God may for a time disregard increasing wickedness up to a certain point, and even overlook it when it has developed to such an extent as to be incurable, in order that the soul may take its fill of evil, and being glutted with the sin it desires may at last become conscious of its evil plight and hate what it formerly welcomed. A parallel is adduced from "the mixed multitude" when in the wilderness they lusted after the fleshpots of Egypt.[71] The Lord glutted them with the food they desired "for a month of days" until it came out at their nostrils and became loathsome unto them.[72] So also the kind and good God may even be said to "give up" men to their evil passions, in order to satiate them with their lust; that, this life ended, they may no longer wish to return to them, but recognizing their desperate condition may of their own free will come to hate that which they formerly desired and seek for heavenly things.

The chapter ends with a short account of the use of temptation. It reveals character. What our soul has received is unknown to all except God—is unknown even to ourselves; but it is manifested by means of temptations. Temptations when they come

70 XXIX, 13.   71 Num. 11:4–6.
72 Num. 11:18–20.

make it plain to us of what sort we are, make known the hidden
things of the heart. This is clearly stated in Scripture, as, for
example, in the passage in Deuteronomy which says that the
trials in the wilderness were sent in order that the things in
the heart of God's people might be made known.[73] Similarly, the
temptations which beset Eve, Cain, the sons of Noah, Esau, and
Joseph did not for the first time make them what they were seen
to be, but rather manifested the weakness or strength that already lay in their characters. Therefore we must not wait until
the temptations come, but prepare ourselves by the power of
God in the times between temptations, so that we shall not be
proved unready when they come.

DELIVER US FROM THE EVIL ONE

Chapter XXX

The student of Origen will not need to be told that he believed in a personal devil. Consequently, it is clear throughout
the short passage which deals with this petition that he interprets τοῦ πονηροῦ as masculine, with the Revised Version, and
not as neuter with the Authorized Version. The passages of
Scripture used to describe the assaults of the devil are Eph. 6:16
and Job, chs. 1 and 2. Origen expounds "Deliver us from the
evil one" on the same lines as "Bring us not into temptation."
God delivers us from the evil one, not when the enemy or the
ministers of his will in no way attack us, but when we conquer
bravely, taking a firm stand against circumstances. This is
clearly indicated in the Book of Job. The patriarch was delivered
from the evil one, not by immunity from attacks of the devil
(for the Lord gave him authority to attack Job), but by the fact
that in all his trials "Job sinned not before the Lord." The experience of the Saviour in the wilderness likewise illustrates the
meaning of this petition. His deliverance consisted, not in absence of temptation (indeed, he was three times assailed), but in
his conquest over it. As for ourselves, the soul must be prepared
for such attacks, if we are to overcome them. We are to have
within ourselves "rivers of water springing up unto eternal
life,"[74] if we are to quench "the fiery darts of the evil one."[75]
Contemplation of the truth will stamp upon the soul of the
spiritual athlete inspired and saving thoughts for his use in time
of need.

[73] Deut. 8:2, 3, 15.   [74] John 7:38; 4:14.
[75] Eph. 6:16.

COMPARISON WITH THE *De Oratione* OF TERTULLIAN

Origen was not the first of the Fathers to write a treatise on Prayer and the Lord's Prayer, being preceded in this respect by about twenty years by Tertullian, whose work is placed between the limits of 196–203[76] or 200–206.[77] The purpose and scope of the two treatises are so different that any attempted comparison between them is certainly very difficult and may seem to be even misleading. Origen writes, as we have seen, primarily for Christians of standing and intelligence, who were disingenuous enough to propound questions which struck at the very root of the efficacy of prayer. Tertullian wrote for catechumens,[78] who are described in his *De Baptismo* as "those whom the grace of God awaits"; and he assumes without question the *rationale* of prayer. Again, as regards length, Origen's treatise occupies 106 pages of the Berlin *Corpus* of the Fathers, Tertullian's twenty pages only of the Vienna *Corpus*; and the treatments of the Lord's Prayer vary correspondingly in length. But against this disparity in length we must set the fact that Tertullian is as concise as Origen is discursive.

In spite of these differences of approach to the subject, however, a comparison between the two treatises may have its value, since no two men can traverse the same ground without revealing those differences which lie deeper than the mere setting in which their treatment of the theme is found, and also the common ground, great or small, on which, in spite of differences, they stand.

In this particular case, the common ground is by no means large. There are, however, a few points of resemblance between the two treatments of the subject. For both writers the Lord's Prayer is the primary source and model of Christian teaching to which they refer. Again, both writers dwell on what the Sermon on the Mount (Matt. ch. 6) has to say about ostentation and "much speaking" in prayer. The distinctively Christian address of "Father" in prayer is noted by both writers. And they both speak of the proper attitude of mind and disposition of him who comes to prayer. There must be no hatred of our brother, or anger, or even perturbation of mind.[79]

But at the outset of the treatment of the Lord's Prayer itself,

---

[76] Harnack.   [77] Bardenhewer and d'Alès.

[78] "consideremus itaque, benedicti," ch. I. For *benedicti* see *De Baptismo*, XX: "benedicti, quos gratia dei expectat."

[79] Tertullian *De Oratione*, chs. XI, XII.

differences begin to appear. Origen is a critical, textual scholar. He notes that the Prayer, according to the Gospels, was given on two different occasions, and that the text of the two prayers differs considerably. Before he begins his exegesis, he sets out the two texts,[80] and continues to keep their differences before him. Tertullian, on the other hand, ignores the presence of these differences (if he knew of them), and confines his exposition to what is broadly speaking a version of the Matthaean text; although, curiously enough, he begins simply with "Pater,"[81] as does the Lukan text. Even though his version contains at least one feature which must have been abnormal (he places "Thy kingdom come" *after* "Hallowed be thy Name, Thy will be done in heaven and on earth"), he does not comment upon any facts of this kind.

In the exegesis of the Prayer much of the difference in the two writers is to be traced ultimately to a difference in philosophical outlook, conscious in the case of Origen, perhaps unconscious for Tertullian, and particularly in respect of transcendence and immanence, material and spiritual. For Origen[82] the kingdom is above all things immanent and spiritual, and the eschatological aspect is secondary and in the sense that the spiritual apprehension of the truth must go on growing and increasing until the consummation is reached, when that which is perfect is come, and God shall be all in all. Tertullian,[83] on the other hand, emphasizes the literal and eschatological sense of the kingdom of God. It is true that there is never a time when God does not reign; and he reigns in us: but the coming of the kingdom is the coming manifestation of the rule of God. It is future. The souls of the martyrs beneath the altar cry out, "How long?" It is for us a matter of earnest expectation. Tertullian's attitude is definitely "other-worldly." He would approve of the sentiment of the prayer in which we ask God "shortly to accomplish the number of thine elect and to hasten thy kingdom." Christians, he says, are illogical if with the words "Thy kingdom come" on their lips they desire any delay of the final consummation, seeing that now we are in servitude, then we shall reign: "optamus maturius regnare, et non diutius servire."

In expounding the petition "Thy will be done, on earth as it is in heaven," both writers admit that a simple, literal interpretation is on the surface impossible. But when they proceed to consider what the deeper, spiritual meaning of "earth" and

[80] Ch. XVIII.
[82] XXV, 1, 2.
[81] But in *Adv. Prax.*, 23, "Pater noster."
[83] Ch. V.

"heaven" may be, they part company. Tertullian[84] holds that, in this sense, "earth" and "heaven" mean, respectively, "flesh" and "spirit." Origen allegorizes differently. He notes the difficulty arising out of the fact that there are spiritual hosts of wickedness in the heavenly places. "Heaven" may mean, then, "Christ"; while "earth" may be interpreted "the Church."[85] But he goes on to give another, and, it would appear, a preferable interpretation, namely, that setting aside all local and temporal ideas, he that doeth the will of God is "heaven," and persons of bad character are "earth."[86]

In the next petition, even more marked differences of treatment appear. As we have noted, Origen spiritualizes altogether the "daily bread": and in fact calls it a false opinion to hold that material bread is spoken of.[87] Tertullian[88] extols the Divine Wisdom which has so arranged the order of the prayer that after things heavenly should come earthly necessities. This, he points out, is in accordance with the command: "Seek ye first the kingdom, and then these things also shall be added unto you." Having said so much, however, Tertullian goes on to say that "nevertheless we may rather understand 'Give us this day our daily bread' spiritually. For Christ is our Bread, and Christ is Life, and bread is life, and he said 'I am the Bread of life.'" But even on this plane of interpretation differences between the two writers manifest themselves. Tertullian at once speaks of the Eucharist and of the bread of which Christ said, "This is my body." Origen, who has a long disquisition on the petition, never includes in it a reference to the Eucharist: to feed on Christ is to feed on his spiritual teachings.

The remaining two petitions of the Lord's Prayer do not provide much material for the purposes of comparison, either in respect of agreement or of disagreement. And so we may pass on to underline an important difference between the two treatises that is to be found throughout them as a whole. Origen speaks almost entirely of private prayer, of individual prayer, although he notes the added value of prayers in common when Christian disciples meet for worship;[89] and he refers very seldom to the ordinances of the Church.[90] Tertullian, on the other hand, at the outset of his treatise,[91] places prayer in the context of the Church. Speaking of the opening words of the Lord's Prayer, he says, "In the Father the Son is invoked; for 'I,' saith

[84] Ch. IV.   [85] XXVI, 4.   [86] XXVI, 6.
[87] XXVII, 1.   [88] Ch. VI.   [89] XXXI, 5.
[90] See pp. 201 f.   [91] Ch. II.

he, 'and the Father are one'" (notably different from Origen, who allows prayer in the proper sense of the term to be addressed to the Father only).[92] Then, rather naïvely, he adds, "Nor is even our mother the Church passed by, if, that is, in the Father and the Son is recognized the mother, from whom arises the name both of Father and Son." Accordingly in the course of the treatise, and especially when he comes to speak of the manner and posture and place of prayer, he has many references to Church ordinances and seasons and customs—the liturgical setting of prayer. He speaks of Eucharist and the words "This is my body,"[93] of the kiss of peace, and about communicating on station days.[94] Later on, he mentions the singing of the Psalms and the liturgical use of Alleluia.[95] Speaking of the question of kneeling at prayer,[96] he mentions that though some refrained from kneeling on Saturdays, the tradition he has received is that we do not kneel on Sundays or in the *Spatio Pentecostes* (? interval between Easter and Pentecost) "quae eadem exultationis sollemnitate dispungitur." We are, however, to kneel on fasts and station days; and we ought to prostrate ourselves before God every day, or certainly when we pray the first thing in the morning. *Per contra*, when Origen[97] is discussing this question, he speaks only of kneeling as a symbol of the man who is abject and submissive, and says nothing about kneeling in church.

Again, when we compare passages which cite the Scriptures as proving the power and efficacy of prayer, we discover a difference of outlook between the two writers. We have seen[98] what Origen's treatment of "Give us this day our daily bread" is, and also how he contrasts the Old Testament with its record of material benefits vouchsafed through prayer with the purely spiritual objects, the "great and heavenly things," for which a Christian ought to pray. In fact, when he says[99] that prayers similar to those which brought blessing to Old Testament saints are answered also today, he is not referring to the same kind of answer but to a spiritualized version of it. Tertullian's treatment of this matter is different. The concluding chapter[1] of his *De Oratione* is an eloquent description of the power and efficacy of prayer. Like Origen he contrasts Old Testament with Christian prayers. "Prayer in olden times, indeed, used to free from fires and from beasts and from famine" (he is probably referring to

---

[92] XV, 1. [93] Ch. VI. [94] Chs. XVIII, XIX.
[95] Chs. XXVII, XXVIII. [96] Ch. XXIII.
[97] XXXI, 3. [98] Pp. 218 ff., 263–266.
[99] XIII, 3. [1] XXIX.

Dan., chs. 3 and 6, and I Kings, ch. 18, with James 5:17,18)
"but how far more fully operative is Christian prayer! It does
not station the angel of dew in mid fires,[2] nor stop the mouths of
lions nor transfer to the hungry the rustics' meal;[3] it has no
grace given it to remove any sense of suffering; but it supplies
with endurance those who are suffering, feeling, grieving." But
this spiritual power, this ability to endure, be it noted, is given
because of the presence of material afflictions or tortures, it is
not a defence against the unseen powers of evil, as Origen would
interpret. And again, according to Tertullian, "Is it any wonder
if prayer knows how to extort the rains[4] of heaven, which was
once able to procure its fires?"[5] And this is *natural* rain, *not* "the
rain of the soul,"[6] which according to Origen is the fulfilment
of which the rain procured by the prayer of Elijah is the type.
Further, in conclusion, among the many benefits resulting from
Christian prayer Tertullian reckons many which concern the
body: prayer is able "to recall the souls of the departed from the
very path of death, to renew the weak, to heal the sick, to purge
them that are possessed of devils, to open prison bars, to loose
the bonds of the innocent."

Finally, it is impossible to avoid contrasting the general outlook of Tertullian upon Christianity and the particular subject
of prayer with that of Origen. For Tertullian Christianity is a
spiritual law and discipline with its prescribed duties. When we
pray, we obey an order (*praeceptum*) of God, and when we call
him Father we acknowledge his authority (*potestas*).[7] It is not
indeed that Tertullian hankers after Judaism. *That* indeed has
passed away: the gospel is the fulfiller[8] of the whole ancient
system. But in its place have come the commandments of God
in Christ, including particularly his command concerning
prayer and its prescribed form; and our mother the Church
(deduced by Tertullian as a natural consequent of Father and
Son)[9] also prescribes services and forms and customs. The whole
setting of the treatise is placed in the sphere of spiritual duty.
The life of the household the Church is conceived after the

---

[2] Origen also refers to the "whistling dewy wind" (Dan. 3:49, 50, LXX),
which tempered the fire for the Three Holy Children.

[3] Bel and the Dragon 33.

[4] A reference to the story (*Apologeticus*, V; Eusebius, *H.E.*, V, 5) of the
"Thundering Legion," when Christians in the army of Marcus Aurelius
by means of prayer brought down a refreshing shower upon soldiers who
were in danger of perishing by thirst.

[5] II Kings 1:10 ff.   [6] XIII, 5.   [7] Ch. II.

[8] Ch. I.   [9] Ch. II.

manner of domestic life in a Roman household, where the
patria potestas was a living reality, setting a rule and standard for
all its members. In that setting there is little room or desire to
dwell upon matters which might weaken the sense of prescribed
duty, such as differences in the text of Holy Scripture, criticism
and interpretation of the Bible, possible objections, alternative
renderings, speculations, and insoluble problems. With all of
these, on the contrary, Origen is pre-occupied. It is part of his
conception of Christianity, which is, to apprehend the truth of
Christ and to feed upon his teachings. If Tertullian's watchword is "duty," Origen's is "understanding," though not simply
understanding that is intellectual but including also mystical
apprehension and self-devotion which issues in a Christian way
of life.

Thus in less than two hundred years profound differences of
outlook had manifested themselves in Christianity. Carthage
and Alexandria are in the same continent. About a thousand
miles of coastline separate them one from the other. But Tertullian and Origen inhabit a different world spiritually and
intellectually—a difference that may be expressed in various
ways, as for example by saying that the one was Latin, the other
Greek, the one authoritative, the other speculative, the one ex-
clusive, the other comprehensive, the one reactionary, the other
liberal. "Quid Athenis et Hierosolymis?"[10] cries Tertullian.
"What have Athens and Jerusalem in common?" And he proceeds, "Away with those who put forward a Stoic, a Platonic, a
dialectic sort of Christianity! We have no need for curious
speculation, once we have accepted Christ Jesus, nor for inquiry
after receiving the gospel. Once we believe, we desire no further
belief. For our belief is this, that there is nothing which we
ought to believe besides."

It is better frankly to acknowledge that these two extreme
types of Christianity emerged early in its history, and have continued ever since, than to attempt a formal reconciliation between them. If we will allow room for them both in a Catholic
Church, we shall serve the Church better than by seeking for
them a common denominator. Perhaps it is necessary to say this
today: for we live at a time when "pattern" has become a
"blessed" word in theology. By using it, some lull themselves
into the comfortable frame of mind which sees a uniformity in
Christian faith and practice which does not in fact exist. "Pattern" is a tendentious, a misleading, but nevertheless for many,

10 *De Praescriptione,* 7.

a soporific word. It persuades those who use it into a totalitarian kind of belief that all happens "according to plan." In comparing these two treatises of Tertullian and Origen, the present writer makes no attempt to establish a common "pattern" between them. He has pointed out a few similarities of thought and treatment. But the two works, as well as the two authors, differ *toto caelo*. They exhibit, not a "pattern," but the "much variegated wisdom of God."[11]

TEXT, TRANSMISSION, MANUSCRIPTS, AND EDITIONS

That the treatise *On Prayer* has come down to us at all must be regarded as a fortunate circumstance. As we have seen,[12] certain passages in the work were accounted heretical, and this in turn doubtless affected its transmission from early times, quite apart from the general destruction of Origen's manuscripts as a result of the controversies of which he was the storm centre. In fact, we are ultimately dependent for the Greek text upon a single MS. which has had a precarious history and might well have never survived its chequered fortunes. And there is no Latin translation of the *De Oratione* as there is of so many of Origen's other works. There are indeed few references to the treatise in the extant literature of the early Church. The *Apologia pro Origene*, written conjointly by Pamphilus and Eusebius c. 308, "because of the fault-finders,"[13] mentions it as extant. It is true that we possess this Apology only in the Latin translation of Rufinus (and that, too, of the first book only), but there is no reason, but rather the contrary, why Rufinus should have included a reference to the book if he did not find it in the original. This translation was made in 398. The reference is as follows:[14] "Denique in tam multis et tam diversis eius libris nusquam omnino invenitur ab eo liber proprie de anima conscriptus, sicut habet vel de Martyrio, vel de Oratione, vel de Resurrectione."[15] There is no reference to the *De Oratione* in the list of Origen's works to be found in Jerome, *Ep.*, XXXIII, *ad Paulam*.[16] But Jerome is here chiefly concerned to enumerate Origen's labours in Biblical exegesis: "qui tanto in sanctarum scriptarum commentariis sudore laboravit, ut iuste adamantis nomen acceperit." Therefore his omission to mention the treatise is not conclusive of his ignorance of its existence; in fact, he does not mention the *Contra Celsum* either. Nor does it follow that

---

[11] Eph. 3:10. [12] See pp. 187 ff. [13] Eusebius, *H.E.*, VI, 33:4.
[14] Ch. 8. [15] Routh, *Reliquiae Sacrae*, IV, 379. [16] *C.V.*, LIV, 253 ff.

Gregory and Basil did not know the *De Oratione* because they did not include a passage from it in the *Philocalia*. This work mainly consists of passages which exemplify Origen's power of resolving difficult questions arising out of the Holy Scriptures.[17]

The synodical letter of Theophilus of Alexandria, a bitter opponent of Origen, "ad Palestinos et ad Cyprios episcopos missa" (c. 400) and translated by Jerome,[18] mentions the *De Oratione* expressly when it includes among the errors of Origen what he wrote about praying to the Father only: "cum legeretur . . . in alio libro, qui 'de oratione' scribitur: non debemus orare filium, sed solum patrem, nec patrem cum filio, obturavimus aures nostras et tam Origenem quam discipulos eius consona voce damnavimus, ne et modicum fermentum totam massam corrumperet." Again, in another, a paschal, letter, also translated by Jerome,[19] Theophilus attacks at greater length the same point in Origen's teaching. He places Origen on a level, in this respect, with Pharaoh, who said, "I know not the Lord."[20] "Nec est aliud dicere 'nescio Dominum' quam hoc, quod dicit Origenes, 'non est orandus filius.'" Inasmuch as Christ is the Son of God it follows as a right and proper consequence that he is to be invoked, and prayer is to be made to him, as indeed we are taught in the Scriptures to do (Acts 7:60; Phil. 2:10). The first of these quotations is an unhappy one from the point of view of Theophilus's criticism, as Origen expressly quotes these words of Stephen ("Lord, lay not this sin to their charge") as an example of *intercession* (which he distinguishes from *prayer* in the full sense of the term) being rightly made to the Son.[21] Origen, says Theophilus, does not believe in the Deity of the Son: "itaque nec deum credit Origenes filium dei, quem non putat adorandum." The name of divinity that he gives him is only an empty name. He thinks that he understands the meaning of the Scriptures, but he does not hear what Moses says against him. "Whosoever curseth God shall bear his sin; he that nameth the name of the Lord shall surely die; the whole congregation shall stone him."[22]

Acquaintance with the *De Oratione* has been claimed for Ambrose, in virtue of certain passages in the *De Sacramentis*[23] and *De Fide*;[24] see note on XXVII, 9. There are marked differences, however, between Ambrose and Origen.

17 γραφικῶν ζητημάτων καὶ ἐπιλύσεων.
18 Jerome, *Ep.*, XCII (*C.V.*, LV, 148, 149).
19 *Ibid.* (*Ep.*, XCVI), 172 ff.   20 Ex. 5:2.   21 See p. 269.
22 Lev. 24:15, 16.   23 V, 24, VI, 22.   24 III, 127.

The writings and pronouncements of the Emperor Justinian in the sixth century afford evidence of his knowledge of the *De Oratione*, in so far as he finds in it the idea that the resurrection body is spherical. In his Epistle to Mennas, Patriarch of Constantinople, he says:[25] "For he [sc. Origen] says that in the resurrection men's bodies are raised spherical. O! the folly and stupidity of this crazy fellow, this expounder of Greek opinions! Darkened in his understanding, and eager to mix up myths with the Christian faith, he aimed at casting insult upon the very hope and salvation of Christians, that is, the resurrection promised to us, not even reverencing the resurrection of the Lord . . . For if, as Origen madly supposes, the body of the Lord was spherical, how was he able to show the piercings of his hands and feet, or the wound in his side? Or how could he eat, or be recognized at all by his disciples? And how also could the bodies of the saints, which were raised after the Lord's resurrection and seen in the holy city, have been known by others, if they were really in a form different from that which they had in life?"

The Epistle to Mennas concludes with a series of ten anathemas against Origen's teachings, of which the following is the fifth:[26] "If anyone says or holds that at the resurrection men's bodies are raised spherical, and does not acknowledge that we are raised upright, let him be anathema." A similar condemnation is to be found in the tenth of the Fifteen Anathemas against Origen, discovered by Peter Lambeck, the Librarian of Vienna, towards the end of the seventeenth century, which some hold to have been adopted by the Fifth General Council, but others, more probably, assign to a "Home Synod," that is, a Synod held in 543 at Constantinople of the bishops of the locality.[27] The translation of this Anathema runs as follows: "If anyone shall say that after the resurrection the body of the Lord was ethereal and spherical in form, and that such shall be the bodies of all after the resurrection; and that after the Lord himself shall have rejected his true body and after the others who rise shall have rejected theirs, the nature of their bodies shall be annihilated: let him be anathema."

On the other hand, Photius[28] refers to an anonymous defender of Origen. "The counts on which he asserts that he [sc. Origen] was falsely accused are fifteen in number, which he declares to be mere slanders. . . . He is charged with teaching

---

[25] *P.G.*, LXXXVI (1), 973.
[26] *Ibid.*, 989.   [27] Hefele, IV, 221 ff.; *N.P.N.F.*, XIV, 316 ff.
[28] *Library*, I, 117, ed. J. H. Freese, 206.

that prayer should not be offered to the Son, and that he is not absolutely good." It is probable that this is a reference to the teaching of the *De Oratione*, because although Origen elsewhere in his writings[29] says that prayer should be addressed to the Father it is only in the present treatise that he enjoins prayer—in the proper sense of the term—to the Father *alone*, that is to say, in so many words.

It is not surprising, therefore, that under this barrage of criticism, although it was directed against at the most two points in the treatise, its circulation came almost to an end. In fact it is preserved for us in a single MS., which if it had been lost—and it might well have been—no trace or fragment or copy of the work would now remain. This MS. is now in the Library of Trinity College, Cambridge (B.8.10: formerly styled "Holmiensis"),[30] known under the symbol T, written on paper, of the fourteenth or fifteenth century. Apart from eight inconsiderable lacunae near the beginning, it contains the whole of the treatise. Bound together with it is another work of Origen, his Commentary on Matthew, written in another, older hand.

The scribe of T appears to have been a conscientious person, for where the text he was copying was missing or illegible, he leaves in every case just so much empty space as seems necessary to him, so that he could eventually later on supply the missing words from another codex. Lacunae falling at regular intervals are found at the beginning of the MS., pointing to the fact that in the archetype the first or last lines of a page were partly or wholly destroyed, or rendered illegible, by some cause, probably damp. It cannot now be determined to what century this archetype belonged; but Koetschau[31] argues that not many intermediaries lay between it and T, since the text has been handed down in comparatively good order.

T has had an interesting, but precarious, history. When the cathedral library of Worms was plundered by soldiers, it was purchased from them for a small sum by a person named Rumfius, physician to Elizabeth, Queen of the Bohemians. He brought it from Germany to The Hague, where it passed from his possession to that of the famous scholar Isaac Voss, who in turn brought it to Sweden, where it was lodged along with other manuscripts in the library at Stockholm. There, some

---

[29] See pp. 346 ff.
[30] So-called, because it was once lodged in the Library of Holmia (Stockholm).   [31] I, lxxxvii.

twenty years after Voss had acquired it, another scholar, Peter
Daniel Huet, came across it in the Library and made a copy
of it in the year 1652. Subsequently Voss allowed the use of the
MS. to Herbert Thorndike (1598–1672), fellow of Trinity
College, who was contemplating an edition of the complete
works of Origen.[32] It remained in Thorndike's possession.
Later on he bequeathed it to the Library of his College.

The transcript made by Huet is known as Cod. Parisin.
Suppl. Gr. Nr. 534.

The concluding part of the treatise *On Prayer* (from XXXI, 1
to XXXIII, 3) has been separately handed down in another MS.
(Cod. Parisin, Gr. Nr. 1788, Colbert 3607, cited as "Col"),
written, according to a subscription written in Greek, by a
monk named Gennadius, in the year 1440. A note, written in
a hand of the fifteenth century, gives the following facts concerning the history and ownership of the codex (which is of a
miscellaneous character, containing several works) of which
this fragment forms part, namely, that it came originally from
Constantinople, having been purchased, after the capture of
that city, by a certain man named Luke Zonaras, who was from
"the wholly wretched and miserable island of Lesbos." It remained in his possession until the taking of this island (i.e., in
the year 1462), when it passed into the hands of one Sophianus
of Phocia,[33] and then finally into those of Sophianus the writer
of the note. The first editor to use this fragment was Delarue
(see below), who believed that it was a valuable help in the
restoration of that part of the text of the treatise which it contains. But Koetschau[34] has shown that the most of the variants
of Col from T are scribal errors and omissions, due to negligence
or wilful alteration, and that Col has never more to offer, but
in numerous passages less, than T, and that in fact in T we see
the text from which Col is derived. This view is confirmed by
the fact that T and Col have certain mis-readings in common.
"Further, the scribe of Col behaves throughout in so inconsistent and arbitrary a manner, that one need not, in order to
expose his many faults, interpose an intermediary between T
and Col." Since, then, T and Col are not independent, and

---

[32] T. A. Lacey in his *Herbert Thorndike*, pp. 25 ff. mentions many Greek and
Latin Fathers whom Thorndike cites, but Origen is not among them. But
B. F. Westcott (*D.C.B.*, IV, 141) notes that Thorndike had indeed contemplated an edition of Origen's works, but had abandoned the project.
because *inter alia* he had learned of Huet's intention to carry out a similar
task.   [33] In Asia Minor.   [34] I, lxxxv.

since Col, as we have seen, originally came from Constantinople, it is not unlikely that T also had its habitat there, and hence also in all likelihood its place of origin. Perhaps the passage I quoted earlier[35] in this section from Photius may be significant in this connection. If in Constantinople of the ninth century there were known to be apologists of Origen's treatise, it is likely enough that a MS. containing it would escape the harsher fate that fell upon its fellows in other parts of the world.

The following are the editions of this treatise that have been published up till now.

1. *Editio Princeps*. Printed and published in Oxford in the year 1682. The editor is anonymous. In his *Praefatio* he says that he has given a transcript (*apographum*) of that manuscript "which is now preserved at Cambridge in the Library of the College of the holy Trinity," of whose existence Voss had made him aware. This codex, he remarks, is "non admodum feliciter descriptus," it contains considerable lacunae, and is so full of abbreviations that it required "an interpreter rather than a reader" to transcribe it. A Latin translation is added, in which the editor acknowledges the help he had received from Gale,[36] who not merely translated the Greek text supplied him by the editor, but also reviewed suspected passages by reference to T: so that the Latin translation, as corrected by Gale, is often a substantial improvement.

2. Next in order of time is the edition of the Treatise published at Basle by J. R. Wetstein, the elder, in 1694. The improvement in this edition over its predecessor is mainly due to the fact that Gale's recension of Codex T is utilized. The exemplar of the Oxford edition used by Wetstein is now in the Library of Göttingen University. It contains in the margin Gale's collation of each passage. But it will be seen from what follows that much further work had yet to be done on the text. Indeed the "Master of a College in Cambridge," referred to in the following paragraph, scathingly speaks of "the Basil Edition" as "being a mere repetition of the Oxford, bating a few alterations of little moment, some for the better, some for the worse."

3. First in order of merit among early editions is that of William Reading (London, 1728). This edition is dedicated to Baron Roger Meredith, who is described as *ornatissimus vir*. Its special value lies in the fact that Reading made use of a fresh collation of T and Notes by an anonymous scholar—in fact, a

[35] P. 232.   [36] I.e., Thomas Gale, Dean of York (c. 1635–1702).

new edition of the book—which were sent to Reading by "the Master of a College in Cambridge," whom Reading describes in his Preface as *vir singularis eruditionis, animique in me bene-volentissimi*, with permission to publish them, if he thought fit, without however disclosing the name of the donor. The reason for all this secrecy is not apparent. In any case, the work of the anonymous scholar, included in this edition, was the most valu-able contribution to the criticism of the *De Oratione* that had so far been made. Not only did he collate Codex T more systematic-ally and thoroughly than either of his two predecessors, but by his notes, which are the result of genuine scholarship and of knowledge in particular of the writings of Origen, he contri-buted, even more than Richard Bentley did, to the purifying and emendation of the text.

4. Charles Delarue in his edition of Origen's Works (Vol. I, pp. 196–272, Paris, 1733) reproduced the text of Wetstein's edition, but also utilized an—admittedly insufficient—collation of Codex T, which "John Walker, an English presbyter," had made for him. He also examined the fragment contained in Codex Paris. no. 1788 ("col"). He added a Latin translation, made by Claudius Fleury for Huet. But a more momentous addition appeared in the footnotes, which give the ingenious, though often audacious, conjectural emendations of Richard Bentley.

5. Charles Henry Edward Lommatzch, who published a recension of the work of Delarue in twenty-five volumes, gives the text of the *De Oratione* in Vol. XVIII, pp. 82–297 (Berlin, 1844). This differs only in a few places in the text from that of Delarue; and whereas Delarue had printed the critical notes of the anonymous scholar at the end of his first volume, Lom-matzch adds these to each respective passage of the text.

6. The edition used in preparing this translation is that of Paul Koetschau (Leipzig, 1899) in the Berlin *corpus* of the Fathers entitled *Die griechischen christlichen Schriftsteller der ersten drei Jahrhunderte*. The Introduction to "Die Schrift von Gebet" is in Vol. I of Origen's Works, pp. lxxv–xcii, the text in Vol. II, pp. 297–403. This edition, which is a worthy contribution to modern scholarship and to the series in which it is included, is based on a new collation of Codex T made by C. J. Bellairs Gaskoin. It is indispensable to a critical study of the treatise. Koetschau has been careful to give as accurately as possible the number of letters or lines to be estimated for each of the lacunae in T. His *apparatus criticus* gives full information concerning not

only variants but also emendations of the Anonymous, Bentley, and others. He says, however, that "from the text in T, I have departed only seldom and for compelling reasons."[37] From this point of view it is not surprising that Koetschau often, and to the mind of the present writer too frequently, dismisses proposed emendations with the terse formula "ohne Grund." This, however, does not seriously impair the value of Koetschau's text, of which every serious student of the *De Oratione* must be conscious. I must personally acknowledge my own indebtedness to his edition, not only throughout this book, but especially in writing this section of the Introduction and the section which deals with the occasion of the treatise. Koetschau stands out among those who in the last three hundred years have laboured to make this work of Origen accessible in scholarly form. It appears here in an English translation, which, it is hoped, will not be found entirely inadequate. But the translator must conclude, as Origen himself does, by acknowledging the difficulty of the task as a ground for asking the indulgence of the reader.

[37] I, xc.

On Prayer

THE TEXT

Introduction

Chapters I and II

I, 1. Inasmuch as the greatest themes surpass man's understanding, and transcend exceedingly our perishable nature, it is impossible for the reason of the race of mortals to grasp them; nevertheless this becomes possible by the will of God, in the abundant and immeasurable grace of God that is poured forth by him upon men, through Jesus Christ, who ministers unto us his unsurpassable grace, and through his fellow-worker the Spirit. Certainly, it is impossible for human nature to acquire that wisdom by which "all things" have been "established"[1] (for, according to David, God "made all things in wisdom"[2]). What is impossible, however, becomes possible through our Lord Jesus Christ, who "was made unto us wisdom from God, and righteousness and sanctification and redemption."[3] "For what man shall know the counsel of God? Or who shall conceive what the Lord willeth?" Because "the thoughts of mortals are timorous, and our devices are prone to fail. For a corruptible body weigheth down the soul, and the earthy frame lieth heavy on a mind that is full of cares. And hardly do we divine the things that are on earth. But the things that are in the heavens, who ever yet traced out?"[4] Nevertheless, this impossibility becomes possible by "the exceeding grace of God."[5] For he who "was caught up" into "the third heaven"[6] "traced out"[7] perchance the things in the three heavens, because he had "heard unspeakable words, which it is not lawful for a man to utter."[8] But who can say that it is possible for "the mind of the Lord"

---

[1] Cf. Heb. 3:4. [2] Ps. 104:24. [3] I Cor. 1:30.
[4] Wisdom of Solomon 9:13–16. [5] II Cor. 9:14.
[6] II Cor. 12:2. [7] Wisdom of Solomon 9:16.
[8] II Cor. 12:4.

to be "known"[9] by man? Nevertheless, even this God bestows through Christ,[10] [who says, "Ye are my friends, if you do the things which I command you. No longer do I call you servants; for the servant knoweth not what his lord doeth: but I have called you friends; for all things that I have heard from my Father I have made known unto you."[11] They who hear the gospel rejoice] when it teaches them the will of their Lord, no longer willing to be Lord, but changing to be a friend for those to whom he was formerly Lord. Nevertheless, "since none among men knoweth the things of a man, save the spirit of the man, which is in him, even so the things of God none knoweth, save the Spirit of God."[12] But if "none knoweth the things of God, save the Spirit of God," it is impossible for man to "know the things of God." Consider also, however, how it becomes possible. "But we," he says, "received not the spirit of the world, but the spirit which is of God; that we might know the things that are freely given to us by God. Which things also we speak, not in words which man's wisdom teacheth, but which the Spirit teacheth."[13]

II, 1. Probably, however, most godly and laborious Ambrose, and most modest and brave Tatiana (for whom, it can be said, "it" has "ceased to be after the manner of women," as "it" had "ceased to be with Sarah"[14]), you are somewhat at a loss why, when the subject before us is prayer, we should begin by speaking of the things which though impossible for men yet become possible by the grace of God. One of these impossible things, having regard to our weakness, is, I believe, to give a clear, exact and appropriate account of the whole matter of prayer, how we ought to pray, what things we ought to say to God in prayer, and what times are more suitable than others for prayer[15] . . . [we know that Paul] who because of "the exceeding greatness of the revelations" took care "lest any man should account of" him "above that which he seeth" him "to be, or heareth from"[16] him, confessed that he did "not know" how "to pray as" he "ought"[17]; for as concerning what ought

---

[9] Cf. Rom. 11:34; I Cor. 2:16 (Isa. 40:13).
[10] A lacuna of three and a half lines occurs here in the MS. T, which Koetschau conjecturally fills up as above.
[11] John 15:14, 15. [12] I Cor. 2:11.
[13] I Cor. 2:12, 13. [14] Gen. 18:11.
[15] A lacuna of four and one-fifth lines (about 300 letters) occurs here in the MS. Doubtless at this point Origen referred to the need for divine grace to help him in his task, as we find him doing lower down in this chapter (sect. 6). [16] II Cor. 12:7, 6. [17] Rom. 8:26.

to be prayed for, he says, "we know not as we ought." So it is necessary not only to pray, but also to pray "as we ought," and to pray for what we ought. For it is not enough that we should be able to pray for what we ought, unless in addition we possess the "as we ought." And what does the "as we ought" profit us, if we do not know how to pray for what we ought?

2. Now, of these two things the one, that is to say, "what we ought," is concerned with the words of prayer; the other, "as we ought," with the condition of him who is praying. Examples of "what we ought" are: "Ask for the great things, and the little things shall be added unto you"[18]; and "Ask for the heavenly things and the earthly things[19] shall be added unto you"[20]; and "Pray for them that despitefully use you"[21]; and "Pray ye therefore the Lord of the harvest, that he send forth labourers into his harvest"[22]; and "Pray that ye enter not into temptation"[23]; and "Pray ye that your flight be not in the winter, neither on a sabbath"[24] and "And in praying use not vain repetitions"[25]; and any other sayings like these. An example of "as we ought" is: "I desire therefore that the men pray in every place, lifting up holy hands, without wrath and disputing. In like manner also that women adorn themselves in modest apparel, with shamefastness and sobriety, not with braided hair, or gold, or pearls, or costly raiment; but (which becometh women professing godliness) through good works."[26] Instruction on "as we ought" is also to be found in the passage: "If therefore thou art offering thy gift at the altar, and there rememberest that thy brother hath aught against thee, leave there thy gift before the altar, and go thy way, first be reconciled to thy brother, and then come and offer thy gift."[27] For what greater gift can a reasonable creature[28] present to God than a sweet-savoured[28a] word of prayer, offered by one whose conscience is void of the foul savour that comes from sin? Further instruction on "as we ought" is: "Defraud ye not one the other, except it be by consent for a season, that ye may give yourselves unto prayer, and may be together again, that Satan rejoice not over you[29] because of your incontinency."[30] From this it follows

18 See note.   19 Cf. John 3:12.   20 Cf. Matt. 6:33; Luke 12:31.
21 Luke 6:28.   22 Matt. 9:38; Luke 10:2.
23 Luke 22:40 (Matt. 26:41; Mark 14:38).
24 Matt. 24:20 (Mark 13:18).   25 Matt. 6:7.
26 I Tim. 2:8–10.   27 Matt. 5:23, 24.
28 Cf. Rom. 12:1.   28a Cf. Eph. 5:2; Phil. 4:18.
29 The usual reading is "tempt you not": see note.
30 I Cor. 7:5.

that "as we ought" is hindered unless in the performance of the
ineffable mysteries of marriage due regard is paid to gravity,
infrequency and absence of passion: for the "consent" here
mentioned does away with the disorder of passion, removes
"incontinency," and hinders the joy that Satan takes in another's ill. In addition to these passages, instruction on "as we
ought" is to be found in the saying: "If we stand praying, forgive, if ye have aught against anyone."[31] Also the passage in
Paul, "Every man praying or prophesying, having his head
covered, dishonoureth his head. But every woman praying or
prophesying with her head unveiled dishonoureth her head,"[32]
is indicative of "as we ought."

3. Paul knew all these passages, and could quote a great
many more besides from the Law and the Prophets and from
their fulfilment,[33] the Gospel, and give a varied exposition of
each of them; nevertheless it is out of a true as well as a modest
disposition that he says (for in spite of all this knowledge he saw
how far off he was from knowing what we ought to pray for "as
we ought"): "As touching what we ought to pray for, we
know not as we ought."[34] And, in addition to this saying, he also
indicates the means whereby what is lacking is supplied for the
man who though ignorant renders himself worthy to have what
is lacking in himself supplied: for he says, "The Spirit himself
maketh intercession" to God "with groanings which cannot be
uttered; and he that searcheth the hearts knoweth what is the
mind of the Spirit, because he maketh intercession for the saints
according to the will of God."[35] Now "the Spirit" who "cries"
in "the hearts" of the blessed ones, "Abba, Father,"[36] knowing
full well the groanings "in this tabernacle,"[37] that they are capable of weighing down those who have fallen or transgressed,
"maketh intercession" to God "with groanings which cannot be
uttered,"[38] and out of his great kindness and sympathy receives
our groanings. And when, in accordance with the wisdom that is
in him, he sees "our soul humbled to the dust"[39] and confined
in "the body of humiliation,"[40] "he maketh intercession" to God,
using no ordinary "groanings," but certain "which cannot be
uttered," which appertain to those "unspeakable words, which
it is not" possible "for a man to utter."[41] In very truth, this
Spirit, not content simply to intercede with God, intensifies the

31 Mark 11:25: see note.   32 I Cor. 11:4, 5.   33 Cf. Matt. 5:17.
34 Rom. 8:26.   35 Rom. 8:26, 27.   36 Gal. 4:6.
37 II Cor. 5:4.   38 Rom. 8:26.   39 Ps. 44:25.
40 Phil. 3:21.   41 II Cor. 12:4.

A.C.—16

intercession and "intercedes exceedingly."[42] I imagine that he does this for those who are conquering exceedingly, such as Paul was when he says, "Nay, in all these things we conquer exceedingly."[43] Probably, he merely "intercedes" for those who, on the one hand, are not so great as "to conquer exceedingly," and yet, on the other, are not such as to be conquered, but rather are conquering.

4. Related to the text "we know not what" we ought "to pray for as we ought; but the Spirit intercedes exceedingly" to God "with groanings which cannot be uttered,"[44] is the text: "I will pray with the spirit, and I will pray with the understanding also: I will sing with the spirit, and I will sing with the understanding also."[45] For neither can our understanding pray, unless previously the Spirit prays, hearkening[46] as it were to it, nor likewise can it sing and hymn the Father in Christ with rhythm, melody, measure and harmony, unless the Spirit, who "searcheth all things, yea, the deep things of God,"[47] first praise and hymn him, whose "deep things" he has "searched," and, so far as he is able,[48] apprehended.

"One of the disciples" of Jesus (being conscious in himself, as I suppose, of human weakness in its ignorance concerning how one ought to pray, and recognizing this especially when he heard the wise and great words uttered by the Saviour in prayer to his Father), "when" the Lord "ceased" praying, said: "Lord, teach us to pray, even as John also taught his disciples." The following is the full context of the saying: "And it came to pass, as he was praying in a certain place, that when he ceased, one of his disciples said unto him, Lord, teach us to pray, even as John also taught his disciples"[49] to pray.[50] . . . Is it then that a man, brought up in the instruction of the Law and in hearing the words of the Prophets, and a constant frequenter of the synagogues, did not know how to pray at all, until he saw the Lord praying "in a certain place"? It would be absurd to assert this. Undoubtedly he was accustomed to pray in the Jewish fashion; but he saw that he needed greater knowledge in the matter of prayer. Moreover, what did "John teach his disciples" concerning prayer, as they came "unto him" to be "baptized"

---

[42] Rom. 8:26: Origen here makes the point that Paul does not simply say ἐντυγχάνει (as in v. 27), but ὑπερεντυγχάνει. The English Bible versions do not attempt to reproduce this distinction.   [43] Rom. 8:37.
[44] Rom. 8:26.   [45] I Cor. 14:15.   [46] See note.
[47] I Cor. 2:10.   [48] See note.   [49] Luke 11:1.
[50] A lacuna of two and a half lines occurs here in the MS., probably containing a citation of Matt. 3:5, 6.

from "Jerusalem, and all Judaea, and the region round about,"[51] unless it was that, being "much more than a prophet,"[52] he saw certain things concerning prayer, which, I dare say, he delivered secretly, not to all those who were being baptized, but to those who were under instruction as disciples for baptism?

5. Such prayers, being truly spiritual (for the Spirit prays in the hearts of the saints), have been recorded, and they are filled with unutterable and marvellous teachings. An example, in the First Book of the Kingdoms, is the prayer of Hannah,[53] which is given in part (for the whole prayer, "when she continued praying before the Lord, speaking in her heart," has not been written down).[54] In the Psalms, the sixteenth Psalm is entitled, "A Prayer of David," and the eighty-ninth, "A Prayer of Moses, the man of God," and the one hundred and first, "A Prayer of the poor man, when he is uncared for, and pours forth his petition before the Lord."[55] Such prayers, since they were truly prayers which came into being and were spoken by the Spirit, are filled with the teachings of the wisdom of God; so that one may say of the things that they set forth: "Who is wise, and he shall understand these" prayers? "and prudent, and he shall know" them?[56]

6. Since, therefore, to treat of prayer is so weighty a task that it requires the illumination of the Father for this very thing, and the teaching of his first begotten Word, and the operation of the Spirit that we may understand and speak worthily of so weighty a matter, I pray as a man (for I do not hold that I am able of my own self to treat of prayer) before I begin to speak on the subject of prayer, that the Holy Spirit may be vouchsafed to me, so that a very full and spiritual word may be bestowed upon me, and the prayers recorded in the Gospels made plain. Let us now then begin the subject of prayer.

Discussion on Prayer in General

CHAPTERS III TO XVII

The words "Euche" and "Proseuche" (Chapters III and IV)

III, 1. The word "prayer" (*euche*) occurs for the first time, so far as my observation goes, when "Jacob," flying from the

---

[51] Matt. 3:5, 6.   [52] Matt. 11:9.   [53] I Sam. 1:11–13.
[54] So Koetschau emends the text of T.
[55] These Psalms are numbered in the English Bible 17, 90, and 102, respectively.   [56] Hos. 14:9.

wrath of his "brother Esau, departed into Mesopotamia" in accordance with the counsel of Isaac and Rebecca.[57] The passage runs as follows: "And Jacob prayed a prayer, saying, if God the Lord will be with me, and will keep me in this way that I go, and will give me bread to eat, and raiment to put on, and will bring me back again in safety to my father's house, then shall the Lord be unto me for God. And this stone, which I have set up for a pillar, shall be unto me God's house: and of all that thou shalt give me, I will surely give the tenth unto thee."[58] . . .[59]

2. Here we should note that the word "prayer" (*euche*), which often has a different meaning from *proseuche*, is used of a person who promises in prayer to do this or that, if so be that he obtains these things from God. But the term is also employed in its customary usage: as, for example, we find it so used after the plague of frogs, the second in order of the ten.[60] . . . "Pharaoh called for Moses and Aaron, and said, Pray the Lord for me, and let him take away the frogs from me and my people; and I will let the people go, that they may sacrifice to the Lord."[61] And if anyone finds it hard to believe, because the expression "pray" is Pharaoh's, that it has the usual sense, as derived from "prayer," in addition to the sense previously mentioned, he should note the passage which follows: "And Moses said unto Pharaoh, Appoint unto me when I shall pray for thee and for thy servants and for thy people, that the frogs be destroyed from thee and from thy people and out of thy houses, and remain in the river only."[62]

3. Observe that in the case of "the lice," the third plague, neither does Pharaoh request a prayer to be made, nor does Moses pray.[63] But in the case of "the swarm of flies,"[64] the fourth, he says, "Pray therefore for me to the Lord"; on which occasion "Moses said, I will go out from thee and I will pray unto God, and the swarm of flies will depart from Pharaoh and his servants and his people, tomorrow."[65] And a little further down,

---

57 Cf. Gen. 27:41–45.
58 Gen. 28:20–22.
59 A lacuna of two lines occurs here in T, which perhaps contained another example from the Scriptures of "prayer."
60 A lacuna of two lines occurs here in T, which Koetschau supplies after this manner: "when Pharaoh commanded Moses and Aaron to pray to the Lord for him, that he should take away from him and his people the frogs which covered everything. The passage is as follows:"
61 Ex. 8:8.   62 Ex. 8:9.   63 Ex. 8:16–19.
64 Ex. 8:20–32.   65 Ex. 8:25, 28 (LXX).

"And Moses went out from Pharaoh, and prayed unto God."[66] And again, while at the fifth and sixth plagues[67] neither did Pharaoh request a prayer to be made nor did Moses pray, at the seventh "Pharaoh sent, and called for Moses and Aaron, and said unto them, I have sinned this time: the Lord is righteous, and I and my people are wicked. Pray therefore unto the Lord, and let there be an end to voices of God and hail and fire."[68] And a little lower down, "Moses went out of the city from Pharaoh, and spread abroad his hands unto the Lord: and the voices ended."[69] Why it is not said, "And he prayed," as on the former occasions, but "he spread abroad his hands unto the Lord," must be considered more suitably at another time. Also, at the eighth plague Pharaoh says, "And pray unto the Lord your God, and let him take away from me this death. And Moses went out from Pharaoh and prayed unto God."[70]

4. We have said that the word *euche* is often used not in the accustomed manner, as for example with reference to Jacob.[71] Also, in Leviticus, "The Lord spake unto Moses, saying, Speak to the children of Israel, and thou shalt say unto them, Whosoever shall vow a vow, as being an estimation of his soul to the Lord, the estimation of the male, from twenty years old to sixty years old, even his estimation shall be fifty shekels of silver by holy weight."[72] And in Numbers, "And the Lord spake unto Moses, saying, Speak to the children of Israel, and thou shalt say unto them, When either man or woman shall vow solemnly[73] a vow to make a separation for himself to the Lord, he shall be separated from wine and strong drink,"[74] and so forth, with reference to him who is called a Nazirite. Then, a little lower down, "And he shall sanctify his head on that day in which he was sanctified to the Lord for the days of his vow."[75] And again, a little lower down, "This is the law of him who hath vowed, in whatsoever day he shall fulfil the days of his vow."[76] And again, a little lower down, "And after that he who hath vowed shall drink wine. This is the law of him who hath vowed, whosoever shall vow to the Lord his gift as concerning his vow, apart from whatsoever his hand shall find

[66] Ex. 8:30.   [67] Ex. 9:1-12.   [68] Ex. 9:27, 28.
[69] Ex. 9:33.   [70] Ex. 10:17, 18.
[71] See III, 2, above: in this section *euche* and the corresponding verb are translated "vow."   [72] Lev. 27:1-3.
[73] Lit. "greatly."   [74] Num. 6:1-3.   [75] Num. 6:11, 12 (LXX).
[76] Num. 6:13.

according to the power of his vow, which he shall vow according to the law of separation."[77] And at the end of Numbers, "And Moses spake unto the heads of the tribes of Israel, saying, This is the thing which the Lord hath commanded. When a man voweth a vow unto the Lord, or sweareth an oath by a bond, or shall make a bond concerning his soul, he shall not cause his word to become void; he shall do according to all that proceedeth out of his mouth. And if a woman voweth a vow unto the Lord, or bindeth herself by a bond, being in her father's house, in her youth; and if her father heareth her vows, and her bonds wherewith she hath bound her soul, and if her father holdeth his peace, all her vows shall stand, and every bond wherewith she hath bound her soul shall remain with her."[78] And subsequently he lays down certain laws concerning such a woman. The same meaning is to be found in Proverbs: . . . ["It is a snare] to a man rashly to sanctify anything of his own; for after he hath vowed cometh repentance"[79]; and in Ecclesiastes: "Better is it that thou shouldest not vow, than that thou shouldest vow and not pay"[80]; and in the Acts of the Apostles: "There are with us four men which are under a vow of their own act."[81]

IV, 1. It has seemed to me not unreasonable to distinguish first between the two meanings of the word *euche* in the Scriptures, and likewise also of the word *proseuche*. For indeed this word, in addition to its common and customary, frequently found, usage, also occurs in the unusual sense to us of *euche*,[82] in what is said concerning Hannah in the First Book of the Kingdoms: "And Eli the priest sat upon a seat by the door posts of the temple of the Lord. And she was in bitterness of soul, and prayed [*proseuxato*] unto the Lord, and wept sore. And she vowed a vow [*euche*], and said, O Lord of hosts, if thou wilt indeed look on the affliction of thine handmaid, and remember me, and not forget thine handmaid, and wilt give unto thine handmaid the seed of a man, then I will give him

---

[77] Num. 6:20, 21.   [78] Num. 30:1–4.
[79] Prov. 20:25. Before this quotation there is a lacuna of one and three-fifths lines in T, which Koetschau conjecturally fills with two other quotations from Proverbs, as follows: "A sacrifice of a peace offering is with me; this day do I pay my vows" (7:14); and "A foolish son is the shame of his father; unholy are the vows of a hired mistress" (19:13 (LXX)); and "It is a snare," etc.
[80] Eccl. 5:5.
[81] Acts 21:23: see note for text.
[82] The text of Koetschau is followed here.

unto the Lord as a gift all the days of his life, and there shall no razor come upon his head."[83]

2. Here it would not be unconvincing to note the phrases "prayed unto the Lord" and "vowed a vow" and say that, if she did the two things, that is to say, "prayed unto the Lord, and vowed a vow," perhaps the word "prayed," on the one hand, occurs in the sense we usually give to the noun *euche* while, on the other hand, "she vowed a vow" has the meaning of the word as it occurs in Leviticus and Numbers.[84] For "I will give him unto the Lord as a gift all the days of his life, and there shall no razor come upon his head" is not a *proseuche* in the proper sense of the term, but rather that "vow" (*euche*) such as Jephtha vowed in these words: "And Jephtha vowed a vow unto the Lord, and said, If thou wilt indeed deliver the children of Ammon into mine hand, then it shall be that whosoever cometh forth of the doors of my house to meet me, when I return in peace from the children of Ammon, even he shall be the Lord's, and I will offer him up for a burnt offering."[85]

Objections to Prayer (Chapter V)

V, 1. If it is necessary, then after this, to set forth, as you have bidden us, the plausible arguments first of those who think that nothing is effected by prayers, and therefore affirm that it is superfluous to pray, we shall not refuse to do this also according to our ability, employing the term "prayer" now in its simpler and more ordinary sense.[86] . . . This opinion is so disreputable and lacking in distinguished supporters, that practically no one can be found among those who admit Providence and place God over the universe who rejects prayer. It is the tenet either of those who are downright atheists and deny the existence of God, or else of those who go as far as to accept the name of God but do away with his Providence. I would go further and say that the power that works in opposition,[87] desiring to attach the most iniquitous opinions to the name of Christ and to the teaching of the Son of God, has even been

---

83 I Sam. 1:9–11.
84 Cf. Lev. 27:2; Num. 6:2, 4, 6, 7, 9, 12, 13, 18, 19, 21 (LXX); 30:3–15.
85 Judg. 11:31.
86 A lacuna of two lines in T follows, which Koetschau fills up conjecturally thus: "For there are some who do not even accept prayer in this sense, but rather make mock of those who pray, and desire to do away completely with any kind of prayer whatsoever."
87 Cf. II Thess. 2:4, 9.

able to persuade some that they ought not to pray. The champions of this opinion are those who completely reject objects of sense, and use neither Baptism nor Eucharist, and slanderously affirm that when the Scriptures speak of "praying" they do not mean this, but teach something with quite a different meaning.

2. The following are the arguments, conceivably, of those who set at naught prayers (that is to say, of those who place God over the universe and say that there is a Providence; for there is no question now of examining the statements of those who reject God or Providence altogether): "God" knows "all things before they be,"[88] and nothing which happens is known to him for the first time when it happens, as if it were not known before this. What need is there, then, to offer up a prayer to him who before it was prayed knows what we lack? "For the heavenly Father knoweth what things" we "have need of before" we "ask him."[89] It is reasonable that he who is the Father and Creator of the universe, who "loveth all things that are, and abhorreth none of the things which" he "hath made,"[90] should dispense what is for the well-being of each one without being prayed to; just as a father does, who protects his little ones and does not wait upon their requests, either because they are unable to ask at all, or because through ignorance they often wish to receive things that are clean contrary to their profit and advantage. And we human beings are much further off from God than mere children are from the mind of their parents.

3. Now it is probable that the future is not only known beforehand to God but also predetermined, and that nothing comes to pass which has not been predetermined by him. For example, if one were to pray that the sun should rise, he would be regarded as a foolish fellow, for requesting that something should happen through his prayer which would happen in any case without his prayer. So also a man would be senseless to imagine that his prayer caused things to happen which would without doubt have taken place had he never prayed. To give another example, it would be unsurpassable folly for a man who was troubled by the scorching sun at the summer solstice to imagine that by his prayer the sun could be shifted back among the vernal constellations, so that he might enjoy a temperate atmosphere. In like manner, for a man to suppose that by prayer he will escape from necessary happenings incidental to the human race, would be to surpass every form of melancholy madness.

[88] Susanna 42.   [89] Matt. 6:8.   [90] Wisdom of Solomon 11:24.

4. Moreover, if "the wicked are estranged from the womb,"[91] and the righteous man is "separated from" his "mother's womb,"[92] and if, "the children being not yet" even "born, neither having done anything good or bad, that the purpose of God according to election might stand, not of works, but of him that calleth,"[93] it is said, "The elder shall serve the younger,"[94] in vain do we pray concerning remission of sins or the reception of "the Spirit of might,"[95] in order that we may "have might for all things, Christ strengthening us."[96] For if we are "sinners," we "are estranged from the womb"[97]; but if we were "separated from" our "mother's womb,"[92] the best things will fall to our lot, even though we should not pray. What prayer did Jacob offer before he was born, that it should be prophesied of him that "he shall prevail" over Esau, and that his brother "shall serve"[98] him? What sin did Esau commit, that he should be "hated"[99] before he was born? Or why does Moses pray, as we find in the eighty-ninth Psalm, if God is his "refuge before the mountains" were established "and the earth and the world formed"[1] . . .[2]

5. Moreover, concerning all those that shall be saved it is recorded in the [Epistle] to the Ephesians that "the Father chose" them "in him, in Christ, before foundation of the world," that they "should be holy and without blemish before him, having foreordained" them "in love unto adoption as sons through Christ unto himself."[3] Either then a man is one of those "chosen before the foundation of the world," and it is impossible for him to fall from this "election,"[4] and therefore there is no need for him to pray; or else he has not been "chosen" neither "foreordained," and it is in vain for him to pray: even were he to pray ten thousand times, he would not be heard. For "whom" God "foreknew," them "he also foreordained to be conformed to the image" of the glory "of his Son. And whom he foreordained, them he also called; and whom he called, them he also justified: and whom he justified, them he also glorified."[5] Why does Josiah weary himself, or wherefore when he prays does he take thought whether or no he shall be heard,[6] when many generations previously it was prophesied of him by name, and it was not

[91] Ps. 58:3. [92] Cf. Gal. 1:15. [93] Rom. 9:11.
[94] Gen. 25:23 (Rom. 9:12). [95] Isa. 11:2.
[96] Cf. Phil. 4:13. [97] Cf. Ps. 58:3.
[98] Gen. 25:23. [99] Mal. 1:3 (Rom. 9:13). [1] Ps. 90:1.
[2] A lacuna of one and three-sevenths lines occurs here in T, in all likelihood containing another of these rhetorical questions.
[3] Eph. 1:3–5. [4] Rom. 9:11. [5] Rom. 8:29, 30.
[6] Cf. II Kings 22:11–13, 18, 19; 23:3 ff.

only foreknown but also foretold in the hearing of many what
he would then do?[7] Why, too, should Judas pray, so that "his
prayer be turned into sin," it having been previously an-
nounced, from the times of "David," that he would lose "his
office," and that "another" would "take" it in his stead?[8] And
since God is unchangeable and has predetermined everything
that is, and abides in what he has pre-arranged, it is obviously
inconsistent to pray with the idea of altering his plan by prayer,
or of intreating him as one who has not pre-arranged it but
awaits each one's prayer. This would be to make prayer the
reason why God arranges what is fitting for him who prays, and
settles then what is deemed proper, as if it had not already been
foreseen by him.

6. Let the position be stated now in the very words of the
letter you addressed to me. They are as follows: "First: if God
knows the future beforehand, and it must come to pass, prayer
is vain. Secondly: if all things happen according to the will of
God, and if what is willed by him is fixed, and nothing of what
he wills can be changed, prayer is vain." It is useful, I think, to
decide these points as a preliminary to solving the difficulties
which cause insensibility in regard to prayer.

Answer to these objections (Chapters VI to VIII, 1)

VI, 1. Of things that are moved,[9] some derive from without
that which moves them, as for example things that are without
life, held together merely by their form, and things that are
moved by nature and soul, which are moved now and then not
as such, but in a manner similar to things that are held together
merely by their form. For stones and pieces of wood, which are
cut out of the quarry or have lost the power of growing, being
held together merely by their form, derive from without that
which moves them; moreover the bodies of living creatures and
the produce of what has been planted, when they are changed
in position by something, are not so changed *qua* living creatures
or plants, but similarly to stones and to pieces of wood which
have lost the power of growth; and even if they are moved in
virtue of the fact that all bodies as they decay are in a state of
flux, this motion which they have is inseparably connected with
their state of decay.

In the second place, and distinct from the foregoing, are
things that are moved by their own inherent nature or soul,

---

[7] Cf. I Kings 13:1–3.   [8] Ps. 109: 7, 8; Acts 1:16, 20.   [9] See note.

which are said to be moved "out of themselves" by those who use the words in their proper sense. A third kind of movement is that which takes place in living creatures, which is called movement "from within themselves"; but I think that the movement of rational beings is movement "through themselves." But if we take away from the living creature this movement "from within itself," it can no longer be conceived of as a living creature, but it will be like either a plant, which is moved merely by nature, or a stone, which is propelled by an external force. But if a thing is inseparably connected with its own movement, since we have called this movement "through itself," of necessity it must be rational.

2. Therefore, they who hold that we have no free will,[10] necessarily take up an extremely foolish position: in the first place, that we are not living creatures; and in the second, that neither are we possessed of reason, but moved, as it were, by some external moving force, and therefore it can in no wise be said of us that we do what we are reckoned to do. Let a man pay particular attention to his own experience and see if it is not impudent for him to affirm that he does not of himself will, or of himself eat, or of himself walk, or of himself assent to or accept any opinions of any sort, or of himself dissent from others as false. On the assumption that free will is not preserved, a man cannot possibly adopt an attitude towards certain opinions, supported though they may be ten thousand times by skilful and plausible arguments, nor, similarly, can one adopt an attitude in regard to human affairs. Who takes up the position that nothing may be apprehended? Or who lives in suspense of judgment about everything whatsoever? Who does not rebuke his servant, when he imagines negligence on the part of a slave? And who is there, who does not accuse a son for failing to render what is due to parents, or does not blame and censure as guilty of a disgraceful act the adulterous wife? For the truth forces and compels us, in spite of thousands of plausible arguments, to take action and to praise and to censure on the assumption that free will is safeguarded, and deserves our praise or blame.

3. If then free will is preserved, with its countless tendencies towards virtue or vice, and, again, towards what is fitting or what is not fitting, it must needs be that this, with all else, has been known to God, before it come to pass, "from the creation"[11] and "the foundation of the world,"[12] of what sort it shall be;

---

[10] See note.   [11] Cf. Rom. 1:20.
[12] Cf. Matt. 25:34; Luke 11:50; Heb. 4:3; 9:26; Rev. 13:8; 17:8.

and in everything which God arranges beforehand in accordance with what he has seen concerning each act of free will, he has so arranged it that that which is to happen in virtue of his providence, and also that which is to come to pass in the train of future events, will be the due result of each movement of the free will. But the foreknowledge of God is not the cause of all future events or of future actions performed by us of our free will and mere motion. Even if, for the sake of argument, God were not to know the future, we should not for that reason lose the power of accomplishing or willing this or that. From foreknowledge, however,[13] it follows that each act of free will is adapted to such an arrangement of the whole as the settled order of the universe demands.

4. If then each act of free will has been known to him, it is a reasonable consequence that what has been foreseen by him is arranged by Providence suitably for every single person, and that it is understood beforehand[14] what so-and-so will pray for, his kind of disposition, the nature of his faith, and what he desires to happen to him; and, this being understood beforehand, some sort of arrangement as this will accordingly have been made in the disposing of things: "I will hear this man who will pray intelligently, for the very prayer's sake which he will pray; but this man I will not hear, either because he will be unworthy to be heard, or because he will pray[14] for things which are neither profitable for him who prays, nor proper for me to grant; and for this prayer (let us say) of so-and-so I will not hear him; but for that, I will hear him." (If anyone is disturbed by the thought that things have been determined by necessity because God, who knows the future beforehand, cannot lie, it should be said to such a one that this very thing is assuredly known to God, that such and such a man does not assuredly and firmly desire what is better, or that he will so will what is worse that he will be incapable of changing towards what is preferable.) And again, "I will grant this or that to this man who will pray, because it is meet for me to do this for a man who will pray blamelessly and will not prove careless in the matter of prayer; and when he shall pray for a certain time, I will bestow this or that upon him 'exceeding abundantly above' what he 'asks or thinks,'[15] for it is meet for me to overpass him in good deeds and to supply him with more than he has been able to ask for. Moreover, to such a one, destined to become such as this, I will send this ministering angel, to be his fellow-

[13] Reading πλήν.   [14] Adopting the reading of Bentley.   [15] Eph. 3:20.

worker unto salvation from such a time onward, and to continue with him until such a time. To another, destined to become greater than the first, I will send this angel (let us say), who is more honourable than the other. And as for this third, who after embracing higher teaching is about to grow somewhat weaker and turn backwards to worldly things, from him I will remove this mightier fellow-worker: and when he has departed, some inferior power, seizing the occasion to assault him in his slackness, will now deservedly come upon him, and finding him given over and ready to sin, will incite him to such and such sins."

5. It is in some such way as this that he who orders beforehand the universe will say: "Amon will beget Josiah, who will not emulate the evil deeds of his father, but will find the path that leads on to virtue, and with the help of those that shall be his fellows will prove to be a good and worthy man, and will 'break down the altar' of 'Jeroboam' that was iniquitously built.[16] And I know also that Judas, when my Son has come to sojourn among mankind, at the beginning will be a good and worthy man, but afterwards will turn aside and fall into the sins that are common to man, on account of which he will rightly suffer such and such things." (And this foreknowledge, perhaps in respect of all things but certainly in respect of Judas and other mysteries, appertains also to the Son of God, who saw in his understanding of the future circle of events Judas and the sins that would be committed by him: so that with direct apprehension, and before Judas was born, he said by the mouth of David, "O God, pass not over in silence my praise,"[17] and so forth.) And knowing the future, and what power[18] for godliness Paul will have, "by myself," he says,[19] "or ever I create the world or set my hand to begin to make it, I will choose out him, and as soon as he is begotten I will provide him with those powers that work together for the salvation of men, 'separating' him 'from' his 'mother's womb,'[20] and permitting him at first in his youthful and ignorant zeal under the cloak of godliness to 'persecute'[21] them that have believed on my Christ, and to keep 'the garments' of them that 'were stoning' my servant and 'martyr Stephen,'[22] so that, when this wanton outburst of youth is over, starting again and changing for the better he should 'not glory before'[23] me, but rather say, 'I am not meet to be

---

16 II Kings 23:15; cf. II Kings 21:24; 22:2.   17 Ps. 109:1.
18 Lit. "tension."   19 The words "he says" are inserted by Koetschau.
20 Gal. 1:15.   21 Acts 9:5.   22 Acts 7:59; 22:20.
23 I Cor. 1:29.

called an apostle, because I persecuted the church of God,'[24] and, perceiving the bounty that should come to him after the errors committed in youth under the cloak of godliness should say, 'by the grace of God I am what I am,'[25] and being prevented by the conscience still with him of what he had done in the impulse of youth, he will not be 'exalted overmuch by reason of the exceeding greatness of the revelations'[26] that will be manifested to him by an act of bounty."

VII. And with regard to prayer concerning the rising of the sun,[27] the following may be said. Even the sun has a certain free will, inasmuch as it, along with the moon, praises God. For he says, "Praise ye him, sun and moon."[28] And it is clear that this also applies to the moon and consequently all the stars: for he says, "Praise him all ye stars and light."[28] As therefore we have said[29] that God uses to the full the free will of each thing upon earth, and has fittingly disposed them to meet a certain need of the things upon earth, so it must be supposed with regard to the free will of the sun and moon and stars, firmly fixed and wisely established, that he has disposed "all the host of heaven"[30] and the course and movement of the stars harmoniously with the whole universe. And if I do not pray in vain concerning some other thing that has free will, much more is this true concerning the free will of the stars that circle in the heaven conformably to the safety of the whole universe. And yet it must be said concerning those on earth, that certain impressions arising from attendant circumstances induce our instability or inclination to the worse[31] course, so as to do or say such and such things. But in regard to those in the heaven, what impression can arise to divert or remove from that course which is beneficial to the universe any of those beings who possess a soul that is perfected by reason and alien to the influence of these impressions, and make use of a body whose quality is etherial and absolutely pure?

VIII, 1. Moreover, it is not unreasonable to use some such illustration as this to encourage the practice of prayer and discourage the neglect of prayer. As it is not possible to beget a child without a woman and the possession of the necessary powers of begetting, so a man may not obtain this or that, unless he has prayed in such a way, with such a disposition, with

[24] I Cor. 15:9.   [25] I Cor. 15:10.   [26] II Cor. 12:7.
[27] See V, 3.   [28] Ps. 148:3.   [29] See VI, 3.
[30] Deut. 4:19.
[31] Reading χεῖρον, with Bentley: the MSS. have "better course."

such a belief; and if before the prayer he has not lived in such a manner. Therefore, "vain repetitions" ought not to be "used,"[32] nor ought we to ask for little things,[33] nor ought we to pray concerning earthly things, nor ought we to come to prayer in "wrath"[34] and with agitated thoughts; indeed, without purity a man cannot secure the giving of himself to prayer,[35] nor can he who prays obtain forgiveness of sins, unless "from" his "heart" he "forgives his brother"[36] who has committed a fault and asks to receive pardon.

Advantages of Prayer (Chapters VIII, 2, to X, 2)

In my opinion benefit often accrues to him who prays as he ought or endeavours as far as in him lies to do so. In the first place, without doubt he whose mind is set on prayer is in some sense profited merely by the settled condition involved in praying, when he has disposed himself to approach God and speak in his presence as to one who watches over him and is present. For just as certain impressions and recollections of this or that sully the thoughts that have been involved in these impressions, in connection with the subjects of these recollections; in the same way we must believe that it is profitable to recollect God in whom we have put our trust, who perceives the secret movements of the soul, when it composes itself to please him who "trieth the hearts and searcheth out the reins"[37] as one who is present and spies out and anticipates every purpose. For if, for the sake of argument, he who sets his mind to prayer obtains no benefit beyond this, it is to be observed that he who thus devoutly disposes himself at the time of prayer profits in no ordinary way. And if this happens often, how many sins it prevents and how many good deeds it promotes, is known by experience to those who have given themselves continually to prayer. For if the calling to mind and reminiscence of an illustrious man who has profited by wisdom stirs us up to emulate him and often checks evil impulses, how much more does the calling to mind of God, the Father of the universe, together with prayer to him, benefit those who are confident in themselves that they stand before and speak to God as one who is present and hears?

IX, 1. What we have said must be proved from the divine Scriptures on this manner. He who prays ought to "lift up holy

[32] Matt. 6:7.   [33] See II, 2.   [34] I Tim. 2:8.
[35] Cf. I Cor. 7:5.   [36] Matt. 18:35.
[37] Cf. Ps. 7:9; Jer. 11:20; 17:10; Rom. 8:27; Rev. 2:23.

hands"[38] by forgiving everyone who has sinned against him,[39] having removed from his soul the feeling of "wrath,"[38] and being angry with no one. Again, in order that his mind may not be distracted by other thoughts, he ought to forget, during the time when he prays, all things outside his prayer (how could such a one be other than most blessed?), as Paul teaches in his first [epistle] to Timothy, saying, "I desire therefore that the men pray in every place, lifting up holy hands without wrath or disputings."[40] Moreover, a woman, especially when praying, ought to be sedate and modest in soul and body, reverencing God above all things when she prays, having banished from the ruling reason every licentious and womanish recollection, adorned not "with braided hair and gold or pearls or costly raiment, but" with the things which it "becomes a woman professing godliness" to be "adorned" (could anyone doubt, I wonder, that such a woman who has thus given herself to prayer would be manifestly blessed merely as a result of such an attitude?), as Paul taught in the same epistle, saying, that "women in like manner adorn themselves in modest apparel, with shamefastness and sobriety; not with braided hair, and gold or pearls or costly raiment, but (which becometh women professing godliness) through good works."[41]

2. The prophet[42] David also has much to say concerning the blessings that the saint has in prayer. And it is not irrelevant to quote the following, so that we may clearly see that the greatest benefits result from the attitude of, and preparation for, prayer, considered simply by themselves, of the man who has dedicated himself to God. He says, then: "Unto thee have I lifted up mine eyes, O thou that dwellest in the heaven"[43]; and, "Unto thee have I lifted up my soul, O God."[44] When the eyes of the understanding are lifted up, away from converse with earthly things and occupation with material impressions, and when they are elevated so high that they can transcend created things and fix themselves solely upon the contemplation of God and of reverent and seemly intercourse with him who hears, it must needs be that the eyes themselves derive the greatest benefit, when "with unveiled face they reflect as a mirror the glory of the Lord, and are transformed into the same image from glory to glory."[45] For they then partake of a kind of divine spiritual effluence, as is indicated in the words: "the light of thy

---

[38] I Tim. 2:8.
[39] Cf. Matt. 6:12, 14; Luke 11:4.
[40] I Tim. 2:8.
[41] I Tim. 2:9, 10.
[42] Cf. Acts 2:30.
[43] Ps. 123:1.
[44] Ps. 25:1, 2.
[45] II Cor. 3:18.

countenance, O Lord, was signed upon us."[46] Moreover, when
the soul is lifted up and follows the spirit and severs itself from
the body—and not only follows the spirit but also dwells in it,
as is indicated in the words: "Unto thee have I lifted up my
soul"[47]—it must needs be that laying aside the nature of a soul
it becomes spiritual.

3. And if to bear no malice is the greatest exçellence, as
would appear from the prophet Jeremiah, when he says that
the whole law is summed up in it: "I commanded not" these
things "to your fathers" when they were coming forth "out of
Egypt," but "I commanded this,"[48] "Let no one bear malice
against his" neighbour "in" his "heart"[49]; and if putting aside
such malice in coming to prayer we observe the commandment
of the Saviour, when he says, "If ye stand praying, forgive, if ye
have aught against anyone,"[50] it is clear that in so doing, as we
stand to pray, we have already obtained the greatest blessings.

X, 1. The foregoing has been said on the supposition that
even if no other result followed our prayers, we gain the greatest
blessings when we understand how to pray as we ought and when
we carry this out. And it is clear that he who thus prays will
hear "while" he "is yet speaking," perceiving, by the power of
him who "hears in heaven,"[51] the "Here I am," having cast
aside, before he prayed, all dissatisfaction concerning Providence. This is indicated in the words: "If thou take away from
thee the yoke, the putting forth of the hand and the word of
murmuring."[52] He who is well pleased with what happens has
been set free from every kind of "yoke," nor does he "put forth
the hand" against God, when he orders what he wills for our
training; nor yet again does he "murmur" in his secret thoughts
apart from an utterance that men can hear. This murmuring is
like that of wicked servants who do not openly cavil at their
masters' orders. Thus do they murmur who do not dare audibly
or whole-heartedly to speak evil of Providence for what has
happened; they wish as it were to escape the notice even of the
Lord of the universe as concerning those things at which they
are displeased. I think that this is the point of the words in the
Book of Job: "In all these happenings did not Job sin with his
lips before God"[53]; it having been written of the previous trial,[54]
"In all these happenings did not Job sin before God."[55] That

46 Ps. 4:6.   47 Ps. 25:1.   48 Cf. Jer. 7:22, 23.
49 Zech. 7:10.   50 Mark 11:25.   51 I Kings 8:30.
52 Isa. 58:9.   53 Job 2:10.
54 Adopting, with Koetschau, a slight change of text.   55 Job 1:22.

this ought not to occur the saying in Deuteronomy ordains:
"Beware that there be not a hidden word in thine heart, a lawless thing, saying, The seventh year is at hand,"[56] and so forth.

2. He then that so prays receives such benefit that he is made
more capable of union with him who "has filled the world,"
even "the Spirit"[57] of the Lord, and with him who has "filled"
all "the earth" and "the heaven," who speaks thus through the
prophet: "Do not I fill heaven and earth, saith the Lord?"[58]
And further, by means of the purification mentioned above,[59]
he will participate in the prayer of the Word of God, who stands
in the midst even of those who know him not, and never fails
the prayer of anyone, but prays to the Father along with him
whose mediator he is. For the Son of God is the "high priest"[60]
of our offerings and "an Advocate with the Father,"[61] praying
on behalf of those who pray, pleading along with those who
plead: nevertheless, he will not pray as on behalf of his own for
those who do not pray continually through him, nor will he be
"an Advocate with" God as on behalf of his very own for those
who do not obey his teachings that one "ought always to pray,
and not to faint."[62] For, it is said, "he spake a parable" that one
"ought always to pray, and not to faint. There was in a city a
judge,"[63] and so forth. And in a previous passage, "And he said
unto them, Which of you shall have a friend, and shall go unto
him at midnight, and say unto him, Friend, lend me three
loaves; for a friend of mine is come to me from a journey, and I
have nothing to set before him."[64] And, a little further on, "I say
unto you, though he will not rise and give him, because he is
his friend, yet because of his importunity he will rise and give
him as many as he needeth."[65] Who is there who believes in the
unerring utterance of Jesus, who would not be stirred up to
instant prayer by his saying, "Ask and it shall be given you, for
everyone that asketh receiveth"[66]? since the "kind Father,"[67]
when we ask him for "the living bread"[68] (not "the stone"[69]
which the adversary[70] desires for the food of Jesus and his disciples) gives to them who have "received the spirit of adoption"
from "the Father"[71]; and "the Father gives the good gift,"[72]
"raining it from heaven,"[73] to them that ask him.

[56] Deut. 15:9.   [57] Wisdom of Solomon 1:7.   [58] Jer. 23:24.
[59] See VIII, 1.   [60] Heb. 2:17, etc.   [61] I John 2:1.
[62] Luke 18:1.   [63] Luke 18:1, 2.   [64] Luke 11:5, 6.
[65] Luke 11:8.   [66] Matt. 7:7, 8; Luke 11:9, 10.   [67] Luke 6:35.
[68] John 6:51.   [69] Cf. Matt. 4:3; Luke 4:3; Matt. 7:9; Luke 11:11.
[70] Cf. Zech. 3:1.   [71] Rom. 8:15.
[72] Cf. Matt. 7:11; Luke 11:13.   [73] Ex. 16:4.

The angels, as well as Christ, pray with us (Chapter XI)

XI, 1. Not only does the high priest pray along with those that genuinely pray, but also the angels "in heaven," who rejoice "over one sinner that repenteth more than over ninety and nine righteous persons, which need no repentance,"[74] and so do also the souls of the saints who have fallen asleep before us. This is indicated in the following references. On the one hand, Raphael offered for Tobit and Sarah a reasonable sacrifice[75] to God.[76] For after the prayer of both, "the prayer of both," the Scripture says, "was heard before the glory of the great Raphael, and he was sent to heal them both."[77] And Raphael himself, when disclosing the mission that he had as an angel to them both by God's command, says, "And now, when thou didst pray, and Sarah thy daughter in law, I did bring the memorial of your prayer before the Holy One."[78] And a little lower down: "I am Raphael, one of the seven angels, which present [the prayers of the saints],[79] and go in before the glory of the Holy One."[80] Certainly, according to the word of Raphael, "good is prayer with fasting and alms and righteousness."[81] On the other hand, "Jeremiah" is represented in the Books of the Maccabees as "of venerable age and exceeding glory," so that "wonderful and most majestic was the dignity around him,"[82] and "stretching forth his right hand, he delivered to Judas a sword of gold."[83] To whom bore witness another of the saints who have fallen asleep before us, saying, "This is he who prayeth much for the people and the holy city, Jeremiah the prophet of God."[84]

2. Since knowledge is disclosed to them that are worthy in this present life "through a mirror" and "in a riddle," but is revealed hereafter "face to face,"[85] it is indeed absurd not to employ this analogy in thinking also of the other virtues; for what has been prepared for in this life is properly perfected hereafter. Now according to the divine word one of the chiefest virtues is love to one's neighbour.[85a] And we must hold that the saints who have fallen asleep before us exercise towards those who are struggling in this life much more than do they who are compassed about with human weakness and are struggling in

74 Luke 15:7.   75 ἱερουργίαν.   76 Cf. Tobit 12:12.
77 Tobit 3:16, 17.   78 Tobit 12:12.
79 The words in brackets are absent from the MS. T, but are found in the
   LXX.   80 Tobit 12:15.   81 Tobit 12:8.
82 II Maccabees 15:13, 14.   83 II Maccabees 15:15.
84 II Maccabees 15:14.   85 I Cor. 13:12.
85 Cf. Matt. 5:43, 44; Luke 6:35; 10:27 etc.

company with feebler folk. It is not only in this life that the words: "If one member suffereth, all the members suffer with it"; and "if one member is honoured, all the members rejoice with it"[86] may be applied to those who love the brethren; for it can be fittingly said also of the love that animates those outside this present life, "anxiety for all the churches. Who is weak, and I am not weak? who is made to stumble, and I burn not?"[87] Christ also acknowledges as concerning each of the saints that are "sick" that he is "sick" likewise, and that he is "in prison," and that he is "naked, a stranger," and "an hungred" and "thirsty."[88] What reader of the Gospel does not know that Christ refers to himself the happenings of the faithful and reckons their sufferings as his own?

3. If "angels" of God "coming to" Jesus "ministered unto him,"[89] we must not suppose that this ministry of angels to Jesus was only for the short period of his bodily sojourn among men, since he is still "in the midst of" believers, not as "sitting at meat," but "as serving."[90] How many angels therefore may there be ministering to Jesus as he seeks to "gather together the children of Israel one by one"[91] and muster them of "the Dispersion,"[92] and as he saves them that fear and call upon him?[93] Do not they, even more than the apostles, work together for the increase and multiplying of the Church (for certain rulers of the churches are called "angels"[94] by John in the Apocalypse)? It is not in vain that "the angels of God ascend and descend upon the Son of man,"[95] being seen by those whose eyes have been "enlightened" with "the light of knowledge."[96]

4. At the actual time of prayer, being reminded by him who prays of what he needs, the angels do all in their power to bring it to good effect in virtue of the general command which they have received. Let me use the following illustration to commend my thought on this matter. Suppose that a physician with a regard for righteousness was present when a sick man was praying concerning his health; and that he knew how to heal the disease concerning which this man was offering up his prayer. It is clear that the physician will be moved to heal the man who prayed, perhaps not unreasonably supposing that this very thing was in the mind of God when he gave ear to the prayer of him who prayed to him for the removal of the disease. Or sup-

---

86 I Cor. 12:26.   87 II Cor. 11:28, 29.   88 Cf. Matt. 25:35–40.
89 Matt. 4:11.   90 Luke 22:27.   91 Isa. 27:12.
92 Cf. John 7:35; 10:16; 11:52.   93 Cf. Acts 2:21; Rom. 10:12, 13.
94 Rev. 1:20, etc.   95 John 1:51.   96 Hos. 10:12 (LXX).

pose that a man abundantly possessed of the means of livelihood and liberally disposed should hear the prayer of a poor man as he offers his petition to God for his needs: it is plain that he too will fulfil for the poor man the substance of his prayer, thus becoming a minister of the Father's will, who brings together to the same place at the time of the prayer both him who is about to pray and also him who is able to supply the request and unable because of his kindly disposition to disregard him who stands in need of such and such things.

5. We need not suppose that these happenings, when they occur, come by chance, since he who "has numbered the hairs of the head"[97] of the saints fittingly brings together at the time of the prayer to hear it him who is to act as the minister of the man who seeks the benefit from God and the man who truly stands in need. In the same way we are to assume that the angels, who watch over things and minister to God, are at times brought into the presence of this or that man who is praying, in order that they may join in the requests that he is making in his prayer. And indeed "the angel" of each one and of the "little ones" in the Church, "always beholding the face of the Father which is in heaven,"[98] and gazing upon the divinity of him who created us, joins in our prayers and co-operates as far as possible in the objects for which we pray.

Our whole life ought to be a prayer (Chapters XII to XIII, 1)

XII, 1. Moreover, I hold that the words of the prayer of the saints are filled with power, especially when "praying with the spirit" they "pray with the understanding also."[99] This last is like a light shining from the mind of him who is praying, and going forth from his mouth, to weaken by the power of God the spiritual poison injected by hostile powers into the reason of those who neglect prayer, and do not observe the saying "pray without ceasing"[1] spoken by Paul in conformity with the exhortations of Jesus. It goes forth like a dart from the soul of the saint who prays, sent on its way by knowledge and reason or by faith,[1a] and inflicts a wound for the destruction and overthrow of the spirits that are at enmity with God, and desire to cast around us the bonds of sin.

2. That man "prays without ceasing"[1] (virtuous deeds or commandments fulfilled being included as part of prayer) who

---

[97] Matt. 10:30; Luke 12:7.   [98] Matt. 18:10.   [99] I Cor. 14:15.
[1] I Thess. 5:17.   [1a] Following an emendation of the text.

combines with the prayer the needful deeds and the prayer with the fitting actions. For thus alone can we accept "pray without ceasing"[2] as a practicable saying, if we speak of the whole life of the saint as one great unbroken prayer: of which prayer that which is commonly called prayer is a part. This ought to be engaged in not less than three times every day, as is clear from the case of Daniel, who when great danger hung over him "prayed three times a day."[3] "Peter" also, "going up to the housetop about the sixth hour to pray," when also he saw the "vessel let down"[4] from heaven, "let down by four corners,"[5] is evidence for the middle one of the three prayers, while the one before it is spoken of by David, "In the morning shalt thou hear my" prayer,[6] "in the morning will I order [my prayer] unto thee and will look up"[7]; and the final one is indicated in the words "the lifting up of my hands as the evening sacrifice."[8] Indeed we shall not fittingly pass even the night time without this prayer: for David says, "At midnight did I rise to give thanks unto thee for the judgments of thy righteousness"[9]; and "Paul," as is stated in the Acts of the Apostles, "about midnight" in company with "Silas," at Philippi, "was praying and singing hymns unto God," so that even the "prisoners listened to them."[10]

XIII, 1. Now if Jesus prays, and does not pray in vain, obtaining through prayer what he asks for (and perhaps he would not have received it without prayer), which of us may neglect prayer? For Mark says, "In the morning, a great while before day, he rose up and went out, and departed into a desert place, and there prayed."[11] And Luke: "And it came to pass, as he was praying in a certain place, that when he ceased, one of his disciples said unto him"[12]; and elsewhere: "and he continued all night in prayer to God."[13] And John records his prayer thus: "These things spake Jesus; and lifting up his eyes to heaven, he said, Father, the hour is come; glorify thy Son, that thy Son also may glorify thee."[14] Also, the saying of the Lord "I knew that thou hearest me always,"[15] recorded by the same writer, shows that praying "always" is "always" heard.

2 I Thess. 5:17.   3 Dan. 6:10.
4 Perhaps *descending* should be read (Acts 10:11).
5 Acts 10:9–11.   6 The Hebrew and LXX have "voice."
7 Ps. 5:3.   8 Ps. 141:2.
9 Ps. 119:62.   10 Acts 16:25.
11 Mark 1:35.   12 Luke 11:1.
13 Luke 6:12.   14 John 17:1.
15 John 11:42.

Examples from Scripture of answered prayer (Chapter XIII, 2)

2. But why need I tell the tale of those who have obtained the greatest blessings from God by praying as they ought? Each one can collect for himself from the Scriptures many examples. Hannah ministered to the birth of Samuel, who was reckoned along with Moses,[16] when, having no child, she prayed in faith to the Lord.[17] Hezekiah, when as yet he was childless, on learning from Isaiah that he was about to die, prayed,[18] and has been given a place in the genealogy of the Saviour.[19] Again, when the people [of the Jews] were about to be destroyed as a result of the plot of Haman under a single decree, the prayer with fasting of Mordecai and Esther was heard, and it gave birth to "the" joyful "day of Mordecai"[20] among the people,[21] an addition to the feasts established by Moses. Judith, moreover, when she had offered up a holy prayer overcame Holophernes with the help of God, and a woman of the Hebrews single-handed brought shame upon the house of Nebuchadnezzar.[22] Also, Ananias, Azarias, and Misael in due answer to their prayer were sent "a whistling dewy wind" which prevented "the flame of fire" from exerting its power.[23] And the mouths of the Babylonians' "lions in the den" were stopped by the prayers of Daniel.[24] And Jonah too did not despair of being heard from "the belly of the great fish" which "swallowed" him, and when he came out from the belly of the fish he fulfilled what was lacking of his prophecy concerning the Ninevites.[25]

Similar prayers are also answered today (Chapter XIII, 3–5)

3. How many things could each of us tell of, had we the desire, out of a thankful remembrance of benefits conferred upon us, to offer praises to God concerning them? Souls that have long been sterile, perceiving the barrenness of their own reason and the sterility of their own mind, have by the Holy Spirit through persistent prayer conceived and given birth to saving words filled with perceptions of truth. How many enemies have been destroyed, when time and again myriads of a hostile power fought against us and sought to turn us from the divine faith? Then we took heart of grace because "some" trust "in chariots" and "some in horses," but "we" calling upon "the name of the

16 Jer. 15:1; cf. Ps. 99:6.   17 I Sam. 1:9 ff.
18 Cf. II Kings 20:1 ff.; Isa. 38:1 ff.   19 Matt. 1:9, 10.
20 II Maccabees 15:36.   21 Cf. Esth. 3:6, 7; 4:16, 17; 9:26–28.
22 Judith 13:4–10.   23 Dan. 3:24, 49, 50 (LXX).
24 Dan. 6:16, 22.   25 Jonah 1:17; 2:1; 3:1–4.

Lord"[26] perceive that truly "an horse is a vain thing for safety."[27] Moreover, he who puts his trust in praise to God oftentimes brings to nought "the chief captain"[28] of the adversary, even that deceitful and plausible word, which causes many to cower for fear, even of those who are reckoned faithful. For Judith signifies praise. What need is there also to speak of the numbers of those who have often encountered trials, hard to overcome, more searing than any flame, and yet have suffered therein no hurt, but have passed through them quite unharmed, not even receiving in the ordinary way the harm of "the smell of the" enemy's "fire."[29] Moreover, how many wild beasts, enraged against us, even evil spirits and cruel men, have they fallen in with, and by their prayers often stopped their mouths, so that they could not fasten their teeth upon those of us who have become "the members of Christ"?[30] Often for each of the saints "the Lord hath broken the great teeth of the lions," and "they have melted away as water that passeth by."[31] And we have often known those who had fled from the commandments of God and were "swallowed up"[32] of death, which in days gone by had power over them, who through repentance were saved from utter disaster, because they did not despair of the possibility of salvation even when held fast "in the belly of"[33] death. For "death, prevailing, swallowed them up; and God hath taken away again every tear from off every face."[34]

4. I consider that, after giving a list of those who have been benefited by prayer, it has been most necessary to add this, in order to turn away from prayer for trivial and earthly things earnest seekers after spiritual life in Christ, and to exhort the readers of this book to the pursuit of things mystical, of which the aforesaid were types. For prayer concerning the spiritual and mystical blessings that we have indicated above, is always and in every case brought to good effect by him who "does not war according to the flesh,"[35] but who "by the spirit mortifies the deeds of the body,"[36] those who seek out and establish the higher sense being preferred to those who appear to receive benefits prayed for according to the letter. And in our case we must make it our endeavour that the soul[37] be not childless or barren, as we listen to the spiritual law with spiritual ears: so

26 Ps. 20:7. 27 Ps. 33:17. 28 Judith 2:4, etc.
29 Dan. 3:27. 30 I Cor. 6:15. 31 Ps. 58:7, 8.
32 Jonah 2:1, 2. 33 Jonah 2:1, 2. 34 Isa. 25:8.
35 II Cor. 10:3. 36 Rom. 8:13.
37 "soul" is supplied from a conjecture of Bentley.

that putting aside childlessness or barrenness we may be heard
as Hannah and Hezekiah were, and may be delivered from
enemies that plot against us, even the spiritual forces of evil, as
Mordecai and Esther and Judith were. And since "Egypt" is
"an iron furnace,"[38] being a symbol of every terrestrial place,
let every one who has escaped from the evil in human life, and
has not been set on fire by sin, nor had his heart full of fire like a
furnace, give thanks no less than they did who were tried in a
"fire of dew."[39] Moreover, let him who has been heard when in
his prayer he said "deliver not to the wild beasts the soul that
hath acknowledged thee,"[40] and has suffered no hurt "from the
adder and the basilisk," because Christ has enabled him to
"tread upon" them, and has "trampled under foot the lion and
the dragon,"[41] and has used the good "power given" by Jesus
"to tread upon serpents and scorpions and over all the power of
the enemy,"[42] and has been in no wise harmed by such like—
let such a one give greater thanks than Daniel did, inasmuch as
he has been delivered from more fearful and harmful wild
beasts. And further, he who is persuaded of what "great fish"
that which "swallowed" Jonah is the type,[43] and comprehends
that it is the one spoken of by Job, "Let him curse it that curses
the day, who is ready to overpower the great fish,"[44] if at any
time he should happen to find himself because of disobedience
"in the belly of the fish"[45]; let him repent and pray, and he shall
go forth therefrom; and going forth and continuing to obey the
commandments of God he shall be able in "the kindness" of
"the Spirit"[46] to prophesy to the Ninevites that are perishing
even now and become for them a cause of salvation, if he is not
displeased at the "goodness of God" and does not seek that his
"severity"[47] should continue towards them that repent.

5. The greatest thing that Samuel is said to have wrought by
prayer, this in the spiritual sense it is possible for every one who
is genuinely devoted to God to accomplish even now, since he
has become worthy of being heard. For it is written: "And now
stand, and see this great thing, which the Lord doeth before
your eyes. Is it not wheat harvest today? I will call upon the
Lord, and he will give thunder and rain." Then, after a little:
"And Samuel called," he says, "unto the Lord, and the Lord
gave thunder and rain that day."[48] For to every saint and to the

---

[38] Deut. 4:20.　　[39] Dan. 3:49, 50 (LXX).　　[40] Ps. 73:19 (LXX).
[41] Ps. 91:13.　　[42] Luke 10:19.　　[43] Jonah 1:17.
[44] Job. 3:8.　　[45] Jonah 2:1.　　[46] Gal. 5:22.
[47] Rom. 11:22 (cf. Jonah 4:1, 2).　　[48] I Sam. 12:16–18.

genuine disciple of Jesus it is said by the Lord: "Lift up your eyes and look on the fields, that they are white already unto harvest. He that reapeth receiveth wages, and gathereth fruit unto life eternal."[48a] Verily at that season of harvest "the Lord doeth a great thing before the eyes" of them that hear the prophets. For when he who has been adorned with the Holy Spirit has "called unto the Lord," God gives from heaven "thunder, and rain" that refreshes the soul, so that he who was formerly in wickedness might "greatly fear the Lord"[49] and the minister of the benefit wrought by God, manifested as reverend and venerable in that his prayer is heard. And Elijah also opened "the heaven," after it had been "shut up" by the divine word for "three years and six months"[50] because of transgressions. And this good result follows always for everyone whomsoever who through prayer receives the rain of the soul, having been formerly deprived of it by reason of sin.

Prayer: (a) Content, (b) Forms, (c) To whom addressed (Chapters XIV to XVII)

XIV, 1. Having thus expounded the benefits which come to the saints from prayer, let us go on to observe the saying: "Ask for the great things, and the little things shall be added unto you" and "Ask for the heavenly things, and the earthly things shall be added unto you."[51] It is clear that all symbolical and typical things are "small" and "earthly" in comparison with the true and spiritual things. And in all likelihood the divine word, in exhorting us to imitate the prayers of the saints, so that we may obtain in truth what they obtained in figure,[52] indicates the "heavenly" and "great" things by means of matters connected with "earthly" and "little" things, saying: "Ye who desire to be spiritual ask in prayer, so that having received them as 'heavenly' ye may inherit the kingdom of heaven, and as 'great' ye may enjoy the greatest blessings; but the 'earthly' and 'little' things, of which ye are in want for bodily necessities, the Father will supply unto you in accordance with the measure of your need."

2. Since the apostle in the First Epistle to Timothy uses four nouns with reference to four matters closely connected with the subject of prayer, it will be useful to quote his saying exactly and to see if we rightly take each of the four in its proper sense. He

[48a] John 4:35, 36.
[50] Luke 4:25; cf. James 5:17, 18.
[52] A textual emendation has been adopted: see note.

[49] I Sam. 12:16–18.
[51] See II, 2.

says as follows: "I exhort, therefore, first of all, that supplications, prayers, intercessions, thanksgivings, be made for all
men,"[53] and so forth. I consider, then, that a "supplication" is
a petition offered with entreaty for the obtaining of something
which a person lacks; a "prayer" is offered in a dignified manner with ascription of praise by some one concerning matters of
importance; an "intercession" is a request to God for certain
things made by one who possesses more than usual confidence;
"thanksgiving" is an acknowledgement, with prayer, that blessings have been obtained from God, the greatness of that for
which acknowledgement is made having been recognized, or
else the apparent greatness to him who has been benefited of the
benefit that has been conferred upon him.

3. Examples of the first of these terms are as follows: (1) The
word of Gabriel to Zacharias when he had prayed, as we may
suppose, concerning the birth of John, which runs thus: "Fear
not, Zacharias: because thy supplication is heard, and thy wife
Elisabeth shall bear thee a son, and thou shalt call his name
John."[54] (2) What is written in Exodus in connection with the
making of the calf, after this manner: "And Moses made supplication before the Lord God and said, Why doth thy wrath, O
Lord, wax hot against thy people, which thou hast brought
forth out of Egypt with great power?"[55] (3) In Deuteronomy:
"And I made supplication before the Lord the second time, as
at the first, forty days and forty nights; I did neither eat bread
nor drink water; because of all your sins which ye sinned."[56]
(4) In Esther: "Mordecai made supplication to God, calling
to mind all the works of the Lord, and he said, Lord, Lord,
King, ruling over all things"[57]; and Esther herself "made supplication to the Lord, the God of Israel, and said, Lord, our
King."[58]

4. Examples of the second term for prayer are as follows:
(1) In Daniel: "And Azarias stood up and prayed thus, and
opened his mouth in the midst of the fire and said."[59] (2) Tobit:
"And I prayed in sorrow, saying, Thou art righteous, O Lord,
and all thy works; all thy ways are mercy and truth, and thou
judgest true and righteous judgment for ever."[60] But since "they
of the circumcision"[61] have obelized the passage in Daniel, as

---

[53] I Tim. 2:1.   [54] Luke 1:13.   [55] Ex. 32:11.   [56] Deut. 9:18.
[57] Esth. 13:8, 9 (R.V. and Vulg.); 4:17 a, b (LXX).
[58] Esth. 14:3 (R.V. and Vulg.); 4:17 k, l (LXX).
[59] Dan. 3:25 (LXX).   [60] Tobit 3:1, 2.
[61] Acts 10:45; 11:2; Rom. 4:12; Gal. 2:12; Col. 4:11; Titus 1:10.

not found in the Hebrew, and since they reject the book of Tobit as uncanonical, I will quote (3) from the First Book of the Kingdoms the passage about Hannah: "And she prayed unto the Lord, and wept sore. And she vowed a vow and said, O Lord of hosts, if thou wilt indeed look on the affliction of thine hand-maid,"[62] and so forth. (4) In Habakkuk: "A prayer of Habak-kuk the prophet, with a song.[63] O Lord, I have heard thy voice, and was afraid: O Lord, I perceived thy works and was as-tounded; in the midst of two living creatures thou shalt be known, when the years draw nigh thou shalt be observed."[64] This passage is an excellent illustration of the definition of prayer, because it is offered with an ascription of praise by him who prayed. (5) Moreover, in the Book of Jonah: "Jonah prayed unto the Lord his God out of the fish's belly, and he said, I called in my affliction unto the Lord my God, and he heard me; out of the belly of hell thou heardest my crying, even my voice. Thou didst cast me forth into the depths of the heart of the sea, and the rivers were round about me."[65]

5. An example of the third term for prayer is to be found (1) with the Apostle, when with good reason he places "prayer" within our power, but "intercession" within the power of the Spirit, since he is greater and has "boldness toward"[66] him with whom he intercedes. "For we know not how to pray," he says, "as we ought; but the Spirit himself maketh intercession exceedingly to God with groanings which cannot be uttered. And he that searcheth the hearts knoweth what is the mind of the Spirit, because he maketh intercession for the saints."[67] The Spirit "intercedes exceedingly" and "intercedes"; but we "pray." (2) Intercession also seems to me to be involved in what is said by Joshua about the sun standing still in Gabaoth: "Then spake Joshua to the Lord, in the day when God delivered the Amorites into the hand of Israel, when he destroyed them in Gabaoth, and they were destroyed from the face of the children of Israel. And Joshua said, Let the sun stand still upon Gabaoth, and the moon in the ravine of Edom."[68] (3) And in Judges, I think that Samson intercedes when he said, "Let my soul die along with the Philistines," when "he leaned with all his might; and the house fell upon the lords, and upon all the people that were therein."[69] And though it is not stated that Joshua and Samson "interceded," but that they "spoke," what they said

---

[62] I Sam. 1:10, 11.   [63] See note.   [64] Hab. 3:1, 2.
[65] Jonah 2:1, 2, 3.   [66] Cf. I John 3:21.   [67] Rom. 8:26, 27.
[68] Josh. 10:12.   [69] Judg. 16:30.

seems to me to be "intercession," which in my opinion is different from "prayer," if we use the terms in their proper sense.

An example of "thanksgiving" is to be found in our Lord's words, "I thank[70] thee, O Father, Lord of heaven and earth, that thou didst hide these things from the wise and understanding, and didst reveal them unto babes."[71] For *exhomologoumai* has the same meaning as *eucharisto*.

6. Now, supplication and intercession and thanksgiving may not unsuitably be addressed to holy men also; but two of them (I mean intercession and thanksgiving) not only to the saints but also to other men,[72] while supplication is addressed to the saints only, if, for example, a Paul or a Peter can be found, in order that they may help us by making us worthy to receive the "authority" given to them "to forgive sins."[73] Nevertheless, if we wrong someone who is not a saint, it is permitted to us, conscious of our sin against him, to supplicate such a one also, that he may pardon our wrongdoing. And if these may be addressed to holy men, how much more may thanksgiving be made to Christ, who has wrought such benefits for us by the will of the Father? Moreover, we may intercede with him, as Stephen did when he said, "Lord, lay not this sin to their charge"[74]; and imitating the father of him who was "epileptic," say, "I beseech" thee, Lord, "have mercy," either on "my son,"[75] or on myself, or on any one whomsoever.

XV, 1. If we understand what prayer is, perhaps we ought not to pray to anyone born [of woman], nor even to Christ himself, but only to the God and Father of all, to whom also our Saviour prayed, as we have mentioned before,[76] and teaches us to pray.[77] For when he heard "Teach us to pray," he did not "teach" them "to pray"[78] to himself, but to the Father, saying, "Our Father which art in heaven,"[79] and so forth. For if, as is shown elsewhere, the Son is different from the Father in person and in subject,[80] we must pray either to the Son and not to the Father, or to both, or to the Father alone. Now, everyone without exception will agree that it would be most absurd to pray to the Son and not to the Father, and that to maintain this would be contrary to revealed truth. If we were to pray to both, this would involve making our requests in the plural, saying in our

---

[70] ἐξομολογοῦμαι.   [71] Matt. 11:25; Luke 10:21.
[72] Text as emended by Klostermann.   [73] Cf. Matt. 9:6; John 20:23.
[74] Acts 7:60.   [75] Matt. 17:15; Luke 9:38.
[76] See XIII, 1.   [77] Cf. Matt. 6:5 ff.; Luke 11:1 ff.
[78] Luke 11:2.   [79] Matt. 6:9.   [80] See note.

prayers "provide ye," "do ye good," "supply ye," "save ye," and so on: this would be in itself incongruous, nor can anyone give an instance from the Scriptures of any persons using this mode of expression. It remains, therefore, to pray only to God the Father of all, but not apart from the high priest,[81] who was "appointed"[82] by the Father "with the taking of an oath," in accordance with the words "he sware and will not repent himself, thou art a priest for ever after the order of Melchizedek."[83]

2. When therefore the saints give thanks in their prayers to God, they acknowledge his favours through Christ Jesus. And as it is not fitting that a man who prays with due care should pray to him who prays but rather to him whom our Lord Jesus has taught us to call upon in prayer, even the Father, so also no prayer should be offered to the Father apart from him, as he himself shows us clearly when he says, "Verily, verily, I say unto you, If ye shall ask anything of my Father, he will give it you in my name: ask, and ye shall receive, that your joy may be fulfilled."[84] For he did not say, "Ask me," nor yet, "Ask the Father" simply, but, "If ye shall ask anything of my Father, he will give it you in my name." For until Jesus had given this teaching, no one had "asked the Father in the name" of the Son. It was a true saying of Jesus: "Hitherto have ye asked nothing in my name"; and true also the saying: "Ask, and ye shall receive, that your joy may be fulfilled."

3. But if anyone, thinking that he ought to pray to Christ himself, and confused by the meaning of the word "worship," should bring forward to us the saying: "Let all the angels of God worship him"[85] (admittedly in Deuteronomy spoken of Christ), we should say to him that the Church also, named Jerusalem by the prophet, is said to be worshipped by kings and queens, who have become her nursing fathers and mothers. The passage is as follows: "Behold, I lift up mine hand to the nations, and will lift up mine ensign to the isles; and they shall bring thy sons in their bosom, and will lift up thy daughters upon their shoulders. And kings shall be thy nursing fathers, and their queens thy nursing mothers: they shall worship [thee][86] with their face to the earth, and lick the dust of thy feet: and thou shalt know that I am the Lord, and shalt not be ashamed."[87]

4. Without doubt, he who said,[88] "Why callest thou me

---

[81] Heb. 2:17, etc. [82] Heb. 8:3. [83] Heb. 7:20, 21.
[84] John 16:23, 24. [85] Deut. 32:43 (LXX); Heb. 1:6.
[86] "thee," absent from the MS. T, is supplied from the LXX.
[87] Isa. 49:22, 23. [88] For text of this passage, see note.

good? none is good save one, even God, the Father,"[89] might also say, "Why dost thou pray to me? It is right to pray to the Father alone, to whom I also pray: as you learn from the holy Scriptures. For you ought not to pray to him who was 'appointed high priest'[90] on your behalf by the Father and who received from the Father the office of 'advocate,'[91] but rather through the high priest and advocate, who 'can be touched with the feeling of' your 'infirmities,' and 'hath been in all points tempted' as you are, yet because of the gift bestowed on me by the Father 'tempted without sin.'[92] Learn therefore how great a gift you have received from my Father, having 'received' through regeneration[93] in me 'the spirit of adoption,'[94] that you may be called 'sons of God.'[95] For you have read the saying addressed to the Father that was spoken by me concerning you through David: 'I will declare thy name unto my brethren, in the midst of the congregation will I sing thy praise.'[96] It is not reasonable that those who have been deemed worthy to have 'one'[97] Father with him should pray to a brother. Therefore your prayer ought to be offered to the Father alone with me and through me."

XVI, 1. Hearing, then, Jesus saying these things, let us pray to God through him, all saying the same thing, and in no way divided concerning the manner of prayer. Are we not divided, if some of us pray to the Father, others to the Son? Those who pray to the Son, either with the Father or apart from the Father, sin with great simplicity through ignorance of the subject due to lack of examination and inquiry. Let us pray, then, as to God, let us make intercession as to a Father, let us make supplication as to a Lord, let us give thanks as to God and Father and Lord, and in no wise as to the Lord of a slave. For the Father might rightly be reckoned both as Lord of the Son and Lord of them who have become sons through him. As "he is not the God of the dead, but of the living,"[98] so he is not the Lord of ignoble slaves, but of those who are ennobled, who at the beginning, because of their infancy,[99] lived in fear, but afterwards in love serve a happier servitude than that of fear.[1] For it is in the soul, and to him alone who sees the heart, that the marks of God's slaves and of his sons are manifest.

---

[89] Mark 10:18.   [90] Cf. Heb. 8:3.   [91] Cf. I John 2:1.
[92] Heb. 4:15.   [93] Cf. I Peter 1:3, 23.   [94] Rom. 8:15.
[95] Rom. 8:14; Gal. 3:26.   [96] Ps. 22:22 (Heb. 2:12).
[97] Cf. Heb. 2:11.   [98] Mark 12:27; Matt. 22:32; Luke 20:38.
[99] Cf. Gal. 4:1, 3.   [1] Cf. Rom. 8:15; Gal. 4:6, 7.

Prayer for "earthly" and "heavenly" blessings

2. Everyone therefore that asks God for "earthly" and "little" things disregards the command to ask for "heavenly" and "great" things from God, who knows not to grant anything "earthly" or "little." If anyone offers as an objection the things pertaining to the body that were bestowed upon the saints as the result of prayer, and also the evangelical saying[2] which tells us that "earthly" and "little" things are "added" to us, the following reply may be made to him. If some one were to give us a bodily object of any kind whatsoever, we should not say that such a one bestowed upon us the shadow of the bodily object. For in giving the bodily object he did not design to give two things, the object and its shadow, but the design of the giver was to give the bodily object: it followed, however, that with the gift of the object we also received its shadow. Similarly, when our understanding has grown in stature and we note which are the gifts which are pre-eminently given us by God, we shall say that bodily things are the most natural accompaniments of the great and heavenly "spiritual gifts,"[3] "given to each" of the saints "to profit withal,"[4] either "according to the proportion of faith,"[5] or "even as" the Giver "wills."[6] And he wills wisely, even though we cannot assign a cause and reason worthy of the Giver to each of his gifts.

3. The soul of Hannah,[7] therefore, after casting off a certain sterility, has borne more abundant fruit than did her body when it gave birth to Samuel. Hezekiah has begotten more divine children of the mind than ever were begotten of his body by bodily seed. Esther and Mordecai and the people (of the Jews) were more largely delivered from spiritual plots than they were from Haman and those that conspired [with him. And Judith] has destroyed [rather][8] the power of "the prince"[9] who willed to ruin her soul than of the famous Holofernes. Who would not confess that the spiritual blessing which comes upon all the saints (spoken of by Isaac to Jacob in the words: "May God give thee of the dew of heaven"[10]) was bestowed more abundantly upon Ananias and those that were with him than was the material dew which conquered the flame kindled by

---

2 Matt. 6:33.   3 I Cor. 12:1, 4.   4 I Cor. 12:7.
5 Rom. 12:6.   6 I Cor. 12:11.
7 This section takes up again the O.T. references of XIII, 2.
8 The words in square brackets have been supplied to fill up a lacuna in the text.
9 Cf. Mark 3:22; John 12:31; 14:30, 16:11.
10 Gen. 27:28.

Nebuchadnezzar? And the mouths of the invisible lions were stopped for the prophet Daniel, so that they could accomplish nothing against his soul, rather than the mouths of the lions perceived by the senses, of whom everyone who reads this book takes note. Does it not follow[11] that he who has escaped from the belly of the great fish worsted by Jesus our Saviour, which swallows every fugitive from God, becomes a Jonah capable as a saint of receiving the Holy Spirit?

XVII, 1. It is not to be wondered at if to all alike who receive, so to speak, the bodies that cause such shadows, a shadow like to it is not given, and to some no shadow is given at all.[12] Students of the problems connected with sun-dials and with the relation of the shadow to the luminous body are clearly aware of what happens according to latitude.[13] For example, in some latitudes the gnomons give no shadow at a certain season, in others the shadow is short, so to speak, and in others again longer than in others. It is not strange, then, if the design of him who bestows pre-eminent gifts grants them in accordance with certain ineffable, mystic analogies to suit the recipients and the times when these pre-eminent gifts are made; sometimes no shadows at all follow for the recipients, sometimes there are shadows not of all the gifts, but of a few, sometimes they are smaller in comparison with the rest, sometimes larger accompany others. If a man who seeks the rays of the sun has this indispensable thing, he is neither rejoiced nor grieved by the presence or absence of bodily shadows, when having been enlightened he is either deprived of the shadow or has more or less of the shadow. So also, if spiritual things are present to us and we are being enlightened by God in the complete possession of what is truly good, we shall not waste words about the paltry thing which is the shadow. For all material and bodily things, of whatever kind they may be, have the value of an unsubstantial and feeble shadow, and can in no way be compared with the saving and holy gifts of the God of the universe. What sort of comparison can there be between bodily riches and the riches "in all utterance and in all"[14] wisdom? Who that is not a madman would compare health of flesh and bones with a healthy mind and a robust soul and a balanced reason? When all these are duly ordered by a God-given reason, they cause bodily sufferings to become a trifling scratch, so to speak, and indeed, in my opinion, less than a scratch.

[11] See note.
[12] So Bentley emends.
[13] Reading κλίματα for σώματα.
[14] I Cor. 1:5.

A.C.—18

2. He who has perceived what the beauty of the Bride is, whom the Bridegroom,[15] who is the Word of God, loves in the full bloom of the super-celestial and super-mundane beauty of the soul, will be ashamed to honour even with the same name of beauty the bodily beauty of woman or boy or man. Flesh does not contain beauty in the true sense of the word, seeing that all of it is shameful. For "all flesh is" as "grass," and the "glory" of it, which appears in the so-called beauty of women and children, has been compared, according to the word of the prophet, to a "flower," as follows: "All flesh is" as "grass, and all the glory of it is as the flower of grass: the grass withereth, and the flower falleth away: but the word of the Lord remaineth for ever."[16] Again, who would properly continue to use the term "noble birth" as it is commonly employed by men, once he has perceived the noble birth of the sons of God? When the mind has contemplated "a kingdom" of Christ "that cannot be shaken,"[17] it cannot but despise as of no worth or account every kingdom upon earth. When a man sees as clearly as he can (in so far as the human mind still imprisoned in the body is capable) the "host"[18] of angels and the "commanders" among them "of the powers of the Lord,"[19] and archangels and "thrones" and "dominions" and "principalities" and "powers,"[20] and when he comprehends that he can attain to equal honour with them[21] from the Father, it must needs follow that, even though he be feebler than a shadow, he will despise by comparison as utterly mean and of no account the things that foolish men set great store by, and, should he be offered all these things, he will disdain them, so that he may not fail to attain unto the true principalities and diviner powers. We must pray, therefore, we must pray concerning the pre-eminently and truly great and heavenly blessings; and as concerning the shadows that accompany these pre-eminent blessings we must commit this matter to God, who "knows before" we "ask him what things" we "have need of"[22] for the perishable body.

Discussion of The Lord's Prayer
CHAPTERS XVIII TO XXX

XVIII, 1. Enough has been said by us in the foregoing examination of the problem of prayer, "according to the grace

---

15 Cf. John 3:29.   16 Isa. 40:6–8.   17 Heb. 12:28.
18 Luke 2:13.   19 Josh. 5:14.   20 Col. 1:16.
21 Luke 20:36.   22 Matt. 6:8.

given," as we were able to receive it, by "God"[23] through his Christ (and we trust also, in the Holy Spirit—which, if it be so, you who read this book will judge). Now we shall proceed to the next task: for we desire to consider the prayer outlined by the Lord, with what power it has been filled.

The texts of the Lord's Prayer (Chapter XVIII, 2, 3)

2. And first of all we must note that Matthew and Luke might seem to most people to have recorded the same prayer, providing a pattern of how we ought to pray. But the text of Matthew runs as follows: "Our Father which art in heaven, Hallowed be thy name. Thy Kingdom come. Thy will be done, as in heaven, so on earth. Give us this day our daily bread. And forgive us our debts, as we also have forgiven our debtors. And bring us not into temptation, but deliver us from the evil one."[24] Luke's text, on the other hand, runs thus: "Father, Hallowed be thy name. Thy kingdom come. Give us day by day our daily bread. And forgive us our sins; for we ourselves also forgive every one that is indebted to us. And bring us not into temptation."[25]

3. But we must reply to those who take this view, in the first place, that the words, although they have some resemblances, nevertheless appear to differ in other points, as our investigation of them will establish; and, in the second place, that it cannot be the same prayer which was spoken on "the mountain," to which "seeing the multitudes he went up," when, "having sat down, his disciples came unto him, and he opened his mouth and taught them"[26] (for this prayer is found recorded in Matthew in the context of the recital of the Beatitudes and the commandments which follow), and that which, "as he was praying in a certain place, when he ceased," was spoken to "one of his disciples," who had asked to be "taught to pray, even as John also taught his disciples."[27] For how can it be possible that the same words were spoken by themselves apart from any previous inquiry and also delivered at the request of a disciple? Perhaps, however, someone will say to this that the prayers are virtually the same and were spoken as one prayer, on one occasion in an extended address, and on another to one of the disciples who had made the request, probably because he was not present when the prayer recorded in Matthew was spoken, or because he had not retained what was said. Perhaps, however, it is better to take the view that the prayers are different, though

23 I Cor. 3:10.   24 Matt. 6:9–13.   25 Luke 11:2–4.
26 Matt. 5:1, 2.   27 Luke 11:1.

they have some parts common. We searched also the Gospel of Mark, in case the record of something equivalent there should escape us, but we found no trace whatever of the prayer in it.

The Introduction to the Prayer in Matthew (Chapters XIX to XXI)

XIX, 1. Since, as we said above,[28] he who prays must first be settled and disposed in a certain manner and then afterwards so pray, let us consider the words that were uttered by the Saviour on this subject before the prayer as it is given in Matthew. They are as follows: "When ye pray, ye shall not be as the hypocrites; for they love to stand and pray in the synagogues and in the corners of the streets, that they may be seen of men. Verily I say unto you, They have received their reward. But thou, when thou prayest, enter into thine inner chamber, and having shut thy door, pray to thy Father which is in secret, and thy Father which seeth in secret shall recompense thee. And in praying use not vain repetitions, as the Gentiles do: for they think that they shall be heard for their much speaking. Be not therefore like unto them: for your Father knoweth what things ye have need of, before ye ask him. After this manner therefore pray ye."[29]

2. Our Saviour in many places clearly ranks vainglory as a deadly passion: as he has done also here, when he deters us from acting at the time of prayer as hypocrites do. For it is to act the hypocrite to wish to pride oneself before men for piety or liberality. Those who remember the saying, "How can ye believe, which receive glory of" men, "and the glory that cometh from the only God ye seek not?"[30] must despise all glory from men, even though it be reckoned to have been given for a good cause, and must seek the true glory that is properly so-called, which comes from him alone who glorifies him who is worthy of glory in a manner fitting to himself and beyond the deserts of the recipient of glory. And that which would be reckoned as good in itself, and is reckoned to be praiseworthy, is sullied when we do it that we "may have glory of men,"[31] or "that" we "may be seen of men"[32]: therefore no recompense from God follows us for this. For every word of Jesus is true[33]; and, if one may use a forced expression, is truer, when it is spoken with his accustomed oath. He says of those who for the sake of vainglory seem to do good to their neighbour or "pray in the synagogues and the corners of the streets, that they may be seen of men," the same thing: "Verily I say unto you, They have received

[28] VIII, 2–X, 2.   [29] Matt. 6:5–9.   [30] John 5:44.
[31] Matt. 6:2.   [32] Matt. 6:5.   [33] ἀψευδής.

their reward."[34] The "rich man," of whom Luke speaks, received as his reward "the good things in"[35] his own mortal life, and because he had received these he was no longer able to obtain them after this present life. Similarly, he who "has received" his own "reward,"[36] either for giving something to someone or for his prayers, inasmuch as he did not "sow unto the Spirit," but "unto the flesh, shall reap corruption," but "shall" not "reap eternal life."[37] Now that man "sows unto the flesh" who "in the synagogues and the streets, that he may have glory of men, doeth alms" with "a trumpet before" him,[38] or he who "loves to stand and pray in the synagogues and corners of the streets, that" he "may be seen of men"[39] and be reckoned as pious and holy by those who see him.

3. Moreover, everyone who travels along "the wide and broad way that leadeth to destruction,"[40] which has nothing clear or straight but is altogether full of twists and corners (for its straightness has been very much broken into curves), stands in it not otherwise than he[41] who "prays in the corners of the streets,"[42] through love of pleasure frequenting not one but several streets, where are to be found those who are "dying like men"[43] because they have fallen from their deity: who praise and count happy those in the streets who are wont to commit iniquity in their company. And at all times there are many who in their praying are manifestly "lovers of pleasure rather than lovers of God,"[44] in the midst of banquets and at carousals behaving drunkenly in prayer, truly "standing in the corners of the streets" and "praying."[45] For everyone who lives according to pleasure, having loved "the broad" path, has fallen from "the narrow and straitened way"[46] of Jesus Christ—a way with not the slightest bend and absolutely no corners at all.

XX, 1. If there is a difference between the Church and the synagogue (the Church properly so called "not having spot or wrinkle or any such thing," but "being holy and without blemish"[47]: into which neither he that is "born of fornication entereth," nor the "eunuch," nor an "emasculated"[48] person, nor yet "an Egyptian" or "an Idumaean," save that "sons born to them" of "the third generation" may scarcely join "the

34 Matt. 6:2, 5.
35 Luke 16:19, 25.
36 Matt. 6:2, 5.
37 Gal. 6:8.
38 Matt. 6:2.
39 Matt. 6:5.
40 Matt. 7:13.
41 See note.
42 Matt. 6:5.
43 Ps. 82:7.
44 II Tim. 3:4.
45 Matt. 6:5.
46 Matt. 7:13, 14.
47 Eph. 5:27.
48 Deut. 23:1, 2.

assembly,"[49] nor yet the "Moabite" or "Ammonite," unless the tenth "generation" is fulfilled and "the age" is accomplished[50]; the synagogue, on the other hand, being "built" by "a centurion," who did this in the times before the sojourn with us of Jesus, when as yet witness had not been borne to him that he had such "faith" as the Son of God "found not in Israel"[51]), he who "loves to pray in the synagogues" is not far from "the corners of the streets."[52] But the saint is not such a one: for he does not "love [φιλεῖ] to pray," but rather has a deep concern [ἀγαπᾷ] to do so, and not "in synagogues," but in churches, and not "in corners of streets," but in the straightness of "the narrow and straitened way"[53]; nor yet again that he "may be seen of men,"[54] but that he "may appear before the Lord God."[55] For he is a male person, perceiving "the acceptable year of the Lord,"[56] and keeping the commandment which says: "Three times in a year shall all thy males appear before the Lord thy God."[55]

2. We must pay careful attention to "they may be seen,"[54] since "nothing that is seen is good,"[57] being in appearance, as it were, and not truly, deceiving the imagination and not forming a distinct or true image. The actors of a drama in the theatre are not what they say they are or what they appear to be in accordance with the character they assume. Similarly, those who simulate in appearance an impression of the good are not righteous but are actors of righteousness, and are themselves acting in their own theatre, "the synagogues and the corners of the streets."[52] But he who is not an actor, and on the contrary puts aside everything that is not his own, and prepares to delight himself in a place that is greater and far surpasses any of the theatres mentioned above, "enters into" his own "inner chamber, shutting"[58] himself in upon the riches laid up in store,[59] "the treasure of wisdom and knowledge."[60] And never bending outside nor gaping at the things outside, he "shuts" every "door" of the faculties of sense, so that he may not be enticed by the impressions of sense and their image may not penetrate into his mind. Thus he prays to the Father, who does not flee from or abandon such a secret place,[61] but rather "dwells"[62] in it, his only begotten[63] being also present with him. For, says

[49] Deut. 23:7, 8.   [50] Deut. 23:3.   [51] Luke 7:2, 5, 9.
[52] Matt. 6:5.   [53] Matt. 7:14.   [54] Matt. 6:5.
[55] Deut. 16:16.   [56] Isa. 61:2 (Luke 4:19).   [57] Ignatius, *Romans*, 3.
[58] Matt. 6:6.   [59] Cf. I Tim. 6:18, 19.   [60] Col. 2:3.
[61] Cf. Matt. 6:6.   [62] Eph. 3:17.   [63] John 1:14, etc.

he, "I and the Father[64] will come unto him and make our abode with him."[65] It is evident that if indeed we pray thus, we shall make intercession not only with the righteous God but also with the Father, as One who is not absent from his sons but is present in our secret place, and watches over it, and increases what is in "the inner chamber," if we "shut the door"[65a] of it.

XXI, 1. In praying, however, do "not" let "us use vain repetitions,"[66] but rather let us speak to God. Now we "use vain repetitions" when we fail to examine for blemishes either ourselves or the words of prayer we offer up, and so speak of corrupt deeds or words or thoughts, which are mean and blameworthy and alien from the incorruptibility of the Lord. Indeed, he who "uses vain repetitions" in "praying" is actually in a worse case than those who frequent "the synagogues," of whom we spoke above, and in a more grievous condition than they who stand "in the corners of the streets,"[67] since he does not preserve a trace of even a pretence of good. According to the text of the Gospel, they who alone "use vain repetitions" are "the Gentiles,"[68] who have no notion whatever of great and heavenly requests, but offer up every prayer for bodily and outward things. Therefore he who requests things of below from him who dwells in the heaven and above the highest heaven, even the Lord, is like unto a "Gentile using vain repetitions."

2. It seems indeed that he who speaks much "uses vain repetitions," and he who "uses vain repetitions" speaks much. For no material or bodily thing is single: but every one of them, though reckoned single, is split up and cut in pieces and divided into several parts, having lost its unity. Virtue is one, vice is many; truth is one, falsehood is many; the wisdom of God is one, the wisdoms "of this world," and "of the rulers of this world, which are coming to nought,"[69] are many; the word of God is one, those who are estranged from God are many. Therefore no one "shall escape transgression for much speaking,"[70] and no one, though "thinking" that he "shall be heard for" his "much speaking," can be heard thereby. And so our prayers must not "be like unto" the "vain repetitions" or "much speaking" of "the Gentiles,"[71] or to whatever else they may do "after the likeness of the serpent."[72] "For" the God of the saints, being a "Father, knoweth what things" his sons "have

---

64 John 10:30. 65 John 14:23. 65a Matt. 6:6.
66 Matt. 6:7. 67 Adopting an emended text (Matt. 6:5).
68 Matt. 6:7. 69 I Cor. 2:6. 70 Prov. 10:19.
71 Matt. 6:7, 8. 72 Ps. 57:5 (LXX).

need of,"[73] since they are things worthy of the Father's knowledge. But if a man knows not God, and knows not the things of God, he knows not "what things" he "has need of": for the things which he thinks he "has need of" are entirely wrong. On the other hand, he who contemplates what higher and holier things he lacks, will attain to the objects of his contemplation, which are known by God and have been known to the Father or ever the request was made. Having said so much on the passage which precedes the prayer in the Gospel according to Matthew, let us now go on to see the meaning of the prayer itself.

OUR FATHER WHICH ART IN HEAVEN
(Chapters XXII and XXIII)

XXII, 1. *Our Father which art in heaven.*[74] It is worth while examining with unusual care the Old Testament, as it is called, to see if it is possible to find anywhere in it a prayer in which someone calls God "Father." Though we searched to the best of our ability, up to the present we have found none. We do not mean that God is never called "Father," or that those who were wont to believe in God are never styled "sons of God," but that we have not yet succeeded in finding in a prayer that confident affirmation in styling God as "Father" which was made by the Saviour. That God is called "Father," and that those who have drawn nigh to the word of God are called "sons," may be seen from many passages, as for example in Deuteronomy: "Thou hast forsaken the God who begat thee, And hast forgotten the God who nurtureth thee"[75]; and again: "Is not he thy Father that hath bought thee, and hath made thee and established thee?"[76]; and again: "Sons in whom is no faith"[77]; and in Isaiah: "I have begotten and brought up sons, but they have rejected me"[78]; and in Malachi: "A son will honour his father, and a servant his master: and if I am a father, where is mine honour? and if I am a master, where is my fear?"[79]

2. Therefore, even though God is spoken of as "Father," and those begotten by the word of faith in him as "sons," it is not possible to find in the ancients at any rate a firm and unchangeable affirmation of sonship. For example, the passages we have quoted show that those called "sons" are blameworthy: since, according to the apostle, while "the heir is a child, he differeth

---

[73] Matt. 6:8.   [74] Matt. 6:9.   [75] Deut. 32:18.
[76] Deut. 23:6.   [77] Deut. 32:20.   [78] Isa. 1:2.
[79] Mal. 1:6.

nothing from a bond-servant, though he is lord of all; but is under guardians and stewards until the term appointed of the father"[80]; but "the fulness of the time"[81] arrived [82] at the sojourn of our Lord Jesus Christ, when those who desire it "receive the adoption of sons,"[83] as Paul teaches in the following words: "For ye received not the spirit of bondage unto fear; but ye received the spirit of adoption, whereby we cry, Abba, Father."[84] And in the Gospel according to John: "But as many as received him, to them gave he the right to become children of God, even to them that believed on his name."[85] And because of this "spirit of adoption," we learn in the general Epistle of John as concerning those "who are begotten of God" that "whosoever is begotten of God doeth no sin, because his seed abideth in him: and he cannot sin, because he is begotten of God."[86]

3. Nevertheless, if we consider the meaning of the words "When ye pray, say, Father,"[87] as it is written in Luke, we shall hesitate if we are not true sons to address him by this title, lest perchance in addition to our sins we should incur the charge of impiety also. What I mean is something like this. Paul says in his former [epistle] to the Corinthians, "No man can say, Jesus is Lord, but in the Holy Spirit"; and "no man speaking in the Spirit of God saith, Jesus is anathema."[88] He uses "Holy Spirit" and "Spirit of God" as synonymous terms. But what the meaning is of "saying in the Holy Spirit Jesus is Lord" is by no means clear, for countless hypocrites and numbers of heretics use this title, and sometimes even demons when they are overcome by the power that is in the Name. No one will dare to maintain that any of these "says Jesus is Lord in the Holy Spirit." Nor could they even be shown to say "Jesus is Lord," since those only from the heart say, "Jesus is Lord," who while serving the word of God and while engaged in doing anything whatsoever call none other "Lord" save him. If it be such that say, "Jesus is Lord," it may be that everyone who anathematizes the divine Word in transgressing by his own actions cries out: "Jesus is anathema." Therefore, just as such a one says, "Jesus is Lord," and he of an opposite mind, "Jesus is anathema," so also, "whosoever is begotten of God" and "doeth no sin," through partaking of the "seed"[89] of God, which turns him aside from every sin, says by his deeds: "Our Father which art in heaven,"[90]

---

[80] Gal. 4:1, 2.
[81] Gal. 4:4.
[82] Reading ἐνέστη.
[83] Gal. 4:5.
[84] Rom. 8:15.
[85] John 1:12.
[86] I John 3:9.
[87] Luke 11:2.
[88] I Cor. 12:3.
[89] I John 3:9.
[90] Matt. 6:9.

"the Spirit himself bearing witness with" their spirit, "that" they "are children of God," and his "heirs," and "joint-heirs with Christ," since suffering "with him" they have good hope to "be also glorified with him."[91] And in order that such may not only half say, "Our Father,"[91a] "the heart" also, which is the fountain and source of good works, in conjunction with the works "believeth unto righteousness," and in harmony with them "the mouth maketh confession unto salvation."[92]

4. Every deed and word and thought of theirs, having been formed by "the only begotten Word"[93] after his likeness, imitates "the image of the invisible God,"[94] and is "after the image of the Creator,"[95] who "maketh his sun to rise on the evil and the good, and sendeth rain on the just and the unjust,"[96] so that there is in them "the image of the heavenly,"[97] who is himself "the image of God."[94] The saints, therefore, being "an image" of an image (that image being the Son), acquire an impression of[98] sonship, becoming "conformed" not only "to the body of the glory"[99] of Christ, but also to him[1] who is "in the body."[2] They become conformed to him who is in "the body of the glory,"[99] as they are "transformed by the renewing of the mind."[3] If such persons in everything say, "Our Father which art in heaven,"[4] evidently "he that doeth sin," as John says in his general [epistle], "is of the devil; for the devil sinneth from the beginning."[5] And as the "seed" of God, "remaining in him that is begotten of God,"[6] becomes for him who has been conformed[7] to "the only begotten Word"[93] the cause that "he cannot sin,"[6] so in everyone "that doeth sin" the seed of "the devil"[5] is present, and, so long as it is inherent in the soul, prevents him who has it from being able to perform right actions. But since "to this end was the Son of God manifested, that he might destroy the works of the devil," it is possible, by the dwelling in our soul of the Word of God, when "the works of the devil" have been "destroyed,"[8] for the evil seed implanted in us to be done away with, and for us "to become children of God."[9]

5. Do not let us think that we are taught to say actual words at a certain fixed time of prayer. If we understand what has

91 Rom. 8: 16, 17. 91a Matt. 6:9. 92 Rom. 10:10.
93 John 1:14, 18. 94 Col. 1:15. 95 Col. 3:10.
96 Matt. 5:45. 97 I Cor. 15:49. 98 See note.
99 Phil. 3:21. 1 Reading τῷ ὄντι. 2 Cf. II Cor. 12:2, 3.
3 Rom. 12:2. 4 Matt. 6:9. 5 I John 3:8.
6 I John 3:9. 7 Cf. Gal. 4:19. 8 I John 3:8.
9 John 1:12.

been said above[10] in our discussion about "praying without ceasing,"[11] our whole life as we "pray without ceasing" shall say, "Our Father which art in heaven"[12]: its "citizenship" shall in no wise be on earth but in every way "in heaven,"[13] which is the "throne"[14] of God; for the kingdom of heaven is seated in all those who "bear the image of the heavenly,"[15] and therefore are themselves heavenly.

XXIII, 1. But when "the Father" of the saints is said to be "in heaven," we are not to suppose that he is circumscribed in bodily fashion and dwells "in heaven"[12]; otherwise, if the heaven contained him, God would be found less than, because contained by, the heaven: but we must believe that by the ineffable power of his Godhead all things are contained and held together by him. And, speaking generally, sayings which taken literally are supposed by simple folk to assert that God is in a place, must instead be understood in a manner that befit grand and spiritual conceptions of God. Such are the following in the [Gospel] according to John: "Now before the feast of the passover, Jesus knowing that his hour was come that he should depart out of this world unto the Father, having loved his own which were in the world, he loved them unto the end"[16]; and, a little further on, "knowing that the Father had given all things into his hands, and that he came forth from God, and goeth unto God"[17]; and later on, "Ye heard how I said to you, I go away, and I come unto you. If ye loved me, ye would have rejoiced, because I go unto the Father"[18]; and again, later on, "But now I go unto him that sent me; and none of you asketh me, whither goest thou?"[19] If these words are to be taken in a local sense, it is obvious that we must do the same with: "Jesus answered and said unto them, If a man love me, he will keep my word: and my Father will love him, and we will come unto him, and make our abode with him."[20]

2. These sayings do not conceive of a local departure of the Father and the Son to him who loves the word of Jesus, nor are they to be taken in a local sense. But the Word of God, condescending for our sakes and being "humbled,"[21] as concerning his own dignity, when he is among men, is said to "depart out of this world to the Father,"[22] in order that we also may behold

10 Ch. XII.   11 I Thess. 5:17.   12 Matt. 6:9.
13 Phil. 3:20.   14 Cf. Isa. 66:1.   15 I Cor. 15:49.
16 John 13:1.   17 John 13:3.   18 John 14:28.
19 John 16:5.   20 John 14:23.   21 Phil. 2:8.
22 John 13:1.

him there in his perfection, returning again to his own "fulness,"[23] after the emptiness wherewith he "emptied himself"[24]
when he was with us: where also we, using him as our guide,
being "made full,"[25] shall be delivered from all emptiness. Let
the Word of God, therefore, depart to "him that sent him,"[26]
quitting the world, and let him "go unto the Father."[27] And as
for that passage at the end of the Gospel according to John,
"Touch me not; for I am not yet ascended unto the Father,"[28]
let us seek to conceive of it in a mystical sense: the ascent of the
Son "unto the Father,"[27] when conceived of by us with holy
insight in a manner befitting Deity, is an ascent of the mind
rather than of the body.

3. I think it necessary[29] to consider carefully these sayings in
connection with the words "Our Father which art in heaven,"[30]
in order to remove a mean conception of God held by those who
consider that he is locally "in heaven," and to prevent anyone
from saying that God is in a place after the manner of a body
(from which it follows that he is a body)—a tenet which leads
to most impious opinions, namely, to suppose that he is divisible, material, corruptible. For every body is divisible, material,
corruptible. Else, let them tell us that instead of indulging in
vain imaginings they claim to conceive clearly how its nature
can be other than material. Since, however, before the bodily
sojourn of Christ many of the Scriptures[31] seem to say that God
was in a place after a bodily manner, it does not appear to me
to be inappropriate to quote a few passages from them also, in
order to take away all doubtfulness[32] from those whose peculiarity it is, so far as they can, to confine God who is over all in a
small and limited space. And, first, in Genesis, Adam and Eve,
he says, "heard the voice of the Lord God walking in the after-
noon in the garden: and Adam and his wife hid themselves from
the face of the Lord God in the midst of the trees of the garden."[33]
We shall ask those who are unwilling to enter into the treasures
of the passage, and indeed do not even make a beginning by
"knocking at" their "door,"[34] if they can maintain that the Lord
God who "filleth heaven and earth,"[35] who (as they suppose)
uses in bodily fashion "heaven" as his "throne" and "the earth"
as "the footstool of his feet,"[36] is bounded by a place so small in

23 Col. 1:19; 2:9.   24 Phil. 2:7.   25 Col. 2:10.
26 John 16:5.   27 John 14:12, 28.   28 John 20:17.
29 The text lacks this word.   30 Matt. 6:9.
31 Lit. "writings."   32 περισπάσμον, "distraction."   33 Gen. 3:8.
34 Luke 13:25.   35 Jer. 23:24.   36 Matt. 5:34, 35.

comparison with the whole heaven and earth, that what they suppose is a bodily garden is not completely filled by God, but is so much larger than he, that it contains him as he "walks, a sound" being heard from the treading of his feet.[37] And it is still more absurd, according to them, that Adam and Eve, in awe of God because of their transgression, should hide themselves "from the presence of the Lord God in the midst of the trees of the garden."[37] For it is not even said that they so wished to hide themselves, but that in very truth "they were hidden." And how, according to them, can God ask Adam, saying, "Where art thou?"[38]

4. We have treated these matters at length in our commentaries on Genesis. However, so that we may not now pass over in complete silence so important a problem, it will be sufficient to call to mind the saying of God in Deuteronomy[39]: "I will dwell in them, and walk in them."[40] His "walking" in the saints is of the same kind as his "walking" in the garden, every sinner hiding himself from the presence of God[41] and avoiding his visitation and shunning open speech with him. So also "Cain went out from the presence of God, and dwelt in the land of Nod, on the east of Eden."[42] As, therefore, he dwells in the saints, so also in heaven, whether in every saint "bearing the image of the heavenly,"[43] or in Christ, in whom are all the "lights"[44] and "stars"[45] of heaven "who are being saved,"[46] or else he dwells there because of the saints in heaven, in accordance with[47] the saying: "Unto thee did I lift up mine eyes, who dwellest in the heaven."[48] And the passage in Ecclesiastes, "Be not hasty to utter any thing before God: for God is in heaven above, and thou upon earth below,"[49] makes a deliberate distinction between those who are still in "the body of humiliation,"[50] on the one hand, and the angels and holy powers who are uplifted by the aid of the Word,[51] or Christ himself, on the other. For it is not inappropriate that he is properly the "throne" of the Father, allegorically called heaven, while his Church, given the name of "earth," is "the footstool of his feet."[52]

---

[37] Gen. 3:8. [38] Gen. 3:9. [39] See note.
[40] II Cor. 6:16: cf. Lev. 26:12; Deut. 23:14.
[41] Text emended: cf. Gen. 3:8. [42] Gen. 4:16.
[43] I Cor. 15:49. [44] Phil. 2:15.
[45] Dan. 12:3; Rev. 1:20. [46] Acts 2:47; I Cor. 1:18; II Cor. 2:15.
[47] Text emended. [48] Ps. 123:1. [49] Eccl. 5:2.
[50] Phil. 3:21. [51] Adopting an emendation of Koetschau.
[52] Matt. 5:34, 35.

5. So we have added from the Old Testament also a few sayings which are considered to show that God is in a place, in order that we may persuade the reader by every means "according to the power" given unto "us"[53] to understand the divine Scripture in a loftier and more spiritual sense, whenever it seems to teach that God is in a place. And it was fitting to examine these passages in connection with the words: "Our Father which art in heaven"[54]—words which separate the essence of God from all created things. For to those who do not partake [of his essence] there appertains a certain divine glory and power, and—so to speak—an effluence of his deity.[55]

HALLOWED BE THY NAME

(Chapter XXIV)

XXIV, 1. "Hallowed be thy name."[56] He who prays these words either shows that the object of his prayer has not been achieved, or else having attained it he asks that a result not permanent should be maintained.[57] This is evident enough from the passage here, in which according to Matthew and Luke we are commanded to say, "Hallowed be thy name,"[56] as if the name of the Father were not yet hallowed. How, someone might say, can a man ask that the name of God be hallowed, as if it had not been hallowed? What is "the name" of the Father, and what is its hallowing? Let us consider these questions.

2. A "name," then, is a compendious appellation manifesting the individual quality of the being named. For example, Paul the apostle has a certain individual quality: a quality of soul, which makes it of a certain kind; a quality of mind, which makes him capable of contemplating certain kinds of things; a quality of body, which makes it of a certain kind. The individuality of these qualities, which is incommunicable to another (for no being is exactly similar to Paul), is indicated by the name "Paul." But in the case of men, since their individual qualities, as it were, alter, their names also according to Scripture alter suitably; when the quality of Abram changed, he was called Abraham[58]; and when Simon's, he was named Peter[59]; and when Saul's, the persecutor of Jesus, he was called Paul.[60] In the case of God, however, who is in himself unchangeable, and

---

[53] Eph. 3:20.   [54] Matt. 6:9.   [55] Cf. Wisdom of Solomon 7:25.
[56] Matt. 6:9; Luke 11:2.
[57] The text of this passage is uncertain, see note.
[58] Gen. 17:5.   [59] John 1:42; cf. Mark 3:16.   [60] Acts 9:4, 5; 13:9.

remaining always unalterable, there is always one name, by which, as it were, he is called, the "I am" spoken of in Exodus,[61] or something of similar import. Since, then, we all have some conception of God, and form some notions of whatever kind about him, but not all conceive what he is (for these are few, and, if I may say so, fewer than these few are those who comprehend his holiness in all things), we are rightly taught that the idea within us of God is holy, in order that we may see the holiness of him as he creates, foresees, judges, chooses, forsakes, receives, turns away from, deems worthy of honour, punishes each one according to his deserts.

3. In these and in similar expressions, if I may say so, the individual quality of God is characterized—what in my opinion is called the "name of God" in the Scriptures: in Exodus, "Thou shalt not take the name of the Lord thy God in vain"[62]; in Deuteronomy, "Let my speech be waited for as the shower; let my words descend as the dew, as the rain upon the young grass and as the copious rain upon the herb[63]: for I called upon the name of the Lord"[64]; in Psalms, "They shall remember thy name in all generations."[65] He who connects the idea of God with things that are not fitting "takes the name of the Lord God in vain," and he who is able to utter speech as the rain, which works together with them that hear for the fruitfulness of their souls, addressing words full of encouragement like dew, and by the power of edification bringing upon the hearers a most profitable shower of words or a most effectual and copious rain, can do these things because of the "name." Therefore,[66] when a man perceives his need of God the perfecter, he calls by himself upon him who is truly the supplier of the above-mentioned blessings; and everyone who clearly sees also the things of God remembers rather than learns them, even though he may seem to hear them from some one or may think that he discovers the mysteries of godliness.

4. Even as he who prays ought to note what has been said here and ask that "the name" of God "be hallowed," so also it is said in Psalms, "Let us exalt his name together,"[67] the prophet[68] commanding us in full accord with the same mind and the same opinion to haste unto the true and lofty knowledge of the distinctive being of God. For this is to "exalt the name"

---

[61] Ex. 3:14.   [62] Ex. 20:7.   [63] See note.
[64] Deut. 32:2, 3.   [65] Ps. 45:17.   [66] See note.
[67] Ps. 34:3.
[68] So Koetschau emends: cf. Acts 2:30, and also IX, 2, above.

of God "together," when a man partaking of an effluence of
deity "exalts"[69] that very power of God of which he has partaken
inasmuch as he has been raised up by God and has conquered
his foes, who are unable to exult over his fall. This is indicated
in the twenty-ninth psalm by the words: "I will exalt thee, O
Lord, because thou didst raise me up, and not make my foes
to rejoice over me."[70] And a man "exalts" God when he has
dedicated for him a house within himself, as the title of the
psalm has it: "A Psalm: A Song at the Dedication of the
House"; A Psalm of "David."[71]

5. Further, with regard to "Hallowed be thy name" and the
words in the imperative mood that follow, it is to be said that
the translators also frequently use the imperative instead of the
optative mood, as for example in the Psalms: "Let the deceitful
lips be dumb, which speak iniquity against the righteous
man,"[72] instead of "may they be"; and "Let the extortioner
seek out all that he hath, Let him have no helper,"[73] in the one
hundred and eighth, concerning Judas. For the whole psalm is
a request concerning Judas, that this and that may happen to
him. But Tatian, failing to understand that "let there be" does
not always indicate the optative, but sometimes the imperative, formed a most impious conception concerning him
who said, "Let there be light,"[74] even God, as if he were praying
rather than commanding that there should be light: "since,"
as he expresses his godless thought, "God was in darkness." To
him we must say, how will he take the words: "Let the earth
bring forth grass for pasture,"[75] and "Let the water under the
heaven be gathered together,"[76] and "Let the waters bring
forth creeping things, creatures that have life,"[77] and "Let the
earth bring forth a living creature"[78]? Does God really pray
that "the water under the heaven" should "be gathered together
into one meeting place" in order that he may stand upon a firm
foundation? Or, does he pray "Let the earth bring forth" in
order that he may partake of the things that are brought forth
from the earth? What need has he similar to the need for light
on the part of creatures in the water and winged creatures or
creatures on dry land, that he should also pray concerning these?
But if, according to this author, it would be absurd to pray concerning these—the language used being in the imperative—may

69 Ps. 34:3.   70 Ps. 30:1.   71 Ps. 30 (title).
72 Ps. 31:18.   73 Ps. 109:11, 12.   74 Gen. 1:3.
75 Gen. 1:11.   76 Gen. 1:9.   77 Gen. 1:20.
78 Gen. 1:24.

not a like thing be said about the saying "Let there be light,"[79] since it is not in the optative but in the imperative? I have thought it necessary, since the prayer is expressed in the imperative, to call to mind his various interpretations for the sake of those who have been deceived into accepting his impious teaching. Once upon a time we ourselves came in contact with these persons.

THY KINGDOM COME

(Chapter XXV)

XXV, 1. "Thy kingdom come."[80] If "the kingdom of God," according to the word of our Lord and Saviour, "cometh not with observation: neither shall they say, Lo, here! or, Lo, there!" but "the kingdom of God is within us"[81] ("for the word is very nigh, in" our "mouth, and in" our "heart"[82]), it is evident that he who prays that "the kingdom" of God should come prays with good reason that the kingdom of God should spring up and bear fruit and be perfected in him. For every saint who takes God as his king and obeys the spiritual laws of God dwells in himself as in a well-ordered city, so to speak. Present with him are the Father and Christ who reigns with the Father in the soul that has been perfected, in accordance with the saying which I mentioned a short time ago: "we will come unto him, and make our abode with him."[83] (And I think that by God's kingdom is meant the blessed state of the reason and the ordered condition of wise thoughts; while by Christ's kingdom is meant the words that go forth for the salvation of those who hear them and the works of righteousness and the other virtues which are being accomplished: for the Son of God is "Word"[84] and "righteousness."[85]) But every sinner is under the tyranny of "the prince of this world,"[86] since he does not hand himself over to him "who gave himself for" us sinners, "that he might deliver us out of this present evil world," and "deliver us out of" it "according to the will of our God and Father,"[87] as is stated in the [Epistle] to the Galatians. He who is under the tyranny of "the prince of this world"[88] through deliberate sin is also ruled over by sin: therefore we are bidden by Paul no longer to submit ourselves to "sin" which desires to "reign" over us; and

---

79 Gen. 1:3.

81 Luke 17:20, 21.

83 John 14:23.

85 I Cor. 1:30.

87 Gal. 1:4.

80 Matt. 6:10; Luke 11:2.

82 Deut. 30:14; cf. Rom. 10:8.

84 Cf. John 1:1, 14.

86 Ignatius, *Ephesians*, 19.

88 Ignatius, *Ephesians*, 19.

indeed we are commanded in these words: "Let not sin therefore reign in our mortal body, that we should obey the lusts
thereof."[89]

2. But some one will say with regard to these two petitions,
that is to say, "Hallowed be thy name" and "Thy kingdom
come,"[90] that if he who prays prays in order to be heard, and is
in fact at some time heard, it is evident that, in accordance with
what has been said above, "the name" of God will "be hallowed" at some time for some one, for whom also "the kingdom"
of God will be present. But if these things come about for him,
how shall he still fittingly pray concerning things that are present already as if they were not present, saying, "Hallowed be
thy name; Thy kingdom come"? The reply to this must be as
follows. He who prays to obtain "the word of knowledge" and
"the word of wisdom"[91] will always fittingly pray for these
things, for he will always go on receiving more and more
intuitions of "wisdom" and "knowledge" as his prayers are
continually heard, howbeit he will "know in part" as much as
he is able to receive in this present life; but "that which is perfect, doing away that which is in part, shall then be made manifest when, "face to face,"[92] the mind without sense perception
comes in contact with spiritual realities. Similarly, "that which
is perfect" in the "hallowing" of the "name" of God for each
of us and in the coming of his "kingdom" cannot be, unless
there "come" also "that which is perfect"[93] as concerning
"knowledge" and "wisdom,"[94] and, it may be, the other virtues
also. And we go on our journey "unto perfection,"[95] if "stretching forward to the things which are before" we "forget the
things which are behind."[96] As we advance unceasingly "the
kingdom of God" that is in us[97] will reach its highest point, when
that which was spoken by the apostle is fulfilled, that Christ,
when all enemies "have been subjected unto him," shall
"deliver up the kingdom to God, even the Father, that God
may be all in all."[98] Therefore, "praying without ceasing,"[99]
with a disposition of the mind that is being deified by the Word,
let us say to "our Father which is in heaven, Hallowed be thy
name; Thy kingdom come."[1]

3. Moreover, concerning "the kingdom" of God this distinc-

---

89 Rom. 6:12.
92 I Cor. 13:9, 10, 12,
95 Heb. 6:1.
97 Cf. Luke 17:21.
99 I Thess. 5:17.

90 Matt. 6:9; Luke 11:2.
93 I Cor. 13:10.
96 Phil. 3:13.
98 I Cor. 15:23–25, 28.
1 Matt. 6:9, 10.

91 I Cor. 12:8.
94 I Cor. 12:8.

tion must also be made, that, as there is no "fellowship" between "righteousness and iniquity," and no "communion"
between "light and darkness," nor any "concord" between
"Christ and Beliar,"[2] so the kingdom of God cannot co-exist
with the kingdom of evil. If therefore it is our will to be under
the reign of God, "let not sin" in any wise "reign in" our
"mortal body,"[3] neither let us obey its commandments, when
it urges our soul to do "the works of the flesh"[4] and things that
are alien from God. Rather, "mortifying the members which
are upon the earth,"[5] let us bring forth "the fruits of the
Spirit,"[6] so that the "Lord" may "walk in"[7] us as in a spiritual
"garden,"[8] reigning alone over us with his Christ, "sitting" in
us "at the right hand of" that spiritual "power"[9] which we pray
to receive, and seated "until" all his "enemies" within us become "the footstool of" his "feet,"[10] and "all rule and authority
and power" is "abolished"[11] from us. For it is possible that these
things should come to pass for each of us, and that the "last
enemy" should be "abolished, even death,"[12] so that in our
case also it may be said by Christ, "O death, where is thy sting?
O Hades, where is thy victory?"[13] Even now therefore let our
"corruptible put on" sanctification in holiness and all purity and
"incorruption, and" let "the mortal"[14] clothe itself, when
"death" has been "abolished,"[12] with the Father's "immortality,"[14] so that we may be reigned over by God and even
now share in the good things of "regeneration"[15] and
resurrection.

THY WILL BE DONE, AS IN HEAVEN, SO ON EARTH

(Chapter XXVI)

XXVI, 1. "Thy will be done, as in heaven, so on earth."[16]
Luke passes over these words in silence, and after "Thy kingdom
come" places "Give us day by day our daily bread."[17] Therefore let us examine the words cited above, as found in Matthew
alone, agreeably with preceding context. Let us who pray,
being still "on earth," and understanding that "the will" of
God is "done in heaven" by all those who dwell[18] in heaven,
pray that "the will" of God may be "done" in all things by us

2 II Cor. 6:14, 15.   3 Rom. 6:12.   4 Gal. 5:19.
5 Col. 3:5.   6 Gal. 5:22.   7 II Cor. 6:16.
8 Cf. Gen. 3:8.   9 Cf. Matt. 26:64; Mark 14:62; Luke 22:69.
10 Ps. 110:1.   11 I Cor. 15:24.   12 I Cor. 15:26.
13 I Cor. 15:55.   14 I Cor. 15:53.   15 Cf. Matt. 19:28.
16 Matt. 6:10.   17 Luke 11:2, 3.   18 τοῖς οἰκείοις.

also "on earth" even as it is by them: which things will come to pass if we do nothing contrary to his "will." But whenever "the will" of God is accomplished by us who are "on earth as it" in fact is "in heaven," we are made like unto those in heaven, inasmuch as we "bear" as they do "the image of the heavenly,"[19] and shall "inherit the kingdom" of heaven,[20] while those who come after us "on earth" will pray to be made like unto us who are "in heaven."

2. But the words "as in heaven, so on earth," to be found in Matthew alone, can be taken with all three clauses, with the result that we are commanded thus to say in the prayer: "Hallowed be thy name, as in heaven, so on earth; Thy kingdom come, as in heaven, so on earth; Thy will be done, as in heaven, so on earth." For "the name" of God has been "hallowed" by those "in heaven," and "the kingdom" of God has come for them, and "the will" of God has been "done" in them: all these things are lacking to us who are "on earth," yet they can become ours as we make ourselves worthy to gain the hearing of God concerning them all.

3. But, with reference to "Thy will be done, as in heaven, so on earth," some one may ask as follows: How has "the will" of God been "done in heaven," where there are "the spiritual hosts of wickedness,"[21] whence it comes to pass that "the sword" of God shall be "filled with blood" even "in heaven"[22]? If we pray that "the will" of God be "done on earth as" it is done "in heaven," perhaps we may without knowing it pray that these opposing forces may remain "on earth," to which they came from "heaven"; for there are many evil things "on earth" because of "the" victorious "spiritual hosts of wickedness"[21] which are "in the heavenly places." Anyone, however, will easily resolve the question by allegorizing "heaven," and saying that it is Christ, and that the Church is "earth" (for who is so worthy to be "the throne of God" as Christ? and what is "the footstool of his feet"[23] equally with the Church?); and that every member of the Church ought to pray that he may so achieve[24] "the" Father's "will" as Christ achieved[24] it, who came to "do the will"[25] of his Father and "accomplished"[25a] it in its entirety. For it is possible by being "joined unto" him to become "one spirit"[26] with him, in this way achieving[24] "the will," in order that "as" it has been accomplished "in heaven," so it may also

---

[19] I Cor. 15:49.
[22] Isa. 34:5.
[25] John 4:34.
[20] Cf. Matt. 25:34.
[23] Matt. 5:34, 35.
[25a] Cf. John 17:4.
[21] Eph. 6:12.
[24] See note.
[26] I Cor. 6:17.

be accomplished "on earth." For, according to Paul, "he that is joined unto the Lord is one spirit."[26] And I think that this interpretation will not be lightly dismissed by anyone who pays careful attention to it.

4. But an objector to it will quote the saying of the Lord after the resurrection to "the eleven disciples," to be found at the close of this Gospel: "All authority hath been given to me as in heaven so also on earth."[27] For having "authority" over the things "in heaven," he says that there has been added authority "on earth," the things in heaven having been formerly enlightened by the Word, but at "the end of the world"[28] the things "on earth" also will imitate the perfect state of the things "in heaven" over which the Saviour received "authority." Therefore, as it were, by means of prayer he wishes to take as his fellow workers before the Father those who are being "made disciples" by him, in order that he may bring the things "on earth" (in like manner as the things "in heaven" which have been subjected to truth and the Word), when they are emended by the "authority," which he received "as in heaven so" also "on earth," to the blessed end that awaits whatsoever has been placed under his authority. But he who maintains that the Saviour is "heaven" and the Church "earth," alleging that "the firstborn of all creation,"[29] on whom the Father rests as on a throne, is "heaven," would find that the "man" whom he put on, when he had fitted him for that power by having "humbled himself" and "becoming obedient unto death,"[30] said after the resurrection, "All authority hath been given unto me as in heaven so also on earth,"[31] the "man" as Saviour having received "authority" over the things "in heaven," as things that appertain to "the only begotten,"[32] in order that he may share them with him, being mingled with his deity and united with him.

5. It still remains to resolve the second difficulty put forward, namely, how "the will" of God is "in heaven," when there are "the spiritual hosts of wickedness in the heavenly places"[33] wrestling against those "on earth." The question may be resolved in this way. It is not because of place but of choice that he who is still "on earth" has his "citizenship in heaven,"[34] "lays up treasure in heaven,"[35] has his heart "in heaven, bears the image of the heavenly,"[36] and "is" no longer "of the

---

27 Matt. 28:16, 18.   28 Matt. 28:20.   29 Col. 1:15.   30 Phil. 2:8.
31 Matt. 28:18.   32 John 1:14, etc.   33 Eph. 6:12.   34 Phil. 3:20.
35 Matt. 6:20; cf. Luke 12:33.   36 I Cor. 15:49.

earth"[37] nor "of the world"[38] below, but of heaven and of the heavenly world that is "better"[39] than this one. Similarly, "the spiritual hosts of wickedness" that still reside "in the heavenly places,"[39a] having their "citizenship[39b] on earth," and, by the evil designs wherewith they wrestle against men, "laying up treasure on earth,"[40] "bearing the image of the earthy,"[40a] such as he who "was first formed by the Lord, having been made for the angels to play with,"[41] are not heavenly, nor do they dwell "in heaven" because of their evil disposition. When, therefore, it is said, "Thy will be done, as in heaven, so on earth,"[42] it is not to be reckoned that they are "in heaven," since they have fallen in mind with him who "fell from heaven" after the manner of "lightning."[43]

6. And perhaps when our Saviour says that we ought to pray that "the will" of the Father be "done, as in heaven," so in like manner "on earth," he is not in any way bidding prayers to be made for those who are in a place "on earth," in order that they are to be made like unto those who are in a heavenly place; but his command to pray arises from his desire that all the things "on earth," that is to say, inferior things, suited to those of the earth, should be made like unto better things, that have their "citizenship in heaven,"[44] that is, to all things that have become "heaven." For he who sins, wheresoever he may be, is "earth,"[45] and, unless he repent, will be returning somehow to his kindred [earth].[46] But "he that doeth the will of God[47] and does not disobey the saving spiritual laws is "heaven." If, therefore, we are still "earth" because of sin, let us pray that the "will" of God may extend to us also for our correction, in like manner as it reached those before us who became "heaven" or were "heaven." And if we are reckoned by God not as "earth" but as already "heaven," let us make our request that the "will" of God may be fulfilled "on earth" (I mean, persons of bad character) in like manner as it is "in heaven," for the heaven-making (if I may use the expression) of earth, so that there may no longer be any "earth," but all things may become "heaven." For if, according to this interpretation, the "will" of God is so "done on earth as in heaven," the earth will not remain earth. To take a clearer example. If the "will" of God were to be

---

[37] John 3:31.   [38] John 15:19.   [39] Cf. Heb. 11:16.
[39a] Eph. 6:2.   [39b] Phil. 3:20.   [40] Matt. 6:19.
[40a] I Cor. 15:49.   [41] Job 40:19 (LXX).   [42] Matt. 6:10.
[43] Luke 10:18.   [44] Phil. 3:20.
[45] Adopting a conjecture of Bentley.   [46] Cf. Gen. 3:19.   [47] I John 2:17.

"done" for the licentious as it had been "done" for the temperate, the licentious will be temperate; or, if the "will" of God were so to be "done" for the unjust as it had been "done" for the just, the unjust will be just. Therefore, if the "will" of God is "done on earth as in heaven," we shall all be "heaven": for "the flesh," which does "not profit,"[48] "and blood," which is akin to it, "cannot inherit the kingdom of God,"[49] but they would be said to inherit it, were they to change from flesh and earth and dust[50] and blood to the heavenly substance.

GIVE US THIS DAY OUR DAILY BREAD
(Chapter XXVII)

XXVII, 1. "Give us this day our daily bread,"[51] or, as Luke has it, "Give us day by day our daily bread."[52] Since some suppose that we are told to pray concerning material[53] bread, it is right to refute here their false opinion and to establish the truth concerning "the daily bread." We must therefore say this to them. How can he, who tells us that we ought to ask for "heavenly things" and "great things,"[54] forget as it were in their case his own teaching and command them to address to the Father an intercession concerning an "earthly" and "small thing," seeing that the bread that is distributed for our flesh is not "heavenly" neither is it a "great" request to pray concerning it?

2. But we, following him as Teacher, will quote at some length the teaching he gives us concerning bread. He says in the Gospel according to John to them who had "come to Capernaum" to "seek" him[55]: "Verily, verily, I say unto you, Ye seek me, not because ye saw signs, but because ye ate of the loaves, and were filled."[56] For he who "eats of the loaves" that were blessed by Jesus, and is filled with them, "seeks" rather to comprehend more perfectly[57] the Son of God, and hastens unto him. Therefore, well does he command them, saying: "Work not for the meat which perisheth, but for the meat which abideth unto eternal life, which the Son of man shall give unto you."[58] Whereupon, when those who heard him inquired, saying, "What must we do, that we may work the works of God? Jesus answered and said unto them, This is the work of God,

---

48 John 6:63. 49 I Cor. 15:50. 50 Cf. Gen. 2:7.
51 Matt. 6:11. 52 Luke 11:3. 53 Lit. "bodily."
54 See II, 2. 55 John 6:24. 56 John 6:26.
57 Lit. "exactly," "accurately." 58 John 6:27.

that ye believe on him whom he hath sent."[59] Now, "God sent his word, and healed them"[60] (as it is written in Psalms), that is to say, those who had been sick: they who believe on that Word "work the works of God," which are "meat abiding unto eternal life."[61] And "my Father," says he, "giveth you the true bread out of heaven. For the bread of God is that which cometh down out of heaven, and giveth life unto the world."[62] Now, "true bread" is that which nourishes "the" true "man," who has been "made in the image of God,"[63] and he who is nourished with it also becomes "after the likeness"[64] of the Creator. But what is more nourishing to the soul than the Word, and what is more precious to the mind of him who makes room for it than the Wisdom of God? And what is more appropriate to the rational soul than truth?

3. But if anyone offer an objection to this and say that he would not have taught us to ask for "the daily bread" as if for some other bread, let such a one observe[65] that in the Gospel according to John also he speaks in one place of it as some other than he, and in another place that he himself is the bread; of some other, as follows: "Moses gave you the bread out of heaven, not the true" bread, "but my Father giveth you the true bread out of heaven"[66]; of himself, he says to those who "said" to him, "Evermore give us this bread, I am the bread of life, he that cometh to me shall not hunger, and he that believeth on me shall never thirst."[67] And a little further on: "I am the living bread which came down out of heaven: if any man eat of this bread, he shall live for ever: yea and the bread which I will give is my flesh, which I will give for the life of the world."[68]

4. Since every kind of food is called "bread" in Scripture (as is evident from what is written concerning Moses: "He did not eat bread forty days and did not drink water"[69]), the Word which nourishes is varied and diverse, for not all are able to be nourished by the solidity and vigorous force of the divine teachings. Therefore, desiring to command a disciplined[70] diet adapted to those who are more perfect, he says, "The bread which I will give is my flesh, which I will give for the life of the world."[71] And a little further on: "Except ye eat the flesh of the

---

59 John 6:28, 29.   60 Ps. 107:20.   61 John 6:28, 27.
62 John 6:32, 33.   63 Gen. 1:26, 27; cf. Col. 3:9, 10.
64 Gen. 1:26.   65 Lit. "hear."
66 John 6:32.   67 John 6:34, 35.   68 John 6:51.
69 Deut. 9:9.   70 Lit. "athletic."   71 John 6:51.

Son of man and drink his blood, ye have not life in yourselves. He that eateth my flesh and drinketh my blood hath eternal life; and I will raise him up at the last day. For my flesh is meat indeed, and my blood is drink indeed. He that eateth my flesh and drinketh my blood abideth in me, and I in him. As the living Father sent me, and I live because of the Father; so he that eateth me, he also shall live because of me."[72] This is the "true meat, the flesh" of Christ, which being the "Word" hath "become flesh," as it is said, "the Word became flesh."[73] When we [ate and[74]] drank him, "he also dwelt among us." But whenever he is "distributed,"[74a] then is fulfilled: "we beheld his glory."[73] "This is the bread which came down out of heaven: not as the fathers did eat, and died: he that eateth this bread shall live for ever."[75]

5. Paul, speaking to the Corinthians as to "babes" and "walking after the manner of men," says, "I fed you with milk, not with meat; for ye were not able" to bear it: "nay, not even now are ye able; for ye are yet carnal"[76]; and in the [Epistle] to the Hebrews: "And ye are become such as have need of milk, not of solid food. For everyone that partaketh of milk is without experience of the word of righteousness; for he is a babe. But solid food is for full-grown men, even those who by reason of use have their senses exercised to discern good and evil."[77] And I think that the words "One man hath faith to eat all things: but he that is weak eateth herbs"[78] were not said by him principally concerning bodily nourishment, but concerning the words of God that nourish the soul: the most believing and perfect man being able to partake of all things (whom he indicates in the words "one man hath faith to eat all things"), the weaker and less perfect being content with simpler teachings which do not produce in him full vigour (and this person he means to point out when he says "but he that is weak eateth herbs").

6. And I think that the saying of Solomon in Proverbs teaches us that he who cannot receive the stronger and more important points of doctrine because of his simplicity (but not, however, holding erroneous opinions), is to be preferred to him who though more skilful and quick-sighted and giving greater thought to things, yet fails to see clearly what concerns the peace and harmony of the whole. His saying is as follows:

[72] John 6:53–57. [73] John 1:14.
[74] Supplied in the text by Koetschau. [74a] John 6:11.
[75] John 6:58. [76] I Cor. 3:1–3. [77] Heb. 5:12–14.
[78] Rom. 14:2.

"Better a dinner of herbs where friendship and grace are than a stalled ox and hatred therewith."[79] Certainly, we have often accepted a private and simpler entertainment served with a good conscience, when we were the guests of those who could not offer us more, preferably to high-flown words "exalted against the knowledge of God,"[80] which with much persuasiveness proclaim a doctrine foreign to the Father of our Lord Jesus who has given "the law" and "the prophets."[81] Therefore, in order that we may not be sick of soul through lack of nourishment, nor "die to"[82] God because of "a famine" of "the word of the Lord,"[83] let us ask from the Father "the living bread,"[84] which is the same as "the daily"[85] [bread], obeying our Saviour as teacher, putting our faith in him, and living more wisely.[86]

The word ἐπιούσιος

7. We must now consider what is the meaning of "daily" (*epiousion*). And first, it ought to be known that this word *epiousios* is not employed by any of the Greeks or learned writers, nor is it in common use among ordinary folk; but it seems likely to have been coined by the evangelists. At any rate, Matthew and Luke are agreed about it, both using it with no difference. The translators of the Hebrew [Scriptures] have done the same kind of thing in other cases. For example, what Greek ever used the words *enotizou*[87] or *akoutieis*[88] instead of "receive into the ears" or "shall make to hear" respectively? There is a word similar to *epiousion*, in the writings of Moses, spoken by God: "And ye shall be unto me a peculiar [*periousios*] people."[90] And it seems to me that each of the two words is derived from *ousia*, the one meaning the bread that comes together into substance, the other indicating the people dwelling around substance and partaking of it.

8. The word "substance" (*ousia*) in its proper sense is commonly used of incorporeal things by those who maintain that the reality of incorporeal things is primary, such things having stable existence, not admitting of addition nor suffering diminution. (For this is the characteristic of bodies that they are susceptible of increase and wasting because they are in a state of flux and need a sustaining force to come upon them and nourish them: if at a given time they receive more than they lose,

---

79 Prov. 15:17. 80 II Cor. 10:5. 81 Matt. 5:17. 82 Rom. 14:8.
83 Amos 8:11. 84 John 6:51. 85 Matt. 6:11; Luke 11:3.
86 δεξιώτερον. 87 Cf. Job 33:1, 31; 34:16; 37:14; Isa. 1:2.
88 Ps. 50:10 (LXX): see note. 90 Ex. 19:6, 5.

there is an increase; but, if less, a decrease. Sometimes it may happen that because nothing at all comes upon them they are in a state of absolute decrease, so to speak.) But those who hold that the reality of incorporeal things is secondary and that of corporeal things is primary, define substance as follows. Substance is the prime matter of existents, and the source of existents; the matter of bodies, and the source of bodies; of things named, and the source of things named; or it is the first substrate, without quality, or the antecedent of existents; or that which receives all changes or alterations but is itself subject to no alteration according to the proper notion of the term; or else that which persists through all alteration or change. For such people substance is without quality or characteristic form according to the proper notion of the term, and has no determined size, but as a suitable place, so to speak, is inherent in every quality. They formally define as qualities energies and actions in which it has happened that there are movements and stationary conditions; they say that substance according to the proper notion of the term does not partake of any of these, but that it is always inseparable from some one of them, and is none the less affected by and receptive of every expression of activity, according as that acts or changes. For the tension that accompanies substance and permeates it in every part is the cause of every quality and of whatever adaptations of it there may be. They say that substance is in every part subject to change and divisible, and that any substance may be compounded with any other, and still form a unity.

9. Since in our discussion of the word "substance" (*ousia*), necessary because of the terms "daily (*epiousios*) bread" and "peculiar (*periousios*) people," we have shown that the different meanings of *ousia* are to be distinguished, and since in the preceding discussion we saw that the "bread" for which we are to ask is "spiritual", we must needs form a conception of the *ousia* which is akin to that of the "bread." The bodily bread which is distributed for the body of him who is nourished thereby passes into his "substance." Similarly, "the living bread" which has "come down out of heaven,"[91] being distributed for the mind and the soul, imparts a share of its peculiar power to him who has willingly accepted the nourishment that comes from it: and thus the bread which we ask for will be *epiousios*. And again, according to the quality of the food, whether it be "solid" and adapted to athletes, or of a milky or herbal kind, he who is

[91] John 6:51.

nourished acquires different forces, so also it follows that, when the word of God is given either as "milk" suitably for "babes," or as "herbs" suitably for them that are "weak,"[92] or as "flesh"[93] seasonably for those who are contesting, each of those who are nourished, in proportion as he has offered himself to the word, can accomplish this or that thing, or becomes such or such a person. There is, however, so-called food which is harmful, another kind which produces disease, and yet another which cannot be given at all: and all these may be transferred by analogy to the different kinds of so-called teachings regarded as nourishing. Therefore *epiousios* bread is that which is best adapted to the reasonable nature and akin to it in its very substance: it provides at once health and vigour and strength to the soul and imparts a share of its own immortality (for the word of God is immortal) to him who eats of it.

10. This *epiousios* bread seems to me to have been called in Scripture by another name, "the tree of life," to which he who "puts forth his hand, and takes" of it, "shall live for ever."[94] And by a third name this "tree" is called the wisdom of God by Solomon, in these words: "She is a tree of life to all them that lay hold upon her, and is safe for them that stay themselves as upon the Lord."[95] And since the angels also are nourished by the wisdom of God, and from the contemplation of truth and wisdom receive strength to carry out their special tasks, it is said in Psalms that the angels also are nourished, and that the men of God who are called Hebrews share this food with the angels, and so to speak feast together with them. Such a statement is "Man did eat angels' food."[96] Our mind is not so poverty-stricken as to think that the angels always partake of and are nourished by some such bodily food as we are told came down from heaven upon those who had gone forth out of Egypt,[97] or that this was the bread which the Hebrews partook of with the angels, who are the "ministering spirits"[98] of God.

11. As we discuss the *epiousios* bread and the tree of life and the wisdom of God and the food that men and angels had in common, it is not out of place to pay attention also to the "three men" of whom Genesis writes, who turned in and lodged with Abraham and partook of "three measures of fine flour kneaded" for the "making" of "cakes baked in the ashes."[99] Perhaps this is to be taken quite figuratively: for the saints are able to partake

92 Cf. Heb. 5:12–14; Rom. 14:2. 93 John 6:51.
94 Gen. 2:9; 3:22. 95 Prov. 3:18. 96 Ps. 78:25.
97 Ex. 16:12–16. 98 Heb. 1:14. 99 Gen. 18:2–6.

on occasion of spiritual and reasonable food not only in company with men but also with diviner powers, either for their own benefit or in order to display what great nourishment they are able to procure for themselves; and angels are glad and are nourished by such a display, and they become the more ready to co-operate in every way and in the sequel to conspire for further and greater understanding on the part of him who gladdens and, so to speak, nourishes them with the nutriment of teachings formerly prepared.[1] And it is not to be wondered at if a man feeds angels, for indeed even Christ acknowledges that he "stands at the door and knocks," so that he may "come in" to him who has "opened" it for him and "sup with him"[2] of the things that he has; afterwards he will share what is his own with him who has first entertained, according to his ability, the Son of God.

12. He who partakes of the *epiousios* "bread strengthens" his "heart"[3] and becomes a son of God; but he who participates in "the dragon" is none other than "the Ethiopian"[4] spiritually, himself changed into a serpent because of the toils of the dragon,[5] so that, even when he says he wishes "to be baptized,"[6] he hears the reproach of the Word against him, "Serpents,[7] offspring of vipers, who warned you to flee from the wrath to come?"[8] And David says this concerning the body of the dragon that was feasted upon by the Ethiopians: "Thou brakest the heads of the dragons upon the water: thou didst smite the head of the dragon in pieces[9]; thou gavest him to be meat to the peoples, the Ethiopians."[10] And if it is not incongruous, since the Son of God subsists substantially, and the adversary[11] also subsists, that either of them should be the food of this or that, why should we hesitate to admit, in the case of all powers greater or inferior and in the case of man, that every one of us can be nourished by them all? For example, when "Peter" was about to have fellowship with the "centurion Cornelius" and those who gathered together with him "in Caesarea," and afterwards to impart of the words of God "to the Gentiles also," he saw the "vessel let down by four corners from heaven, in which" were "all manner of fourfooted beasts and creeping things and beasts of the earth";

---

1 Text emended by Delarue.
3 Ps. 104:15; cf. James 5:8; I Thess. 3:13.
5 Cf. Rev. 12:9.
7 Matt. 23:33.
9 This clause is found in Codex ℵ (LXX).
11 Cf. Zech. 3:1.

2 Rev. 3:20.
4 Ps. 73:13, 14 (LXX).
6 Luke 3:7.
8 Matt. 3:7; Luke 3:7.
10 Ps. 73:13, 14 (LXX).

and when, having been bidden to "rise" and "kill and eat," he excused himself, saying, Thou knowest "that never hath anything common or unclean entered into my mouth," he was commanded "not to call any man common or unclean," in that what was "cleansed" by God ought "not" to be "made common" by Peter. For the saying is: "What God hath cleansed, make not thou common." Therefore the clean and unclean meats according to the law of Moses, distinguished under the names of several animals, and bearing an analogy to the different characters of creatures of reason, teach us that some are nourishing for us, while others are the opposite, until "God," having "cleansed"[12] them, makes them all nourishing, even those of "every kind."[13]

Today

13. This being so, and there being such a variety of meats, the one that surpasses all that have been named is the *epiousios* bread, concerning which we ought to pray that we may be deemed worthy of it, and by feeding on "God the Word" who was "in the beginning with God"[14] may be deified. But someone will say that *epiousios* is formed from *epienai*,[15] so that we are bidden to ask for the bread appropriate to the coming age, in order that God by anticipation may give us it now, with the result that what is to be given tomorrow, so to speak, should be given us "today," "today" signifying the present age, and "tomorrow" the coming age. But the former interpretation[16] being in my judgment the better, let us consider the meaning of the "today" as it is found in the passage in Matthew, or the "day by day" which is written in Luke. It is a frequent custom in the Scriptures to call the whole age "today," as for example in the words: "He is the father of the Moabites unto this day,"[17] and "He is the father of the Ammonites unto this day,"[18] and "This saying was spread abroad among the Jews until this day,"[19] and in the Psalms, "Today if ye shall hear his voice harden not your hearts."[20] And in Joshua there is a very clear instance of this manner of speech: "Depart not from the Lord this day."[21] And if all this age is "today," perhaps the past age is "yesterday." This usage occurs in my opinion in Psalms, and in Paul in the

12 Acts 10:1, 9, 11–15, 24, 34, 45; 11:8, 9.   13 Matt. 13:47.
14 John 1:1.   15 I.e., "to come close after."
16 I.e., deriving it from *ousia*.   17 Gen. 19:37.
18 Gen. 19:38.   19 Matt. 28:15.
20 Ps. 95:7, 8.   21 Cf. Josh. 22:16, 18.

Epistle to the Hebrews: in Psalms thus, "A thousand years in thy sight are but as yesterday, which is past"[22] (this is perhaps the famous period of a thousand years, which is likened to "yesterday" as distinct from "today"); and in the apostle it is written, "Jesus Christ is the same yesterday and today, yea and for ever."[23] And there is nothing wonderful in the fact that with God the whole age is reckoned as the space of one of our days: and in my view, as even less.

14. And we have to consider if the words written of feasts or solemn assemblies that take place according to "days" or "months" or "seasons" or "years"[24] are to be referred to ages. For if "the law" has "a shadow of the things to come,"[25] it must needs be that the many sabbaths are a "shadow" of so many days and that the new moons come round in intervals of time, being the result of the conjunction of some moon or other with a certain sun. Now if the "first month" and the "tenth" day "until the fourteenth" and the feast of unleavened bread from "the fourteenth until the one and twentieth"[26] contain "a shadow of things to come,"[25] "who is wise"[27] and so great "a friend" toward God[28] as to perceive the "first" of many months, and the "tenth day" of it, and so forth? What ought I to say of the feast of the "seven weeks"[29] and of "the seventh month"[30] (of which the new moon is a day "of trumpets," but "on the tenth, a day of atonement"[31]—things known to God alone who has laid down laws concerning them? And who has so entered into "the mind of Christ"[32] that he can understand the seven years of the freedom of the Hebrew servants and "the release" of debts and the relief from tillage of the Holy Land?[33] And there is also what is called the Jubile over and above the feast of seven years,[34] but what it is clearly or what are the true laws to be fulfilled in it no one can even so much as imagine, save he who has contemplated the Father's will concerning his ordinances in all the ages in accordance with "his unsearchable judgments and his ways past finding out."[35]

15. I have often found myself at a loss, when I bring together two conflicting apostolic sayings, how it is "the end of the ages" in which "once" Jesus "hath been manifested to put away sins,"

22 Ps. 90:4.   23 Heb. 13:8.   24 Cf. Gal. 4:10.
25 Heb. 10:1.   26 Ex. 12:2, 3, 6, 15, 18.   27 Hos. 14:9.
28 Cf. James 2:23.   29 Deut. 16:9.   30 Lev. 16:29 etc.
31 Lev. 23:24, 27.   32 Cf. I Cor. 2:16.
33 Cf. Ex. 21:2; Lev. 25:4-7, 10-17; Deut. 15:1-3.
34 Cf. Lev. 25:8 ff.; 27:17 ff.   35 Rom. 11:33.

if there are "ages to come" which shall be after this one. His sayings are as follows: in the Epistle to the Hebrews, But now "once at the end of the ages hath he been manifested to put away sins by the sacrifice of himself"[36]; and in the Epistle to the Ephesians, "That in the ages to come he might shew the exceeding riches of his grace in kindness towards us."[37] If I may offer a conjecture on so great a matter, I think that, as the last month is the end of the year, after which the beginning of another month ensues, so it may be that, since several ages complete as it were a year of ages, the present age is "the end," after which certain "ages to come" will ensue, of which the age to come is the beginning, and in those coming ages God will "shew the riches of his grace in kindness": when the greatest sinner, who has spoken ill of the Holy Spirit[38] and is under the power of sin throughout the present age, will, I know not how, be under treatment from beginning to end in the ensuing age that is to come.

16. He therefore who sees these things, and perceives in his mind a week of ages that he may contemplate a holy sabbath rest,[39] and a month of ages, that he may see the holy new moon of God, and a year of ages, that he may understand the feasts of the year, when "all the males" must appear before "the Lord God,"[40] and the years proportioned to so large a number of ages, that he may comprehend the holy seventh year, and the seven weeks of ages, that he may sing the praises of him who has laid down laws so great—such a one will go on to ask, how can he regard lightly the smallest portion of an hour of a day of so great an age, and shall he not rather do everything, in order that after his preparation here he may be found worthy to attain to the *epiousios* bread in the day that is called "today," and receive it also "day by day," it now being clear from the foregoing what the "day by day" is? He who prays "today" to God who is from infinite to infinite, not only concerning "today," but also in some sort concerning "day by day," will be able to receive from him who can bestow "exceeding abundantly above all that we ask or think,"[41] even—if I speak in hyperbole—what is beyond "things which eye saw not" and beyond "things which ear heard not" and beyond things which "entered not into the heart of man."[42]

17. It has seemed to me very necessary to discuss these ques-

[36] Heb. 9:26. [37] Eph. 2:7. [38] Cf. Matt. 12:31.
[39] Cf. Heb. 4:9. [40] Deut. 16:16. [41] Eph. 3:20.
[42] I Cor. 2:9.

tions, in order that a conception may be formed of "today" and "day by day," when we pray that the *epiousios* bread may be given us from his Father. Nevertheless, if we examine the "our" in the latter work[43] first, when it is said, not, "Give us this day our daily bread,"[44] but, "Give us day by day our daily bread,"[45] the question must be examined how this "bread" is "ours." Certainly the apostle teaches that "whether life, or death, or things present, or things to come, all"[46] are the saints'. Concerning which it is not necessary to speak at present.

FORGIVE US OUR DEBTS

(Chapter XXVIII)

XXVIII, 1. "And forgive us our debts, as we also have forgiven our debtors"[47]; or, as Luke, "And forgive us our sins; for we ourselves also have forgiven[48] every one that is indebted to us."[49] Concerning "debts" the apostle also says, "Render to all their debts, tribute to whom tribute is due; fear to whom fear; custom to whom custom; honour to whom honour; owe no man anything save to love one another."[50] We "owe" therefore, having certain duties not only in the matter of giving but also in gentle speech and in certain particular actions, and we also "owe" it to others to have a certain kind of disposition towards them. "Owing" these things we either repay them by fulfilling what is commanded by the divine law, or by despising the wholesome word and failing to repay we remain in "debt."

2. A similar thing must be observed in our "debts" to the brethren, that is to say, to those who have been born again with us in Christ according to the word of godliness and share with us fathers and mothers. There is also a "debt" to citizens, and another, common, "debt" to all men, particularly strangers and also those who have attained the age of fathers,[51] and still another to certain whom it is reasonable to honour as sons or as brethren. He therefore who omits to pay "debts" to the brethren remains a "debtor" in respect of what he has not done. And so, if even we fail in anything that is due from us to men as concerning the spirit of kindly wisdom, our "debt" becomes greater. Moreover, "we are debtors" in what we owe to ourselves in so using the body that we do not waste its strength

---

43 I.e., Luke.   44 Matt. 6:11.   45 Luke 11:3.
46 I Cor. 3:22.   47 Matt. 6:12.
48 So the text here: but see XVIII, 2.   49 Luke 11:4.
50 Rom. 13:7, 8.   51 Reading text as emended by Klostermann.

through love of pleasure; and we are debtors to observe this care also for the soul, and to show forethought for the acuteness of the mind, and for the word, that it may be without sting and helpful and in no way "idle."[52] In fact whenever we fail to pay what is owing to us by ourselves, our debt becomes heavier.

3. And above all, since we are the "workmanship"[53] and "thing formed"[54] of God that surpasses all else, "we owe" it to maintain a certain disposition towards him, and that love which is "with all the heart, and with all the strength, and with all the mind"[55]; which things if we do not rightly perform, we remain "debtors" to God, sinning towards the Lord. And who in that case will pray for us? For "if a man sinning sin against a man, they will even pray for him. But if he sin against the Lord, who will pray for him?"[56] as Eli says in the first [book] of the Kingdoms. Moreover, since Christ bought us "with his own blood,"[57] "we are debtors," even as every servant is the "debtor" of him who bought him for so much a sum of money as was given for him. We also incur a debt to "the Holy Spirit," which is paid when we do not "grieve" him, "in whom ye were sealed unto the day of redemption,"[58] and if we do not "grieve" him we bear the fruits which are demanded of us, since he is present with us and "quickeneth"[59] our soul. And even though we do not know precisely, who is "the angel" of each of us who "beholds the face of the Father in heaven,"[60] at any rate it is manifest to each one of us when he reflects upon it that we are "debtors" to him also for certain things. And moreover, if we are in "a theatre" of "the world and angels and men,"[61] we ought to know that, as he who is in "a theatre" is a debtor to say or do such and such things in the sight of the spectators, which if he fails to do he is punished for having insulted the whole "house," so also we "owe" to the whole "world, and to" all the "angels, and to" the race of "men" those things which, if we are willing, we shall learn from wisdom.

4. But apart from these more general considerations, there is a certain "debt" due from a widow for whom the Church provides, and another due from a deacon, and another from a presbyter, but the "debt" due from a bishop is the heaviest, since it is demanded of him by the Saviour of the whole Church,

---

52 Matt. 12:36.   53 Eph. 2:10.   54 Rom. 9:20.
55 Cf. Mark 12:30.   56 I Sam. 2:25.
57 Cf. Acts 20:28; Rev. 5:9; I Peter 1:18, 19.   58 Eph. 4:30.
59 John 6:63; cf. II Cor. 3:6.   60 Matt. 18:10.
61 I Cor. 4:9.

and retribution follows if it be not paid. Also, the apostle speaks of a certain "debt" common to husband and wife, saying, "Let the husband render unto the wife her debt: and likewise the wife unto the husband."[62] And he goes on to say, "Defraud ye not one another."[63] And what need is there for me to speak, when the readers of this book can make up their own reckonings from what has been said previously—which "debts" if we fail to pay we shall be kept in prison, or if we pay shall be set free? Howbeit, in life there is not an hour of the night or the day that we do not "owe" something.

5. Now, in "owing" a debt either a man pays or else refuses payment. And he can pay during his lifetime, and he can also refuse payment. And some indeed "owe no man anything"[64]; while others pay the greater part and owe a little, and others again pay a little and owe the greater part. And there may be a man who pays up nothing and owes everything. Of course, he who pays all, so as to owe nothing, achieves this result at some time or another, and he needs a period of grace[65] concerning his former debts: which grace can reasonably be obtained by a man who has made it his aim to be in the position at a certain date of not owing anything which has not been paid when the debt falls due. But actual transgressions, being engraved upon our reason, become of themselves[66] "the written bond against us,"[67] by which we shall be judged, like books testified under the hand of all, so to speak, which shall be brought forward when "we shall all stand before the judgment-seat"[68] "of Christ; that each one may receive the things done in the body, according to what he hath done, whether it be good or bad."[69] As concerning these debts it is also said in Proverbs, "Do not give thyself for security, thou who respectest thy person: for if thou hast not whence to pay, they will take thy bed from under thy ribs."[70]

6. Now, if we "are in debt" to so many, assuredly some "are" also "in debt" to us. Some "are in debt" to us as to men, others as to citizens, others again as to fathers and some as to sons, and, yet again, as wives to husbands or as friends to friends. Whenever, therefore, out of our numerous "debtors" some show remissness about paying back what is due to us, we shall act with fellow-feeling and not bear malice towards them, remembering

---

[62] I Cor. 7:3. [63] I Cor. 7:5. [64] Rom. 13:8.
[65] See note. [66] Reading αὐταί for αὗται.
[67] Col. 2:14. [68] Rom. 14:10. [69] II Cor. 5:10.
[70] Prov. 22:26, 27.

our own debts, how often we have failed to pay them, not only
to men but also to God himself. For when we remember those
to whom we were in debt yet did not pay, but refused payment
as the time went on during which we ought to have done this or
that to our neighbour, we shall be gentler towards those who
have incurred a debt to us and have not paid what is due: and
especially will this be so if we do not forget our transgressions
against God and the "iniquity" we "have spoken on high,"[71]
either in ignorance of the truth or in discontent at the misfortunes which have fallen to our lot.

7. If we are unwilling to be gentler towards those who have
incurred a debt with us, we shall suffer what he did who would
not concede the "hundred pence" to his "fellow-servant."[72]
This man, who had himself previously received a concession,
according to the parable in the Gospel,[73] his master reproached,[74] and exacted from him what had been previously
conceded, saying to him, " 'Thou wicked and slothful servant,'[75]
'shouldest not thou have had mercy on thy fellow-servant, even
as I had mercy on thee?'[76] Cast ye him into prison, 'till he pay
all that is due.'" And then the Lord went on to say, "So shall
also my heavenly Father do unto you, if ye forgive not every one
his brother from your hearts."[77] Certainly, those who say that
they repent of the sins they have committed against us must be
forgiven, even though the debtor does this frequently: for "if,"
he says, "thy brother sin against thee seven times in a day, and
seven times turn, saying, I repent; thou shalt forgive him."[78] It
is not we who are harsh towards those who do not repent;
rather, such persons are wicked to their own hurt: for "he that
refuseth correction hateth himself."[79] And even in the case of
such persons, every means must be sought to care for him who
is so completely perverted that he does not even perceive his
own wicked deeds, but is drunk with a drunkenness more deadly
than that of wine—that which comes from the darkening power
of wickedness.

8. When Luke says, "Forgive us our sins"[80] (since the sins
arise from our being in debt and not paying), he says the same
thing as Matthew; but Luke seems not to give room for him who
wishes to forgive repentant debtors only, saying that it has been
laid down by the Saviour that we ought in the prayer to add:

[71] Ps. 73:8.　　　　　[72] Matt. 18:28.　　　　[73] Matt. 18:23–35.
[74] Reading ὀνειδίσας: see note.　　[75] Matt. 25:26.
[76] Matt. 18:33.　　　[77] Matt. 18:34, 35.　　[78] Luke 17:3, 4.
[79] Prov. 15:32.　　　[80] Luke 11:4.

"for we ourselves also forgive everyone that is indebted to us."[80]
Certainly, we all have power "to forgive" the sins committed
against us: this is clear from the words "for we ourselves also
forgive everyone that is indebted to us."[80] But he who is inspired by Jesus, as the apostles were, and can be known "by the
fruits,"[81] as one who has received the Holy Spirit and has become "spiritual"[82] by being "led by the Spirit" as a "son of
God"[83] to do everything in accordance with reason—such a
one "forgives" whatever God forgives and "retains"[84] such
sins as are incurable; and even as the prophets serve God in
speaking not the things of their own but of the divine will, so
also he serves him who alone "hath power to forgive,"[85] even
God.

9. In the Gospel according to John the following is said concerning the forgiveness of sins by the apostles: "Receive ye the
Holy Ghost: whose soever sins ye forgive, they are forgiven
unto them; whose soever sins ye retain, they are retained."[84] If
one were to take these words without due consideration, one
might lay a charge against the apostles for not "forgiving" all,
in order that sins might "be forgiven" to all, but "retaining the
sins" of some, so that they are "retained" on their account and
with God. But it is useful to take an illustration from the Law so
as to understand the forgiveness of sins that comes from God to
men through men. The priests according to the Law are prohibited in the case of certain sins from offering a sacrifice that
the faults may be forgiven those for whom the sacrifices are
made. And though the priest has power to offer as concerning
certain involuntary or voluntary faults,[86] he actually does not
offer "burnt offering and sin offering"[87] for adultery or voluntary murder or any other more grievous transgression. In like
manner, therefore, the apostles also, and those likened to the
apostles, being priests of the "great high priest,"[88] having received knowledge of the healing that comes from God, know,
being taught by the Holy Spirit, concerning what sins they
ought to offer sacrifices, and when, and in what manner, and
they understand concerning what sins they ought not to do this.
Eli the priest, for example, learning that his sons Hophni and
Phinehas were sinning, since he was unable to help them to
secure forgiveness of their sins, acknowledged in these words the

81 Matt. 7:16, 20.   82 I Cor. 2:15.   83 Rom. 8:14.
84 John 20:23.   85 Matt. 9:6.
86 Adopting an emendation of Koetschau.   87 Ps. 40:6.
88 Heb. 4:14.

hopelessness of achieving it: "for if a man sinning sin against a man, they will even pray for him: but if a man sin against the Lord, who will pray for him?"[89]

10. Certain persons, I know not how, arrogating to themselves powers beyond the priestly office, perhaps because they have no accurate grasp of the knowledge that a priest should possess, boast that they are able to pardon even idolatry and to forgive adultery and fornication, on the ground that by means of the prayer offered for those who have committed these deeds even "the sin unto death" is absolved. For they do not read the words: "There is a sin unto death: not concerning this do I say that he should make request."[90] And we must not pass over in silence that bravest of men, Job, who said as he was offering "sacrifice for" his "sons": "It may be that my sons have thought evil of God in their mind."[91] For he offered the sacrifice in a case where it was doubtful if sins had been committed, and that too where the sins had not even reached as far as the lips.

BRING US NOT INTO TEMPTATION

(Chapter XXIX)

XXIX, 1. "And bring us not into temptation, but deliver us from the evil one."[92] But the words "But deliver us from the evil one" are not found in Luke.[93] It is, I think, a question that deserves discussion (unless the Saviour commands us to pray for the impossible), how we can be bidden, when the whole of men's "life on earth is a temptation,"[94] to pray that we enter "not into temptation." For inasmuch as we are on earth "compassed about with"[95] "the flesh"[96] "that warreth"[97] "against the Spirit,"[96] "the mind" of which "is enmity against God," and "cannot" in any wise "be subject to the law of God,"[98] we are "in temptation."

2. That the whole of human "life upon earth" is "a temptation" we learn from Job, as follows: "Is not the life of men upon earth a temptation?"[94]; and from the seventeenth Psalm the same thing is indicated in the words: "In thee I shall be delivered from temptation."[99] And Paul also writing to the Corinthians says that God grants, not that they should not be

89 I Sam. 2:25.   90 I John 5:16.   91 Job. 1:5.
92 Matt. 6:13.   93 Luke 11:4.   94 Job. 7:1.
95 Heb. 5:2.   96 Gal. 5:17.
97 Cf. James 4:1; I Peter 2:11.   98 Rom. 8:7.
99 Ps. 17:30 (LXX).

tempted but, that they should "not be tempted" beyond their power, saying, "There hath no temptation taken you but such as man can bear: but God is faithful, who will not suffer you to be tempted above that ye are able; but will with the temptation make also the way of escape that ye may be able to endure it."[1] For whether "the wrestling"[2] is with "the flesh" that "lusteth"[96] and "warreth"[97] "against the Spirit,"[96] or with "the soul of all flesh"[3] (which is synonymous with the guiding principle, called the heart, which dwells in the body)—of whatever kind "the wrestling"[4] is for those who are "tempted" with "temptations such as man can bear"[5]; or whether the contests we undergo are "against the principalities" and "the powers" and "the world-rulers of this darkness" and "the spiritual hosts of wickedness" and we are as mightily striding and perfectly trained athletes, no longer "wrestling against flesh and blood,"[4] nor proved by "temptations such as man can bear"[5] (for these are already "trodden under foot")[6]: in either case we have not been delivered from temptation.

3. How then does the Saviour bid us pray not to enter "into temptation," when in some sense God tempts all? For "remember," says Judith, not only to the elders of that day but also to all those who read her book, "all the things which he did to Abraham, and all the things in which he tempted[7] Isaac, and all the things which happened to Jacob in Mesopotamia of Syria, when he kept the sheep of Laban his mother's brother. For the Lord, who scourgeth them who come near unto him to admonish them, doth not take vengeance on us as he tried them in the fire, to search out their hearts."[8] And David also shows in a general way concerning all righteous persons when he says, "Many are the tribulations of the righteous"[9]; and the apostle in the Acts, "Through many tribulations we must enter into the kingdom of God."[10]

4. And if we do not understand a point which escapes many people in connection with praying not to enter "into temptation," now is the time to say that the apostles frequently failed to be heard when they prayed: for they suffered countless trials in their life-time, "in labours more abundantly, in stripes more abundantly, in prisons above measure,[11] in deaths oft"; and Paul on his own account "of the Jews five times received forty

---

[1] I Cor. 10:13.   [2] Eph. 6:12.   [3] Lev. 17:11.
[4] Eph. 6:12.   [5] I Cor. 10:13.   [6] Ps. 91:13.
[7] R.V. "tried."   [8] Judith 8:26, 27 (with variants).
[9] Ps. 34:19.   [10] Acts 14:22.   [11] The reading also of Codex ℵ.

stripes save one, thrice was" he "beaten with rods, once was" he "stoned, thrice" he "suffered shipwreck, a night and a day was" he "in the deep,"[12] a man "pressed on every side" and "perplexed" and "pursued" and "smitten down"[13]; and he confesses that "even unto this present hour we both hunger, and thirst, and are naked, and are buffeted, and have no certain dwelling-place; and we toil, working with our own hands: being reviled, we bless; being persecuted, we endure; being defamed, we intreat."[14] Now if the apostles in praying have failed to be heard, what hope is there for anyone inferior to them of gaining the ear of God to his prayer?

5. The words in the twenty-fifth Psalm, "Examine me, O Lord, and prove[15] me; try as by fire my reins and my heart,"[16] might reasonably be supposed by some one who did not grasp accurately the meaning of the Saviour's command to be opposed to what our Lord taught concerning prayer. But when did anyone think that he was outside the range of "temptations such as man can bear,"[17] in the knowledge that the sum total of them had been completed? What season is there, during which anyone light-heartedly thinks that he has not to struggle to avoid future sin? Is anyone "needy"? Let him take care lest he "steal" and "use profanely the name of the Lord."[18] Is he, on the other hand, rich? Let him not presume. For "when" he "is full," he may "become a liar," and being lifted up "say, Who seeth me?"[19] And certainly Paul, "rich in all utterance and all knowledge,"[20] was not delivered from the danger of sinning, through being on that account "exalted overmuch," but he needed "a thorn of Satan buffeting" him, "that" he "should not be exalted overmuch."[21] And should anyone be conscious of his own superiority and eagerly expect freedom from ills,[22] let him read what is stated in the Second Book of Chronicles concerning "Hezekiah," who is said to have fallen from "the pride of his heart."[23]

6. But if, since we have not said more about the poor man, anyone should presume that there is no temptation attached to poverty, let him know that the plotter plots "to cast down the poor and the needy"[24]; and especially since, as Solomon says,

[12] II Cor. 11:23–25.   [13] II Cor. 4:8, 9.   [14] I Cor. 4:11–13.
[15] Or "tempt."   [16] Ps. 26:2.
[17] I Cor. 10:13: for reading, see note.
[18] Prov. 24:32 (30:9, R.V.).   [19] Prov. 24:32 (30:9, R.V.).
[20] I Cor. 1:5.   [21] II Cor. 12:7.
[22] Following an emendation of Koetschau.
[23] II Chron. 32:25, 26.   [24] Ps. 37:14.

"the poor man submitteth not to threatening."[25] What need is there to speak of those who because of material riches, which they have failed to administer well, have received the place of punishment allotted to the "rich man" in the Gospel,[26] and of those who bear their penury ignobly and live in a lower and more servile fashion than is "becoming" for "saints,"[27] and so have fallen from the heavenly "hope"?[28] Neither are they who are between these on either side, riches and poverty, entirely freed from sinning because of their moderate possessions.

7. But a man healthy in body and in good condition supposes that he is beyond all temptation because of this very health and good condition. To whom else attaches the sin of "destroying the temple of God,"[29] except it be to those who are in good condition and healthy? No one will dare to say what may be said on this topic because the matter is evident to all. Has a sick man, then, escaped the incitements to "destroy the temple of God,"[30] seeing that he has at that time full opportunity for receiving impure thoughts? What need is there also to speak of the other things that trouble him, unless "with all watchfulness" he "keep the heart"?[31] For many, when they are overcome by misfortunes and do not know how to bear sicknesses bravely, have as a result of their sickness suffered damage in the soul rather than in the body. And many also in fleeing ignominy have been ashamed to bear nobly the name of Christ, and so have fallen into eternal shame.

8. A man thinks that he may safely rest free from temptation when he has been glorified among men. But how can the saying, "They have received their reward" from "men,"[32] be anything but a hard one, spoken as it was to those lifted up by the glory bestowed upon them by the multitude as for some good thing? And how can they fail to be censured by the words: "How can ye believe, which receive glory one of another, and the glory that cometh from the only God ye seek not?"?[33] And what need is there for me to recount the falls through pride of those reckoned highborn, and the fawning submission, due to lack of *savoir-faire*, towards their supposed superiors on the part of those who are accounted lowborn—a submission which separates from God those who lacking genuine friendship lay pretence to

25 Prov. 13:8.
26 Cf. Luke 16:19, 22–24.
27 Cf. Eph. 5:3.
28 Cf. Col. 1:5.
29 I Cor. 3:17.
30 I Cor. 3:17.
31 Prov. 4:23.
32 Matt. 6:2.
33 John 5:44.

the most beautiful thing to be found among men, namely, charity?

9. "The" whole "life," therefore, "of man upon earth is temptation,"[34] as we have said before.[35] Accordingly let us pray to be "delivered"[36] from temptation, not in the sense of not being tempted (for that is impossible, especially for those "on earth"[37]) but in the sense of not being overcome when we are tempted. In my opinion, he who is overcome in being tempted "enters into temptation,"[38] being held fast in its meshes. These meshes, because of those who were caught in them aforetime, the Saviour entered: "Glancing through the meshes," as it is said in the Song of Songs, "he replies" to those who were caught by them aforetime and who "entered into temptation," and "he says" to her who is his bride: "Rise up, come, my near one, my fair one, my dove."[39] And I will add the following to show that every time is a time of temptation for men: not even he who "meditates" on "the law" of God "day and night"[40] and exercises himself to fulfil the saying "the mouth of the righteous will meditate wisdom,"[41] is delivered from being tempted.

10. What need is there also to speak of those who though giving themselves up to the study of the divine Scriptures have misinterpreted the statements of the Law and the Prophets and have given themselves up to godless and impious, or else to stupid and ridiculous, doctrines; for it would seem that very many who cannot rightly be charged with neglect of these writings have nevertheless fallen into this kind of error? And the same thing has happened to many in the case also of the apostolic and evangelical writings, when in their own folly they invent a Son or a Father other than him whom the saints speak of as God and conceive of in accordance with the truth. For he who fails to think truly concerning God or his Christ has fallen away from "the true God"[42] and his only begotten.[43] But him whom his folly has invented, supposing him to be Father and Son, he does not truly worship. This happens to him because he has failed to recognize the "temptation" that lurks in reading the holy [Scriptures], neither has he armed himself for a contest which was at that very time upon him, nor stood firm.

11. We ought therefore to pray, not that we may not be

---

[34] Job. 7:1.   [35] Section 2, above.   [36] Matt. 6:13.
[37] Matt. 6:10.   [38] Matt. 26:41, etc.   [39] Song of Songs 2:9, 10.
[40] Ps. 1:2.   [41] Prov. 10:31 (for reading, see note).
[42] I John 5:20.   [43] John 1:14, etc.

tempted (for that cannot be), but that we may not be encompassed by temptation, a thing that happens to those who are held fast by it and overcome. Since, then, outside the prayer it is written "not to enter into temptation"[44] (the meaning of which is clear enough from what has been said), but in the prayer we are to pray to God the Father "bring us not into temptation"[45]: it is worth while to see how we may conceive of God leading "into temptation" him who did not pray or him whose prayer was not heard. For inasmuch as he who is conquered "enters into temptation," it is incongruous to think that God leads anyone "into temptation," in the sense of giving him up to be conquered. And the same incongruity remains however we interpret the words: "pray not to enter into temptation." For if it is an evil to fall "into temptation"—a thing we pray that we may not suffer—it must needs be absurd to think that the good God, who "cannot bring forth evil fruit,"[46] encompasses anyone with evil.

12. In this connection, then, it is useful to quote what is said by Paul in the [Epistle] to the Romans, as follows: "Professing themselves to be wise, they became fools, and changed the glory of the incorruptible God for the likeness of an image of corruptible man, and of birds, and fourfooted beasts, and creeping things. Wherefore God gave them up in the lusts of their hearts unto uncleanness, that their bodies should be dishonoured among themselves."[47] And a little further on: "For this cause God gave them up unto vile passions: for their women changed the natural use into that which is against nature: and likewise also the men, leaving the natural use of the woman, burned,"[48] and so forth. And again, a little further on: "And even as they refused to have God in their knowledge, God gave them up unto a reprobate mind, to do those things which are not fitting."[49] All these things, however, must be put to those who divide the Godhead, and it must be said to them, since they suppose that the good Father of our Lord is other than the God of the Law: if the good God leads "into temptation" him whose prayer is not answered, and if the Father of the Lord gives up "in the lusts of their hearts" those who had previously sinned "unto uncleanness, that their bodies should be dishonoured among themselves," and if, as they say, having done with judgment and punishment, he "gives them up unto vile passions" and "unto a

---

44 Luke 22:40 (Matt. 26:41; Mark 14:38).
45 Matt. 6:13; Luke 11:4.   46 Matt. 7:18.
47 Rom. 1:22–24.   48 Rom. 1:26, 27.   49 Rom. 1:28.

reprobate mind, to do those things which are not fitting," would not those who were not "given up" to them by "God" have been "in the lusts of their hearts," and would not those who were not "given up" to them by "God" have fallen "into vile passions," and would not those who came under this condemnation fall "into a reprobate mind" apart from being "given up" unto it by "God"?[50]

13. I know well that these observations will trouble the persons in question exceedingly, in that they have imagined a God other than the creator of heaven and earth because they find many such things in the Law and the Prophets and have taken offence against him as not good who utters such sentiments. Confronted, however, with the difficulties arising out of the words: "Bring us not into temptation," because of which we quoted the text from the apostle, let us now consider if we can find an adequate solution of these contradictions. I verily believe that God orders every rational soul with a view to its eternal life, and that it always maintains its free will, and of its own motion either mounts ever higher and higher until it reaches the pinnacle of virtue, or on the contrary descends through carelessness to this or that excess of wickedness. When a rapid and brief cure causes some to regard lightly, as easily cured, the diseases into which they have fallen, so that after being restored to health they fall the second time into the same condition: in such cases God will with good reason disregard their increasing wickedness to a certain point, and even overlook it when it has developed in them to such an extent as to be incurable, in order that continuance in the evil may cause them to take their fill and be glutted with the sin they desire: thus they may become conscious of their harmful condition and hate what they formerly welcomed, and so when they are healed they can possess more securely the health that comes to their souls by being healed. So it was once upon a time with "the mixed multitude that was among" the children of Israel. They "fell a lusting, and the children of Israel also sat down and said, Who shall give us flesh to eat? We remember the fish that we did eat in Egypt for nought, and the cucumbers, and the melons, and the leeks, and the onions, and the garlic: but now our soul is dried away; we have nought save this manna to look to."[51] Then a little further on it is said: "And Moses heard them weeping throughout their families, every man at his door."[52] And again a little further on the Lord says to Moses:

[50] Rom. 1:26, 28.   [51] Num. 11:4–6.   [52] Num. 11:10.

"And thou shalt say unto this people, Sanctify yourselves against tomorrow, and ye shall eat flesh. Ye shall not eat one day, nor two days, nor five days,nor ten days, nor twenty days; for a month of days ye shall eat, until it come out at your nostrils; and it be loathsome unto you; because that ye have rejected the Lord which is among you, and have wept before him, saying, Why came we forth out of Egypt?"[53]

14. Let us therefore look at this account, to see if it serves you with a useful parallel in resolving the difficulty that lies in the words "Bring us not into temptation" and in the texts from the apostle. "The mixed multitude that was among" the children of Israel, having "fallen a lusting, wept, and the children of Israel"[54] with them. And it is clear that so long as they had not the things that they desired, they could not be satiated with them nor cease from their evil state. But the kind and good God, in giving them that which they desired, did not wish so to give it as to leave in them desire. Therefore it says that they did not eat the "flesh one day"[55] (for their evil state would have remained in a soul inflamed and set on fire by the meat, if they had partaken of it for only a little while): indeed he did not give them that which they desired for "two days" alone. But in his wish to satiate them with it, he does not give a promise, as it were, but rather threatened with his intended gifts him who is able to understand, saying, Ye shall spend "not five days" only eating "the flesh," not even twice that number, nor even twice that number again, but "ye shall eat" for so long a time, eating meat for a whole month, until that which ye deemed good, and your blameworthy and shameful desire concerning it, "come out at your nostrils" with a "loathsome" effect.[56] And [this I will do] that ye may have desire no longer when I rid you of life, and thus coming forth, as men purified from desire and remembering through what afflictions you were freed from it, you may be able either to fall into it no more, or else, if this should at any time come to pass, only after a long lapse of time, when you have forgotten what you suffered because of your desire: in which case, if you do not take heed to yourselves and receive the word that rids you perfectly of every kind of mishap, and so fall into evil, and afterwards desire earthly things and again ask to receive for the second time your desires, you may then, having come to hate that which you did desire, be able to retrace the path towards beauty and that heavenly food, which you once despised when you yearned after evil things.

[53] Num. 11:18–20. [54] Num. 11:4. [55] Num. 11:18, 19. [56] Num. 11:20.

15. Like sufferings will befall those who having "changed the glory of the incorruptible God for the likeness of an image of corruptible man, and of birds, and fourfooted beasts, and creeping things," are "given up," through abandoning him, "in the lusts of their hearts unto uncleanness, that their bodies should be dishonoured."[57] By giving it to a lifeless and senseless body they have degraded the name of him who has bestowed upon all sensible and rational creatures not only the power of sense but also that of reasonable sense, and, in the case of some also, of perfect and virtuous sense and perception. And with good reason such persons are given up by the God they have abandoned, being in turn abandoned by him, "unto vile passions, receiving that recompense of error which was due," in the itch of the pleasure they loved.[58] For "that recompense of error which is" their "due" falls to their lot when they are "given up unto vile passions" rather than when they are purged with the wise fire[59] or made to pay in "prison" every debt up to "the last farthing."[60] For when they are "given up" to "vile passions," not only those according to nature but also many of those that are "against nature," they are defiled and made gross by the flesh, so that we might say they no longer possess a soul or mind, but become altogether flesh. But in the fire and the "prison" they do not receive "the recompense of error," but rather a benefaction to cleanse them from the evils committed in their "error," together with salutary sufferings that follow lovers of pleasure: thus they are delivered from all the filth and blood with which they had been so filthied and defiled that they could not even think about being saved from their own perdition. For God "shall wash away the filth of the sons and the daughters of Sion, and shall purge the blood from the midst of them, by the spirit of judgment and the spirit of burning."[61] For "he goes forth as the fire of a foundry and as the lye of fullers,"[62] washing and cleansing them who are in need of such healing remedies, because they did not will determinedly "to have God in their knowledge." When they are willingly given over to these remedies they will hate their "reprobate mind."[63] For God does not wish that good should come to anyone as of necessity, but of free will. Perhaps there are some who from their long association with evil will come to perceive its ugliness

---

[57] Rom. 1:23, 24.
[59] φρονίμῳ πυρί: see note.
[61] Isa. 4:4.
[63] Rom. 1:28.

[58] Rom. 1:26, 27.
[60] Matt. 5:25, 26.
[62] Mal. 3:2

with difficulty, and turn away from it as from something that has falsely been supposed to be beautiful.

16. It is to be noted if it was for this reason that God "hardens the heart of Pharaoh,"[64] that he might be able to say what he said when he was not hardened: "the Lord is righteous, and I and my people are wicked."[65] But he needed to be hardened still further and still further to suffer certain things, in order that too rapid a cessation of the hardening should not cause him to despise the hardening as an evil, and should not render him many times more worthy to be hardened. If, then, "not unjustly are the nets spread for birds,"[66] as is said in Proverbs, but if on the contrary with good reason God "brings into the snare," according to him who said, "Thou broughtest us into the snare,"[67] and if "without" the will of "the Father" not even the cheapest of winged creatures, the "sparrow,"[68] falls "into the snare" (for when it falls "into the snare" it does so for this reason that it did not make good use of the power given by its wings to fly aloft), let us pray that we may never do anything worthy of being "brought into temptation" by the just judgment of God: for everyone is so brought who is "given up unto vile passions," and everyone who, "inasmuch as he refused to have God in himself," is "given up unto a reprobate mind, to do those things which are not fitting."[69]

17. The use of temptation is as follows. What our soul has received is unknown to all save God—is unknown even to ourselves; but it is manifested by means of temptations: so that it may be no longer unknown what kind of persons we are, but rather that we should also know ourselves and be aware, if we will, of our own faults and give thanks for the good results manifested to us of temptations. That temptations, when they come, come to make it plain to us of what sort we are, or to "make known" the hidden things "in" our "heart,"[70] is established by the saying of the Lord in Job and what is written in Deuteronomy, as follows: "Dost thou think that I have answered thee save that thou mayest appear righteous?"[71] and in Deuteronomy thus, "He humbled thee and suffered thee to hunger, and fed thee with manna," and led thee in "the wilderness, wherein were biting serpent and scorpion and thirst," in order that "the things in thy heart might be made known."[72]

---

[64] Cf. Ex. 9:12, 35; 10:1, 20, 27; 11:10.   [65] Ex. 9:27.
[66] Prov. 1:17.   [67] Ps. 66:11.   [68] Matt. 10:29.
[69] Rom. 1:24, 26, 28.   [70] Cf. Deut. 8:2.   [71] Job 40:8 (LXX).
[72] Deut. 8:3, 15, 2.

18. And if we wish also to have reminders from history, we should know that the mind of Eve did not become easily persuaded and feeble when she disobeyed God and listened to the serpent: but rather it was proved to be so beforehand, the serpent approaching her for this very reason, that his own insight perceived her weakness.[73] Neither did wickedness first arise in Cain when "he slew"[74] his brother (for even before that "God which knoweth the heart"[75] "had not respect unto Cain and to his sacrifices"[76]); but his badness came to light when he killed Abel. Again, had not "Noah drunk of the wine" which he had tilled and "become drunken" and had he not "been uncovered," neither, on the one hand, would the hastiness of action of Ham and his impiety towards his father, nor, on the other, the grave and respectful behaviour of his brothers to their parent, have been manifested.[77] And the plot of Esau against Jacob seemed to have as its pretext the taking away of "the blessing"[78]; but before this his soul had the "roots" of being a "fornicator" and "profane person."[79] And we should not have known the splendour of Joseph's self-control, who was prepared against the assaults of any desire, had not his mistress become enamoured of him.[80]

19. Therefore, in the times between successive temptations, we ought to take a firm stand against what is impending, and prepare ourselves for anything that may possibly happen, so that, whatever it may be, we shall not be proved unready, but shall be made manifest to have disciplined ourselves with the utmost care. For that which is lacking through human weakness, though we do everything within our power, "God will supply,"[81] who "maketh all things to work together for good to them that love" him, "to them whom according to"[82] his infallible foreknowledge he has foreseen what they shall be in themselves.

DELIVER US FROM THE EVIL ONE

(Chapter XXX)

XXX, 1. It seems to me that Luke in the words: "Bring us not into temptation"[83] has virtually taught also "Deliver us from the evil one."[84] Probably to "the disciple,"[85] inasmuch as

---

73 Cf. Gen. 3:1–5.   74 Gen. 4:8.   75 Acts 15:8.
76 Gen. 4:5.   77 Gen. 9:20–23.   78 Gen. 27:41.
79 Heb. 12:15, 16.   80 Gen. 39:7 ff.   81 Phil. 4:19.
82 Rom. 8:28.   83 Luke 11:4.   84 Matt. 6:13.
85 Luke 11:1.

he had already profited,[86] the Lord spoke the more concise saying, but to the many, who were in need of clearer teaching, that which was plainer. But God "delivers us from the evil one," not when the enemy that wrestles against us[87] in no way attacks us by any of his methods whatsoever or by the ministers of his will, but when we conquer bravely, taking a firm stand against circumstances. It is thus that we understand also the saying: "Many are the afflictions of the righteous, and he delivereth them out of them all."[88] For God "delivereth" from "afflictions," not where there are no longer "afflictions" (seeing that Paul says, "afflicted on every side,"[89] as never not "afflicted"), but when "afflicted" by the help of God we are "not straitened"[89]: to be afflicted, according to a customary Hebrew usage, indicates a critical happening which occurs independently of choice, while to be "straitened" is a matter of choice, when a man is conquered by affliction and gives in to it. Therefore Paul well says: "Afflicted on every side, yet not straitened."[89] And I think that the saying in Psalms is similar to this: "In affliction thou didst set me at large."[90] For by the co-operation and presence of the Word of God, who encourages and saves us, the gladness and cheerfulness of our mind that comes to us from God in the season of critical circumstances is termed enlargement.

2. Similarly is to be understood the "deliverance" of anyone "from the evil one." For God "delivered" Job, not by the devil not receiving authority to involve him with this or that temptation (for he did receive it),[91] but by the fact that "in all these happenings Job sinned not before the Lord,"[91a] but was shown to be righteous: He who said: "Doth Job fear God for nought? Hast thou not fortified what is outside and what is within his house and what is outside all that he hath round about? His works thou hast blessed and his cattle thou hast made abundant upon the earth. But put forth thine hand and touch all that he hath, verily he will curse thee to thy face"[92]—he who said this was put to shame, as having thereby uttered a falsehood against Job: who after so many sufferings does not, as the adversary says, "curse" God "to" his "face," but even when given up to the tempter continues blessing God, and rebukes his wife when she says: "Speak a word to the Lord, and die,"[93] chiding her

---

[86] Sc., by our Lord's teaching. [87] Cf. Eph. 6:11, 12.
[88] Ps. 34:19. [89] II Cor. 4:8. [90] Ps. 4:1.
[91] Job. 1:12. [91a] Cf. Job 1:22 [92] Job. 1:9–11.
[93] Job 2:9.

and saying, "Thou hast spoken as one of the foolish women: if we have received good at the hand of the Lord, shall we not endure evil"?[94] And the second time also the devil spake concerning Job to the Lord, "Skin for skin, all that a man hath will he give for his life. Only put forth thine hand and touch his bones and his flesh: verily, he will curse thee to the face."[95] Howbeit, conquered by this champion of virtue, he was shown to be a liar: for though undergoing the most severe sufferings Job remained "not sinning with his lips before God."[96] And having undergone two wrestlings and conquered, Job did not sustain a third contest of this sort: for it must needs be that the threefold wrestling was reserved for the Saviour, such as is recorded in the three Gospels,[97] our Saviour as man being seen to have conquered the enemy three times.

3. Having carefully examined these words and given them our personal scrutiny in order that we may intelligently ask God that we "enter not into temptation"[98] and that we be "delivered from the evil one"[99] and having become worthy through hearing God of being heard by him: let us when tempted beseech him that we be not put to death, and when attacked by "the fiery darts of the evil one"[1] that we be not set on fire by them. All they are set on fire by them whose hearts, according to one of the twelve [prophets], have become "like an oven."[2] But they are not set on fire who with "the shield of faith quench all the fiery darts"[1] that are sent against them by "the evil one"[99]; so often as they have within themselves "rivers of water springing up unto eternal life,"[3] which do not allow the dart of the evil one to prevail, but easily bring it to nought by the flood of inspired and saving thoughts, which are stamped by the contemplation of the truth upon the soul of him who trains himself to be spiritual.

Supplement to General Discussion on Prayer
CHAPTERS XXXI TO XXXIII

Disposition and Posture in Prayer (Chapter XXXI, 1–3)

XXXI, 1. After this it does not seem to me to be out of place, in order to complete our discussion of the problem of prayer, to treat in an elementary manner of the disposition and the posture which he who prays ought to have, and the place, where he

---

[94] Job 2:10.   [95] Job 2:4, 5.   [96] Job 2:10.
[97] Cf. Matt. 4:1–11; Luke 4:1–13.
[98] Matt. 26:41; Mark 14:38; Luke 22:40.   [99] Matt. 6:13.
[1] Eph. 6:16.   [2] Hos. 7:6.   [3] John 7:38; 4:14.

ought to pray, and the direction in which he ought to look if no
obstacle opposes, and the specially suitable time for prayer, and
any other similar matters. The matter of disposition is to be referred to the soul, the matter of posture to the body. Thus Paul
says, as we mentioned above,[4] in describing the disposition,
that prayer should be made "without wrath and disputing"; in
describing the posture, "lifting up holy hands."[5] This, it seems
to me, has been taken from the Psalms, as follows: "The lifting
up of my hands as an evening sacrifice."[6] Concerning the place:
"I desire therefore that the men pray in every place."[7] Concerning the direction, in the Wisdom of Solomon: "That it
might be known that we must rise before the sun to give thee
thanks, and must plead with thee before the dawning of the
light."[8]

2. It seems to me therefore that he who is about to come to
prayer, if he withdraws and prepares himself for a little while,
will be more earnest and attentive in regard to his prayer as a
whole. He should put aside every kind of distraction[9] and disturbance of mind, and recollect as far as possible the greatness
of him to whom he comes, and that it is a sacrilege to approach
him lightly and carelessly and with a kind of disdain; and he
should cast off all alien thoughts. Thus ought he to come to
prayer, as it were stretching out the soul before the hands, and
directing the mind to God before the eyes; and before he stands
raising up from the ground the reason and making it to stand
towards the Lord of all. All malice towards anyone who appears
to have wronged him he should cast aside in so far as he wishes
God to bear no malice towards himself, since he has injured and
sinned against many a neighbour, or else is conscious of deeds
of various kinds that he has committed contrary to right reason.
Neither ought he to doubt that, as there are countless attitudes
of the body, that attitude in which the hands are stretched out
and eyes lifted up is to be preferred to all others, since the body
brings to prayer the image, as it were, of the qualities suitable
to the soul. We mean, however, that these attitudes should be
given preference unless an obstacle opposes. For where there is
an obstacle it is permissible on an occasion to pray suitably in a
sitting position, on account of a disease of the feet that may not
be disregarded, or even lying down, through fever or some such
sickness. And also, on account of circumstances, if we are sailing,

---

[4] Chs. II and IX.   [5] I Tim. 2:8.   [6] Ps. 141:2.
[7] I Tim. 2:8.   [8] Wisdom of Solomon 16:28: see note.
[9] Adopting emendation of Bentley.

let us say, or if our business does not allow us to withdraw and offer the prayer that is due, it is permitted to pray without even seeming to do so.

3. And as for kneeling, that it is necessary when one is about to accuse oneself of his sins before God, supplicating him for healing therefrom and for forgiveness thereof, it ought to be known that it is a symbol of the man who is abject and submissive. Paul says, "For this cause I bow my knees unto the Father, from whom every family in heaven and on earth is named."[10] Spiritual kneeling, so named because every creature falls down before God "in the name of Jesus" and humbles himself before him, appears to me to be indicated in the words: "That in the name of Jesus every knee should bow, of things in heaven and things on earth and things under the earth."[11] It is not by any means to be supposed that the bodies of heavenly beings are so fashioned as to possess bodily knees; for it has been shown by those who have treated of these matters carefully that their bodies are spherical.[12] He who does not wish to admit this will admit at any rate that each limb has its uses, so that nothing they possess has been fashioned to no purpose by God; unless indeed he shamelessly contradicts reason. Such a one will blunder in either case. Either he will affirm that the limbs of their body have been made by God to no purpose and not for their proper function; or else he will say that even in the case of heavenly bodies the viscera and the "intestinum rectum" perform their special uses. It would lead to a very absurd conclusion to suppose that these organs had merely a surface like man's, after the manner of a statue, but no longer any depth as well. So much for my examination of the subject of kneeling and my recognition that: "in the name of Jesus every knee" shall "bow, of things in heaven, and things on earth, and things under the earth."[13] Moreover, what is written in the prophet, "Unto me every knee shall bow,"[14] has the same significance.

The Place of Prayer (Chapter XXXI, 4–7)

4. And concerning the place, it should be known that every place is suitable for prayer by him who prays well. For, "In every place offer incense to me, saith the Lord"[15]; and "I desire therefore that the men pray in every place."[16] But in order that he may perform the act of prayer in quiet without distrac-

---

10 Eph. 3:14, 15.   11 Phil. 2:10.   12 See note.
13 Phil. 2:10.   14 Isa. 45:23.   15 Mal. 1:11.
16 I Tim. 2:8.

tion, each one can select in his own house, if possible, a place set apart, of a sacred character, if I may so express it, and thus pray. In addition to his general inquiry concerning it, he will take care that in this place, where he prays, no crime has at any time been committed or anything done contrary to right reason. It is as if he had made not only himself but also the place of his prayer such that the visitation of God will not rest upon it. And as I look into this matter still further, concerning the place of prayer, I must mention an opinion which may seem rather severe; but which, perhaps, a careful examination will show to be not negligible. It is a question whether it is a holy and pure thing to intercede with God in the place where sexual intercourse occurs—I do not mean unlawful intercourse, but that which is allowed by the apostolic word, "by way of permission, not of commandment."[17] For if it is not possible to "give" oneself "unto prayer" as one ought, "unless" given over to it "by consent for a season,"[18] perhaps the same consideration should be applied, if possible, to the place.

5. There is a place of prayer which has charm as well as usefulness, the spot where "believers" come together "in one place,"[19] and, it may be, angelic powers also stand by the gatherings of believers, and the power of the Lord and Saviour himself, and holy spirits as well, those who have fallen asleep before us, as I think, and clearly also those who are still in this life, although "how" it is not easy to say. As concerning angels, we must reckon the matter in this way. If "the angel of the Lord encampeth round about them that fear him, and will deliver them"[20]; and if Jacob tells the truth not only about himself but also about all who are devoted to God, when he says to him who understands it, "the angel who delivers me from all evil,"[21] it is probable that, when numbers are come together genuinely for the praise of Christ, each one's "angel" who is "round about" each of "them that fear [God] encamps"[20] with that man whom he is charged to guard and keep: so that when the saints are gathered together there is a double church, the one of men, the other of angels. And if Raphael says of Tobit by himself, that he had offered up his "prayer" for "a memorial" and, after him, the prayer of "Sarah," who later on became his "daughter-in-law" through her marriage to Tobias[22]: what is to be said of that occasion when numbers journey together and come together as a body in Christ "in the same mind and in the same

[17] I Cor. 7:6. [18] I Cor. 7:5. [19] Cf. Acts 2:1, 44.
[20] Ps. 34:7. [21] Gen. 48:16. [22] Tobit 12:12; 3:16, 17.

judgment"?[23] As concerning the power of the Lord being present with the Church, Paul says, "Ye being gathered together, and my spirit, with the power of our Lord Jesus: the power of the Lord Jesus"[24] being associated not only with the Ephesians[25] but also with the Corinthians. And if Paul while still clothed with a body held that it co-operated with his spirit in Corinth,[26] we must not give up the belief that so also the blessed ones who have departed come in the spirit more quickly than he who is in the body to the assemblies of the Church. Therefore we must not despise the prayers that are made there, since they have a singular value for him who joins genuinely in common worship.

6. Even as the power of Jesus, the spirit of Paul and of such as he, and "the angels of the Lord encamping round about"[27] each of the saints joins in meeting and assembly with those who are genuinely gathered together, so also, one must venture to conjecture, if there be someone, unworthy of a holy angel, who gives himself up to an angel of the devil[28] through his sins and wicked disregard of God, such a one, if there be a few like him, will not for long escape the notice of the angels, who serve the divine will and watch over[29] the Church and they will bring the faults of such a one to the knowledge of the majority. But if such persons are numerous and assemble together after the manner of human associations for the carrying out of worldly business, they will not be watched over.[30] This is indicated in Isaiah when the Lord says, "not even if ye come to appear before me"[31]; for, he says, "I will turn away mine eyes from you: yea, when ye make many prayers, I will not hear you."[32] For perhaps instead of the aforesaid company of holy men and blessed angels, again a double gathering comes together, of wicked men and bad angels; and of an assembly composed of such it might be said by holy angels and devoted men, "I have not sat with a vain council, and with transgressors I will not enter. I hate the congregation of evil-doers, and with the wicked I will not sit."[33]

7. It is for this reason, I think, that those who in Jerusalem and all Judaea have multiplied sins have become subject to their enemies, because the peoples in abandoning the law have been abandoned by God and the angels who were their shield

---

[23] I Cor. 1:10.   [24] I Cor. 5:4.   [25] See note.
[26] Cf. I Cor. 5:3, 4.   [27] Ps. 34:7.
[28] Adopting an emendation of the Anonymous.
[29] Adopting emendation.   [30] I.e., by the good angels.
[31] Isa. 1:12.   [32] Isa. 1:15.   [33] Ps. 26:4, 5.

and the holy men who were their saviours. Thus, even whole assemblies were at times left to encounter trials: so that "even that which" they "seem to have was taken away from"[34] them. Like "the fig tree" which had been "cursed," which was taken away even "from the roots," because it had not given "fruit" to Jesus when he was "hungry," so also they were "withered,"[35] losing any little vital power of faith that they had. So much, it seems to me, I must say in discussing the place of prayer and in showing the superiority of the place where the saints meet when they assemble devoutly together in church.

The Superiority of Prayer towards the East (Chapter XXXII)

XXXII. A few words also must now be said about the direction towards which he who prays should look. There are four cardinal points, north, south, west, and east. Who would not at once agree that the east clearly shows the direction we ought to face when praying, symbolically of the soul looking to the "rising"[36] of "the true light"?[37] But if someone should prefer to offer his intercessions towards the opening of his house, in whatever direction the doors of the dwelling face, on the plea that the heaven-ward aspect is more compelling than looking towards the wall, should it happen that the openings of the building are not towards the east, we may reply to him that it is by convention that the doors of men's dwelling-places face in this or that direction, but that by nature the east has been given a preference over the other points of the compass, and nature ought to be placed before convention. Further, suppose that a man wishes to pray on a plain. Why on that reasoning should he pray towards the east rather than towards the west? But if reason dictates that the east is to be preferred in that case, why should this not be done everywhere? So much for this matter.

The Subjects of Prayer (Chapter XXXIII)

XXXIII, 1. Before bringing this treatise to an end, I think I ought to say something about the subjects of prayer. It seems to me that four subjects, which I have found here and there throughout the Scriptures, may be outlined, and that every one should form his prayer accordingly. The subjects are these. At the beginning and preamble of the prayer, so far as possible, God is to be glorified, through Christ glorified together with him,

---

[34] Luke 8:18.   [35] Mark 11:12–14, 21.   [36] Luke 1:78.
[37] John 1:9.

in the Holy Spirit hymned together with him. And next in order after this each one must offer general thanksgiving including blessings bestowed on many besides himself, together with those he has personally obtained from God. After thanksgiving, it seems to me that he ought to accuse himself bitterly before God of his own sins, and then ask God, first for healing that he may be delivered from the habit that causes him to sin, and secondly for forgiveness of the past. After confession, it seems to me that in the fourth place he should add his request for great and heavenly things,[38] his own and general, and also for his family and his dearest. And finally he should bring his prayer to a close glorifying God through Christ in the Holy Spirit.

2. These subjects of prayer, as we said before, we found in one place or another of the Scriptures. The subject concerned with giving glory to God is thus expressed in the one hundred and third Psalm: "O Lord, my God, how greatly art thou magnified! Thou art clothed with praise and majesty; who coverest thyself with light as with a garment; who stretchest out the heavens like a curtain, who layeth the beams of his chambers in the waters; who maketh the clouds a place for his feet, who walketh upon the wings of the winds; who maketh winds his messengers, his ministers a flame of fire: who layeth the foundations of the earth to remain stedfast; it shall not be removed for ever and ever. The deep is his covering as a vesture: the waters shall stand upon the mountains. At thy rebuke they shall flee: at the voice of thy thunder they shall be afraid."[39] And the greater part of this Psalm contains a glorification of the Father. And each one can collect many other passages for himself, and he will thus see how widely the subject of glorification is dispersed.

3. As for thanksgiving, this example may be cited from the second [book] of the Kingdoms. After the promises made to David through Nathan,[40] David was astonished at the gifts of God, and is reported to have given thanks for them in these words: "Who am I, O Lord my Lord, and what is my house, that thou lovedst me thus far? And I was made little in thy sight, my Lord, and thou hast spoken concerning the house of thy servant for a long time to come; but this is the law of man, O Lord my Lord. And what can David say more unto thee? And now thou knowest thy servant, O Lord. For thy servant's sake thou hast done it, and according to thine heart hast thou

38 See II, 2.   39 Ps. 104:1-7.   40 II Sam. 7:1-17.

wrought all this thy greatness to make it known unto thy servant, that he may magnify thee, O Lord my Lord."[41]

4. An example of confession: "From all my transgressions deliver me"[42]; and elsewhere: "My wounds stink and are corrupt, because of my foolishness. I am pained and bowed down to the uttermost: I go mourning all the day long."[43]

5. Of requests, in the twenty-seventh Psalm: "Draw me not away with sinners, and with workers of iniquity destroy me not"[44]; and like words.

6. And having begun by glorifying God it is fitting to conclude and bring the prayer to an end by glorifying him, hymning and glorifying the Father of the universe through Jesus Christ in the Holy Spirit, "to whom be the glory for ever."[45]

Conclusion
CHAPTER XXXIV

XXXIV. Thus, according to my ability, I have wrestled with the problem of prayer, and the prayer that is found in the Gospels,[46] and the preceding context in Matthew,[47] on your behalf,[48] my very studious and true brethren in godliness, Ambrose and Tatiana. And I do not despair that, if you "stretch forward to the things which are before" and "forget the things which are behind,"[49] and pray for us as we are engaged in these studies, I can obtain from God, the giver, greater and diviner gifts for these tasks, and receiving them I shall be able to treat again of these same matters with greater breadth and elevation and clarity. For the present, however, you will read this book with indulgence.

41 II Sam. 7:18–22.   42 Ps. 39:8.   43 Ps. 38:5, 6.
44 Ps. 28:3.   45 Rom. 16:27.
46 Matt. 6:9–13; Luke 11:2–4.   47 Matt. 6:5–8.   48 Reading ὑμῖν.
49 Phil. 3:13.

On Prayer

NOTES

Title On Prayer] A Title is wanting in Codex T. There can, however, be little or no doubt that "On Prayer" is correct. In the course of the work Origen himself speaks of its subject as περὶ εὐχῆς (II, 1); and in his *Apologia pro Origene* (as translated by Rufinus) Pamphilus writes (ch. VIII): "Denique in tam multis et tam diversis eius libris nusquam omnino invenitur ab eo liber proprie *De anima* conscriptus, sicut habet vel *De Martyrio*, vel *De Oratione*, vel *De resurrectione*" (*P.G.*, XVII, 603). Cf. also the title of the fragments in Codex Col. (see Introduction, p. 234) containing the last part of the treatise: τοῦ ὠρϊγένους τὸ τῆς εὐχῆς ἀκροτελεύτϊον.

I, 1. *"a corruptible body weigheth down the soul,"* etc.] Thus, at the outset of his treatise Origen states in the words of the Wisdom of Solomon his philosophical position, akin to that of Plato (*Phaedo*, XXX, 81C), concerning the relation of the soul to the body. This was fundamental in all Origen's thinking.

I, 1. *"the things that are in the heavens, who ever yet traced out?"*] The impossibility of knowing God, apart from revelation, is yet another fundamental conviction. De Faye, III, 31, 32: "Origène élève son Dieu audessus de toute pensée. Il le relègue dans une insondable abstraction." See Introduction, p. 189.

I, 1. *God bestows through Christ, who says,* etc.] I have included in this case in the text the conjectural filling up of the lacuna by Koetschau, since a quotation from John 15:14, 15 is obvious, being demanded by the words that follow. The sentence "They who hear the gospel . . . of whom he was formerly Lord" follows an emendation by F. Leo (in Hautsch, *T.U.*, XXXIV, 155), accepted by Koetschau in his translation.

II, 1. *Ambrose*] Further details concerning this man may be

330

found in *D.C.B.*, I, 90–91, and Lawlor and Oulton, *Eusebius*, II, 213 f. It is sufficient here to note that his association with Origen had a profound effect upon them both. Origen reclaimed him from heresy. Ambrose, on his part, encouraged Origen in his literary labours, and generously out of his own means, which were abundant, supplied him with equipment for them. The epithet "most laborious," which Origen here applies to Ambrose, is by no means otiose. His zeal and industry were so intense that even the indefatigable Origen called him playfully his "task-master" or "slave-driver" (ἐργοδιώκτης: Ex. 3:7; 5:6–14). Ambrose communicated in writing to Origen the questions about prayer (V, 6) which gave rise to this treatise. See Introduction, p. 182.

II, 1. *Tatiana*] Nothing is known about this woman. Ambrose associated her with himself, apparently, in the questions about prayer. Some have supposed her to be Ambrose's sister (the name of his wife was Marcella: see Origen, *Ep. ad Africanum*, *sub fin.*). She was evidently a person of somewhat mature age. The epithet "very brave" may suggest constancy in time of persecution.

II, 2. *"Ask for the great things, and the little things shall be added unto you"*] An *Agraphon*, or extra-canonical saying, attributed by some writers in the early Church to our Lord. Origen goes on: "and 'Ask for the heavenly things and the earthly things shall be added unto you.'" But it is not clear whether he intends both parts to be regarded as one or two separate sayings. The latter part has echoes of John 3:12 combined with Matt. 6:33 and Luke 12:31. Clement of Alexandria (*Strom.*, I, 24:158, 2) refers to the earlier part only: "Of the kingly office one portion is divine, that which appertains to God and his holy Son, by whom are supplied both the good things of the earth and besides perfect felicity as well. For 'Ask,' he says, 'for the great things, and the little things shall be added unto you.'" Cf. Eusebius, *In Psalm.*, 16:2: "This also the Saviour taught, saying, 'Ask for the great things, and the little things shall be added unto you.'" On the interpretation of "the great" and "the little" things Clement and Origen are at one. Clem., *Strom.*, IV, 6:34, 6, says, "Seek ye first the kingdom of heaven and the righteousness: these are great things; the small things, appertaining to this life, shall be added unto you." Origen (*contra Celsum*, VII, 44) declares that the Christian prays for no trivial blessings, "for he has learnt from Jesus to seek for nothing little, that is, an object of the senses, but to seek only the great and truly divine things, such as are given by God to help to lead us on to that blessedness that is to be found with him through his Son, the Word, who is God"; and he develops this thought in XIV, 1, of this treatise (see p. 266). Some modern scholars have also reckoned this *agraphon* as an indubitable saying of the Lord, e.g., Resch, *Agrapha*, 230, "Es ist ein sehr gut beglaubigtes Herrenwort," and Ropes, *Sprüche Jesu*, 140, "Dieser Spruch kann gewiss als eine treue Wiedergabe eines Lehrspruches Jesu gelten." See *H.D.B.*, article "Agrapha" in extra volume; B. Jackson, *Twenty-five Agrapha*, 29 ff. For the sentiment, cf. Plato, *Apology*, XVII.

II, 2. *"that Satan rejoice not over you"*] ἵνα μὴ ἐπιχαρῇ ὑμῖν ὁ σατανᾶς. The usual reading in I Cor. 7:5 is: ἵνα μὴ πειράζῃ ὑμᾶς ὁ σατανᾶς. Von Soden notes this variant; but it seems to have escaped the attention of English scholars. That it is not a scribal error in T is plain from the words of Origen that follow: "the joy that Satan takes in another's ill." In spite of its weak attestation, there are two points that may be urged in favour of ἐπιχαρῇ ὑμῖν being the true reading: (1) it would be fatally easy for a scribe to alter ἐπιχαρῇ to πειράζῃ in a reference to Satan; and (2) if Paul wrote ἐπιχαρῇ it would give additional point to I Cor. 13:6: ἡ ἀγάπη . . . οὐ χαίρει ἐπὶ τῇ ἀδικίᾳ.

II, 2. *"If ye stand praying"*] Mark 11:25. Here and in IX:3 Origen reads "If ye stand" instead of "Whensoever ye stand," which is found in all the other textual authorities, except the Bohairic and the Sahidic versions, which also read "if." For posture in prayer, see XXXI, 2.

II, 4. *hearkening as it were to it*] Reading, with Bentley, ἐπηκόῳ for ὑπηκόῳ, which usually means "obeying" although it can also mean "hearkening."

II, 4. *him, whose* deep things, etc.] An emendation of Bentley is followed.

II, 4. *so far as he is able*] ὡς ἐξίσχυσε. The words, taken in their literal meaning, would indicate that the Spirit cannot fully fathom the deep things of God. If so, they must be added to those expressions used by Origen which indicate a doctrine of the Holy Spirit that falls short of the Catholic Faith. On the other hand, in *De Princ.*, I, 3, 4 (as translated by Rufinus), in which the reference to I Cor. 2:10 again occurs, Origen says: "As the Son, who alone knows the Father, reveals him to whom he will, so the Holy Spirit, who alone searches the deep things of God, reveals God to whom he will." The knowledge and power of revelation possessed by the Holy Spirit is parallel to that possessed by the Son, and he has it in virtue of his own being. It may be, however, that Origen draws a subtle distinction between "knowing the Father" (the peculiar property of the Son) and "searching the deep things of God" (the peculiar property of the Spirit), and suggests that the latter involves a less complete understanding than does the former. And we cannot be sure that Rufinus has not doctored this passage in the interests of orthodoxy. Certainly, *In Joh.*, II, 10, 11 (ed. Brooke) is on different lines. There Origen raises the question whether since it is said that all things were made through the Son, the Holy Spirit is one of them; and after some hesitation (in the course of which, however, he affirms his belief in three Hypostases) he slips into an affirmative answer, and comes to the conclusion that the Holy Spirit is one of the "all things" inferior (*ὑποδεεστέρων*) to him through whom all things were made.

II, 4. *not to all those who were being baptized*] It is a favourite thought of Origen that there are two classes of believers, a higher and a lower, and that the former alone are capable of receiving esoteric teaching. Here he suggests that the same distinction was to be found in John's, as it was afterwards in Christian, disciples.

II, 6. *I pray as a man*] The punctuation and construction of the rest of this sentence is not self-evident: but I have followed Koetschau as giving the clearest sense.

II, 6. *the prayers recorded in the Gospels*] Origen held (XVIII, 2, 3) that the versions of the Lord's Prayer in Matthew and Luke represent two different prayers.

III, 1. *occurs for the first time, so far as my observation goes*] For another statement, involving a similar, but even greater amount of, search, see XXII, 1. Such investigation must, under the literary conditions of the time, have been very laborious. But we now know that Christians of Origen's day had several books of the Bible combined in codex or book form, as for example in the Chester Beatty Biblical Papyri. And this must have made the task of such an examination of the Scriptures much lighter than if separate rolls had to be handled.

III, 2. *is also employed in its customary usage*] i.e., simply as "prayer," with no suggestion of "vow."

III, 2. *in addition to the sense previously mentioned*] i.e., the sense of "vow" (as at the beginning of this section).

III, 3. *"I will go out from thee,"* etc.] In this quotation two similar verses of the LXX (Ex. 8:25, 28) are combined in a manner that suggests that Origen was relying on his memory.

III, 4. *is often used not in the accustomed manner*] i.e., it is used in the sense of "vow" (as in Gen. 28:20–22), and not simply as "prayer."

III, 4. "*There are with us four men which are under a vow of their own act*"] The reading followed by the Revised Version in Acts 21:23 is: "We have four men which have a vow on them." The reading "of their own act" (lit. "by themselves") appears to be "Alexandrian," being read by Codices ℵ and B and by the two Egyptian versions, as well as by Origen. It makes good sense, showing that the men in question had taken upon them their vow independently of Paul's intervention.

IV, 1. *to distinguish*, etc.] Trench (*Synonyms of the New Testament*, 188) justly points out that this long discussion of Origen on *euche* and *proseuche* has no great value. It amounts to no more than this. The customary meaning of both words is "prayer": III, 2 (*euche*); IV, 2 (*proseuche*). But in both cases the meaning "vow" is sometimes found, although of *euche* many more instances of this sense are given than there are of *proseuche*: indeed only one passage, I Sam. 1:9–11, is cited for *proseuche* = vow, and in it the verb (*proseuxato*), not the noun, is used.

V, 1. *the plausible arguments first of those*, etc.] Origen's friends placed before him two arguments against prayer (see section 6 of this chapter): (1) that God has foreseen the future, and it must come to pass; (2) man has no free will, since God's will cannot be changed. The conclusion on both suppositions is that prayer is in vain. Before he deals with these objections, Origen mentions in passing (section 1) a third class of objectors who reject prayer altogether because they are atheists or do not believe in Providence. He then proceeds to deal with argument (1) in sections 2–5. In ch. VI he begins a discussion of objection (2). A clearer arrangement would have been to place V, 6, at the beginning of the chapter.

V, 1. *lacking in distinguished supporters*] Origen means that there is no sect of philosophers which admits God and Providence and at the same time rejects prayer altogether, although it may doubt its efficacy.

V, 1. *deny the existence of God*, etc.] There is an echo of this aspect of Origen's teaching in the Panegyric of Gregory addressed to Origen, ch. XIII (*P.G.*, X, 1088; *A.N.L.*, VI, 34): "He [Origen] deemed it right for us to study philosophy in such wise, that we should read with utmost diligence all that has been written, both by the philosophers and by the poets of old, rejecting nothing, and repudiating nothing . . . except

only the productions of the atheists, who, in their conceits, lapse
from the general intelligence of man, and deny that there is
either a God or a Providence." In *contra Celsum*, II, 13, Origen
says that the Epicureans "completely reject" Providence.

V, 1. *to persuade some that they ought not to pray*] Perhaps this is
a direct reference to Clement of Alexandria, *Strom.*, VII, 41,
who speaks of the followers of the heresy of Prodicus as holding
that one "ought not to pray"—περὶ τοῦ μὴ δεῖν εὔχεσθαι—the
same phrase as Origen uses here.

V, 1. *those who completely reject objects of sense, and use neither
Baptism nor Eucharist*] That such persons were to be found in the
early Church is clear from Irenaeus, *Haer.*, I, 14:3 (Harvey),
who speaks of a section of the gnostics, called the Marcosians,
who reject baptismal rites, affirming that "the mystery of the
ineffable and invisible power ought not to be performed by
visible and corruptible things, nor the mystery of beings who are
inconceivable and incorporeal by material objects of sense."
And Tertullian (*De Baptismo*, 1) states that the Cainites rejected
Baptism. The persons referred to by Ignatius (*Smyrn.* 6), who
"abstain from Eucharist and prayer," did not apparently abstain altogether from this sacrament, but established a sacrament of their own apart from the Church (see Lightfoot's note
ad. loc.). In *contra Celsum* II, 13, Origen says of the Peripatetic
philosophers that they maintain prayers to be of no avail
and sacrifices offered as to a Divinity.

V, 2. *"abhorreth none of the things,"* etc.] Wisdom of Solomon
11:24. This appears to be the source of the words in the Collect
of Ash Wednesday: "Almighty and everlasting God, who hatest
nothing that thou hast made."

V, 2. *much further off from God*] i.e., from the mind of God.
See Introduction, p. 189.

V, 3. *melancholy madness*] Origen uses the corresponding verb
in *contra Celsum*, II, 60, where he co-ordinates it with "being out
of one's mind and delirious."

V, 4. *"good or bad"*] In this quotation from Rom. 9:11 Origen
reads φαῦλον for "bad" with א AB, etc., *v.l.*, κακόν.

V, 4. *in vain do we pray concerning . . . the reception of the Spirit
of might*] It is noteworthy that this form of the doctrine of pre-
destination gives rise to the same difficulties concerning the
reception of grace as Calvinism afterwards occasioned.

V, 4. *why does Moses pray*] The title of Ps. 89 (LXX) in both
Hebrew and LXX is: "A Prayer of Moses, the man of God."

V, 5. *"in him, in Christ"*] Eph. 1:4. Either "in Christ" is a gloss which has subsequently got into the text, or it is added by Origen from the preceding verse of Ephesians by way of explanation.

V, 5. *one of those "chosen"*] So Bentley emends the text of T.

V, 5. *"conformed to the image" of the glory "of his Son"*] Origen apparently quotes from memory. The words "of the glory" are not in Rom. 8:29, but in Phil. 3:21; "conformed to," being in both texts, has given rise to the confusion.

V, 5, *many generations previously it was prophesied of him by name*] The passage in I Kings 13:2 is without analogy in Hebrew prophecy, in that 350 years before its fulfilment it gives a specific and detailed prediction of what a person named (Josiah) would do.

V, 5. *why should Judas pray*, etc.] This passage throws light upon the manner of interpreting the Old Testament in the time of Origen. Psalm 109 is regarded, not as indicating a set of circumstances which afterwards were seen to be applicable to the case of Judas, but as referring in the first instance to Judas, so much so that the actions of Judas, historically considered, are predestined by the prophecy. Origen indicates in *contra Celsum*, II, 11, that he himself took a similar view of the Psalm, although he rejected the predestinarian views founded upon it. Cf. also *De Orat.*, VI, 5; XXIV, 5.

V, 6. *you addressed*] "You" is singular. Ambrose wrote the letter, although Tatiana was associated with it.

V, 6. *the future . . . must come to pass . . . what is willed by him is fixed*] It is not clear if Ambrose (and Tatiana) put forward these difficulties as their own or as suggested to them by others. It is significant, however, that Ambrose was formerly a gnostic. Eusebius (*H.E.*, VI, 18:1) says he was a follower of Valentinus, Jerome (V.1, 5, 6) that he was a Marcionite. For the gnostics denied moral freedom and held predestinarian views (see de Faye, III, 179 ff.; Bigg, 243 ff.). Probably, therefore, even if the difficulties about prayer that Ambrose puts forward were not held by him at the time of writing, they had been difficulties for him once; and it is more than likely that he still had friends in gnostic circles who would press him for an answer to these questions.

V, 6. *insensibility*] Greek ἀποναρκᾶν, lit. "to be numb": the effect, it was supposed, of being touched by the ναρκή, the electric rayfish.

VI, 1. *Of things that are moved*, etc.] As in *De Princ.*, III, 1, 2, Origen bases the reality of free will on the faculty of motion. In order to demonstrate this, he arranges objects into three (or four) classes, as follows:

(1) (a) Things without life, held together merely by their form (e.g., stones cut out of the quarry, wood that has lost the power of growing).

(b) Bodies of living creatures and growing plants when moved, not *qua* living creatures or plants, but by an external force, or when moved in virtue of the fact that they are in a state of decay and, consequently, of flux.

(2) Inanimate things (ἄψυχα: *De Princ.*, III, 1:2) moved by their own inherent nature or soul, i.e., "out of themselves" (ἐξ ἑαυτῶν), e.g., a growing plant.

(3) Animate things (ἔμψυχα), living creatures (ζῷα), moved "from within themselves" (ἀφ' αὐτῶν). The impulse of the spider to weave a web, or of a bee to produce wax, are examples of this (*De Princ.*). [In *De Principiis* Origen, while maintaining the distinction between classes (2) and (3), also groups them together as objects which are moved "in themselves" (ἐν ἑαυτοῖς).]

(4) Rational creatures, which are moved "through themselves" (δι' αὐτῶν). In this case the movement and the mover are inseparably connected.

In the *De Oratione* Origen does not distinguish formally between classes (3) and (4); perhaps because he is anxious to point out, as he does, that to deny free will to us would be to deny that we are even living creatures (class 3), much less creatures of reason (class 4).

This argument from the power of self-motion is clearly derived, ultimately, from Plato (cf. *Phaedrus*, 245C *et seq.* and *Laws*, X, 893B *et seq.*), who regards it as constituting the essential character of the soul. On this point Plato was criticized by Aristotle (*De Anima*, I, ch. III).

VI, 1. *held together merely by their form*] Cf. Marcus Aurelius, *Meditations*, VI, 14, and Sextus Empiricus, *adv. Math.*, VIII, 2, for a very similar phrase.

VI, 1. *moved by their own inherent nature and soul*] Cf. Proclus, *Inst.*, 20.

VI, 2. *that we have no free will*] Lit. "that nothing is in our power." We have translated the phrase τὸ ἐφ' ἡμῖν ("that which is in our power") as free will in this section, in VI, 3, 4, and in ch. VII. It is found frequently also in *contra Celsum*, (I, 66; II, 20; IV, 3, 67 (*bis*), 70; V, 21). The plural, τὰ ἐφ' ἡμῖν, occurs in *contra Celsum*, V, 21, and *De Orat.*, VI, 3.

By the phrase the Stoics meant the inner court of judgment, that in a man which has the power to accept or reject certain impressions; and Origen took it over from them in the sense of the power of judgment or choice, as for example the power to resist evil passions and refrain from evil actions. The possession of this power was held to be open to question in Origen's day by the Sceptics: cf. Sextus Empiricus, *Outline of Pyrrhonism*, III, 70, "And if anyone should seek refuge in the notions of 'impulse' and 'purpose,' we must remind him of the controversy about 'What is in our power,' and how it is still unsettled, since hitherto we have failed to find a criterion of truth." This quotation suggests, which is indeed a fact, that by this time the phrase had become through usage a recognized term, so much so indeed that it signified generally the power of choice, and could be used of a third person, in which case the "our" had no significance. Thus we have in ch. VII (beginning) τοῦ ἡλίου ἐφ' ἡμῖν, "the free will of the sun," and later on in the chapter "the free will of the sun and moon and stars"; and in *contra Celsum*, I, 66, τὸ ἐφ' ἡμῖν 'Ηρώδου, "the free will of Herod." See de Faye, III, 182 ff., who translates the phrase: "ce qui dépend de nous."

VI, 2. *Let a man pay particular attention*, etc.] So in almost the same words Origen begins a similar line of argument in *De Princ.*, III, 1:4 (*C.B.*, XXII, 198).

VI, 2. *Some external moving force . . . assent to or accept*] Following emendations adopted by Koetschau in his translation.

VI, 2. *in suspense of judgment*] ὡς ἐπέχων. This was a characteristic feature of the philosophy of the sceptics. Cf. Sextus Empiricus (c. 200 A.D.) *Outlines of Pyrrhonism*, I, 10: "'Suspense' [ἐποχή] is a state of mental rest as a result of which we neither deny nor affirm anything."

VI, 2. *and deserves our praise or blame*] I read τοῦ for τούτου with Wendland. For "praise or blame" cf. Plato, *Laws*, 639C.

VI, 3. *the train of future events*] τὸν εἱρμὸν τῶν ἐσομένων. Origen uses the same phrase in a similar argument in *In Rom.*, I (*Philocalia*, 227, 229).

VI, 4. *"I will hear this man,"* etc.] This is not the only passage in which Origen adopts the method of putting his own conception of the mind of God into words as if spoken by God himself or Christ: cf. XIV, 1; XV, 4; XXIX, 14.

VI, 4. *some inferior power . . . will now deservedly come upon him*] Reading ἤδη for ἤδε ἡ with Koetschau in his translation.

VI, 5. *power for godliness*] "Power" is literally "tension."

Origen borrowed this term from the Stoics (see XXVII, 8, and especially the reference of Plutarch to Cleanthes in note there, p. 367). According to them "tension" when imparted to the soul was the cause of virtues and vices. Origen points out that in Paul it was an enablement towards virtue.

VII, 1. *Even the sun has a certain free will,* etc.] This passage must be read in the context of Origen's belief that the sun and moon and the host of heaven were rational beings and possessed of souls. Justinian, *Ep. ad Mennam* (*P.G.*, LXXXVI, 971; cf. *C.B.*, XXII, 91), criticized Origen for saying that "the heaven and the sun and the moon and the stars and the waters that are above the heavens are living creatures [ἔμψυχα] and are rational powers of a sort." Cf. *De Princ.*, I, 7:4 (as restored from Jerome: see *C.B.*, XXII, 90): "the sun too and moon and the other stars are living creatures [*animantia*]; indeed, just as we men because of certain sins are encompassed with bodies which are gross and fat, so also the luminaries have received such and such bodies, so that they shine more or less brilliantly; and demons because of graver transgressions are clothed with a transitory body." Cf. also *contra Celsum*, V, 11: "being persuaded that the sun himself and the moon and the stars pray to the God of the universe through his only-begotten Son, we judge it improper to pray to those beings who themselves offer up prayers." See also Danièlou, *Origène*, III, 1. Origen was not alone among the Fathers in holding this opinion: see Bigg, 242.

VII, 1. *certain impressions*] φαντασίαι, here translated "impressions," also occurs in this treatise in VI, 2; VIII, 2 (*bis*); IX, 2; XX, 2 (*ter*); XXI, 1. It is not an easy word to translate in every case. Aristotle (*De Anima*, III, 3) contrasts it with sense-perception (αἴσθησις); and he defined it as "that faculty in respect of which an image or mental picture presents itself before us." As used in the *De Oratione* the "impression" may be of good or evil. "Imagination," "thought," "notion," have also been used to translate the word. Marcus Aurelius (*Meditations*, V, 16) employs it in a famous sentence: "the soul takes its dye from the thoughts" (βάπτεται ὑπὸ τῶν φαντασιῶν ἡ ψυχή). Origen followed Epictetus and the Stoics in holding that by virtue of the possession of free will a man could discriminate between "impressions," as they presented themselves to him, and either accept or reject them. See de Faye, III, 183 ff.

VII, 1. *the worse course*] This emendation (in place of "the better course") seems necessary, since Origen is contrasting beings on earth with heavenly beings who cannot be diverted from the right course.

VIII, 1. *"vain repetitions"*] See note on XXI, 1.

VIII, 1. *nor ought we to come to prayer in wrath*] Five times in this treatise (cf. also II, 2; IX, 1 (*bis*); XXXI, 1) Origen makes this point, with a reference to I Tim. 2:8. Perhaps the bitter experience he had recently gone through at Alexandria caused him to emphasize it. See Introduction, p. 176.

VIII, 2. *God ... who ... is present*] Three times in this section Origen lays stress upon the need of remembering the presence of God when praying. The fact throws light upon the mystical side of his nature. Though for him God is transcendent, philosophically speaking, it is of the essence of his religion to realize God's nearness.

VIII, 2. *spies out and anticipates every purpose*] Cf. Clement of Alexandria, *Strom.*, VII, 7:36, 37, for the belief concerning God and his presence entertained by the true gnostic.

VIII, 2. *if the calling to mind ... of an illustrious man*] Cf. Clement of Alexandria, *Strom.*, VII, 7:35, where a similar line of thought is followed.

IX, 1. *"disputings"*] Here and In *Joh.*, XXVIII, 5, and In *Jerem. hom.*, V, 9, Frag. no. lxviii (*C.B.*, VI, 39, 231) Origen quotes I Tim. 2:8 with the plural (διαλογισμῶν), as vouched for by the corrector of ℵ, and Bohairic and Syriac versions and other authorities. In *De Orat.*, II, 2, and XXXI, 1, he reads the singular.

IX, 1. *"and gold"*] Twice in this section, in quoting I Tim. 2:9, Origen reads καὶ χρυσῷ. Variant readings are ἤ for καὶ and χρυσίῳ ("wrought gold") for χρυσῷ.

IX, 2. *When the eyes of the understanding are lifted up*, etc.] This eloquent passage is paralleled, though not equalled, in In *Joh.*, XXVIII, 4, and *contra Celsum*, VII, 44 (end). Cf. also Clement of Alexandria, *Strom.*, VII, 3:13.

IX, 2. *they partake of a kind of divine spiritual effluence*] See XIX, 3, note.

IX, 2. *"was signed upon us"*] The Hebrew of Ps. 4:7(b) is, "Lift the light of thy countenance upon us," the verb "lift" being connected with a root meaning "banner" or "standard." Hence Symmachus translated it "makes a sign." The LXX, reading the passive (*niphal*) of the verb, has "was signed"; and Origen applies it to the spiritual impress upon the mind of him who contemplates God.

IX, 2. *laying aside the nature of a soul it becomes spiritual*] So also in *In Joh.*, I, 28, Origen speaks of a man's soul becoming mingled with his spirit, with the result that he becomes spiritual.

IX, 3. *Jeremiah*] Origen apparently quotes from memory. There is nothing about bearing no malice in the passage of Jeremiah (7:22, 23) to which he refers. The words: "Let no one bear malice against his neighbour in his heart" are a loose reference to Zech. 7:10: "Let no one bear malice in your hearts as concerning the evil done by his brother." Another explanation of the confusion is that the shorthand writer may himself have been confused and have failed to reproduce Origen's dictation accurately. But there are other indications (see XXVIII, 7; XXX, 3; XXXI, 7) that Origen relied too much on his recollection of Scripture passages.

IX, 3. *putting aside such malice in coming to pray*] Perhaps here again we may find an echo of the wrongs Origen suffered before leaving Alexandria. See VIII, 1, note.

IX, 3. *"If ye stand praying"*] See note on II, 2.

X, 1. *"while" he "is yet speaking"*] This reference to Isa. 58:9 occurs also in a similar connection in *In Joh.*, XXVIII, 6, and in Clement of Alexandria, *Strom.*, VII, 7:49 (end).

X, 1. *by the power of him who "hears in heaven"*] An emendation of the Anonymous, who reads ἐν οὐρανῷ for ἐνορῶν with a reference I Kings 8:30.

X, 1. *it having been written of the previous trial*] Koetschau thus emends the text of T, which runs, "it having been written of the trial before it."

X, 2. *who stands in the midst even of those who know him not*] An allusion to John 1:26, which, together with Jer. 23:23, 24, is also referred to in *contra Celsum*, V, 12, where Origen says that the Christ of God is present, not only with those who cleave to him, but also everywhere with those who know him not.

X, 2. *"at midnight"*] The reading of T μεσονύκτιον appears to be a mistake for μεσονυκτίου, as the Anonymous notes.

XI, 1. *the angels . . . the souls of the saints*] Cf. XXXI, 5, where there is also a reference to the Book of Tobit. See also *contra Celsum*, VIII, 34.

XI, 1. *Tobit*] Here and in *contra Celsum*, V, 19, the name is spelt Τωβῆτ.

XI, 1. *"the Scripture says"*] Tobit 3:16, 17. But in XIV, 4, Origen notes that "they of the circumcision . . . reject the book of Tobit as uncanonical." The citations from Tobit in this section follow the text of B and A, not that of ℵ.

XI, 1. *"Jeremiah"*] An example of a departed saint who prays for those on earth. II Maccabees 15:14 is also quoted for the same purpose in *In Joh.*, XIII, 58.

XI, 2. *what had been prepared for*, etc.] I follow the text as emended by the Anonymous.

XI, 2. *one of the chiefest virtues*] Cf. XXIX, 8 (end): "the most beautiful thing to be found among men, namely, charity."

XI, 2. *Christ also acknowledges*, etc.] For a similar thought and reference to the parable of the sheep and the goats, cf. *In Jerem. hom.*, XIV, 7 (*C.B.*, VI, 112).

XI, 3. *How many angels*, etc.] The Anonymous scholar observes that the question is not the *number* of angels but their ministry. He would therefore read πῶς οὐκ for πόσους—it must be that angels work more for the building up of the Church than did the apostles; and he refers to *contra Celsum*, VIII, 34, and *In Joh.*, XXXII, 17.

XI, 3. *Do not they, even more than the apostles, work together*] This passage does not fully express Origen's thought concerning the relationship of angels to churches. Not only do angels help the apostles to carry out the work of evangelization, but they are the heads in the invisible order of the churches as the apostles (and the bishops) are in the visible sphere. When the Apocalypse speaks of angels of churches, invisible rulers are indicated. Thus each church possesses at one and the same time a visible bishop and an invisible angel. "One might almost say, if we follow Scripture, that there are two bishops for each church: the one perceptible and visible and the other invisible [νοητός]. And just as a man, if he has faithfully exercised the charge committed to him is praised: so also an angel" (*In. Luc. hom.*, XIII; *C.B.*, XXXV, 91). Cf. *In. Num. hom.*, XI, 4 (*C.B.*, XXX, 82 ff.). See also J. Danièlou, *Origène*, 240.

XI, 4. *the general command*] See Heb. 1:7, 14. Angels are ministers (λειτουργοί) of God, and are sent forth for the salvation of believers.

XI, 5. *joins in our prayers*] Cf. *contra Celsum*, VIII, 64.

XII, 1. *the exhortations of Jesus*] E.g., Luke 18:1, "men ought always to pray, and not to faint," and 21:36, "watch ye at every season, making supplication."

XII, 1. *It goes forth . . . or by faith*] The text as emended by the Anonymous scholar has been followed. The general sense of the passage is not in doubt, and even Koetschau admits that some emendation is necessary. T has: "It goes forth like a dart from the soul of him who prays by knowledge and reason or by faith from the saint."

XII, 2. *virtuous deeds or commandments being included as part of prayer*] Cf. *In Matt.*, XVI, 22 (*C.B.*, XL, 551) "'My house shall be called the house of prayer.' For there should be nothing else in the Church besides prayer, every good deed also inviting the attention of God, being reckoned as prayer by God, in accordance with which the saying 'pray without ceasing' becomes possible." It is clear, therefore, that Origen did not regard the contemplative life and the practical life as distinct.

XII, 2. *three times every day*] Cf. Clement of Alexandria, *Strom.*, VII, 40.

XII, 2. "*In the morning*," etc.] In this quotation from Ps. 5:3 Origen apparently alters "voice" (Hebrew and LXX) to "prayer" in the first half of the verse. In the second half the object of "I will order" has to be supplied from the sense; and the Revised Version adds "my prayer."

XIII, 1. *perhaps he would not have received it without prayer*] Cf. *In Joh.*, XIII, 1: "The opinion may perhaps be held that no one who does not ask it receives the heavenly gift. Certainly, in the psalm the Father urges the Son himself to ask that it shall be given him, even as the Son similarly teaches us, saying: 'The Lord said unto me, Thou art my Son, ask of me and I will give thee the heathen for thine inheritance, and the utmost parts of the earth for thy possession.'"

XIII, 2. *Samuel, who was reckoned along with Moses*] Cf. *In I Sam. hom.*, XXVIII, 3 (*C.B.*, VI, 285): "Moses who has been coupled with Samuel, according to the saying [Jer. 15:1]."

XIII, 2. *Hezekiah, when as yet he was childless*] Origen bases this statement on the prayer of Hezekiah, when he was recovered of his sickness, as given in the LXX of Isa. 38:19, "From henceforth I will beget children, who shall proclaim thy righteousness, O Lord of my salvation," a passage which Origen quotes in *contra Celsum*, VIII, 46. The Hebrew Scriptures speak of one child—Manasseh—born three years after the illness of his father (II Kings 20:6; 21:1).

XIII, 2. "a whistling dewy wind"] πνεῦμα δρόσου διασυρίζον. A detail wholly absent from the Hebrew, which is found in the Greek versions, LXX, and Theodotion, of Dan 3:50. The phrase is referred to again in XIII, 4, "fire of dew," and also in XVI, 3, "the material dew which conquered the flame kindled by Nebuchadnezzar." Tertullian, *De Oratione*, XXIX, also refers to "the angel of dew in mid-fires" ("roris angelum in mediis ignibus": *P.L.*, I, 1195).

XIII, 3. *have they fallen in with*, etc.] This is the reading of T.

Probably read "have we fallen in with, and by our prayers," etc.

XIII, 4. *"Egypt" is "an iron furnace," being a symbol, etc.*] Cf. *In Jerem. hom.*, IX, 2 (*C.B.*, VI, 66).

XIII, 4. *of what great fish . . . type, etc.*] Similarly in *In Levit. hom.*, VIII, 2 (*C.B.*, XXIX, 397 f.) Origen speaks of the "great fish" which swallowed Jonah as the type of that referred to in Job 3:8, and identifies it with the devil.

XIII, 5. *"this great thing, which the Lord doeth before your eyes"*] I Sam. 12:16. Here and lower down in this section Origen reads "doeth" for "will do" of the LXX. It being wheat harvest, i.e., May–June, it was a season when thunder and rain were almost unknown in Palestine. Such a period is likened by Origen to a period of spiritual drought when the "thirsty soul" longs for the "refreshing grace" of God.

XIV, 1. *so that we may obtain in truth what they obtained in figure*] I follow the emendation of the Anonymous. T has "so that we may ask them" (sc. "the prayers"), which is obviously corrupt. "The prayers of the saints" here mentioned are clearly the prayers of the Old Testament saints, which Origen refers to in XIII, 2. They prayed for, and obtained, material blessings: but Christians can command spiritual blessings of which the former are but a symbol and type.

XIV, 1. *will supply unto you*] So Bentley and the Anonymous read, emending T which has "may supply unto you." If the reading of T is retained, the construction is "so that . . . the earthly and little things . . . the Father may supply," etc.

XIV, 2. *four nouns, etc.*] See Introduction, pp. 206 f.

XIV, 2. *in a dignified manner*] Greek μεγαλοφυέστερον. The word is not easy to translate, but its meaning here may be illustrated from *contra Celsum*, IV, 31: "stately and dignified [σεμνὸν καὶ μεγαλοφυὲς] is this prohibition of theirs 'Lift not thine eyes up to heaven,' etc. [Deut. 4:19]."

XIV, 3. *Examples of the first of these terms*] i.e., of "supplication," the object of which, according to Origen, is "the obtaining of something which a person lacks." But only in the case of the first of the four examples given is the object indicated.

XIV, 4. *obelized*] The obelus was one of the critical signs used from the third or second century B.C. by the grammarians of Alexandria, and said to have been first employed by Aristarchus in connection with his edition of Homer. The word means "a spit," and it was usually represented by a straight line——, with or without accompanying dot or dots ——. It was

originally used to mark passages which the critic wished to censure. In the *Hexapla* Origen prefixed the obelus to words or lines
which were wanting in the Hebrew; and this is precisely the
meaning of the verb "obelize" here. See H. B. Swete, *Introduction to the Old Testament in Greek*, 69 ff.

XIV, 4. *"with a song"*] LXX: μετά ᾠδῆς (Hab. 3:1). The
Hebrew is *al Shigionoth* (Revised Version "set to Shigionoth").
This word is apparently the plural of *Shiggaion*, found in the
title of Psalm 7, and usually held to denote a poem of a wild,
passionate character with rapid changes of rhythm. But the
LXX read, doubtless correctly, *al Neginoth* (as in the title
of Psalm 4, etc.) "with music of stringed instruments." In
Hab. 3:19 the LXX translation of *al Neginothai* is ἐν τῇ ᾠδῇ
αὐτοῦ.

XIV, 4. *"in the midst of the two living creatures"*] So the LXX
reads in Hab. 3:2. The Hebrew has "in the midst of the years."
In *De Princ.*, I, 3, 4 (*C.B.*, XXII, 53) Origen states it as his
opinion that the two living creatures (ζῴων) are the Son and the
Holy Spirit. Justinian fastened on this passage (*Ep. ad Mennam*:
P.G., LXXXVI, 983) as implying Origen's belief that the Son
and the Holy Spirit were created beings; but he failed to prove
his assertion. See the note of the Anonymous in the edition of
W. Reading, pp. 73, 74. This note, incidentally, indicates how
clearly the Anonymous perceived the untrustworthiness of
Rufinus's translations: "si qua omnino fides Interpreti Rufino
sit habenda."

XIV, 4. *an excellent illustration of the definition of prayer*] But on
his own definition "prayer," for Origen, includes "a request to
God for certain things." There is, however, no such request in
Hab., ch. 3, which is an example of the wider use of the term
"prayer" in the Old Testament as an elevation of the mind to
God which does not necessarily include petition.

XIV, 5. *intercession*] Though I have retained this translation
of ἔντευξις, the Greek word does not necessarily involve what
the English does, namely prayer in relation to others. But it implies, as Origen correctly observes, a free, confident approach
to God. See Trench, *Synonyms of the New Testament*, 189 f.

XIV, 5. *intercedes exceedingly*] See footnote in text of II, 3.

XIV, 5. *if we use the terms in their proper sense*] It is essential to
bear in mind, if we are to follow Origen's argument, how he
defines "prayer" in section 2 of this chapter.

XIV, 6. *supplication . . . addressed to holy men also*] The text of
T reads simply "men"; but some alteration is required in view

of the words "if these may be addressed to holy men" lower down in this section.

XIV, 6. *other men*] Here also T reads "men." Koetschau, following Klostermann, inserts "other." The Anonymous suggests "all men."

XIV, 6. *supplication is addressed to the saints only*] The reference is obviously to living saints. Note the words: "If, for example, a Paul or a Peter can be found" (εἴ τις εὑρεθείη Παῦλος ἢ Πέτρος) —*not* "Paul or Peter." The interpretation of G. Dix, *The Shape of the Liturgy*, 346, appears to be incorrect.

XIV, 6. *Making us worthy to receive the authority*] Light is thrown upon this passage by XXVIII, 9. The apostles received through the Holy Spirit the authority to forgive sins. Others like them ("a Paul or a Peter"), who are led by the Spirit as sons of God, have a similar authority. Like the prophets they are speaking not the things of their own but of the divine will. See W. H. Frere in *The Early History of the Church and Ministry*, ch. V, p. 292.

XIV, 6. *Stephen*] Acts 7:60. But in the previous verse we read of him "calling upon (the Lord) saying, Lord Jesus, receive my spirit"—clearly a "prayer."

XV, 1. *but only to the God and Father of all*] For this limitation concerning prayer (in the proper sense of the term according to Origen), see Introduction, pp. 187 f., 231.

Cf. *contra Celsum*, V, 4: "Every supplication and prayer and intercession and thanksgiving is to be offered to God who is over all through the high priest who is above all the angels, the living Word and God. But we shall supplicate the Word himself and intercede with him and give thanks, yes and pray also, if we are able to pay attention to the correct use and the abuse of terms concerning prayer." The concluding words, if they are to be brought into line with *De Orat.*, XV, 1, must mean that "prayer" in the looser, but not in the stricter, sense may be addressed to Christ.

On similar lines is *contra Celsum*, VIII, 13: "We worship the one God and his one Son and Word and Image with entreaties and requests according to our ability, bringing our prayers to the God of the universe through his only-begotten: to whom first we offer them, counting him worthy who is the propitiation for our sins to bring as a high priest our prayers and sacrifices and intercessions to the God who is over all."

A less decisive passage is *contra Celsum*, V, 11 (end): "And although one may not be so great (as the sun), nevertheless let such a one pray to the Word of God as able to heal him, and much more to his Father, who sent his Word to them of old time and healed them and delivered them from their afflictions."

On the other hand, a different point of view is indicated in *In Rom.*, VIII, 5: "If therefore Enoch and Moses and Aaron and Samuel called upon the Lord, and he heard them, doubtless they called upon Christ Jesus as Lord: and if to call upon the name of the Lord and to pray to the Lord are one and the same thing, as God is called upon, Christ is to be called upon; and as God is prayed to, so also Christ is to be prayed to; and as we offer prayers to God the Father first of all, so also to the Lord Jesus Christ; and as we offer requests to the Father, so we offer requests to the Son also; and as we offer thanksgiving to God, so also we offer thanks to the Saviour" (*P.G.*, XIV, 1165 f.). But as this passage is found only in the Latin translation of Rufinus, it may have been altered in the interests of orthodoxy. The Anonymous, however, in a learned and able note (Reading, 78 f.), confining himself to a consideration of those passages in which the Greek is extant, endeavours to make Origen consistent with himself. He maintains that in the passage of the *De Oratione* Origen is speaking of Christ only under the aspect of "high priest and advocate" (see XV, 4), and therefore insists that Christ *qua* mediator is not to be prayed to; but that when Origen is referring to Christ as Word or Son of God (e.g., in *contra Celsum* V, 4 and V, 11) he says something different. The Anonymous also draws attention to the limited connotation of the word "prayer" as used in the *De Oratione* here.

XV, 1. "*Teach us to pray*" . . . "*Our Father*," etc.] Origen here confuses Matthew and Luke. The words "Teach us to pray" come from Luke 11:2, but "Our Father," etc., from Matt. 6:9. Indeed, in XVIII, 2, Origen gives the text of the prayer in Luke as "Father, Hallowed be thy name," etc.

XV, 1. *the Son is different from the Father in person and subject*] ἕτερος . . . κατ᾽ οὐσίαν καὶ ὑποκείμενόν (-ός τ) ἐστιν ὁ υἱὸς τοῦ πατρός. Apparently Origen uses οὐσία here in the sense of Person (that which distinguishes the Son from the Father); as he also does in *In Joh.*, II, 23, where he argues that because the Son is called light and the Father is called light, it does not follow that the Son is not in οὐσία (i.e., Person) different from the Father. Cf. also *In Joh.*, I, 28 *fin.* and *contra Celsum*, VI, 64. ὑποκείμενος is similarly used in *In Jerem. hom.*, VIII, 2 (*C.B.*, VI, 57). A similar use of the term οὐσία appears in Eusebius, *H.E.*, VI, 33, in describing the heresy of Beryllus of Bostra, whom Origen converted to orthodoxy. On the other hand, οὐσία and ὑποκείμενος are distinguished in *In Joh.*, X, 37, οὐσία meaning "essence," and ὑποκείμενος "person" or "subject." See Bigg, 203 (note), Bethune Baker, 149, F. Prat, *Origène* 172.

XV, 1. *in accordance with the words "he sware"*] The Anonymous would read "the Lord sware" following Ps. 109:4 (LXX) and Heb. 7:21.

XV, 2. *it is not fitting that a man . . . should pray to him who prays*] Cf. *contra Celsum*, V, 11.

XV, 2. *had given this teaching*] An emendation of the Anonymous, followed by Koetschau. T reads "shall give."

XV, 2. *no one had "asked the Father"*] In XXII, 1, Origen points out that nowhere in the Old Testament is God called "Father" in prayer.

XV, 3. *named Jerusalem*] Actually "Sion" is the word used (Isa. 49:14).

XV, 4. *he who said . . . might also say*] This emendation by Delarue makes it clear that the words put into the mouth of the Son, which follow, are merely hypothetical.

XV, 4. *"Why callest thou me good?"*] This quotation from Mark 10:18 is a favourite one with Origen when he touches on the subordination of the Son to the Father. Cf. *contra Celsum*, V, 11; *In Joh.*, I, 35; II, 13; XIII, 36; also VI, 47; XIII, 25; *Exhort.* 7. See H. B. Swete, *ad loc.*

XV, 4. *"one" Father with him*] Reading αὐτῷ for αὐτῶν with Bentley and the Anonymous.

XV, 4. *to the Father alone with me and through me*] i.e., in company with me (as your brother) and through me (as your mediator).

XVI, 1. *either with the Father or apart from the Father*] Cf. the letter of Theophilus Alex., as translated by Jerome (*C.V.*, LV, 148, 149) "cum legeretur . . . in alio libro, qui 'de oratione' scribitur: 'non debemus orare filium, sed solum patrem, nec patrem cum filio,' obturavimus aures nostras," etc. See Introduction, p. 231.

XVI, 2. *the command to ask for "heavenly" and "great" things*] Cf. *In Matt.*, XVI, 28 (*C.B.*, XL, 571).

XVI, 2. *the shadow of the bodily object*] The illustration may be found puzzling if it is not perceived that in the case of a human giver "the bodily object" is the important thing, "the shadow," which it casts, is unimportant; but in the case of the divine Giver, the heavenly, spiritual gifts are what really matter, the earthly blessings are the "shadows" of the heavenly things, and are quite inferior. It is the will of God to give us heavenly things: the bodily blessings, which are "added" (Matt. 6:33), are merely their natural accompaniments.

XVI, 3. *material dew*] See note on XIII, 2.

XVI, 3. *Does it not follow*, etc.] A free translation is given of this sentence, following an emendation of Bentley. In any case, Origen's meaning is clear. Jonah and his physical deliverance is typical of the spiritual deliverance of those who look to Jesus as Saviour.

XVI, 3. *the great fish*] i.e., allegorically, the devil, with reference to Job 3:8, as is apparent from *In Joh.*, I, 17, and *De Princ.*, IV, 5 (*C.B.*, XXII, 300).

XVII, 1. This chapter is an example of the imperfect arrangement, due no doubt to its hasty composition, that is to be found here and there in the *De Oratione*. Obviously it ought to follow XVI, 2, immediately. In that section, *q.v.*, Origen speaks of the "shadows," i.e., earthly blessings, which accompany, as a natural consequence, spiritual blessings. He now qualifies this statement. Just as in some latitudes and at some times the gnomon of the sun-dial gives no shadow, or a greater or less shadow, so God's spiritual gifts are sometimes accompanied by no earthly blessings or only to a more or less degree. This will cause the spiritually minded man no real concern. He who rejoices in the sunlight will pay no attention to the presence or absence of a shadow on the dial; neither should we, in the presence of God's spiritual gifts, take thought concerning material blessings, whether they be given or not.

XVII, 1. *problems connected with sun-dials*] Cf. Pliny, *Nat. Hist.*, II, (72) 74–(76) 78, where the variations, according to latitude, of shadows on the sun-dial are discussed.

XVII, 2. *"a kingdom" of Christ "that cannot be shaken"*] Cf. Heb. 12:28. An emendation of Bentley. T reads "a kingdom of Christ of those who reign," which has been emended to "a kingdom of Christ, king of those who reign" (Klostermann), with reference to I Tim. 6:15, and "a kingdom of Christ who reigns" (Anonymous).

XVIII, 1. *you who read this book will judge*] The gift of the Spirit for discernment being the possession of all Christians (cf. I Cor. 2), the readers of the *De Oratione* will be able to discover if it possesses the marks of the spirit.

XVIII, 1. *outlined*] ὑπογραφεῖσαν, i.e., written as a model or example of prayer. The verb is used for tracing letters for

children to write over: cf. I Pet. 2:21, "leaving us an example
(ὑπογραμμὸν)."

XVIII, 1. *with what power it has been filled*] Origen examines
the text of the Lord's Prayer from no merely critical or intellectual standpoint: for him its inspiration, in the sense of power
to inspire, is paramount. Cf. John 20:31: "These are written
. . . that believing ye may have life in his name." See also H. de
Lubac, *Histoire et Esprit*, 125 ff.

XVIII, 2. *The text of Matthew . . . Luke's text*] See Introduction, pp. 213 f.

XVIII, 3. *It is better to take the view that the prayers are different*]
Origen forms this judgment simply from the prayers as they lay
before him in the Gospels, and from this point of view his conclusions are reasonable and sound. We should today approach
the problem rather from the findings of source-criticism of the
Gospels, the Jewish antecedents of the Prayer, and its liturgical
use in the primitive Church, laying less stress than Origen does
upon its context in the Gospels. It is easier, therefore, for us to
hold the view that an original nucleus transmitted from the
Lord has resulted in two different forms, one of which has become almost universal under the influence of liturgical tradition.

XVIII, 3. *we searched also*] For a similar kind of search, see
XXII, 1.

XIX, 1. *must first be settled and disposed*, etc.] Cf. VIII, 2–
X, 2. It is not surprising that Origen, as a master of the spiritual
life, lays stress on this; but it is characteristic of him that he
seeks for and cites Scriptural support for his view.

XIX, 2. *his accustomed oath*] A heightened description of the
formula "Verily, I say unto you," which occurs some seventy
times in the Gospels.

XIX, 2. *"They have received their reward"*] The verb used in
Matt. 6:2, 5, is ἀπέχουσι, which means, in the light of its usage
in papyri, "they have given their receipt"—and therefore
cannot claim anything further in that respect.

XIX, 2. *he did not "sow unto the Spirit"*] The passage in Gal.
6:6–10 has much in it about doing good to others, and its reward. And this suggests to Origen its co-ordination with the
passage in Matt. ch. 6, referred to in the previous note.

XIX, 3. *stands in it*, etc.] The text followed is that as emended
by Koetschau ("if any alteration is necessary"), except that he
takes "through love of pleasure" with the preceding clause. T
has: "stands in it not well, praying in the corners of the streets,
through love of pleasure frequenting not one but several

streets." Bentley conjectured: "stands in it, praying not otherwise in the corners of the streets than through love of pleasure
frequenting," etc. The Anonymous conjectured: "in which he
stands not well who prays in the corners of the streets through
love of pleasure," etc. At the background of these references to
"twists" and "corners" and "not one but several streets" is the
Greek idea, to which Origen gives expression in XXI, 2, that
virtue is one, vice is many.

XIX, 3. *fallen from their deity*] In *contra Celsum*, III, 37,
Origen says that Christians through the only-begotten God the
Word "partake of deity"; and in *De Orat.*, XXIII, 5, he speaks
of those "to whom appertains a certain divine glory and power
and—so to speak—an effluence of his deity." Again, in
XXIV, 4, we read, "when a man partaking of an effluence of
deity exalts that very power of God of which he has partaken."
See also IX, 2, and XXV, 2.

XX, 1. *a difference between the Church and the synagogue*] The
point of this strange and rambling argument is that, according
to the Scriptures, from the "church" (the *ecclesia* of the LXX of
Deut. 23:2) the type of person there mentioned and strangers
were excluded, because it was holy and without blemish; but
the "synagogue" could be built by a Gentile (Luke 7:5). This
indicates the inferiority of the synagogue, and so to "the
synagogue" is given that moral connotation which in the previous section is given to "the corners of the streets." Historically
considered, the basis of this distinction is that Christians took
over as the name of their society the word *ecclesia* from the Jews,
leaving almost entirely to their use the word "*synagogue*."

XX, 1. *love . . . has a deep concern*] There is clearly a distinction here between the meaning of φιλεῖ and ἀγαπᾷ, whether
or not such a distinction holds generally. φιλεῖ has in this passage a definite suggestion of natural desire and of self-pleasing
—a meaning that is helped out by the wider context, in which
(XIX, 3) we read of "love of pleasure" *(φιληδονία)* and "lovers
of pleasure" *(φιλήδονοι)*. ἀγαπᾷ, on the other hand, describes
the desire of a person whose thoughts are centred, not on self or
his fellow-men, but on God, and who seeks to tread the narrow
way of self-discipline.

XX, 1. *that he "may appear before the Lord God"*] i.e., as a true
Israelite who belongs to the *ecclesia*, which is now the Christian
Church.

XX, 1. *he is a male person*] The Christian corresponds to the
male under the Old Covenant, who was required to appear

before the Lord, since in prayer he appears not unto men to pray but unto God.

XX, 2. *nothing that is seen is good*] A textual quotation from Ignatius, *Romans*, 3. Koetschau refers to several passages in Origen (*contra Celsum*, IV, 93; VII, 13; VIII, 13, 36; *Exhort.*, 12) in which he detects echoes of Ignatius; but strangely enough he fails to note this direct quotation.

XX, 2. *The actors of a drama in a theatre*] The illustration is doubtless suggested by the fact that the word ὑποκριτὴς which occurs in Matt. 6:5 in the sense of "hypocrite" also means "actor." Cf. XXVIII, 3.

XX, 2. *he "shuts" every "door" of the faculties of sense*] Cf. IX, 2.

XXI, 1. *do not let us use vain repetitions*] We have kept the Authorized Version and Revised Version rendering of Matt. 6:7, although it is doubtful if it is correct, and still more doubtful if it expresses the meaning that Origen took out of *battologia*. Both here and in VIII, 1 (*q.v.*), he connects the word, at any rate in part, with the practice of asking God for "bodily" or "outward" or "earthly" things. On the contrary, in prayer we are to "speak to God," that is to him, as we are taught in the Lord's Prayer, who is "our Father, which art in heaven"; and since he is "in heaven" we shall ask him for "heavenly things." *Battologia*, therefore, includes (*a*) asking for the wrong things and (*b*) forgetfulness of the true character of him to whom we pray. Possibly Origen would not disagree with Hesychius, who defined it as *argologia*, "idle speech."

XXI, 1. *examine for blemishes*] μωμοσκοποῦντες. In the LXX μῶμος is a flaw or blemish which vitiates a person or thing for holy purposes. The use of the verb is confined to Jewish (e.g., Philo) and Christian writers. It is suitable in this context because Origen goes on to speak of "the words of prayer offered up (ἀναπεμπομένους)," and this verb is used in the Martyrdom of Polycarp, in Justin Martyr, and in the Greek Liturgies, as well as in Clement of Alexandria and Origen, of offering up prayer to the throne of grace. (Lightfoot on *Mart. Polyc.*, XV).

XXI, 2. *he who speaks much*] With a reference to "much speaking" in Matt. 6:7. It is clear from this section that "much speaking" is "ill speaking." And indeed in a fragment from his Commentary on John (Brooke, II, 230; *Philocalia*, ed. J. Robinson, 45) Origen says that "he who utters anything whatever that is foreign to godliness speaks much." The moral connotation which he places upon "much speaking" is obviously connected with the conception in his mind (see the note following) that vice is many.

XXI, 2. *virtue is one, vice is many*] A characteristically Platonic doctrine. Cf. *Rep.*, IV, 445c: "while there is only one form of virtue, there are infinite varieties of vice." Similar statements about the unity of virtue may be found in, e.g., *Prot.*, 329cd, *Meno* 72c. Any virtue we attempt to explain must, according to Plato, be defined as "the knowledge of what is good"; so that every virtue "seems on examination to cover the whole field of the conduct of life, and none can be in principle distinguished from any other" (A. E. Taylor, *Plato, The Man and His Work*, 64). Cf. Xenophon, *Mem.*, III, 9:5: "[Socrates] said that justice and every other virtue is wisdom." The Pythagoreans had also held the unity of virtue; but Aristotle, who criticized on this point Platonic doctrine (*Pol.*, I, 13), praises them at the expense of the Platonists, in that they, *sc.* the Pythagoreans, made the One good, instead of the good one (*Eth. Nic.*, I, 4:1096b). Thus, in constructing (after the fashion of the time) a double column of good and bad things, respectively, (see Lightfoot on Gal. 4:25), they would place "the one" and "the good" in the same column, and "the many" and "the bad," opposite them, in the other (Aristotle, *Met.*, I, 5:986a). Platonists, on the contrary, as Origen does here, would head one column "The One" and the other "The Many," and place underneath good things and bad things, respectively. In other words, Origen follows the Platonists in making the good an abstract unity. Possibly Paul had this idea of "the one" and "the many" in his mind when he spoke (*pace* the English Litany) of *the fruit* of the Spirit and *the works* of the flesh (Gal. 5:19, 22).

XXI, 2. *after the likeness of the serpent*] The reference is to the LXX of Ps. 57:4, 5: "Sinners were estranged from the womb, they went astray from the belly, they spoke falsehood; their mind is after the likeness of the serpent." The words "falsehood" and "estranged," which occur earlier in this section, seem to have suggested to Origen's too susceptible mind their use in this Psalm, and so led him to refer to the "serpent," which otherwise appears inconsequential.

XXII, 1. *the Old Testament, as it is called*] The phrase may suggest that "Old Testament" was not yet an absolutely settled title for the first portion of the Bible. In the previous century, however, c. 170, Melito of Sardis had spoken of "the books of the Old Testament" (*ap.* Eusebius, *H.E.*, IV, 26, 14), and by Origen's time "Old Testament" must have been well on the way to general acceptance as a description of the writings embodying the "covenant" that God had made with his ancient people Israel. Tertullian testifies for Latin Christianity to the title, e.g., in *Adv. Marc.*, IV, 22 (*P.L.*, II, 414): "oportebat in eo suggestu consignari novum testamentum, in quo conscriptum vetus fuerat."

XXII, 1. *a prayer in which someone calls God "Father"*] Cf. *In Joh.*, XIX, 5: "Though there are countless prayers to be found written in the Psalms and the prophets and also in the law, we did not find a single one in which God is addressed as Father." For another passage, emphasizing the distinctive Fatherhood of God under the Christian Dispensation, see *In Matt.*, XVII, 36 (*C.B.*, XL., 702).

XXII, 1. *we searched to the best of our ability*] Cf. also XVIII, 3, "We searched the Gospel of Mark," and III, 1, "the word 'prayer' occurs for the first time, so far as my observation goes." This "searching of the Scriptures" must have been a laborious task under the conditions of Origen's time, and affords eloquent testimony to the pains he took to ensure that his theology was formed on the usage of the Bible.

XXII, 2. *those called "sons" are blameworthy*] Sections 1 and 2 of this chapter, if read by themselves, might suggest the view that Christian sonship involves complete freedom from sin; for on the one hand Origen contrasts it with what is implied in passages of the Old Testament where God rebukes his sons, and, on the other, he quotes the words of John, "whosoever is begotten of God doeth no sin." Other passages from his writings, however, modify or even oppose this inference. In *In Matt.*, XIX, 23 (*C.B.*, XL, 416 ff.), Origen contrasts the washing of regeneration by water and spirit with the eschatological regeneration spoken of in Matt. 19:28. The former cleanses from defilement, so that he who is born from above is pure, "if I may make so bold to say", "in a glass darkly"; but he who comes to the other regeneration will be absolutely pure (καθαρώτατος) from defilement and will see "face to face." In the washing of regeneration we are buried through baptism with Christ; but in the regeneration at the last day we shall be conformed to the body of Christ's glory. *In Jesu Nave hom.*, XXI, (*C.B.*, XXX, 431), of which the Latin is extant, is more decisive: "I do not think that anyone's heart can become so pure that the thought of evil never stains it." See J. Danièlou, *Origène*, 72 f.; Bigg, 250.

XXII, 3. *"no man speaking in the Spirit of God"*] So the Anonymous reads for "no man speaking in the Holy Spirit," rightly, as the next line shows.

XXII, 3. *numbers of heretics use this title*] Origen is thinking especially of the followers of Marcion, Basilides, and Valentinus, of whom he says (*In Jerem. hom.*, X, 5: *C.B.*, VI, 75 f.): "They name the name of Jesus, but they do not possess Jesus; for they do not confess him as they ought."

XXII, 4. *acquire an impression of sonship*] ἀπομάττονται υἱότητα. The verb is used of "taking an impression of," as a sculptor would do. Those who are called to be sons of God bear the image or likeness of the Son of God, who is himself the image of the invisible God.

XXII, 4. *but also to him who is "in the body"*] T has ἀλλὰ καὶ ὄντι ἐν τῷ σώματι. The emendation τῷ ὄντι of the Anonymous seems necessary to make sense. The sons of God are not only united with and therefore conformed to the glorified body of Christ, but also to Christ in his glorified body. This is accomplished, as Origen points out in the next sentence, by the renewing of their mind: so that mind as well as body bears the impress of the divine image.

XXII, 5. *the kingdom of heaven is seated in all those*, etc.] According to Origen the kingdom of heaven or of God is preeminently immanent and spiritual. See XXV, 1.

XXIII, 1. *we are not to suppose that he is circumscribed in bodily fashion*] Cf. section 3; and for other early statements of the immensity of God, see Hermas, *Shepherd*, Mand. 1; Clement of Alexandria, *Strom.*, VII, 35; Novatian, *De Trinitate*, XII.

XXIII, 1. *"Jesus answered and said unto them"*] John 14:23. This is an unique reading. All other textual authorities read "said unto him" (i.e., unto Judas, not Iscariot, in reply to his question).

XXIII, 3. *a tenet which leads to most impious opinions*] Both here and elsewhere Origen vehemently rejects the notion that God has a body. He deals with this opinion in the first chapter of the *De Principiis* and also in *In Joh.*, XIII, 21–25; *contra Celsum*, III, 75; VI 70, 71; VIII, 49; *In Gen.*, I, 13; as well as in this passage. It is not hard to understand how such a notion was absolutely opposed to Origen's philosophy. But the vigour with which he attacks it suggests, what is indeed a fact, that he is opposing actual persons who held it. These were of two classes. There were the simple-minded, matter-of-fact Christians who interpreted everything in the Scriptures literally, and when they read in them that God was in a place, or that he had hands or arms, or that he was a consuming fire, they pictured him as corporeal in his nature. The Origenistic conception of God was one of the chief causes of conflict between the Greek and the literalistic Coptic monks in Egypt in the fourth century. See O. Chadwick, *John Cassian*, 15 ff. On the other hand, there were the Stoics, who were in part materialists, and conceived of a material force inherent in things. The followers of Zeno and Chrysippus, for example, and their idea that God has a body, are explicitly refuted in *contra Celsum*, VIII, 49. See de Faye, III, 27 ff. (See also Introduction, pp. 193 f.)

XXIII, 3. *what they suppose is a bodily garden*] Origen similarly allegorizes the Garden of Eden in *De Princ.*, IV, 2 *fin.* (cf. *Philocalia*, 24 f.); *contra Celsum*, IV, 39.

XXIII, 3. *they were hidden*] Gen. 3:8, according to the LXX. The Hebrew has "hid themselves."

XXIII, 4. *We have treated these matters at length in our commentaries on Genesis*] See Introduction, p. 181, and Koetschau, I, lxxvi, who holds that the exegesis of Gen. 3:8, 9, can hardly have stood earlier than in the ninth book of the Commentaries on Genesis. Eusebius (*H.E.*, VI, 24:2) says that the first eight books were written at Alexandria. It follows, therefore, that the later books were written after the removal to Caesarea (231 or 232), and the composition of the *De Oratione* must be placed subsequently to that date.

XXIII, 4. *Deuteronomy*] A slip on the part of Origen. "I will dwell in them, and walk [in them]" is from II Cor. 6:16, where Paul seems to be referring confusedly to several Old Testament passages. "I will walk in you" occurs in Lev. 26:12; "the Lord thy God will walk in thy camp" in Deut. 23:14. Origen again quotes "I will dwell and walk in them," but this time without giving a reference, in *In Matt.*, X, 15 (*C.B.*, XL, 20).

XXIII, 4. *every sinner hiding himself from the face of God*] This emendation of the Anonymous, with ref. to Gen. 3:8, is supported by *In Jerem. hom.*, XVI, 4 (*C.B.*, VI, 136): "Wicked men hide themselves from the face of God."

XXIII, 4. *As he dwells in the saints, so also in heaven*] Cf. Clement of Alexandria, *Ecl. Proph.*, 52 (*C.B.*, XVII, 151): "The Lord is properly called the heavens, next those who were first created, after them the holy men who lived before the Law, such as the patriarchs, then the apostles also."

XXIII, 4. *or else he dwells*, etc.] The text is doubtful. T reads "or else he dwells because of the saints according to the saying: 'Unto thee, etc.'"; Bentley, "or else because the saints dwell in heaven. Now the saying: 'Unto thee, etc.'"; the Anonymous followed by Koetschau, "or else he dwells there because of the saints in heaven, in accordance with the saying: 'Unto thee, etc.'" (i.e., inserting the words "there" and "in accordance with"). Koetschau points out that the quotation "Unto thee, etc." goes with what precedes and not with what follows.

XXIII, 4. *by the aid of the Word*] T has "by the aid and the Word."

XXIII, 4. *Christ . . . heaven . . . his Church . . . earth*] For these identifications, see further XXVI, 3.

XXIV, 1. The general meaning of the opening sentence is not in doubt, but how best to emend the text of T is uncertain. I have added the words "He who prays," as suggested by the Anonymous, and read "either . . . or" with Bentley instead of "some times . . . at other times."

XXIV, 2. *the I am*] T has ὤν, which has been emended to ὁ ὤν in accordance with the LXX of Ex. 3:14.

XXIV, 3. *young grass*] Greek ἄγρωστις, lit. "dog's-tooth grass."

XXIV, 3. *copious rain*] Greek νιφετός, "snowstorm," which seems quite unsuitable, unless the word is used simply for "rain," for which there is some authority in Nonnus. I have accordingly translated it "copious rain," since the Hebrew word (pl.), of which νιφετός is the translation, is derived from a root meaning "much or many," and is interpreted as "copious showers" by Brown, Driver, and Briggs.

XXIV, 3. *Therefore, when a man perceives*] I read διὰ τοῦτο for ταῦτα, as suggested by the Anonymous scholar.

XXIV, 3. *remembers rather than learns them*] This is perhaps the only passage in Origen's works where he hints at the Platonic doctrine of Anamnesis, namely, that "learning is nothing but reminiscence" (*Phaedo*, 72 E; cf. *Meno*, 81 D). If Origen lays little emphasis upon this doctrine, Clement of Alexandria expressly denies it in *Ecl. Proph.*, 17 (*C.B.*, XVII, 141): "God made us not pre-existing. For if we had pre-existed, we should also of necessity know whence we are, and how and for what purpose we have come hither."

XXIV, 4. *partaking of an effluence of deity*] Cf. IX, 2; XXIII, 5; XXIV, 4; and XIX, 3 (note).

XXIV, 5. *the translators*] i.e., the Septuagint.

XXIV, 5. *Tatian*] An Assyrian by birth, a disciple of Justin Martyr, who having been converted to Christianity composed c. 165 an *Oratio ad Graecos*, in which he ridiculed polytheism and Greek philosophy. His *Diatessaron* or Harmony of the Four Gospels dates from c. 170. Returning to the East after many travels, he founded the school and sect of the Encratites, whose tenets included a rejection of the use of wine and flesh and matrimony. They celebrated the Eucharist in water only, hence they were called Aquarii. The date of his death is uncertain.

Origen (*contra Celsum*, I, 16) refers to the "very great learning" that Tatian displayed in his *Oratio ad Graecos*, and there is another reference, though not by name, to this treatise in *contra Celsum*, IV, 67. But in *contra Celsum*, VI, 51, the idea that "Let there be light" is to be taken as if it were a wish and in the optative mood, is associated with a "pestilent heresy," although Tatian is not mentioned, as he is here, in the same connection. Tatian is also mentioned with disapprobation for this interpretation of Gen. 1:3 by Clement of Alexandria in the *Ecl. Proph.*, 38:1 (*C.B.*, XVII, 148).

XXIV, 5. *his godless thought, "God was in darkness"*] We are not told why Tatian held this idea. It may be, however, that believing, with other gnostics, that the supreme God was inscrutable he interpreted the creation story in such a way as to assign the creation of light (whereby God was revealed) to a subordinate aeon. God, therefore, expressed a *wish* "Let there be light," and until his wish was carried out by another he himself "was in darkness."

XXV, 1. *but the kingdom of God is within us*] The variations from the text of Luke 17:21 ("but" instead of "for behold," and "us" instead of "you") are not to be regarded as variant readings. It is evident that Origen does not here quote exactly (he changes the order of the Greek in the preceding verse). The significant point of the quotation for him is "*within* you (us)": ἐντὸς ὑμῶν, as is clear from the exposition that follows in this section. Origen, therefore, does not agree with those modern commentators who, in defiance of what seems to be the plain meaning of ἐντός, interpret it, with the margin of the Revised Version, as "in the midst of" or "among." For Origen the kingdom is first and foremost immanent and spiritual. Cf. "In our hearts all-sovereign reign" in Archbishop Whately's hymn: "Thou to whom all power is given"—a paraphrase of the Lord's Prayer.

XXV, 1. *the saying which I mentioned a short while ago*] In XX, 2.

XXV, 1. *the reason*] Lit. "the ruling principle"—a favourite Stoic term.

XXV, 1. *Christ's kingdom*] Cf. *In Jerem. hom.*, XIV, 5

(*C.B.*, VI, 110 f.): "Jesus Christ uprooted the kingdoms of sin and overthrew the dwellings of iniquity and made instead of these kingdoms righteousness and truth to reign in our souls."

XXV, 1. "*the prince of this world*"] ὁ ἄρχων τοῦ αἰῶνος τούτου, an expression which occurs twice in this section, and also in *contra Celsum*, IV, 93; VIII, 13, 36, is apparently derived from Ignatius, *Ephesians*, 19. See also note on XX, 2.

XXV, 2, 3. See Introduction, pp. 216 f. The kingdom, though immanent and present, is as yet imperfectly realized within us. It must be developed, and also be made perfect at the consummation of all things.

XXV, 2. *is being deified*] Cf. XXVII, 13, and *Exhort.*, 25 (end), in which passages, as here, the word θεοποιεῖσθαι is used. W. R. Inge, *Christian Mysticism*, 13 (see also pp. 356–368), remarks that "St. Augustine is no more afraid of *deificari* in Latin than Origen of θεοποιεῖσθαι in Greek. The subject is one of primary importance to anyone who wishes to understand mystical theology; but it is difficult for us to enter into the minds of the ancients who used these expressions, both because θεός was a very fluid concept in the early centuries, and because our notions of *personality* are very different." See note on XIX, 3.

XXV, 3. "Beliar"] This spelling is supported by the best textual authorities in II Cor. 6:15; and Origen so spells the name here and also in *contra Celsum*, VI, 43; *In Joh.*, XIX, 21; XXXII, 24, 30

XXV, 3. "*the fruits of the Spirit*"] Paul speaks of the fruit (sing.) of the Spirit. Origen falls into the same inaccuracy as the English Litany.

XXV, 3. *the good things of regeneration*] i.e., the regeneration referred to in Matt. 19:28.

XXVI, 1. *Luke passes over these words in silence*] It is noteworthy that Origen seems to be unaware of the existence of MSS. containing "Thy will be done, as in heaven, so on earth" in the text of Luke 11:3, inasmuch as these words are found in the Codex א (? of Egyptian origin) and the Bohairic version.

XXVI, 2. *can be taken with all three clauses*] F. H. Chase, *The Lord's Prayer in the Early Church* (*Texts and Studies*, vol. I, no. 3, pp. 40, 41), gives reasons for holding that the words "as in heaven, so on earth" may appropriately be construed with "Hallowed be thy name" and "Thy kingdom come" as well as with "Thy will be done." It is natural that the thought of God as "Father" and "in heaven" "should exercise a continuous influence on the petitions which immediately follow, rather than it should at once fall into the background to re-appear at a later part of the prayer." Further, many passages of Scripture which speak of the coming of the Kingdom are in harmony with this interpretation, as for example, I Chron. 29:11; Dan. 2:44; 7:14; Matt. 3:2; 16:28; Luke 11:20; 17:20; 22:29; Rev. 11:15. Chase, however, does not notice that Origen had suggested it. Bengel on Matt. 6:10 quotes from the *Catechismus Romanus* put forth by the Council of Trent: "Pastoris erunt partes monere fidelem populum verba illa 'sicut in coelo, et in terra,' ad singulas referri posse singularum (trium) primarum postulationum, ut, 'Sanctificetur nomen tuum, sicut in coelo, et in terra.' Item, 'adveniat regnum tuum, sicut in coelo, et in terra'. Similiter, 'Fiat voluntas tua, sicut in coelo, et in terra.'"

XXVI, 3. *achieve the Father's will as Christ achieved it*] The verb is χωρεῖν, which, when used transitively, usually means "to contain," "to have room for," and hence "to be capable of," and (as apparently here) "to fulfil." But the expression is somewhat strange.

XXVI, 4. An objector urges that if you allegorize "heaven" as "Christ" and "earth" as "the Church," how can Christ say after the resurrection, "All authority hath been given to me as in heaven so also in earth"? Origen replies, in effect, that it was Christ as man who said this: as man he co-ordinates himself with his disciples for the work of bringing things on earth under the subjection of God, and as man united with the Word he has received authority over the things in heaven.

XXVI, 4. *being mingled with his deity*] A similar passage is *In Joh.*, I, 32: "the man of the Son of God, who has been mingled with his deity."

XXVI, 5. *the second difficulty*] See section 3 of this chapter.

XXVI, 5. *he who was first formed by the Lord, having been made for the angels to play with*] Job 40:19 (LXX). The reference is to the "behemoth" (v. 15, according to the Hebrew: the LXX has wild beasts). *Behemoth* is the intensive plural of *behemah*, "cattle": the idea that it was the first animal formed is an inference from Gen. 1:24, where "cattle" is the first living creature named. It is usually identified with the hippopotamus. The latter half of Job 40:19 is corrupt. That behemoth was made for the angels to play with (according to LXX) is an idea paralleled in 41:5: "Wilt thou play with him [i.e., leviathan, the crocodile] as with a bird?" Cf. also Ps. 104:26, which may be rendered: "There is leviathan, whom thou hast formed to play with him." It is clear from *In Joh.*, XX, 22, that Origen allegorizes the beast referred to in Job 40:19 as the devil, who is the prototype of those who are of the earth earthy.

XXVI, 5. *have fallen in mind*] Cf. Milton, *Paradise Lost*, I, 254:

> The mind is its own place, and in itself
> Can make a Heav'n of Hell, a Hell of Heav'n.

A similar line of thought is found in *In Jerem. hom.*, VIII, 2 (*C.B.*, VI, 57, 58).

XXVI, 6. *he who sins, wheresoever he may be, is earth*] A convincing emendation of Bentley. Cf. "he that doeth the will of God is heaven." T has "wheresoever there is earth."

XXVII, 2. *to comprehend more perfectly*] The line of thought here indicated is characteristic. As those who had been fed with material food by Jesus were urged by him to seek for the meat which abideth unto eternal life, so we, when we read of "bread" in the Lord's Prayer, must not rest upon the thought of a material substance, but rather understand it in a higher and spiritual sense. See section 5.

XXVII, 3. The argument that it is unwarrantable to suppose that "the daily bread" is Christ because the phrase seems to speak of some other bread, is countered by an appeal to the language of John 6. In that chapter sometimes, e.g., in v. 32, the "bread" is spoken of as other than Christ, yet other passages (e.g., v. 35) make it clear that the "bread" is Christ.

XXVII, 3. *"which I will give for the life of the world"*] John 6:51. Note that here and in the following section Origen (or the MS. T) by including the words "which I will give" before "for the life of the world" follows the reading of the Textus Receptus.

XXVII, 4. *every kind of food is called bread,* etc.] A very similar passage occurs in *In Joh.*, X, 17.

XXVII, 4. *ate and drank him*] In supplying the words "ate and" Koetschau refers to the text quoted above: "Except ye eat the flesh of the Son of man and drink his blood," etc.

XXVII, 4. *whenever he is distributed*] A reference to John 6:11: "having given thanks he distributed to them that were set down."

XXVII, 5. *Paul, speaking to the Corinthians . . . and in the Epistle to the Hebrews*] The views of Origen on the authorship of Hebrews are sometimes misrepresented. It is true that in an excerpt from his homilies on that Epistle, quoted by Eusebius, *H.E.*, VI, 25:11–14, Origen gives it as his own opinion that "the thoughts are the apostle's, but the style and composition belong to one who called to mind the apostle's teachings, and, as it were, made short notes of what his master said." "But who wrote the epistle, in truth God knows." It has been hastily concluded from this that Origen "rejected" the Pauline authorship of Hebrews. But that is not so. The words "who wrote the epistle" mean "who penned the actual words of the epistle." Not only in this passage of the *De Oratione* but frequently elsewhere in his other writings Origen explicitly ascribes Hebrews to Paul: e.g. (to mention only passages in which the original Greek is extant), *In Joh.*, I, 22; II, 10, 11, 17; X, 14; XIII, 33; XX, 32; XXXII, 28; *contra Celsum*, III, 53; *De Orat.*, XXVII, 5, 13; *Exhort.*, 44; also in *In Joh.*, I, 2, 18 and *De Princ.*, IV, 13, 24, where the Epistle is ascribed to "the apostle," and by implication also in *De Orat.*, XXVII, 15, where "two apostolic sayings" are quoted from Ephesians and Hebrews. In this Origen followed the view generally held in the Eastern Church of his day. Dionysius of Alexandria took the same view in his letter to Fabius, Bishop of Antioch (Feltoe, p. 8).

XXVII, 6. *a doctrine foreign to the Father of our Lord Jesus who has given the law and the prophets*] A thinly veiled reference to the Marcionites, who held that the God of the Old Testament was other than the Father of the Lord Jesus Christ. See also XXIX, 10, 13.

XXVII, 7. *this word "epiousios"*, etc.] That *epiousios* is not a literary Greek word is undisputed, as Origen says. Strictly speaking he does not affirm that neither is it ever used colloquially, but only that it is "not in common use among ordinary folk." The suggestion, however, that the evangelists coined the word, and the two examples of "biblical" words that he gives from the LXX, would appear to indicate that apart from its use in the Lord's Prayer he was otherwise quite unfamiliar with it. But an apparent example of the use of the word in a papyrus account book came to light when Flinders Petrie published in 1889 a volume entitled *Hawara, Biamu and Arsinoe*. The text of this document is also given in F. Preisigke, *Sammelbuch griechischen Urkunden aus Agypten*, I, 5224. An item in these accounts is ½ obol for επιουσι . . ., which doubtless should be completed ἐπιουσίων. The original document appears to have been since lost. On the derivation and meaning of the word, see note lower down. G. Klaffenbach (*Museum Helveticum*, vol. VI, Fasc. 4 (1949), pp. 216 ff.) believes that the true reading of an inscription (no. 419) discovered in Lindos (1902–1914), and edited by C. Blinkenberg, is τῷ ἱερεῖ τᾶς ᾿Αθάνας ἐπιουσίῳ, "the next-following priest of Athene." W. Bauer *Wörterbuch zum Neuen Testament* (1952), *s.v.* σήμερον, accepts this. It would seem, however, to the present writer that further corroboration of this reading is necessary.

XXVII, 7. *it seems likely to have been coined by the evangelists. At any rate, etc.*] Observe that Origen expresses himself cautiously. But the previous note would seem to show that his suggestion is incorrect. If *epiousios* was in use as a non-literary word, no explanation is required for its appearance in the forms of the Lord's Prayer as used by Greek-speaking Christians of the first century. The word may have been chosen by the author of Q as the translation of an Aramaic original, and subsequently taken over by both Matthew and Luke. On the other hand, if the Lord's Prayer in these Gospels is derived from two independent forms of oral tradition (as it may well be), and not based upon a common written document, the use of *epiousios* in both would strongly suggest its use also in the common speech. It may be an accident that we do not happen to have discovered another example of it in a papyrus of a non-literary character. In literary documents we could not expect to find it.

XXVII, 7. *enotizou*] The verb ἐνωτίζεσθαι occurs about thirty-seven times in the LXX and once (Acts 2:14) in the New Testament. The second person present imperative ἐνωτίζου is found in Job 33:1, 31; 34:16; 37:14; Isa. 1:2. The word appears to be a "Biblical" creation for the purpose of rendering the Hiphil of the Hebrew verb *'azan*, "to give ear." But it is also used in the LXX as the translation of other Hebrew verbs. Some scholars have questioned the view that the translators of the LXX coined the word. But until examples, which are not yet forthcoming, for its use elsewhere have been produced, Origen's statement must be allowed to stand. See H. St. J. Thackeray, *A Grammar of the Old Testament in Greek*, 267; J. H. Moulton and J. Milligan, *The Vocabulary of the Greek Testament, s.v.*

XXVII, 7. *akoutieis*] T reads in the passage: τίς γάρ ποτε Ἑλλήνων ἐχρήσατο . . . τῇ "ἀκουτίσθητι" ἀντὶ τοῦ . . . "ἀκοῦσαι ποιεῖς"; ἰσομοία τῇ "ἐπιούσιον" προσηγορία ἐστὶ κτλ. Obviously, emendation is necessary: for (1) neither ἀκουτίσθητι nor any form of the passive ἀκουτίζειν (a "Biblical" word, like ἐνωτίζεσθαι) occurs in the LXX; and (2) the explanation "thou makest to hear" does not in any case fit it. Koetschau, perversely retaining ἀκουτίσθητι, emends the explanation to ἀκούεσθαι ποίει σε "make thee to be heard." The Anonymous scholar reads ἀκούτισον (which occurs in the LXX in S. of Sol., 2:14; 8:13) and ἀκοῦσαι ποίει. I suggest ἀκουτιεῖς (Ps. 50 (51):10 "thou shalt make (me) to hear"), and ἀκοῦσαι ποιήσεις; ὁμοία for ἀκοῦσαι ποιεῖς; ἰσομοία. A dittography may lurk in -θητι ἀντὶ; and ἰσομοία is a suspiciously rare word, whereas ὅμοιος is common in Origen.

XXVII, 7. *periousios*] This word occurs in the LXX in Ex. 19:5; 23:22; Deut. 7:6; 14:2; 26:18, always as the translation of *segullah*, a special or peculiar possession (in Deut. the Vulg. translates *peculiaris*). In the Hebrew it is preceded only in Deuteronomy by the word *'am*, "people": but the LXX in every case, both in Exodus and Deuteronomy, renders λαὸς περιούσιος; and probably *'am* should be restored in the passages in Exodus (see A. H. McNeile on Ex. 19:5). *Periousios* literally means "that which is over and above" (from *peri* and the verb "to be"), hence "specially acquired," with a meaning similar to the classical ἐξαίρετος. Although no clear example of the adjective has been found in the papyri, there are many examples of the substantive *periousia*, meaning "superfluity," "abundance." (J. B. Lightfoot on *I Clem.*, LXIV; F. J. A. Hort on I Pet. 2:9; W. Lock on Tit. 2:14; Moulton and Milligan, *s.v.*)

XXVII, 7. *each of the two words is derived from "ousia"*] For the derivation of *periousios*, see above. That *epiousios* is derived from *ousia*, substance or being, is very unlikely. The only meaning quotable in the New Testament (Luke 15:12, 13) or the papyri for *ousia* is "property" or "estate"; and in any case it is unlikely that the philosophical meaning would be present in a word employed in so simple and ordinary a context as the Lord's Prayer. Two other derivations are possible. (1) *epienai* "to come close upon" (Latin *instare*): *epiousios* bread meaning the bread of the "immediately following" day (cf. Acts 16:11); or, if the prayer were used in the morning, the bread of "that same day." This is preferable to (2), the derivation from *epi* (*ten*)*ousan* (the participle of the verb "to be"), in which case *epiousios* bread would be the bread for "the (day) that is," i.e., for "the current day": but no instance of this phrase, in which "day" has to be supplied, is forthcoming. The general meaning of *epiousios artos* appears in the Latin *diaria* (found in a wall-inscription at Pompeii), i.e., daily rations for slaves, soldiers, etc. (J. H. Lightfoot, *On a fresh Revision of the New Testament*, pp. 217 ff.; J. H. Moulton, *A Grammar of New Testament Greek*, II, 313 f.; Moulton and Milligan, *s.v.*; T. W. Manson, *The Mission and Message of Jesus*, 461; G. Kittel, *Theologisches Wörterbuch zum N.T.*, *s.v.*)

XXVII, 8. *The word "substance" ("ousia") in its proper sense is commonly used*, etc.] This section describes the views on "substance" of two different schools of philosophy: (1) the Platonists, who held that substance is immaterial, and (2) the Stoics, who held that substance is the prime matter of existents.

XXVII, 8. *the reality of incorporeal things is primary*] Cf. Plato, *Phaedrus*, 247 C, "The colourless, formless, and intangible truly existing substance, with which all true knowledge is concerned, holds this region (*sc.* above the heavens] and is visible only to the mind"; *Timaeus*, 34C, "God made the soul to be older than the body and prior in birth and worth"; *Laws*, X, 892A, "the soul is older than the body"; *Laws*, X, 892C, "By 'nature' they mean the origin of things primary; but if soul shall be shown to have been produced first (not fire or air, but soul first and foremost): then it would most truly be spoken of as a superlatively 'natural' existence"; *Laws*, X, 896C, "we find soul to be prior to body, and body secondary and posterior." Ps.-Plutarch, *De Placitis Philosophorum*, I, 10: "Pythagoras and Aristotle [affirm] that the first causes are incorporeal."

XXVII, 8. *state of flux*] Cf. H. Diels, *Doxographi Graeci*, 307: "The disciples of Thales and Pythagoras and the Stoics hold that matter is changeable and variable and alterable and in a state of flux." Hippolytus, *Philosophumena*, I, 23:1, 2 (*C.B.*, XXVI, 27): "The sect of philosophers called 'of the Academy' ... whose founder was Pyrrho, [affirm] that all substance is in a state of flux and changeable and never remains in the same place."

XXVII, 8. *if . . . they receive more*, etc.] Cf. Timaeus Locrus, περὶ ψυχᾶς καὶ κόσμω, ch. XIV (Teubner, p. 417): "All nourishment is brought to the body from the heart as its root through the belly as its channel; and if the body receives more moisture than that which flows off, there is said to be an increase; but, if less, a wasting."

XXVII, 8. *those who hold that the reality . . . of corporeal things is primary*] Plutarch, *Epit.*, I, 11 (Diels, 310): "The Stoics [affirm] that all causes are bodily"; cf. *Epit.*, IV, 20 (Diels, 410): "The Stoics say that the voice is a body: for everything that does or makes is a body." Hippolytus, *Philosophumena*, I, 21:1 (*C.B.*, XXVI, 25), refers to the tenet of the Stoics that "the body is the purest of all things." Aëtius, I, 3:25 (*Stoicorum Veterum fragmenta*, ed. J. von Arnim, I, 24): "Zeno the son of Mnaseas of Citium says that God and matter are the first principles of which the one is the cause of action, the other of being acted upon." Theodoret, *Graecarum affectionum curatio* (*P.G.*, LXXXIII, 901): "Zeno of Citium, the son of Mnaseas, the disciple of

Crates, who began the Stoic heresy, said that God and matter are first principles."

XXVII, 8. *the prime matter of existents*] Stobaeus, *Ecl.*, I, 11:5a (Diels, 457; von Arnim, I, 24): "Zeno affirms that substance is the prime matter of existents, and that as a whole it is eternal and becomes neither greater nor less."

XXVII, 8. *subject to no alteration*] See the last note in this section.

XXVII, 8. *substance is without quality or characteristic form*] Cf. *contra Celsum*, III, 41: "Let him attend to what is said by the Greeks concerning matter without quality in the proper sense of the term"; *contra Celsum*, IV, 56: "the same matter underlying all bodies is without quality or characteristic form in the proper sense of the term"; cf. also *contra Celsum*, IV, 61. Timaeus Locrus, ch. I (Teubner, p. 407): "he said that this matter is eternal, not indeed immovable, but without shape in itself or characteristic form, yet receiving every kind of shape."

XXVII, 8. *is inherent in*] Or, perhaps better, "underlies," reading ὑπόκειται with the Anonymous.

XXVII, 8. *movements and stationary conditions*] κινήσεις καὶ σχέσεις. These two terms are not seldom found in opposition in Stoic writers, e.g., in Marcus Aurelius, *Meditations*, XI, 2: "So too with the dance, if thou do the like for each movement and stationary condition," and in Plutarch, *Quaestionum Convivalium*, 747C (IX, 2): "Dancing consists of movements and stationary conditions."

XXVII, 8. *is none the less affected by*] Reading εἶναι, παθητὴν δὲ οὐδὲν with von Arnim, II, 115.

XXVII, 8. *receptive of every expression of activity*] Cf. *contra Celsum*, IV, 57: "That the underlying matter is receptive of those qualities which the Creator wishes [to bestow] is firmly held by all of us who accept Providence."

XXVII, 8. *the tension*] ὁ τόνος. A force, according to the Stoics, in nature and man. It was regarded as holding the universe together: cf. Marcus Aurelius, *Meditations*, VI, 38: "Meditate often on the intimate union and mutual interdependence of all things in the universe. For all things are after a manner mutually intertwined, and accordingly all things are dear to one another. For they follow in order one upon another because of the movement resulting from tension [διὰ τὴν τονικὴν κίνησιν] and like spirit and the unification of all substance [τὴν ἕνωσιν τῆς οὐσίας]." In the soul, "tension," imparted to it by atmospheric substance therein existing, was the cause of virtues and vices. See note on VI, 5, and Plutarch *De Stoicorum Repugnantiis*, 7 (Teubner, VI, 218): "Cleanthes .. says that 'tension' is a stroke of fire, and if there is enough of it in the soul to master circumstances, it is called force and power." See de Faye, III, 123 ff.

XXVII, 8. *substance is in every part subject to change and divisible*] If this is consistent with what has been said of substance above, it must refer to that part of the definition of it which says that it "persists through all alteration or change." Stobaeus, *Ecl.*, *I*, 11:5a (Diels, 457; von Arnim, I, 24): "According to Zeno substance is the prime matter of all existents, and as a whole it is eternal, neither greater or less. But its parts do not always remain the same, but are divided and commingle with one another. Through it runs the Logos of the universe, which some call fate, just as seed does in the act of generation." Cf. also Cicero, *Acad.*, I, 7: "subjectam putant omnibus sine ulla specie, atque carentem omni illa qualitate . . . materiam quandam, e qua omnia expressa atque effecta sint; quae una omnia accipere possit, omnibusque modis mutari, atque ex omni parte."

XXVII, 9. *the living bread which has come down out of heaven, being distributed for the mind and the soul*] So also Ambrose, *De Sacramentis*, V, 24, referring to this clause in the Lord's Prayer, says: "It is not the bread which passes into the body, but that bread of eternal life, which supports the substance of the soul. Therefore in Greek it is called *epiousion*." J. H. Srawley in his note, *ad. loc.*, thinks that Ambrose is here dependent upon Origen.

XXVII, 9. *either as "milk" . . . or as "herbs" or as "flesh"*] Whereas Ambrose interprets the bread of the Eucharist, given for the faithful "daily," Origen's treatment is definitely non-sacramental. To feed on the living bread of Christ is to feed on his spiritual teachings. And these, according to Origen's favourite thought, must be adapted to the several capacities of the hearers. See Introduction, p. 199.

XXVII, 9. *There is so-called food which is harmful*] Cf. *In Joh.*, XIII, 33: "There is also a kind of food which is harmful, such as we hear of in the fourth Book of the Kingdoms, when certain persons said to Elisha 'There is death in the pot, O man of God'" (II Kings 4:40).

XXVII, 10. "*and is safe for them that stay themselves as upon the Lord*"] Some MSS. of the LXX in Prov. 3:18 omit "is safe." The Hebrew has: "And happy is every one that retaineth her."

See C. H. Toy, *ad loc.*, in the *I.C.C.* for readings underlying the Greek translation.

XXVII, 10. *or that this was the bread*] So the Anonymous emends (ἄρτου for τούτου).

XXVII, 11. *teachings formerly prepared*] This slight emendation of Delarue brings out clearly the connection with what has gone before. As the angels partook of the meal that had been prepared for them, so they are also nourished from the store of spiritual things that the saint has to offer them.

XXVII, 11. *even Christ acknowledges*] An example of Origen's penetrating analysis of the words of Scripture, in this case of Rev. 3:20. Origen points out that in the feast here mentioned Christ is both guest and host: he sups with the man, and the man with him; indeed, according to the order of the words, it is the man who first entertains the Son of God. This thought of a mutual giving and receiving as between God and man runs through this and the preceding section, and emerges clearly in the "entertainment" that Abraham provides for the angels who lodged with him.

XXVII, 12. *he who participates "in the dragon,"* etc.] A reference, as is made explicit, to the LXX of Ps. 73:13, 14, which has "dragon" for "leviathan" and "the peoples of the Ethiopians" for "the people inhabiting the wilderness." The "dragon" is interpreted in the light of Rev. 12:9, where it is identified with "the old serpent, he that is called the Devil and Satan," or, as Origen says lower down, "the adversary." A similar interpretation is found in Theophilus Alex., *Ep. pasch.*, as translated by Jerome (*P.L.*, XXII, 782; *C.V.*, LV, 170): "The food of all the wicked is the accursed Devil himself, as the prediction of the prophet proclaims, 'Thou didst give him as food to the people of Ethiopia.'"

XXVII, 12. *the Ethiopian spiritually*] This use of νοητός is common in Origen. Cf. *De Princ.*, IV, 25 (*Philocalia*, p. 31): "If then the prophecies concerning Judaea and concerning Jerusalem and Israel and Judah and Jacob, since we do not take them in a fleshly sense, suggest some such mysteries, it would follow that the prophecies also concerning Egypt and Egyptians, and Babylon and Babylonians, and Tyre and Tyrians, and Sodom and Gomorrah and the rest of the nations, do not tell simply of these Egyptians and Babylonians and Tyrians and Sidonians in a bodily sense. For if there are Israelites in the spiritual sense of the term, it follows that there are also Egyptians and Babylonians in the spiritual sense of the term."

XXVII, 13. *may be deified*] The text of T reads "may deify," which has been corrected into the passive by another hand. The thought (for which see also XXV, 2, note) is appropriate to this discussion, which is based on the assumption that the *epiousios* bread has a kinship in substance with him who eats it. Cf. XXVII, 2 (end): "True bread is that which nourishes the true man, who has been made in the image of God, and he who is nourished with it also becomes after the likeness of the Creator"; XXVII, 9 (end): "*Epiousios* bread is that which is best adapted to the reasonable nature and akin to it in its very substance: it provides at once health and vigour and strength to the soul and imparts a share of its own immortality (for the Word of God is immortal) to him who eats of it."

XXVII, 13. *some one will say that "epiousios" is formed from "epienai"*] See note on XXVII, 7, p. 364.

XXVII, 13. *this is perhaps the famous period of a thousand years*] A reference to Rev. 20:4–6. The period was "famous" because of the controversy that centred around it in the Church even from early times. Among holders of millenarian views prior to or contemporary with Origen were Papias, Justin Martyr, Irenaeus, Tertullian, and Hippolytus, all of whom interpreted the passage of a literal reign of Christ on earth (although it is to be noted that the author of Revelation does not use the words "on earth"). Naturally, Origen spiritualized the passage after the Alexandrine manner; and subsequently Dionysius of Alexandria (*ap.* Eusebius, *H.E.*, VII, 25) followed on the same lines. But the details of Origen's interpretation are not clear. He regards, however, the "thousand" years as past already and to be contrasted with "today." Possibly in some work which is now lost he had discussed the passage more fully.

XXVII, 13. *the whole age is reckoned as the space of one of our days*] Cf. *In Matt.*, XV, 31 (*P.G.*, XIII, 1344 f.; *C.B.*, XL, 442): "See if we can speak of the whole present age as in a sense a day."

XXVII, 14. *perceive the "first"*] The Greek is simply "see," which apparently here means to "see the inner meaning of." An exceptionally spiritual man may, according to Origen, understand the significance of the numbers mentioned in connection with the feast of unleavened bread: but no man can understand such deeper mysteries as underlie the feast of the seven weeks, and so forth. The same thought is found in the passage from *In Matt.* quoted in the last note.

XXVII, 14. *save he who has contemplated the Father's will*] i.e.,

A.C.—24

the Logos. Cf. *In Joh.*, II, 2: "He would not have remained God, did he not remain in the unceasing contemplation [θέᾳ] of the Father's abyss"; *In Joh.*, XXXII, 28: "For in my opinion no one except his Son can grasp [χωρῆσαι] the full effulgence of the whole glory of God." As regards the former of these quotations, Origen explains elsewhere (*In Matt.*, XV, 31: *P.G.*, XIII, 1345; *C.B.*, XL, 444) that by "abyss" he means profundity of thought.

XXVII, 15. *two conflicting apostolic sayings*] Note that Origen believed the author of Hebrews and the author of Ephesians to be the same person. See on XXVII, 5. A similar juxtaposition of these two sayings is to be found in *In Matt.*, XV, 31 (*P.G.*, XIII, 1346f; *C.B.*, XL, 445).

XXVII, 15. *"to put away sins"*] All textual authorities read "sin" in Heb. 9:26 except the Codex Claromontanus (D2) which supports Origen here. But in the passage in *In Matt.* referred to in the last note Origen has the singular. This is also read in the Latin of *De Princ.*, II, 35: "ad refellendum peccatum."

XXVII, 15. *be under treatment*] It is implied that this disciplinary process will be successful in delivering even the greatest sinner from his sin. Cf. *In Joh.*, XIX, 14; *contra Celsum*, V, 16, and *In Matt.*, XV, 31.

XXVII, 16. *it now being clear . . . what the "day by day" is*] The present age is "today," and of this it is possible to form some conception, just as we can also of single "days" under the Mosaic dispensation (see note on section 14) and how they are a shadow of the good things to come. It follows, therefore, that "day by day" refers to the succeeding ages, when this age is over, when the riches of God's grace, at present uncomprehended, will be manifest. These wonders were symbolized in the old law by the larger measures of time, the weeks and months and holy seventh year and so forth; and he who can contemplate such mysteries may in some sort enter into the secrets of the "day by day," that is, of the super-abundance of the blessings that God will bestow in those far-stretching ages of grace.

XXVII, 17. *how this "bread" is "ours"*] i.e., how the bread of the succeeding ages can be ours. Origen points out that "things to come" as well as "things present" belong to the saints.

XXVIII, 1. *"have forgiven"*] ἀφήκαμεν: probably from Matt. 6:12: for in XVIII, 2, where he gives the whole prayer from Luke he reads ἀφίεμεν.

XXVIII, 1. *in gentle speech*, etc.] Origen's emphasis upon the law of love in this treatise is noteworthy in view of the bitter experiences he had recently passed through in the *fracas* with Demetrius of Alexandria. See Introduction, p. 176.

XXVIII, 2. *those who have been born again*] Cf. XV, 4 (Christ speaks) "having received the spirit of adoption through the being born again in me."

XXVIII, 3. *the whole "house"*] i.e., the whole body of spectators.

XXVIII, 4. *"debt" due from a widow*] Cf. I Tim. 5:3–16.

XXVIII, 5. *so as to owe nothing*] Cf. *In Jerem. hom.*, XIV, 4.

XXVIII, 5. *period of grace*] This seems to be the sense required from the Greek ἀφέσεως, which signifies rather "remission."

XXVIII, 5. *being engraved upon the reason*] Cf. *In Jerem. hom.*, XVI, 10: "Having committed the sin, I have its stamp [τύπον], and the stamp of the sin which has been sinned is written in my soul."

XXVIII, 5. *the written bond*] The same expression is used of the debt incurred by sinners in *In Jerem. hom.*, XV, 5.

XXVIII, 7. *reproached*] T reads ἐνειλήσας, which according to the unsupported statement of Hesychius may mean "fined" or "punished." The Anonymous prefers ἀπειλήσας, "threatened." Neither of these gives the required sense. I suggest ὀνείδισας, "reproached."

XXVIII, 7. *"Thou wicked and slothful servant"*] A slip on the part of Origen. These words occur in the parable of the Talents (Matt. 25:26), *not* in the parable of the Unmerciful Servant.

XXVIII, 8. *he says the same thing as Matthew*] i.e., "forgive us our debts, as we also have forgiven our debtors" (Matt. 6:12).

XXVIII, 8. *but Luke seems not to give room*] The Greek is "who seems not to give room." To refer the "who" to Matthew, as some commentators have done, leads to confusion. Origen's point is that Luke says, "we ourselves also forgive *everyone* that is indebted to us," thereby seeming to exclude those who wish, in accordance with other passages of Scripture, to forgive repentant sinners only.

XXVIII, 8. *as the apostles were*] Similarly in XIV, 6, he speaks of saints who may be regarded as "a Paul or a Peter."

XXVIII, 8. *in speaking not the things of their own*] Cf. II Peter 1:21.

XXVIII, 9. *The priests according to the Law are prohibited*] A distinction between voluntary and involuntary faults is a familiar feature of the law. See Leviticus, ch. 4, and Numbers, ch. 15. For "presumptuous sins" (Ps. 19:13) no sacrifice was available. "The soul that doeth aught with a high hand, whether he be homeborn or a stranger, the same blasphemeth the Lord; and that soul shall be cut off from among the people. Because he hath despised the word of the Lord, and hath broken his commandment; that soul shall be utterly cut off, his iniquity shall be upon him" (Num.15:30, 31).

XXVIII, 9. *though the priest has power*, etc.] A difficult sentence. Translated as in the text, it simply outlines the distinction above. But the negative may be taken with both clauses: "the priest having no power to offer . . . actually does not offer." This means that in certain cases of voluntary or trivial sins no offering is *prescribed*: but in the graver transgressions the absence of a sacrifice is explicitly indicated. Regarding such trivial sins undealt with by the law, two opinions obtained among the Rabbis: the majority holding that no sacrifice was required; one Rabbi (Levi Barcinonensis), however, maintaining that there were three faults, namely, blasphemy, neglect of circumcision, and failure to observe the Passover rightly, which though incurred involuntarily could not be expiated by sacrifice. See Reading, note, pp. 177, 178.

XXVIII, 10. *Certain persons*, etc.] At the general background of this passage lies the disciplinary action of the early Church, with its varying degrees of severity. The more rigorous view, which Origen from temperament and training would obviously support, found its Scriptural warrant in such passages as I John 5:16 (quoted here), Hebrews 6:4–6; 10:26–30, and possibly also II Peter 2:20–22, but this epistle from its late date and weak attestation can scarcely have exerted much influence (it is, however, referred to by Hippolytus in *Philosophumena*, IX, 7, of lapses on the part of Christians). It also finds expression in the *Shepherd* of Hermas, which, however, allows one post-baptismal fall, but not a second, and in Irenaeus, *Haer.*, IV, 42:4, Tertullian *De Baptismo*, 8. Clearly, the more rigorous view concerning post-baptismal sin must have had regard to major offences only, and so a distinction between "deadly" and "venial" sins became soon apparent. Origen's own view on this matter is indicated in several passages in his writings, e.g., *In Lev. hom.*, XV, 2 (end): "In gravioribus enim criminibus semel tantum poenitentiae conceditur locus; ista vero communia, quae frequenter incurrimus, semper poenitentiam recipiunt, et sine intermissione redimuntur" (*C.B.*, XXIX, 489); *contra Celsum*, III, 51: "They [*sc.* the Christians] lament as dead those who have been vanquished by licentiousness or some foul wickedness, since

they are lost and dead to God"; and in *In Matt.*, XIII, 30
Origen distinguishes between lesser and graver sins ("murder,
or poisoning, or pederasty, or anything of that sort"), the latter
being such as those which the law in Numbers 18:22 describes
as "death-bearing." But, quite clearly, a particular instance of
disciplinary laxity is referred to in this passage ("certain persons"), and this has been usually identified (see Introduction,
p. 180) with the controversy that took place at the end of the
second and the beginning of the third century, and is associated
in the first instance with the name of Pope Zephyrinus (197–
217), but more particularly with his successor Callistus (217–223),
who apparently went much further in the matter of laxity than
Zephyrinus had done. The "rigorist" champion at Rome was
Hippolytus, whose *Philosophumena* or *Omnium haereseum refutatio*
refers disparagingly to Zephyrinus and contains a scathing
description of the career of Callistus before he became Pope,
and of his disciplinary action after it. It has in fact been held
that the controversy produced a schism in the Roman Church
with Hippolytus as anti-pope of the opposite faction. The difficulty in holding this view is that Jerome, though he knew Hippolytus was "bishop of some church" adds "the name of the city I
have not been able to learn" (*De Viris Illustribus*, 61). Origen
could not have been unaware of this controversy, for Jerome
(*ibid.*) also says that in one of his works, *On the praise of our Lord
and Saviour*, Hippolytus "indicates that he is speaking in the
Church in the presence of Origen." (The Greek version has it
that Hippolytus was speaking in church after the manner of
Origen and in his presence.) Origen paid his visit to Rome
about 212 (see H. J. Lawlor, *Eusebius*, II, 201), and we cannot
suppose that his contact with Hippolytus consisted merely in
hearing him preach in church. Zephyrinus was then Pope; but
as we have noted Hippolytus's criticism did not leave him un-
spared—on the contrary he represents him as deceived by
Callistus and in close connection with him (*Philosoph.* IX, 6, 7,).
Further, the controversy (and the schism, if it existed) continued after the death of Callistus, for Hippolytus says that his
"school continues, preserving its customs and traditions, not
discerning with whom they ought to communicate, but indis-
criminately offering communion to all." This subsequent period
would involve the episcopate of Urban (223–230) and probably also that of his successor Pontianus.

XXVIII, 10. *perhaps because they have no accurate knowledge*]
Hippolytus says that Zephyrinus was "an ignorant and

unlearned man and unskilled in ecclesiastical definitions" (*Philo-soph.*, IX, 11)—the passage referring more particularly to theological definition concerning the godhead. This opinion is supported by a remark of Rufinus in his translation (or para-phrase) of Eusebius, *H.E.*, VI, 29:4. This chapter recounts a "surprise" election to the bishopric of Rome. A certain Fabian had come from the country for the election. No one thought of him as the future bishop; but during the proceedings a dove lighted on his head, and this omen secured his election "by acclamation." Rufinus adds, from his own stock of knowledge, to this account: "Some tell this story of Fabian, others of Zephyrinus"; and the coupling of the two in this connection suggests that Zephyrinus, like Fabian, had no great reputation for learning.

XXVIII, 10. *boast that they are able to pardon*] Tertullian *De Pudicitia*, 1 (*P.L.*, II, 980f.) speaks of something much more definite than a boast: "Audio etiam edictum esse propositum, et quidem peremptorium. Pontifex scilicet maximus, quod est, episcopus episcoporum, edicit: 'Ego et moechia et fornicationis delicta poenitentia functis demitto.' O edictum, cui adscribi non poterit, Bonum factum."

XXVIII, 10. *idolatry . . . adultery and fornication*] In the Decian persecution, which took place later, "idolatry" on the part of Christians consisted in offering incense at a pagan altar (see J. E. B. Mayor on Tertullian, *Apol.*, p. 351), or in taking part in pagan sacrifices by tasting the victim's flesh, or in pro-ducing a certificate, often procured by collusion, that such an act had been performed (see Benson, *Cyprian*, 80, 81). Cyprian (*Ep.*, 8:2) and Dionysius of Alexandria (*ap.* Eusebius, *H.E.*, VI, 45) use the word in this sense, and there is no reason to think that any other meaning should be attached to it here: indeed, since the time of Trajan the approved form of profession of paganism was to take part in sacrifice. The conditions on which such lapsed Christians should be re-admitted, if at all, to com-munion was one of the major disciplinary problems with which the Church of the middle of the third century had to wrestle. But this was subsequent to Zephyrinus or Callistus, and there is no suggestion by Hippolytus that they made concessions to such offenders. The *De Pudicitia* of Tertullian, whether directed against Zephyrinus or Callistus, argues that adultery and fornication ought to exclude from communion equally with idolatry and murder (chs. 5, 12), and therefore seems to imply that the Pope's laxity consisted in this only, that he was willing to re-admit to communion, in peace, the adulterer and the fornicator. But Tertullian's treatise is dated between 217 and 222; and in the interval between the date of its composition and that of the *De Oratione* (233–234) wider concessions may have been made by subsequent Popes (note that Origen uses the plural in this connection—"certain persons"), involving those guilty of "idolatry." With regard to the concessions made by Callistus concerning adultery and fornication, G. Dix argues (*The Apostolic Tradition,* XVIII) with plausibility that all that the Pope did was to recognize as marriage in the sight of the Church something that could not be so recognized in the eyes of the law, namely, a permanent union between a woman and a slave.

XXIX, 1. *"bring us not into temptation"*] "Temptation" and "tempt" in the Greek and English Bibles are used in two senses, of (*a*) a solicitation to evil and (*b*) a testing or trial. In modern English sense (*a*) predominates; and so in Genesis 22:1 the Revised Version translates "God did prove [Authorized Version 'tempt'] Abraham," in order to avoid misapprehension; for in the sense of solicitation to evil "God tempteth no man" (James 1:13). A similar aim in early times appears to underlie the gloss on this petition "ne nos patiaris induci" (Tertullian and Cyprian). In expounding it Origen takes "temptation" in its most inclusive sense, as is evident from the opening section of the chapter. The whole life of man upon earth is a testing ground; and he is also in his inner nature subject to the solicitations to evil that come from "the flesh." Such being the case, why are we taught to pray: "Bring us not into temptation"? Are we not praying for the impossible? Origen's answer is given in section 9. We pray to be delivered from temptation, not in the sense of not being tempted, but in the sense of not being overcome by temptation.

XXIX, 1. *"life upon earth is a temptation"*] Job 7:1. The Hebrew has "warfare," "hard service."

XXIX, 2. *"In thee I shall be delivered from temptation"*] Ps. 17:30 (LXX). "Temptation" (πειρατήριον) is the same word as in Job 7:1, above. The Hebrew is: "By thee I run upon a troop," i.e., attack a hostile, marauding army.

XXIX, 2. *"the soul of all flesh"*] i.e., the blood (Lev. 17:11). "The soul [Revised Version 'life'] of all flesh is the blood thereof" (LXX). There is therefore here a *metalepsis* or compound figure, by which "blood" is used to indicate both "soul" (which resides in it) and "heart" (the fount of both "soul" and "blood"). Origen means that our wrestling is with the soul, the guiding principle of the animated body, called the heart because out of it come the evil passions (see Mark 7:21), against which the spirit of man wars.

XXIX, 2. *the guiding principle*] τὸ ἡγεμονικὸν. Cf. *In Joh.*, II, 35: "In the heart is the guiding principle." The idea is borrowed from the Stoics, who held that the dominant part of the soul, the guiding principle or reason, as well as other parts, had their centre in the heart (Zeller, *Stoics and Epicureans*, 214).

XXIX, 3. *bid us pray not to enter "into temptation"*] Although ostensibly Origen is commenting upon the petition in the Lord's Prayer ("bid us pray"), his mind seems to have travelled on to Matt. 26:41, and parallels, "Watch and pray, that ye enter not into temptation."

XXIX, 3. *Judith*] T reads "Judaea." This quotation from Judith 8:26, 27, varies somewhat from the text as given by Rahlfs. Origen: "For the Lord, who scourgeth them who come near unto him to admonish them, doth not take vengeance on us." Rahlfs: "Because the Lord hath not taken vengeance on us, but scourgeth them who draw near unto him to admonish them."

XXIX, 4. *"in stripes more abundantly, in prisons above measure"*] The text of Origen here agrees with that of the first hand of Codex ℵ. The Revised Version, in accordance with Codex B, reads "in prisons more abundantly, in stripes above measure."

XXIX, 5. *outside the range of "temptations such as man can bear"*] πειρασμῶν ἀνθρωπίνων. I read this in place of π. ἀνθρώπους ("when did anyone think that men were outside the range of temptations"), which gives a poor sense.

XXIX, 5. *eagerly expect freedom from ills*] T reads "by ills," which Koetschau emends as above.

XXIX, 5. *in the sense of not being overcome when we are tempted*] This is the explanation also of Dionysius of Alexandria (Feltoe, 247), who appears to be dependent upon Origen in this point, and also in the meaning of "enter into temptation."

XXIX, 9. *"Glancing through the meshes"*] The Revised Version of S. of Sol. 2:9 has: "He sheweth himself ["glanceth", margin] through the lattice." This description of the beloved in the Song of Songs easily lent itself to a mystical interpretation. The Midrash applies the words to the *Shechinah* peering through the outstretched hand of the priest when blessing the people (the Hebrew word for "glanceth" signifying "to sparkle"). Origen's explanation is suggested to him by the LXX for "lattice," namely, τῶν δικτύων, which, while found in the sense of "lattice-work," more usually means "meshes" or "toils" of a net. Hence it is but a step, in Origen's mind, to apply the phrase to the meshes of temptation into which the Saviour willingly entered for our sakes. An amplified, though similar, interpretation is found in his Commentary on the Song of Songs, Book III (*C.B.*, XXIII, 199, 200, 203, and especially 222). The *retia* are there the "laquei tentationum et decipulae insidiarum diaboli," which man cannot overcome by himself but needs a greater and stronger than he to break them down and open up the way. Therefore, the Saviour, before he was united with his Bride the Church, was tempted by the devil, that he might overcome the *retia tentationum*, and passing through them call to his Bride to "rise up" and "come."

XXIX, 9. *"the mouth of the righteous will meditate wisdom"*] Revised Version, "bringeth forth," margin, "buddeth with": the Hebrew verb elsewhere meaning "to sprout," "to grow."

XXIX, 10. *they invent a Son or a Father*] The Marcionites are no doubt intended. A similar passage is *contra Celsum*, VIII, 16, in which Origen speaks of those "who deny the Creator, and make to themselves another god under a new form, having merely the name of god, to whom they give themselves as being superior to the Creator," and with them are to be classed "any one there may be who says that the Son and Lord is mightier than God who rules all things." For further reference to Marcionites, see XXIX, 12, 13.

XXIX, 11. *the meaning of which is clear enough from what has been said*] See section 9, above: "he who is overcome in being tempted enters into temptation," and also below in section 11: "he who is conquered enters into temptation."

XXIX, 12. *divide the Godhead*] Origen again reverts to the Marcionites, who supposed that there were two Gods, the one the just God of the law, the other the good God of the gospel. The same phrase occurs in *In Jerem. hom.*, IX, 1: "There will be those who divide the Godhead which is prior to the coming of the Saviour, as they suppose, from the Godhead proclaimed by Jesus Christ. But we know one God both then and now." The same "division" into "just" and "good" is discussed in *De Princ.*, II, 5:1. Cf. Irenaeus, *Haer.*, III, 40:2: "Marcion igitur ipse dividens Deum in duo, alterum quidem bonum, et alterum iudicialem dicens, ex utrisque interimit Deum."

XXIX, 13. *these observations will trouble the persons in question*

exceedingly] Because Origen's quotations here are taken from the
New Testament, and from Paul, whom the Marcionites held in
special honour (see E. C. Blackman, *Marcion and his influence*,
ch. 6). They could not therefore be attributed to the "just" God
of the Old Testament.

XXIX, 13. *an adequate solution of these contradictions*] In section
11 Origen has said that "it is incongruous to think that God
leads anyone into temptation, in the sense of giving him up
(παραδόντα) to be conquered." How then can Paul say (section
12) in regard to certain persons that "God gave them up
(παρέδωκεν) in the lusts of their hearts unto uncleanness," that
"God gave them up unto vile passions," that "God gave them
up unto a reprobate mind"? A partial answer to this difficulty
is given at the end of section 12, namely, that such people, even
if God had not "given them up," would still have been in the
lust of their hearts, and have fallen into vile passions and into
a reprobate mind. But in sections 13–15 Origen's real solution is
disclosed, which incidentally involves several of his fundamental
convictions. These are (1) God orders every rational soul with
a view to its eternal life; (2) the soul always maintains its free
will; (3) probation continues after death; (4) God's punishment
is always remedial, not penal. A quickly cured sin might lead
the sinner into further carelessness. So God may "give up" the
sinner unto his vile passions, so that continuance in the evil may
cause him to take his fill of wickedness and be so glutted with it,
that when this life is over he may desire his sin no longer and
retrace the path to heavenly things. An illustration is chosen
from the Book of Numbers, where God sent the Israelites, who
had lusted for flesh, such a glut of food as should eventually
become loathsome to them.

XXIX, 13. *have taken offence against him as not good*] Cf. *In
Jerem. hom.*, I, 16: "Had the wretched heretics understood this,
they would not be continually saying to us: 'You see the God of
the Law, that he is fierce and inhuman'"; *In Jerem. hom.*, XII, 5:
"The heretics say, 'Do you see what kind of a person the
Creator is?—the God of the prophets who says, "I will not spare
and I will not pity them in their destruction"? How can he be
good?'"

XXIX, 13. *a rapid and brief cure*] Origen employs the same
thought to God's treatment of his people Israel in *contra Celsum*,
V, 31.

XXIX, 14. *afterwards desire earthly things*] The Anonymous
scholar, quoted by Reading, *ad loc.*, (196 f.) shows that γένεσις

here means "terrena illa, quae ad victus delicias pertinet, quales erant carnes, quarum cupiditate flagarbat populus Israeliticus," giving several examples of this usage; e.g., *contra Celsum* VIII, 60 (*bis*), 62.

XXIX, 14. *you may then, having come to hate,* etc.] Some emendation seems necessary to clarify the conclusion of this very lengthy and difficult and complicated sentence: accordingly I have adopted the addition of "you may be able" in this place, suggested by the Anonymous, and also his alteration of "they yearned" into "you yearned."

XXIX, 15. *the wise fire*] This phrase occurs several times in Clement of Alexandria: *Paed.*, III, 8:44 (of the Sodomites), "God pouring forth a little of his wise fire upon their wantonness"; *Strom.*, VII, 6:34, 4, "We say that the fire purifies not the flesh but sinful souls, not an all-devouring and vulgar fire, but 'the wise fire' as we call it, the fire that 'pierceth the soul' which passes through it"; *Ecl. Proph.*, XXV, 4, "Fire is conceived of as a beneficent and strong power, destroying what is base, preserving what is good; therefore this fire is called 'wise' by the prophets" (Isa. 4:4; Mal. 3:2). Cf. also Origen, *In Ezech. hom.*, 1:3, "quis est ignis sic sapiens?" and Minucius Felix, XXXV, 3, who speaks of the fire of hell as *sapiens ignis*.

XXIX, 15. *in the fire and the prison they do not receive the recompense of error*] The real punishment of sin, according to Origen, is to be enslaved by sin. God's punishments, spoken of under the symbols of "fire" (see previous note) and "prison," are remedial. See next note.

XXIX, 15. *a benefaction*] So Origen also describes God's disciplinary action in *contra Celsum*, IV, 12, 13, 21; V, 15; *In Jerem. hom.*, II, 2, 3; XVI, 6, as for the benefit of the sinner.

XXIX, 15. *God does not wish,* etc.] Cf. *In Jerem. hom.*, XX, 2: "God does not rule as a tyrant, but as a king; and when so doing he does not compel [βιάζεται], but persuades, and desires that those under him should willingly yield themselves to his direction, so that the good of no one should come by necessity, but of his free will." Clement of Alexandria, *Strom.*, VII, 42:4: "For neither is God good involuntarily as the fire is warming (but in him the imparting of good things is voluntary); nor on the other hand shall he who is saved be saved involuntarily." *Ep. ad Diognetum*, VII, 3–5, especially the words: "Compulsion [βία] is not an attribute of God." Irenaeus, *Haer.*, IV, 59: "Vis a Deo non fit," and V, 1:1 "Deum suadentem et non vim inferentem."

XXIX, 16. *God "hardens the heart of Pharaoh"*] Cf. what Origen says on this subject in *De Princ.*, III, 1:7 ff. (*C.B.*, XXII, 204 ff.), and in *In Exod. hom.*, IV (*C.B.*, XXIX, 171 ff.).

XXIX, 16. *not unjustly are the nets spread for birds*] The Greek for "nets" is δίκτυα, recalling the "meshes" of temptation spoken of in section 9.

XXIX, 16. *the sparrow falls into the snare*] So also in *contra Celsum*, VIII, 70, apparently under the influence of Ps. 66:11: but Matt. 10:29 has "fall to the ground."

XXIX, 19. *who "maketh all things to work together for good"*] In the usual form which this passage takes (Authorized Version and Revised Version) "work together" (συνεργεῖ) is intransitive and its nominative is "all things." But frequently (though not always), as here, Origen cites a text which has πάντα συνεργεῖ ὁ θεός: "God maketh all things to work together" (so margin of Revised Version). This reading is supported by A and B and some of the Egyptian versions. See Sanday and Headlam on Rom. 8:28.

XXX, 1. *Luke . . . has virtually taught also "Deliver us from the evil one"*] Because, as Origen has maintained (XXIX, 11), the prayer, "Bring us not into temptation," really means, "May we not be encompassed or overcome by temptation." It is unnecessary to labour the point that Origen takes τοῦ πονηροῦ as masculine, not neuter, since the whole chapter, and especially the quotations from Job and Eph. ch. 6, imply belief in a personal devil.

XXX, 1. *by a customary Hebrew usage*] The root of the Hebrew word translated "afflictions" in Ps. 34:19 means "evil," "distress," or "calamity."

XXX, 1. *as never not "afflicted"*] The phrase translated "afflicted on every side" in II Cor. 4:8 is literally "afflicted in every thing."

XXX, 1. *to be "straitened" is a matter of choice*] This is questionable. The word in II Cor. 4:8 means: "not in hopeless straits," "not in a situation from which there is no way out." Here the question of choice does not seem to be involved, although Paul's courage in adverse circumstances is manifest. But in II Cor. 6:12, "ye are straitened in your own affections," Paul clearly attributes to the Corinthians something that they might have avoided.

XXX, 1. *is termed enlargement*] A good illustration of Origen's words is to be found in Ps. 18:18, 19: "They came upon me in the day of my calamity: But the Lord was my stay. He brought

me forth also into a large place (LXX, 'into enlargement')."
Cf. also Ps. 118:5; 119:45.

XXX, 2. *"curse" God "to" his "face"*] Job 2:9. But the word
translated "curse" (Revised Version "renounce") is in the LXX
and the Hebrew "bless." It must be supposed that the word
"curse" stood originally in the Hebrew text, and was altered
subsequently from motives of reverence, but in defiance of the
sense of the passage, to "bless."

XXX, 2. *recorded in the three Gospels*] A slip on the part of
Origen. Mark does not record three temptations.

XXXI, 1. *before the dawning of the light*] Wisdom of Solomon
16:28. This is the reading of a corrector of Codex א. But the
sense demands the usual reading "towards the dawning of the
light," i.e., the East.

XXXI, 2. *every kind of distraction*] This is the emendation by
Bentley of T, which has "every kind of temptation" (περισπα-
σμὸν for πειρασμὸν). Koetschau goes as far as to acknowledge
that the conjecture is "nicht ohne Wahrscheinlichkeit."

XXXI, 2. *before the hands . . . before the eyes*] "Before" is best
taken as temporal, as it must certainly so be taken in "before he
stands," etc. The preferable attitude of the body in prayer is
indicated lower down in this section—standing, with hands
outstretched and eyes uplifted; and inasmuch as the soul
takes precedence over the body, so also the soul, the mind
and the reason should symbolically anticipate the movements of the body. See the article *Orant, Orante*, with numerous
illustrations of this attitude in prayer, by H. Leclercq in
D.A.C.L.

XXXI, 2. *the hands are stretched out*] So also Tertullian, *Apol.*,
30, speaks of Christians in prayer *manibus expansis*. J. E. B.
Mayor, *ad loc.*, gives many references to this practice.

XXXI, 3. *"I bow my knees unto the Father"*] After these words
the "received text" adds "of our Lord Jesus Christ," which
Origen omits with א A B C P Boh Aeth Jerome (expressly) and
other authorities. The corrector of א inserts them.

XXXI, 3. *it has been shown . . . that their bodies are spherical*]
Many of the Greek philosophers from early times held that the
cosmos and celestial bodies were spherical. Xenophanes (sixth
century B.C.) affirmed that God, and Parmenides (born c. 510
B.C.) that "the whole," was of this shape (see Hippolytus,
Philosoph., I, 11, 14). Plato, *Timaeus*, 33B (trans. R. G. Bury),
says: "Now for that Living Creature which is designed to embrace within itself all living creatures the fitting shape will be

that which comprises within itself all the shapes that are; wherefore he wrought it into a round [κυκλοτερές], in the shape of a sphere [σφαιροειδές], equidistant in all directions from the centre to the extremities, which of all shapes is the most perfect and the most self-similar; since he deemed that the similar is infinitely fairer than the dissimilar." The same view was taken by Aristotle (e.g., *De Anima*, I, 2), and also Theophrastus (c. 371–c. 287 B.C.), who attached a spherical shape to the "first principle." Another holder of this opinion used to be cited in "Timaeus Locrus," *Concerning the World-Soul and Nature* (printed in Teubner texts after the *Timaeus* in Vol. IV of Plato's Dialogues) II, 94D: but this work is now held to be spurious and to be probably dated not earlier than first century A.D. (J. Burnet, *Early Greek Philosophy*, 280). H. Chadwick, however, has pointed out (*The Harvard Theological Review*, Vol. XLI, No. 2) that there is no specific reference in this passage of the *De Oratione* to the resurrection or the resurrection body; and that Justinian, in criticizing Origen on this matter (see Introduction, p. 232), may have attributed to Origen himself the views of some of his followers.

XXXI, 3. *It would lead to a very absurd*] This sentence is designed to refute a further line of argument which might be put forward, namely, that though it is true that celestial bodies could have no uses for all the organs of an earthly body, they might have the appearance of possessing all these organs. This, says Origen, would be to liken them to a hollow statue, with surface but no depth.

XXXI, 4. *every place is suitable for prayer*] Cf. *contra Celsum*, VII, 44: "A Christian, even an ordinary Christian, is persuaded that every place forms part of the universe, and the whole world is God's temple. And so, praying in every place, shutting the eyes of sense, and raising upwards the eyes of the soul, he climbs above the whole universe. Neither does he pause at the vault of heaven, but passes in thought into the region beyond the heaven, being led on his way by the divine Spirit, and having thus as it were travelled beyond the universe, he offers up his prayer to God for no trivial blessings." A similar thought inspires Clement of Alexandria to one of his most eloquent passages (*Strom.*, VII, 35): "Such is he who believes God is everywhere present, and does not suppose him to be shut up in a certain definite place. . . . Accordingly all our life is a festival: being persuaded that God is everywhere present on all sides, we praise him as we till the ground, we sing hymns as we sail the

sea, we feel his inspiration in all that we do" (Hort and Mayor).
Cf. *Strom.*, VII, 43.

XXXI, 4. *the visitation of God will not rest upon it*] Here
"visitation" ἐπισκοπή connotes "searching inquisition," "punishment," as sometimes in the Old Testament (Isa. 10:3; Jer.
6:15; 10:15; Ecclesiasticus 18:20).

XXXI, 4. "*by consent for a season*"] Here Origen harks back
to a passage (II, 2) at the beginning of the treatise where he
also quotes I Cor. 7:5.

XXXI, 5. *clearly also those who are still in this life*] Origen's
confident assertion is based on the quotation from I Cor. 5:4
which follows later, in which Paul says that though absent in
the flesh he will be present in the spirit at a gathering of the
Christian Church.

XXXI, 5. *each one's angel*] For the belief that each Christian
has a guardian angel, see also VI, 4, XI, 5, and Introduction,
p. 195.

XXXI, 5. *there is a double church*] The same words occur in *In
Luc. hom.*, XXIII (*C.B.*, XXXV, 156): "Ego non ambigo et in
coetu nostro adesse angelos, non solum generaliter omni ecclesiae,
sed etiam singillatim, de quibus Salvator ait *Angeli eorum semper,
vident faciem Patris mei qui in caelis est.* Duplex hic adest ecclesia,
una hominum, altera angelorum." The following quotation
from C. H. Boutflower, domestic chaplain to Bishop Westcott
(*Life and Letters of B. F. Westcott*, by A. Westcott, II, 372) may be
relevant. "Finding the Bishop struggling late and minutely one
night over the draft of a service for the Dedication of Gifts in
some humble church, his Chaplain said, 'Well, my Lord, that
congregation will not be a critical one: they are accustomed to
anything.' With a gentle, surprised smile, such as Elisha's
might have been at Dothan, the Bishop looked up from his
desk and said, 'You forget: *who* are "the congregation"? *We* are
only an infinitesimal part of it.'"

XXXI, 5. *Raphael says of Tobit*] Cf. XI, 1, where the book
of Tobit is also used to enforce teaching about angels.

XXXI, 5. *who later on became his daughter-in-law*] T has "who
became his subsequent [ὑστέρας] daughter-in-law": but Tobias
had no wife before Sarah. Koetschau emends to ὑστέρως.

XXXI, 5. *being associated not only with the Ephesians*] Paul
wrote his first Epistle to the Corinthians from Ephesus (I Cor.
16:8).

XXXI, 5. *his spirit in Corinth*] Probably we should adopt the
emendation of the Anonymous "his spirit for those in Corinth."

XXXI, 6. *who has given himself up to the angel of the devil*] A brilliant emendation of the Anonymous, who reads ἐπιδῷ for ἐπί τῷ, and cites parallels for the thought from Origen and Hermas.

XXXI, 6. *the angels . . . watch over the Church*] T has: "the divine will watching over the Church," which the Anonymous rightly emends. Cp. XI, 5; "the angels who watch over."

XXXI, 6. *for the carrying out of worldly business*] Like those who met in the Temple to buy and sell (Matt. 21:12).

XXXI, 7. *the fig tree . . . was taken away from the roots*] But the fig tree was not taken away (ἀρθείσῃ), it was withered away (ἐξήρανται): Mark 11:21; and Origen says immediately afterwards "so also they were withered." Emendations suggested are ἀσθείσῃ (from ἄζομαι) Oxford ed.; ξηρανθείσῃ, Anonymous; αὐανθείσῃ, Koetschau. If ἀρθείσῃ was in the original text of the treatise, it may be due to a mistake of the stenographer in taking down Origen's words; or it may be a slip on the part of Origen, occasioned by the occurrence of ἄρθητι in the following context (Mark 11:23: "Whosoever shall say unto this mountain, 'Be thou taken up,'" etc.). But Origen discusses fully the incident of the fig tree and its "withering away" in *In Matt.*, XVI, 26 (*C.B.*, XL, 562).

XXXI, 7. *in church*] ἐν ἐκκλησίᾳ, i.e., in assembly, when Christians are gathered together, especially for worship. It is the usage of Paul in I Cor. 11:18; 14:19, 28, 35, and is based on the Old Testament use of qāhāl, "assembly," "convocation," of which ἐκκλησία is normally the rendering in the LXX.

XXXII. *the east . . . the direction we ought to face when praying*] Turning to the east when making supplication or offering sacrifice was a common custom in pre-Christian times. Cf. Sophocles *O.C.*, 477 (with R. C. Jebb's note); Vergil, *Aeneid*, XII, 172; Tacitus, *Hist.*, III, 24; Philo, *De V.C.*, 3. Probably it was taken over thence without more ado by the Christian Church. At any rate some of the early Fathers in their more candid moments confessed that they knew of no definite Scriptural sanction for the custom. Origen, *In Num. hom.*, V (*C.B.*, XXX, 26): "Sed et in ecclesiasticis observationibus sunt nonnulla huiusmodi, quae omnibus quidem facere necesse est, nec tamen ratio eorum omnibus patet. Nam quod, verbi gratia, genua flectimus orantes et quod ex omnibus coeli plagis ad solam orientis partem conversi orationem fundimus, non facile cuiquam puto ratione compertum." Basil, *De Spiritu Sancto*, 66: "What writing taught us to turn to the east in prayer?" Other early references to the custom are Clement of Alexandria, *Strom.*, VII, 7, 43; Tertullian, *Adv. Valent.*, 3; *Apol.*, 16 (where T. says that because they turned to the east in prayer Christians were suspected of worshipping the sun). Nevertheless, while the origin of the custom must be sought in times before Christ, Christian writers were unable to resist the temptation to find support for it in a mystical interpretation of certain passages of Scripture. Thus, Origen, *In Levit. hom.*, IX, 10 (*C.B.*, XXIX, 438) says: "Ab oriente tibi propitiatio venit; inde est enim vir, cui 'Oriens nomen' est [Zech. 6:12] . . . Imitaris ergo per hoc, ut ad orientem semper adspicias, unde tibi oritur 'sol iustitiae'" [Mal. 4:2]. Another text is adduced in support of the practice in *Didascalia Apostolorum*, ch. XII (ed. R. H. Connolly, 119, 120): "For it is required that you pray toward the east, as knowing that which is written 'Give ye glory to God, who rideth upon the heaven of heavens towards the east' [Ps. 67 (68):33]." Yet another passage of Scripture is laid hold of by Gregory of Nyssa, *In Oratione Dominica*, V (*P.G.*, XLIV, 1184), where the argument is that since Paradise was in the east (Gen. 2:8), therefore when we turn to the east in prayer, we ask the second Adam to restore to us what the first Adam lost. At a much later date (? c. 743), John of Damascus, *De Fide Orthodoxa*, IV, 12 (*P.G.*, XCIV, 1133–1136) repeats the texts from Zechariah, Malachi, and Genesis and adds other reasons for the custom, namely, that when Christ was on the Cross, his face was turned to the west, hence when we adore him we turn to the east; and that when he ascended into heaven, he was borne towards the east, and so will come in like manner: quoting Matt. 24:27.

Candidates for baptism faced west when they were renouncing Satan; in professing the Creed they faced east, "the region of light," where God had planted Paradise. (Cyril, Hieros., *Cat. Myst.*, I; *P.G.*, XXXIII, 1068, 1073). Cf. also Ambrose, *De Mysteriis*, II; Jerome, *Comment. in Amos*, III, 6 (*P.L.*, XXV, 1068). On the general subject of praying eastwards, see Bingham, *Antiquities of the Christian Church*, 517, 653; "Orientation," in *D.A.C.L.*, by H. Leclercq.

XXXII. *by convention . . . by nature*] θέσει . . . φύσει. A Stoic antithesis. Diogenes Laërtius, VII, 128 quotes Chrysippus as saying that τὸ δίκαιον is "by nature" and not "by convention": see J. von Arnim, *S.V.F.*, III, 76. Strabo, *Geographica*, II, 3:7, contrasts φύσις with "custom" and "training," and in the same section speaks of a certain question as "a mere matter of argument" (θετική).

XXXIII, 1. *God is to be glorified*, etc.] Cf. the concluding words of this section "glorifying God through Christ in the Holy Spirit." Although Origen is speaking of private prayer, it seems almost certain that he has in mind a liturgical formula corresponding to the *Gloria Patri*. At a later date Basil, *De Spiritu Sancto*, in discussing different forms of this formula, seems to imply (section 71) that "in the Holy Spirit" was the most usual ending. He refers, however, to two forms of doxology, both of which he used in public worship, sometimes glorifying God the Father "in fellowship with [μετὰ] the Son, together with [σὺν] the Spirit," and at others using the prepositions (as Origen here) "through" the Son and "in" the Holy Spirit. Basil's preference is for the former of these two forms, since he wrote subsequently to the Arian heresy, and it was desirable not to give a loophole to those who denied that the Son and the Holy Spirit are co-essential with the Father. He proceeds to cite many authorities in the past who used the phrase "together with the Holy Spirit," among them "Origen in many of his expositions of the Psalms." (I have failed to find an example of this in the extant fragments of this work.) Basil then goes on to say of Origen (ch. 73) that "the opinions he held concerning the Holy Spirit were not always and everywhere sound; nevertheless in many passages even he reverently recognizes the force of established usage, and expresses himself concerning the Spirit in terms consistent with true religion" (*N.P.N.F.*, VIII, 46).

XXXIII, 2. *"how greatly art thou magnified"*] B and ℵ omit "how."

XXXIII, 2. *"majesty"*] This is the reading of A. The first hand of ℵ reads "goodliness."

XXXIII, 2. *"a flame of fire"*] So the second hand of A, instead of "a flaming fire."

XXXIII, 2. *"who layeth the foundations*] So A: *v.l.*, "he laid the foundations."

XXXIII, 3. *through Nathan*] διὰ τοῦ Νᾶθαν. This is an emendation for διὰ τοῦ θανάτου (*sic*) of T, the scribe of which the Anonymous calls "half asleep": *semisomnis librarius*.

XXXIII, 3. *"I was made little"*] This is also the reading of B. A reads "it was made little."

XXXIII, 3. *"thou knowest thy servant, O Lord"*] This is the reading of T in this place, and also of B and A in the LXX. Rahlfs, however, gives "my Lord" as the reading of Origen's recension.

XXXIII, 3. *"For thy servant's sake"*] Here again T gives a reading not in accordance with the Origenist text, which according to Rahlfs has "On thy account."

XXXIII, 5. *"Draw me not away with sinners"*] This is the reading of Codex ℵ. *v.l.*, "Draw not my soul away with sinners."

XXXIV. *on your behalf*] If this reading is correct, it refers more particularly to Origen's answer to "the problem of prayer" which had been posed to him by his two friends (V, 6). That Origen, however, gave the subject a much wider treatment than "the problem" demanded, may suggest that he felt his friends needed to be brought on much further on the whole subject and practice of prayer. This may also be suggested in the quotation from Phil. 3:13 which follows.

XXXIV. *very studious*] Lit. "very fond of learning," an epithet that was certainly deserved by Ambrose. See Introduction, p. 182.

XXXIV. *pray for us*] With a Christian tactfulness worthy of Paul, Origen gives the impression that it is he who needs his friends' prayers.

XXXIV. *to treat again of these matters*] We have no reason to think that Origen ever wrote again specifically on the subject of prayer. The *De Oratione* was in fact no mean contribution to it, and was much fuller than the treatises of Tertullian and of Cyprian which preceded and followed it, in point of time. The apologetic tone of the concluding words: "you will read this book with indulgence," if not merely a conventional phrase, may point to the haste, and consequent defects in arrangement, of which Origen was conscious as he surveyed his completed task.

Exhortation to Martyrdom

INTRODUCTION

EARLY IN A.D. 235 THE SOLDIER MAXIMIN LED A successful revolt against the regime of Severus Alexander, last of the Syrian emperors, who was killed on the Rhine frontier. Severus Alexander had been friendly to the Church. His wife, Mamaea, when on one occasion she was staying at Antioch, had sent for Origen and asked him theological questions.[1] According to the *Historia Augusta* there was a private chapel in the imperial household containing statues of past emperors and great men of history, including Apollonius of Tyana, Orpheus, Abraham, and Christ.[2] It was in reaction against this policy of friendliness to the Church that Maximin began to persecute the Christians. Only the clergy were attacked. The church historian Eusebius of Caesarea says that Maximin, "through ill will towards the house of Alexander, since it consisted for the most part of believers, raised a persecution, ordering the leaders of the church alone to be put to death, as being responsible for the teaching of the gospel."[3] At Rome Bishop Pontianus and Hippolytus were deported to Sardinia.[4]

At the threat of persecution Origen wrote his *Exhortation to Martyrdom* for his rich patron, Ambrose, who was in deacon's orders, and for Protoctetus, a presbyter of the church at Caesarea in Palestine. The *Exhortation* shows signs of having been written in haste, and Origen shows little concern for style or ordered arrangement. The style is in places verbose, and for a modern reader Origen's characteristic habit of quoting a text

[1] Eusebius, *H.E.*, VI, 21:3–4.
[2] S. H. A., Lampridius, *Vita Severi*, 29.
[3] Eusebius, *H.E.*, VI, 28; cf. *Chronic.*, p. 216, ed. Helm.
[4] *Liber Pontificalis*, I, p. 4, ed. Duchesne.

388

from the Synoptic Gospels in all its possible forms must seem pedantic and irritating. Nevertheless the work is of high interest, because of the insight it gives us into the spirit of the early Church under the immediate stress of persecution.

Chapters 1–5 are an introduction in the form of an exposition of Isa. 28:9–11. This is followed by a warning against idolatry and apostasy (Chapters 6–10) and an exhortation to stand firm (Chapters 11–21). The example of the Maccabean martyrs, which exercised great influence on early Christian ideas of true martyrdom, is held up in Chapters 22–27. Origen then writes of the value of death by martyrdom, and of baptism of blood as conferring remission of all sins (Chapters 28 ff.). He emphasizes the absolute dividing line between the Christian and the world (34 ff.) which means that there can be no compromise. Chapters 45–46 (cf. 5) deal with the lax views of those who sought to rationalize the attitude of compromise with the State, saying that a mere name is nothing, and that to swear by the *Tyche* of the emperor is not a significant act. This tendency appears in many gnostic sects such as the Simonians (Origen, *contra Celsum*, VI, 11), and the followers of Prodicus (Tertullian, *Scorpiace*, 15). The view that apostasy is a matter of moral indifference is also attributed to Basilides.[5] The school of Valentine was particularly exercised by the question; Clement of Alexandria[6] preserves Heracleon's interpretation of Luke 12:11–12. Confession before the authorities, he says, is to be made only "if necessary and if reason demand."

Origen's closing section (Chapters 47 to end) consists of a final exhortation to courage.

Origen's *Exhortation* is an outstanding witness to the dignity which the early Church attributed to martyrdom.[7] It was the highest ambition of Ignatius of Antioch to be torn to pieces by wild beasts at Rome. No higher reward could be reserved for the Christian than the martyr's crown. No epithet was too exalted for him. Thus for Tertullian the glory of the church at Rome consisted precisely in the fact that Peter and Paul had

---

[5] Agrippa Castor in Eusebius, *H.E.*, IV, 7:7; Origen, *Hom. in Ezech.*, III, 4; *Comm. Ser. in Matt.*, 38. Possibly this represents the view of the later followers of Basilides, rather than Basilides himself; at any rate, it is difficult to see how this can be reconciled with the statements of Basilides cited by Clement (*Strom.*, IV, 83).

[6] *Strom.*, IV, 71.

[7] For the following, cf. H. Delehaye, *Les Origines du Culte des Martyrs* (2nd edition, 1933). E. Lucius, *Die Anfänge des Heiligenkults* (1904), remains of high value.

died there during the Neronian persecution. Naturally therefore a martyr's death was accepted with joy. *Deo gratias,* said
Cyprian of Carthage as the proconsul pronounced the death-
sentence.

Above all, the Gospel saying (Luke 12:11–12) was a guaran-
tee that the martyr before his judges was possessed by the Holy
Spirit. It is scarcely surprising that exaggerated claims were
made by those who had boldly confessed their faith. As vehicles
of the Spirit they surely had power to remit sins to the lapsed,
an attitude of mind which caused Cyprian much trouble.
Zealots would do all in their power to provoke the authorities,
and measures had to be taken by church authorities to deny the
title of martyr to the provocative. Such men were regarded as
suicides. The confessor in prison could be sure of the assiduous
visits of the faithful who would bring him food and kiss his
chains. Lucian's satire on *The Death of Peregrinus* is a vivid contemporary caricature of these attentions and the abuse to which
they could easily lead.

By death the martyr was assured of an absolute remission of
all his sins. Even a catechumen, not yet baptized in water, could
have all stain of sin washed away by the baptism of blood,[8] and
could enter Paradise in white robes. There he joined with all
other martyrs and confessors in interceding for the Church on
earth.[9]

On the anniversary of his "birthday," i.e., the day when he
entered the life of the world to come, the faithful would gather
at his tomb outside the city, and a sermon would be preached
on the theme of his noble witness to Christ. Local churches
carefully preserved records of the date of each martyr's "birthday," and the lists they made were the first church calendars.
The earliest surviving calendar is that used by the church at
Rome in the middle of the fourth century.

It is only natural that sometimes the instinct for revenge took
hold of the martyrs, although this is usually sublimated to the
next world with the threat of worse punishment for the per-
secutors there. This psychological reaction seems to have contributed substantially to the lurid nature of some Christian
language about hell, and that this is a *vera causa* in Tertullian's

---

[8] Cf. Origen, *Exh. Mart.*, 30, 39.
[9] Cf. Origen, *Exh. Mart.*, 37–38. Tertullian held that while all other
Christians remained in Hades till the last judgment, martyrs were at
once admitted to paradise. See J. H. Waszink's commentary on Tertullian, *de Anima,* 55.

mind is obvious from the well-known last chapter of his *De Spectaculis*. The idea is implied in the common notion that at the last day the martyr will sit in judgment on those who were his judges on earth (cf. Origen, *Exh. Mart.*, 28).

The particular value of martyrdom consisted in that the martyr knew himself to be in mystical union with his Lord in his passion. Origen, when seventeen years of age, had lost his father in the persecution of Septimius Severus, and was only prevented from going out to martyrdom himself by the fact that his mother concealed his clothes (Eusebius, *H.E.*, VI, 2:5). This experience he never forgot. Origen always prized persecution because it revealed who in the Church were true believers. Writing in the period of peace before the Decian persecution broke out, he looks wistfully back to the days of conflict with the government: "That was the time when Christians really were faithful, when the noble martyrdoms were taking place, when after conducting the martyrs' bodies to the cemeteries we returned thence to meet together, and the entire church was present without being afraid, and the catechumens were being catechized during the very time of the martyrdoms and while men were dying who had confessed the truth unto death. . . . Then we knew and saw wonderful and miraculous signs. Then there were true believers, few in number but truly faithful, treading the strait and narrow way which leads to life. But now when we have become many, . . . out of the multitude who profess piety there are extremely few who are attaining to the election of God and to blessedness."[10] Only the martyr, felt Origen, truly followed Christ and was in union with him. The disciple who takes up his cross and follows Jesus attains, he says, to an immediate knowledge of God whom he sees face to face.[11] This is a belief fundamental to Origen's ideas about the nature of the Church and of the spiritual life. It is for this reason that Origen's *Exhortation to Martyrdom* is so moving a document, and tells us so much of the spirit of the early Church.

The *Exhortation to Martyrdom* is preserved in two Greek manuscripts at Paris and Venice: Codex Paris. Suppl. Gr., 616, dated 1339 (of this there are also two copies), and Codex Venet.

---

10 *Hom. in Jerem.*, IV, 3.
11 *Exh. Mart.*, 13. The importance of this background for understanding Origen's mystical language is admirably brought out by J. Lebreton, "La source et le caractère de la mystique d'Origène," in *Analecta Bollandiana*, LXVII (= *Mélanges Paul Peeters*, I), 1949, pp. 55–62. The language of "deification" is applied to the martyrs in *Exh. Mart.*, 25.

Marc., 45, of the fourteenth century.[12] The standard critical edition of the text, which is here translated, is that of Paul Koetschau in the Berlin Academy corpus (1899). Koetschau also produced a German translation in 1926, with some valuable textual notes (*Bibliothek der Kirchenväter*, Band 48). A French translation by G. Bardy appeared in 1932. Both of these translations I have found useful in revising my own.

[12] The Venice manuscript belonged to Cardinal Bessarion and contains a remarkable note in his hand expressing the fervour of his admiration for Origen which had led him to seek everywhere for copies of his works. See Koetschau's edition, p. xvii.

Exhortation to Martyrdom

THE TEXT

1. "You who have been weaned from milk, who have been drawn away from the breast: expect tribulation upon tribulation, expect hope upon hope; a little longer, a little longer, because of the scorn of lips, by another tongue."[1]

And you, most reverend Ambrose, and most religious Protoctetus, as being no longer carnal, nor being babes in Christ,[2] who have advanced in your spiritual age,[3] and have no more need of milk but of solid food,[4] are according to Isaiah's words as "those who have been weaned from milk" and "drawn away from the breast." Hear how the prophet foretells for athletes who have been weaned not merely tribulation but a "tribulation upon tribulation." But he who does not refuse tribulation upon tribulation, but accepts it like a noble athlete, immediately receives also "hope upon hope" which he will enjoy after but a short time of the tribulation upon tribulation. For that is the meaning of "a little longer, a little longer."

2. Even if we are scorned and despised by those who treat us as blasphemers and fools, and who are strangers to the language of the holy scriptures, let us remember that the hope upon hope, which after a little while will be given to us, is to be given "because of the scorn of lips, by another tongue." And who would not gladly receive tribulation upon tribulation if he is at once to receive also hope upon hope, reckoning with Paul that "the sufferings of this present time," by which as it were we buy our salvation, "are not worthy to be compared with the glory which shall be revealed to us"[5] by God? So much the more, in fact, since "our light affliction which is but for a moment" (light not

---

[1] Isa. 28:9–11.   [2] Cf. I Cor. 3:1.   [3] Cf. Luke 2:52.
[4] Heb. 5:12.   [5] Rom. 8:18.

merely in words, but also in fact for those who are not depressed by the difficulties) "works in us a weight of eternal glory"[6] which is greater in proportion to the severity of the affliction. This is true if at the very moment when we are attacked by those who afflict us and desire, so to speak, to press down our souls, we turn our mind away from the troubles and fix our gaze not on the tribulations that are upon us, but on the rewards which by God's grace are laid up for those who have striven lawfully[7] in Christ because they have borne affliction patiently. For God multiplies the benefits and grants far greater favours than are deserved by the distress experienced by the man who fights through it. This is in character for him who makes his gifts not in any miserly fashion, but with generosity and understanding to those who to the best of their ability have shown by their scorn for their "earthen vessel"[8] that they love him with all their soul.

3. I think that they love God with all their soul who with a great desire to be in union with God withdraw and separate their soul not only from the earthly body but also from everything material. Such men accept the putting away of the body of humiliation[9] without distress or emotion when the time come for them to put off the body of death by what is commonly regarded as death. Then they may be heard to pray with the apostle saying: "O wretched man that I am, who shall deliver me from this body of death?"[10] Who among those who groan in this tabernacle because they are weighed down by the corruptible body[11] will not also first give thanks saying: "Who shall deliver me from this body of death?" He sees that by his confession[12] he has been delivered from the body of death and with holy lips will cry: "Thanks be to God through Jesus Christ our Lord."[13] If this seems difficult to anyone, it is because he has not been "athirst for the living God, the strong God," nor has he longed for God "like as the hart desires the water springs." Nor has he said: "When shall I come and appear in the presence of God?" Nor has he considered in his mind as the prophet did when it was said to him every day, "Where is thy God?" and he poured out his heart upon himself, and rebuked it because it was still weak, overcome by sadness, and distressed, saying:

---

6 II Cor. 4:17. 7 II Tim. 2:5. 8 II Cor. 4:7.
9 Phil. 3:21. 10 Rom. 7:24.
11 II Cor. 5:4; Wisdom of Solomon 9:15.
12 Read with Koetschau's translation: ὁμολογίας.
13 Rom. 7:25.

"For I shall pass through in the place of the wonderful tabernacle as far as the house of God, with a voice of rejoicing and of confession of a festal sound."[14]

4. I beseech you, therefore, throughout the present conflict to remember the great reward laid up in the heavens for those who are persecuted and reviled for righteousness' sake and for the Son of Man's sake,[15] and that you rejoice and be glad and exult just as the apostles rejoiced when on one occasion they were "counted worthy to suffer insults for his name."[16] And if sometimes you feel anguish in your soul, may the mind of Christ within us speak to the soul, even though desire does everything possible to confuse even this mind of Christ, saying: "Why art thou sad, O my soul? And why do you disquiet me? Put thy trust in God, for I will make confession of him."[17] And again, I pray that our souls may never be troubled, but that, even before the tribunals and before the swords unsheathed to behead us, they may be kept by the peace of God which passes all understanding[18] and may enjoy tranquillity, reckoning that those who are absent from the body are present with the Lord[19] of the universe himself. But if we have not such courage as to remain always without anxiety, at least let the distress of our soul be not displayed nor apparent to the pagan onlookers, that we may be able to defend ourselves to God saying to him: "O God, my soul is vexed within me."[20] The Word exhorts us to remember also the words of Isaiah as follows: "Fear not the reproach of men, and be not cast down by their contempt."[21] Moreover, since God manifestly watches over the movement of the heaven and the stars in it and over that which takes place by his divine arrangement in earth and sea, in the birth and nourishment of all kinds of animals and in the origin and growth of all plants, it would be absurd for us to shut our eyes and not to look to God, but in fear to turn our eyes upon men who will shortly die and be handed over to the punishment they deserve.

5. God once said to Abraham: "Get out of thy land."[22] Perhaps it will shortly be said to us: "Get out of the earth altogether." And it will be good to obey the command, so that God may quickly show us the heavens in which is the kingdom of heaven as it is called. We can readily perceive that life is full of conflicts and of men engaged in a struggle concerning the

---

[14] Ps. 42 (41):2–3, 11–12. [15] Cf. Matt. 5:10–12; Luke 6:23.
[16] Acts 5:41. [17] Ps. 42 (41):6, 12. [18] Phil. 4:7.
[19] II Cor. 5:8. [20] Ps. 42 (41):6–7. [21] Isa. 51:7.
[22] Gen. 12:1.

various different virtues. Many who do not belong to the portion of God[23] appear to have fought to attain self-control, and some have died a heroic death because of their loyalty to the common Master of all men. Men eminent in philosophical inquiry have been anxious to be prudent; men who have made it their purpose to live rightly have devoted themselves to righteousness. Indeed, each virtue is opposed either by "the carnal mind" or by many attacks from external sources. But the only people to fight for religion are "the elect race, the royal priesthood, the holy nation, a people for God's possession."[24] The rest of mankind do not even try to make it appear that, if there is persecution of religious people, they intend to die for religion and to prefer death rather than deny their religion and live. And each one of those who wish to be members of the elect race is convinced that at all times, even when he is attacked by those who are supposed to be polytheists but are really atheists, he must listen to God, who says, "Thou shalt have none other gods but me,"[25] and "The name of other gods ye shall not remember in your hearts, nor mention with your mouth."[26] Accordingly, such people "believe in God with the heart unto righteousness, and with the mouth make confession unto salvation."[27] They are aware that they are not granted righteousness until they so believe in God that their heart remains unmoved, and that they will not be saved unless their word corresponds to their inner conviction. They deceive themselves who suppose that it is sufficient for the attainment of the end in Christ if with the heart they believe unto righteousness, omitting the words "but with the mouth confession is made unto salvation." Indeed, I would go so far as to say that it is better to honour God with lips when one's heart is far from God[28] than to honour him with the heart and not to make confession with the mouth unto salvation.

6. God who commands, "Thou shalt not make for thyself an idol nor any image of anything,"[29] and so on, appears to distinguish between "Thou shalt not bow down to them" and "Thou shalt not worship them." Accordingly, perhaps he who believes in idols may worship them, but he who does not believe in them, moved by cowardice to make a pretence which he calls accommodating himself,[30] so as to seem to be religious like the

23 Cf. Deut. 32:9. 24 Ex. 19:6; I Pet. 2:9. 25 Ex. 20:3.
26 Ex. 23:13. 27 Rom. 10:10. 28 Isa. 29:13.
29 Ex. 20:4-5.
30 Cf. Origen, contra Celsum, VII, 66, with my note thereon. For the attitude of the gnostic sects in time of persecution see above, Introduction, p. 389.

multitude, does not worship the idols, but only bows down to them. And I would say that those who abjure Christianity at the tribunal, or even before arriving there, do not worship the idols, but only bow down to them, taking the name of the Lord and applying the word "God" to vain and lifeless matter. In their matter also the people "defiled with the daughters of Moab"[31] bowed down to idols but did not worship them. At any rate Scripture says in these very words: "They called them to the sacrifices of their idols, and the people ate of their sacrifices and bowed down to their idols and were initiated into Beelphegor."[32] Notice that it does not say, "And they worshipped their idols." For it was impossible that after such remarkable signs and wonders they should be persuaded in an instant by the women with whom they committed fornication to believe that the idols were gods. Perhaps in the same way also at the making of the calf in Exodus they bowed down, but did not worship the calf which they had watched being made.[33]

We must therefore regard the present temptation as a trial and test of our love for God. "For the Lord tempts you," as it is written in Deuteronomy, "to know whether you love the Lord your God with all your heart and with all your soul."[34] But you, when you are tempted, "will follow the Lord your God and will fear him and keep his commandments," especially noting the precept, "Thou shalt have none other gods but me," and you "will hear his voice and obey him" who takes you from this earthly region and attaches you to himself for "the increase of God"[35] in him, to use the apostle's language.

7. But if "every evil word is an abomination to the Lord thy God,"[36] what abomination must be the evil word of denial and the evil word that calls upon another god, and the evil oath by the "fortune" of men, a word that corresponds to no reality.[37] When this oath is required of us, let us remember him who taught us: "But I say unto you, Swear not at all."[38] For if he who swears by heaven insults the throne of God, and if he who swears by earth utters blasphemy by making a god of what is called "God's footstool," and if he who swears by Jerusalem sins even though it is a city of a great King, and if he who swears by his own head[39] is doing wrong: how great a sin must we think it

31 Num. 25:1.   32 Num 25:2–3.   33 Ex. 32:8.
34 Deut. 13:3–4.   35 Col. 2:19.
36 Cf. Matt. 12:36; Prov. 15:26.
37 See Origen, *contra Celsum*, VIII, 65, with my note thereon.
38 Matt. 5:34.   39 Matt. 5:35–6.

to swear by some man's fortune? At that time let us also bear in
mind the word: "For every idle word you shall give account in
the day of judgment."[40] For what other word is so idle as the
oath of denial?

But it is probable that the enemy wishes to use every argument in his power to make us worship the sun or the moon or all
the host of heaven.[41] But we will reply that the word of God
"has not commanded this." We ought on no account to worship
the creatures in the presence of the Creator[42] who is sufficient
for and anticipates the prayer of all. Nor indeed would the sun
himself wish to be worshipped by those who belong to the portion of God,[43] and probably not even by anyone else. But he
might imitate him who said, "Why do you call me good? There
is none good but the one God the Father,"[44] and, as it were, say
to him who desires to worship him: "Why do you call me God?
There is one true God. And why do you bow down to me?
'Thou shalt worship the Lord thy God and him only shalt thou
serve.'[45] I also am a created being. Why do you wish to worship
one who himself offers worship? I also worship and serve God
the Father and in obedience to his commands I am made subject to futility on account of him who put me in subjection in
hope, and I shall be liberated from the bondage of corruption,
even though I am now bound to a corruptible body, into the
liberty of the glory of the children of God."[46]

8. It is only to be expected that some prophet of impiety (and
perhaps not merely one but several) will tell us some alleged
"word of the Lord, which the Lord has not commanded,"[47] or
put out as a "word of wisdom"[48] something quite alien to wisdom, to slay us with the word of his mouth. But we, even at that
very moment when the sinner confronts us, should say: "But
like a deaf man I heard not, and like a dumb man who opens
not his mouth; and I became like a man who cannot hear."[49]
Deafness to blasphemous words is excellent when we have no
hope of correcting those whose words are evil.

9. It is well for us to reflect, at the moments when we are
tempted to do wrong, upon that which God desires to teach us
when he says: "I the Lord thy God am jealous."[50] In my opinion

[40] Matt. 12:36.   [41] Deut. 17:3.   [42] Rom. 1:25.
[43] Deut. 32:9.
[44] Mark 10:18; Luke 18:19. Cf. Origen, contra Celsum, V, 11; de Orat., XV, 4.
(above, p. 271).
[45] Matt. 4:10.   [46] Rom. 8:20–21.   [47] Deut. 18:20, 22.
[48] I Cor. 12:8.   [49] Ps. 38:13–14.   [50] Ex. 20:5.

just as the husband who is concerned to help his bride to live chastely, to bring all her affection towards her husband and to take every precaution to avoid another man, if he is wise, will show some jealousy and will adopt this attitude to his bride as a precautionary remedy: so also the Lawgiver (especially if it be clear that he is "the firstborn of all creation"[51]) says to the soul betrothed to God that he is jealous. His purpose is to separate the hearers from all fornication with daemons and with the supposed gods. It is as a jealous God that he says of those who have in any way gone a-whoring after other gods: "They provoked me to jealousy against that which is not God, they made me wrathful against their idols. And I will provoke them to jealousy with people who are not a nation, I will make them wrathful against a foolish nation. For the fire is kindled from my anger, and it shall burn to the bottom of Hades."[52]

10. If it is not for his own sake that the husband, wise and without passion, seeks to turn his betrothed from all defilement, it is for her sake; because he sees her defilement and impurity he will do all in his power to cure and convert her. To her free will he will speak words to dissuade her from fornication. What worse pollution for the soul can one imagine than to call upon another God and not to confess the one true and only Lord? I believe that just as "he who is joined to a harlot is one body,"[53] so also he who confesses faith in any god, especially at a time of persecution and trial of faith, is mingled and united with the god whom he confesses. He who denies is separated by the very act of denial like a cutting sword, from him whom he denies; he suffers alienation and is severed from him whom he has denied. Consider therefore the scripture: "Whosoever confesses me before men, him shall I confess before my Father in heaven, [and whosoever denies me before men him shall I deny before my Father in heaven.]"[54] This implies that it necessarily and inevitably follows that he who confesses is confessed and he who denies is denied. The very Logos and very Truth might say both to him who confesses and him who denies: "The measure you apply to others is the measure that shall be applied to you."[55] You therefore who have measured with the measure of confession of faith in me and have fulfilled[56] the measure of the confession, will receive the measure of my confession, "shaken

---

51 Col. 1:15.   52 Deut. 32:21–22.   53 I Cor. 6:16.
54 Matt. 10:32–33. The second half (verse 33) is lacking in the manuscripts, but appears to be necessary for the sense of the passage.
55 Luke 6:38.   56 Cf. Matt. 23:32.

together, pressed down, and running over" which shall be given into your bosom.[57] But you who have measured with the measure of denial and have denied me shall receive the measure of my denial of you, corresponding to the denial you have made of me.

11. Let us in this way consider how the measure of confession may be filled up or how it may be not filled but left deficient. If throughout the time of trial and temptation we give no place in our hearts to the devil,[58] who wishes to defile us with evil thoughts of denial or hesitancy or some plausible argument which may tempt us to the very opposite of martyrdom and perfection; and if, furthermore, we pollute ourselves by not a word contrary to our profession, and if we bear all the adversaries' reproach and mockery and laughter and slander, and the pity which they think they have for us, imagining us dupes and fools and calling us deluded; if, moreover, we are not distracted or held even by affection for our children or for their mother or for one of those whom we regard as our dearest friends in this life, so as to value their possession and to prize our earthly life, but turn away from these ties and become wholly dedicated to God and to living in his company and presence that we may share communion with his only-begotten Son and those who participate in him[59]: then I would affirm that we have fulfilled the measure of the confession. But if we fall short even in any one point, we have not fulfilled it, but have defiled the measure of our confession and have adulterated it with something foreign. In that case we shall be lacking, in the same way as those who have built upon the foundation wood, or hay, or stubble.[60]

12. We must also realize that we have received the so-called covenants of God on conditions, set forth in the agreements which we made with him when we first took upon us to live the Christian life. And among the terms of our agreement with God was the entire way of life set forth in the gospel which says: "If any man will follow me, let him deny himself and take up his cross and follow me. For whosoever wishes to save his life shall lose it, and whosoever loses his life for my sake, he will save it."[61] And often we have been filled with enthusiasm on hearing the words: "For what shall it profit a man if he gain the whole world and lose his own soul? Or what shall a man give in exchange for his soul? For when the Son of Man shall come in the glory of his

[57] Luke 6:38.   [58] Eph. 4:27.   [59] Cf. Heb. 3:14.
[60] I Cor. 3:12.   [61] Matt. 16:24–25.

Father with his angels, even then shall he render to each man according to his work."[62]

That it is necessary to deny oneself and take up one's cross and follow Jesus is recorded not merely by Matthew, whose text we have been quoting, but also by Luke and Mark. Hear the words of Luke: "He said to them all, If any man wishes to follow me, let him deny himself and take up his cross and follow me. For whosoever wishes to save his life shall lose it; but whosoever shall lose his life for my sake, he shall save it. For what will it profit a man if he gain the whole world and lose or forfeit himself?"[63] Mark says: "And calling the crowd with his disciples, he said to them, If any man wishes to follow me, let him deny himself and take up his cross and follow me. For whosoever wishes to save his life shall lose it; and whosoever shall lose it for the gospel's sake shall save it. But what shall it profit a man if he gain the whole world and lose his own soul? For what shall a man give in exchange for his soul?"[64]

Long ago we ought to have denied ourselves, saying, "It is no longer I who live."[65] Now it is revealed whether or not we have taken up our cross and followed Jesus. This will have happened if Christ is living in us. If we wish to save our soul, so that we may receive it back as better than a soul,[66] let us lose it even by martyrdom. For if we lose it for Christ's sake, throwing it at his feet in dying for him, we acquire its true salvation. But if we do the opposite, then we shall hear that it does not profit one who gains the whole material world at the price of losing or forfeiting himself. Once a man has lost his own soul or forfeited it, even if he gain the whole world, it will not be possible for him to pay anything in exchange for the soul he has lost. For the soul created in the image of God[67] is more precious than anything material. One person alone has been able to pay the price of our soul which was previously lost, he who bought us with his own precious blood.[68]

13. With profound meaning Isaiah says: "I gave Egypt for

---

[62] Matt. 16:26–27.   [63] Luke 9:23–25.   [64] Mark 8:34–37.
[65] Gal. 2:20.
[66] That is, as *nous*. Cf. Origen, *de Principiis*, II, 8:3: "The soul when saved remains a soul no longer." Origen explains that *psyche*, which with other ancient writers he connected with the Greek word for growing cold, is not a suitable term for a rational being that has recovered the warmth of its love for God lost by the Fall. *Hom. in Lucam*, XXXVI (on Luke 17:33): ". . . let us lose our soul that by cleaving to the Lord we may be transformed into one spirit."
[67] Gen. 1:27.   [68] I Pet. 1:19.

thy ransom, and Ethiopia and Syene for thee, for thou wast precious in my sight."[69] The right meaning of this and other such sayings you will understand if you have a desire for knowledge in Christ and even now wish to surpass that which is seen "through a glass, darkly," and hasten towards him who has called you. Then as never before you will comprehend "face to face,"[70] as friends of the heavenly Father who is your teacher. Friends know not by obscure hints, or by mere knowledge of sounds and words, symbols and types, but by a real awareness through which they attain to the nature of the intelligible world and to the beauty of the truth. If you believe that Paul was caught up to the third heaven, and was caught up to Paradise and heard unspeakable words which man cannot utter,[71] you will accordingly realize that you will have immediate knowledge of more and greater matters than the unspeakable words revealed to Paul. For after receiving them he descended from the third heaven, whereas after you have acquired this knowledge you will not descend again, if you take up your cross and follow Jesus whom we have as "a great high priest who has passed through the heavens."[72] And if you do not fall away from those who follow him you yourselves shall pass through the heavens, passing not merely above earth and the mysteries of earth, but even above the heavens and their mysteries. For in God there are treasured up much greater visions than these, which no being with a material body can perceive before it is separated from every contact with matter. For I am persuaded that God is keeping and storing in himself far greater wonders than are seen by sun, moon, and the choir of stars, and even by the holy angels whom God made "spirit" and "flame of fire,"[73] so that he may reveal them when the whole creation is liberated from the bondage of the enemy to the liberty of the glory of the children of God.[74]

14. And to those exalted heights[75] the ascent will be quickly made by one of those first martyrs, who have a Christian love of learning surpassing many others. But you, devout Ambrose, can see by close study of the gospel saying that probably nobody at all, or at any rate only very few, will attain to an exceptional and transcendent wealth of blessedness. You yourself will attain to this if you pass through the conflict without hesitating. The

---

[69] Isa. 43:3–4. [70] I Cor. 13:12. [71] II Cor. 12:2, 4.
[72] Heb. 4:14. On this passage cf. Introduction, p. 391.
[73] Ps. 104 (103):4; Heb. 1:7. [74] Rom. 8:21.
[75] Read with Koetschau's translation: ἐπ' ἐκεῖνα.

words read as follows: Peter once said to the Saviour, "Behold we have left all and followed you. What shall our reward be? Jesus said to them" (that is the apostles) "Verily I say to you that you who have followed me, in the regeneration when God [76] shall sit upon the throne of his glory, shall yourselves sit upon twelve thrones judging the twelve tribes of Israel. And everyone who has left brothers or sisters or children or lands or houses for my sake, shall receive manifold reward and shall inherit everlasting life." [77] On account of these words I pray that even if I possessed as many earthly possessions as you do, or even more than that, I may become a martyr for God in Christ that I may receive manifold, [78] or as Mark says "a hundredfold," [79] which is far more than the little we leave behind, which if we are called to martyrdom is multiplied a hundred times.

Therefore if I am to be a martyr, I would wish to leave children and lands and houses that with "the God and Father of our Lord Jesus Christ, from whom all fatherhood in heaven and earth is named" [80] I may be called father of children many times more numerous and holy or, to give an exact figure, of a hundred times more children. If there are fathers such as are mentioned in the words spoken to Abraham, "But thou shalt go to thy fathers in peace, having lived to a good old age," [81] someone might say (whether the suggestion is right or wrong I do not know): Perhaps there are fathers who once bore witness and left children, and in exchange for these they have become the fathers of the patriarch Abraham and of other patriarchs; for it is probable that those who have left children by bearing their witness become fathers not of infants but of fathers.

15. If anyone who as it were desires the greatest gifts, and blesses the martyrs as rich men and fathers who will beget a hundred times more children and will receive a hundred times more lands and houses, asks if it is reasonable that they should obtain a far larger inheritance in the spiritual world than those who were poor in this life, my reply to him is this. Just as those who have endured torments and agony have shown a more distinguished virtue by their martyrdom than those who have not been tried in this way, so also those who besides their normal attachment to the material world and for this life have cut free from very strong worldly ties because of their profound love for

---

[76] We expect "the Son." Elsewhere Origen quotes this text in the usual form. [77] Matt. 19:27-29.
[78] Matt. 19:29. [79] Mark 10:30. [80] Eph. 3:15.
[81] Gen. 15:15. Cf. Origen, *Dial. c. Heracl.*, p. 166, Scherer (below, p. 452).

God and true grasp of "the word of God which is living and active and sharper than any two-edged sword,"[82] are enabled by the act of cutting free from these ties to make for themselves wings like an eagle's, and so to "return to the house of their master."[83] It is right, therefore, that just as those who have not been tried by pain and agony yield first place to those whose patience has been manifested on the rack and by various kinds of torture and by fire, so also we poor men, even if we are martyrs, quite reasonably yield first place to you who for your Christian love for God trample underfoot the deceitful glory that most men seek after, and your great possessions and affection for your children.

16. Notice at the same time the gravity of the scripture which promises multiplication, even to a hundred times, of brothers, children, parents, lands, and homes. But a wife is not included in this list. For scripture does not say: Everyone who has left brothers or sisters or parents or children or lands or houses or a wife for my sake, will receive manifold reward. "For at the resurrection of the dead they neither marry nor are given in marriage, but are as the angels in heaven."[84]

17. The scripture might say to us now what Joshua said to the people when bringing them to settle in the holy land. The text reads as follows: "Now fear the Lord and serve in truth and righteousness."[85] If we are being pressed to idolatry the next words also would be applicable: "Destroy the foreign gods whom your fathers worshipped on the far side of the river and in Egypt, and worship the Lord."[86]

At the beginning when you were to be instructed in the Christian faith it would have been reasonable to say to you: "If you do not wish to serve the Lord, choose you this day whom you will serve, whether the gods of your fathers on the far side of the river or the gods of the Amorites, among whom you inhabit the land." And the catechist might have said to you: "As for me and my house, we will serve the Lord, for he is holy." But now it is

---

[82] Heb. 4:12.   [83] Prov. 23:5.

[84] Matt. 22:30; Mark 12:25. Cf. Jerome, *Comm. in Matt.*, III (Migne, *P.L.*, XXVI, 145 B): "On the ground of this saying [i.e., Matt. 19:29] some believe there will be a thousand years after the resurrection and assert that then we are to be given a hundredfold of all that we have left behind us and everlasting life. They fail to understand that if in reference to other things the promise appears right and proper, yet of wives it is obviously improper, since it implies that if a man has left one for the Lord's sake, he will receive a hundred in the future life."

[85] Josh. 24:14.   [86] Josh. 24:14.

not possible to say this to you. For at that time you said: "God forbid that we should forsake the Lord and serve other gods. The Lord our God, he is God, who brought us and our fathers up out of Egypt and kept us in all the way in which we journeyed." Moreover, in the agreements concerning religion you long ago made this reply to your instructors: "We will serve the Lord, for he is our God."[87] If, then, he who breaks agreements with men is one with whom no peace can be made and who is alien to salvation, what are we to say of those who by denial abrogate the agreements they have made with God and return to Satan whom they renounced at their baptism? To this we should say the words spoken by Eli to his sons: "If a man sins against a man, prayer may be made for him; but if he sins against the Lord, who shall pray for him?"[88]

18. A great audience is gathered to watch you who are engaged in conflict and are called to martyrdom, such as we might compare[89] to the vast crowd that gathers to watch the conflict between famous popular wrestlers. As you fight you may say no less than Paul, "We are become a spectacle to the world and to angels and to men."[90] The whole world, then, and all the angels of the right and left[91] and all men, both those who belong to God's portion[92] and the rest, will be watching us as we fight for Christianity. Either the angels in heaven will rejoice over us, and "the rivers will clap their hands together, and the hills sing for joy," and "all the trees of the plain shall clap their branches,"[93] or, which God forbid, those who rejoice will be the hellish powers that delight in evil. It is not inappropriate to see in a passage from Isaiah[94] what will be said by the powers of Hades to those who have been vanquished and have fallen from their heavenly witness. Their words will make us further tremble at the blasphemy of denial. For I imagine that this will be said to the apostate: "Hell from beneath is moved to meet thee. Risen up for thee are all the giants who have ruled the earth, who have said from their thrones all the kings of the earth. They shall all answer and say to thee." And what shall the vanquished powers say to the vanquished, and those captured by the devil to those captured in apostasy? Shall they not say this: "Even you are captured as we are and you are reckoned one of us." And if a man who has the great and glorious hope

---

87 Josh. 24:15–18.　　　　88 I Sam. 2:25.
89 Read with Koetschau: λέγοιμεν.
91 Cf. my note on Origen, contra Celsum, VI, 27.
93 Ps. 98 (97):8; Isa. 55:12.
90 I Cor. 4:9.
92 Deut. 32:9.
94 Isa. 14:9 ff.

in God is conquered by cowardice or by tortures suffered for his faith in God, he will hear it said: "Thy glory is come down to Hell and thy great joy. Beneath thee they shall spread rottenness and a worm shall be your covering." And if one has held distinguished office in the churches, so that he appears to them as the daystar because his good works shine before men, and if after this in fighting the great fight he has lost the crown of such a throne, he shall hear it said: "How has the daystar, which rose at dawn, fallen from heaven? It has been trampled on the earth." And as by his apostasy he has become like the devil this shall be said to him: "He shall be cast upon the mountains like an abominable corpse with many other dead men pierced by swords who are going down to Hell. Just as a garment defiled with blood shall not be clean, so also thou shalt not be clean." For how shall he be pure who is defiled with blood and murder by the abominable sin of apostasy and is polluted by so terrible a crime?

Let us now show that we have understood the saying: "He who loves his son or daughter more than me is not worthy of me."[95] Let us take care lest there should even be in us any hesitation whether to deny or to confess, lest the word of Elijah be also addressed to us: "How long will you limp from one leg to the other? If the Lord be God, follow him."[96]

19. Probably we shall be reviled by our neighbours and mocked at by some who come round us and shake their heads at us as if we were blockheads. But when this happens we may say to God: "Thou hast made us a reproach to our neighbours, a mockery and a laughing-stock to those round about us. Thou hast made us a byword among the nations, and the peoples shake their heads at us. All the day long my confidence is before me, and the shame of my face has covered me, from the voice of the reviler and accuser, from the face of the enemy and the persecutor."[97] Blessed are we if, when all this happens, we can say to God the words which the prophet boldly applied to this situation: "All these things are come upon us, and we have not forgotten thee, and we have not wronged thy covenant, and our heart has not gone back."[98]

20. Let us remember that while we live this life, we are to think of the ways that lie outside this life, saying to God: "Thou hast directed our paths out of thy way."[99] Now is the time to

[95] Matt. 10:37.
[96] I Kings 18:21.
[97] Ps. 44 (43): 13–16.
[98] Ps. 44 (43):17–18.
[99] Ps. 44 (43):19.

recall the fact that this earth is a place of affliction for the soul in which we are brought low, so that we may say in our prayers: "Thou hast brought us low in the place of affliction and the shadow of death has covered us."[1] And let us boldly say: "If we have forgotten the name of our God, and if we have stretched out our hands to ₍any strange god, shall not God search it out?"[2]

21. Let us so fight as to give a perfect witness not merely in public but also in secret, so that we also may say like the apostle: "This is the ground of our boasting, the witness of our conscience, that in holiness and the sincerity of God we behaved in this world."[3] We may add to the apostle's words that of the prophet: "He himself knows the secrets of our heart,"[4] especially if we are brought to death. Then we may say that which only martyrs can say to God: "For thy sake we are killed all the day long, we are accounted as sheep for the slaughter."[5] If ever "the mind of the flesh"[6] leads us to be afraid of the judges who threaten us with death, we can then say to them the word from Proverbs: "My son, fear the Lord and thou shalt be strong. Fear none but him."[7]

22. This text also is helpful for our present theme. In Ecclesiastes Solomon says: "I praised all the dead more than the living, as many as are alive until now."[8] Who could more justifiably be praised for his death than he who of his own free choice chooses to die for the sake of religion? Such a man was Eleazar "who welcomed death with honour rather than life with pollution and of his own free choice went forward to the instrument of torture." He "with a noble resolution worthy of his ninety years and the eminence of his age and the grey hairs marking the distinction to which he had attained and his noble upbringing since childhood, and even more of the holy laws appointed by God,"[9] said: "It does not become my age to make a pretence, so that many of the young men will suppose that Eleazar at the age of ninety has gone over to a foreign religion. They would be led astray by my pretence and for the sake of a short and brief period of life, and I should win for my old age pollution and disgrace. Even if at the present time I escape the punishment of men, yet I shall not escape the hands of the Almighty, whether alive or dead. Therefore now I will manfully depart this life and show myself worthy of my old age, leaving

1 Ps. 44 (43): 19.   2 Ps. 44 (43):20–21.   3 II Cor. 1:12.
4 Ps. 44 (43):21.   5 Ps. 44 (43):22.   6 Rom. 8:6.
7 Prov. 7:1.   8 Eccles. 4:2.   9 II Maccabees 6:19, 23.

a noble example to the young to encourage them to die eagerly and nobly for the sacred and holy laws."[10]

I beseech you, when you are at the gates of death, or rather of freedom, especially if you are tortured (for it is not to be expected that you will be spared this suffering at the design of the hostile powers), to say this: "To the Lord who has holy knowledge it is known that, though I could have been freed from death, I am enduring cruel bodily pains by scourging, and in my soul I suffer this gladly for fear of him." Such indeed was the death of Eleazar that it was said of him: "He left his death as an example of nobility and a memorial of virtue, not only to the young but also to the nation as a whole."[11]

23. The seven brothers described in the books of Maccabees,[12] whom Antiochus tortured with "whips and scourges" because of their loyal adherence to their religion, constitute a magnificent example of courageous martyrdom to everyone who considers whether he will be inferior to children who not only endured tortures one by one but also showed how stedfastly they adhered to their religion by witnessing the sufferings of their brothers. One of them, who is called in Scripture their spokesman, said to the tyrant: "Why question us? What will you learn? For we are ready to die rather than to transgress the laws of our fathers?" I need not mention what they suffered from heated pans and cauldrons by which they were tortured after each had endured some different torment. For first he who was called their spokesman had his tongue cut out; then his head was scorched, and he endured the scorching as others undergo the circumcision appointed by God's law, believing that even in this way he was fulfilling the intention of the covenant of God.[13] Not content with this Antiochus had his hands and feet cut off while his other brothers and his mother looked on, wanting to punish his brothers and mother by the sight and supposing that he would move them from their resolve by these terrible torments. Indeed, not content with crippling his body by the first tortures, Antiochus ordered him to be put on the fire, while still alive, and fried in the pans and cauldrons. And as the vapour of the flesh of the noble athlete of piety, roasting by the cruelty of the tyrant, spread abroad, the others

---

[10] II Maccabees 6:24–28.   [11] II Maccabees 6:30–31.

[12] II Maccabees 7.

[13] Origen seems to be thinking of the Maccabean martyr's death as the Jewish equivalent of the Christian baptism by blood, baptism being the equivalent under the new covenant of circumcision under the old.

exhorted one another with their mother to die nobly, comforting each other with the thought that God was seeing it all. Sufficient to steel them to endurance was the conviction that the eye of God was upon them in their suffering. And the leader of the athletes of piety exhorted them, being himself encouraged and, so to speak, filled with rejoicing by the heroism of their resistance to such fearful agonies. If we were in such a situation we might well repeat the words they said to each other which read as follows: "The Lord God beholds us and in reality is having compassion on us."

24. After the first had been tested in this manner, as gold is proved in the crucible, the second was brought to the torture. After the ministers of the tyrant's cruelty had torn off his skin with the hair, they called upon him to change his mind, asking their victim if he would eat meat offered to idols before his body was punished limb by limb. When he refused to change his mind, he was led to the next torture and remained stedfast to his last gasp. He in no way broke down or yielded to the torments, but said to the blasphemer: "You criminal, you remove us from this present life, but the King of the world shall raise us up to everlasting life because we have died for his laws."

25. The third also, counting his sufferings as nothing and for his love to God trampling upon them, when told to put out his tongue, did so forthwith and valiantly stretched out his hands, saying, "Because of God's laws I leave these behind me, but I hope to regain from God the rewards he grants to those who have fought for their religion."

Likewise the fourth was tortured and endured the blows saying: "When we die at the hands of men, it is better to look to the hopes we have of God that we shall be raised up by him in a resurrection the tyrant will not know. For he will rise not to life but to reproach and everlasting shame."

Next the fifth was tormented. Looking at Antiochus he reviled him for that his corruptibility had not lessened his pride, and that he supposed tyrannical power held for a few days was great authority. While being tortured he said that his race had not been deserted by God who would inflict far worse torments on Antiochus and his seed.

After him the sixth at the point of dying said: "Do not deceive yourself. We are paying the penalty of our sins, and are enduring these sufferings willingly, in order that by them we may be purified." And he said to the king that he must not imagine that he would go unpunished for daring to fight against God.

For he who fights against those made divine by the Word is fighting God.

26. Lastly Antiochus took the youngest in his hands and, being persuaded that he was a brother of those who counted such terrible agonies for nothing and that he had the same resolve as they, used other methods. He thought he might be won over by exhortations, and swore oaths promising to make him rich and happy if he would abandon his ancestral laws, and to enrol him among the Friends[14] and to entrust him with imperial offices. But as he had no success whatever and the young man did not even listen to his words as being alien to his resolve, he appealed to his mother, exhorting her to advise the boy to save himself. But she while agreeing to persuade her son to do what he wanted, mocked the tyrant by giving her son many exhortations to endurance, so that the boy did not wait for the punishment to be brought to him, but took the initiative and called to the torturers saying: "What are you waiting for? Why are you so slow? For we obey the law given by God. We must not accept a command contrary to God's words." Moreover like a king pronouncing sentence on those subject to his judgment he pronounced sentence against the tyrant, being judge of him rather than being judged by him. And he told him that for having raised his hands against the children of heaven he would not escape the judgment of Almighty God who sees everything.

27. At that moment one could have seen how the mother of these heroes, for her hope in God, bravely bore the torments and deaths of her sons. For the dew of piety and the cool breath of holiness did not allow to be kindled within her her maternal instinct which in most mothers faced with such severe pains would have been a burning fire. I believe that this story which I have quoted from the Scripture in abbreviated form is most valuable for our purpose. It enables us to see how piety and love for God, in face of the most painful agonies and the severest torments, is far more powerful than any other bond of affection. This love for God and human weakness cannot dwell together in us. Weakness is exiled and altogether driven out of our soul and is rendered entirely impotent where a man can say, "The Lord is my strength and my song" and "I can do all things through Christ Jesus our Lord who strengthens me."[15]

28. The value of martyrdom and the boldness it gives us

14 A title of honour given to the highest royal officials.
15 Ps. 118 (117):14; Phil. 4:13.

before God we can also learn from this consideration. The saint
who possesses a certain ambition and desires to offer something
in return for the benefits that come to him from God, asks what
he can do to the Lord for all that he has received from him. And
he finds that a man with a grateful heart can render to God
nothing else capable of being as it were a counterweight to his
benefits except a martyr's death. For in the 115th Psalm there
is first the question: "What shall I render to the Lord for all the
benefits he has done to me?" The answer to him who asks what
he should render to the Lord for all the benefits he has received
from him reads as follows: "I will take the cup of salvation and
will call upon the name of the Lord."[16] "The cup of salvation"
is the usual name for martyrdom, as we find in the gospel. For
when those who are ambitious for greater honour desire to sit
on the right and left of Jesus in his kingdom, the Lord says to
them, "Can you drink of the cup that I drink?"[17] By "cup" he
means martyrdom. This is clear from the saying, "Father, if it
be possible, let this cup pass from me. Nevertheless, not my will
but thine be done."[18] We learn, besides, that he who drinks
of that cup that Jesus drank will sit and rule and judge with the
King of kings.[19] This, then, is the cup of salvation, and he who
receives it will call upon the name of the Lord. "And everyone
that calls upon the name of the Lord shall be saved."[20]

29. But perhaps on account of the words "Father, if it be
possible, let this cup pass from me," someone who did not examine the meaning of Scripture closely might think that, as it
were, even the Saviour was afraid in the hour of the passion.[21]
But if he was afraid, one might say, who ever was courageous?
In the first place, we will ask those who hold this view of the
Saviour if he was inferior to him who said: "The Lord is my
light and my salvation; whom shall I fear? The Lord is the pro-
tector of my life, of whom shall I be afraid? When evil men
approached me to eat up my flesh, those who persecuted me and
my enemies were struck with weakness and fell. If a host should
be drawn up against me, my heart shall not be afraid. If war
should rise up against me, then will I be full of hope."[22] But

---

[16] Ps. 116 (115):3-4.   [17] Matt. 20:22; Mark 10:38.   [18] Mark 14:36.
[19] Cf. I Cor. 6:2; Hippolytus, *in Dan.*, II, 37; Cyprian, *Ep.*, 6; Dionysius of
Alexandria, in Eusebius, *H.E.*, VI, 42:5.
[20] Joel 2:32.
[21] Cf. Celsus in Origen, *contra Celsum*, II, 24: "Why then does he utter loud
laments and wailings, and pray that he may avoid the fear of death, saying
something like this, 'O Father, if this cup could pass by me'?"
[22] Ps. 27 (26):1-3.

perhaps these words reported by the prophet are spoken by none other than the Saviour, since by reason of the light and salvation given to him by the Father he fears no man, and because of the protection granted by God he is afraid of none. His heart was in no way fearful when the entire host of Satan was drawn up against him. When war rose up against him, his heart hoped in God, being filled with his holy doctrines. It would not be in character for the same person to say in a cowardly spirit, "Father, if it be possible, let this cup pass from me," and to say courageously, "If a host be drawn up against me, my heart shall not be afraid."

Lest we miss some point in the passage, notice the express designation of "the cup" in the three evangelists. According to Matthew the Lord said: "Father, if it be possible, let this cup pass from me." Luke has: "Father, if it be thy will, take this cup away from me." Mark has: "Abba, Father, all things are possible to thee; take this cup away from me."[23] Consider, then, seeing that any martyrdom by death suffered for any cause whatever is called a cup, whether you could affirm that it is not martyrdom in general that he is putting from him when he says, "Let this cup pass from me" (otherwise he would have said, "Let the cup pass from me"), but perhaps only this particular kind. Consider also the possibility that the Saviour had in mind the various kinds of cup, so to speak, and the possible results of each one, and, because by a certain very profound wisdom he understood the differences, asked that this kind of martyr's death might be avoided, while secretly he made request for another which would have been even more of an ordeal, so that by a different cup he might achieve an even wider diffusion of benefits which would reach more people. This, however, was not the will of the Father who with a wisdom greater than the will of his Son and a vision wider than the Saviour's was controlling events to follow an ordered path. It is at any rate clear that in the Psalms the cup of salvation is the death of the martyrs. That is why "I will take the cup of salvation and will call upon the name of the Lord" is followed by the words: "Precious in the Lord's sight is the death of his saints."[24] To us, then, as God's saints who are not unworthy, there comes a precious death, in that our death is of some special significance if it is endured for the sake of Christianity and piety and holiness.

30. Let us also remember the sins we have committed, that remission of sins cannot be obtained without baptism, that

[23] Matt. 26:39; Luke 22:42; Mark 14:36.   [24] Ps. 116 (115):13, 15.

according to the laws of the gospel it is not possible again to be baptized with water and the Spirit for remission of sins, and that a baptism of martyrdom has been given to us. That this name is given to it is clear from the fact that after the saying: "Can you drink of the cup that I drink?" there follow the words "Or be baptized with the baptism that I am baptized with?"[25] And elsewhere it is said: "I have a baptism to be baptized with, and how am I straitened until it be accomplished."[26] Consider whether, just as the Saviour's death brought purification to the world, the baptism of martyrdom may also by the service of those who undergo it bring purification to many. Just as those who attend at the altar according to the Law of Moses thought they obtained remissions of sins for the Jews by the blood of bulls and goats,[27] so the souls of those "who have been beheaded for the testimony of Jesus"[28] do not attend in vain at the heavenly altar, but mediate remission of sins to those who pray. At the same time we know that, just as the high priest, Jesus Christ, offered himself in sacrifice,[29] so the priests, whose high priest he is, offer themselves in sacrifice and therefore appear by the altar in their proper place. Those priests who are blameless and offer blameless sacrifices used to serve the worship of God; but those who were at fault, as Moses set out in Leviticus,[30] were banished from the altar. Who then is the blameless priest who offers a blameless offering other than he who holds fast the confession and fulfils every requirement made by the doctrine of martyrdom? This point we have discussed above.[31]

31. Let us not be surprised that the wonderful blessedness of the martyrs who enjoy deep peace and calm and rest has to be begun in apparently dark and, so to speak, wintry weather. It is by journeying in this life on the strait and narrow way[32] in winter that each one of the blessed will have to show what ability he has gained for following the right road; so that after this life there may be fulfilled the word in the Song of Songs spoken to the bride who has come through the winter: "My beloved, she says, answers and says to me, Arise, come my friend, my lovely, my dove. Behold, the winter is past, the rain has dispersed and gone away."[33] You also should remember that you cannot hear that "the winter is past" unless you have battled bravely and manfully with the present winter. After the

25 Mark 10:38.   26 Luke 12:50.   27 Heb. 9:13; 10:4.
28 Rev. 20:4; 6:9.   29 Heb. 5:1; 7:27; 8:3; 10:12.
30 Lev. 21:17–21.   31 Chapter 11.   32 Matt. 7:14.
33 S. of Sol. 2:10–11.

winter is past and rain has gone away and dispersed the flowers
will appear. "Planted in the house of the Lord they shall flower
in the halls of our God."[34]

32. And this we know, that if we have been persuaded by
Jesus to forsake the idols and polytheistic atheism, the enemy
cannot persuade us to commit idolatry, but he wants to compel
us. And on this account he brings this pressure to bear on those
over whom he has power, and either makes martyrs or idolaters
of those who are tempted by him. Frequently even now he says:
"All these things will I give you if you will fall down and worship me."[35] Let us therefore take heed lest we commit idolatry
and subject ourselves to daemons. "For the gods of the heathen
are daemons."[36] What a terrible thing it is when a man forsakes
Christ's easy yoke and light burden[37] and again subjects himself
to the yoke of daemons, and bears a burden of the gravest sin
after we have known that the heart of idol-worshippers is ash,
and their life more worthless than dust,[38] and after we have
spoken the words "How false are the idols our fathers possessed;
and there is none among them that can make it rain."[39]

33. It was not merely in ancient times that Nebuchadnezzar
set up the golden image, nor merely then that he threatened
Ananias, Azarias, and Misael that if they would not bow down,
he would cast them into the fiery furnace.[40] Even now Nebuchadnezzar is saying the very same thing to us, the true Hebrews,
whose home is in the next world.[41] But we, that we may experience the heavenly dew which quenches all fire in us and refreshes our mind, let us imitate those holy men lest even now
Haman may wish you Mordecais to bow down to him, and you
reply to him, "I will not place the glory of men higher than the
glory of the God of Israel."[42] Let us destroy Bel by the word of
God and kill the dragon with Daniel,[43] that when we draw near
to the mouths of lions we can suffer no harm from them, and
that only those responsible for our present conflict may be eaten
up by the lions which cannot consume us. Let us be encouraged
by the fact that among the good deeds of Job we read these
words: "If[44] I laid my hand on my mouth to kiss, let this also be

---

[34] Ps. 92 (91):13.   [35] Matt. 4:9.   [36] Ps. 96 (95):5.
[37] Matt. 11:30.   [38] Wisdom of Solomon 15:10.
[39] Jer. 16:19; 14:22.   [40] Dan. 3:1 ff.
[41] Philo. *Migr. Abrah.*, 20, similarly explains the word "Hebrews"; also
Origen, *Comm. in Matt.*, XI, 5.
[42] Esth. 4:17 (LXX), in English Apocrypha, 13:14.
[43] Bel and the Dragon, 22 ff.   [44] Read with Koetschau: ⟨εἰ⟩ ἐπιθείς.

reckoned to me as the greatest crime."[45] For it is probable that they will require us to put our hand on our mouth to give a kiss.

34. This also let us notice, that the Saviour's prophecies about martyrdom do not occur in the words he addressed to the multitude, but to the apostles. For after Scripture has first said: "Jesus sent out these twelve commanding them, Do not go into the way of the Gentiles" and so on, there follow these words: "Beware of men; for they shall deliver you to the councils, and shall beat you in their synagogues. And you shall be led before governors and kings for my sake, for a witness to them and to the Gentiles. But when they give you up, do not be anxious how or what you should speak. For it is not you that speak, but the Spirit of the Father speaking in you. Brother shall betray brother to death, a father his child, and children shall rise up against their parents and have them killed. And you shall be hated by all men for my name's sake. But he who endures to the end shall be saved. When they persecute you in one city flee to the next, and if they chase you out of that, escape to another. Verily I say to you, you shall not complete all the cities of Israel before the Son of man come."[46]

And Luke writes as follows: "When they bring you before synagogues and rulers and authorities, do not be anxious how you should reply or what you should say. For the Holy Spirit will teach you in that hour what you ought to say." And after other sayings: "Settle it therefore in your hearts not to meditate beforehand how to answer. For I will give you a mouth and wisdom which all your adversaries shall not be able to withstand or gainsay. But you shall be delivered up even by parents and brethren and kinsfolk and friends, and some of you they shall cause to be put to death, and you shall be hated by all men for my name's sake. And not a hair of your head shall perish. In your patience possess your souls."[47] This is Mark's account: "When they lead you to judgment and deliver you up, do not be anxious beforehand or meditate beforehand; but speak that which is given you in that hour. For it is not you that speak but the Holy Spirit. And brother shall deliver up brother to his death, and the father his child; and children shall rise up against parents and cause them to be put to death. And you shall be hated by all men for my name's sake. But he that endures to the end shall be saved."[48]

[45] Job 31:27–28. The kiss required is an act of loyalty to the heathen god.
[46] Matt. 10:5, 17–23.   [47] Luke 12:11–12; 21:14–19.
[48] Mark 13:11–13.

The following exhortations to martyrdom in Matthew are not addressed to any but the twelve. We too must hear them, and by so doing we shall be brothers of the apostles who heard them and be numbered with the apostles. The passage reads as follows: "Fear not those who kill the body but are not able to kill the soul; fear rather him who can destroy both soul and body in Gehenna." And after this the Lord teaches us that it is not without divine providence that anyone comes to face the conflict of martyrdom. For he says: "Are not two sparrows sold for a farthing? Yet not one of them will fall to the earth without the Father who is in heaven. The hairs of your head are all numbered. Fear not therefore. You are of more value than many sparrows. Everyone who confesses me before men will I also confess before my Father who is in heaven. But whosoever shall deny me before men, him will I also deny before my Father who is in heaven."[49] Luke's words are to the same effect: "This I say to you, my friends. Fear not those who kill the body and after that have power to do nothing further. I will show you whom you shall fear. Fear him who after killing you has power to cast you into Gehenna. Yea, I say to you, Fear him. Are not five sparrows sold for two farthings? Yet not one of them is forgotten before God. But even the hairs of your head are all numbered. Fear not therefore. You are of more value than many sparrows. And I say to you: Everyone who confesses me before men, the Son of man will also confess before the angels of God. But he who denies me before men shall be denied before the angels of God."[50] And in another place: "Whosoever is ashamed of me and of my words, of him shall the Son of man be ashamed when he comes in his glory and in that of the Father and the holy angels."[51] In the same sense Mark also wrote as follows: "Whosoever is ashamed of me and my words in this adulterous and sinful generation, of him shall the Son of man be ashamed when he comes in the glory of the Father with the holy angels."[52]

Those who destroy us kill the life of the body. That is the meaning of the saying: "Fear not those who kill the body," which Matthew and Luke have in identical wording. For after they have killed the body, even if they wish they have no power to kill the soul. Nor have they power to do anything further. For how is it possible to destroy a soul which by the very act of confession is given life? Witness to it is given by him who exhorts us to martyrdom in Isaiah, and by his Son, according to the

[49] Matt. 10:28–33.   [50] Luke 12:4–9.   [51] Luke 9:26.
[52] Mark 8:38.

Scripture: "Be my witnesses and I will be your witness, saith the Lord God, and the Son whom I have chosen."[53]

Notice this also, that it is not to Jesus' servants but to his friends[54] that he gives this commandment: "Fear not those who kill the body and after that have power to do nothing further." We must fear, therefore, him who is able to destroy both soul and body in Gehenna. He alone, after killing us, has power to cast into Gehenna. Indeed he will cast there those who are terrified by those who kill the body and those who do not fear him who is able to destroy both soul and body in Gehenna, and who, after killing us, has power to cast us into Gehenna. If anyone's hairs are numbered, this is obviously true of those who are executed for Jesus' sake. We, then, will make confession in the Son of God even before those who are men and not gods, so that he whom we confess may reply to us by confessing us before his God and Father, he himself confessing in heaven the man who has confessed him on earth.

35. Who on considering this will not cry out with the apostle: "The sufferings of this present time are not worthy to be compared with the glory that shall be revealed to us"?[55] Is not confession before the Father much greater than confession before men? And is not the confession made in heaven by him who is confessed far superior to the confession on earth of the Son of God made by the martyrs? Let anyone who thinks of denying him before men bear in mind the words of him who does not err: "I also will deny him before my Father who is in heaven."

Matthew's text has: "I also will confess him before my Father who is in heaven," while Luke has: "The Son of man will also confess him before the angels of God."[56] I ask, therefore, whether the firstborn of all creation, the image of the invisible God,[57] will confess the man who confesses him before his Father in heaven, while he who was "born of the seed of David according to the flesh,"[58] and is therefore Son of man, and was born of a woman[59] who was herself human, and on this account is given the title of Son of man, whom we understand to be the humanity of Jesus,[60] will confess those who confess him before the angels of God. We might say the corresponding thing of those who deny.

---

[53] Isa 43:10.   [54] Cf. John 15:15.   [55] Rom. 8:18.
[56] Matt. 10:32; Luke 12:8.   [57] Col. 1:15.
[58] Rom. 1:3.   [59] Gal. 4:4.
[60] The Greek phrase is common in Origen for the human nature of Christ; cf. my note in *Harvard Theological Review*, XLI (1948), p. 100, n.30.

We must further consider this point. He who confesses the Son before men, so far as in him lies, commends Christianity and the founder of Christianity before those to whom he makes his confession. But he who is confessed by the firstborn of all creation and the Son of man is commended by the confession of the Son of God and the Son of man to the Father in heaven and the angels of God. But if "it is not he who commends himself who is approved, but he whom the Lord commends,"[61] must we not think him approved who is judged worthy of commendation to the Father in heaven and the angels of God? But if he is approved with those like him whom the Lord has tested by tortures and examinations "as gold in the crucible," and has accepted "as a whole burnt-offering,"[62] what must we say of those who have been shown up in the furnace of persecution and have denied? These, as not being true Christians, are denied before the Father in heaven and before the angels of God by him who denies everyone who deserves it.

36. We have to strive not merely against denial but also lest we feel any shame when the enemies of God suppose that we are suffering shameful indignities. This is particularly applicable to you, holy Ambrose. Honoured and respected by a vast number of cities, you are now, so to speak, walking in the procession bearing the cross of Jesus and following him who leads you before governors and kings, that he himself may go with you and give a mouth and wisdom to you his companion in the fight, Protoctetus, and to those who bear witness with you, who make up that which is lacking in the sufferings of Christ.[63] He will be with you on the way to the paradise of God and will show you how to pass by "the cherubim and the flaming sword which turns and guards the way of the tree of life."[64] Though both of these guard the way of the tree of life, they do so to prevent anyone unworthy from passing through and reaching the tree of life. For the flaming sword will lay hold of those who have built upon the established foundation, Jesus Christ, "wood or hay or stubble,"[65] and the wood, so to speak, of denial which is quickly kindled and burns rapidly. The cherubim will receive those who cannot be caught by the flaming sword because they have built with nothing inflammable, and will conduct them to the tree of life and to all that God

---

[61] II Cor. 10:18. [62] Wisdom of Solomon 3:6. [63] Col. 1:24.
[64] Gen. 3:24. Gregory of Nyssa (*Orat. in XL mart.*, II, Migne, *P.G.*, XLVI, 772 AB) likewise explains that the flaming sword does not exclude everyone, but only the unworthy. [65] I Cor. 3:11–12.

planted in the east and caused to rise up from the earth.[66] Since
Jesus journeys with you to paradise scorn the serpent vanquished and bruised by Jesus' feet, and through him by yours
as well,[67] for he has "given you power to trample on serpents
and scorpions and on every power of the enemy that nothing
should harm you."[68]

37. We must not, therefore, deny the Son of God or be
ashamed of him or his servants or his words, but listen to the
saying, "Whosoever shall deny me before men, him will I also
deny before my Father who is in heaven," and to the saying,
"For whosoever shall be ashamed of me and mine, of him shall
the Son of man be ashamed when he comes in his glory and in
the glory of the Father and the holy angels," and to the words,
"For whosoever is ashamed of me and my words in this
adulterous and sinful generation, of him shall the Son of man
also be ashamed when he comes in the glory of the Father with
the holy angels."[69]

Jesus once "endured the cross and despised the shame" and
therefore "sat down at the right hand of God."[70] His followers
also who despise the shame will sit with him and reign in heaven
with him who came to bring peace not on the earth but in the
soul of his disciples, and to bring on the earth a sword.[71] For
since "the word is God is living, and active and sharper than
any two-edged sword, and penetrates to the separating of soul
and spirit, the joints and the marrow, and is a judge of the
thoughts and intents of the heart,"[72] he rewards our souls,
particularly at this present time, with the peace that passes all
understanding,[73] which he left to his apostles.[74] But he has
thrust a sword between the image of the earthy and the image
of the heavenly,[75] so that now he takes the heavenly part of us
that afterwards, if we no longer deserve to be divided into two
parts, he may make us entirely heavenly.

And he came to cast not merely a sword on the earth but also
fire. Of this he said: "I wish it were already kindled."[76] Let this
fire, therefore, be kindled in you, consuming every earthly and
carnal thought. Show all zeal to be baptized now with the
baptism concerning which Jesus was "straitened until it be
accomplished." And you [Ambrose], since you have wife and
children and brothers and sisters, remember the words: "If any

66 Gen. 2:8–9. 67 Rom. 16:20. 68 Luke 10:19.
69 Matt. 10:33; Luke 9:26; Mark 8:38. 70 Heb. 12:2; 8:1.
71 Matt. 10:34. 72 Heb. 4:12. 73 Phil. 4:7.
74 John 14:27. 75 I Cor. 15:49. 76 Luke 12:49–50.

man comes to me and does not hate his father and mother and wife and children and brothers and sisters, he cannot be my disciple."[77] Both of you [Ambrose and Protoctetus] remember the saying: "If any man comes to me and does not hate his own soul," in addition to those already mentioned, "he cannot be my disciple."[78] So hate your own soul that by your hatred you may preserve it to everlasting life. "For," he says, "he who hates his own soul in this world shall preserve it to everlasting life."[79] Accordingly, hate your soul for the sake of everlasting life in the sure conviction that it is a good and valuable hatred which Jesus teaches us to have. Just as we have to hate our soul to preserve it to everlasting life, so also must you [Ambrose], who have wife and children and brothers and sisters, hate them. You will thus help those you hate, since by the very act of hating them you become a friend to God and receive the freedom to benefit them.

38. But at the same time remember him who prays in spirit for the children left by the martyrs for the sake of their love for God, and said: "Redeem the children of those condemned to death."[80] Only realize that it is not the children of the flesh who are children of God,[81] and that, just as it is said to the descendants of Abraham: "I know that you are Abraham's seed"[82] and "if you were Abraham's children, you would do the works of Abraham,"[83] so also it will be said to your children: I know that you are Ambrose's seed, and if you are Ambrose's children you will do the works of Ambrose. No doubt they will do them, for you will help them more after dying a martyr's death than if you had remained with them. For then you will love them with greater knowledge and pray for them with deeper understanding if you find that they are your children and not merely your seed. Take now upon your lips the words: "He who loves son or daughter more than me is not worthy of me," and "He who finds his soul shall lose it, and he who loses his soul for my sake shall find it."[84]

39. By your readiness for martyrdom give place to the Spirit of your Father who speaks in those delivered up for the sake of religion.[85] If you know yourselves to be hated and reviled and

---

[77] Luke 14:26.   [78] Luke 14:26   [79] John 12:25.
[80] Ps. 79 (78):11.   [81] Rom. 9:8.   [82] John 8:37.
[83] John 8:39, similarly quoted in *Hom. in Ezech.*, IV., 8, where Origen attacks fools who say, "In the future each one of us will be able by our prayers to deliver from Gehenna anyone he likes," forgetting that a martyr only benefits me if I live rightly.
[84] Matt. 10:37, 39.   [85] Matt. 10:20.

thought to be blasphemers, then take to heart the words: "On this account the world hates you, because you are not of this world. If you were of this world, the world would love its own."[86] Already you have endured many reproaches and many dangers for Christ's sake since the time when you first believed. Advance by enduring to the end. For "he who endures to the end shall be saved."[87] Know that according to Peter you will rejoice "though now for a short time, if need be, you are grieved by various temptations, that the testing of your faith, which is far more valuable than perishable gold which is tried by fire, may be found to deserve praise and glory and honour at the revelation of Jesus Christ."[88] Understand the word "grieved" to mean suffering physical pain, as is clear from the words "In grief shalt thou bear children."[89] For a woman giving birth to a child suffers no grief whatever, but physical pain.

To Christ's disciples this word was helpful: "Love not the world, neither the things that are in the world. If any man loves the world, the love of the Father is not in him. For all that is in the world, the lust of the flesh and the lust of the eyes and the pride of life, is not of the Father but is of the world. And the world passes away and its lust."[90] Accordingly, do not love that which is transitory, but by doing God's will become worthy to be one with Son and Father and Holy Spirit, in accordance with the Saviour's prayer "that they also may be one in us as I and thou are one."[91] How many days of life can one gain by loving the world or the things that are in the world, while losing or destroying one's own soul and carrying a conscience burdened by a heavy load and weighed down by the guilt of apostasy? Let us each remember how often we have been in danger of dying in the ordinary way, and reckon that we may have been preserved in order that baptized in our own blood and washed from all sin we may dwell beside the heavenly altar with our comrades in the fight.[92]

40. If, however, any man is led to yield by a great love for this life or by lack of courage in face of the torments or by the seemingly persuasive arguments used by those who would persuade us to choose the evil course, and denies the one God and his Christ, and confesses the daemons or "fortunes,"[93] let him realize that when he prepares "a table for the daemon," and "fills the cup to fortune," he "forsakes the Lord and forgets his

86 John 15:19.   87 Matt. 10:22; 24:13.   88 I Pet. 1:6-7.
89 Gen. 3:16.   90 I John 2:15-17.   91 John 17:21-22.
92 Rev. 6:9.   93 Cf. Chapter 7, above.

holy mountain." These charges against him are set forth by Isaiah as follows: "Ye who forsake me and forget my holy mountain and prepare a table for the daemon and fill the cup to fortune, I will deliver you to the sword, ye shall all fall slain. For I called you and ye did not listen. I spoke and ye disobeyed and did evil before me and chose that which was not my will. Therefore thus saith the Lord: Behold my servants shall eat, but ye shall be hungry. Behold, my servants shall drink, but ye shall be thirsty. Behold, my servants shall be glad, but ye shall be ashamed. Behold, my servants shall rejoice with gladness, but ye shall cry out for the pain of your heart and shall groan for the distress of your spirit. For ye shall abandon my name for the satisfaction of my elect, but you shall the Lord destroy." [94] Moreover, if we understand what the table of the Lord is, and desire to partake of it, let us know this: "You cannot partake of the table of the Lord and the table of daemons." [95] Further, if we understand the meaning of the words "I shall not henceforth drink of the fruit of this vine until that day when I drink it new in the kingdom of heaven," [96] and if we wish to be found in the company of those who drink with Jesus, let us pay heed to this: "You cannot drink the cup of the Lord and the cup of daemons." [97]

John the son of thunder says: "He who denies the Father and the Son: everyone who denies the Son has not the Father. He who confesses the Son has the Father also." [98] Who that understands this truth will not be afraid to say that he is not a Christian, and thus deny the Son, since by his denial he will not have the Father? And who would not be led to confess himself a Christian by words and deeds, so that he might have the Father also? For those who make such a confession have the Father.

41. If we have passed from death to life [99] by our transition from unbelief to faith, let us not be surprised if the world hates us. [1] For no one who has not passed from death to life, but remains in death, can love those who have passed from the dark house of death, so to speak, to the buildings full of the light of life built of living stones. [2] For us Jesus laid down his life. [3] Let us therefore lay down ours, I will not say for his sake but for our own, and I think also for those who will be edified by our

94 Isa. 65:11–15.
96 Matt. 26:29.
98 I John 2:22–23 (Mark 3:17).
1 John 15:18.
3 I John 3:16.

95 I Cor. 10:21.
97 I Cor. 10:21.
99 John 5:24; I John 3:14.
2 John 8:12; I Pet. 2:5; Eph. 2:20–22.

martyrdom. For us Christians the time of boasting is at hand. For the apostle says: "Not only so, but we also make our boast in our tribulations, knowing that tribulation effects patience, and patience experience, and experience hope; and hope is not put to shame; only let the love of God be poured out in our hearts by the Holy Spirit."[4] While Paul may say, "If after the manner of men I have fought with wild beasts at Ephesus,"[5] we could say, "If after the manner of men I have been executed in Germany."[6]

42. If "as the sufferings of Christ overflow, so through Christ consolation also overflows,"[7] let us gladly accept the sufferings of Christ so that they overflow in us, if at least we desire the abundant consolation which is received by all who mourn,[8] though probably not in equal measure. For if the consolation were equal for all, Scripture would not have said: "As the sufferings of Christ overflow to us, so also our consolation overflows." Those who share in sufferings will also share in consolation in proportion to the sufferings that they share with Christ. This you learn from him who with full conviction said: "For we know that as you are partakers of the sufferings so also do you share in the consolation."[9]

God says by the prophet: "In an acceptable time have I heard thee and in a day of salvation have I succoured thee."[10] What other time is so acceptable as that when, for our faith towards God in Christ, we are brought in procession under arrest in the world, and are led away to die, though the triumph is ours rather than theirs? For the martyrs in Christ put off with him the principalities and powers and join in his triumph[11]; as they share in his sufferings, so also they share in the benefits of his sufferings. These include triumphing over principalities and powers which shortly you shall see vanquished and put to shame. What is the day of salvation so much as the day we are delivered from this life? But I beseech you, "Give no offence in anything"[12] lest through you the presbyterate or the diaconate be found at fault, "but in all things commend yourselves as the ministers of God." "In much patience," say, "And now what is my patience? Is it not the Lord?"[13] "In tribulations" be persuaded that "many are the tribulations of the righteous."[14] "In

---

[4] Rom. 5:3–5. [5] I Cor. 15:32.
[6] The emperor Maximin was in Germany at the time of writing.
[7] II Cor. 1:5.   [8] Matt. 5:4.   [9] II Cor. 1:7.
[10] Isa. 49:8; II Cor. 6:2.   [11] Col. 2:15.   [12] II Cor. 6:3 ff.
[13] Ps. 39 (38):7   [14] Ps. 34 (33):19.

necessities" let us ask for blessedness as a necessity for us. "In
afflictions" let us unfailingly walk upon the strait and narrow
way that we may attain to life.[15] If it is needful, let us also commend ourselves "by scourgings, by imprisonments, by riots, by
labours, by watchings, and by fastings." For behold the Lord is
here with his reward in his hand to render to each man
according to his works.[16]

43. Let us now show that we have desired "knowledge" for
the sake of the works befitting that knowledge. Let there be
manifested in us complete "purity" from all defilement by any
sort of sin. As sons of a longsuffering God and brethren of a long-
suffering Christ let us be "patient" in all misfortunes. "For a
longsuffering man has much to think about; the pusillanimous
man is a prodigious fool."[17] If one must commend oneself "by
the armour of righteousness on the right hand and on the left,"
and if we have commended ourselves by "honour" and have not
been made proud by it, let us now even endure "dishonour."
And if we have behaved worthily to deserve a "good reputation"
and if we have enjoyed such a reputation, let us now tolerate
the "evil report" of the impious. Moreover, if as "true" men
we have been admired by lovers of truth, now let us laugh if
someone says we are "mistaken." Because we have been
delivered from many dangers many have said that we were
"known of God." But now let anyone say that we are "unknown," when probably we are in fact even better known.
Bearing whatever comes, we are afflicted but not put to death,
and while rejoicing are likened to men who are grieved.[18]

44. Paul somewhere says to those who have endured suffering
at the first, exhorting them to be patient under the second
attack of danger for the sake of the word, as they were under the
first: "Remember the former days when after you were enlightened, you endured a severe struggle of suffering, being
partly an object of public ridicule and affliction, and partly
being associated with those who were being thus treated. Moreover, you sympathized with those in prison, and gladly accepted
the plunder of your property, knowing that you have a better
possession that lasts. Do not, then, abandon your confidence
which carries with it great rewards. For you need patience."[19]

[15] Matt. 7:14.
[16] Isa. 40:10; 62:11; Ps. 62 (61):12; Rom. 2:6; Rev. 2:23; 22:12.
[17] Prov. 14:29.
[18] The language of this, as of the preceding chapter, is drawn from II Cor.
6:3–10.   [19] Heb. 10:32–6.

Let us also now endure a severe struggle of suffering, being an object of public ridicule and affliction, and accepting gladly the plunder of our property. For we are convinced that we have a better possession, not earthly nor even material, but invisible and immaterial. For we make our aim not the things that are seen, seeing that they are transitory while the immaterial things are eternal.[20]

45. Some do not consider the truth concerning daemons, namely that if they are to remain in this gross air near the earth they need food from sacrifices and so keep where there is always smoke and blood and incense.[21] Accordingly, they hold it a light and indifferent matter to offer sacrifice. To this we would say that if those who provide food for thieves and murderers and barbarian enemies of the great king are punished as offenders against society, how much more would they be most justly punished who by sacrificing to the ministers of evil give them food which maintains them in the region near the earth; and particularly so if they have learnt that "he who sacrifices to other gods except to the Lord alone shall be destroyed"[22] and nevertheless sacrifice to those responsible for the evils upon earth. Indeed, I think that because of the misdeeds committed by the daemons who work against mankind those who feed them with sacrifices are no less responsible than the daemons who commit wicked deeds. For both the daemons and those who keep them on earth have injured men in like degree, since without the smoke and sacrifices and the food thought to be suited to their bodies the daemons would not be able to subsist.

46. Some, again, think that names are given by an arbitrary convention and have no natural attachment to the things they describe.[23] They think it is of no consequence if a man says, "I worship the supreme God whether his name is Zeus or Zen," or if he says, "I honour and venerate the sun or Apollo, and the moon or Artemis, and the spirit in the earth or Demeter,

---

[20] II Cor. 4:18.

[21] For sacrifices as the food of daemons, cf. my note on Origen, *contra Celsum*, III, 28; for the view that they cause earthly disasters such as famine, drought, flood, and earthquake, cf. *contra Celsum*, VIII, 31.

[22] Ex. 22:20 (19).

[23] The arguments of this chapter recur in *contra Celsum*, I, 24; V, 45. Aristotle held that names were given by an arbitrary human determination. The Stoics held that names were given "by nature," "the first utterances (of the first men) being imitations of the things described and so becoming their names." Probably the view combated by Origen was advanced by gnostic sects who wished to provide a rational justification of yielding to authority in time of persecution.

and whatever else the Greek wise men say." To them we must reply that the question of names is very profound and obscure. He who understands it will see that, if names were a matter of mere human convention, those beings we call daemons, or other powers unperceived by us, would not obey those who, while thinking of them in their minds, use their names as if they had been given by an arbitrary convention. But in fact certain sounds and syllables which are pronounced with or without aspiration, with either long or short vowel-sound, control those who are invoked probably by some natural power imperceptible to us. If this is so, and names are not a matter of arbitrary convention, the supreme God ought not to be invoked by any name except those used by Moses and the prophets and our Saviour and Lord himself, such as Sabaoth, Adonai, Shaddai, and again, God of Abraham, God of Isaac, and God of Jacob. "For this," he says "is an everlasting name and a memorial to generations of generations."[24] It is not surprising if the daemons attribute their own names to the supreme God so that they may be worshipped as the supreme God. But this is foreign to our Moses and the prophets and to Christ, the law's fulfilment, and to his apostles. We have felt it necessary to say this lest anyone should trick us in argument or in even the least degree defile our reasoning. These considerations must be carefully weighed if we are to give our opponents no opportunity for a subtle attack.

47. Furthermore, a man may still love life even though he has attained a conviction that the essence of the rational soul has a certain kinship with God.[25] For both are intellectual and invisible and, as decisive reasoning proves, incorporeal. But why did our Maker implant in us a longing for religious communion with him, so that even in the erring he preserves certain traces of the divine will,[26] if it were not possible and attainable for the rational beings to apprehend that which they long for by nature? And it is clear that just as each of our members has some ability for which it is naturally fitted, the eyes to see visible things, and the ears to hear sounds, so the mind is for intelligible things and God who transcends them. Why, then, do we hesitate and doubt to put off the corruptible body that hinders us and weighs down the soul, the "earthly tabernacle" that fills the

[24] Ex. 3:15.
[25] This is Platonic language; cf. Celsus in Origen, contra Celsum, I, 8, with my note thereon.
[26] Origen frequently denies total depravity: cf. contra Celsum, II, 11.

mind full of many anxieties,[27] and to be set free from our ties and to retire from the stormy waves that are the lot of flesh and blood? For then we may enjoy with Christ Jesus the rest which accompanies blessedness, and contemplate him in his wholeness, the living Word. Fed by him and comprehending the manifold wisdom in him, and being stamped with the very truth, we may have our minds enlightened by the true and unfailing light of knowledge and have the vision of those things which by that light can be seen by eyes illuminated by the commandment of the Lord.[28]

48. Long ago we heard Jesus' words, and it is now in the distant past that we were made disciples of the gospel, and all built for ourselves a house. Where we have built, whether we have dug deep and founded it on the rock, or on the sand without any foundation, the present struggle will show. For a storm is imminent bringing rain and rivers and winds, or, as Luke says, flood-water.[29] When these break upon the house, either they will not be able to shake it, and the house will not fall for the reason that it is built upon the rock, on Christ, or they will show up the weakness of the building which will fall under the blows of the tempest. May this never happen to our buildings. A fall by apostasy is very great, or, as Luke says, great is the ruin of the building that lacks any foundation. Therefore let us pray that we may be like the wise man who built his house on the rock. Against such a house there may come the rain from the spiritual powers of evil in the heavens or the rivers from the world-rulers of this darkness[30] or the flood-water of the spirits beneath the earth. Let them break themselves on our building founded on the rock, not only that the house may not fall but that it may not be shaken in the least, and that it may be rather they than we who suffer from their onslaught. Let each one of us say as he strikes the hostile powers, "So I fight, but not as a man beating the air."[31]

49. Moreover, since "the sower went forth to sow," let us show that our soul has received his seed, not as those by the way-side, nor as those on rocky ground, nor as the thorns, but as the good soil. Because the word of Jesus did not come by the way-side or among thorns, so much as in us lies let us make our boast in the Lord. For we have understood the message. Wherefore the evil one has not snatched away the seed sown in our

27 Wisdom of Solomon 9:15.   28 Cf. Ps. 19 (18):8; Eph. 1:18.
29 Matt. 7:24–27; Luke 6:48–49.   30 Eph. 6:12.
31 I Cor. 9:26.

heart. That the seed was not sown among thorns, many will bear witness to us, seeing that neither the care of this world nor the deceitfulness of riches nor the pleasures of this life have been able to hinder the word of God in our souls. It remains for men to doubt whether God's word, so far as we have received it, has fallen in rocky ground or on good soil. For tribulation and persecution have arisen on account of the word, and there has come upon us a time of great temptation, when he whose seed has been sown in rocky ground, and those who have not dug deep and received Jesus into the depths of their soul, will be shown up. But he who has understood the word bears fruit and holds the word to the end, producing a hundredfold in patience.[32]

We hear how Scripture speaks of those who stumble in time of tribulation or persecution after they have seemed to receive the holy teaching with joy. They stumble because they have no root but believe only for a time. According to Matthew the text reads: "He who was sown on rocky ground, this is he who hears the word and at once receives it joyfully. But he has not root in himself and endures only for a time. When tribulation or persecution arise because of the word, immediately he stumbles."[33] According to Mark: "These are they who are sown on stony ground, who when they hear the word at once receive it joyfully; and they have no root in themselves, but endure only for a time. When tribulation and persecution arise because of the word, immediately they stumble."[34] According to Luke: "But those on the rock are they who when they hear receive the word joyfully; and these have no root, who for a time believe and in time of temptation fall away."[35] But concerning those who bring forth good fruit Scripture teaches as follows: "He who is sown on the good soil, this is he who hears the word and understands it, who bears fruit and produces it, some a hundredfold, some sixty, some thirty."[36] Or, "And those are they who were sown upon the good soil, who hear the word and accept it and bear fruit, thirtyfold, and sixtyfold, and a hundredfold."[37] Or, "But that in the good soil, these are they who in an honest and good heart hear the word and hold it fast, and bring forth fruit with patience."[38]

Since then according to the apostle "you are God's planting, God's building,"[39] planted in the good soil, built on the rock, as

---

[32] See Matt. 13:3 ff.; Mark 4:4 ff ; Luke 8:5 ff.   [33] Matt. 13:20-21.
[34] Mark 4:16-17.   [35] Luke 8:13.   [36] Matt. 13:23.
[37] Mark 4:20.   [38] Luke 8:15.   [39] I Cor. 3:9.

God's building let us stand unshaken before the storm and as God's planting let us not think of the evil one, nor of tribulation or persecution which are arising because of the word, nor of the care of this world or the deceitfulness of evil or the pleasures of this life. Let us despise all these, and take the spirit of wisdom which is free from anxiety[40] and hasten to obtain the wealth that has no deceitfulness, and let us go to the pleasures, so to speak, of "the paradise of luxury."[41] In every distress let us reckon that "our present light affliction which lasts but a moment results in an eternal weight of glory beyond all estimation, if we fix our eyes not on the things that are seen but on those that are unseen."[42]

50. Let us also be aware that the word concerning Abel who was killed by the wicked murderer Cain applies to all whose blood is unjustly shed. "For the words "The cry of thy brother's blood calls to me from the ground"[43] we may consider to be applicable also to each of the martyrs; the cry of their blood calls to God from the ground.

Perhaps also just as we have been redeemed by the precious blood of Jesus,[44] Jesus who has received the name that is above every name,[45] so also some are redeemed by the precious blood of the martyrs. And they themselves are exalted more than they would have been if they had been just men but had not been martyrs. For it is with reason that a martyr's death is called "exaltation," as is clear from the saying: "If I be exalted from the earth, I will draw all men to me."[46] Let us also, therefore, glorify God exalting him by our own death, since by his death the martyr will glorify God; we learn this from the words of John: "This he said signifying by what death he would glorify God."[47]

51. This exhortation which I have written for you is the best of which I am capable. I pray it may be of assistance to you in the present conflict. If, expecially now when you are worthy to see more of the mysteries of God, you can apprehend greater and richer truths, more valuable for the present crisis, so that you look down on my poor efforts as childish and simple, I myself hope that this will be your experience. What is important for you is that you should be helped not by me but from any source whatever. God grant that you may be helped by words more divine and full of understanding, surpassing all human nature, and by the wisdom of God.

[40] Wisdom of Solomon 7:23.
[41] Gen. 3:23.
[42] II Cor. 4:17–18.
[43] Gen. 4:10.
[44] I Pet. 1:19.
[45] Phil. 2:9.
[46] John 12:32.
[47] John 21:19.

Dialogue with Heraclides

INTRODUCTION

EARLY IN AUGUST 1941 THE BRITISH ARMY HAD some caves cleared of rubbish at Tura, south of Cairo, to make a store for ammunition. This led the discovery of a small library of works, written on papyrus, by Origen and Didymus the blind. The papyri appear to have been written late in the sixth century. Both Origen and Didymus were condemned as heretical at Justinian's Council of Constantinople in 553, and it is very possible that the cache was made in consequence of the resulting proscription. Of the works of Origen the most important is the only one so far published, the *Dialogue with Heraclides*. The present translation is made from the splendid edition produced by the French papyrologist M. Jean Scherer. Nothing was previously known of the existence of this work. No work of Origen is more obviously authentic.

The *Dialogue* consists of the minutes of a discussion held at a synod of bishops summoned to discuss the opinions of a certain Bishop Heraclides whose orthodoxy has been called in question. No indication is given of the place and date, and it seems that some preliminary matter is missing at the beginning. Perhaps other parts of the discussion did not interest the sixth-century copyist so much as the part in which Origen played the leading role.

Origen frequently took part in theological disputations. He disputed with Jewish Rabbis on a number of occasions.[1] Eusebius of Caesarea had before him the minutes of a discussion, held some time between 238 and 244 with Beryllus, Bishop of Bostra in Arabia, whose monotheistic theology led him to deny the pre-existence and independent *hypostasis* of the Son. Origen

[1] Cf. Origen, *contra Celsum*, I, 45, with my note thereon.

430

won over Beryllus to his own more pluralistic doctrine of God.[2] Eusebius also mentions another "synod of no small dimensions" in Arabia to which Origen was invited to debate with some who taught that the soul dies with the body at death and only comes to life with the body at the resurrection.[3] Similar questions are ventilated in the *Dialogue with Heraclides*, but it would be risky to identify our *Dialogue* with the debate of the Arabian synod. This Arabian synod may with more probability be identified, if at all, with Origen's discussion with "the other Heraclides and Celer his predecessor" mentioned in the *Dialogue with Heraclides* (below, p. 444). Origen says that at this earlier debate controversy had become so acute that he had almost withdrawn altogether. But his opponent had eventually come round to his view.

Origen's fame brought him frequent invitations to go and explain to other churches the finer points of theology. On one occasion it led to serious trouble. About A.D. 229 he was invited to Greece to dispute with a certain Valentinian named Candidus; it was when he was on his way there that he was ordained presbyter at Caesarea in Palestine.[4] Candidus defended the Valentinian doctrine that salvation and damnation are determined by nature, not by will; and to prove his point, he observed that the devil was wholly wicked and could not be saved. Origen replied that if the devil fell by his own free will, it must at least be possible for him to choose right and to be saved.[5] A garbled version of the debate was published by Candidus. The imputation to Origen of the doctrine that the devil will be saved caused no little consternation at Alexandian, where Bishop Demetrius was already vexed by his ordination at Caesarea. He evidently wrote an angry letter to Palestine. The Palestinian bishops hastily wrote to Origen at Athens telling him of the general consternation and asking for an authentic copy of the dispute with Candidus. Formal censure was passed upon Origen at Alexandria, though the bishops of Palestine, Arabia, Phoenicia,

---

[2] Eusebius, *H.E.*, VI, 33. The minutes were also known to Jerome, (*de Vir. Inl.*, 60). They also contained some discussion of the soul of Christ, but to what purpose is not clear (Socrates, *H.E.*, III, 7:6).

[3] Eusebius, *H.E.*, VI, 37.

[4] Eusebius, *H.E.*, VI, 8:4; 23:4; Jerome, *de Vir. Inl.*, 54; Pamphilus, *ap.* Photius, *Bibl.*, 118. See above, p. 175.

[5] Origen elsewhere expresses this view: cf. *de Princ.*, III, 6:5; I, 6:3; *Comm. in Ep. ad Titum* (V, 290, Lommatzsch). Rufinus has reshaped *Comm. in. Ep. ad Rom.*, VIII, 8 (VII, 247, Lommatzsch), to give explicit denial of the possibility.

and Achaea (the scene of his recent visit) significantly refused to agree to the sentence.[6] We have substantial fragments of an impassioned letter written by Origen to his friends at Alexandria, in which with crushing irony (similar in tone to that used about Demetrius at the beginning of the sixth book of the *Commentary on St. John*) he observes that he would not revile the devil any more than the bishops who have condemned him.[7] Such unfortunate experiences explain the caution shown by Origen in the conference with Heraclides.

It is not impossible that the bishop Demetrius mentioned in the *Dialogue with Heraclides* is none other than the Bishop of Alexandria; if so, the *Dialogue* must be earlier than A.D. 230. It is also possible that "the beloved Dionysius" is the future Bishop of Alexandria. But this is not really probable. The Maximus of the *Dialogue* may be the successor of Beryllus of Bostra, who took part in the Origenist synod at Antioch at 268 which condemned Paul of Samosata. If so, the *Dialogue* must be placed later in Origen's career, and occurred at a synod in Arabia. The later date has received more support, and seems to be more likely.

The *Dialogue with Heraclides* is concerned with three main subjects. The chief concern of the synod was the orthodoxy of Bishop Heraclides, and the synod is evidently held in his church. The bishops did not, perhaps, trust their own powers to deal with such advanced theological questions, and called in Origen

---

[6] Jerome, *Ep.*, 33:5.

[7] Sources: Rufinus, *de Adulteratione librorum Origenis* (*P.G.*, XVII, 624–626), with the corrections of Jerome, *Apol. adv. Rufin.*, II, 18–19. Photius (*Bibl.*, 118) summarizes the account of Demetrius' condemnation of Origen given by Pamphilus' *Apology*. The tendency of Pamphilus is to play down doctrinal issues, and to make it appear that Demetrius' ground of complaint was the irregularity of Origen's ordination (*a*) as having been done in Palestine without his consent, (*b*) as being contrary to church law, prohibiting the ordination of the mutilated. The same tendency is clear in Eusebius (*H.E.*, VI, 8:4–5), who says that Demetrius was envious of Origen's fame and so objected to the technical validity of his ordination. Jerome, writing before he joined the anti-Origenist camp, similarly says that the censure passed upon Origen at Rome was "not on account of any doctrinal innovation, not for any heresy, as rabid dogs are now alleging against him, but because they could not endure the magnificence of his eloquence and knowledge" (*Ep.* 33:5). The majority of modern writers have accepted the thesis of Pamphilus and Eusebius that Demetrius' condemnation was based not on a doctrinal issue but on mere matters of church discipline. The evidence of Rufinus and Jerome's *Apology* seems clearly to tell against it. Cf. C. C. Richardson, "The Condemnation of Origen," in *Church History*, VI (1937), pp. 50–64.

to help them. Just as at Antioch in A.D. 268 the presbyter Mal-
chion is asked to conduct the cross-examination of Paul of
Samosata, so Origen questions Heraclides; it is he who deter-
mines the form in which the questions are put, so that Heraclides
finds himself arguing on Origen's ground. We cannot tell how
he would have expressed his theology if he had been left to
himself. The laity are present in the church, as also they were
at Antioch in 268.

Heraclides begins by assuring the synod that he too is ready
to agree to the Logos theology of the Fourth Gospel (John
1:1–3). It seems that in the immediately preceding discussion,
not copied by the scribe, this text has been quoted against him.
He follows this with a credal statement. It is now time for
Origen to begin his cross-examination, which is designed to
elicit from Heraclides a confession of the pre-existence and
independent existence of the Son.

The theology of the Greek apologists is marked by a strong
emphasis on the independent *hypostasis* of the Son in relation to
the Father. Justin Martyr had spoken of the Son as "another
God." From the last decade of the second century the Logos
theology of the apologists met with strong opposition from those
who felt that it was incompatible with monotheism. Two courses
were open to the critics. *Either* they could say that Jesus was
God without qualification; the person of Christ is the person of
God; if Christ suffered, then God suffered. *Or* they could say
that Jesus was a man like other men, but indwelt by the spirit of
God to a unique degree. The former view was later known in the
East as Sabellianism, in the West as Patripassianism. The latter
view is usually called Adoptianism by modern writers (it has
no ancient equivalent title). Origen's theology, as set forth to
Heraclides, is intended to steer a middle course between Scylla
and Charybdis. The one party, he says, abolishes the distinct
personality of the Son in relation to the Father, and thus virtually does away with the Father as well, since if the Son is not
distinct the Father cannot be Father. The other party denies
the deity of Christ. Only the doctrine that the Logos is both
separate from and one with the Father avoids heresy. It is clear
that for Origen the independence of the Son is theologically
prior to his oneness with the Father. He begins by thinking of
two Gods and then tries to explain how they are one, never
vice versa. In other writings he does not shrink any more than
in the *Dialogue with Heraclides* from affirming that there are
two Gods, though as here he usually adds some qualifying

434   ORIGEN

phrase.[8] He pursues Heraclides with politely relentless questioning until he has to agree, despite all his reluctance, that there
are two Gods. Heraclides at once adds: "The power is one."[9]
And even Origen deems it wise to take the edge off his sharply
ditheistic statement so scandalous to the brethren.

The controversy in Heraclides' church seems to have centred
on the prayers used at the eucharist. Origen appeals to the
universal usage of the Church to make offering to God through
Jesus Christ. This is no double offering to two Gods, but "to
God through God." The theology of prayer here implied is set
forth at greater length in Origen's treatise on Prayer.[10] Here
he insists that the church of Heraclides must show its unity
with all other churches by adhering to the customary, agreed
formulas of prayer. If it fails to do so, "it will give rise to
fresh disputes."[11]

In the second section of the *Dialogue* Origen turns to deal
with an objection raised, it appears, at some earlier stage of the
conference by Maximus, concerning the Christological implications of the Logos doctrine. If Jesus Christ is God in his very
essence (οὐσιωδῶς), what is to be said of the reality of his body
and in particular of his death? Could the body of God become
a corpse?[12] Origen states his beliefs: If the body of Christ did
not truly die and rise again, it cuts at the root of the Church's
faith in the resurrection of believers.[13] Maximus is asked if he is
satisfied (the text is again corrupt, but this seems to be required
by the context). Maximus' reply shows a fear, significant for the
atmosphere of the synod, lest the fact of his raising a question
may impugn his reputation for orthodoxy. His question is only

[8] Cf. Origen, de Oratione, XV, 1; contra Celsum, V, 39; VI, 61; VII, 57;
   Comm. In Ev. Jo., II, 2; X, 37 (21).
[9] The language is reminiscent of Hippolytus who uses the same phrase to
   qualify ditheistic statements; contra Noetum, 7, 11 (Schwartz, pp. 10, 24;
   13, 3).
[10] See contra Celsum, V, 4-5; VIII, 26; and Prof. Oulton's notes on de
   Oratione, XV–XVI (above, pp. 346–48). It is noteworthy that Paul of
   Samosata disapproved of prayer to Christ (Eusebius, H.E., VII, 30:10).
   E. C. Ratcliff (J.T.S., XXX (1929), pp. 23–32, cited by A. D. Nock,
   Amer. Journ. Arch., LV (1951), 284) argues that originally the East Syrian
   eucharistic liturgy was addressed to Christ, not the Father.
[11] This is the general sense of a passage which is badly corrupted and was
   unintelligible to the original scribe.
[12] The connection of thought at this point in the Dialogue is not immediately
   obvious; the view expressed above seems to be the simplest interpretation.
[13] Similar insistence on the reality of Christ's material body as necessary for
   human salvation in Origen's Commentary on Galatians, cited in Pamphilus'
   Apology (XXIV, 365 ff., Lommatzsch).

a request for information: "I need the help of my brother and instruction on this point." The difficulty about Origen's view, as he sees it, is this. Jesus said: "Father, into thy hands I commend my spirit." The divine nature returned to the Father. What power, then, was it which opened the tomb and raised up the flesh?

Origen replies by appealing to the Pauline trichotomy of I Thess. 5:23: "May God sanctify your spirit and your soul and your body." The spirit Jesus committed to the Father was not the Holy Spirit, but his human spirit. For the Logos took to himself the entire constitution of man, body, soul, and spirit. "The whole man would not have been saved unless he had taken upon him the whole man"—a sentence which anticipates the standard anti-Apollinarian argument of the fourth century. Thus Christ's human body, soul, and spirit were separated at the Passion. The spirit was temporarily entrusted to the Father, the soul descended to Hades, the body remained in the tomb. They were reunited shortly after the Resurrection, though not at the actual moment of the Resurrection as is proved by the words to Mary Magdalene (John 20:17): "Touch me not, for I am not yet ascended to the Father." He did not wish her to touch him before he had reclaimed the spirit left in temporary deposit with the Father. He appeared to his disciples after all three elements of his humanity had been reunited.

Origen has now said his say on all the questions of doctrine which had been the immediate subject of controversy in Heraclides' church. After a homily on the equal importance of orthodoxy and right conduct, he invites questions on any other points of theology.

The question is put by Dionysius: "Is the soul the blood?" From the text in Lev. 17:11, "The soul of all flesh is blood," supported by Deut. 12:23, some were evidently drawing the conclusion that the soul was material, and was corrupted with the body in the grave.[14] With such explicit texts of Scripture to explain away Origen finds himself extremely embarrassed. He is most reluctant to speak, especially with uninstructed laymen present, lest he should be casting his pearls before swine. His lengthy reply (so long that some of his audience cease to pay attention in their impatience) is that Scripture often uses

[14] Similar beliefs were refuted by Origen at the Arabian synod mentioned by Eusebius (*H.E.*, VI, 37) though we are not told that the Leviticus text played any part in the discussion there. For a comparable discussion, cf. Tertullian, *de Anima*, 53.

physical terms to describe spiritual realities. Therefore, "blood" in the Leviticus text cannot possibly mean blood. A certain Bishop Philip has been absent and so has missed Origen's discourse. As he enters the synod, Bishop Demetrius summarizes the debate for him: "Brother Origen teaches that the soul is immortal." The implication, which is not lost on Origen, is that he is suspected of being more a Platonist than a truly Biblical theologian in his doctrine of the soul. He answers that his appeal is not to the Greeks but to the Scripture. It is, however, difficult to see that his involved discussion of the various meanings of "death" is of any value in answering the point. The argument here shows him at his weakest, content merely to assert, and to conceal his embarrassment with verbiage.

Origen ends with a final peroration, similar in tone to the *Exhortation to Martyrdom*.

The text of the *Dialogue with Heraclides* is edited with a French translation, introduction, and notes by Jean Scherer: *Entretien d'Origène avec Héraclide et les évêques, ses collègues sur le Père, le Fils, et l'Âme* (Cairo, 1949).

For discussions of the text consult the following: B. Capelle, "L'Entretien d'Origène avec Héraclide," in *The Journal of Ecclesiastical History*, II (1951), pp. 143–157; H. C. Puech, "Les nouveaux écrits d'Origène et de Didyme découverts à Toura," in *Revue d'histoire et de philosophie religieuses*, XXXI (1951), pp. 293–329; J. Crehan, "The Dialektos of Origen and John 20:17," in *Theological Studies*, XI (1950), pp. 368–372; B. Capelle, "Origène et l'oblation à faire au Père par le Fils, d'après le papyrus de Toura," in *Revue d'histoire Ecclésiastique* XLVII (1952), pp. 163–171; G. Kretschmar, "Origenes und die Araber," in *Zeitschrift für Theologie und Kirche* L (1953), pp. 258–279.

For reviews of Scherer's edition see G. W. H. Lampe in *Journal of Theological Studies*, New Series, I (1950), pp. 105–107; L. Früchtel in *Theologische Literaturzeitung*, 1950, cols. 504–506 (with some venturesome emendations of the text); A. D. Nock in *American Journal of Archaeology*, LV (1951), pp. 283–284.

The fundamental paper on the Toura find as a whole is that of O. Guéraud, "Note préliminaire sur les papyrus d'Origène découverts à Toura," in *Revue de l'histoire des religions*, CXXXI (1946), pp. 85–108.

In the present translation the page numbers of Scherer's edition of the Greek text are noted in the margin.

Dialogue of Origen with Heraclides and the Bishops with him concerning the Father and the Son and the Soul [1]

THE TEXT

After the bishops present had raised questions concerning the faith of the 118
bishop Heraclides, that he might confess before all the faith which he
held, and after each one had said what he thought and asked questions,
Heraclides said:

I also believe what the sacred Scriptures say: "In the beginning was the Word, and the Word was with God, and the Word
was God. He was in the beginning with God. All things were
made by him, and without him nothing was made." [2] Accordingly, we hold the same faith that is taught in these words, and
we believe that Christ took flesh, that he was born, that he went 120
up to heaven in the flesh in which he rose again, that he is sitting
at the right hand of the Father, and that thence he shall come
and judge the living and the dead, being God and man.

Origen said: Since once an inquiry has begun it is proper to
say something upon the subject of the inquiry, I will speak. The
whole church is present and listening. It is not right that there
should be any difference in knowledge between one church and
another, for you are not the false church.

I charge you, father Heraclides: God is the almighty, the
uncreated, the supreme God who made all things. Do you hold
this doctrine?

Heracl.: I do. That is what I also believe.

Orig.: Christ Jesus who was in the form of God, [3] being other

---

[1] The original scribe only wrote the title in the final colophon at the end of
the work: "Dialogues of Origen: with Heraclides and the bishops with
him." A later reviser added to this final colophon "Concerning the Father
and the Son and the Soul" and also inserted this full title at the head of
the work.

[2] John 1:1–3.   [3] Phil. 2:6.

437

than the God in whose form he existed, was he God before he came into the body or not?

123   *Heracl.:* He was God before.

Orig.: Was he God before he came into the body or not?

Heracl.: Yes, he was.

Orig.: Was he God distinct from this God in whose form he existed?

Heracl.: Obviously he was distinct from another being and, since he was in the form of him who created all things, he was distinct from him.

Orig.: Is it true then that there was a God, the Son of God, the only begotten of God, the firstborn of all creation,[4] and that we need have no fear of saying that in one sense there are two Gods, while in another there is one God?

Heracl.: What you say is evident. But we affirm that God is the almighty, God without beginning, without end, containing all things and not contained by anything[5]; and that his Word is the Son of the living God, God and man, through whom all things were made,[6] God according to the spirit, man inasmuch as he was born of Mary.[7]

Orig.: You do not appear to have answered my question. Explain what you mean. For perhaps I failed to follow you. Is the Father God?

Heracl.: Assuredly.

Orig.: Is the Son distinct from the Father?

Heracl.: Of course. How can he be Son if he is also Father?

124   *Orig.:* While being distinct from the Father is the Son himself also God?

Heracl.: He himself is also God.

Orig.: And do two Gods become a unity?

Heracl.: Yes.

Orig.: Do we confess two Gods?

Heracl.: Yes. The power is one.

Orig.: But as our brethren take offence at the statement that there are two Gods, we must formulate the doctrine carefully, and show in what sense they are two and in what sense the two are one God. Also the holy Scriptures have taught that several things which are two are one. And not only things which are two, for they have also taught that in some instances more than two, or even a very much larger number of things, are one. Our

---

[4] Col. 1:15.
[5] A theological commonplace; cf. Origen, *de Princ.*, I, 3:3, etc.
[6] John 1:3.   [7] Cf. Rom. 1:3.

present task is not to broach a problematic subject only to pass it by and deal cursorily with the matter, but for the sake of the simple folk to chew up, so to speak, the meat, and little by little to instil the doctrine in the ears of our hearers. . . . Accordingly, there are many things which are two that are said in the Scriptures to be one. What passages of Scripture? Adam is one person, his wife another. Adam is distinct from his wife, and his wife is distinct from her husband. Yet it is said in the story of the creation of the world that they two are one: "For the two shall be one flesh."[8] Therefore, sometimes two beings can become one flesh. Notice, however, that in the case of Adam and Eve 126 it is not said that the two shall become one spirit, nor that the two shall become one soul, but that they shall become one flesh. Again, the righteous man is distinct from Christ; but he is said by the apostle to be one with Christ: "For he that is joined to the Lord is one spirit."[9] Is it not true that the one is of a subordinate nature or of a low and inferior nature, while Christ's nature is divine and glorious and blessed? Are they therefore no longer two? Yes, for the man and the woman are "no longer two but one flesh," and the righteous man and Christ are "one spirit." So in relation to the Father and God of the universe, our Saviour and Lord is not one flesh, nor one spirit, but something higher than flesh and spirit, namely, one God. The appropriate word when human beings are joined to one another is flesh. The appropriate word when a righteous man is joined to Christ is spirit. But the word when Christ is united to the Father is not flesh, nor spirit, but more honourable than these —God. That is why we understand in this sense "I and the Father are one."[10] When we pray, because of the one party let us preserve the duality, because of the other party let us hold to the unity. In this way we avoid falling into the opinion of those who have been separated from the Church and turned to the illusory notion of monarchy, who abolish the Son as distinct from the Father and virtually abolish the Father also. Nor do 128 we fall into the other blasphemous doctrine which denies the deity of Christ. What then do the divine Scriptures mean when they say: "Beside me there is no other God, and there shall be none after me," and "I am and there is no God but me"?[11] In these utterances we are not to think that the unity applies to the God of the universe . . . in separation from Christ, and

---

[8] Gen. 2:24; Matt. 19:5.
[9] I Cor. 6:17. Cf. *contra Celsum*, II, 9; VI, 47; *Comm. in Matt.*, XIV, 16.
[10] John 10:30.   [11] Isa. 43:10; Deut. 32:39.

certainly not to Christ in separation from God. Let us rather say that the sense is the same as that of Jesus' saying, "I and my Father are one."

It is necessary to study these doctrines because there has been much disturbance in this church. Often people write and demand a signature of the bishop and of those they suspect, asking that they should give their signatures in the presence of all the people, that there may be no further disturbance or dispute about this question. Accordingly, with the permission of God and secondly of the bishops, thirdly of the presbyters, and also of the people, I will again say what I think on this subject.

130 Offering is universally made to Almighty God through Jesus Christ inasmuch as, in respect of his deity, he is akin to the Father. Let there be no double offering, but an offering to God through God. I shall seem to be speaking in a daring manner. When we pray let us abide by the agreements.[12] If the word: "Thou shalt not respect the person of man, nor allow thyself to be impressed by the person of the mighty"[13] is not realized . . . If this is not realized . . . these agreements, it will give rise to fresh disputes. . . . If a man is a bishop or a presbyter, he is not a bishop, he is not a presbyter. If he is a deacon, he is not a deacon, nor even a layman. If he is a layman, he is not a layman, nor is there a meeting of the congregation. If you assent, let these agreed usages prevail.

132   Some people raise the objection that, with reference to the problem of deity, while I have thus attributed deity to Jesus Christ substantially, I have professed before the church my faith that at the resurrection the body which rose had been a corpse.[14] But since our Saviour and Lord took a body, let us

---

12 Origen uses *sunthekai* of the promises and credal confession made in baptism (e.g., *Exh. Mart.*, 12, 17). Cf. Clem. *Strom.* VII, 90. "The terms of the baptismal confession" would perhaps be a possible translation here. But the general idea of this corrupt passage is an appeal to the universal sense of the church. It is likely that Origen means the agreed formulas of liturgical prayer: *lex orandi lex credendi*. Scherer, however, thinks it means the agreements which are to constitute the practical conclusion of the debate.

13 Lev. 19:15. The quotation is odd. Scherer is probably right in taking this to refer to interference in the affairs of the church by powerful people without authority; but the precise sense of the allusion is lost, and the passage, the text of which is more corrupt than any other in the Dialogue, was not understood by the original scribe. The general sense is that if unauthorized people interfere, there will be chaos and the authorized ministry deprived of all meaning.

14 See the Introduction, above p. 434.

examine what the body was. The church alone in distinction from all the heresies that deny the resurrection confesses the resurrection of the dead body. For from the fact that the first-fruits were raised from the dead, it follows that the dead are raised. "Christ the firstfruits"[15]; on that account his body became a corpse. For if his body had not become a corpse, capable of being wrapped in a grave-cloth, of receiving the ointment and all the other things applied to dead bodies, and of being laid in a tomb[16]—these are things that cannot be done to a spiritual body. For it is entirely impossible for that which is spiritual to become a corpse, neither can that which is spiritual become insensible. For if it were possible for that which is spiritual to become a corpse, we would have reason to fear lest after the resurrection of the dead, when our body is raised, according to the apostle's saying, "It is sown animate, it is raised spiritual,"[17] we shall all die. . . . In fact "Christ being raised from the dead dies no more."[18] And not only Christ, but those who are Christ's,[19] when they are raised from the dead, die no more. If you agree to these statements, they also with the solemn testimony of the people shall be made legally binding and established.[20]

What else is there to be said concerning the faith? Do you agree to this, Maximus? Say.

Maximus: May everyone hold the same doctrines as I do. Before God and the Church I both give my signature and make my oath. But the reason why I raised a certain question was in order that I might be in no doubt or uncertainty at all. For the brethren know that this is what I said: "I need the help of my brother and instruction on this point." If the spirit was truly given back to the Father, in accordance with the saying, "Father, into thy hands I commend my spirit,"[21] and if without the spirit the flesh died and lay in the tomb, how was the tomb opened and how are the dead to rise again?

Orig.: That man is a composite being we have learnt from the sacred Scriptures. For the apostle says, "May God sanctify your spirit and your soul and your body," and "May he sanctify you wholly, and may your entire spirit and soul and body be

15 I Cor. 15:12 ff.   16 Cf. Matt. 27:59; Mark 15:46; Luke 23:53.
17 I Cor. 15:44.   18 Rom. 6:9.   19 I Cor. 15:23.
20 The procedure appears to have been that at the end of the synod the doctrinal decisions would have been formally set forth, and the congregation would have declared their adherence thereto.
21 Luke 23:46.

preserved unblameable at the coming of our Lord Jesus Christ."[22]
This spirit is not the Holy Spirit, but part of the constitution of
man, as the same apostle teaches when he says: "The spirit
bears witness with our spirit."[23] For if it were the Holy Spirit
he would not have said: "The spirit bears witness with our
spirit." So then our Saviour and Lord, wishing to save man in
the way in which he wished to save him, for this reason desired
in this way to save the body, just as it was likewise his will to
save also the soul; he also wished to save the remaining part of
man, the spirit. The whole man would not have been saved unless he had taken upon him the whole man. They do away with
the salvation of the human body when they say that the body
of the Saviour is spiritual. They do away with the salvation of
the human spirit, concerning which the apostle says: "No man
knows the things of man except the spirit of man that is in
138 him."[24] . . . Because it was his will to save the spirit of man,
about which the apostle said this, he also assumed the spirit of
man. At the time of the passion these three were separated.
At the time of the resurrection these three were united. At the
time of the passion they were separated—how? The body in the
tomb, the soul in Hades, the spirit was put in the hands of the
Father.[25] The soul in Hades: "Thou shalt not leave my soul in
Hades."[26] If the spirit was put into the hands of the Father, he
gave the spirit as a deposit. It is one thing to make a gift, another
thing to hand over, and another to leave in deposit. He who
makes a deposit does so with the intention of receiving back that
which he has deposited. Why then had he to give the spirit to the
Father as a deposit? The question is beyond me and my powers
and my understanding. For I am not endowed with knowledge
to enable me to say that, just as the body was not able to go down
to Hades, even if this is alleged by those who affirm that the body
of Jesus was spiritual,[27] so also neither could the spirit go down

---

[22] I Thess. 5:23. Cf. Origen, de Princ., II, 8:4, where he suggests that Christ's
soul was "a kind of medium between the weak flesh and the willing
spirit."　　　[23] Rom. 8:16.　　　[24] I Cor. 2:11.

[25] J. Crehan, "The Dialektos of Origen and John 20:17," in Theological
Studies, XI (1950), 368–372, compares the Paschal homily ascribed both
to John Chrysostom and Hippolytus, edited by P. Nautin, Homélies
Pascales, I (1950), 185: "The heavens have thy spirit, paradise thy soul
. . . the earth thy body. The indivisible is divided."

[26] Ps. 16 (15):10; Acts 2:27. Cf. contra Celsum, II, 16.

[27] The Marcionites believed that their docetic Christ had descended to
Hades to save all who had resisted the God of the Jews such as the
Sodomites. Cf. contra Celsum, VI, 53, with my note thereon.

to Hades, and therefore he gave the spirit to the Father as a deposit until he should have risen from the dead. . . . After he had entrusted this deposit to the Father, he took it back again. When? Not at the actual moment of the resurrection, but immediately after the resurrection. My witness is the text of the gospel. The Lord Jesus Christ rose again from the dead. Mary met him and he said to her: "Touch me not."[28] For he wished anyone that touched him to touch him in his entirety, that having touched him in his entirety he might be benefited in body from his body, in soul from his soul, in spirit from his spirit. "For I am not yet ascended to the Father." He ascends to the Father and comes to the disciples. Accordingly he ascends to the Father. Why? To receive back the deposit.

All the questions about the faith which disturbed us have been examined. But we must realize that at the divine tribunal we are not judged for faith alone,[29] as if our life were left unexamined, nor for our life alone, as if our faith were not subject to scrutiny. We are justified on the ground that both are correct. We are punished for both if both are incorrect. There are some, however, who will not be punished for both, but for one of the two: some for their faith because it is defective, but not because their life is lacking in right conduct; others, again, will not be punished for their faith, but will be for their life, on the ground that they have lived a life contrary to right reason. My opinion is that in the Proverbs of Solomon these two kinds (I mean that which concerns our belief and knowledge and that which concerns our manner of life) are mentioned by Solomon in the following words: "Who shall boast that he has a pure heart? Or who shall present himself saying that he is free from sins?"[30] The difference between these we take to be this: the "heart" means the thought, the "sins" refer to actions. "Who shall boast that he has a pure heart" which is undefiled by the knowledge falsely so-called,[31] undefiled by falsehood? Or "who shall present himself saying that he is free from sins," having done nothing amiss in his practical conduct? If then we wish to be saved, let us not be concerned about faith to the neglect of practical conduct of life, nor again let us place our confidence in our life. Let us realize, let us comprehend, let us believe that it is on the ground of both that we either receive our acquittal or blessedness, or receive the opposite of these. The things that are liable to punishment, therefore, are not merely the terrible

140

142

28 John 20:17. 29 Cf. James 2:24.
30 Prov. 20:9. 31 I Tim. 6:20.

and fearful sins which should not even be named,[32] whether
sins of life or of thought, but also sins commonly thought to be
of less importance. That is why, it seems, the apostle puts side
by side with acts which are abominable, infamous, and revolting
(if I may so say) things which are regarded by most people as of
little significance. What does he say? "Be not deceived; neither
fornicators, nor adulterers, nor effeminate men, nor homosexuals, nor thieves, nor drunkards, nor revilers, shall inherit
the kingdom of God."[33] You see that together with such gross
sinners as the homosexual person, the effeminate man, the
adulterer, the fornicator, he enumerates the drunkard, the
reviler—sins thought by all of us to be of small account, so that
we may be taught that it is not for the great sins alone that we •
are excluded from the kingdom of God, but also for these which
are commonly supposed to be of minor significance. Therefore,
let us not revile, nor be drunkards, nor extort, nor steal, nor
do anything wrong, even if we are "deceived."[34]

144   If there is any further point to raise concerning the Rule
of faith, mention it. We will speak still further upon the
Scripture.

   Dionysius said: Is the soul the blood?

   Orig.: It has come to my notice, and I say this with full knowledge of the facts, that some of the folk here and in the neigh-
bourhood suppose that after the soul has departed this life it is
incapable of feeling, but is in the tomb, in the body. And I know
that on this question I was impelled to deal very severely with
the other Heraclides and Celer his predecessor, so severely in
fact that I would have preferred to leave the subject and to go
away.[35] But for the sake of honour and for the subject under
debate he summoned us to deal with it. We agreed to discuss

---

[32] Eph. 5:3.

[33] I Cor. 6:9–10. Cf. Origen, *in I Cor.*, XXVI (Jenkins, *J.T.S.*, IX (1908),
367): "Most of us can know in our consciences that we are not guilty of
these vices; but with regard to those that follow, even I myself fear lest I
may be guilty of the other sins. . . ."

[34] This strange phrase is explained by *Hom. in Jerem.*, XX, 3, where Origen
says that I Cor. 6:9–10 might cause those who do not understand that
God's punishments are purifying to lose heart. "For which of us is not
aware in his conscience of having drunk not wisely and too well? Which
of us is pure from theft . . .?" The truth that minor sins are punished by
God no less than serious vices is a mystery which providentially is not
understood by the ignorant multitude of believers who, if they were not
deceived, would abandon hope, not realizing that God's punishments and
harsh words are remedial and not retributive.

[35] Cf. Introduction, above p. 431.

the matter; he made a statement . . .[36] how the former cleared himself before us, as though before God, by his orthodox[37] statements.

Accordingly, the question posed by the beloved Dionysius forces our hand. I shall first set out the passages which trouble them, lest any one of them be omitted, and by God's permission we will answer each one of them in accordance with your request. The disturbing passage is as follows: "The soul of all flesh is blood." This text has terribly distressed those who have not understood it. Also, "Ye shall not eat the soul with the flesh; pay strict heed to see that you eat no blood; ye shall not eat the soul with the flesh."[38] The disturbing text is this one. For the other distressing texts are far less emphatic in expressing the idea suggested here. For my part, according to my measure of understanding, and praying for assistance in reading the divine words (for we are in need of help lest our minds should conceive ideas diverging from the truth),[39] I have found that incorporeal things are given the same names as all the corporeal things, so that just as corporeal things apply to the outer man, those which are given the same names as corporeal things apply to the inner man. The Bible says that man is two men: "For if our outward man perish, yet our inward man is renewed day by day," and "I rejoice in the law of God after the inward man."[40] These two men the apostle everywhere shows to be distinct. In my judgment he would not have ventured to invent this notion out of his own head, but rather said this because he had clearly understood statements in the Scriptures which are obscurely expressed. Some people imagine that there is a mere repetition when in the story of the creation of the world after the creation of man we read "God took dust of the earth and formed man."[41] The corollary of this interpretation is that it is the body which is the part "after the image,"[42] and that God is given a human form, or that the form of God[43] is shaped like the human body. But we are not so crazy as to say either that

146

---

[36] The sense is not clear and was not understood by the scribe. Whether Heraclides or Celer cleared himself before Origen is obscure.

[37] Reading: φωναῖς πίστεως ὀρθῆς (MS. ὅτι) ὡς πρὸς θεόν.

[38] Lev. 17:11 f; Deut. 12:23.

[39] Origen often says that divine grace and prayer are necessary for interpreting the Scripture rightly. Cf. e.g. *Hom. in Ezech.*, II, 2 .

[40] II Cor. 4:16; Rom. 7:22. For the idea cf. *contra Celsum*, VII, 34; *de Princ.*, I, 1:9: "The names of organs of sense are often applied to the soul." Very similar is *Hom. in Ezech.*, III, 8.

[41] Gen. 2:7.   [42] Gen. 1:26.   [43] Cf. Phil. 2:6.

148 God is composed of a superior and an inferior element so that
that which is in his image is like him in both elements, which
consitute God in his completeness, or that that which is in his
image consisted rather in the inferior part and not in the
superior.[44]

The questions are highly delicate. We need hearers who have
an acute understanding. I therefore charge those who listen to
pay heed to themselves lest they should make me liable to the
accusation of casting holy things to the dogs, to shameless souls.
For the barkers, like dogs, those who think only of fornication
and abuse, do nothing but yelp like dogs, and it is not right for
me to cast holy things before such folk. So also I charge my
hearers that they do not make me liable to the accusation of
150 laying splendid pearls, which we try to collect like good mer-
chants,[45] before people steeped in the impurities of their bodies,
and who are therefore called swine.[46] For I would say that a
person who continually steeps himself and wallows in the filth
of life and makes no attempt to live a pure life, a holy life, is
simply a swine. If then, because the kingdom of heaven is like a
merchant seeking goodly pearls, I find the goodly pearls, and
having bought them at the price of weariness and sleeplessness
I fling them before pleasure-loving souls, and those who are
steeped in the filth of the body and in impurity, then I also
will be a transgressor because I am casting pearls before swine.
But when the swine have got the pearls, because they do
not perceive their beauty nor see their excellence, they
tread them under foot by speaking evil of what was rightly
said, and not only do they trample the pearls under foot, but
they also turn and rend those who supplied them with the
pearls.

I beseech you, therefore, be transformed. Resolve to learn
that in you there is the capacity to be transformed, and to put
off the form of a swine, which is in an impure soul, and the
shape of a dog, which is that of a man who barks and reviles and
pours out abuse. It is also possible to be transformed from the
shape of snakes; for a wicked man is described as a serpent and

---

[44] The text here is corrupt. The later reviser makes corrections rejected by
Scherer, but which seem more satisfactory than his own close adherence
to the original scribe; I have attempted to translate the reviser's text.
The idea is closely paralleled in *contra Celsum*, VI, 63.

[45] Read after Früchtel: πειρώμεθα ὡς καλοὶ ἔμποροι, παρατιθέντες . . . (but
Früchtel needlessly inserts a verb; Origen normally constructs ἐγκαλέω
with a following participle, as here, and p. 152, 18 Sch.).

[46] Matt. 7:6.

"the offspring of vipers."[47] If, then, we are willing to understand that in us there is the power to be transformed from being
serpents, swine, and dogs, let us learn from the apostle that the
transformation depends upon us. For he says this: "We all,
when with unveiled face we reflect the glory of the Lord, are
transformed into the same image."[48] If you are like a barking
dog, and if the Word has moulded and transformed you, you
have been transformed from being a dog to being a man. If you
were impure and the Word came to your soul and you sub-
mitted yourself to the moulding of the Word, you changed from
being a swine to being a man. If you were a savage beast, and 152
heard the Word that tames and softens, that changes you into a
man, by the will of the Word you will no longer be called a serpent, the offspring of vipers. For if it were impossible for these
serpents, serpents in their soul because of wickedness, to be
changed, the Saviour (or John) would not have said: "Do
therefore fruits worthy of repentance."[49] After repentance you
are no longer a serpent, the offspring of vipers.

Since it is our task to speak about man, and to inquire
whether the soul of man is not blood, and since this subject required us to discuss in detail the doctrine of the two men, and
as we have come to a mysterious subject, I beseech you that you
do not cause me to be accused of casting pearls before swine,
of throwing holy things to the dogs, of flinging divine things to
serpents, of giving the serpent a share in the tree of life. That
I may avoid this accusation, be transformed, put off evil, quarrelling, wrath, strife, anger, division of opinion,[50] that there
may not be any further schisms among you but that "you
may be firmly established in the same mind and the same
judgment."[51]

To speak makes me embarrassed, and not to speak makes me
embarrassed. Because of those who are worthy I would speak,
lest I be accused of depriving of the word those able to understand it. Because of the unworthy I shrink from speaking for
the reasons I have given, lest I should be flinging holy things to
dogs and casting pearls before swine. It was the work of Jesus
only to know how to distinguish among his hearers between
those without and those within, so that he spoke to those without in parables, but explained the parables to those who

47 Cf. Matt. 23:33. For the idea cf. Clement, *Protrept.*, I, 4.
48 II Cor. 3:18.
49 Luke 3:8; cf. Matt. 3:8.   50 Cf. Col. 3:8.
51 I Cor. 1:10.

entered into his house.[52] To remain without and to enter into
the house have a mystical meaning. "Why should I judge those
154 that are without?"[53] Every sinner is without. That is why those
without are addressed in parables in case they should be able
to leave the things without and enter within. To enter the house
has a mystical meaning: he who enters Jesus' house is his true
disciple. He enters by holding the doctrine of the church, by
living a life according to the teaching of the church. "Within"
and "without" are spiritual terms.

You see how long an introduction I have given in order to
prepare my hearers. I shrink from speaking. When I am on the
point of speaking I put it off. What is my purpose in doing this?
To shape my discourse so as to heal the souls of my hearers.

At the creation of man, then, there was first created the man
that is "after the image," in whom there was nothing material.
He who is in the image is not made out of matter. "And God
said, Let us make man in our image and likeness, and let them
have dominion"[54] and so on. And when God made man he did
not take dust of the earth, as he did the second time, but he
made him in the image of God. That that which is in the image
of God is understood as immaterial and superior to all corporeal existence not only by Moses but also by the apostle is
shown by his words, as follows: "Putting off the old man with
his deeds and putting on the new which is renewed in the knowledge of him who created him."[55]

Therefore in each one of us there are two men. Why does
Scripture say that the soul of all flesh is blood? It is a great
problem. Just as the outward man has the same name as the
inward man, so also this is true of his members, so that one may
say that every member of the outward man has a name corresponding to what is true of the inward man.

156   The outward man has eyes, and the inward man also is said
to have eyes: "Lighten my eyes lest I sleep in death."[56] This
does not refer to these eyes, nor to physical sleep, nor to
ordinary death. "The commandment of the Lord, luminous,
enlightens the eyes."[57] By keeping the commandments of the
Lord we do not become more sharp-sighted physically but by

[52] Cf. Mark 4:11; Matt. 13:36. Similarly *contra Celsum*, III, 21.
[53] I Cor. 5:12.
[54] Gen. 1:26–27. Origen follows Philo (*Opif.*, 134 ff.; *Leg. Alleg.*, I, 31 f.) in
interpreting Gen. ch. 1 of the creation of the archetypal Image; Gen.
ch. 2 describes the making of material man of the dust of the earth. For
the idea cf. C. H. Dodd, *The Bible and the Greeks* (1935), pp. 145 ff.
[55] Col. 3:9.   [56] Ps. 13 (12):3.   [57] Ps. 19 (18):8.

keeping the divine commands we become more sharp-sighted in mind. The eyes of our inward man see with greater perception: "Open my eyes and I shall comprehend the wonders of thy Law."[58] It is not that his eyes were veiled; but our eyes are our mind. It is for Jesus alone to unveil them, that we may be able to understand the Scriptures and comprehend what is obscurely expressed.

The outward man has ears, and the inward man also is said to have ears. "He that has ears to hear, let him hear."[59] They all had ears as organs of physical sense; but they had not all succeeded in having the inward ears which are purified. To possess the latter sort of ears is not part of our natural constitution; the former are part of our nature. And because the former sort of ears are part of our nature the prophet says, "Hear ye deaf, and ye blind, look and see. Who is deaf but my servants, and who is blind but those who are their lords? Even the servants of God are blinded."[60] That to become deaf is what we bring upon ourselves—let us pay attention: what I am saying will affect all of us; it is necessary to describe the inward man to discover what the blood is—that to become deaf in respect of the inward ears is something we bring upon ourselves, hear the declaration of the prophet: "Sinners are alienated from the womb; they have erred from the womb. They have spoken lies. Wrath is upon them after the likeness of the serpent, like a deaf adder which stops her ears, which does not hear the voice of those who enchant her and the incantation pronounced by a wise man."[61] And all of you also who are aware that you are responsible, if you hear the word and the incantation pronounced by a wise man and listen to the enchanting words, so that he may check your wrath and iniquity, and if, then, you shut your ears, and do not throw them wide open to accept what is said, then to you apply the words: "Wrath is on them after the likeness of the serpent like a deaf adder which stops her ears, which does not hear the voice of those who enchant her and the incantation pronounced by a wise man."

The outward man has nostrils with which to smell, and so perceives good and bad smells; and the inner man with different nostrils perceives the good smell of righteousness and the bad smell of sins. Of the good smell the apostle teaches us when he says, "We are a sweet savour of Christ unto God in every place,

158

---

[58] Ps. 119 (118):18.   [59] Matt. 11:15, etc.
[60] Isa. 42:18.
[61] Ps. 58 (57):3-5. Cf. contra Celsum, IV, 72, and note thereon.

among them that are saved and them that are perishing; to the one a savour of death unto death, to the others a savour of life unto life."[62] And Solomon also says in the Song of Songs, putting the words into the mouth of the daughters of Jerusalem: "After thee we will run to the odour of thy perfumes."[63] As, then, we perceive with our nostrils good and bad smells in the world of sense, so also for the inward man there is a perception of the good smell of righteousness such as the apostle had, and an evil smell of sins, which is possessed by the person whose divine senses are in good health. What is the evil smell of sins? That of which the prophet says this: "My sores have become foul and rotten in face of my foolishness."[64]

The outward man has the sense of taste; and the inner man also has a spiritual taste, of which it is said: "Taste and see that the Lord is kindly."[65]

160 The outward man has physical touch. The inner man also has touch, that touch by which the woman with the issue of blood touched the hem of Jesus' garment.[66] She touched it. For he witnessed to the fact saying, "Who touched me?" Yet just before Peter said to him, "The crowds throng you and you say, Who touched me?" He imagined that those who touched him, touched by physical, not spiritual contact. Those, therefore, who thronged Jesus did not touch him. For they did not touch him by faith. Only the woman, who had a sort of divine touch, touched Jesus and by this was healed. And because she touched him with a divine touch, power went out from Jesus at her divine touch. He says therefore: "Who touched me? For I have felt power to go forth from me." Concerning this more divine touch John says: "And our hands have handled concerning the word of life."[67]

In this way we possess other hands, concerning which it is said: "Let the lifting up of my hands be an evening sacrifice."[68] For it is not when I lift up these hands, while the hands of my soul hang down instead of being lifted up by holy and good works, that the lifting up of my hands becomes an evening sacrifice. I also have feet of a different kind, concerning which Solomon commands me saying, "Let not thy foot stumble."[69]

There is a curious saying in Ecclesiastes. To anyone that does not understand it it will seem meaningless, but it is for the wise man that Ecclesiastes says: "The wise man has his eyes in his

---

[62] II Cor. 2:15–16. [63] S. of Sol. 1:4. [64] Ps. 38 (37):5.
[65] Ps. 34 (33):8; I Pet. 2:3. [66] Luke 8:45–46; Mark 5:29–32.
[67] I John 1:1. [68] Ps. 141 (140):2. [69] Prov. 3:23.

head."[70] In what head? Every man, even the blockhead and the fool, has his bodily eyes in his bodily head. But "the wise man has his eyes" (those of which I have already spoken, which are enlightened by the Lord's commandment[71]) "in his head," in 162 Christ, since "Christ is the head of a man,"[72] the apostle says. The thinking faculty is in Christ.

"My belly, my belly is in pain,"[73] says Jeremiah. In what belly is he in pain? That in which we too feel pain, that by which, when it is in travail bringing the people to birth[74]; "I suffer pain in my belly and my sense"—not these senses, but those of my heart.

Even if I pass on to the fine parts of the body, I see them in the soul under an unfleshly form. "Lord, reprove me not in thine anger; chastise me not in thy anger. Have pity on me, Lord, for I am feeble. Heal me Lord, for my bones are troubled."[75] What bones of the prophet were troubled? The constitution of his soul and the firmness of his mind was troubled, and he implored the Lord for the restoration of those bones. "Our bones are scattered in Hades."[76] What bones of the speaker were scattered in Hades? Consider, I pray you, the sinner, consider his frame in the domain of sin, in the domain of the dead, in the domain of evil, and you will say of such a man that his bones are scattered. "All my bones will say, Lord who is like unto thee?"[77] They are the bones which speak, converse with, and perceive God, whereas these bones are incapable of perception, as is shown by the sons of physicians; when they saw off a man's bones, he does not feel the saw. "All my bones will say, Lord who is like unto thee?" All the bones are those which belong to the inner man.

The inner man has a heart. "Hear me, ye who have lost your heart."[78] They possessed a heart, that of the body; it was not that heart which they lost. But when a man neglects to 164 cultivate his intellectual life, and in consequence of much idleness his thinking capacity has atrophied, he has lost his heart, and it is to such a person that the words are added: "Hear me, ye who have lost your heart."

"The hairs of your head are all numbered."[79] What hairs? Those by virtue of which they were Nazirites in a spiritual sense.

[70] Eccles. 2:14.   [71] Cf. Ps. 19 (18):8.   [72] I Cor. 11:3.
[73] Jer. 4:19.   [74] Cf. Gal. 4:19.   [75] Ps. 6:2–3.
[76] Ps. 141 (140):7.   [77] Ps. 35 (34):10.   [78] Isa. 46:12.
[79] Matt. 10:30.

Thus you have all the parts of the visible body in the inner man. Do not doubt, then, concerning the blood also because it has the same name as physical blood, like the other members of the body. It is that which belongs to the inner man. It is that blood which is poured forth from a sinful soul. For "The blood of your souls shall be required."[80] It does not say "your blood" but "the blood of your souls." And "I will require the blood at the hand of the watchman."[81] What kind of blood does God require at the hand of the watchman, but that which is poured forth from the sinner? Thus the heart of the fool perishes, and it is said, "Hear me, ye who have lost your heart," because there is poured forth the blood and the vital power of the soul.

If one comprehends what the soul is, and that it belongs to the inner man, and that it is in that part there is the element which is "in the image," it is clear that Paul was right when he said: "For it were better to depart and to be with Christ."[82] Before the resurrection the righteous man is with Christ and in his soul he lives with Christ. That is why it is better to depart and to be with Christ. But according to you who say that the soul remains in the tomb with the body, it has not left the body, it does not rest, it does not dwell in the paradise of God, it does not repose in the bosom of Abraham.[83] According to you who 166 maintain such absurd doctrines it would not be better to depart and to be with Christ. For one is not with Christ as soon as one departs if the soul is the blood. If the soul remains in the tombs, how can it be with Christ? But according to my view and that of the word of God, the soul which has departed from the troubles, the sweat, and the body, that which can say, "Lord now lettest thou thy servant depart in peace,"[84] is that which departs in peace and rests with Christ. It is thus that the soul of Abraham understood the words: "As for thee, thou shalt go in peace to thy fathers, having lived to a good old age."[85] He departed to his fathers. What fathers? Those of whom Paul says: "For this cause I bow my knees to the Father of whom all fatherhood is derived."[86] In our view it was in this sense that Aaron was set free.[87] Also it is written in Ecclesiastes concerning the just man who has fought a good fight, who is departing from the fetter of the body, that "From the house of the prisoners he will go forth to be a king."[88] Thus I am persuaded to die for the

---

[80] Gen. 9:5.   [81] Ezek. 33:6.   [82] Phil. 1:23.
[83] Luke 16:23.   [84] Luke 2:29.
[85] Gen. 15:15; cf. *Exh. Mart.*, 14 (above, p. 403).   [86] Eph. 3:14.
[87] Num. 20:29.   [88] Eccles. 4:14.

truth, thus I readily despise what is called death. Bring wild beasts, bring crosses, bring fire, bring tortures. I know that as soon as I die, I come forth from the body, I rest with Christ. Therefore let us struggle, therefore let us wrestle, let us groan being in the body,[89] not as if we shall again be in the tombs in the body, because we shall be set free from it, and shall change our body to one which is more spiritual. Destined as we are to be with Christ, how we groan while we are in the body!

Bishop Philip came in, and Demetrius, another bishop, said: Brother Origen teaches that the soul is immortal.

Orig.: The remark of father Demetrius has given us the starting point for another problem. He asserted that we have said the soul is immortal. To this remark I will say that the soul is 168 immortal and the soul is not immortal. Let us first define the meaning of the word "death," and determine all its possible senses. I will try to show all its meanings not by appealing to the Greeks, but all its meanings as found in the divine Scripture. Perhaps one more learned than I will point out other senses also. But for the present I am aware of three kinds of death. What are these three kinds of death? According to the apostle, a man may live unto God and die unto sin.[90] This death is a blessed thing. A man dies to sin. This death my Lord died. "For in that he died, he died unto sin."[91] I know also another sort of death, according to which a man dies to God; concerning this it was said: "The soul that sins, it shall die."[92] And I know of a third kind of death, according to which we commonly suppose that those who are separated from the body die. For "Adam lived nine hundred and thirty years and died."[93]

There being, then, three kinds of death, let us see whether the human soul is immortal in respect of the three kinds of death, or if not in respect of the three, yet in respect of some of them. The death that is a matter of moral indifference all men die. 170 It is that which we consider dissolution. No soul of man dies this death. For if it did so, it would not be punished after death. It is said: "Men shall seek for death and shall not find it."[94] In this sense every human soul is immortal. But in the other meanings, the soul in one sense is mortal, and blessed if it dies to sin. It is of this death that Balaam spoke when he prophesied, praying by divine inspiration: "May my soul die among the souls of

89 II Cor. 5:2, 4.   90 Rom. 6:2.
91 Rom 6:10.   92 Ezek. 18:4.
93 Gen. 5:5.   94 Rev. 9:6.

the just."[95] Concerning this death Balaam made his astonishing prophecy, and by the word of God he made for himself a splendid prayer. For he prayed that he might die to sin that he might live unto God. And this account he said: "May my soul die among the souls of the just and my posterity be like their posterity." There is another death in respect of which we are not immortal, although we have the power by exercising vigilance to avoid death. And perhaps that which is mortal in the soul is not for ever mortal. For in so far as it gives way to sin, so that the word is realized which says, "the soul that sins, it shall die,"[96] the soul is mortal and dies a real death. But if it is found firmly established in blessedness so that it is inaccessible to death, because it has eternal life, it is no longer mortal but in this sense has even become immortal. How is it that the apostle says of God: "He who alone has immortality"?[97] On investigation I find that Christ Jesus "died for all apart from God."[98] There you have the explanation how God alone has immortality.

172

Let us therefore take up eternal life. Let us take up that which depends upon our decision. God does not give it to us. He sets it before us. "Behold, I have set life before thy face."[99] It is in our power to stretch out our hand, to do good works, and to lay hold on life and deposit it in our soul. This life is the Christ who said: "I am the life."[1] This life is that which now is present in shadow, but then will be face to face.[2] "For the spirit before our face is Christ of whom we may say, In his shadow we shall live among the nations."[3] If the mere shadow of life that is yours offers you so many good things, that shadow which Moses had when he prophesied, that shadow which Isaiah possessed when he saw the Lord Sabaoth sitting upon a throne high and lifted up, which Jeremiah had when he heard the words: "Before I formed thee in the womb, I knew thee, and before thou didst come forth from the womb I sanctified thee," which Ezekiel

---

[95] Num. 23:10. Scherer is no doubt right in explaining the repetition here as originating from a double recension. The second, fuller version was intended to replace the first. It is probable that the two versions arose from two different stenographic reports, and that, if Origen revised the final copy himself, he failed to notice the mistake.

[96] Ezek. 18:4.   [97] I Tim. 6:16.

[98] II Cor. 5:15; Heb. 2:9, which Origen knows in both readings (a) "apart from God," (b) "by the grace of God" (*Comm. in Joann.*, I, 35 (40); XXVIII, 18 (14)). He regarded the first as the correct text.

[99] Deut. 30:15.   [1] John 11:25; 14:6.   [2] I Cor. 13:12.
[3] Lam. 4:20.

had when he saw the Cherubim, when he saw the wheels, the 174
ineffable mysteries[4]: what sort of life shall we live when we are
no longer living under the shadow of life but are in life itself.
For now "our life is hid with Christ; but when Christ, who is our
life, shall appear, then shall we also appear with him in glory."[5]
Let us haste towards this life, groaning and grieving that we are
in this tent, that we dwell in the body. So long as we are present
in the body, we are absent from the Lord.[6] Let us long to be
absent from the body and to be present with the Lord, that
being present with him we may become one with the God of the
universe and his only begotten Son, being saved in all things
and becoming blessed, in Jesus Christ, to whom be the glory and
the power for ever and ever. Amen.

Dialogues[7] *of Origen:*
with Heraclides and the bishops with him,
concerning the Father and the Son and the Soul.

---

[4] Isa. 6:1; Jer. 1:5; Ezek. 1:15; 10:1.
[5] Col. 3:3–4. [6] II Cor. 5:6, 8.
[7] The plural offers no reason for supposing that there was a *collection* of
Origen's discussions, only one of which has been preserved in the present
text. The reviser used the singular in the heading he gave to the work,
and evidently thought that a more appropriate designation. But the
original scribe may have used the plural to refer to the various themes
discussed.

BIBLIOGRAPHY

CLEMENT OF ALEXANDRIA

A. Editions

The standard edition of Clement, which has made all earlier editions antiquated, is that of Otto Stählin in the Berlin Corpus (*Die griechischen christlichen Schriftsteller der ersten drei Jahrhunderte*, 4 vols., Leipzig, 1905–1936). The *editio princeps* was produced by P. Victorius (Florence, 1550), soon followed by that of F. Sylburg (Heidelberg, 1592). Archbishop Potter produced a good edition (Oxford, 1715), reprinted at Venice in 1757, and by several later editors, e.g., F. Oberthür (Würzburg, 1778–1779) who, however, omitted all accents from the Greek text (!); R. Klotz (Leipzig, 1831–1834); Migne, *Patrologia Graeca*, VIII–IX (1857). The edition of W. Dindorf (Oxford, 1869) can only be used by those who are prepared to emend the Greek text as they read.

Of *Stromateis* VII an excellent edition with an English translation (reprinted in the present volume) and provided with an important introduction and commentary was produced by F. J. A. Hort and J. B. Mayor (London, Macmillan, 1902).

B. Literature

Anrich, G., "Clemens und Origenes als Begründer der Lehre vom Fegfeuer," *Theologische Abhandlungen für H. J. Holtzmann* (1902), pp. 97–120.

Bardy, G., *Clément d'Alexandrie* (Paris, 1926).

Bardy, G., "Aux origines de l'école d'Alexandrie," *Recherches de science religieuse*, Vol. XXVII (1937), pp. 65–90.

Bardy, G., "Pour l'histoire de l'école d'Alexandrie," *Vivre et Penser*, 2e série, Paris, 1942, pp. 80–109.

Bigg, C., *The Christian Platonists of Alexandria* (2nd ed., Oxford, 1913).

Buri, F., *Clemens Alexandrinus und der paulinische Freiheitsbegriff* (Zürich, 1939).

Camelot, T., *Foi et Gnose: introduction à l'étude de la connaissance mystique chez Clément d'Alexandrie* (Paris, 1945).

Casey, R. P., "Clement of Alexandria and the beginnings of Christian Platonism," *Harvard Theological Review*, Vol. XVIII (1925), pp. 39–101.

Faye, E. de, *Clément d'Alexandrie* (2nd ed., Paris, 1906).

Lietzmann, H., *The Founding of the Church Universal* (2nd ed., London, 1950) (=*Geschichte der alten Kirche*, II, Leipzig, 1936).

Molland, E., *The Conception of the Gospel in the Alexandrian Theology* (Oslo, 1938).

Mondésert, C., *Clément d'Alexandrie* (Paris, 1944).

Munck, J., *Untersuchungen über Klemens von Alexandria* (Stuttgart, 1933).

Pohlenz, M., "Klemens von Alexandreia und sein hellenisches Christentum," *Nachrichten der Akademie der Wissenschaften in Göttingen* (phil. hist. Kl. 1943, Heft 3).

Quatember, F., *Die christliche Lebenshaltung des Klemens von Alexandrien* (Vienna, 1947).

Rüther, T., *Die sittliche Forderung der Apatheia in den beiden ersten christlichen Jahrhunderten und bei Klemens von Alexandrien* (Freiburg, 1949).

Tollinton, R. B., *Clement of Alexandria: a study in Christian Liberalism* (London, 1914).

Völker, W., *Der wahre Gnostiker nach Clemens Alexandrinus* (Berlin and Leipzig, 1952).

Westcott, B. F., Article "Clement of Alexandria," in *Dictionary of Christian Biography*, Vol. I (1877).

Zahn, T., *Supplementum Clementinum* (Erlangen, 1884).

ORIGEN

A. Editions

Until the present century the standard collected edition of Origen's works was that of Charles Delarue and his nephew Charles Vincent Delarue, published in four volumes in the eighteenth century (1733–1759). This edition, with minor additions, was reprinted by C. H. E. Lommatzsch in twenty-five handy volumes (Berlin, 1831–1848), and with more substantial additions by Migne, *Patrologia Graeca*, Vols. XI–XVIII (Paris, 1857). So far as it is available, the standard edition now is that of the Berlin Corpus, twelve volumes of which have hitherto been devoted to Origen. These include the *contra Celsum, de Oratione*, the *Exhortation to Martyrdom*, the *Homilies* on books of the Old Testament and on St. Luke, and the two great commentaries on St. Matthew and St. John.

B. Literature

Bardy, G., *Origène* (Paris, 1931).

Bigg, C., *The Christian Platonists of Alexandria* (1913).

Butterworth, G. W., *Origen on First Principles* (London, 1936).
Cadiou, R., *Introduction au système d'Origène* (Paris, 1932).
Cadiou, R., *La Jeunesse d'Origène* (Paris, 1935).
Chadwick, H., *Origen: contra Celsum* (Cambridge, 1953).
Danièlou, J., *Origène* (Paris, 1948).
Denis, M. J., *De la philosophie d'Origène* (Paris, 1884).
Faye, E. de., *Origène, sa vie, son œuvre, sa pensée* (Paris, 1923-1928).
Faye, E. de, *Origen and his work* (trans. Fred Rothwell. London, 1926).
Hanson, R. P. C., *Origen's Doctrine of Tradition* (London, 1954).
Harnack, A. von, *Der kirchengeschichtliche Ertrag der exegetischen Arbeiten des Origenes* (Leipzig, 1919).
Karpp, H., *Probleme altchristlicher Anthropologie* (Gütersloh, 1950).
Knox, W. L., "Origen's conception of the resurrection body," *Journal of Theological Studies*, Vol. XXXIX (1938), pp. 247-248.
Koch, Hal, *Pronoia und Paideusis: Studien über Origenes und sein Verhältnis zum Platonismus* (Berlin and Leipzig, 1932).
Lieske, A., *Die Theologie der Logos-Mystik bei Origenes* (Münster, 1938).
Lubac, H. de, *Histoire et Esprit: L'intelligence de l'écriture d'après Origène* (Paris, 1950).
Redepenning, E. R., *Origenes, eine Darstellung seines Lebens und seiner Lehre* (Bonn, 1841).
Völker, W., *Das Vollkommenheitsideal des Origenes* (Tübingen, 1931).
Westcott, B. F., Article "Origenes," in *Dictionary of Christian Biography*, Vol. IV (1887).

INDEXES

General Index

459

Modern Authors

Kahle, P. E., 23
Kern, H., 68
Kirk, K. E., 36
Kittel, 364
Klaffenbach, G., 26, 362
Klostermann, E., 219, 305, 346, 349
Koetschau, P., 180 ff., 392, 394, 402, 405, 414
Kraft, H., 27
Kretschmar, G., 436

Lacey, T., 234
Lambeck, P., 232
Lampe, G. W. H., 436
Lawlor, H. J., 24, 373
Lawlor, H. J. and Oulton, J. E. L., 169 ff.
Lebreton, J., 391
Leclercq, H., 35, 381, 385
Leisegang, H., 26
Liboron, H., 27
Lightfoot, J. B., 24, 335, 352, 353, 364
Lipsius, R. A., 26
Lock, W., 364
Lommatzsch, C. H. E., 236
Lovejoy, A. O., 98
Lubac, H. de, 350
Lucius, E., 389
Lutz, C. E., 33

McNeile, A. H., 364
Magie, D., 26
Manson, T. W., 364
Mayor, J. E. B., 17, 39, 374, 381
Meredith, R., 235
Milton, J., 182, 361
Molland, E., 19
Moulton, J. H. and Milligan, J., 170, 363, 364

Nautin, P., 442
Nilsson, M. P., 26
Nock, A. D., 434, 436

Petrie, Flinders, 362
Prat, F., 348
Preisigke, F., 362
Puech, H. C., 30, 436

Ratcliff, E. C., 434
Reading, W., 235, 345, 347, 378
Resch, A., 151, 332
Richardson, C. C., 432
Robinson, J. A., 170, 352
Rohde, E., 28
Ropes, J. H., 332

Sagnard, F., 17
Salmon, G., 26
Sanday, W. and Headlam, A. C., 380
Scherer, J., 177, 430 ff.
Schultz, W., 26
Schürer, E., 28
Schwartz, E., 81, 434
Srawley, J. H., 332
Stählin, O., 39, 46
Swete, H. B., 15, 345, 348

Taylor, A. E., 353
Telfer, W., 16
Thackeray, H. St. J., 363
Thorndike, H., 234
Toy, C. H., 368
Trench, R. C., 334, 345

Usener, H., 28

Völker, W., 21, 38
Volkmar, G., 26
Voobus, A., 23
Voss, I., 233

Walker, J., 236
Walzer, R., 18, 36
Wendland, P., 338
Westcott, B. F., 184, 234, 383
Wetstein, J. R., 235
Whately, R., 358
Whitham, A. R., 187
Wilamowitz-Moellendorf, U. von, 28, 162
Williams, I., 187
Wissowa, G., 28

Zahn, T., 24
Zeller, E., 376
Ziegler, K., 20
Zonaras, L., 234

BIBLICAL REFERENCES

Genesis
1:3 .... 22, 190, 288, 289, 358
1:9 288

Genesis—continued
1:11 288
1:20 288
1:24 288

Genesis—continued
1:26 .... 296, 445
1:26–27 .... 296, 448
1:27 401

A.C.—30